Jean-Claude Corbeil・Ariane Archambault
ジャン＝クロード・コルベイユ／アリアーヌ・アルシャンボ

オールカラー
英語百科
大図典

日本語－英語

小学館

オールカラー
英語百科大図典

日本語－英語

Jean-Claude Corbeil • Ariane Archambault

ジャン＝クロード・コルベイユ／アリアーヌ・アルシャンボ

編集
発行者: Jacques Fortin
編集局長: François Fortin
ジュニア版編集局長: Caroline Fortin
編集長: Serge D'Amico
ジュニア版編集長: Martine Podesto
ジュニア版副編集長: Johanne Champagne
グラフィック・デザイナー: Josée Noiseux

専門用語検討
Jean Beaumont
Catherine Briand
Nathalie Guillo

イラスト
アート・ディレクター: Jocelyn Gardner
ジュニア版アート・ディレクター: Anouk Noël
Jean-Yves Ahern
Rielle Lévesque
Alain Lemire
Mélanie Boivin
Yan Bohler
Claude Thivierge
Pascal Bilodeau
Michel Rouleau
Carl Pelletier

レイアウト
Jean-François Nault
Jean-Philippe Bouchard
Nathalie Gignac
Kien Tang

文献調査
Gilles Vézina
Kathleen Wynd
Stéphane Batigne
Sylvain Robichaud
Jessie Daigle

データ管理
プログラマー: Daniel Beaulieu

校正
Veronica Schami Editorial Services

制作
Guylaine Houle

プリプレス
Sophie Pellerin
Tony O'Riley

協力
Jean-Louis Martin, Marc Lalumière, Jacques Perrault, Stéphane Roy, Alice Comtois, Michel Blais, Christiane Beauregard, Mamadou Togola, Annie Maurice, Charles Campeau, Mivil Deschênes, Jonathan Jacques, Martin Lortie, Raymond Martin, Frédérick Simard, Yan Tremblay, Mathieu Blouin, Sébastien Dallaisers, Hoang Khanh Le, Martin Desrosiers, Nicolas Oroc, François Escalmel, Danièle Lemay, Pierre Savoie, Benoît Bourdeau, Marie-Andrée Lemieux, Caroline Soucy, Yves Chabot, Anne-Marie Ouellette, Anne-Marie Villeneuve, Anne-Marie Brault, Nancy Lepage, Daniel Provost, François Vézina.

目次

天文学
- 太陽系 6
- 銀河 11
- 天体観測 12
- 宇宙探査 13

地理学
- 大陸の配置 18
- 地図作成法 20

地質学
- 地球の構造 24
- 岩石と鉱石 25
- 地質学的現象 26
- 地球の地形 28

気象学
- 大気圏 32
- 気候 33
- 気象現象 35
- 気象予報 38

自然環境
- 生物圏 40
- 水の循環 42
- 温室効果 43
- 汚染 44
- ごみ[廃棄物]の分別 46

植物界
- 単純な植物 47
- 顕花(けんか)植物 48
- 木／樹木 52

動物界
- 単純な生物と棘皮(きょくひ)動物 ... 56
- 軟体動物 57
- 甲殻類 58
- 蜘蛛類 59
- 昆虫 60
- 軟骨魚 64
- 硬骨魚 65
- 両生類 66
- 爬虫類 67
- 鳥類 72
- 哺乳動物 76

人間
- 人体 90
- 骨格 92
- 歯 94
- 筋肉 95
- 解剖学 96
- 感覚器官 100

食べ物
- 野菜 103
- 豆類 108
- 果物 109
- さまざまな食品 114

衣類と身の回り品
- 衣類 116
- 身の回り品 123

家
- 家屋の外観 134
- 家屋の構成要素 136
- 主な部屋 138
- 家具調度 140
- 台所 143
- 浴室／バスルーム 154
- 照明と暖房 155
- 家事用品と家電製品 159
- 日曜大工 161
- 園芸／ガーデニング 164

科学
- 実験器具 ... 166
- 計測機器 ... 168
- 幾何学 ... 171

エネルギー
- 太陽エネルギー ... 173
- 水力電気 ... 174
- 核エネルギー ... 177
- 風力エネルギー ... 179
- 化石エネルギー ... 180

輸送と重機
- 道路輸送 ... 182
- 鉄道輸送 ... 196
- 海上輸送 ... 200
- 航空輸送 ... 203
- 重機 ... 209

芸術
- 美術 ... 211
- 工芸 ... 214

建築
- 家屋 ... 215
- 建築物の作品 ... 217

音楽
- 楽譜記号 ... 222
- 楽器 ... 224
- 交響[管弦]楽団 ... 234

通信
- 写真 ... 235
- ラジオ ... 237
- テレビ ... 238
- 音声再生装置 ... 241
- ポータブル音響機器 ... 242
- 電話通信 ... 244
- パーソナル・コンピューター／パソコン ... 246
- インターネット ... 248

社会
- 中心街 ... 250
- ターミナルと駅 ... 252
- 商業サービス ... 256
- 安全 ... 262
- 健康 ... 266
- 教育 ... 268
- 娯楽 ... 272

スポーツ
- 体操 ... 274
- 水泳 ... 276
- 海上スポーツ ... 278
- 乗馬スポーツ ... 280
- 正確さを競うスポーツ ... 281
- ウインター・スポーツ ... 284
- 球技 ... 290
- ラケット・スポーツ ... 302
- 格闘技 ... 304
- モーター・スポーツ ... 306
- ローラー・スポーツ ... 307
- 自転車競技 ... 308

レジャーとゲーム
- キャンプ ... 309
- ゲーム ... 313

象徴／シンボル
- 道路標識 ... 317
- 一般的な案内標識 ... 319
- 安全標識 ... 320

索引 ... 321

太陽系 | SOLAR SYSTEM

太陽系は広い宇宙の片隅にあって、太陽という名の恒星、太陽の周りを回る天体から成り立っています。その天体には、合わせて100以上もの衛星を伴った9つの惑星と、何千もの小惑星、何百万もの彗星などがあり、何十億もの小石、塵（ちり）、ガスがその空間を満たしています。

惑星と衛星
PLANETS AND SATELLITES

惑星の軌道
ORBITS OF THE PLANETS

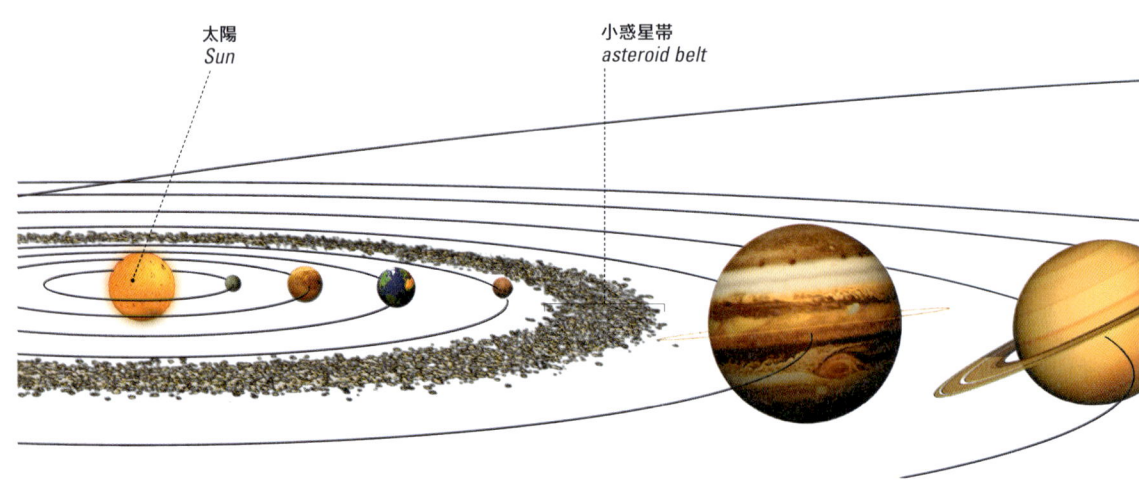

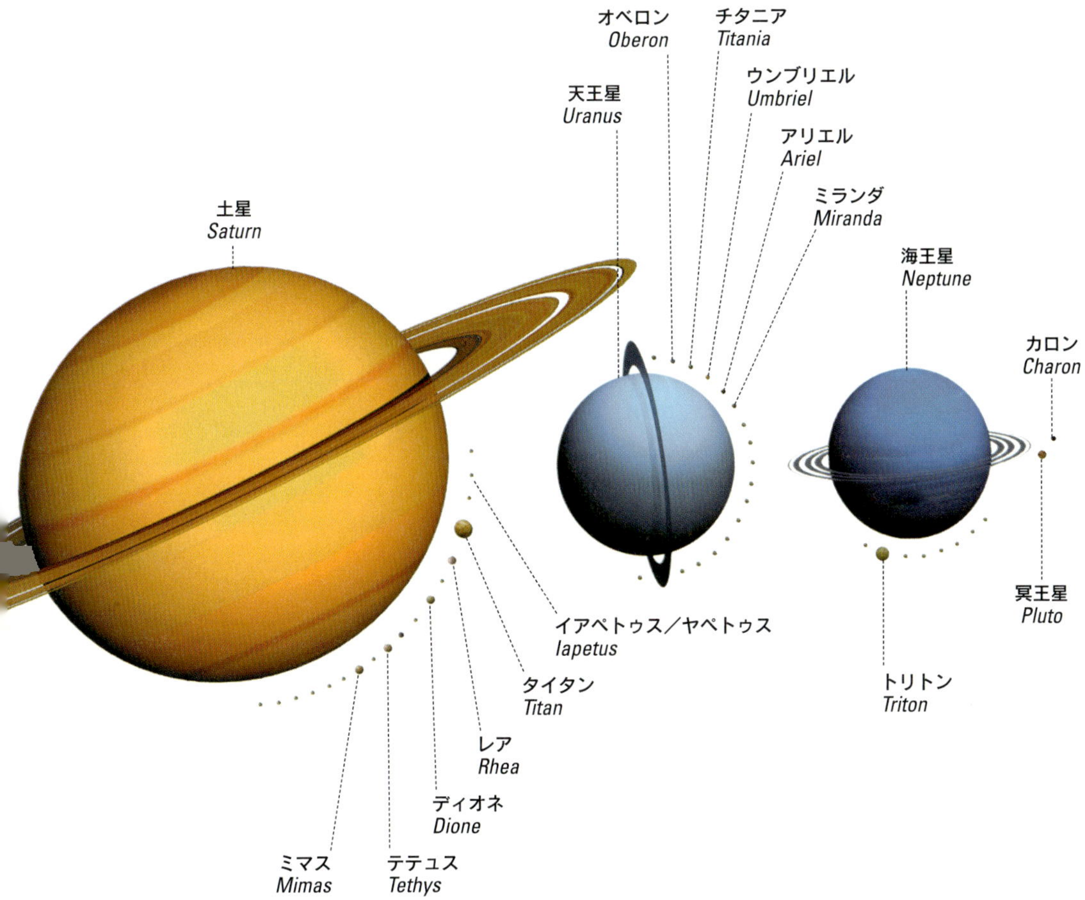

太陽系 | SOLAR SYSTEM

天文学

土星
Saturn

オベロン
Oberon

チタニア
Titania

ウンブリエル
Umbriel

アリエル
Ariel

天王星
Uranus

ミランダ
Miranda

海王星
Neptune

カロン
Charon

イアペトゥス／ヤペトゥス
Iapetus

タイタン
Titan

レア
Rhea

ディオネ
Dione

テテュス
Tethys

ミマス
Mimas

トリトン
Triton

冥王星
Pluto

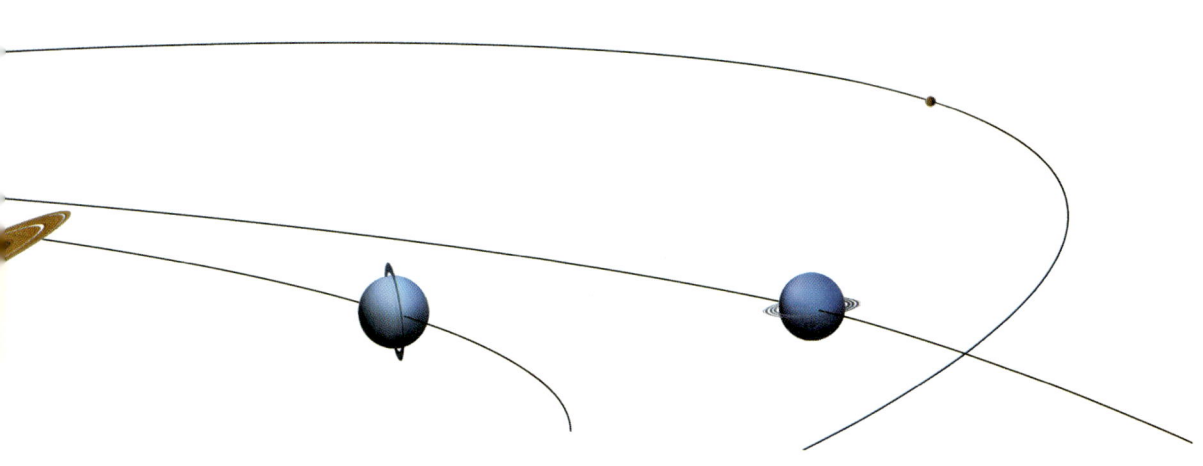

太陽系 | SOLAR SYSTEM

太陽
SUN

天文学

太陽の構造
structure of the Sun

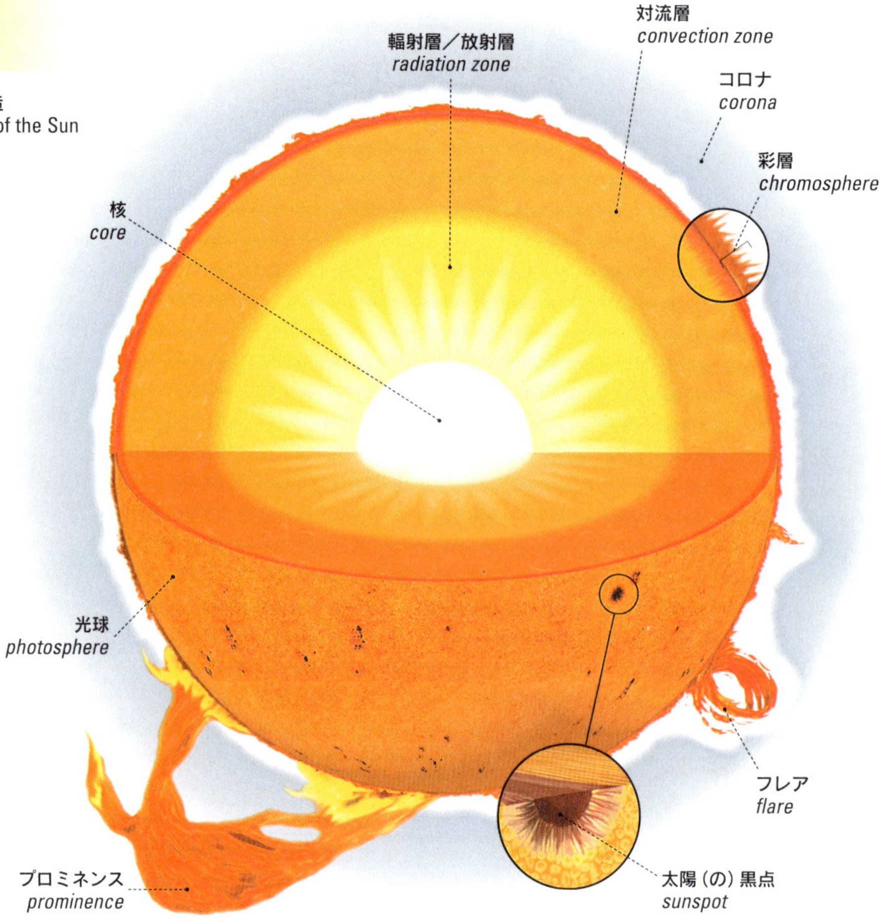

- 輻射層／放射層 / radiation zone
- 対流層 / convection zone
- コロナ / corona
- 彩層 / chromosphere
- 核 / core
- 光球 / photosphere
- プロミネンス / prominence
- 太陽（の）黒点 / sunspot
- フレア / flare

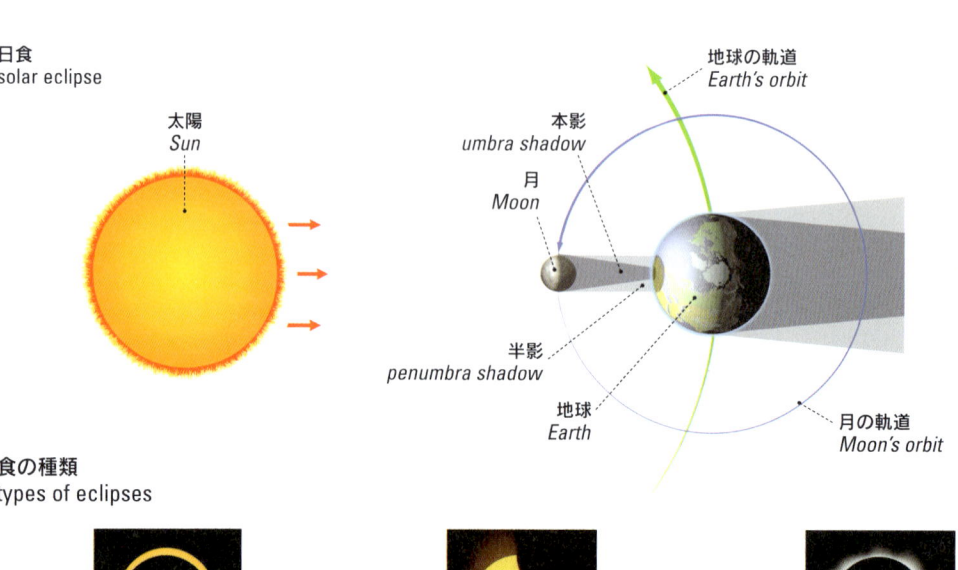

日食
solar eclipse

- 太陽 / Sun
- 地球の軌道 / Earth's orbit
- 本影 / umbra shadow
- 月 / Moon
- 半影 / penumbra shadow
- 地球 / Earth
- 月の軌道 / Moon's orbit

食の種類
types of eclipses

- 金環食 / annular eclipse
- 部分食 / partial eclipse 
- 皆既食 / total eclipse

太陽系 | SOLAR SYSTEM

月
MOOM

月の地形
lunar features

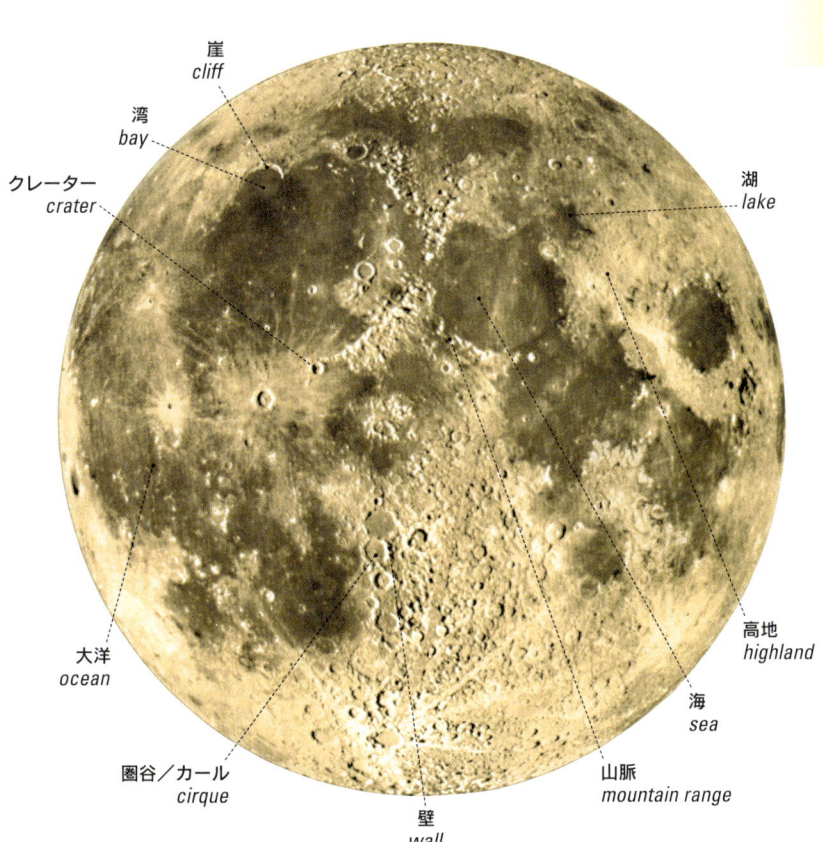

崖 cliff
湾 bay
クレーター crater
湖 lake
大洋 ocean
圏谷／カール cirque
壁 wall
山脈 mountain range
海 sea
高地 highland

月食
lunar eclipse

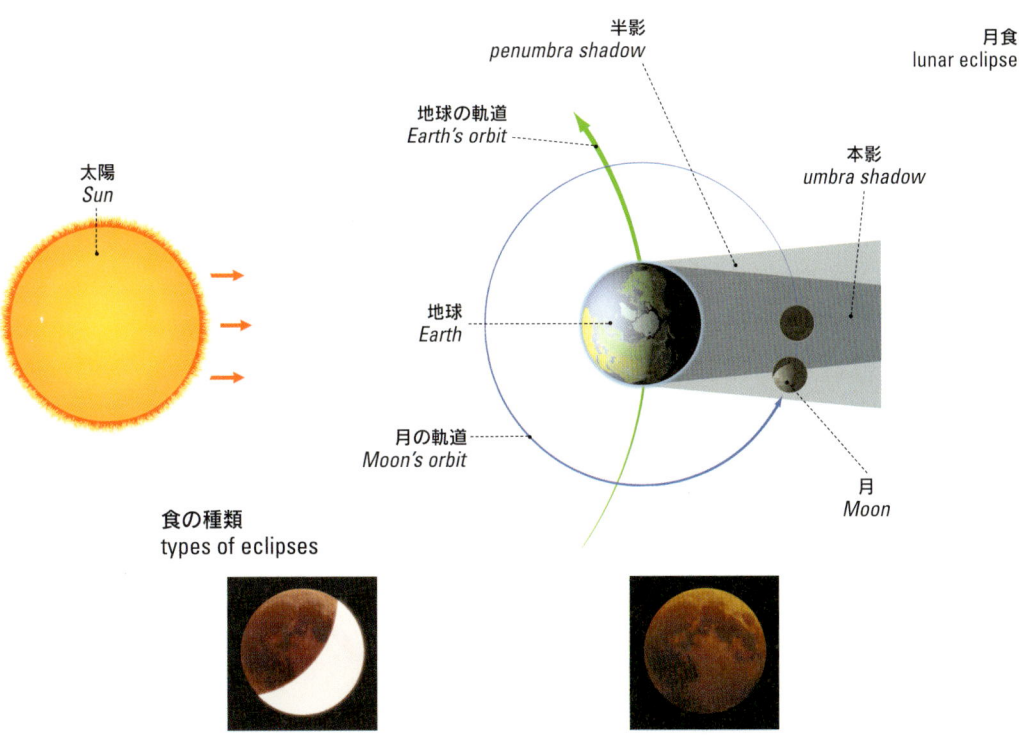

太陽 Sun
半影 penumbra shadow
地球の軌道 Earth's orbit
本影 umbra shadow
地球 Earth
月の軌道 Moon's orbit
月 Moon

食の種類
types of eclipses

部分食
partial eclipse

皆既食
total eclipse

9

太陽系 | SOLAR SYSTEM

月の相
phases of the Moon

新月／朔
new moon

三日月
new crescent

上弦の月
first quarter

十日月
waxing gibbous

満月／望／十五日月
full moon

二十日月
waning gibbous

下弦の月
last quarter

二十六日月
old crescent

彗星
COMET

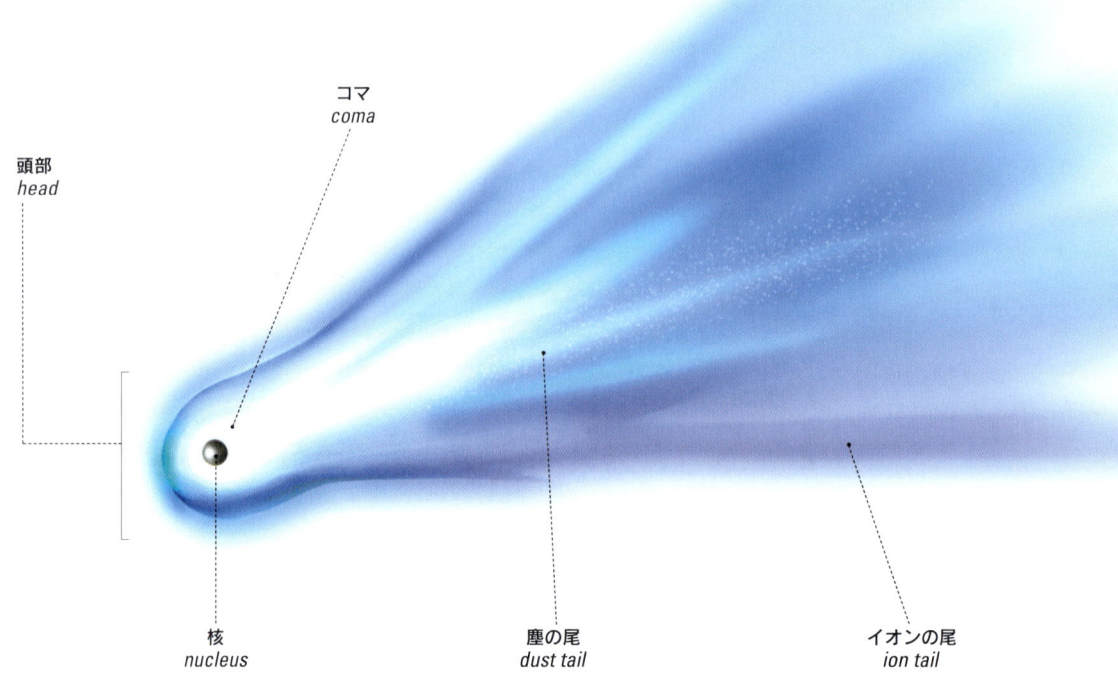

コマ
coma

頭部
head

核
nucleus

塵の尾
dust tail

イオンの尾
ion tail

天文学

銀河 | GALAXY

宇宙には約１,０００億の銀河があり、それぞれが何十億もの星、塵（ちり）、ガスから成り立っています。太陽系は天の川と呼ばれている銀河の端に位置しています。私たちの銀河は地球から見ると、夜空を横切る光の帯のように見えます。この白っぽい帯状の物は２,０００億とも３,０００億とも言われる星の光の集まりなのです。

天の川／銀河
MILKY WAY

天文学

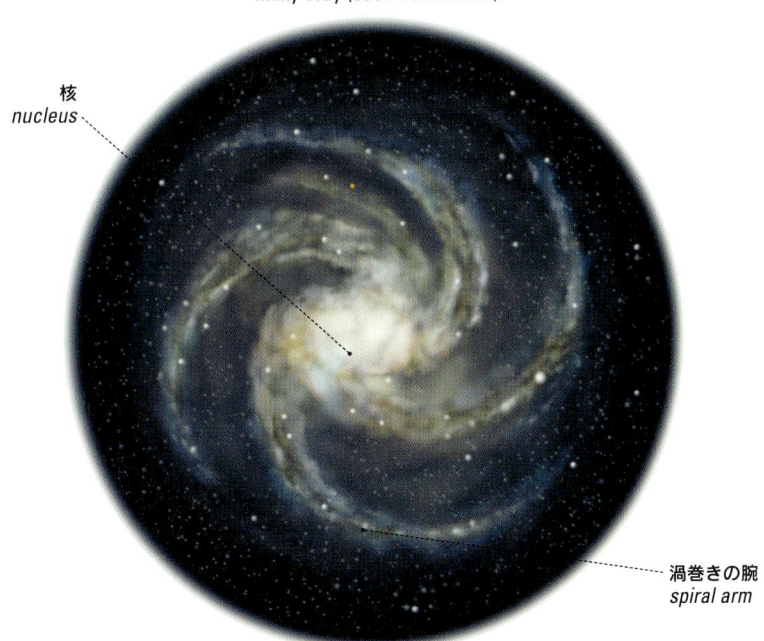

天の川／銀河（上から見た姿）
Milky Way (seen from above)

核 *nucleus*

渦巻きの腕 *spiral arm*

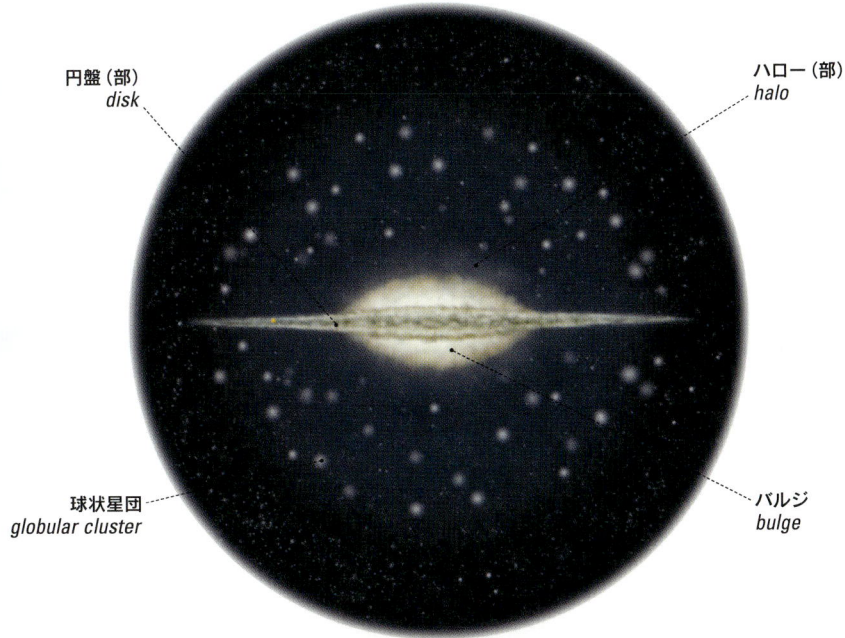

天の川／銀河（横から見た姿）
Milky Way (side view)

円盤（部） *disk*

ハロー（部） *halo*

球状星団 *globular cluster*

バルジ *bulge*

天体観測 | ASTRONOMICAL OBSERVATION

望遠鏡や天体望遠鏡の発明によって私たちの宇宙観は大きく変わりました。レンズや鏡を使った機器で天空の物体から届く光を集めることによって、観測の対象である天体の、膨大で詳細な像を初めて手に入れることができるようになりました。今日では、専門家がより完全な天体望遠鏡モデルの開発に取り組んでいます。

天文学

屈折（式）望遠鏡
REFRACTING TELESCOPE

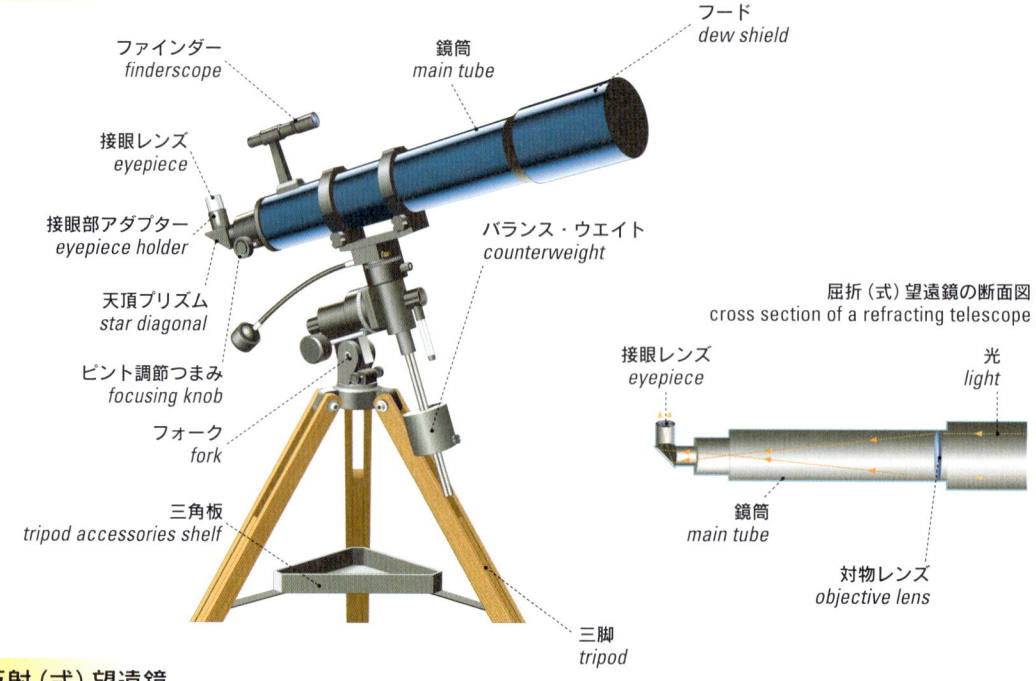

反射（式）望遠鏡
REFLECTING TELESCOPE

宇宙探査 | SPACE EXPLORATION

宇宙探査機は人間が到達できない天体と宇宙空間を探索します。宇宙ロケットやスペースシャトルによって打ち上げられる、さまざまな工夫を凝らしたロボットは現代の探検家と言うことができるでしょう。一回限りのロケットとは違って、スペースシャトルは再利用が可能な乗り物で、さまざまなミッションの中でも未来の国際宇宙ステーション用の機材を運ぶことが期待されています。

宇宙探査機 / SPACE PROBES

天文学

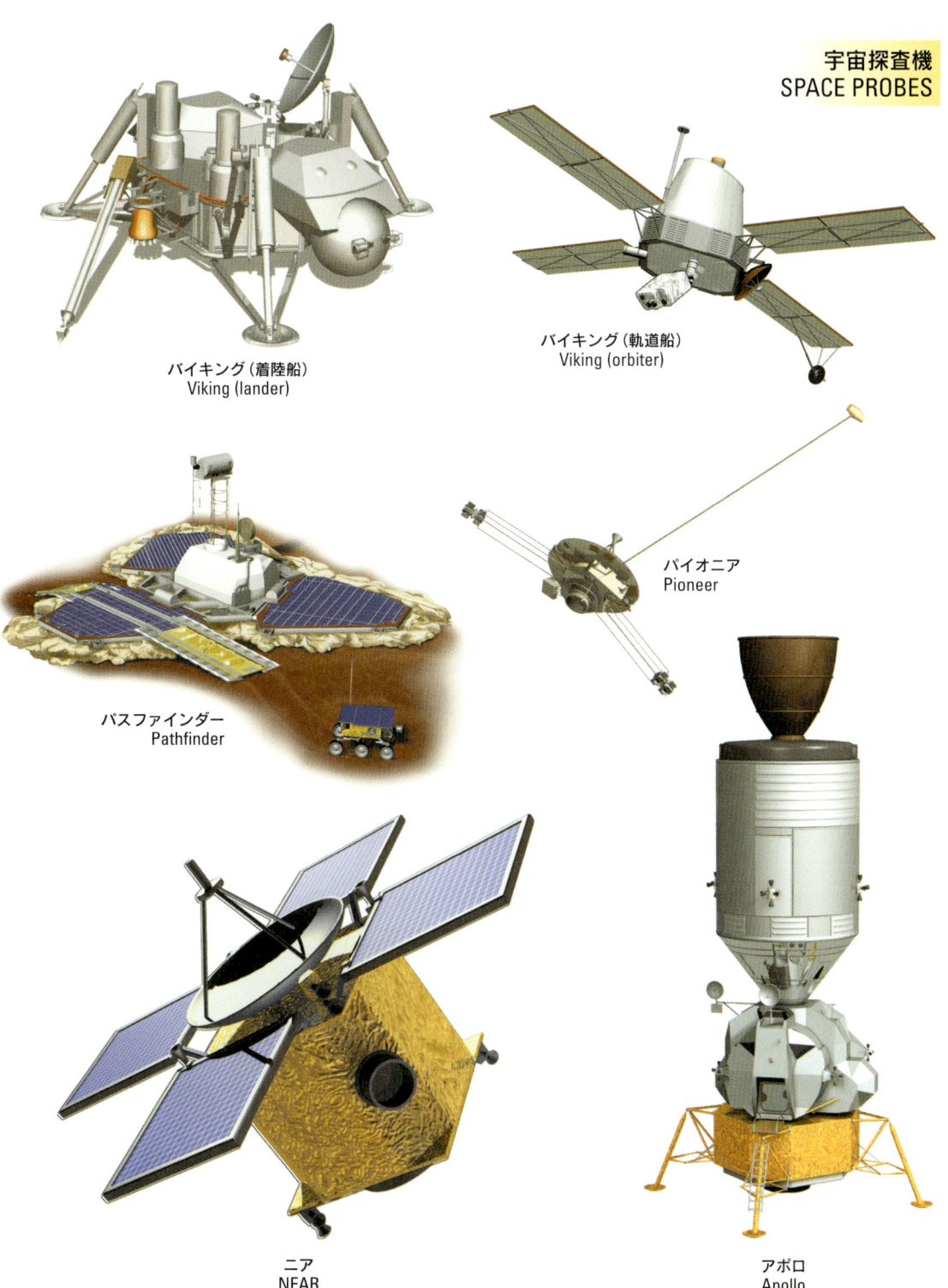

バイキング（着陸船） Viking (lander)

バイキング（軌道船） Viking (orbiter)

パスファインダー Pathfinder

パイオニア Pioneer

ニア NEAR

アポロ Apollo

宇宙探査 | SPACE EXPLORATION

天文学

国際宇宙ステーション
INTERNATIONAL SPACE STATION

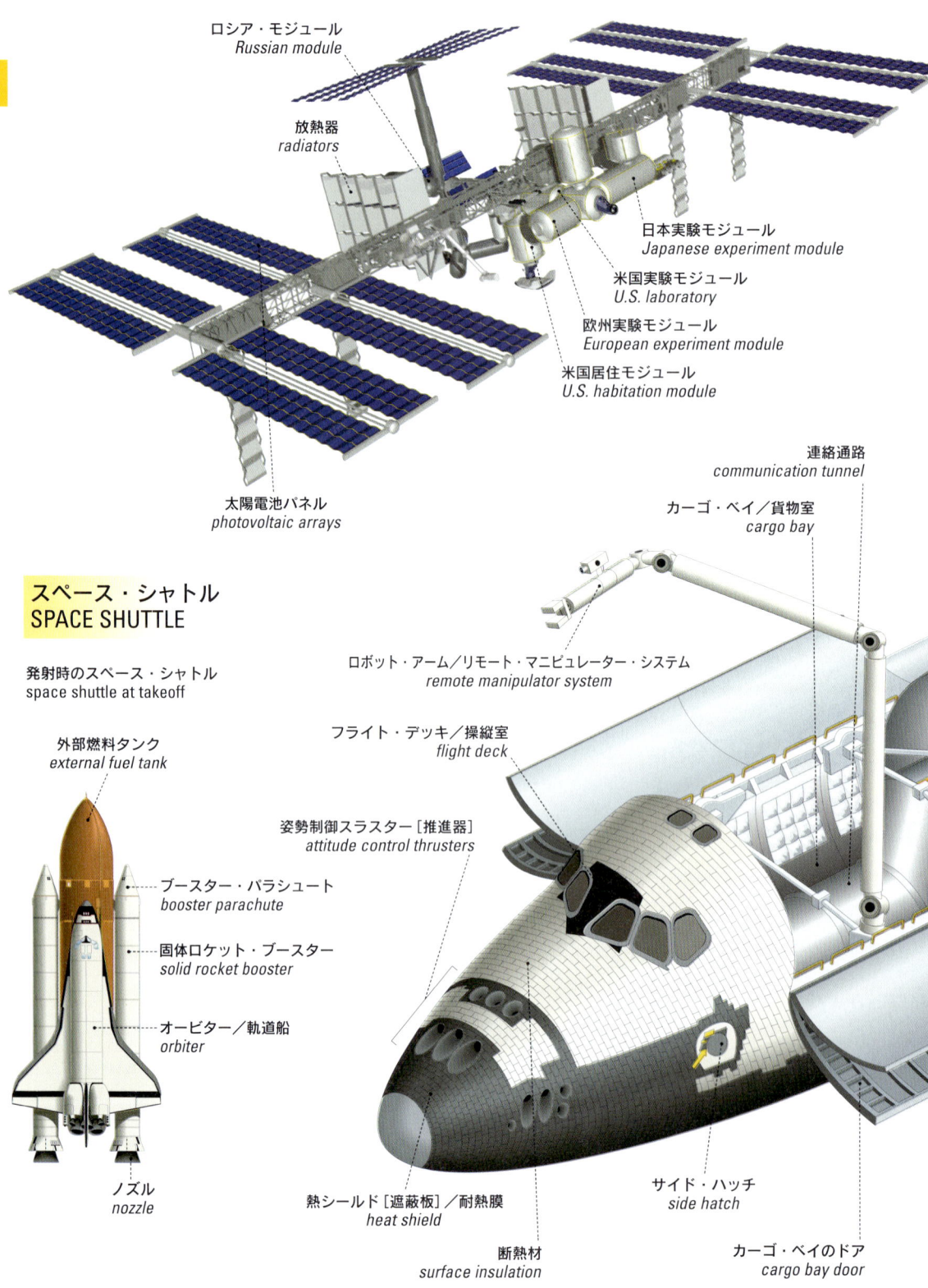

ロシア・モジュール
Russian module

放熱器
radiators

日本実験モジュール
Japanese experiment module

米国実験モジュール
U.S. laboratory

欧州実験モジュール
European experiment module

米国居住モジュール
U.S. habitation module

太陽電池パネル
photovoltaic arrays

連絡通路
communication tunnel

カーゴ・ベイ／貨物室
cargo bay

スペース・シャトル
SPACE SHUTTLE

発射時のスペース・シャトル
space shuttle at takeoff

外部燃料タンク
external fuel tank

ブースター・パラシュート
booster parachute

固体ロケット・ブースター
solid rocket booster

オービター／軌道船
orbiter

ノズル
nozzle

ロボット・アーム／リモート・マニピュレーター・システム
remote manipulator system

フライト・デッキ／操縦室
flight deck

姿勢制御スラスター［推進器］
attitude control thrusters

熱シールド［遮蔽板］／耐熱膜
heat shield

断熱材
surface insulation

サイド・ハッチ
side hatch

カーゴ・ベイのドア
cargo bay door

14

宇宙探査 | SPACE EXPLORATION

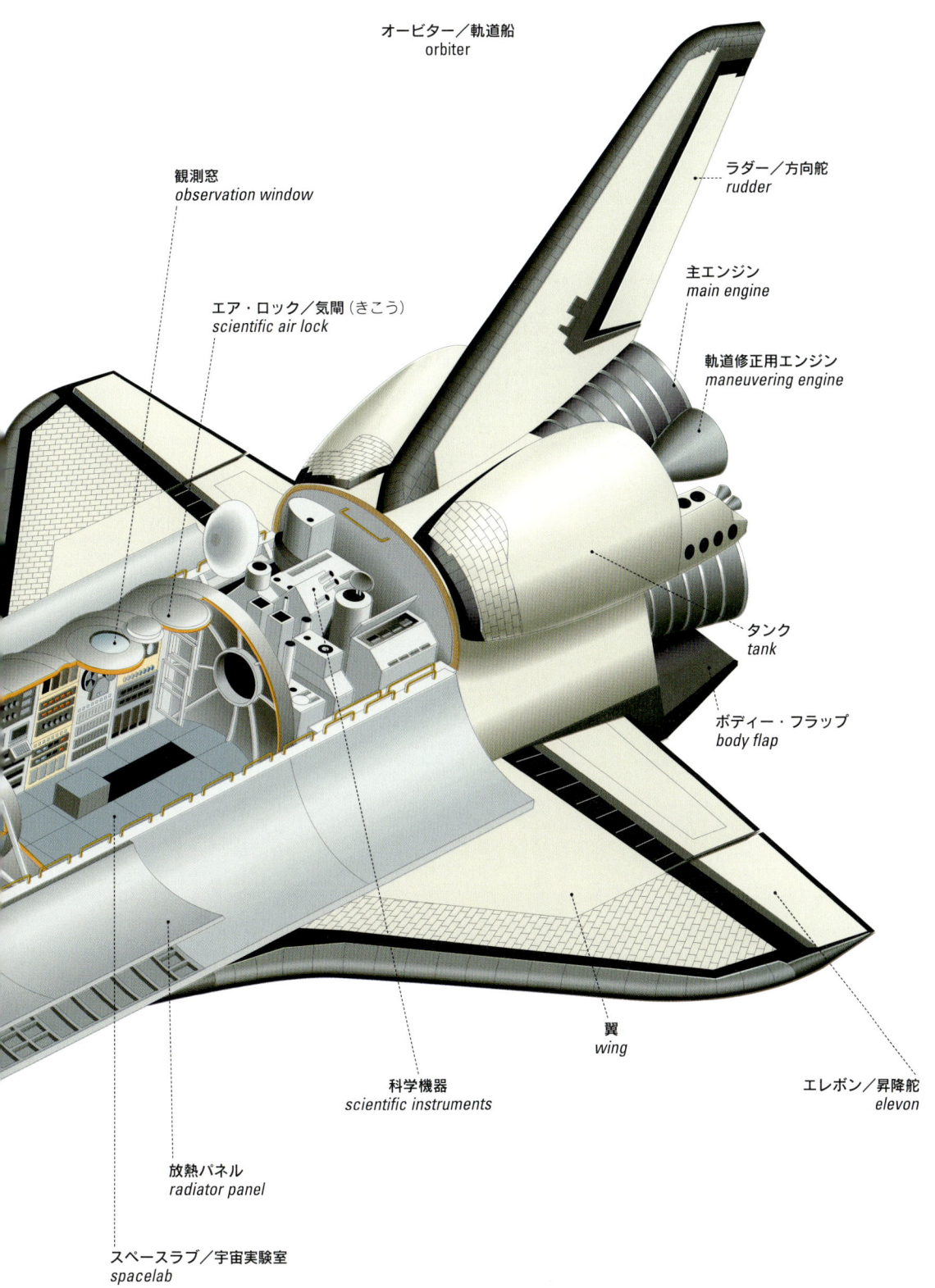

宇宙探査 | SPACE EXPLORATION

打ち上げロケット
SPACE LAUNCHER

天文学

打ち上げロケットの断面図（アリアン5）
cross section of a space launcher (Ariane V)

打ち上げロケットの例
examples of space launchers

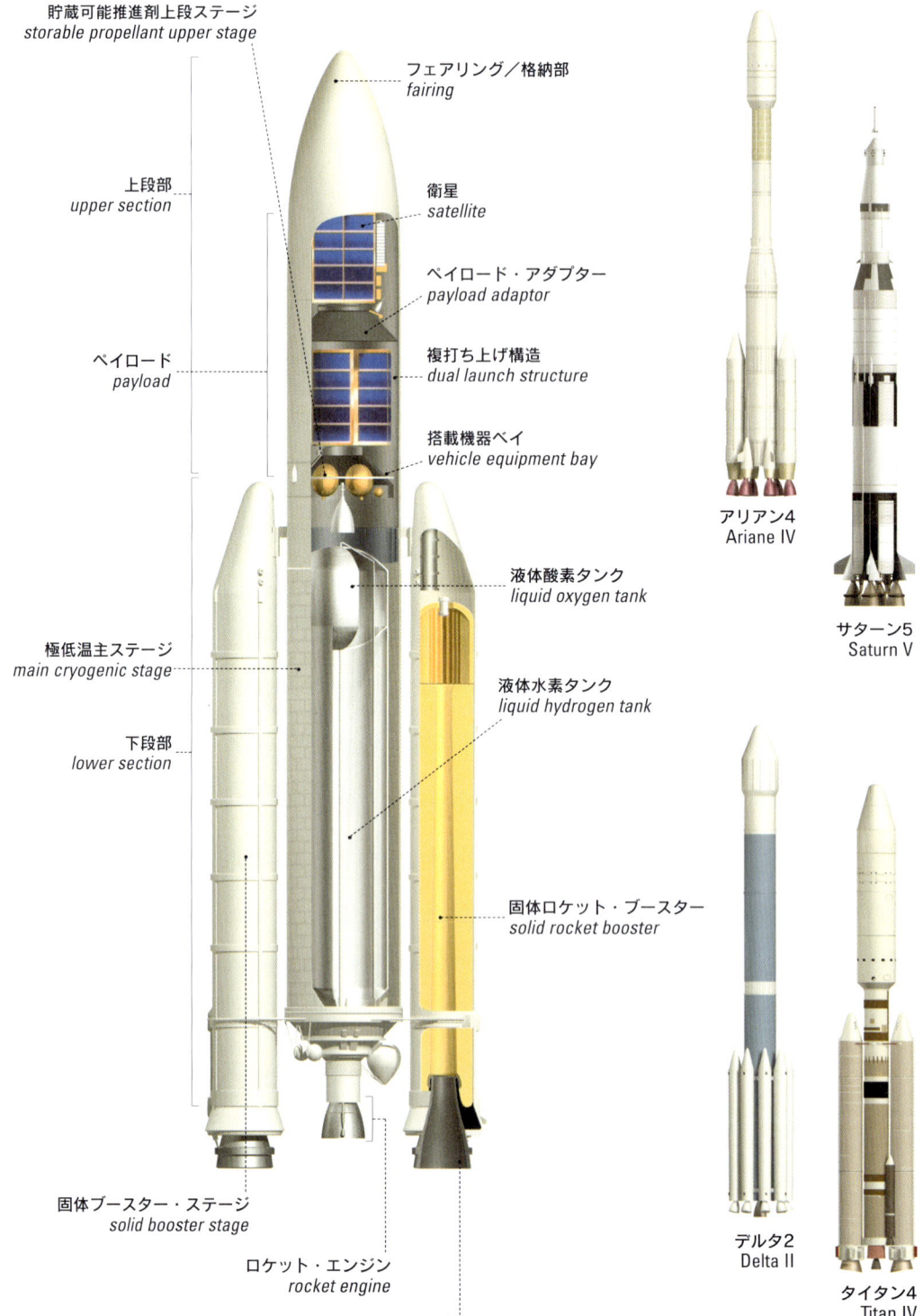

- 貯蔵可能推進剤上段ステージ / storable propellant upper stage
- 上段部 / upper section
- ペイロード / payload
- 極低温主ステージ / main cryogenic stage
- 下段部 / lower section
- 固体ブースター・ステージ / solid booster stage
- ロケット・エンジン / rocket engine
- ノズル / nozzle
- フェアリング／格納部 / fairing
- 衛星 / satellite
- ペイロード・アダプター / payload adaptor
- 複打ち上げ構造 / dual launch structure
- 搭載機器ベイ / vehicle equipment bay
- 液体酸素タンク / liquid oxygen tank
- 液体水素タンク / liquid hydrogen tank
- 固体ロケット・ブースター / solid rocket booster

アリアン4 / Ariane IV

サターン5 / Saturn V

デルタ2 / Delta II

タイタン4 / Titan IV

宇宙探査 | SPACE EXPLORATION

宇宙服／与圧服
SPACESUIT

天文学

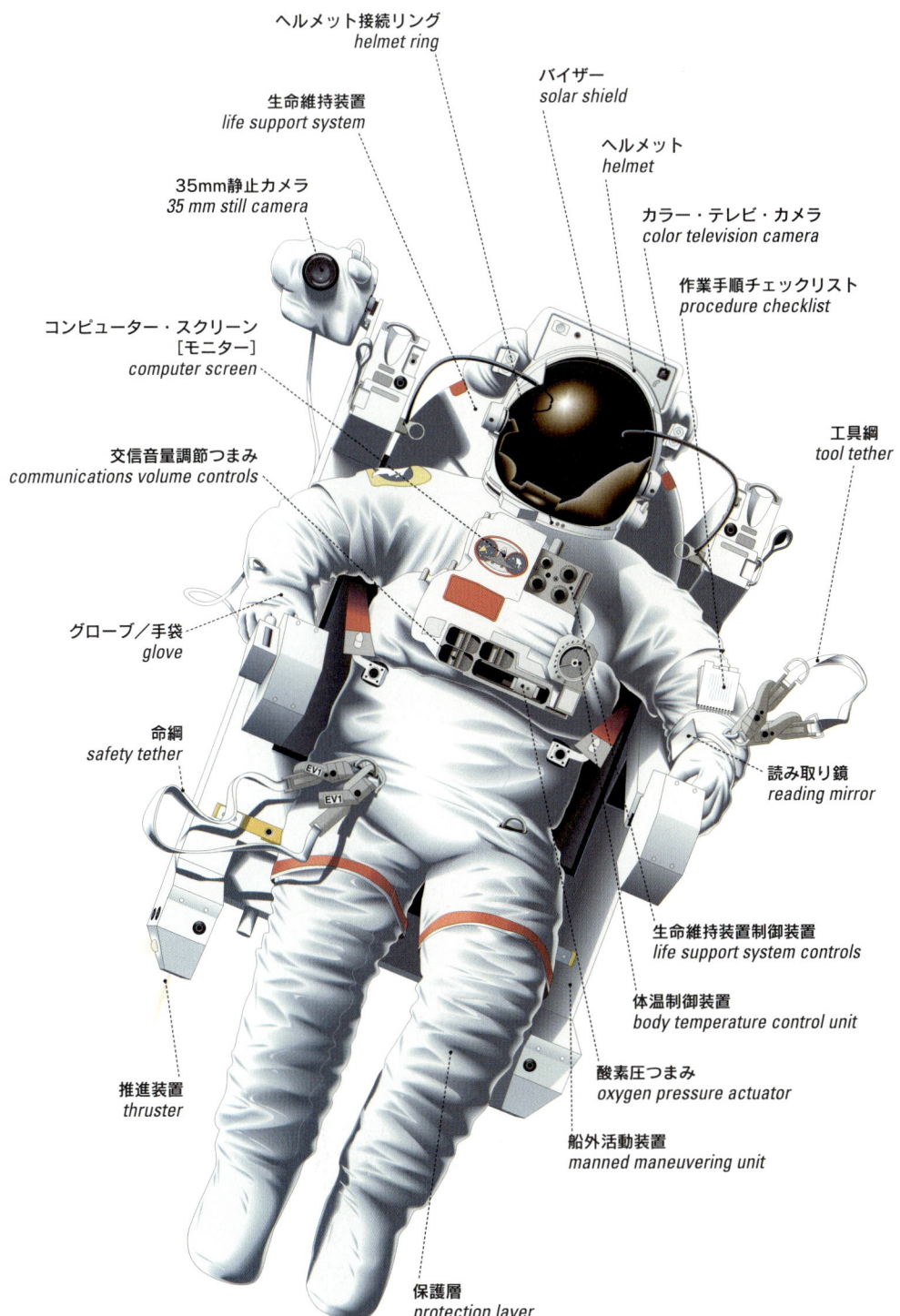

- ヘルメット接続リング / helmet ring
- バイザー / solar shield
- 生命維持装置 / life support system
- ヘルメット / helmet
- 35mm静止カメラ / 35 mm still camera
- カラー・テレビ・カメラ / color television camera
- 作業手順チェックリスト / procedure checklist
- コンピューター・スクリーン［モニター］/ computer screen
- 工具綱 / tool tether
- 交信音量調節つまみ / communications volume controls
- グローブ／手袋 / glove
- 読み取り鏡 / reading mirror
- 命綱 / safety tether
- 生命維持装置制御装置 / life support system controls
- 体温制御装置 / body temperature control unit
- 推進装置 / thruster
- 酸素圧つまみ / oxygen pressure actuator
- 船外活動装置 / manned maneuvering unit
- 保護層 / protection layer

17

大陸の配置 | CONFIGURATION OF THE CONTINENTS

私たちの世界は水で囲まれた7つの大陸から成り立っています。ユーラシア大陸は、ヨーロッパとアジアが結び付いて造られた大陸です。この二つの地域は水で分けられてはいませんが、歴史的な理由から明らかに二つの大陸とみなすことができます。7つの大陸を合わせると、地球の表面の約3分の1を覆うことになります。南極大陸を除けば、すべての大陸に人が住んでいます。

平面投射図／球体平面図
PLANISPHERE

大陸の配置 | CONFIGURATION OF THE CONTINENTS

19

地図作成法 | CARTOGRAPHY

地球の表面を描くために地図作製者は地図を描き、ある地域のさまざまな特長をその上に忠実に移し替えます。地図を製作するためには、まずは長期にわたって調査し、情報をコード化し、ありのままに表現するために、２次元や３次元の投影法を選ばなければなりません。

地理学

地球座標とグリッド法
EARTH'S COORDINATES AND GRID SYSTEMS

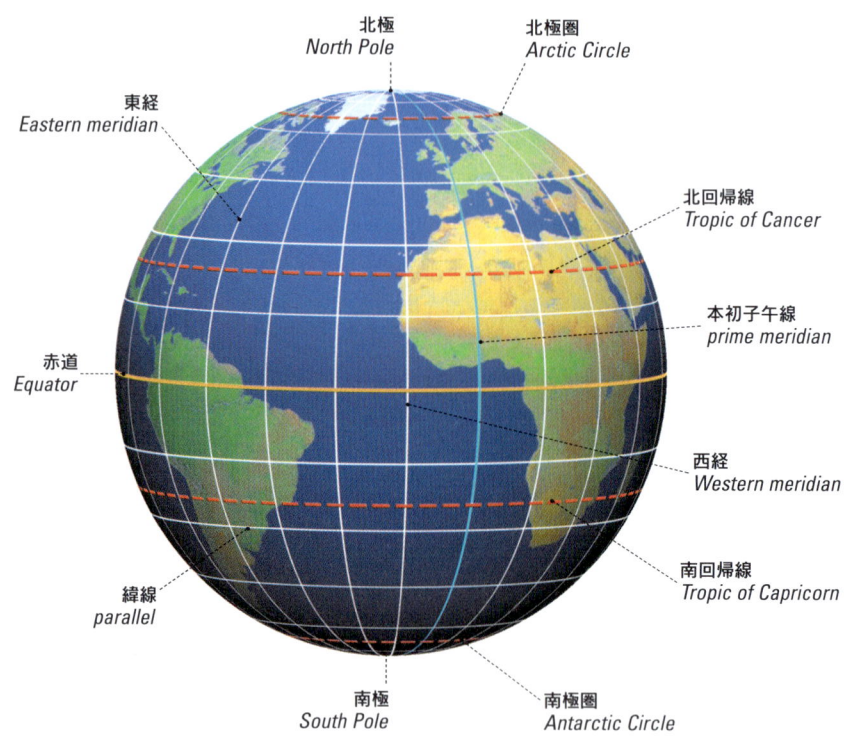

地図作成法 | CARTOGRAPHY

地図投影法
MAP PROJECTIONS

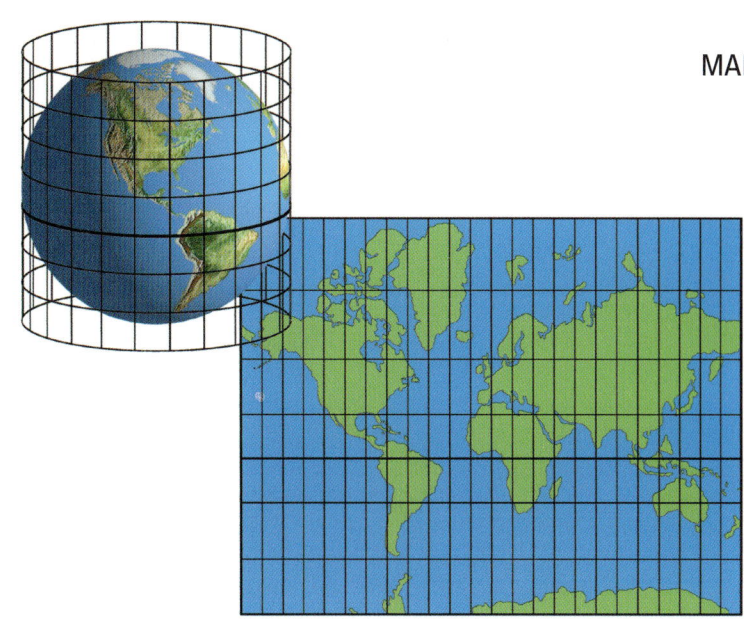

円筒図法
cylindrical projection

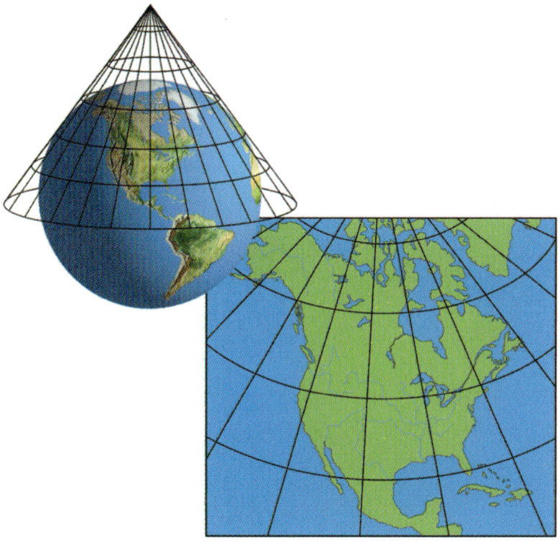

円錐図法
conic projection

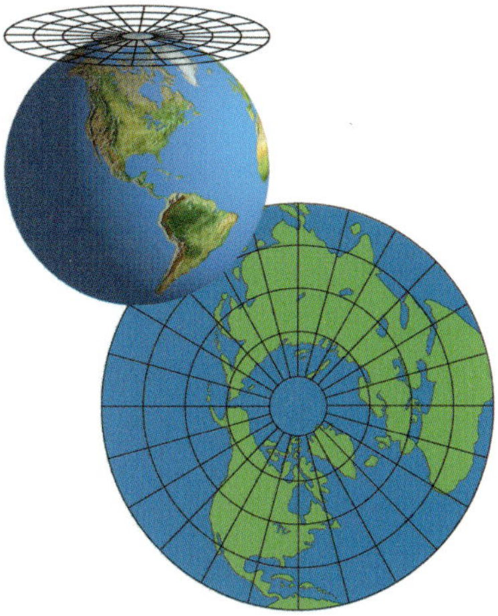

平面図法
plane projection

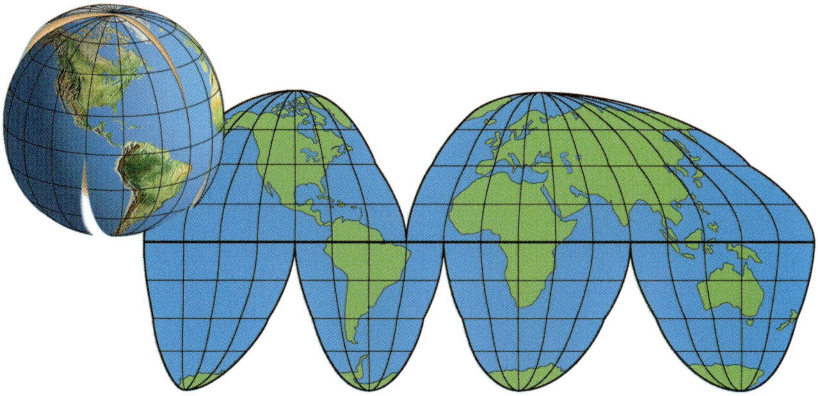

断裂ホモロサイン図法
interrupted projection

地図 MAPS

地勢図
physical map

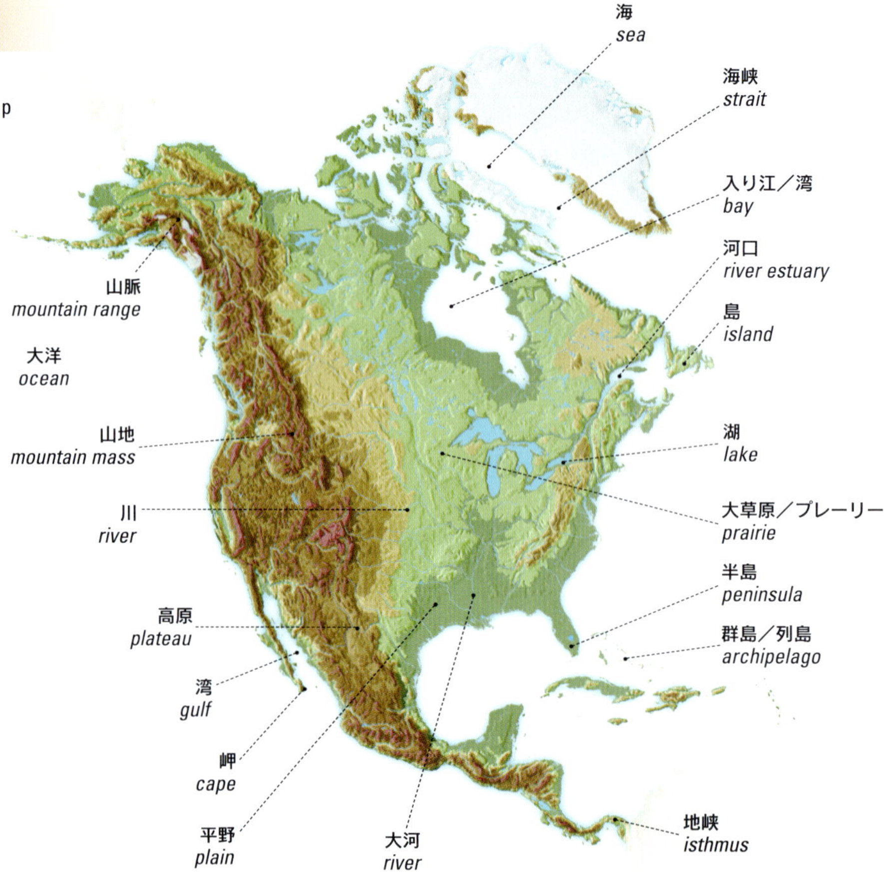
海
sea
海峡
strait
入り江／湾
bay
河口
river estuary
島
island
湖
lake
大草原／プレーリー
prairie
半島
peninsula
群島／列島
archipelago
地峡
isthmus
山脈
mountain range
大洋
ocean
山地
mountain mass
川
river
高原
plateau
湾
gulf
岬
cape
平野
plain
大河
river

行政区画図
political map

州
province
州界
internal boundary
国境
international boundary
都市
city
首都
capital
国
country
州
state
CANADA
UNITED STATES
MEXICO
Edmonton
Calgary
Vancouver
Winnipeg
Seattle
Montréal
Ottawa
Toronto
Detroit
New York
Washington
Chicago
San Francisco
Denver
Los Angeles
San Diego
Atlanta
Dallas
Houston
Miami
Monterrey
Guadalajara
Ciudad de México

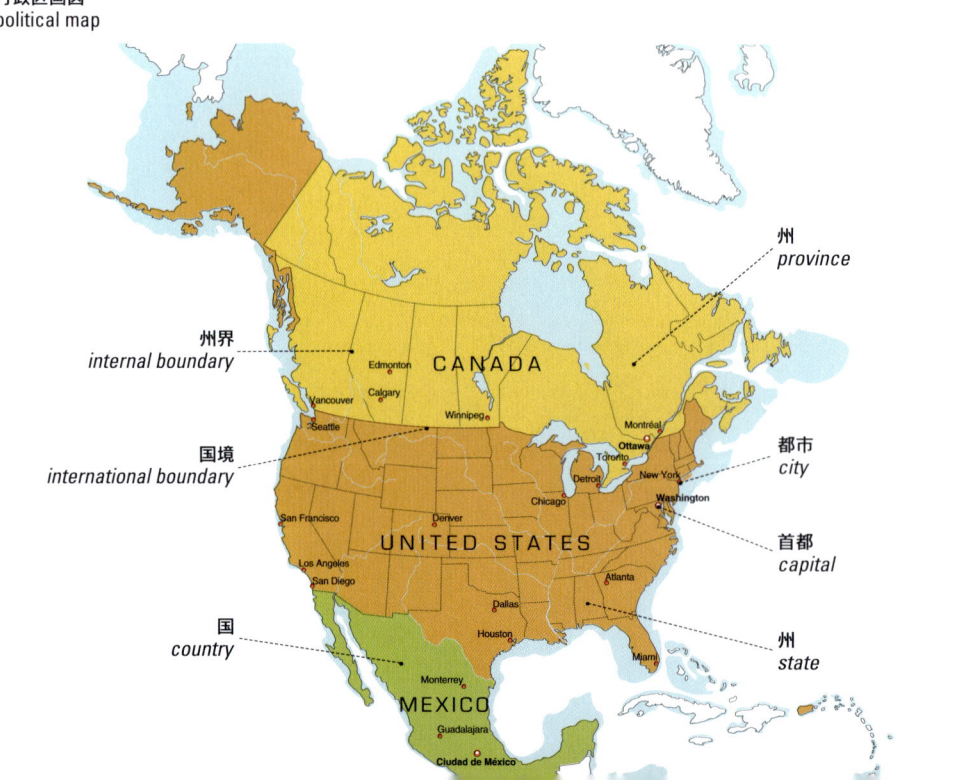

地図作成法 | CARTOGRAPHY

道路地図
road map

幹線道路番号
highway number

幹線道路
highway

レスト・エリア
rest area

サービス・エリア
service area

環状道路
belt highway

二級道路
secondary road

名所
point of interest

道路
road

道路番号
road number

空港
airport

国立公園
national park

景観道路
scenic route

羅牌（らはい）／コンパス・カード
COMPASS CARD

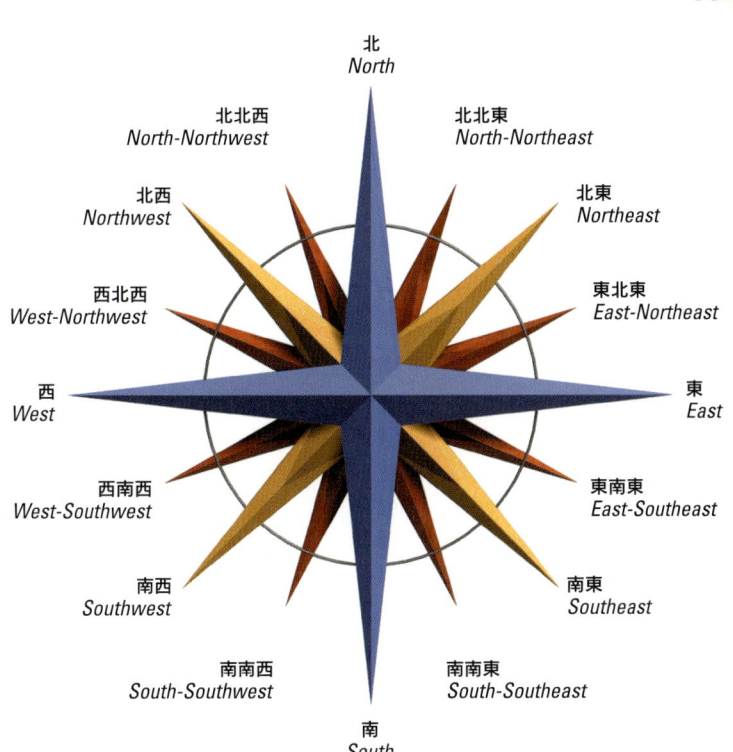

北
North

北北西
North-Northwest

北北東
North-Northeast

北西
Northwest

北東
Northeast

西北西
West-Northwest

東北東
East-Northeast

西
West

東
East

西南西
West-Southwest

東南東
East-Southeast

南西
Southwest

南東
Southeast

南南西
South-Southwest

南南東
South-Southeast

南
South

地球の構造 | STRUCTURE OF THE EARTH

地球の内部を調査するのが不可能だとしても、地表を揺らす地震波の伝わり方を研究することで、地質学者は内部構造を決定することができました。通過する岩や物質によって振動の伝わり方が異なるので、地球は地殻、マントル、核の3つの主な層から成り立っていると推論することができたのです。

地質学

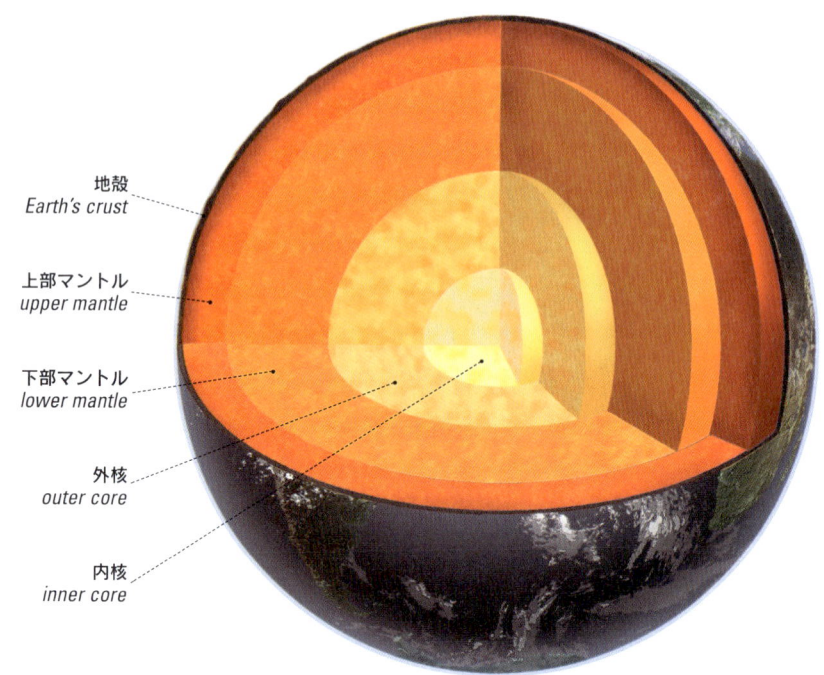

地殻 / Earth's crust
上部マントル / upper mantle
下部マントル / lower mantle
外核 / outer core
内核 / inner core

地殻断面図 / section of the Earth's crust

貫入岩 / intrusive rocks
火山 / volcano
深海底 / deep-sea floor
山脈 / mountain range
海面 / sea level
玄武岩層 / basaltic layer
堆積岩 / sedimentary rocks
変成岩 / metamorphic rocks
花崗岩（かこうがん）層 / granitic layer
火成岩 / igneous rocks

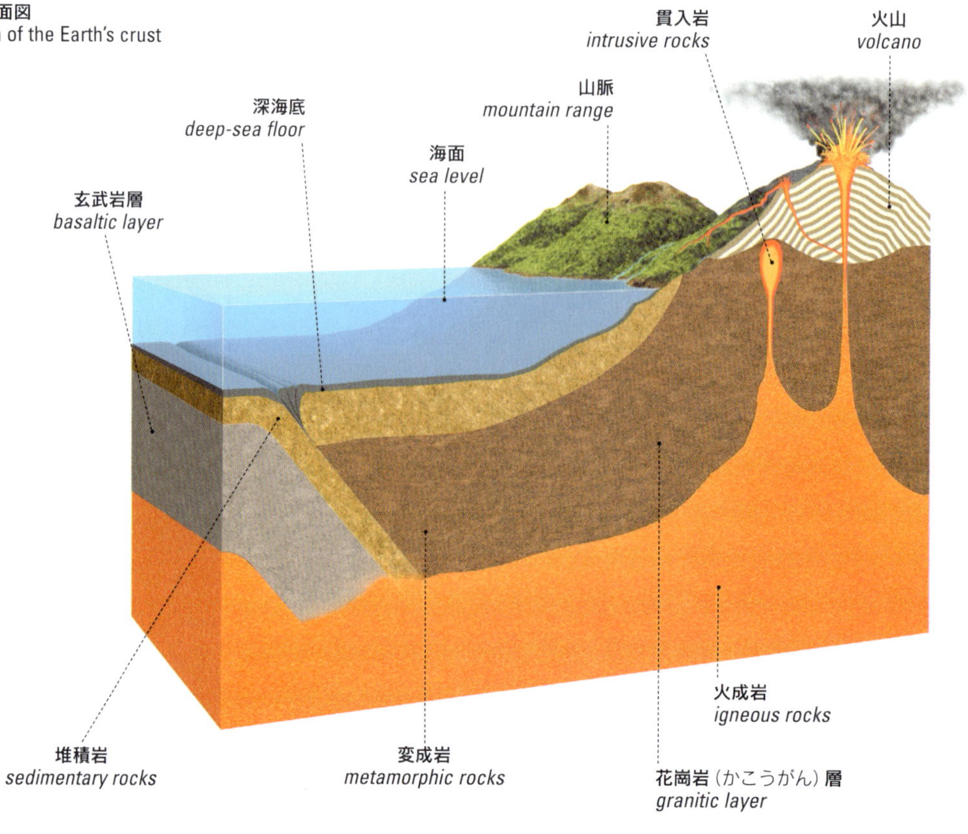

岩石と鉱石 | ROCKS AND MINERALS

地殻はさまざまな原石からできており、どの石も実際には鉱石の寄せ集めです。例えば花崗岩は、石英のような鉱石がたくさん混じった硬い石です。とりわけ色と硬度が異なる鉱石が約3,500存在しています。金やダイヤモンドのような鉱石の多くが、価値が高いために、探し求められています。

地質学

鉱石 minerals

水晶／石英 quartz
銀 silver
金 gold
ダイヤモンド diamond

黒鉛／石墨 graphite
雲母（うんも） mica
孔雀石（くじゃくいし）／マラカイト malachite

岩石 rocks

岩塩 rock salt
砂岩 sandstone
白亜 chalk

石炭 coal
石灰岩 limestone
大理石 marble

粘板岩（ねんばんがん） slate
玄武岩 basalt
花崗岩（かこうがん） granite

地質学的現象 | GEOLOGICAL PHENOMENA

火山と地震は、地球が活動していることを示す、目を見張るべき地質学的な現象と言うことができます。ジグソー・パズルのように地殻は１２のプレートに分かれています。ふつう地震は活動しているプレートがぶつかり合う場所で起こります。プレートの境界線には激しい噴火を引き起こすかもしれない火山が数多く存在しています。

地震 / EARTHQUAKE

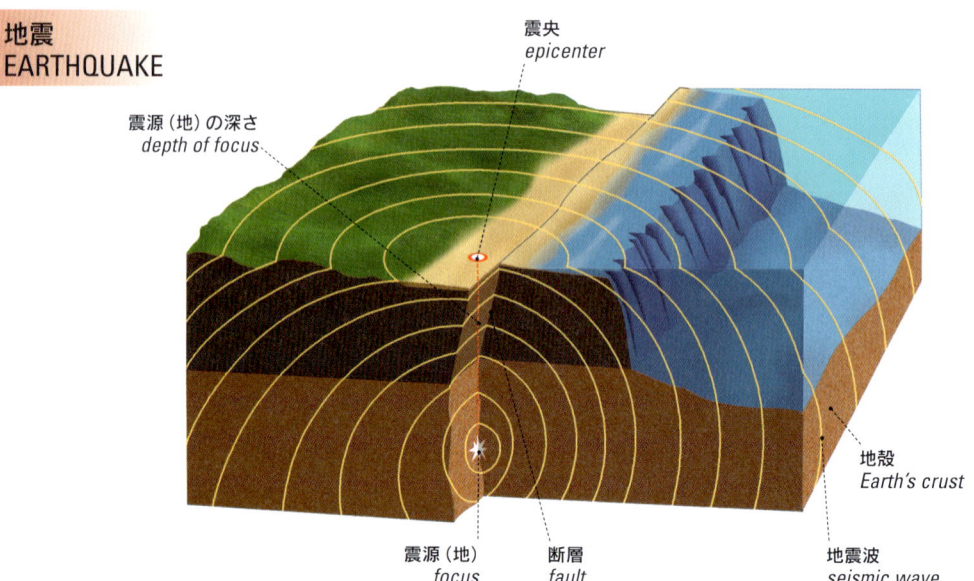

- 震央 / epicenter
- 震源（地）の深さ / depth of focus
- 震源（地） / focus
- 断層 / fault
- 地殻 / Earth's crust
- 地震波 / seismic wave

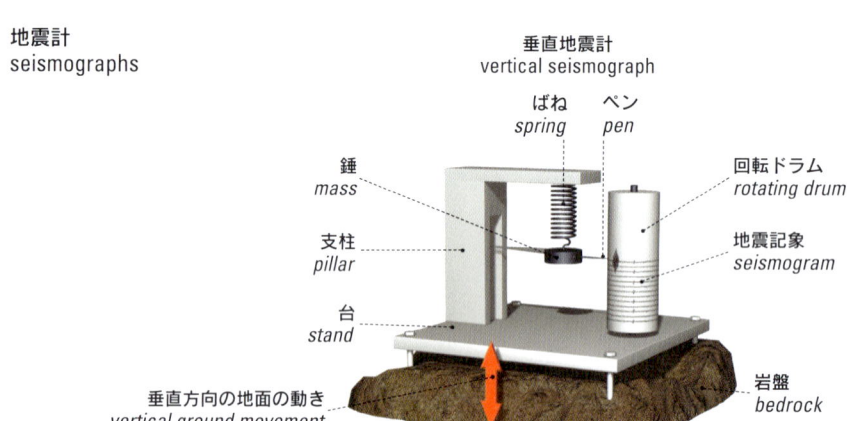

地震計 / seismographs

- 垂直地震計 / vertical seismograph
- ばね / spring
- ペン / pen
- 錘 / mass
- 回転ドラム / rotating drum
- 支柱 / pillar
- 地震記象 / seismogram
- 台 / stand
- 岩盤 / bedrock
- 垂直方向の地面の動き / vertical ground movement

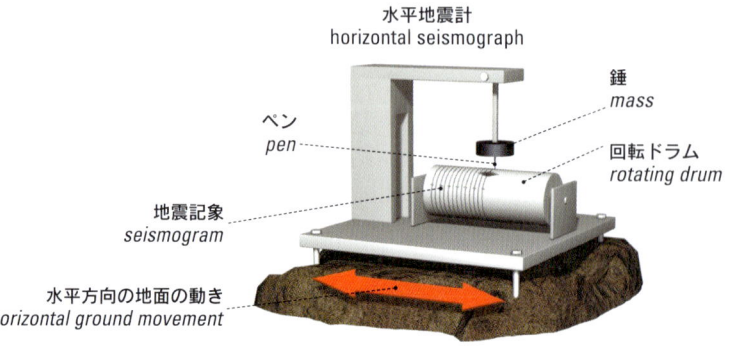

- 水平地震計 / horizontal seismograph
- 錘 / mass
- ペン / pen
- 回転ドラム / rotating drum
- 地震記象 / seismogram
- 水平方向の地面の動き / horizontal ground movement

地質学的現象 | GEOLOGICAL PHENOMENA

火山
VOLCANO

噴火中の火山
volcano during eruption

円錐火山／コニーデ
cone

間欠泉
geyser

噴気
fumarole

火口
crater

火山灰の雲
cloud of volcanic ash

火山弾
volcanic bomb

溶岩層
lava layer

主火道
main vent

副火道
side vent

溶岩流
lava flow

火山灰層
ash layer

餅盤（べいばん）／ラコリス
laccolith

マグマ溜り
magma chamber

岩脈
dike

マグマ／岩漿（がんしょう）
magma

貫入岩床
sill

地質学

火山のタイプ
types of volcanoes

爆発性の火山
explosive volcano

噴火性の火山
effusive volcano

27

地球の地形 | EARTH'S FEATURES

地球が誕生して以来、形成される大洋もあれば、消滅する大洋もありました。山脈は平らになるために地表まで隆起します。一見して私たちの周りの景観に変化は見られないようですが、実際は絶えず変化しているのです。その変化は時として地震のように急激であり、時として国の海岸線を少しずつ変える海水のように緩慢です。

山
MOUNTAIN

地質学

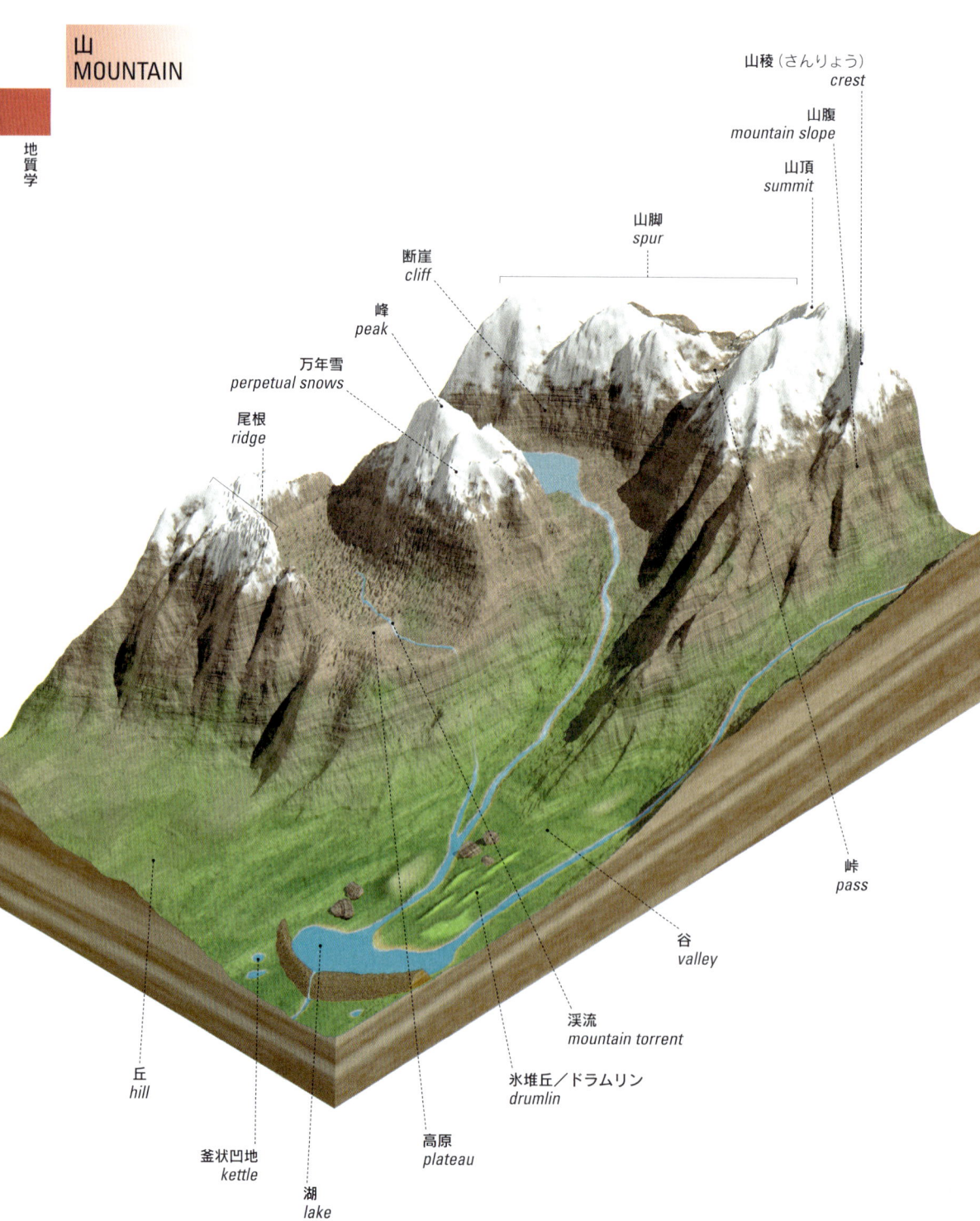

山稜（さんりょう） *crest*
山腹 *mountain slope*
山頂 *summit*
山脚 *spur*
断崖 *cliff*
峰 *peak*
万年雪 *perpetual snows*
尾根 *ridge*
峠 *pass*
谷 *valley*
渓流 *mountain torrent*
氷堆丘／ドラムリン *drumlin*
高原 *plateau*
丘 *hill*
釜状凹地 *kettle*
湖 *lake*

地球の地形 | EARTH'S FEATURES

氷河 / GLACIER

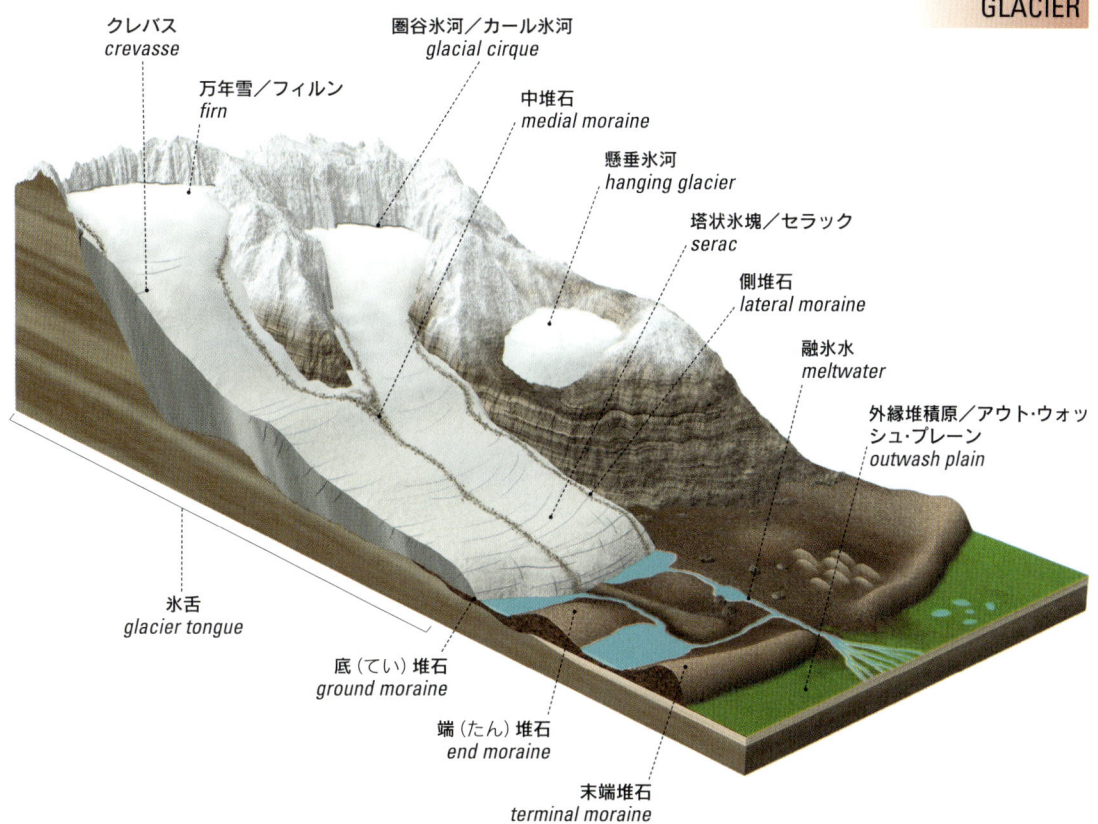

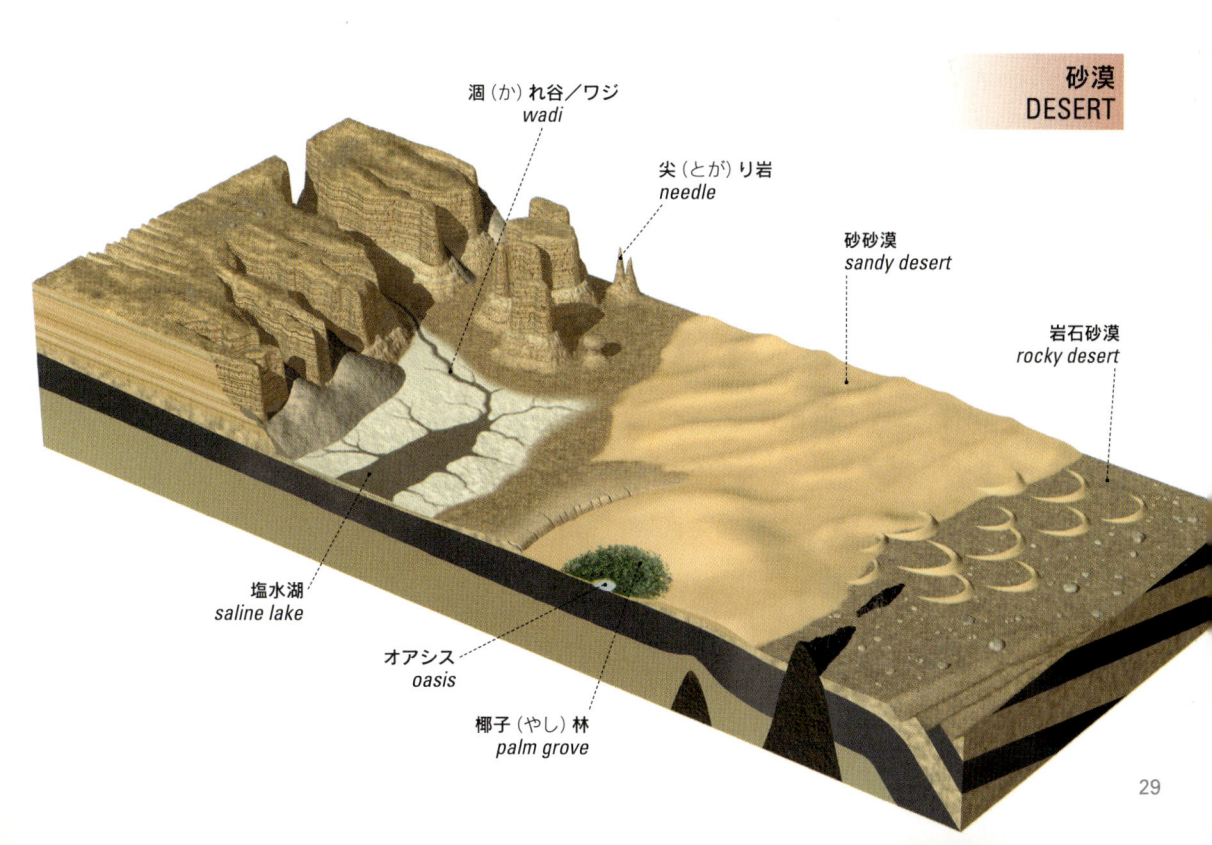

- クレバス / crevasse
- 万年雪／フィルン / firn
- 圏谷氷河／カール氷河 / glacial cirque
- 中堆石 / medial moraine
- 懸垂氷河 / hanging glacier
- 塔状氷塊／セラック / serac
- 側堆石 / lateral moraine
- 融氷水 / meltwater
- 外縁堆積原／アウト・ウォッシュ・プレーン / outwash plain
- 氷舌 / glacier tongue
- 底（てい）堆石 / ground moraine
- 端（たん）堆石 / end moraine
- 末端堆石 / terminal moraine

地質学

砂漠 / DESERT

- 涸（か）れ谷／ワジ / wadi
- 尖（とが）り岩 / needle
- 砂砂漠 / sandy desert
- 岩石砂漠 / rocky desert
- 塩水湖 / saline lake
- オアシス / oasis
- 椰子（やし）林 / palm grove

29

地球の地形 | EARTH'S FEATURES

水流
WATERCOURSE

洞穴
CAVE

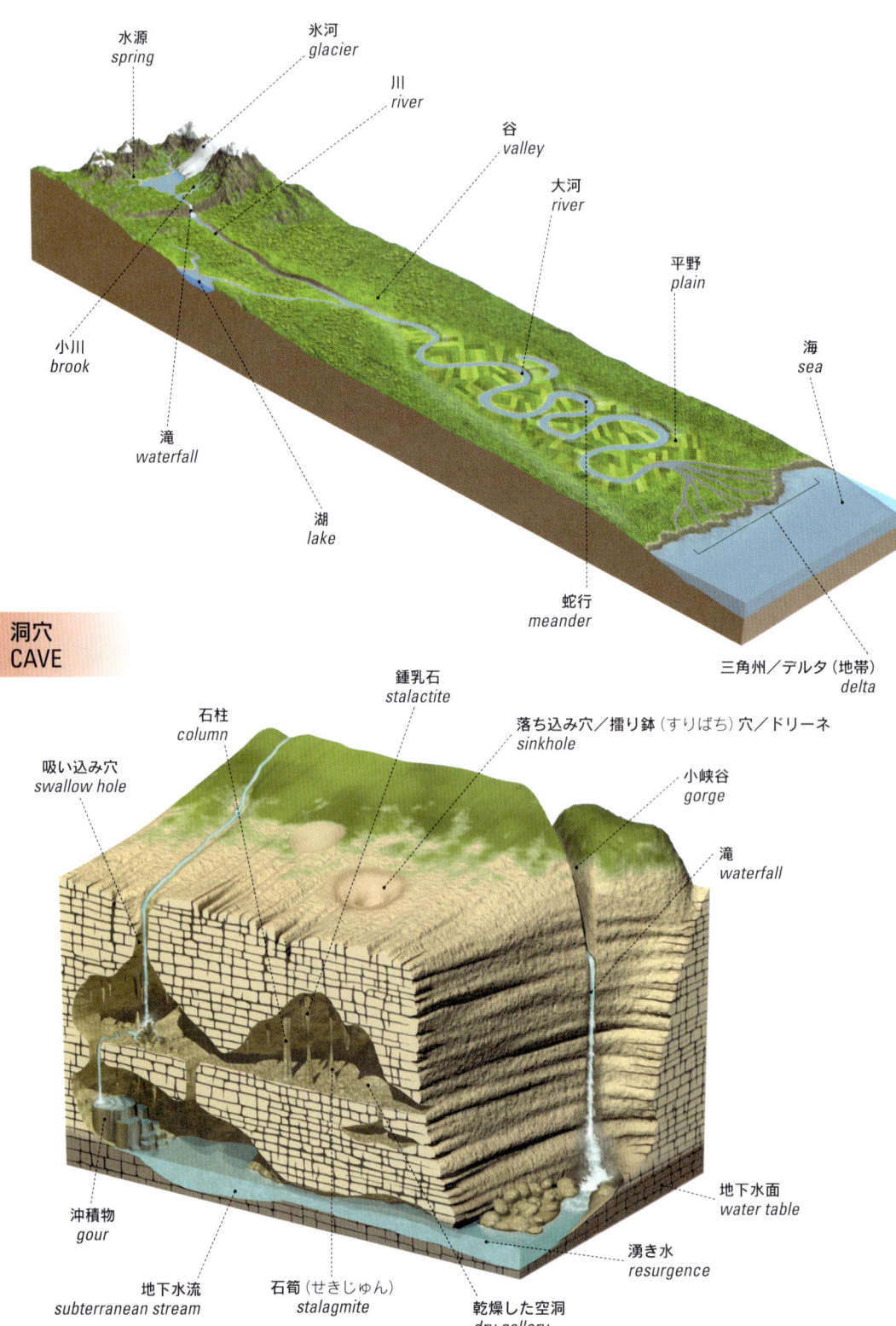

地球の地形 | EARTH'S FEATURES

海岸の地形
COMMON COASTAL FEATURES

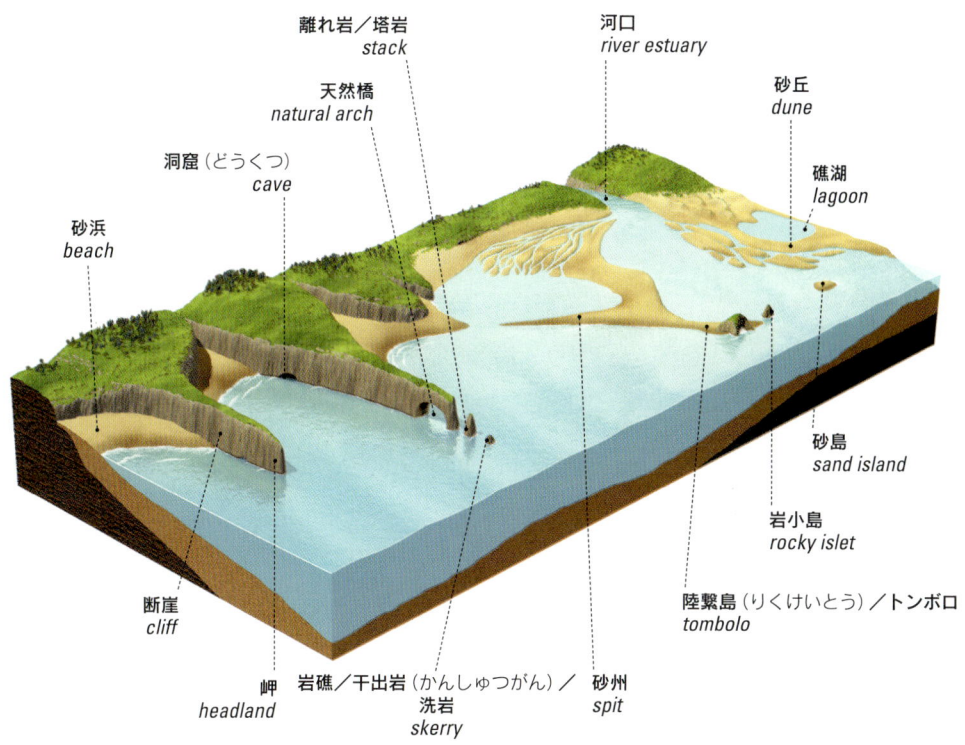

地質学

海岸線の例
examples of shorelines

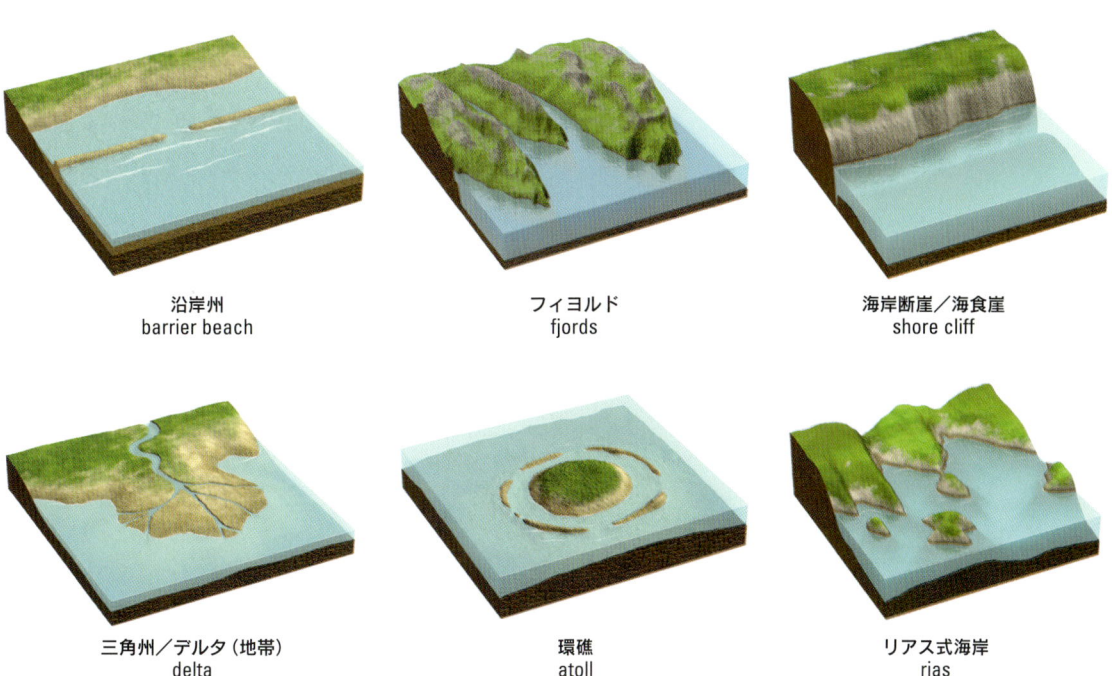

大気圏 | ATMOSPHERE

大気圏とは地球を取り巻く気体の層で、それぞれ地球上の生命を守る役割を担って、連続したいくつかの層から成り立っています。例えば、地球に最も近い対流圏と呼ばれる層は人間が呼吸する空気を含み、風や竜巻といったさまざまな気象学的な現象が起きるのもこの層です。

大気圏の構造
PROFILE OF THE EARTH'S ATMOSPHERE

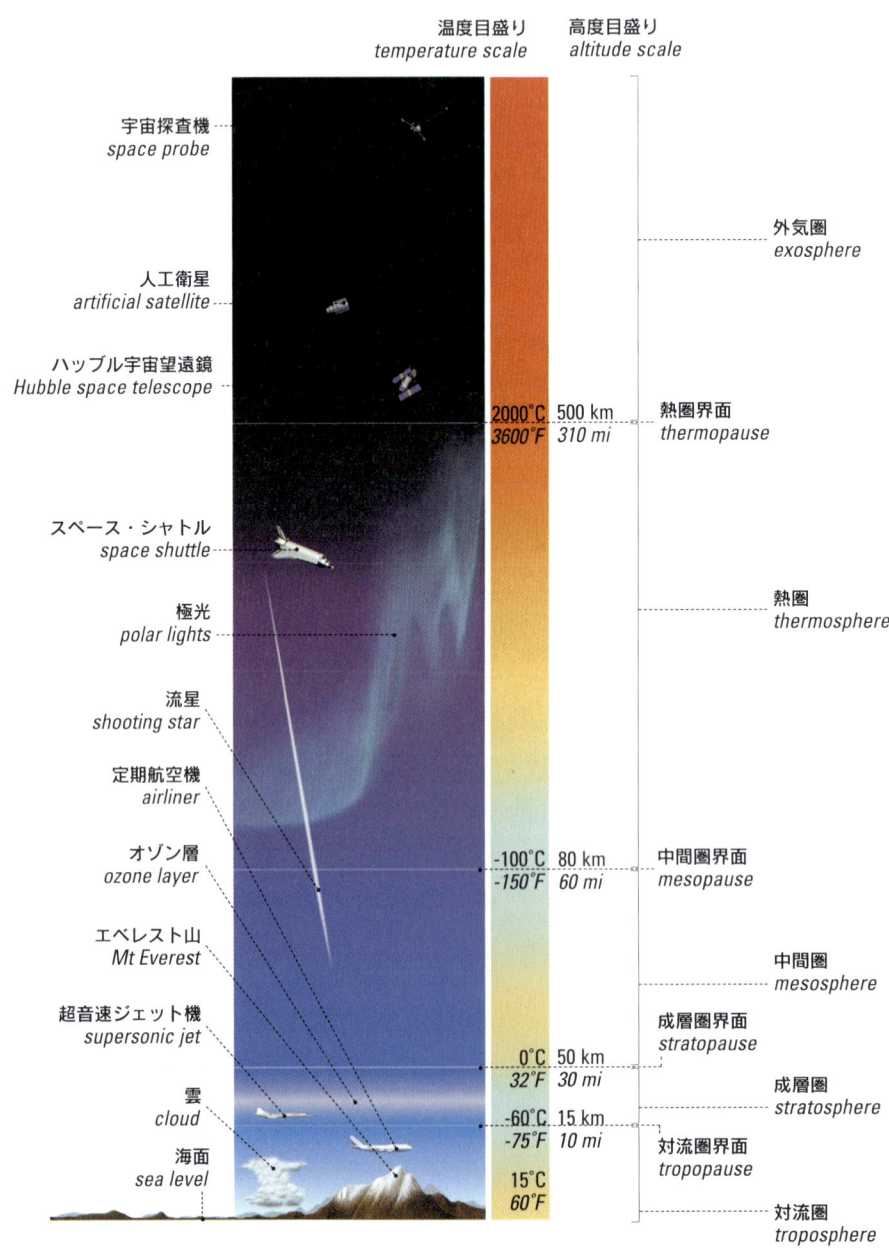

気候 | CLIMATE

気候とは、ある地域に特有の気象学的な状況を集めたものです。地球上の各地域で受け取る太陽エネルギーの量が、その地域の気候を大きく変えます。さらに言えば、地球が少し傾いて太陽の周りを回っているため、北半球や南半球は1年を通して温められたり冷やされたりします。この現象がそれぞれの半球で異なる季節を作り出しているわけです。

季節の移り変わり［循環］
SEASONS OF THE YEAR

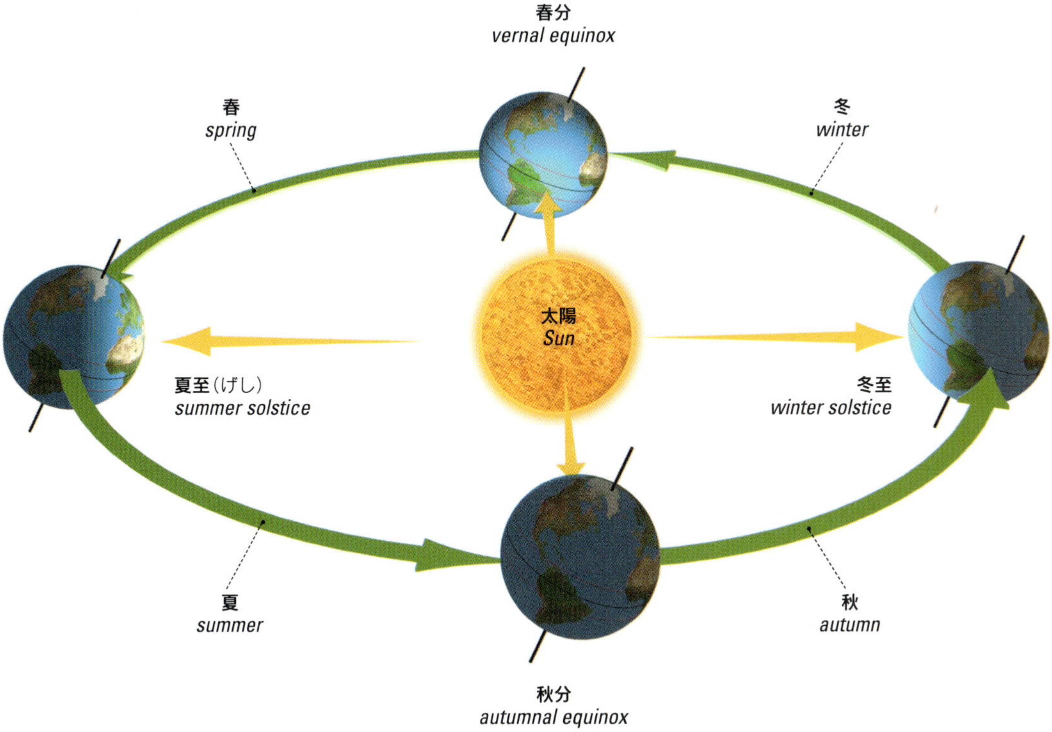

春分 vernal equinox
春 spring
冬 winter
太陽 Sun
夏至（げし） summer solstice
冬至 winter solstice
夏 summer
秋 autumn
秋分 autumnal equinox

亜寒帯気候における季節
seasons in the cold temperate climates

春 spring　夏 summer　秋 autumn　冬 winter

33

気候 | CLIMATE

世界の気候
CLIMATES OF THE WORLD

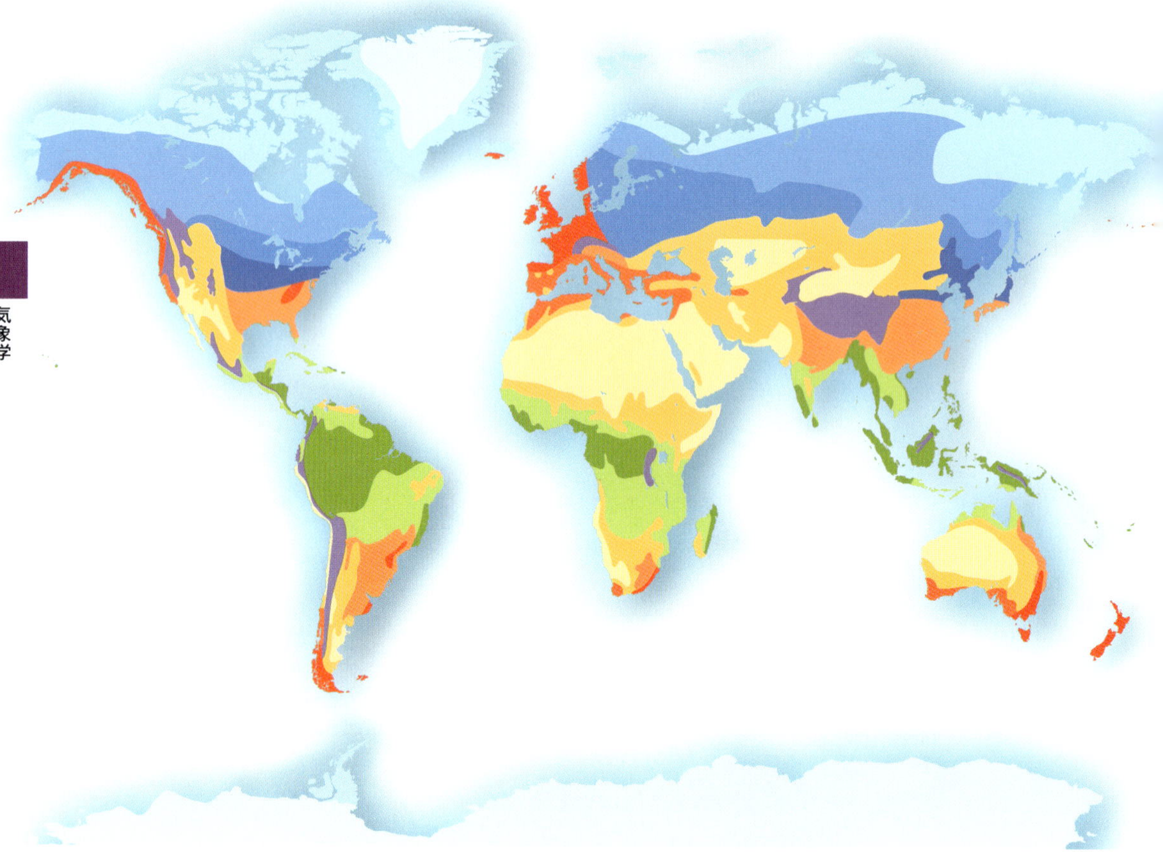

亜寒帯気候／冷帯気候
cold temperate climates

- 湿潤大陸性気候（夏季高温）
  humid continental — hot summer
- 湿潤大陸性気候（夏季温暖）
  humid continental — warm summer
- 亜北極気候
  subarctic

熱帯気候
tropical climates

- 熱帯雨林気候
  tropical rain forest
- 熱帯サバンナ気候
  tropical wet-and-dry (savanna)

乾燥気候
dry climates

- ステップ［草原］気候
  steppe
- 砂漠気候
  desert

亜熱帯気候／温帯気候
warm temperate climates

- 亜熱帯多雨気候
  humid subtropical
- 地中海性亜熱帯気候
  Mediterranean subtropical
- 海洋性気候
  marine

寒帯気候／極気候
polar climates

- ツンドラ気候
  polar tundra
- 氷雪気候
  polar ice cap

高原気候
highland climates

- 高山気候
  highland

気象現象 | WEATHER PHENOMENA

雨のような液体であれ、雪のような固体であれ、降ってくると嵐になることがあります。サイクロンやトルネードのような大気の乱れは、風の強さで区別され、かなりの損害を与えることがあります。このような嵐の中で最も破壊的なものはトルネードですが、発生のメカニズムがまだ解明されていないために、残念ながら予測するのが困難です。

雲
CLOUDS

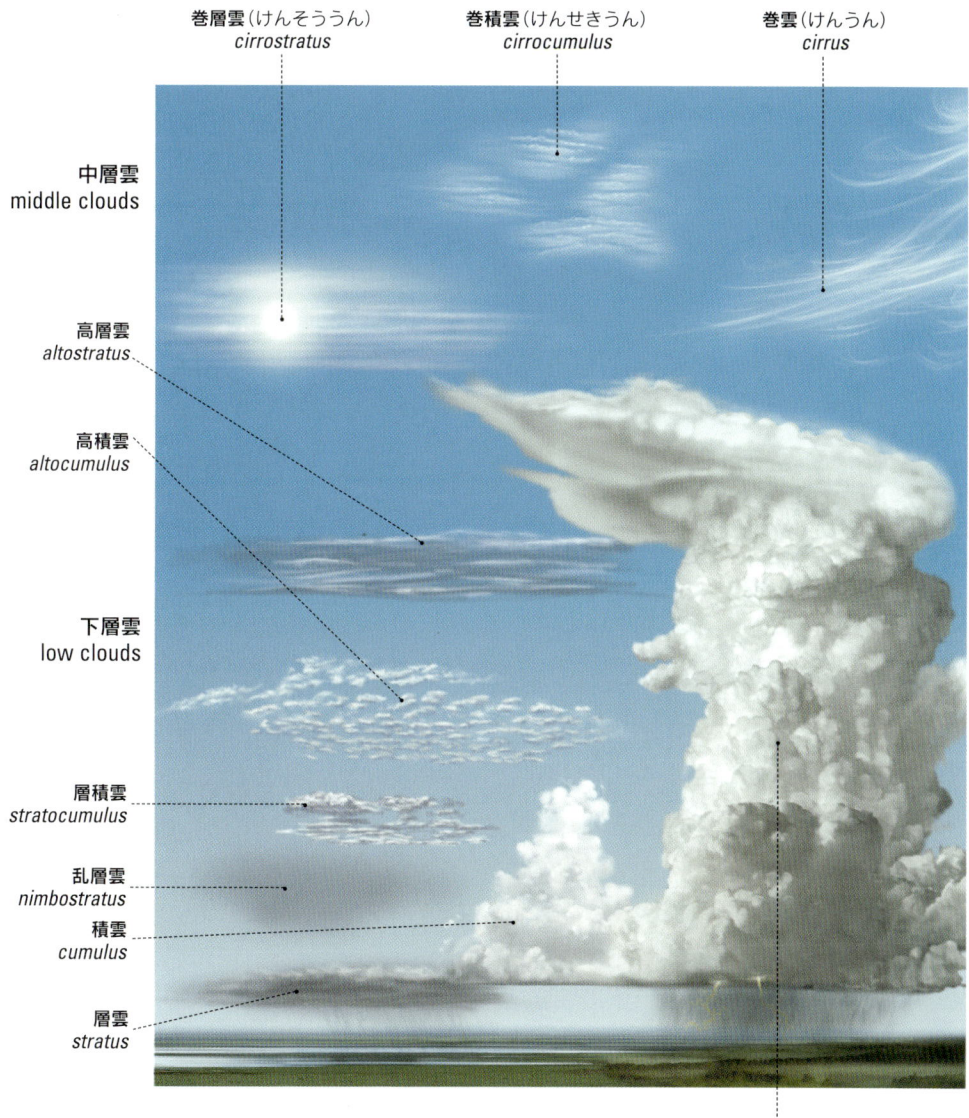

上層雲
high clouds

巻層雲（けんそううん）
cirrostratus

巻積雲（けんせきうん）
cirrocumulus

巻雲（けんうん）
cirrus

中層雲
middle clouds

高層雲
altostratus

高積雲
altocumulus

下層雲
low clouds

層積雲
stratocumulus

乱層雲
nimbostratus

積雲
cumulus

層雲
stratus

積乱雲
cumulonimbus

縦に発達する雲
clouds of vertical development

気象学

気象現象 | WEATHER PHENOMENA

降水
PRECIPITATIONS

霧雨（きりさめ）
drizzle

雨
rain

大雨
heavy rain

露
dew

氷霰（あられ）／霙（みぞれ）
sleet

雪
snow

氷晶雨／着氷性雨
freezing rain

靄（もや）
mist

霧
fog

気象学

雷雨
THUNDERSTORM

稲光／稲妻
lightning

雲
cloud

雨
rain

虹
rainbow

気象現象 | WEATHER PHENOMENA

熱帯性低気圧
TROPICAL CYCLONE

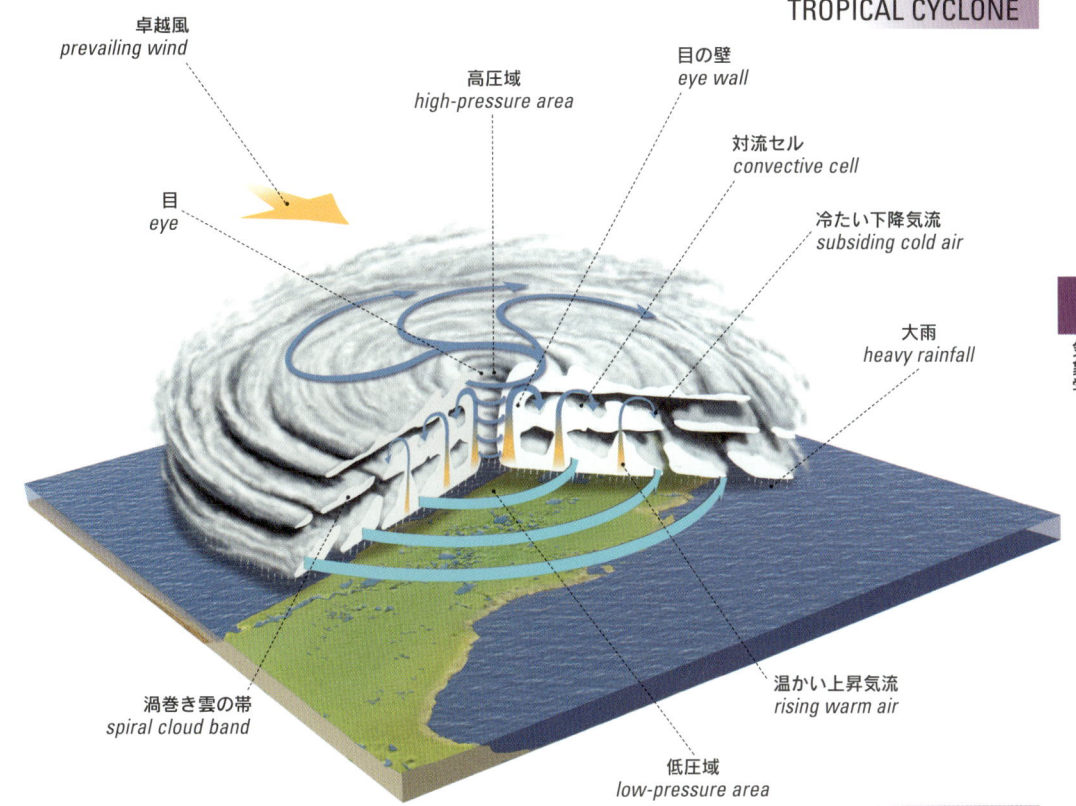

- 卓越風 / prevailing wind
- 高圧域 / high-pressure area
- 目の壁 / eye wall
- 対流セル / convective cell
- 目 / eye
- 冷たい下降気流 / subsiding cold air
- 大雨 / heavy rainfall
- 渦巻き雲の帯 / spiral cloud band
- 温かい上昇気流 / rising warm air
- 低圧域 / low-pressure area

気象学

トルネード
TORNADO

- 破片 / debris
- 漏斗雲 / funnel cloud
- 壁雲 / wall cloud

37

気象予報 | METEOROLOGICAL FORECAST

地上には約１２，０００の測候所があり、備え付けの機器を使って風速、風向、温度、雨量などを毎日測定しています。すべての測定結果は次に世界気象機構に送られます。観測から得られる情報処理サンプルのお陰で、気象学者は中・長期的な天気を予測することができるのです。

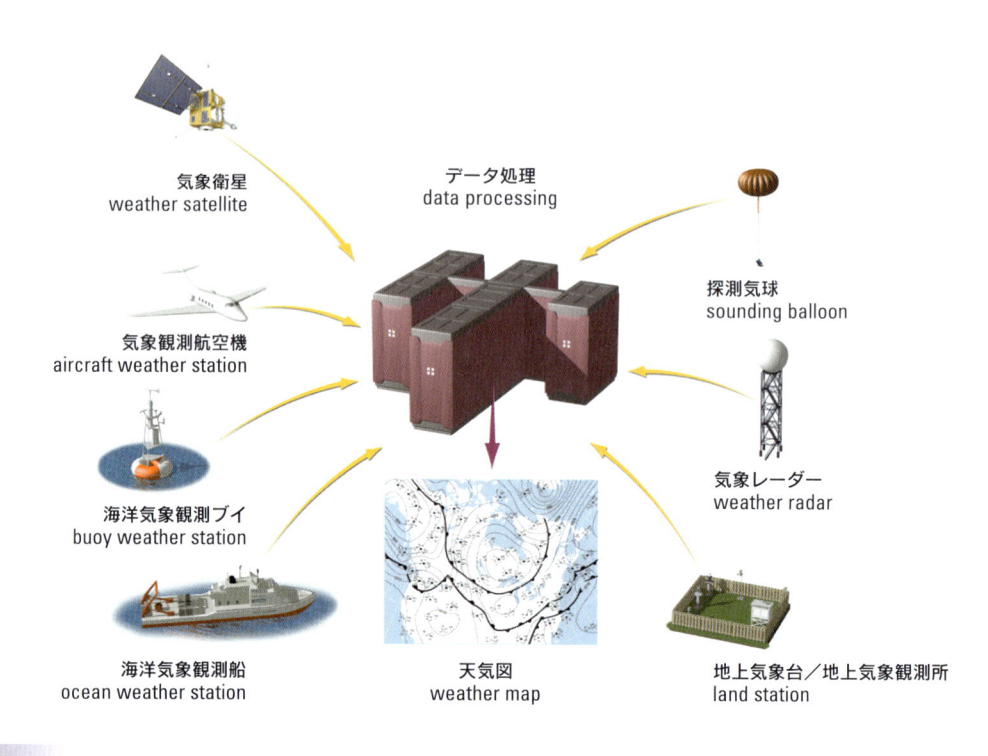

気象学

- 気象衛星 weather satellite
- データ処理 data processing
- 気象観測航空機 aircraft weather station
- 海洋気象観測ブイ buoy weather station
- 海洋気象観測船 ocean weather station
- 天気図 weather map
- 探測気球 sounding balloon
- 気象レーダー weather radar
- 地上気象台／地上気象観測所 land station

測候所 METEOROLOGICAL STATION

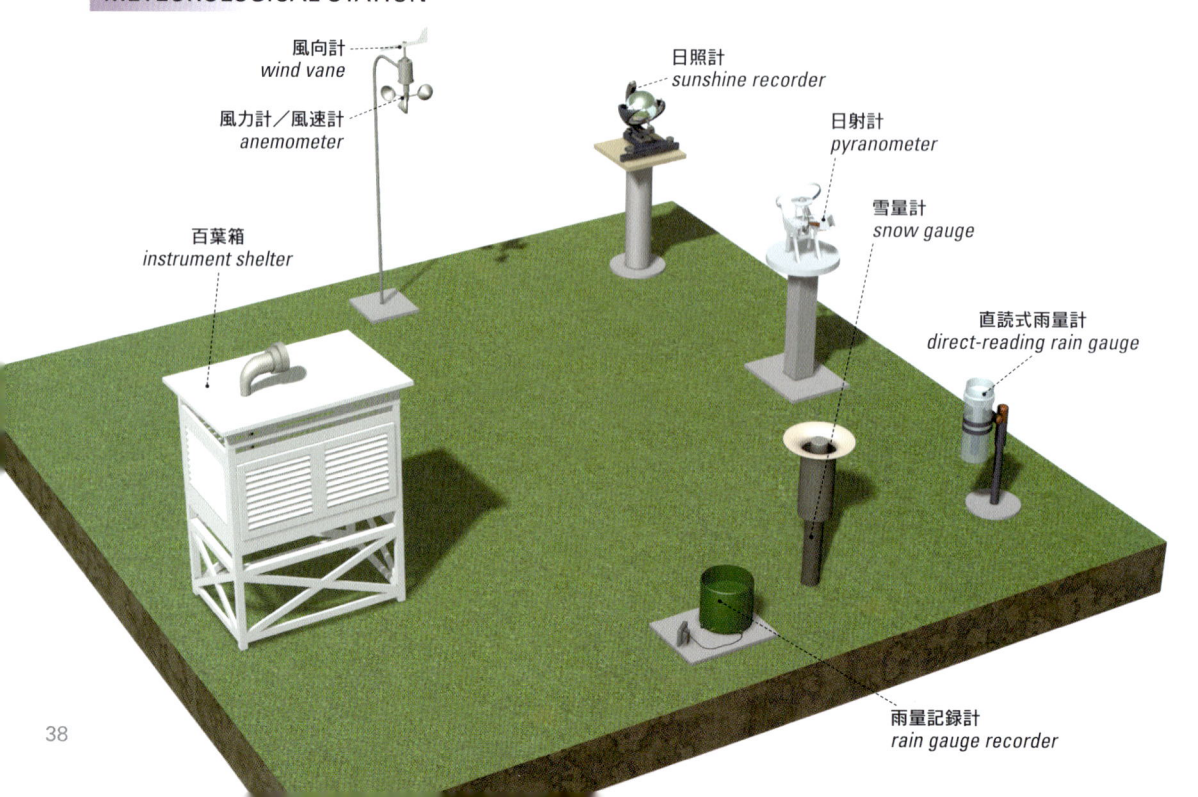

- 風向計 wind vane
- 風力計／風速計 anemometer
- 百葉箱 instrument shelter
- 日照計 sunshine recorder
- 日射計 pyranometer
- 雪量計 snow gauge
- 直読式雨量計 direct-reading rain gauge
- 雨量記録計 rain gauge recorder

気象予報 | METEOROLOGICAL FORECAST

気象測定機器
METEOROLOGICAL MEASURING INSTRUMENTS

気象学

雨量測定
measure of rainfall

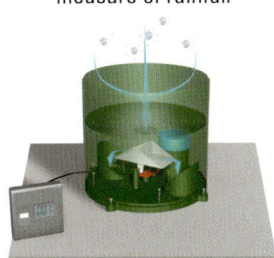

雨量記録計
rain gauge recorder

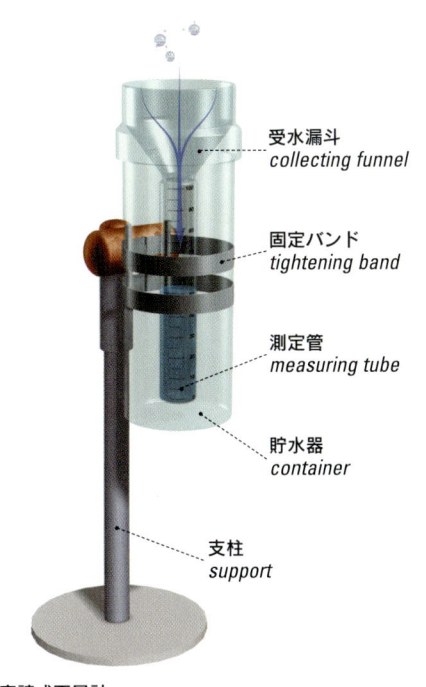

温度測定
measure of temperature

最高温度計
maximum thermometer

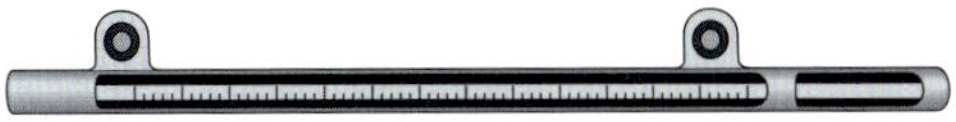

最低温度計
minimum thermometer

受水漏斗
collecting funnel

固定バンド
tightening band

測定管
measuring tube

貯水器
container

支柱
support

直読式雨量計
direct-reading rain gauge

風向測定
measure of wind direction

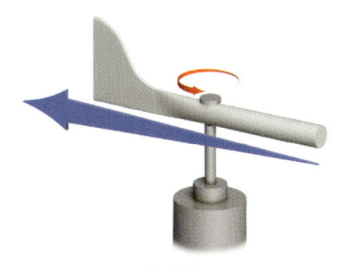

風向計
wind vane

風力測定
measure of wind strength

風力計／風速計
anemometer

気圧測定
measure of air pressure

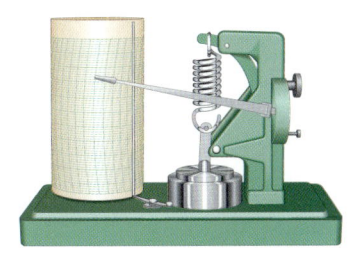

自記気圧計
barograph

湿度測定
measure of humidity

自記湿度計
hygrograph

39

生物圏 | BIOSPHERE

地球上の生命は生物圏と呼ばれている大気、土壌、水から成る環境にしか見られません。地球のこの居住部分は、さまざまな種が環境に適応しながら生きている、込み入った世界を形成しています。あらゆる生物は生き延びるために必要なエネルギーを、摂取する食物から取り出しています。このような食物のつながった関係を食物連鎖と呼んでいます。

植生と生物圏
VEGETATION AND BIOSPHERE

植生分布
vegetation regions

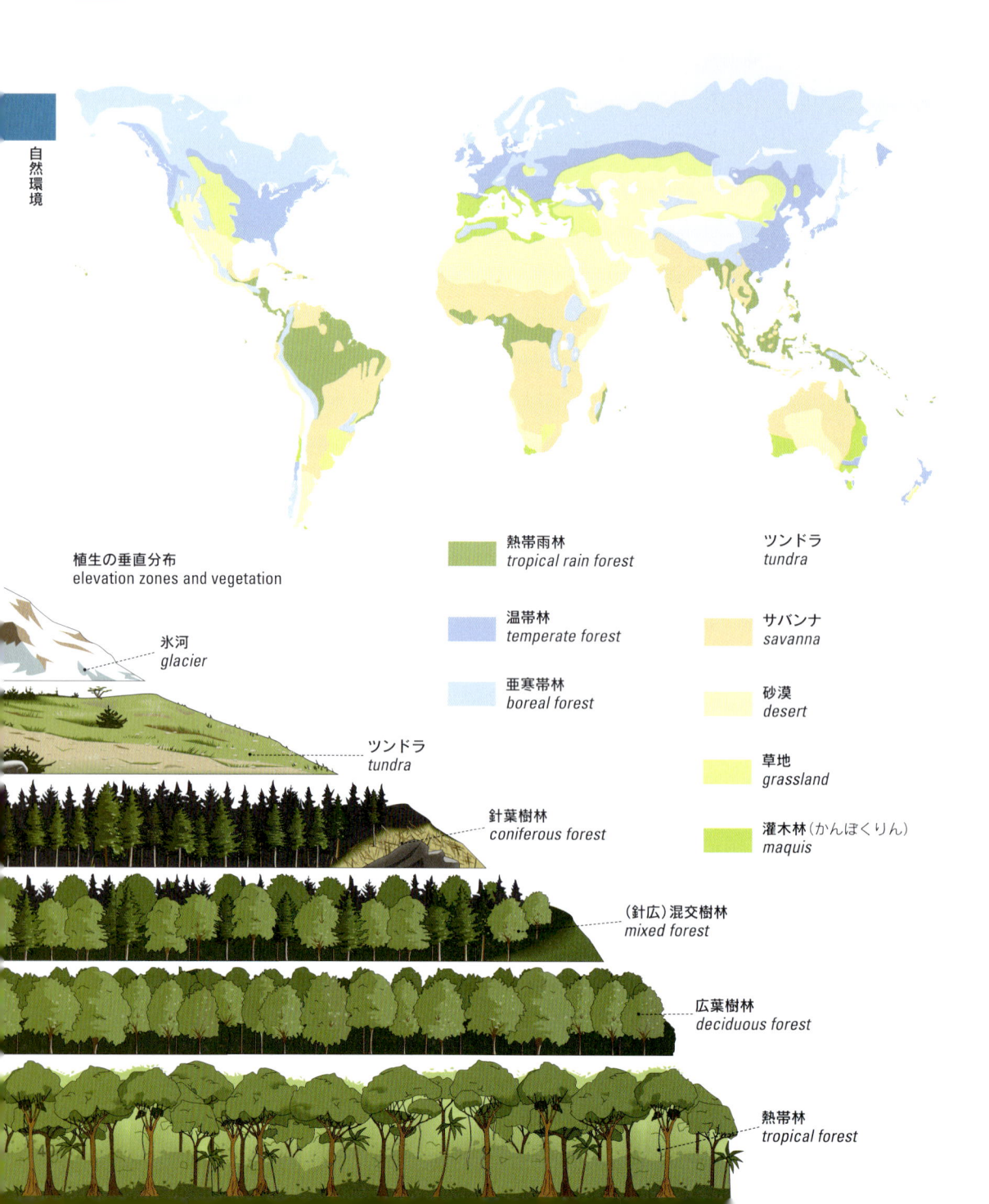

自然環境

植生の垂直分布
elevation zones and vegetation

氷河
glacier

ツンドラ
tundra

針葉樹林
coniferous forest

（針広）混交樹林
mixed forest

広葉樹林
deciduous forest

熱帯林
tropical forest

熱帯雨林
tropical rain forest

温帯林
temperate forest

亜寒帯林
boreal forest

ツンドラ
tundra

サバンナ
savanna

砂漠
desert

草地
grassland

灌木林（かんぼくりん）
maquis

生物圏 | BIOSPHERE

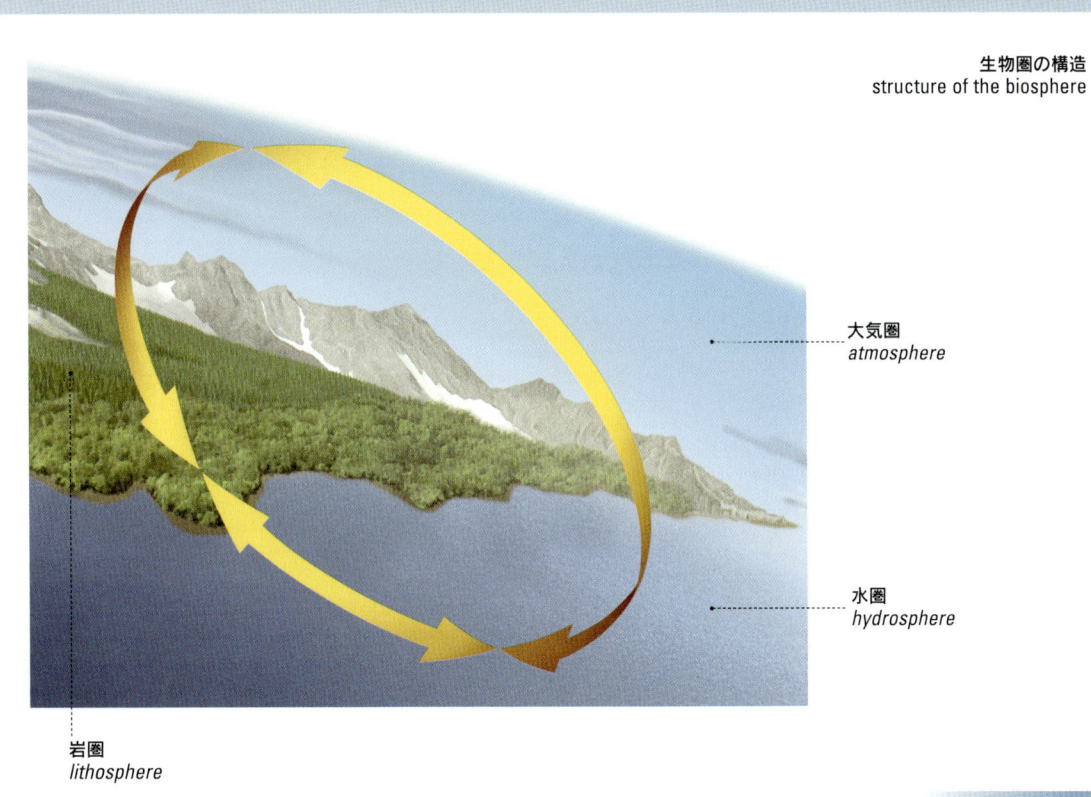

生物圏の構造
structure of the biosphere

大気圏
atmosphere

水圏
hydrosphere

岩圏
lithosphere

自然環境

食物連鎖
FOOD CHAIN

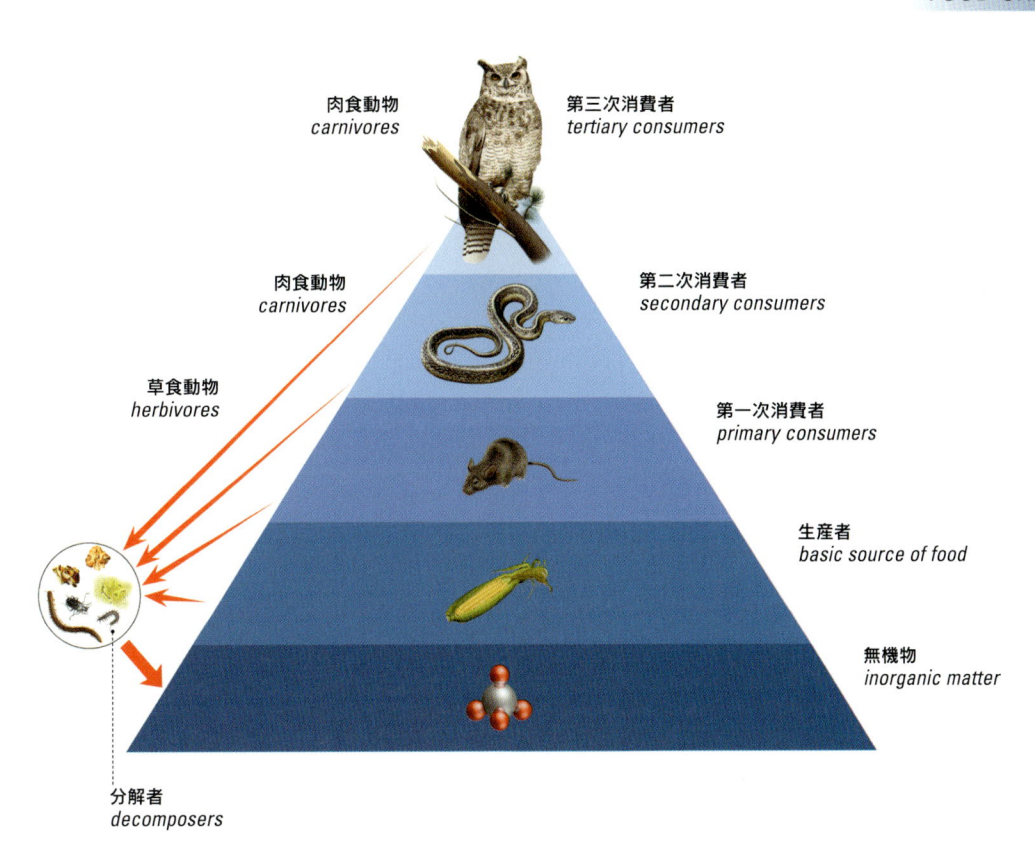

肉食動物
carnivores

第三次消費者
tertiary consumers

肉食動物
carnivores

第二次消費者
secondary consumers

草食動物
herbivores

第一次消費者
primary consumers

生産者
basic source of food

無機物
inorganic matter

分解者
decomposers

41

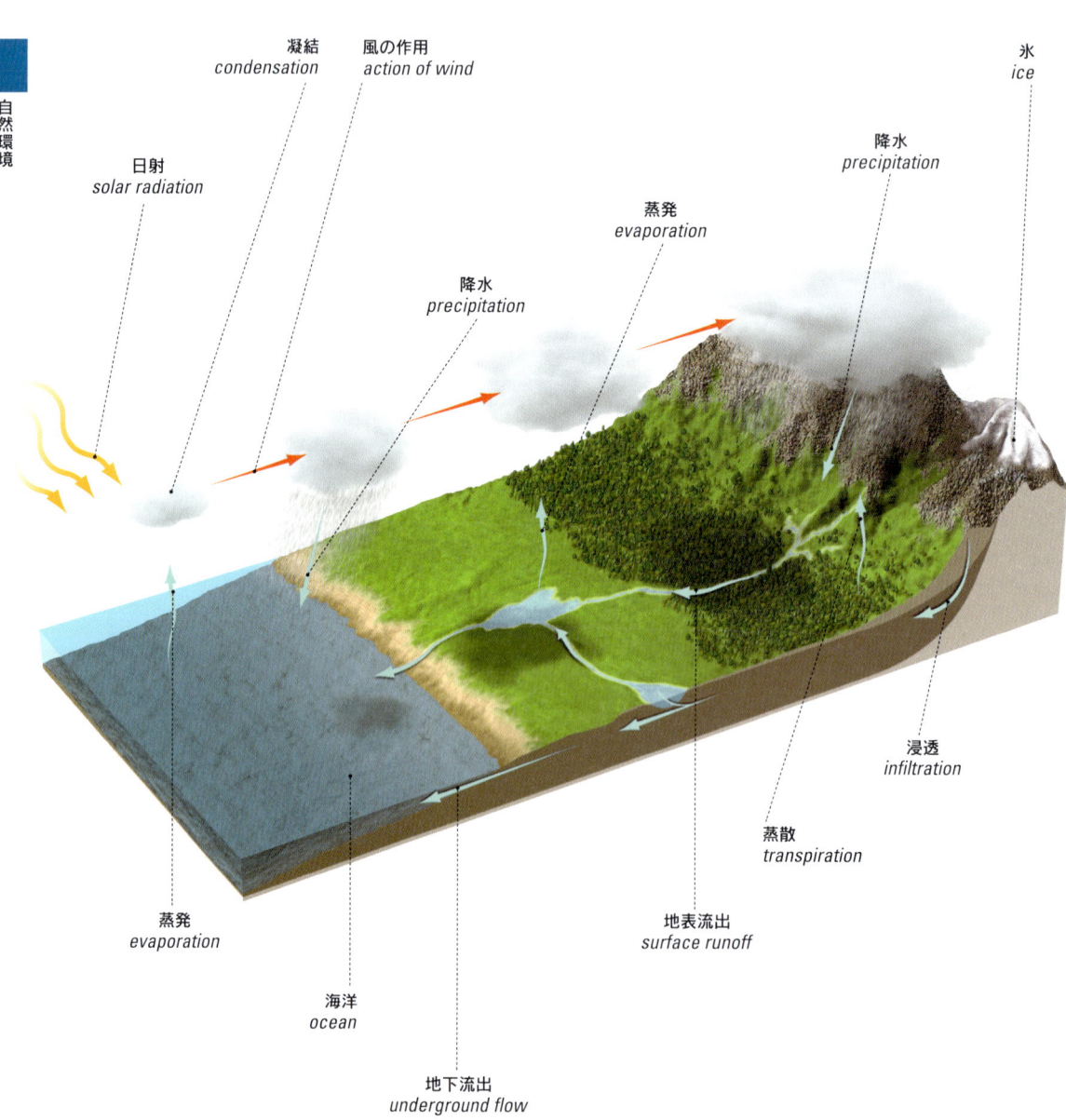

水の循環 | HYDROLOGIC CYCLE

太陽熱は大洋と大気の間で絶えずやり取りされています。大気中の水蒸気は、凝縮して雲になり、降水という形で再び地上に落ちてきます。水は大陸を浸食し、土の中に浸透し、湖や川に流れ、最後に大洋に達します。大量の水が大洋上で蒸発し、大気中に戻ります。これを水の循環と呼んでいます。

自然環境

凝結 condensation
風の作用 action of wind
氷 ice
日射 solar radiation
降水 precipitation
蒸発 evaporation
降水 precipitation
浸透 infiltration
蒸散 transpiration
蒸発 evaporation
地表流出 surface runoff
海洋 ocean
地下流出 underground flow

温室効果 | GREENHOUSE EFFECT

日射の一部は土によって吸収され、熱という形で大気中に投げ返されます。大気中のある種のガスはこの熱を閉じ込める性質を持っています。この自然現象は"温室効果"と呼ばれ、地上の温度を生活に適した温度に保ちます。ある種の人間の営みの結果、ますます大量のガスが温室効果によって大気中に放出され、地球は今日、温暖化に向かっています。

自然環境

自然の温室効果 / natural greenhouse effect

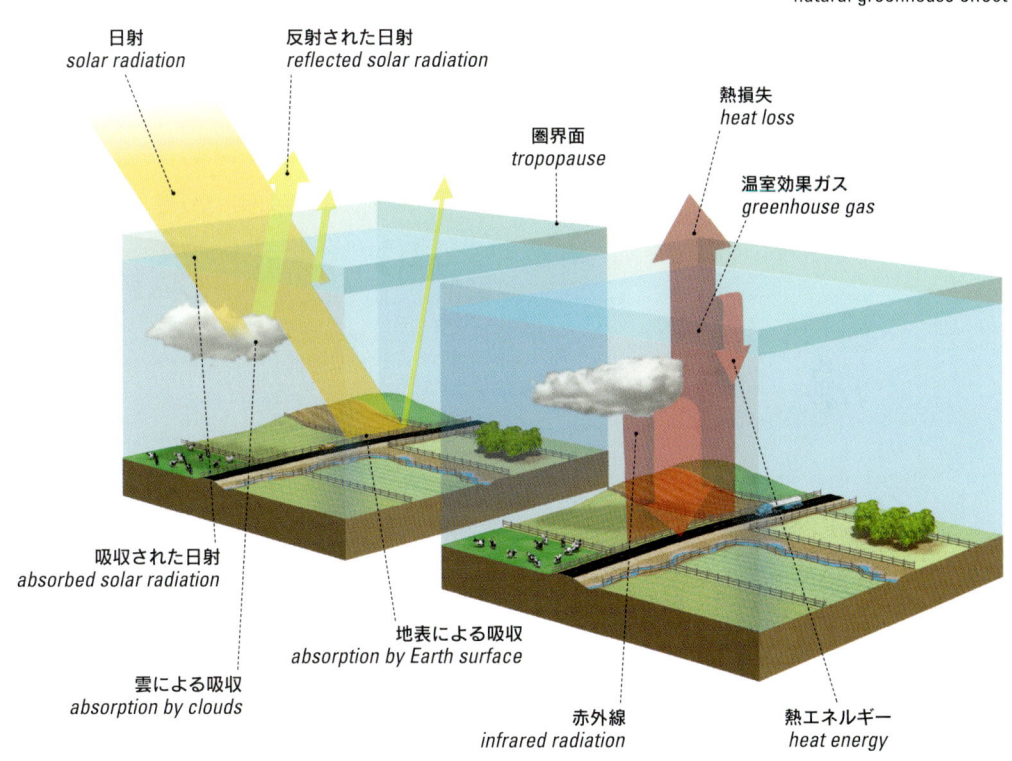

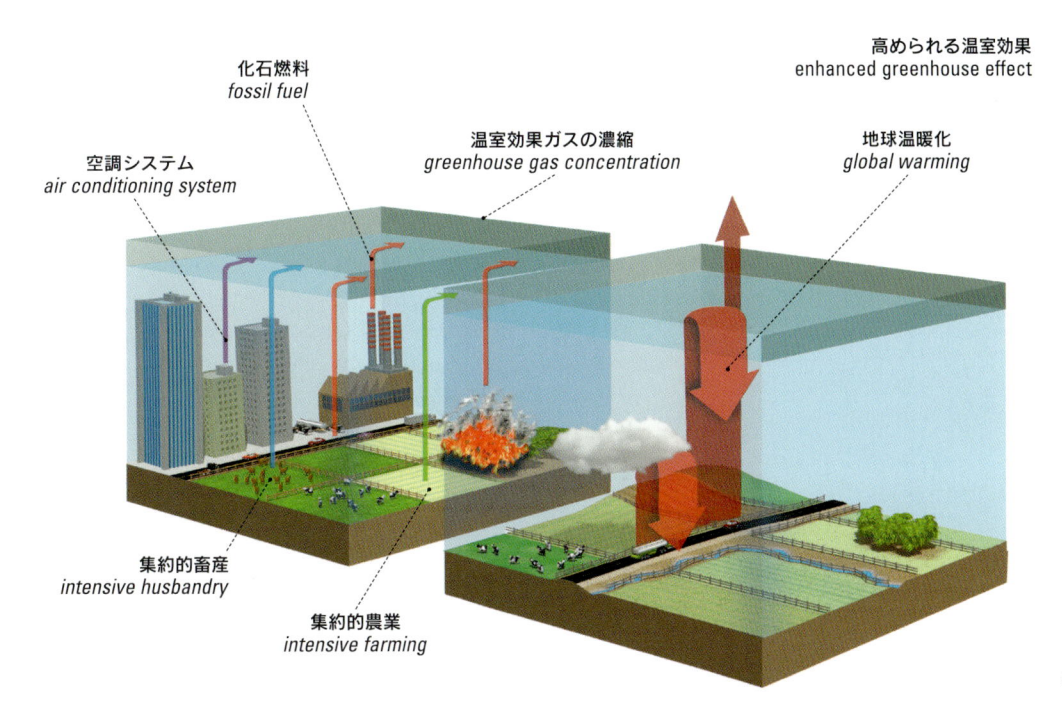

- 日射 / solar radiation
- 反射された日射 / reflected solar radiation
- 圏界面 / tropopause
- 熱損失 / heat loss
- 温室効果ガス / greenhouse gas
- 吸収された日射 / absorbed solar radiation
- 地表による吸収 / absorption by Earth surface
- 雲による吸収 / absorption by clouds
- 赤外線 / infrared radiation
- 熱エネルギー / heat energy

高められる温室効果 / enhanced greenhouse effect

- 化石燃料 / fossil fuel
- 温室効果ガスの濃縮 / greenhouse gas concentration
- 地球温暖化 / global warming
- 空調システム / air conditioning system
- 集約的畜産 / intensive husbandry
- 集約的農業 / intensive farming

汚染 | POLLUTION

工場は大量の化学廃棄物を周囲の環境に放出しています。そのうちのあるものはきわめて有害です。火力発電所と車はこのようにして環境を汚染しています。私たちは幸いなことに、天然資源には限りがあり、空気、土壌、水を汚染すると地球の将来に悪影響を及ぼすことを、いっそう理解し始めています。

自然環境

土壌汚染
LAND POLLUTION

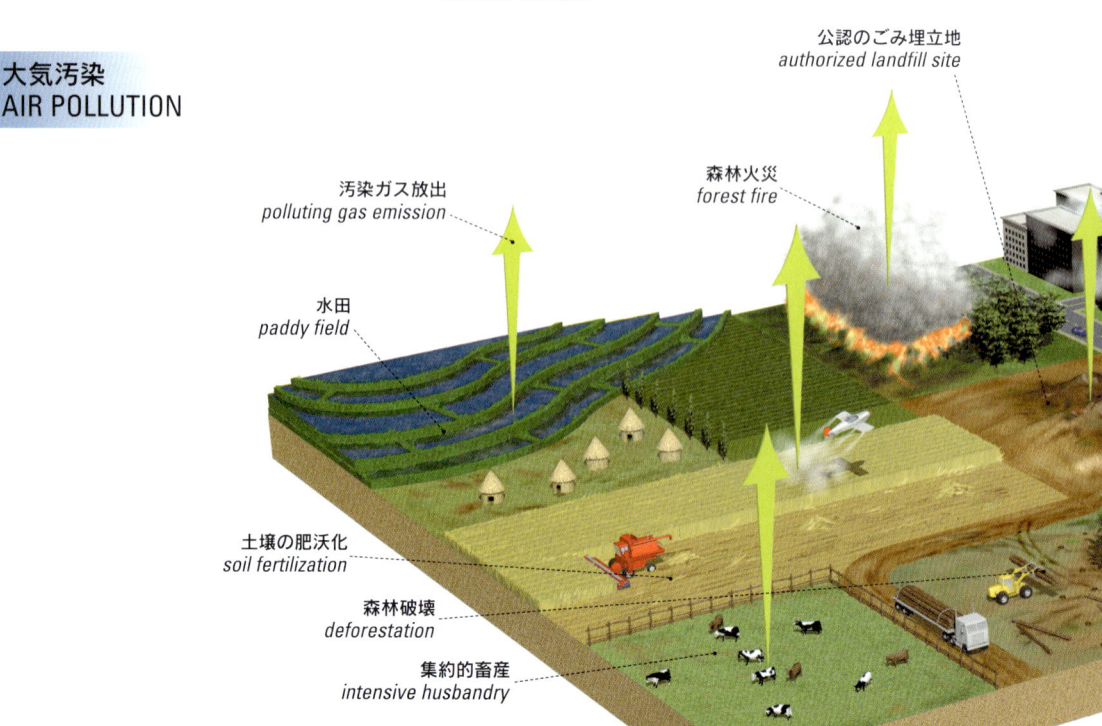

- 化学肥料散布 / fertilizer application
- 生物分解できない汚染物質 / nonbiodegradable pollutants
- 工業汚染 / industrial pollution
- 集約的畜産 / intensive husbandry
- 家庭汚染 / domestic pollution
- 農業汚染 / agricultural pollution
- 公認のごみ埋立地 / authorized landfill site
- 産業廃棄物 / industrial waste
- 殺虫剤 / pesticide
- 家庭ごみ / household waste
- 除草剤 / herbicide
- 殺菌剤 / fungicide
- 廃棄物の層 / waste layers
- 浸透 / intrusive filtration

大気汚染
AIR POLLUTION

- 公認のごみ埋立地 / authorized landfill site
- 汚染ガス放出 / polluting gas emission
- 森林火災 / forest fire
- 水田 / paddy field
- 土壌の肥沃化 / soil fertilization
- 森林破壊 / deforestation
- 集約的畜産 / intensive husbandry

汚染 | POLLUTION

水質汚染
WATER POLLUTION

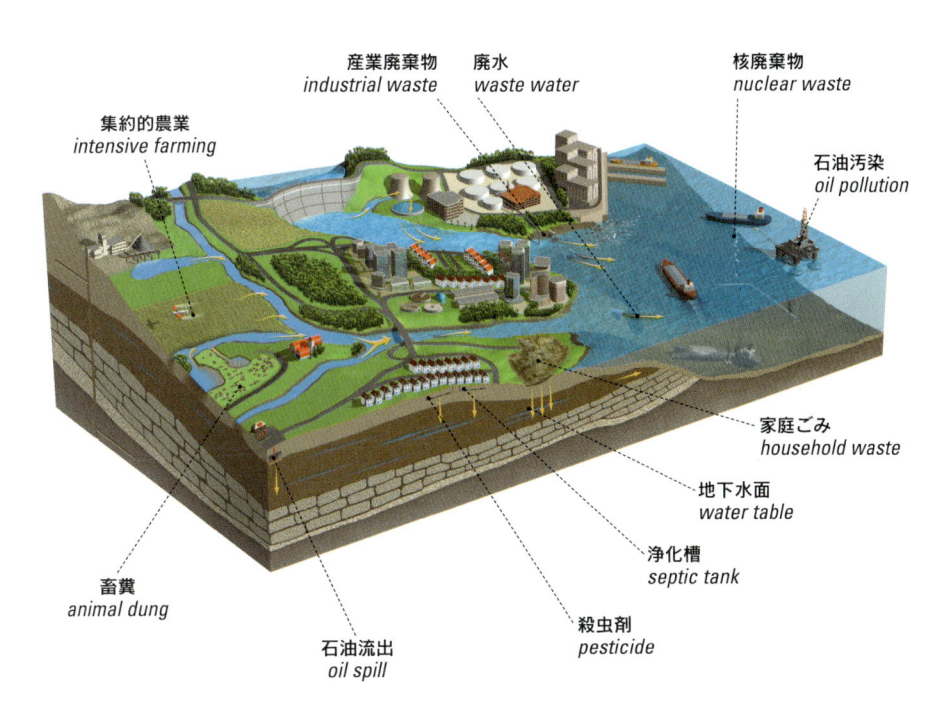

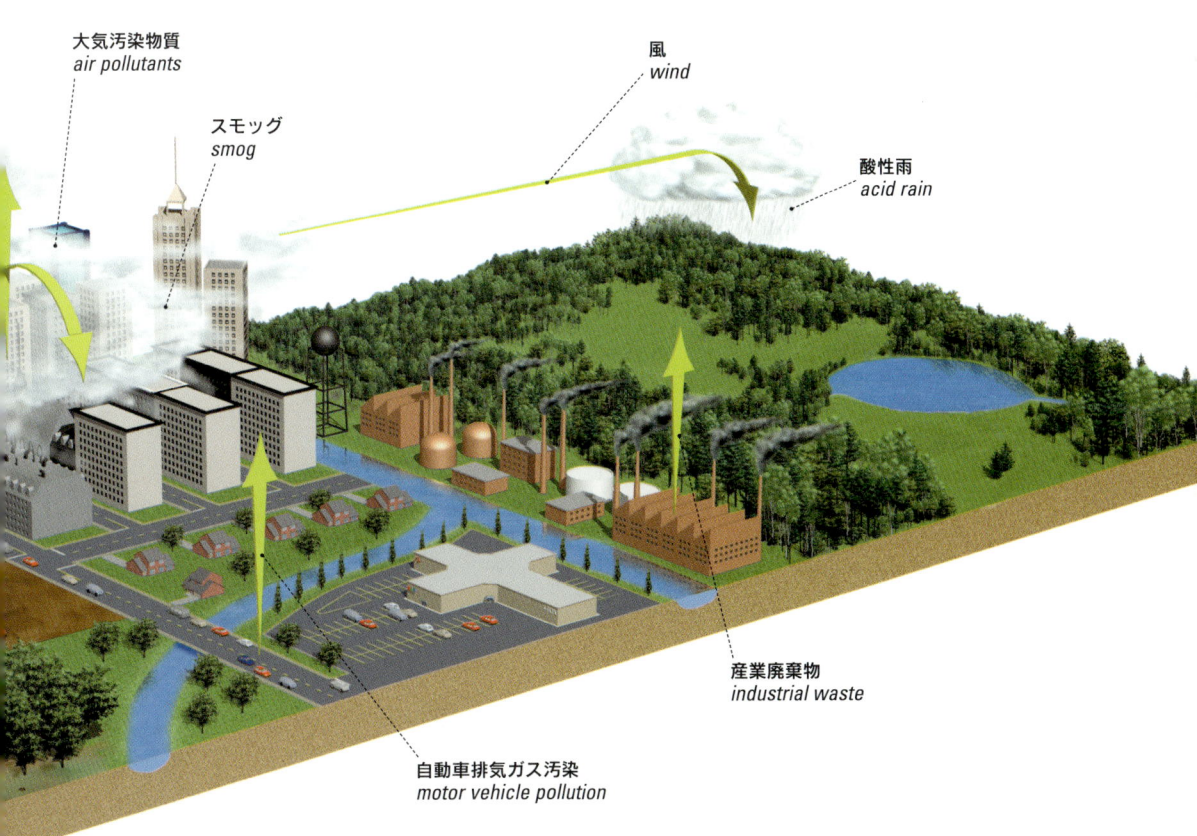

- 産業廃棄物 industrial waste
- 廃水 waste water
- 核廃棄物 nuclear waste
- 石油汚染 oil pollution
- 集約的農業 intensive farming
- 家庭ごみ household waste
- 地下水面 water table
- 浄化槽 septic tank
- 畜糞 animal dung
- 石油流出 oil spill
- 殺虫剤 pesticide

自然環境

- 大気汚染物質 air pollutants
- スモッグ smog
- 風 wind
- 酸性雨 acid rain
- 産業廃棄物 industrial waste
- 自動車排気ガス汚染 motor vehicle pollution

45

ごみ［廃棄物］の分別 | SELECTIVE SORTING OF WASTE

工業国で生み出される家庭のごみの大部分はリサイクルが可能かもしれません。街ではごみの選別収集方法がますます進んできました。ごみは分別工場へ送られ、そこでは係員や機械がガラス、金属、プラスチック、紙といったふうにリサイクル可能な物を選び出し、再びきれいにしたり、加工したりしています。

自然環境

分別工場［センター］
sorting plant

紙とボール紙の分別
paper/paperboard sorting

プラスチックの分別
plastics sorting

ガラスの分別
glass sorting

手作業による分別
manual sorting

破砕機
crusher

分別（ぶんべつ）収集
separate collection

再利用できない残留ごみ
nonreusable residue waste

紙とボール紙の選別
paper/paperboard separation

埋め立て
burial

焼却
incineration

梱包（こんぽう）
baling

コンベヤー・ベルト
conveyor belt

金属の分別
metal sorting

磁石による選別
magnetic separation

圧縮
compacting

光学的分別
optical sorting

細断
shredding

リサイクリング
recycling

紙のリサイクル用コンテナ
paper recycling container

アルミニウムのリサイクル用コンテナ
aluminum recycling container

リサイクル容器
recycling bin

紙の回収箱
paper collection unit

ガラスのリサイクル用コンテナ
glass recycling container

ガラスの回収箱
glass collection unit

単純な植物 | SIMPLE VEGETABLES

もしもすべての植物が植物細胞からできているとしたら、構造はさぞかしいろいろと異なることでしょう。そのような植物の中で最も単純な構造をしているのは藻類、地衣類、蘚類、シダ類、キノコで、葉も花も種もありません。キノコには植物を緑色にする色素、つまり葉緑素が欠けています。このような理由からも生物学者はキノコを別の界に分類しているのです。

植物界

キノコの構造
structure of a mushroom

- 傘 / cap
- つば / ring
- ひだ / gill
- 茎／柄 / stem
- つぼ / volva
- 胞子 / spores
- 菌糸 / hypha
- 菌糸体 / mycelium

キノコ (茸)
MUSHROOM

猛毒キノコ
deadly poisonous mushroom

シロタマゴテングタケ (白玉子天狗茸)
destroying angel

毒キノコ
poisonous mushroom

ベニテングタケ (紅天狗茸)
fly agaric

藻類、地衣類、蘚類、シダ類
ALGA, LICHEN, MOSS, AND FERN

シダの構造
structure of a fern

- 胞子嚢 (ほうしのう) 群 / sorus
- 葉 / frond
- 葉身 / blade
- 羽片 / pinna
- 葉柄 (ようへい) / petiole
- 渦巻き状の若葉 / fiddlehead
- 根茎 / rhizome
- 不定根 / adventitious roots

藻 (類) / alga

蘚類／蘚苔 (せんたい) 類／苔 (こけ) 類 / moss

地衣 (類) / lichen

顕花(けんか)植物 | FLOWERING PLANTS

顕花(けんか)植物は、小さな胚を保護する種子を持っているので、確実に繁殖し続けます。胚は発芽する際に種子に含まれている栄養素を取りながら成長し、早く独立個体になります。私たちに馴染みの植物の多くは、235,000種類以上を数える、きわめて多様なグループに属しています。

植物の構造と発芽
STRUCTURE OF A PLANT AND GERMINATION

植物界

植物の構造
structure of a plant

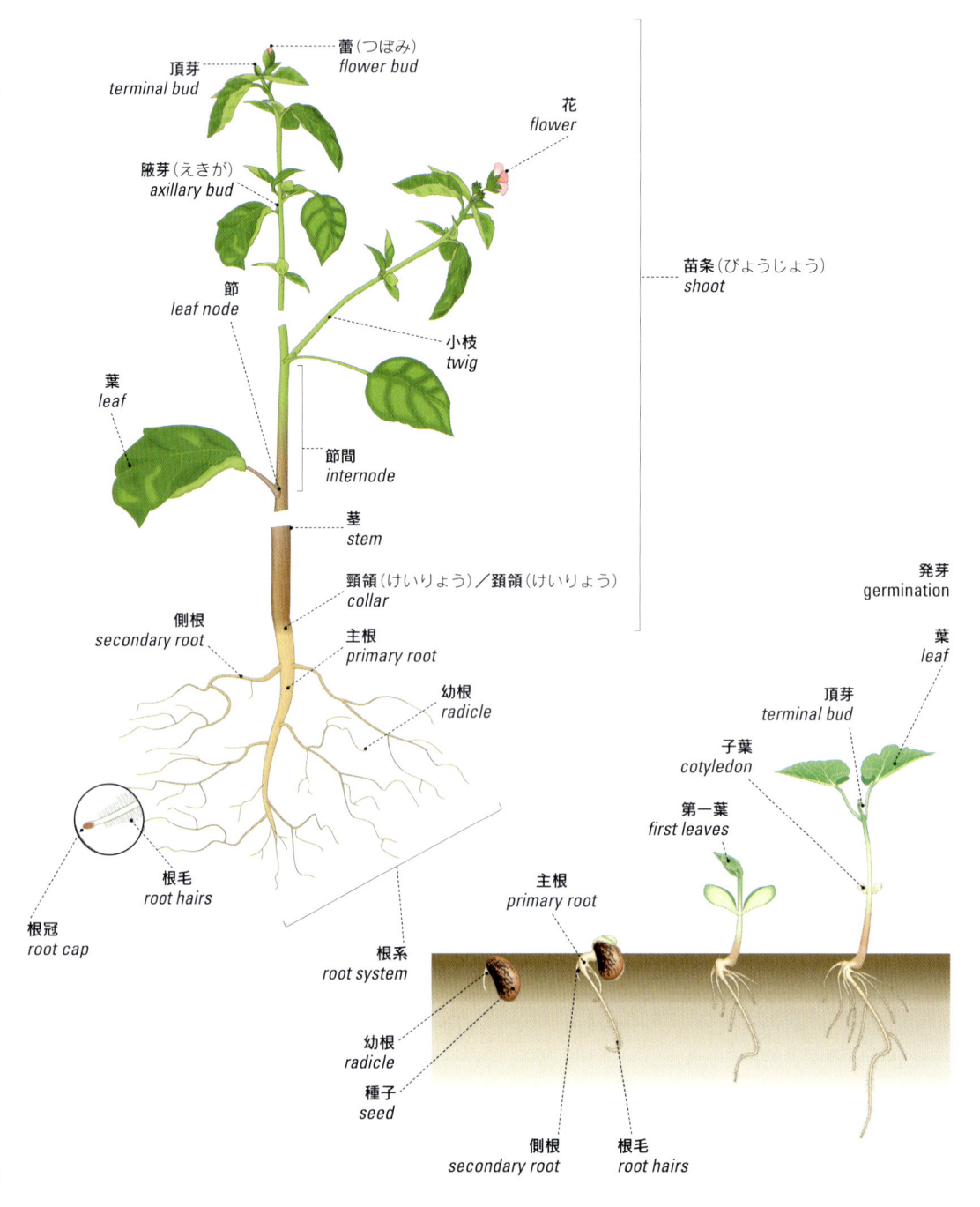

- 頂芽 / terminal bud
- 蕾(つぼみ) / flower bud
- 花 / flower
- 腋芽(えきが) / axillary bud
- 節 / leaf node
- 小枝 / twig
- 苗条(びょうじょう) / shoot
- 葉 / leaf
- 節間 / internode
- 茎 / stem
- 頸領(けいりょう)／頚領(けいりょう) / collar
- 側根 / secondary root
- 主根 / primary root
- 幼根 / radicle
- 根毛 / root hairs
- 根冠 / root cap
- 根系 / root system

発芽 / germination

- 主根 / primary root
- 幼根 / radicle
- 種子 / seed
- 側根 / secondary root
- 根毛 / root hairs
- 第一葉 / first leaves
- 子葉 / cotyledon
- 頂芽 / terminal bud
- 葉 / leaf

48

顕花植物 | FLOWERING PLANTS

葉
LEAF

葉の構造 / *structure of a leaf*

- 葉頂 / *tip*
- 葉縁 / *margin*
- 葉脈 / *vein*
- 中肋／主脈 / *midrib*
- 葉身 / *blade*
- 葉柄（ようへい） / *petiole*
- 托葉 / *stipule*
- 葉鞘（ようしょう） / *sheath*
- 葉腋 / *leaf axil*

単葉 / *simple leaves*
- へら形の / *spatulate*
- 腎（臓）形の / *reniform*
- 線形の / *linear*
- 披針形（ひしんけい）の / *lanceolate*
- 卵形の / *ovate*
- 円形の / *orbiculate*
- 心（臓）形の / *cordate*

複葉 / *compound leaves*
- 三出の／三小葉ある / *trifoliolate*
- 羽状中裂の / *pinnatifid*
- 掌（しょう）状の / *palmate*

葉縁 / *leaf margin*
- 鋸歯（きょし）状の / *dentate*
- （二）重鋸歯状の／複鋸歯状の / *doubly dentate*
- 円鋸歯状の／鈍鋸歯状の / *crenate*
- 毛縁の／繊毛（せんもう）状の / *ciliate*
- 全縁の / *entire*
- 裂片状の／欠刻状の / *lobate*

植物界

49

顕花植物 | FLOWERING PLANTS

花
FLOWER

花の構造
structure of a flower

植物界

柱頭 *stigma*
葯(やく) *anther*
花糸 *filament*
花弁 *petal*
花柱 *style*
花床／花托 *receptacle*
子房 *ovary*
花柄(かへい)／花梗(かこう) *peduncle*
萼片(がくへん) *sepal*
胚珠 *ovule*

花冠 corolla
萼(がく) calyx
雌しべ pistil
雄しべ stamen

花の例
examples of flowers

ラン(蘭) orchid

ユリ(百合) lily

50

顕花植物 | FLOWERING PLANTS

ラッパズイセン（らっぱ水仙）
daffodil

チューリップ
tulip

サクラソウ（桜草）
primrose

ベゴニア
begonia

ヒナギク（雛菊）
daisy

キンポウゲ（金鳳花）
buttercup

スミレ（菫）
violet

スズラン（鈴蘭）
lily of the valley

ケシ（芥子）
poppy

アザミ（薊）
thistle

タンポポ（蒲公英）
dandelion

カーネーション
carnation

クロッカス
crocus

ヒマワリ（向日葵）
sunflower

バラ（薔薇）
rose

植物界

51

木／樹木 | TREE

木とは四方に広がる植物で、大きめの葉を付ける広葉樹と、針のような形をした細い葉を付ける針葉樹の２つに大別されます。針葉樹は、いくつかの例外を除けば冬の間ずっと落葉しないので、常緑樹と呼ばれ、広葉樹は、ふつう冬になる前に落葉するので、落葉樹とも呼ばれています。

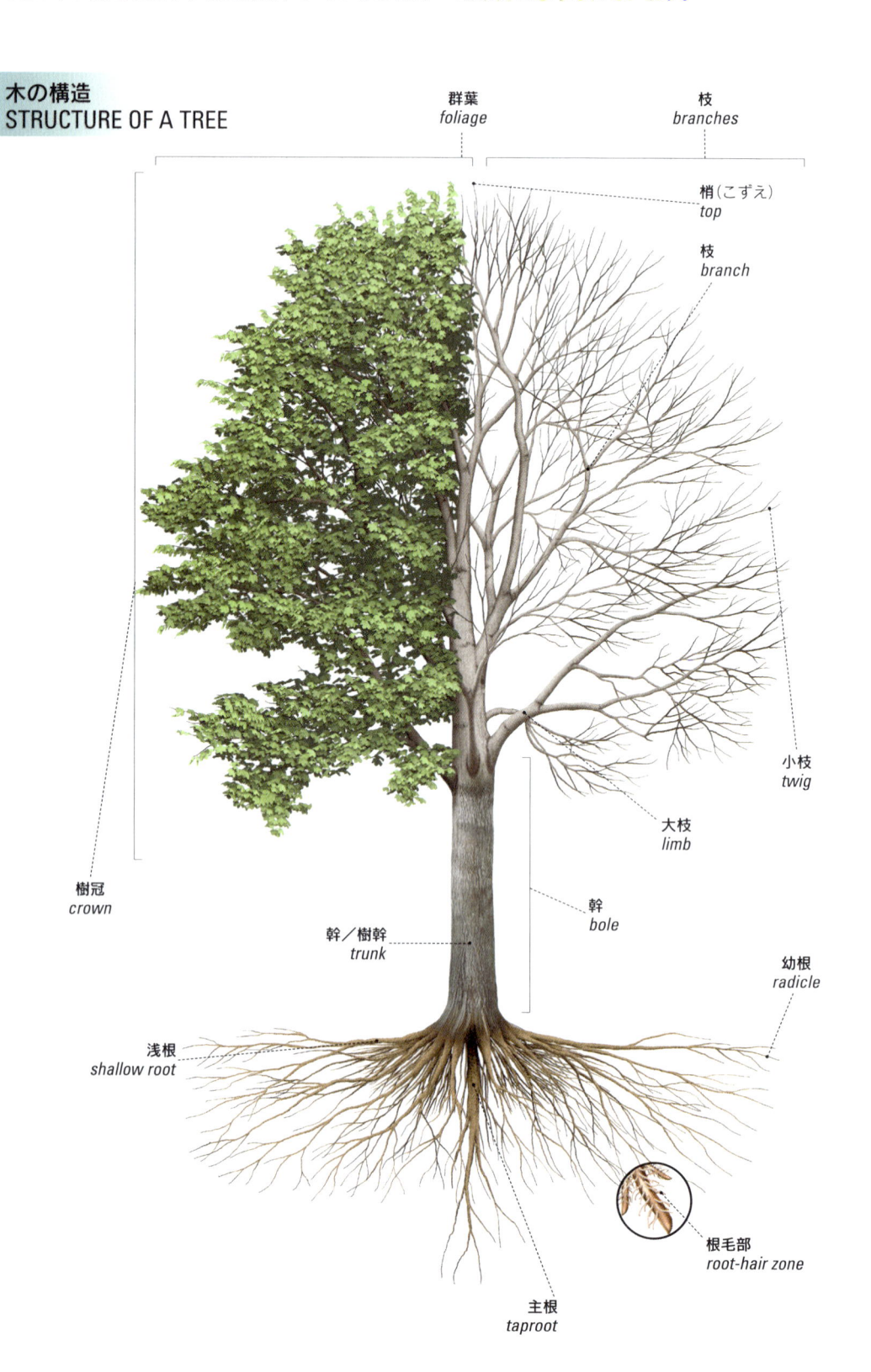

木の構造
STRUCTURE OF A TREE

群葉 / foliage
枝 / branches
梢（こずえ）/ top
枝 / branch
小枝 / twig
大枝 / limb
幹 / bole
幼根 / radicle
樹冠 / crown
幹／樹幹 / trunk
浅根 / shallow root
根毛部 / root-hair zone
主根 / taproot

植物界

木／樹木 | TREE

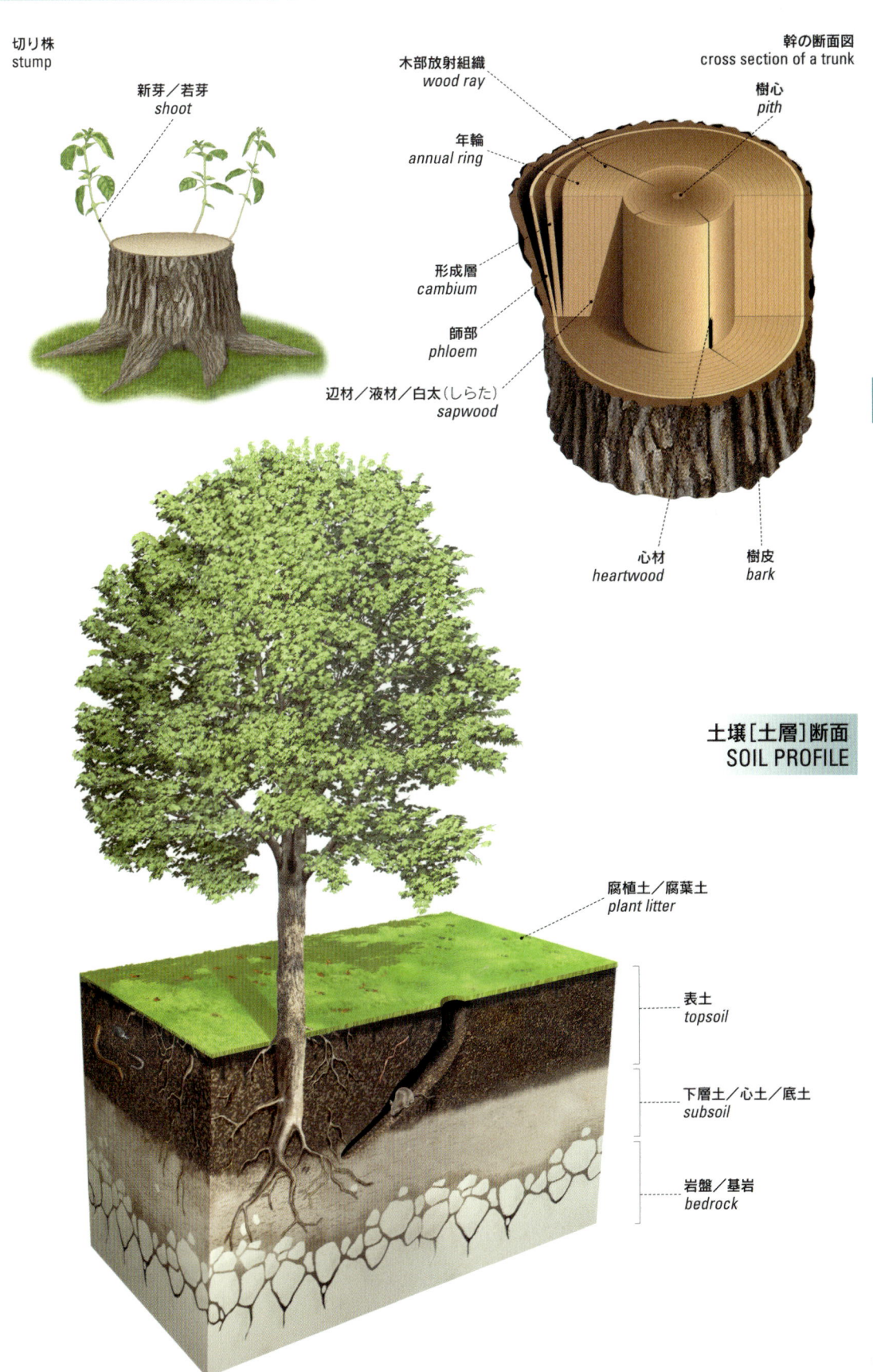

切り株
stump

新芽／若芽
shoot

幹の断面図
cross section of a trunk

木部放射組織
wood ray

樹心
pith

年輪
annual ring

形成層
cambium

師部
phloem

辺材／液材／白太（しらた）
sapwood

心材
heartwood

樹皮
bark

植物界

土壌[土層]断面
SOIL PROFILE

腐植土／腐葉土
plant litter

表土
topsoil

下層土／心土／底土
subsoil

岩盤／基岩
bedrock

木／樹木｜TREE

広葉樹の例
EXAMPLES OF BROADLEAVED TREES

カエデ（楓）
maple

ヤナギ（柳）
willow

オーク
oak

ヤシ（椰子）
palm tree

クルミノキ（胡桃の木）
walnut

ポプラ
poplar

ブナノキ（ぶなの木）
beech

カバノキ（樺の木）
birch

植物界

木／樹木 | TREE

針葉樹の例
EXAMPLES OF CONIFERS

枝
branch

マツ（松）の実
pine seeds

球果
cone

植物界

レバノンスギ（杉）
cedar of Lebanon

カラマツ（唐松）
larch

トウヒ（唐檜）
spruce

モミ（樅）
fir

マツ（松）
pine

55

単純な生物と棘皮(きょくひ)動物 | SIMPLE ORGANISMS AND ECHINODERMS

アメーバやゾウリムシのように単細胞のもの、シロナガスクジラのように何十億もの細胞を数えるもの、これらすべての動物が動物細胞から成り立っています。もしも原生動物を除外し、別の界に分類すると、脊柱があるか否かで、脊椎動物と無脊椎動物の2つのグループに大別できます。もしも海綿動物が無脊椎動物の中でも最も原始的なものとすれば、棘皮(きょくひ)動物はその中で最も進化したものと言うことができます。

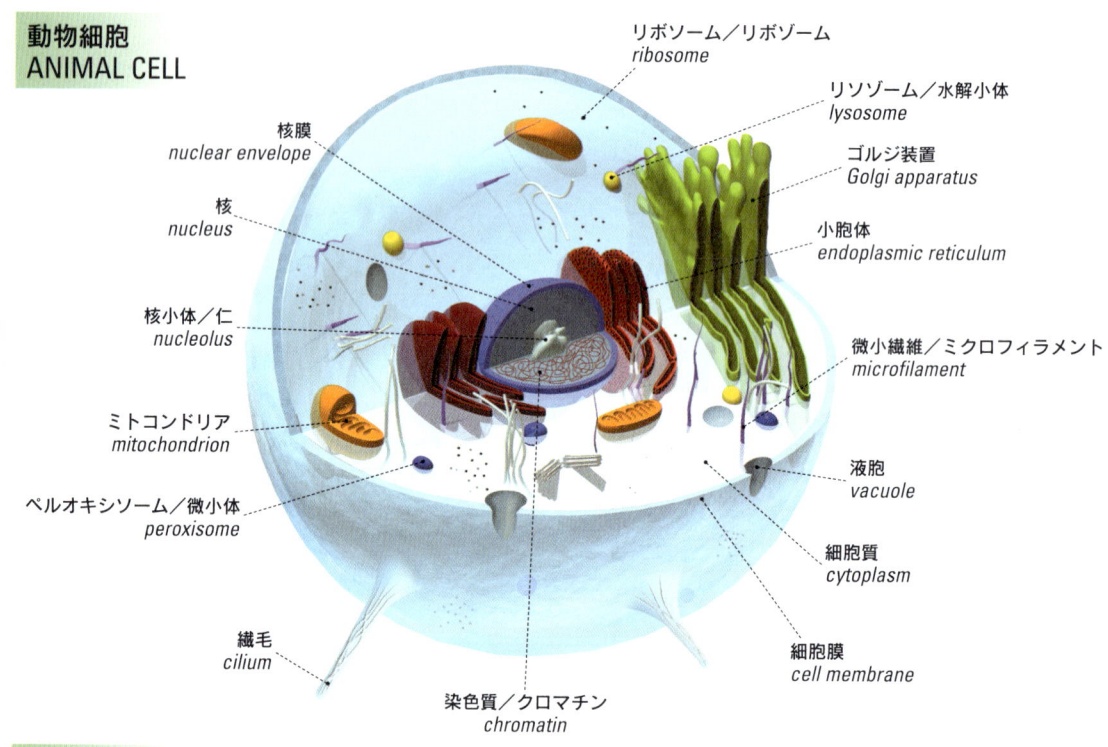

動物細胞 / ANIMAL CELL

- 核膜 / nuclear envelope
- 核 / nucleus
- 核小体／仁 / nucleolus
- ミトコンドリア / mitochondrion
- ペルオキシソーム／微小体 / peroxisome
- 繊毛 / cilium
- 染色質／クロマチン / chromatin
- リボソーム／リボゾーム / ribosome
- リソゾーム／水解小体 / lysosome
- ゴルジ装置 / Golgi apparatus
- 小胞体 / endoplasmic reticulum
- 微小繊維／ミクロフィラメント / microfilament
- 液胞 / vacuole
- 細胞質 / cytoplasm
- 細胞膜 / cell membrane

単細胞動物、海綿動物、棘皮(きょくひ)動物
UNICELLULARS, SPONGE, AND ECHINODERMS

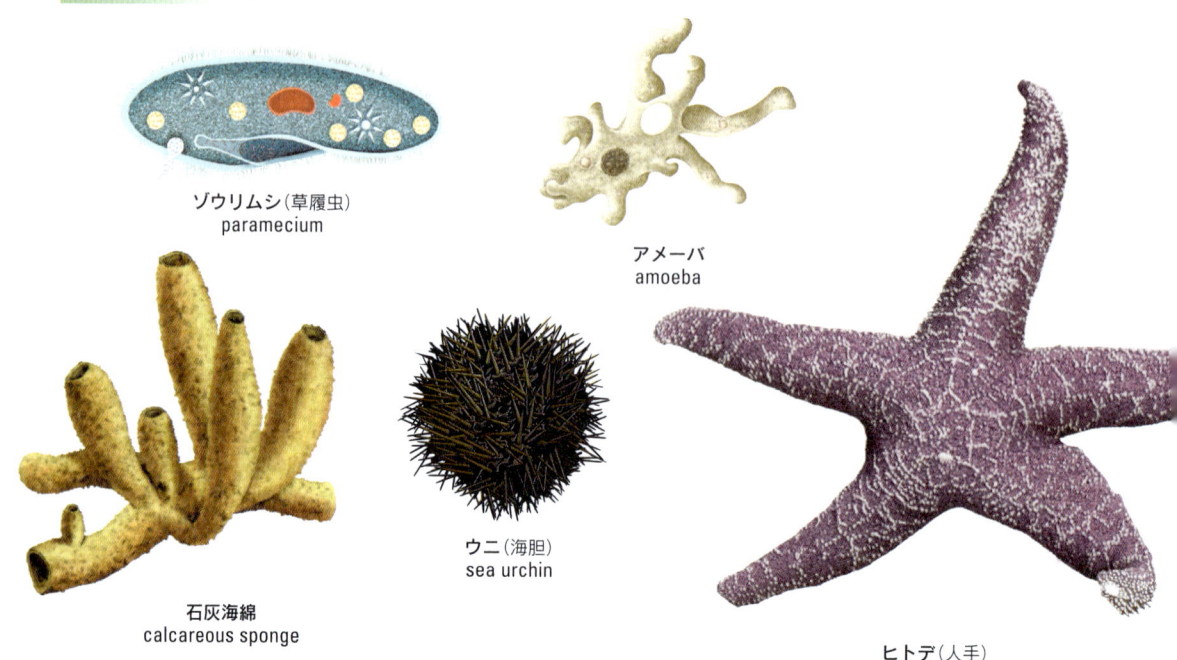

- ゾウリムシ(草履虫) / paramecium
- アメーバ / amoeba
- 石灰海綿 / calcareous sponge
- ウニ(海胆) / sea urchin
- ヒトデ(人手) / starfish

軟体動物 | MOLLUSKS

名前から分かるように、軟体動物は軟らかい体を持っています。しかしながら、骨格のない体は殻に守られていることがよくあります。その種の大部分は水生で、えらで呼吸し、陸生の軟体動物は、カタツムリやナメクジのように肺で呼吸します。無脊椎動物の多くは同時に雄でも雌でもあり、雌雄同体と呼ばれています。

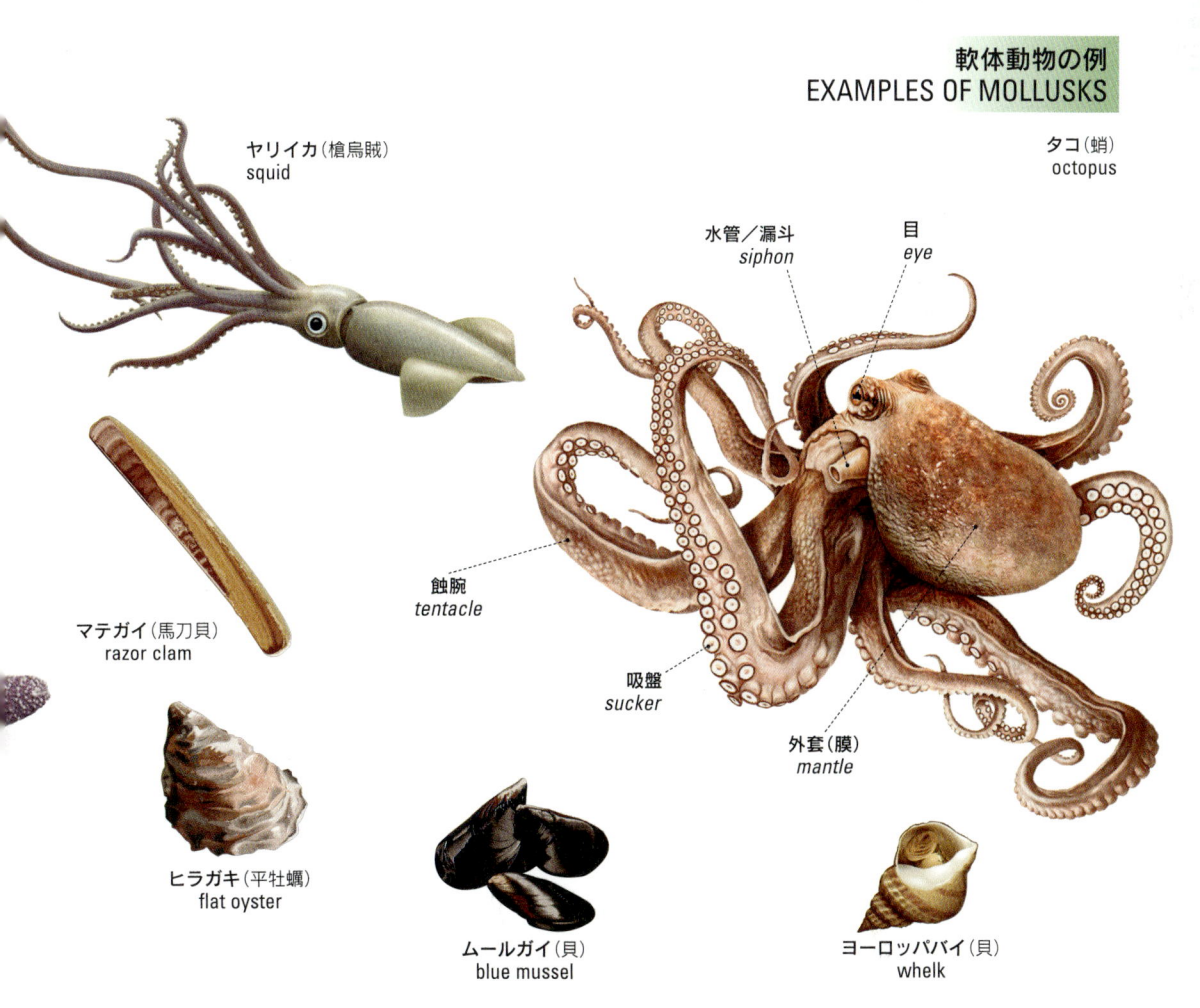

カタツムリ（蝸牛） SNAIL

カタツムリの形態図
morphology of a snail

- 螺層（らそう） whorl
- 成長線 growth line
- 殻頂 apex
- 頭 head
- 目 eye
- 殻 shell
- 眼柄（がんぺい） eyestalk
- 小触角 tentacle
- 腹足 foot
- 口 mouth

軟体動物の例 EXAMPLES OF MOLLUSKS

- ヤリイカ（槍烏賊） squid
- タコ（蛸） octopus
- 水管／漏斗 siphon
- 目 eye
- 触腕 tentacle
- 吸盤 sucker
- 外套（膜） mantle
- マテガイ（馬刀貝） razor clam
- ヒラガキ（平牡蠣） flat oyster
- ムールガイ（貝） blue mussel
- ヨーロッパバイ（貝） whelk

動物界

57

甲殻類 | CRUSTACEANS

エビやカニは、昆虫やクモと同じく脚に関節があるのが特徴で、無脊椎動物の重要なグループの一つである節足動物に属しています。約３０，０００種類のエビやカニは、とりわけ２本の触角と、体を保護するための甲殻、１０本の脚によってほかと区別されます。泳いだり歩いたりするのに役立つ脚の前方に、餌をつかむのに適したはさみが見られます。

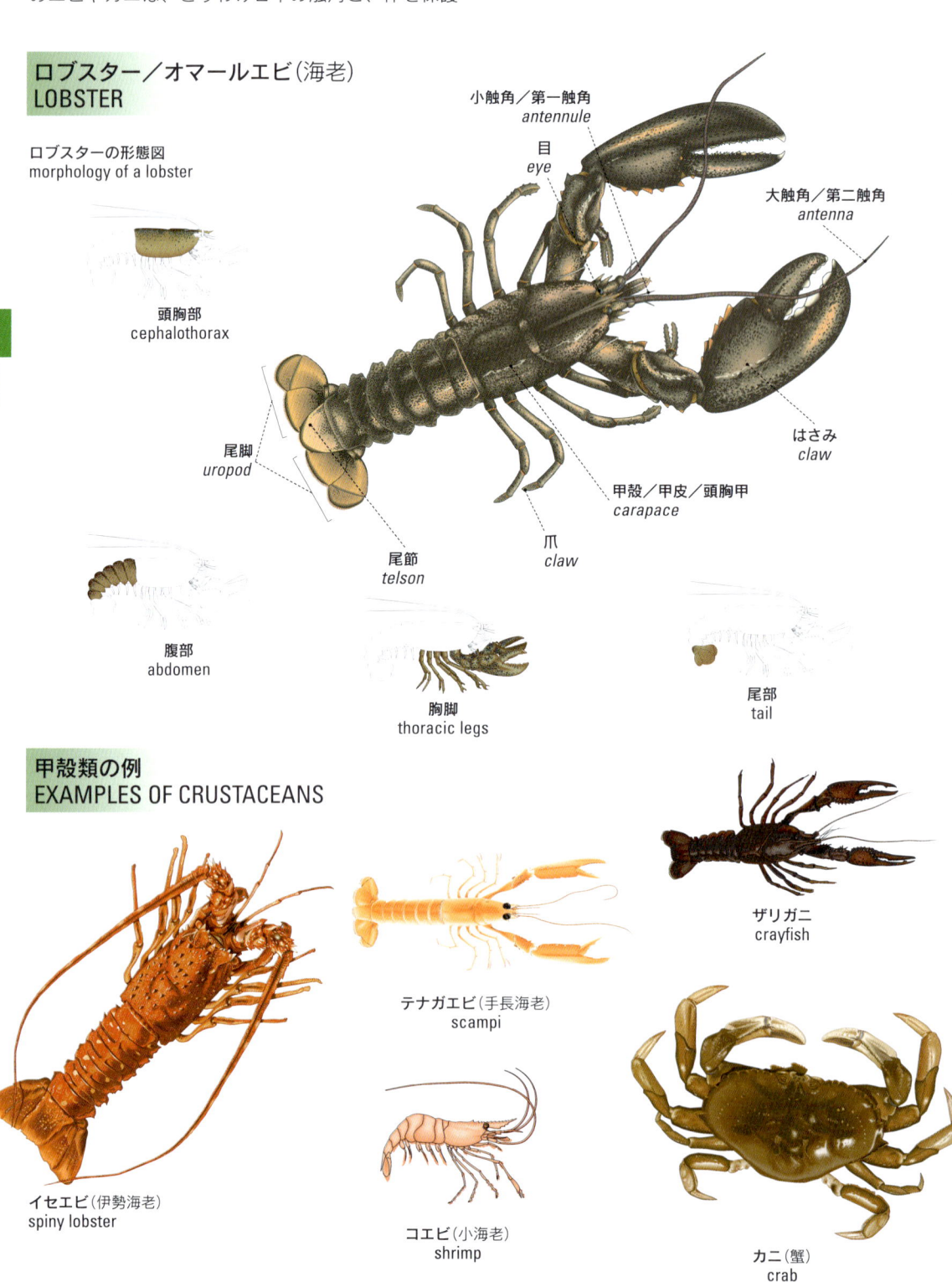

ロブスター／オマールエビ（海老）
LOBSTER

ロブスターの形態図
morphology of a lobster

- 小触角／第一触角 antennule
- 目 eye
- 大触角／第二触角 antenna
- 頭胸部 cephalothorax
- はさみ claw
- 尾脚 uropod
- 甲殻／甲皮／頭胸甲 carapace
- 尾節 telson
- 爪 claw
- 腹部 abdomen
- 胸脚 thoracic legs
- 尾部 tail

甲殻類の例
EXAMPLES OF CRUSTACEANS

- イセエビ（伊勢海老） spiny lobster
- テナガエビ（手長海老） scampi
- ザリガニ crayfish
- コエビ（小海老） shrimp
- カニ（蟹） crab

蜘蛛類 | ARACHNIDS

クモは、50,000種類以上いる無脊椎動物の重要なグループの一つであるクモ類の中で、最も知られた存在です。このクモ類を代表するすべてが獲物をつかむ一対のはさみを口の前方に持っています。昆虫やエビ、カニとは違って、クモ類は触角を持たず、4対の脚によってほかと区別されています。

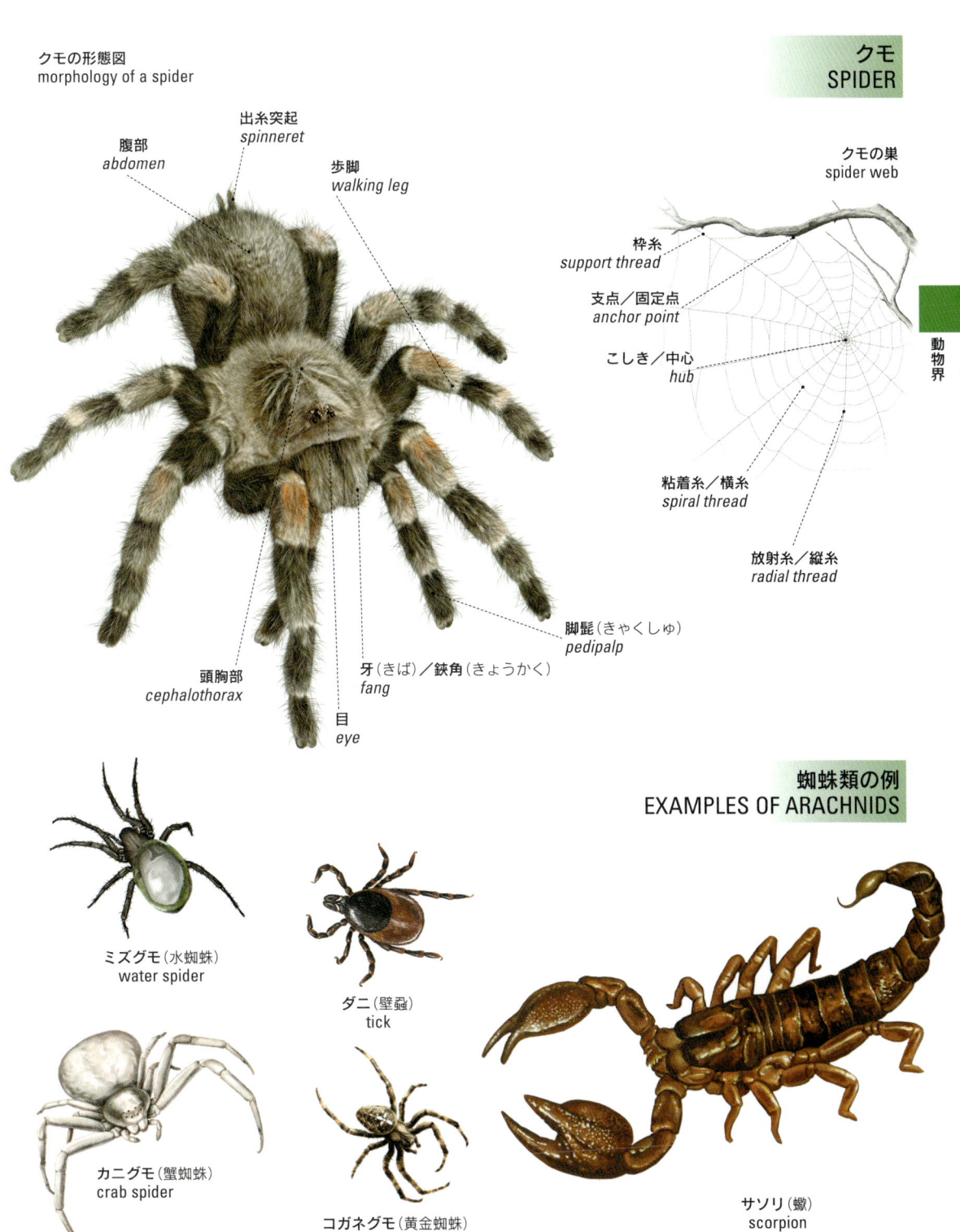

クモ
SPIDER

クモの形態図
morphology of a spider

- 腹部 / abdomen
- 出糸突起 / spinneret
- 歩脚 / walking leg
- 脚髭(きゃくしゅ) / pedipalp
- 牙(きば)／鋏角(きょうかく) / fang
- 目 / eye
- 頭胸部 / cephalothorax

クモの巣
spider web

- 枠糸 / support thread
- 支点／固定点 / anchor point
- こしき／中心 / hub
- 粘着糸／横糸 / spiral thread
- 放射糸／縦糸 / radial thread

蜘蛛類の例
EXAMPLES OF ARACHNIDS

- ミズグモ（水蜘蛛） / water spider
- ダニ（壁蝨） / tick
- カニグモ（蟹蜘蛛） / crab spider
- コガネグモ（黄金蜘蛛） / garden spider
- サソリ（蠍） / scorpion

昆虫 | INSECTS

昆虫は地球上の動物の中でも最も数と種類の多いグループに属し、今日では１００万種類以上を数え、あらゆる環境に適応しています。昆虫は3対の脚を持ち、ほとんどが翅（はね）を持っているところがほかの節足動物とは異なり、飛ぶことができる唯一の無脊椎動物です。

ミツバチ（蜜蜂）
HONEYBEE

ハタラキバチ（働き蜂）の形態図
morphology of a honeybee (worker)

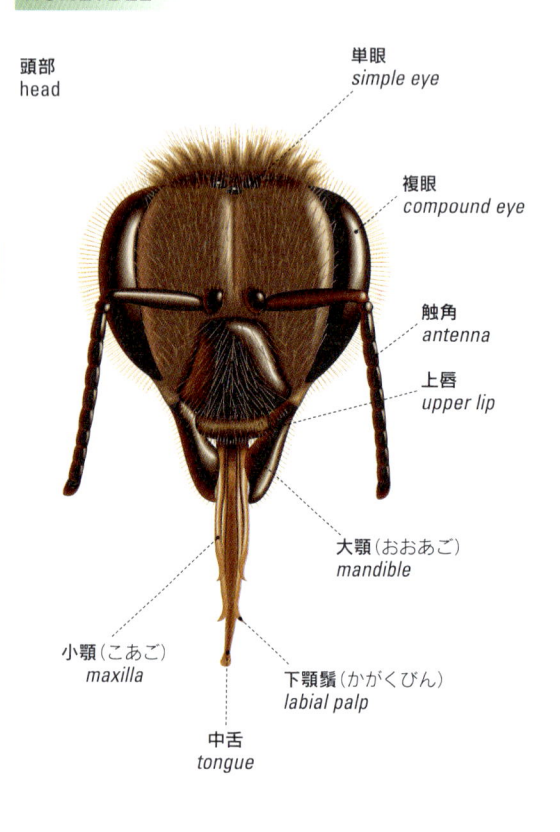

- 頭部 head
- 単眼 simple eye
- 複眼 compound eye
- 触角 antenna
- 上唇 upper lip
- 大顎（おおあご）mandible
- 小顎（こあご）maxilla
- 下顎鬚（かがくひん）labial palp
- 中舌 tongue
- 胸部 thorax
- 触角 antenna
- 口器 mouthparts
- 前脚（まえあし）foreleg
- 中脚（なかあし）middle leg

階級（型）castes

- 女王バチ queen
- 働きバチ worker
- 雄（ミツ）バチ drone

昆虫 | INSECTS

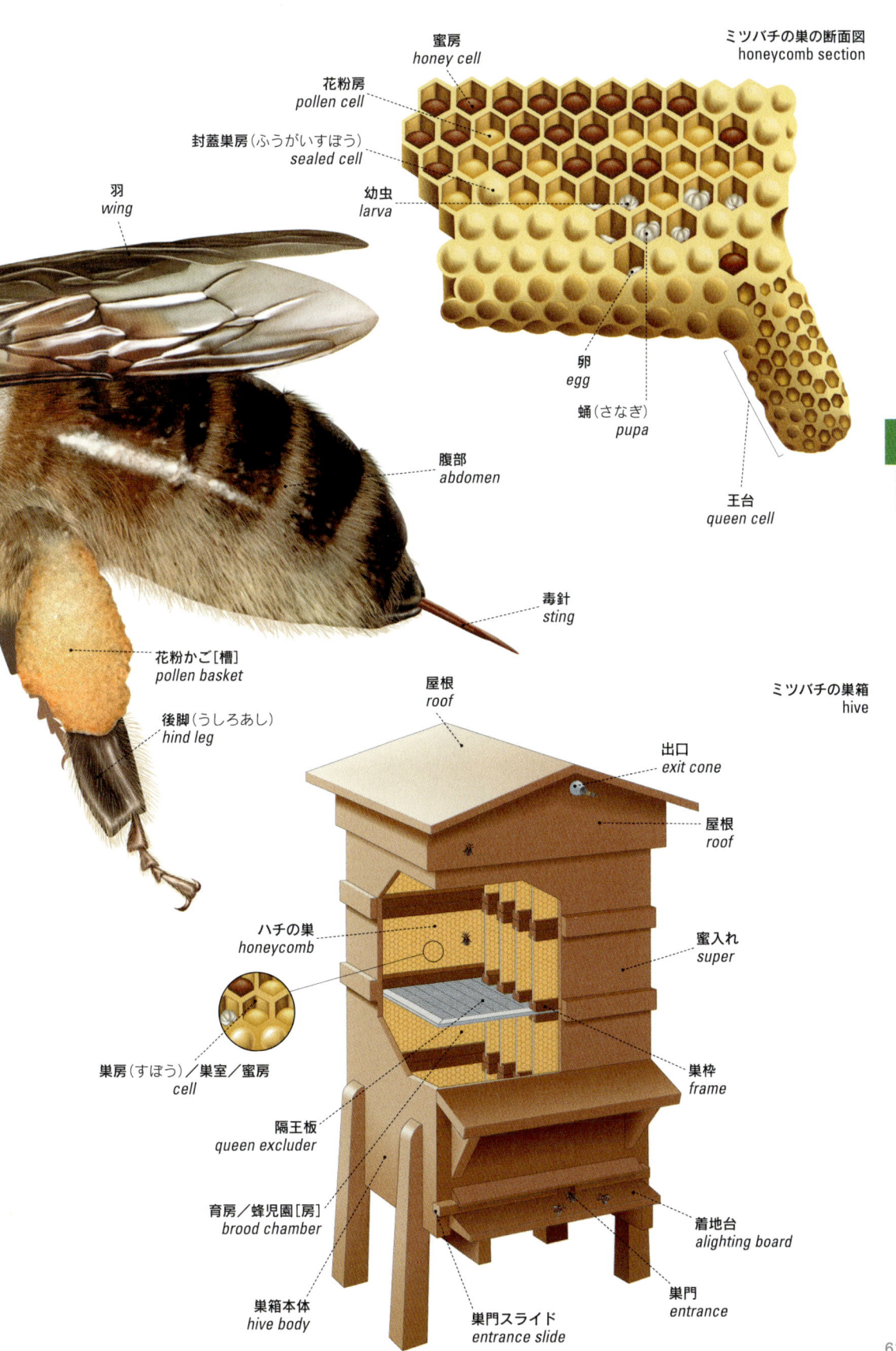

ミツバチの巣の断面図
honeycomb section

- 蜜房 / honey cell
- 花粉房 / pollen cell
- 封蓋巣房（ふうがいすぼう）/ sealed cell
- 幼虫 / larva
- 卵 / egg
- 蛹（さなぎ）/ pupa
- 王台 / queen cell

- 羽 / wing
- 腹部 / abdomen
- 毒針 / sting
- 花粉かご［槽］/ pollen basket
- 後脚（うしろあし）/ hind leg

ミツバチの巣箱
hive

- 屋根 / roof
- 出口 / exit cone
- 屋根 / roof
- ハチの巣 / honeycomb
- 蜜入れ / super
- 巣房（すぼう）／巣室／蜜房 / cell
- 巣枠 / frame
- 隔王板 / queen excluder
- 育房／蜂児圏［房］/ brood chamber
- 着地台 / alighting board
- 巣箱本体 / hive body
- 巣門スライド / entrance slide
- 巣門 / entrance

動物界

昆虫 | INSECTS

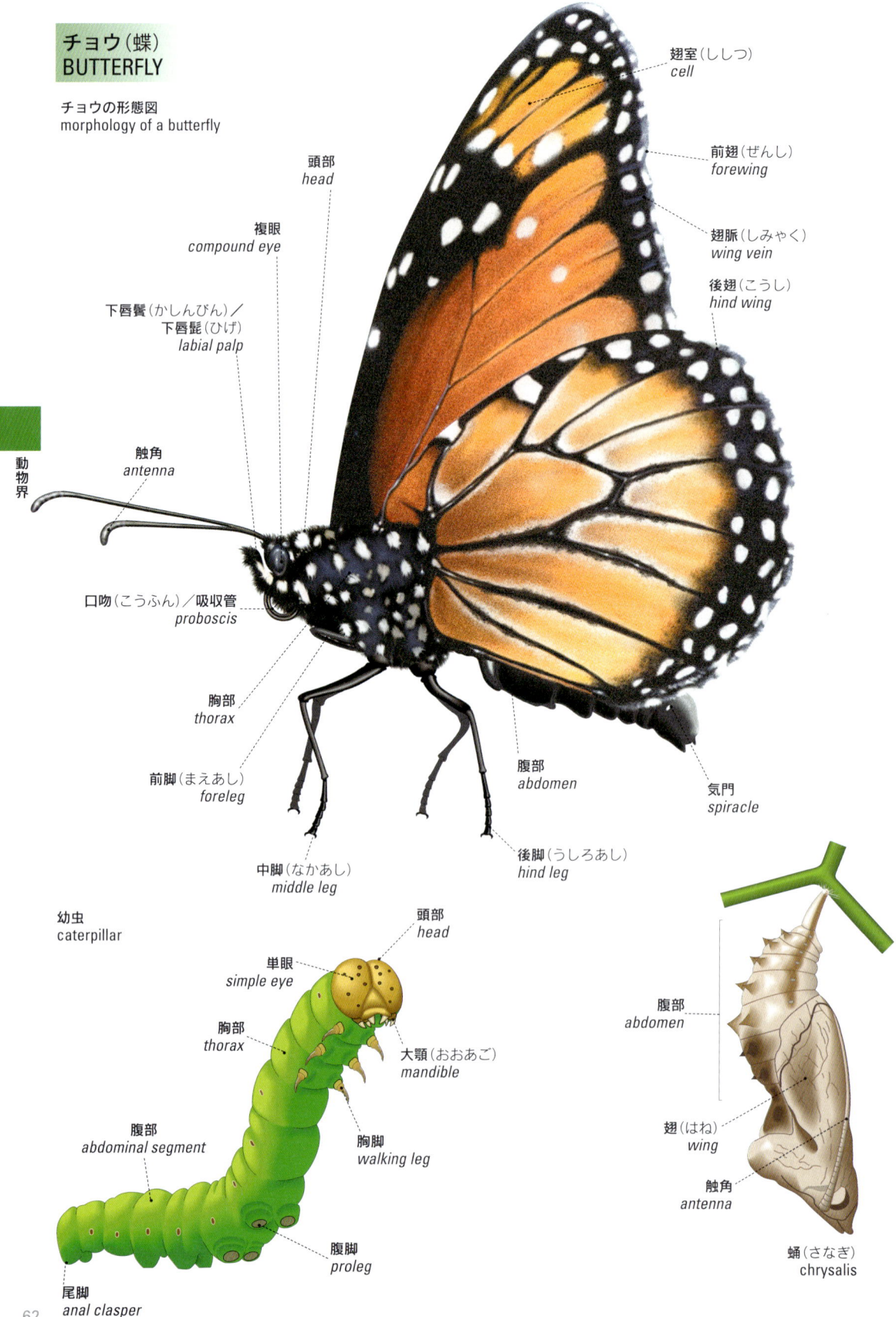

チョウ（蝶）
BUTTERFLY

チョウの形態図
morphology of a butterfly

翅室（ししつ） *cell*

前翅（ぜんし） *forewing*

翅脈（しみゃく） *wing vein*

後翅（こうし） *hind wing*

頭部 *head*

複眼 *compound eye*

下唇鬚（かしんびん）／下唇髭（ひげ） *labial palp*

触角 *antenna*

口吻（こうふん）／吸収管 *proboscis*

胸部 *thorax*

前脚（まえあし） *foreleg*

中脚（なかあし） *middle leg*

腹部 *abdomen*

後脚（うしろあし） *hind leg*

気門 *spiracle*

幼虫 *caterpillar*

頭部 *head*

単眼 *simple eye*

胸部 *thorax*

大顎（おおあご） *mandible*

腹部 *abdominal segment*

胸脚 *walking leg*

腹脚 *proleg*

尾脚 *anal clasper*

腹部 *abdomen*

翅（はね） *wing*

触角 *antenna*

蛹（さなぎ） *chrysalis*

動物界

62

昆虫 | INSECTS

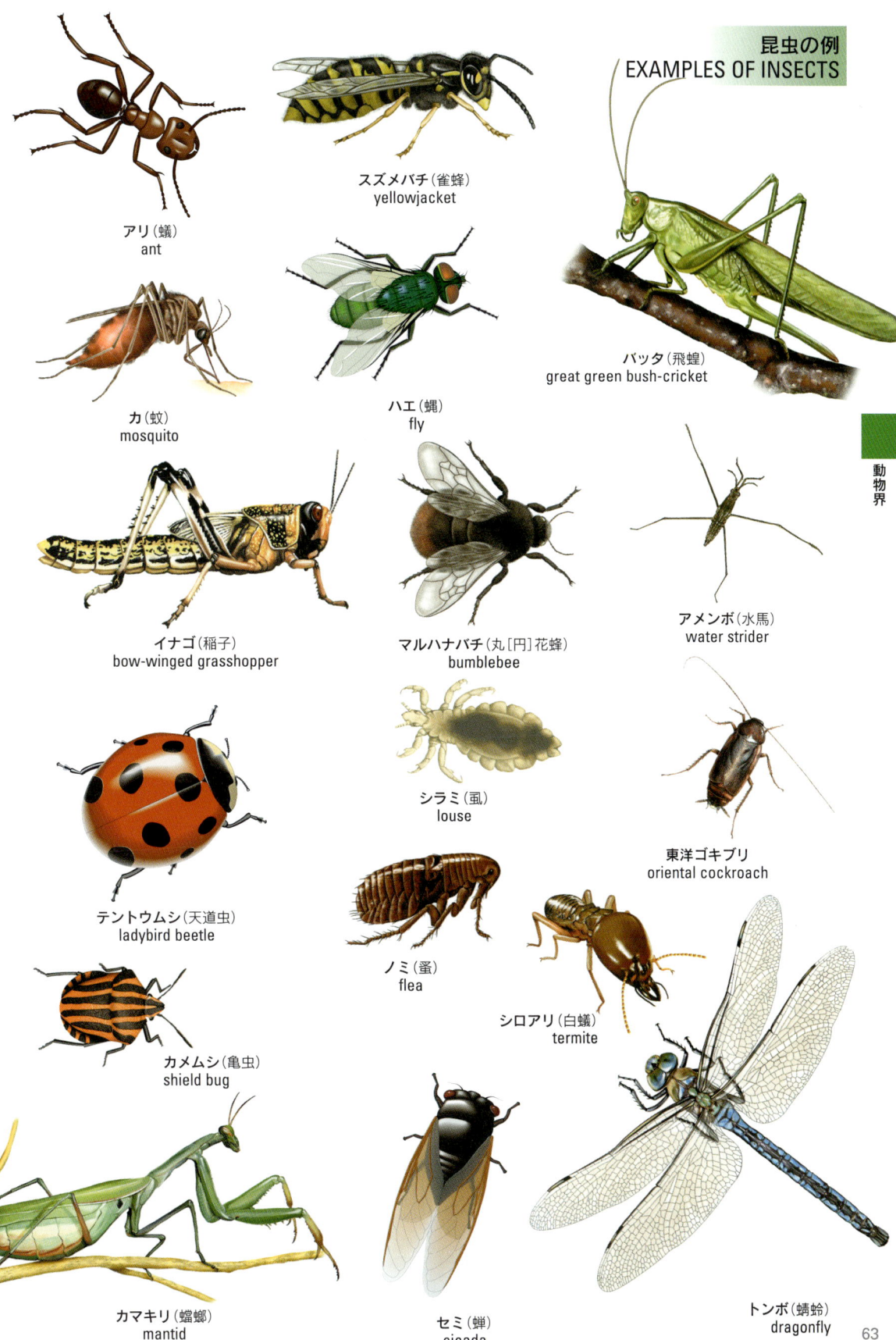

昆虫の例
EXAMPLES OF INSECTS

アリ（蟻）
ant

スズメバチ（雀蜂）
yellowjacket

カ（蚊）
mosquito

ハエ（蝿）
fly

バッタ（飛蝗）
great green bush-cricket

イナゴ（稲子）
bow-winged grasshopper

マルハナバチ（丸[円]花蜂）
bumblebee

アメンボ（水馬）
water strider

テントウムシ（天道虫）
ladybird beetle

シラミ（虱）
louse

東洋ゴキブリ
oriental cockroach

カメムシ（亀虫）
shield bug

ノミ（蚤）
flea

シロアリ（白蟻）
termite

カマキリ（蟷螂）
mantid

セミ（蝉）
cicada

トンボ（蜻蛉）
dragonfly

動物界

軟骨魚 | CARTILAGINOUS FISHES

魚は太古の昔から存在する脊椎動物で、現代の種の大部分は硬骨魚と軟骨魚という2つのグループに大別されます。軟骨魚のグループは、軟骨でできた骨格があるという点でほかと区別され、エイとサメがその代表と言えるでしょう。軟骨魚であれ硬骨魚であれ、すべての魚が細長い体型をして、ひれ、えらを持ち、完全に水生生活に適応しています。

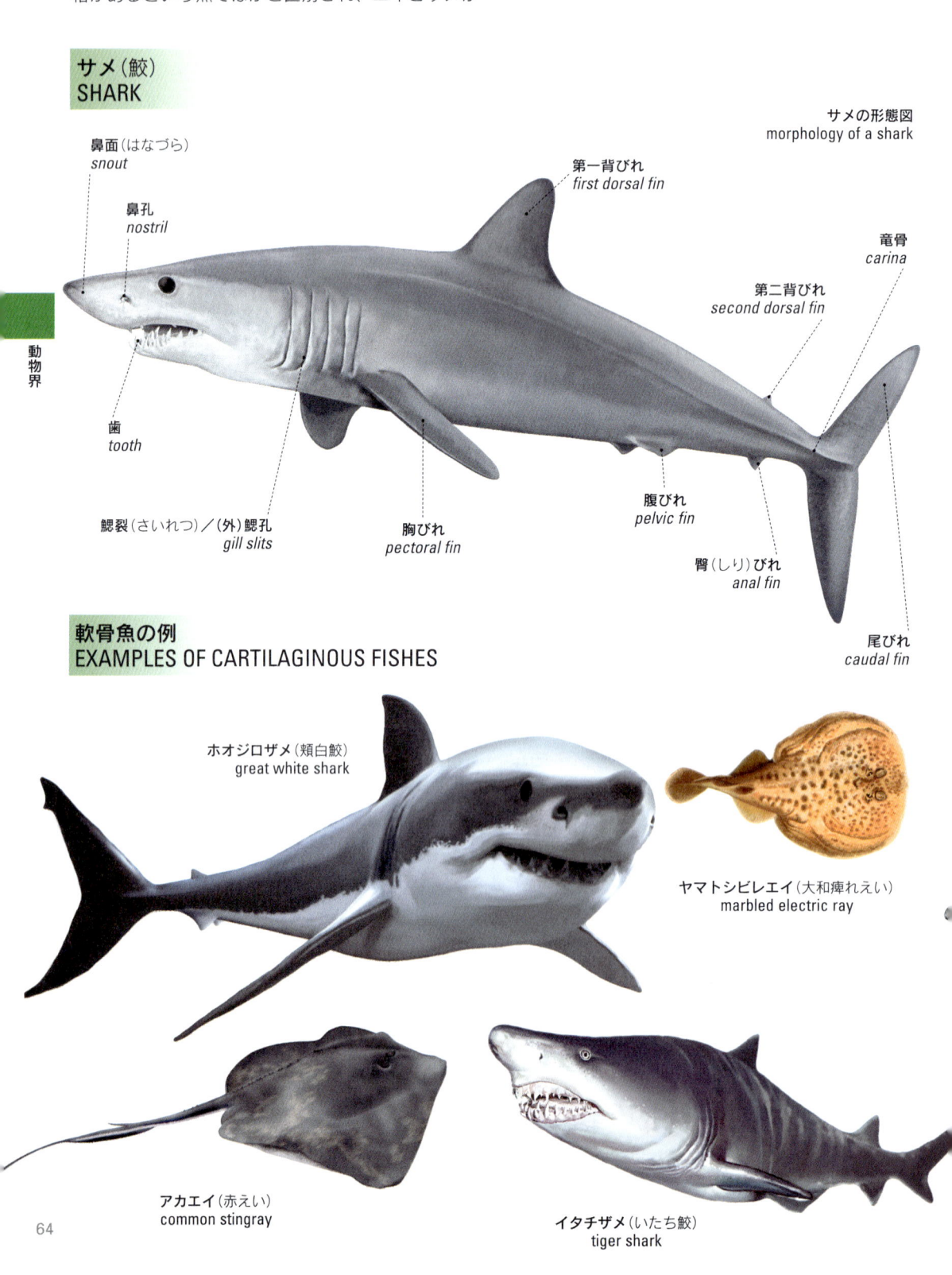

動物界

サメ（鮫）
SHARK

サメの形態図
morphology of a shark

- 鼻面（はなづら） snout
- 鼻孔 nostril
- 第一背びれ first dorsal fin
- 竜骨 carina
- 第二背びれ second dorsal fin
- 歯 tooth
- 鰓裂（さいれつ）／(外)鰓孔 gill slits
- 胸びれ pectoral fin
- 腹びれ pelvic fin
- 臀（しり）びれ anal fin
- 尾びれ caudal fin

軟骨魚の例
EXAMPLES OF CARTILAGINOUS FISHES

ホオジロザメ（頬白鮫） great white shark

ヤマトシビレエイ（大和痺れえい） marbled electric ray

アカエイ（赤えい） common stingray

イタチザメ（いたち鮫） tiger shark

硬骨魚 | BONY FISHES

名前から分かるように、硬骨魚は全体的であれ部分的であれ骨格を持っています。軟骨魚に続いて地球上に現れて以来きわめて進化を遂げた硬骨魚は、今日では２０，０００種類以上を数え、ウナギ、タツノオトシゴ、小さなイワシ、とげのあるひれを持ったスズキと同じくらい種類があります。地球で水生生活が可能な場所なら至る所で硬骨魚は見られます。

スズキ(鱸) PERCH

スズキの形態図
morphology of a perch

- 鰓蓋(えらぶた) operculum
- 棘条(きょくじょう) spiny ray
- 鼻孔 nostril
- 鱗(うろこ) scale
- 軟条 soft ray
- 前上顎 premaxilla
- 側線 lateral line
- 下顎(かがく) mandible
- 上顎(じょうがく) maxilla
- 腹びれ pelvic fin
- 胸びれ pectoral fin
- 臀(しり)びれ anal fin
- 尾びれ caudal fin

動物界

硬骨魚の例 EXAMPLES OF BONY FISHES

- カワカマス(河かます) pike
- メカジキ(眼旗魚) swordfish
- マス(鱒) trout
- カレイ(鰈) common plaice
- ウナギ(鰻) eel
- マグロ(鮪) tuna

両生類 | AMPHIBIANS

両生類の特徴は、水中でも地上でも同様に生活できるところです。両生類は、器用に泳ぐ能力も備えていながら、脚と肺のお陰で水のある場所から陸地に這い上がった最初の脊椎動物でした。よく知られた３,０００種類の大部分は地上の湿った場所や淡水面でよく見られます。

カエル(蛙)
FROG

カエルの形態図
morphology of a frog

- 鼓膜 tympanum
- 胴 trunk
- 上瞼(うわぶた) upper eyelid
- 眼球 eyeball
- 吻端(ふんたん)／鼻先 snout
- 外鼻孔 nostril
- 口 mouth
- 下瞼(したまぶた) lower eyelid
- 前肢(まえあし) forelimb
- 指 digit
- 後肢(うしろあし) hind limb
- 水掻き web
- 水掻きのある足 webbed foot

カエルの一生
life cycle of the frog

卵
eggs

外鰓(がいさい)
external gills

後肢(うしろあし)
hind limb

前肢(まえあし)
forelimb

オタマジャクシ
tadpole

両生類の例
EXAMPLES OF AMPHIBIANS

アマガエル(雨蛙)
tree frog

イモリ(井守)
newt

ヒキガエル(蟇蛙)
common toad

アルプスサラマンダー
alpine salamander

ヒョウガエル(豹蛙)
Northern leopard frog

カエル(蛙)
common frog

爬虫類 | REPTILES

爬虫類は、甲羅や、湿り気を逃がさない鱗状の皮膚、よく発達した肺のお陰で、地上生活に完全に適応した最初の脊椎動物でした。これらの冷血動物がよく知られているのは、長い間失われている"科"、つまり恐竜に負うところが大きいのです。今日では爬虫類として知られている約6,500種類はとりわけ熱帯地方に多く見られます。

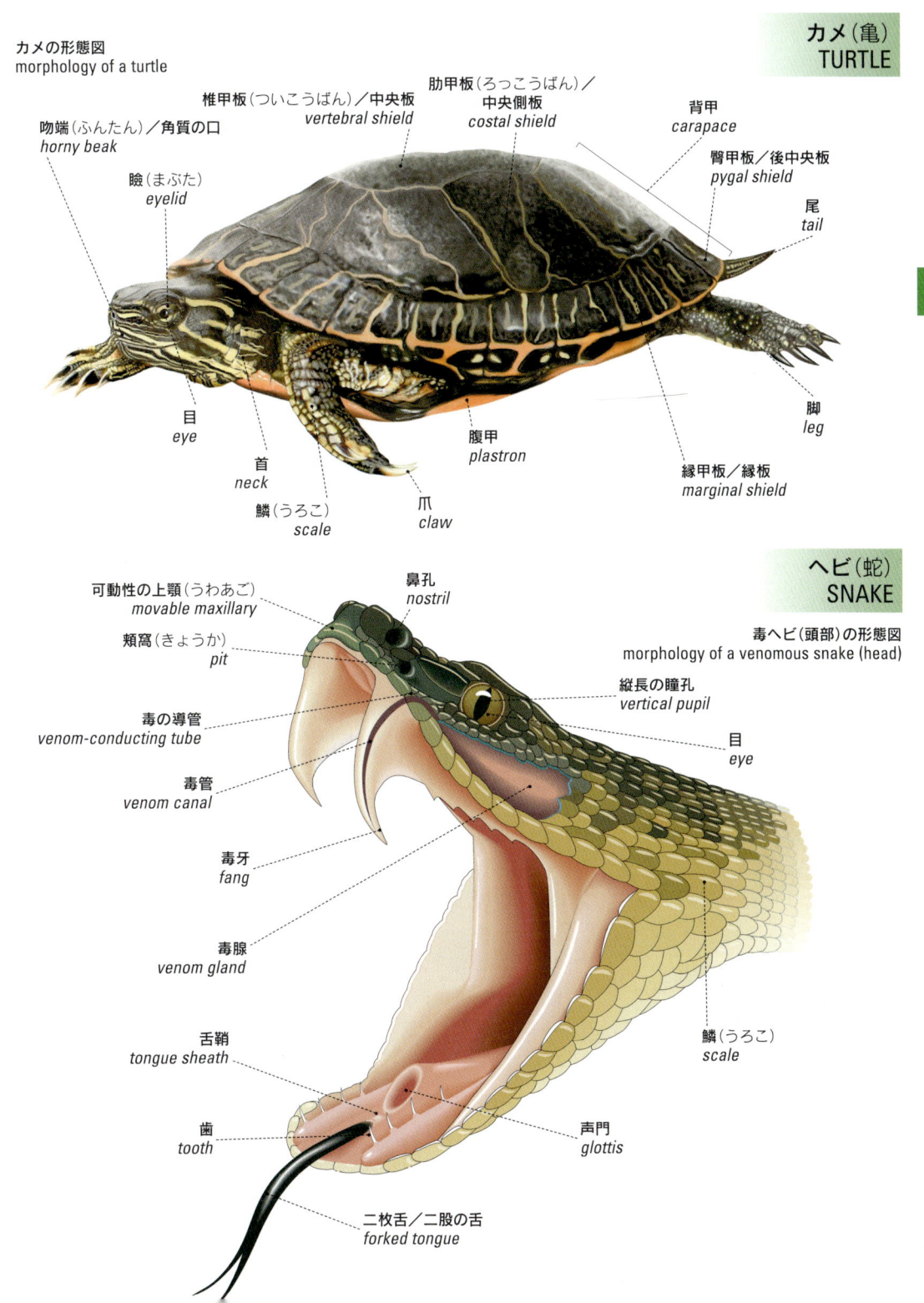

カメの形態図
morphology of a turtle

カメ(亀)
TURTLE

- 椎甲板(ついこうばん)／中央板 vertebral shield
- 肋甲板(ろっこうばん)／中央側板 costal shield
- 背甲 carapace
- 臀甲板／後中央板 pygal shield
- 尾 tail
- 吻端(ふんたん)／角質の口 horny beak
- 瞼(まぶた) eyelid
- 目 eye
- 首 neck
- 鱗(うろこ) scale
- 爪 claw
- 腹甲 plastron
- 縁甲板／縁板 marginal shield
- 脚 leg

ヘビ(蛇)
SNAKE

毒ヘビ(頭部)の形態図
morphology of a venomous snake (head)

- 可動性の上顎(うわあご) movable maxillary
- 頬窩(きょうか) pit
- 毒の導管 venom-conducting tube
- 毒管 venom canal
- 毒牙 fang
- 毒腺 venom gland
- 舌鞘 tongue sheath
- 歯 tooth
- 二枚舌／二股の舌 forked tongue
- 鼻孔 nostril
- 縦長の瞳孔 vertical pupil
- 目 eye
- 鱗(うろこ) scale
- 声門 glottis

動物界

67

爬虫類 | REPTILES

爬虫類の例
EXAMPLES OF REPTILES

オサガメ（長亀）
leatherback turtle

ニシキヘビ（錦蛇）
python

ガーターヘビ（蛇）
garter snake

コブラ
cobra

サンゴヘビ（珊瑚蛇）
coral snake

ガラガラヘビ（蛇）
rattlesnake

ボア
boa

クサリヘビ（鎖蛇）
viper

爬虫類 | REPTILES

オオトカゲ（大蜥蜴）
monitor lizard

カメレオン
chameleon

トカゲ（蜥蜴）
lizard

イグアナ
iguana

アリゲーター
alligator

カイマン
caiman

クロコダイル
crocodile

動物界

爬虫類 | REPTILES

恐竜
DINOSAURS

ステゴザウルス
stegosaurus

スピノサウルス
spinosaurus

動物界

アロサウルス
allosaurus

パラサウロロフス
parasauroloph

ハドロサウルス
hadrosaurus

ディプロドクス
diplodocus

爬虫類 | REPTILES

ティラノザウルス
tyrannosaurus

パキケファロサウルス
pachycephalosaurus

アンキロサウルス
ankylosaurus

ディノニクス
deinonychus

トリケラトプス
triceratops

ブラキオサウルス
brachiosaurus

動物界

鳥類 | BIRDS

コウモリを除けば、鳥は飛ぶことのできる唯一の脊椎動物です。軽い骨格と羽毛に覆われた翼があって、鳥は動物界で最もじょうずに飛べる動物になっています。鳥を科学的に分類しようとすると、例えば羽毛の構造をどうとらえるべきか難しい面があります。そのため私たちは、よく知られた１０，０００種類を単純に水鳥と陸鳥に区別することがあります。

鳥 BIRD

動物界

餌台／餌箱
bird feeder

巣箱
birdhouse

巣
nest

鳥の形態図
morphology of a bird

- 鼻孔 nostril
- 嘴（くちばし） bill
- 顎（あご） chin
- 咽（のど） throat
- 雨覆い（あまおおい） wing covert
- 胸 breast
- 腹 abdomen
- 頸（くび） nape
- 翼 wing
- 第二趾／内趾 inner toe
- 鉤爪 claw
- 第三趾／中趾 middle toe
- 第四趾／外趾 outer toe

卵 egg
- 胚盤 blastodisc
- 卵殻 shell
- 気室 air space
- 卵黄 yolk
- 卵白 albumen

鳥類 | BIRDS

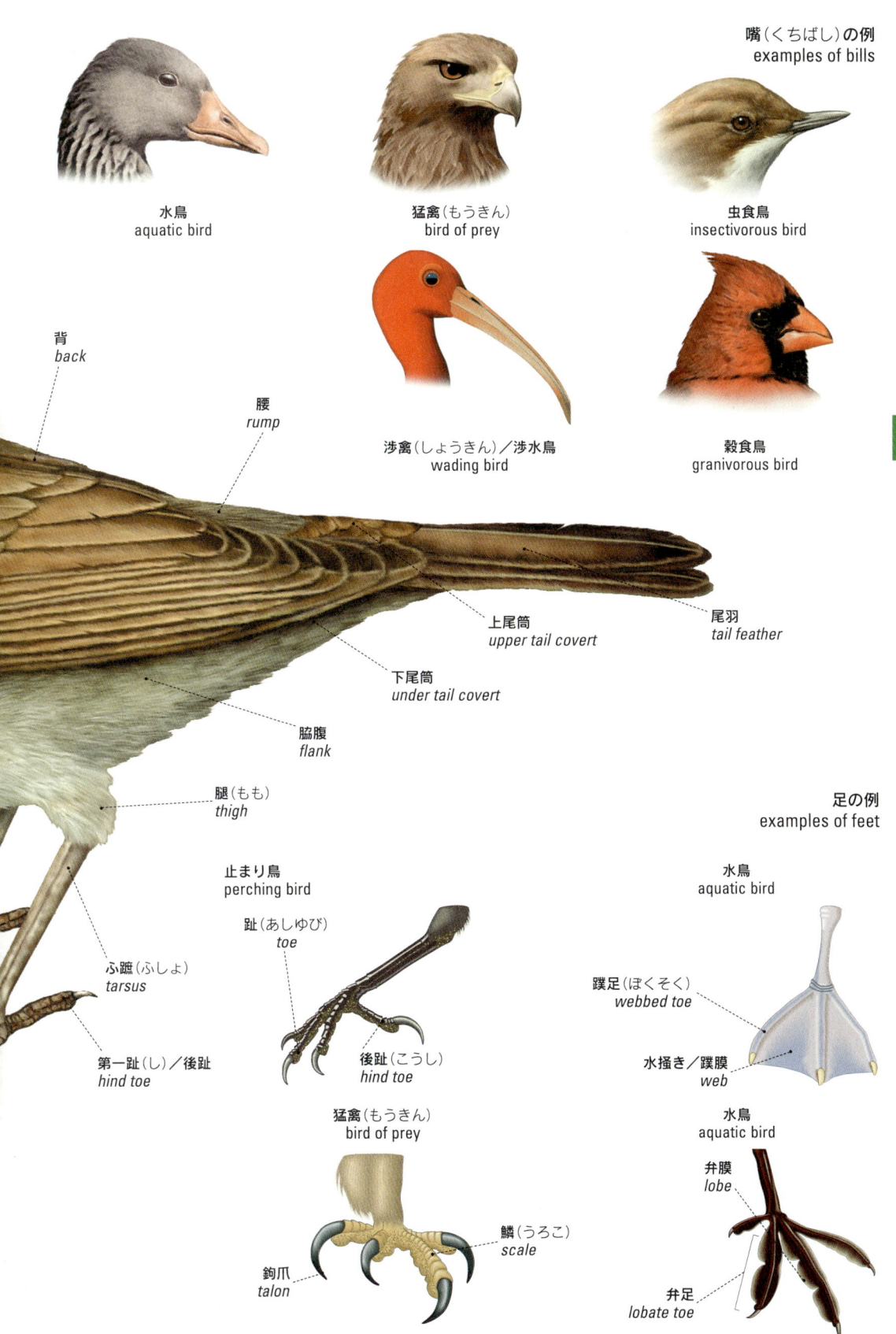

嘴（くちばし）の例
examples of bills

水鳥
aquatic bird

猛禽（もうきん）
bird of prey

虫食鳥
insectivorous bird

涉禽（しょうきん）／涉水鳥
wading bird

穀食鳥
granivorous bird

背
back

腰
rump

上尾筒
upper tail covert

下尾筒
under tail covert

尾羽
tail feather

脇腹
flank

腿（もも）
thigh

足の例
examples of feet

止まり鳥
perching bird

趾（あしゆび）
toe

水鳥
aquatic bird

蹼足（ぼくそく）
webbed toe

水掻き／蹼膜
web

ふ蹠（ふしょ）
tarsus

第一趾（し）／後趾
hind toe

後趾（こうし）
hind toe

猛禽（もうきん）
bird of prey

鱗（うろこ）
scale

鉤爪
talon

水鳥
aquatic bird

弁膜
lobe

弁足
lobate toe

動物界

73

鳥類 | BIRDS

陸生鳥類の例
EXAMPLES OF TERRESTRIAL BIRDS

動物界

ハチドリ（蜂鳥）
hummingbird

カケス（懸巣）
jay

ショウジョウコウカンチョウ（猩々紅冠鳥）
cardinal

ツバメ（燕）
swallow

ゴシキヒワ（五色鶸）
goldfinch

アトリ（花鶏）／フィンチ
finch

カラス（烏）
raven

スズメ（雀）
sparrow

ムクドリ（椋鳥）
starling

アメリカワシミミズク（鷲木菟）
great horned owl

ハト（鳩）
pigeon

ヨーロッパヤマウズラ（山鶉）
partridge

オオハシ（巨嘴鳥）
toucan

ワシ（鷲）
eagle

コンゴウインコ（金剛鸚哥）
macaw

タカ（鷹）
falcon

クジャク（孔雀）
peacock

鳥類 | BIRDS

オンドリ（雄鶏）
rooster

シチメンチョウ（七面鳥）
turkey

ヒヨコ（雛）
chick

ガチョウ（鵞鳥）
goose

ダチョウ（駝鳥）
ostrich

メンドリ（雌鶏）
hen

動物界

水辺の鳥と海辺の鳥の例
EXAMPLES OF AQUATIC AND SHOREBIRDS

ペンギン
penguin

コウノトリ（鸛）
stork

カワセミ（川蝉）
kingfisher

アジサシ（鯵刺）
tern

アヒル（家鴨）
duck

ミヤコドリ（都鳥）
oystercatcher

ペリカン
pelican

フラミンゴ
flamingo

哺乳動物 | MAMMALS

哺乳類の4,600種類の大部分は、毛に覆われた皮膚を見ればすぐに見分けがつきます。すべての雌は乳房から子供に哺乳します。ここから哺乳類という名前が来ています。哺乳類は脊椎動物の中でも最も進化を遂げた動物と言えます。鳥と同様に、哺乳類は体温を一定に保つことができる唯一の動物です。

有袋哺乳動物
MARSUPIAL MAMMALS

カンガルーの形態図
morphology of a kangaroo

- 耳介（じかい） pinna
- 鼻（口部）／鼻面（はなづら）／口吻（こうふん） snout
- 前足／前肢 forelimb
- 鉤爪 claw
- 後ろ足／後肢 hind limb
- 足指 digit
- 毛皮 fur
- 大腿部 thigh
- 育児嚢（のう）／育児袋 pouch
- 足 foot
- 尾 tail

有袋動物の例
examples of marsupials

- オポッサム／フクロネズミ（袋鼠） opossum
- コアラ koala

食虫哺乳動物の例
EXAMPLES OF INSECTIVOROUS MAMMALS

- モグラ（土竜） mole
- トガリネズミ（尖鼠） shrew
- ハリネズミ（針鼠） hedgehog

動物界

哺乳動物 | MAMMALS

齧歯（げっし）類（動物）
RODENTS

ネズミ（鼠）の形態図
morphology of a rat

- 耳介（じかい） pinna
- 毛衣 fur
- 震毛／感覚毛 vibrissa
- 鼻 nose
- 指 digit
- 鉤爪 claw
- 尾 tail

齧歯（げっし）類動物の例
examples of rodents

- ビーバー beaver
- ノネズミ（野鼠） field mouse
- ヤマアラシ（山荒らし） porcupine
- リス（栗鼠） squirrel
- ハムスター hamster
- シマリス（縞栗鼠） chipmunk
- テンジクネズミ（天竺鼠）／モルモット guinea pig
- マーモット groundhog

ウサギ目の動物
LAGOMORPHS

- ノウサギ（野兎） hare
- ナキウサギ（啼兎） pika
- （アナ）ウサギ（（穴）兎） rabbit

哺乳動物 | MAMMALS

肉食哺乳動物（イヌ（犬））
CARNIVOROUS MAMMALS (DOG)

イヌの形態図
morphology of a dog

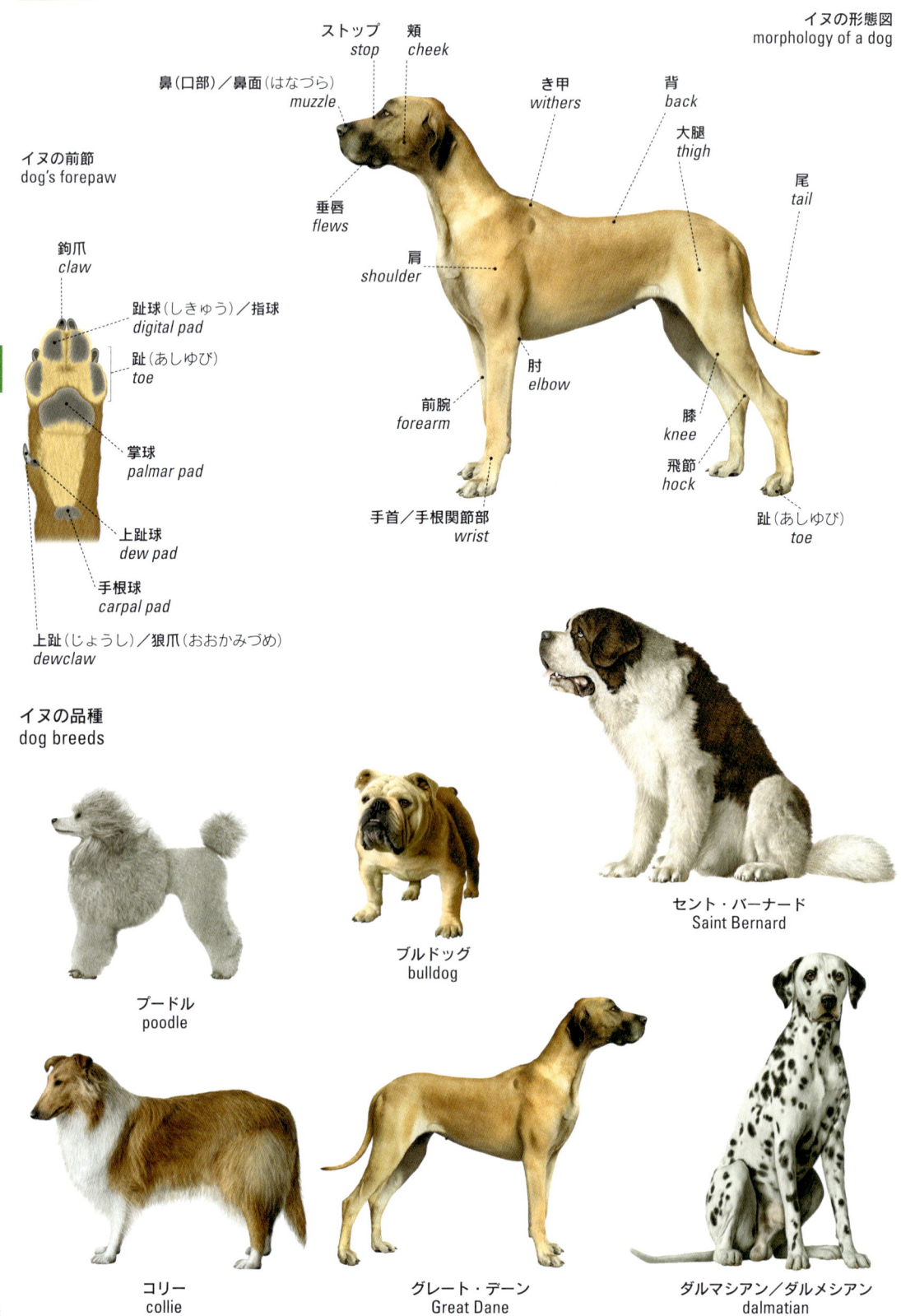

ストップ stop
頬 cheek
鼻（口部）／鼻面（はなづら） muzzle
き甲 withers
背 back
大腿 thigh
尾 tail
垂唇 flews
肩 shoulder
肘 elbow
前腕 forearm
膝 knee
飛節 hock
手首／手根関節部 wrist
趾（あしゆび） toe

イヌの前節
dog's forepaw

鉤爪 claw
趾球（しきゅう）／指球 digital pad
趾（あしゆび） toe
掌球 palmar pad
上趾球 dew pad
手根球 carpal pad
上趾（じょうし）／狼爪（おおかみづめ） dewclaw

動物界

イヌの品種
dog breeds

プードル poodle

ブルドッグ bulldog

セント・バーナード Saint Bernard

コリー collie

グレート・デーン Great Dane

ダルマシアン／ダルメシアン dalmatian

哺乳動物 | MAMMALS

肉食哺乳動物（ネコ（猫））
CARNIVOROUS MAMMALS (CAT)

ネコの形態図
morphology of a cat

- 耳 / ear
- 尾 / tail
- 目 / eye
- 柔毛 / fur

頭部
head

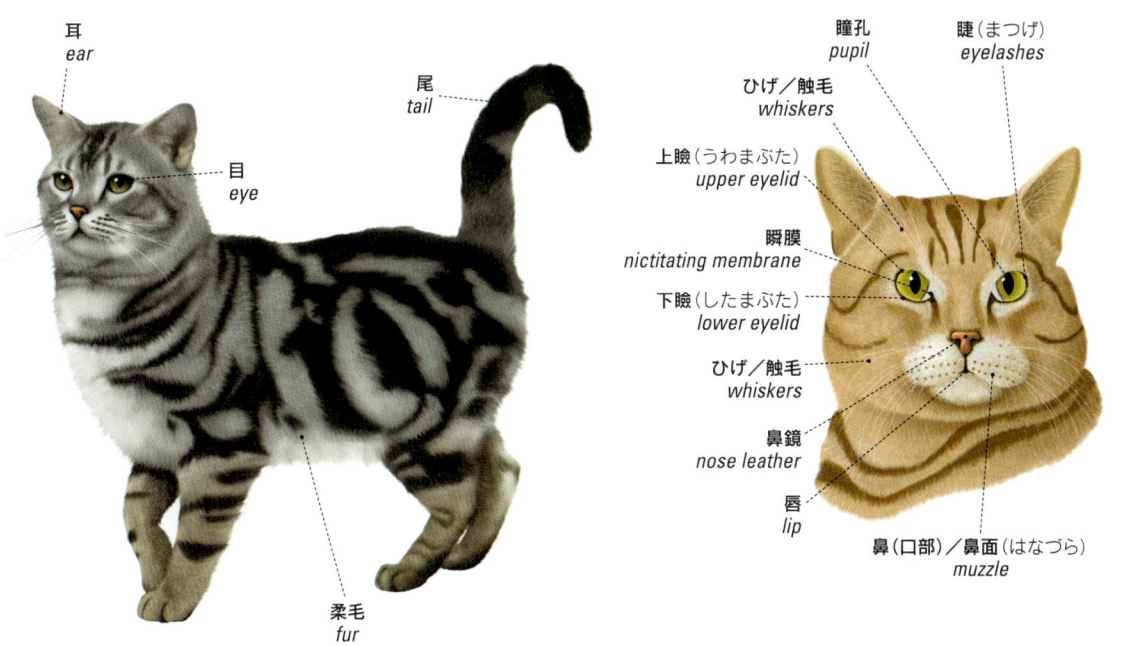

- 瞳孔 / pupil
- 睫（まつげ）/ eyelashes
- ひげ／触毛 / whiskers
- 上瞼（うわまぶた）/ upper eyelid
- 瞬膜 / nictitating membrane
- 下瞼（したまぶた）/ lower eyelid
- ひげ／触毛 / whiskers
- 鼻鏡 / nose leather
- 唇 / lip
- 鼻（口部）／鼻面（はなづら）/ muzzle

動物界

ネコの品種
cat breeds

- アビシニアン / Abyssinian
- マンクス / Manx
- メインクーン / Maine Coon
- ペルシャネコ / Persian
- アメリカンショートヘア / American shorthair
- シャムネコ / Siamese

79

哺乳動物 | MAMMALS

肉食哺乳動物の例
EXAMPLES OF CARNIVOROUS MAMMALS

アナグマ（穴熊）
badger

カワウソ（獺）
river otter

イタチ（鼬）
weasel

ハイイロマングース（灰色）
mongoose

ミンク
mink

ハイエナ
hyena

フェネック
fennec

アライグマ（洗い熊）
raccoon

オオカミ（狼）
wolf

キツネ（狐）
fox

スカンク
skunk

哺乳動物 | MAMMALS

アメリカクロクマ（黒熊）
black bear

ホッキョクグマ（北極熊）
polar bear

ジャガー
jaguar

オオヤマネコ（大山猫）
lynx

ヒョウ（豹）
leopard

動物界

ライオン
lion

トラ（虎）
tiger

チーター
cheetah

81

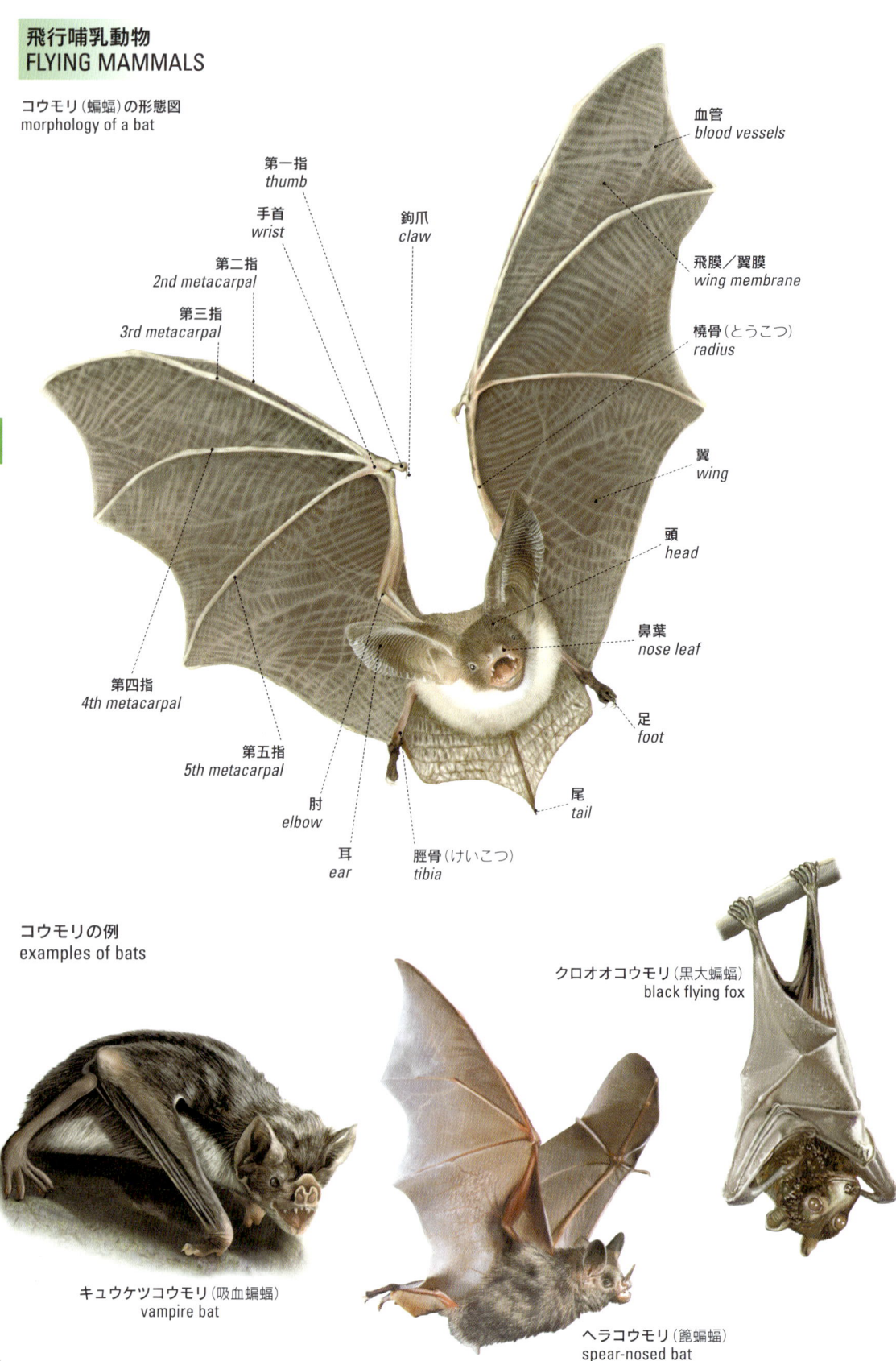

哺乳動物 | MAMMALS

飛行哺乳動物
FLYING MAMMALS

コウモリ（蝙蝠）の形態図
morphology of a bat

- 第一指 / *thumb*
- 手首 / *wrist*
- 第二指 / *2nd metacarpal*
- 第三指 / *3rd metacarpal*
- 鉤爪 / *claw*
- 血管 / *blood vessels*
- 飛膜／翼膜 / *wing membrane*
- 橈骨（とうこつ） / *radius*
- 翼 / *wing*
- 頭 / *head*
- 鼻葉 / *nose leaf*
- 足 / *foot*
- 第四指 / *4th metacarpal*
- 第五指 / *5th metacarpal*
- 尾 / *tail*
- 肘 / *elbow*
- 耳 / *ear*
- 脛骨（けいこつ） / *tibia*

コウモリの例
examples of bats

キュウケツコウモリ（吸血蝙蝠）
vampire bat

ヘラコウモリ（箆蝙蝠）
spear-nosed bat

クロオオコウモリ（黒大蝙蝠）
black flying fox

哺乳動物 | MAMMALS

霊長類
PRIMATE MAMMALS

ゴリラの形態図
morphology of a gorilla

- 顔 / face
- 毛（皮）/ fur
- 腕 / arm
- 手 / hand
- つかむのに適した指 / prehensile digit
- 脚 / leg
- 足 / foot
- ほかの指に対して向かい合わせになる親指 / opposable thumb

動物界

霊長類の動物の例
examples of primates

- テナガザル（手長猿）/ gibbon
- ヒヒ（狒狒）/ baboon
- オランウータン / orangutan
- マカク / macaque
- キツネザル（狐猿）/ lemur
- チンパンジー / chimpanzee

哺乳動物 | MAMMALS

有蹄哺乳動物
UNGULATE MAMMALS

ウマの蹄（ひづめ）
horse's hoof

- 蹄壁 / side wall
- 蹄冠 / coronet
- 蹄尖 / toe
- 蹄球 / bulb
- 鉄唇 / toe clip
- 蹄踵（ていしょう）/ heel
- 馬蹄／蹄鉄 / horseshoe
- 蹄側 / quarter

馬蹄／蹄鉄
horseshoe

- 鉄尾部 / quarter
- 鉄枝 / branch
- 鉄側部 / side wall
- 鉄頭 / toe

ウマ（馬）の形態図
morphology of a horse

- 脾腹（ひばら）／脇腹 / flank
- 腰 / loin
- 背 / back
- 尻 / croup
- 尾 / tail
- 大腿（だいたい）/ thigh
- 後膝（あとひざ）/ stifle
- 下腿（かたい）／脛（はぎ）/ gaskin
- 腹 / belly
- 飛節 / hock
- 蹴爪（けづめ）/ fetlock
- 管（くだ）/ cannon
- 球節 / fetlock joint
- 踵（あくと）／繋（つな）ぎ / pastern
- 蹄冠 / coronet
- 蹄（ひづめ）/ hoof

歩様／歩法
gaits

常歩（なみあし）/ walk

速歩（はやあし）/ trot

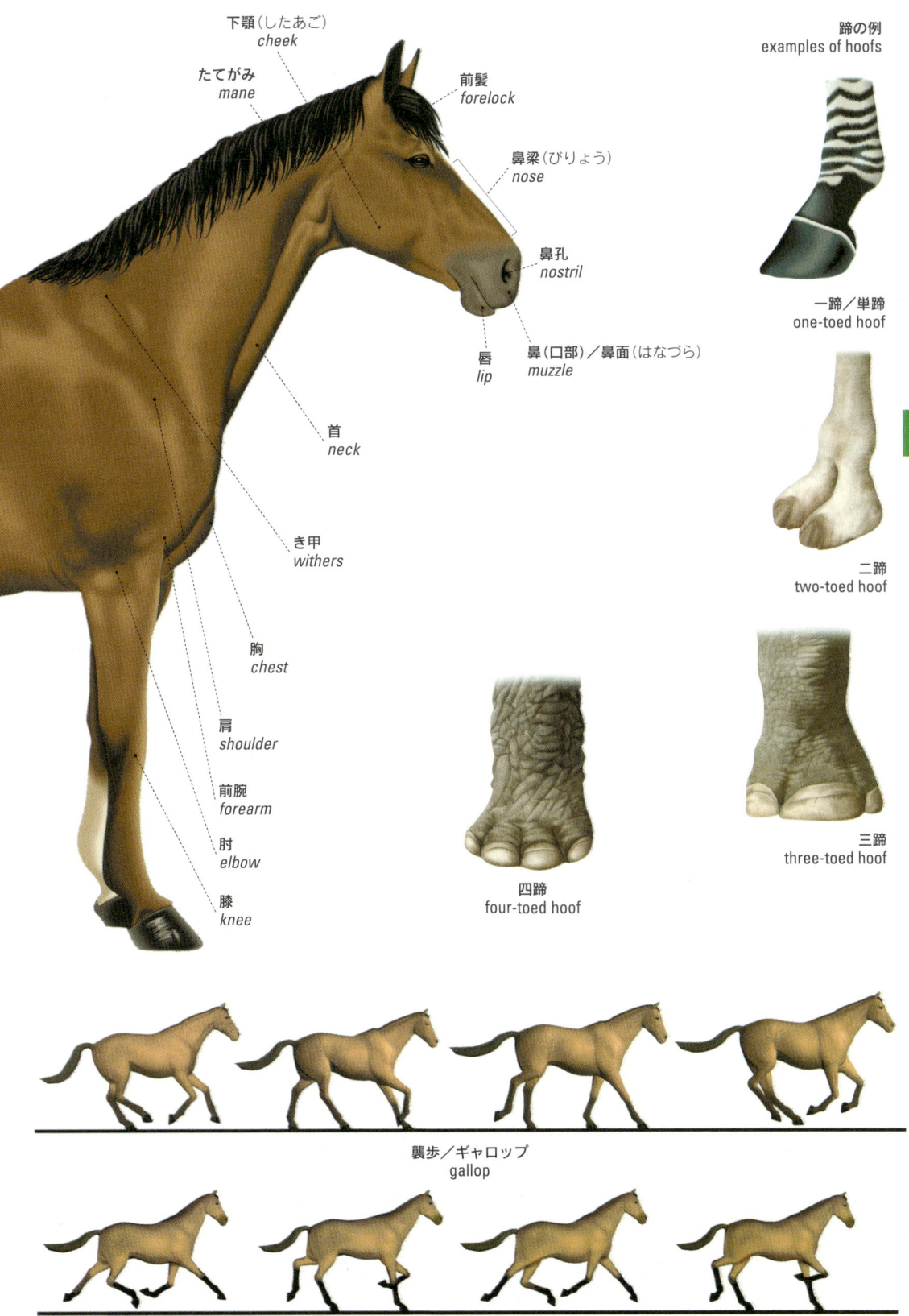

哺乳動物 | MAMMALS

下顎(したあご)
cheek

たてがみ
mane

前髪
forelock

鼻梁(びりょう)
nose

鼻孔
nostril

唇
lip

鼻(口部)／鼻面(はなづら)
muzzle

首
neck

き甲
withers

胸
chest

肩
shoulder

前腕
forearm

肘
elbow

膝
knee

蹄の例
examples of hoofs

一蹄／単蹄
one-toed hoof

二蹄
two-toed hoof

四蹄
four-toed hoof

三蹄
three-toed hoof

動物界

襲歩／ギャロップ
gallop

側対速歩(はやあし)
pace

85

哺乳動物 | MAMMALS

有蹄哺乳動物の例
examples of ungulate mammals

ブタ(豚)
pig

メウシ(雌牛)
cow

ヤク
yak

バイソン
bison

オジロジカ(尾白鹿)
white-tailed deer

ヤギ(山羊)
goat

ヒツジ(羊)
sheep

ムフロン
mouflon

サイ(犀)
rhinoceros

哺乳動物 | MAMMALS

ヒトコブラクダ（単峰駱駝）
dromedary camel

フタコブラクダ（双峰駱駝）
bactrian camel

ロバ（驢馬）
donkey

シマウマ（縞馬）／ゼブラ
zebra

ラマ
llama

カバ（河馬）
hippopotamus

キリン
giraffe

オカピ
okapi

ゾウ（象）
elephant

哺乳動物 | MAMMALS

海棲哺乳動物
MARINE MAMMALS

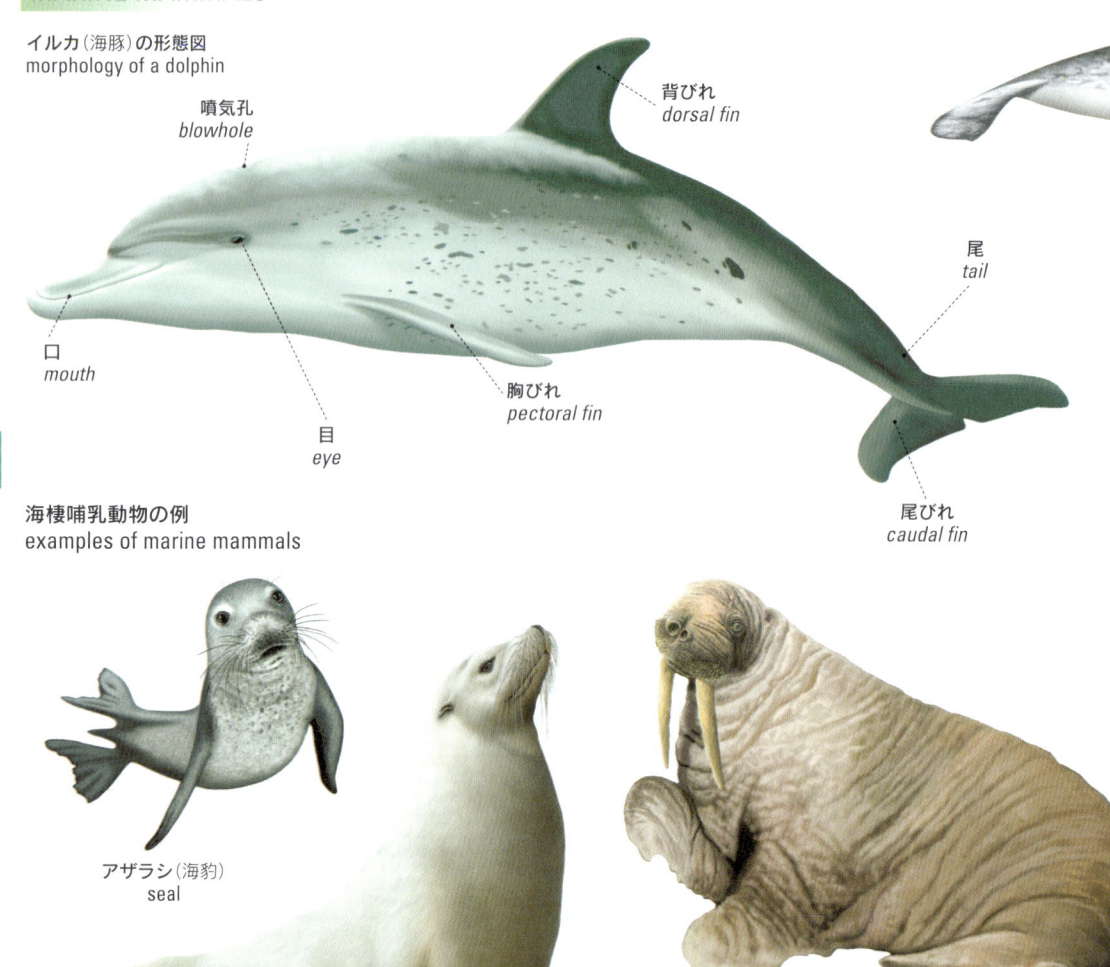

イルカ（海豚）の形態図
morphology of a dolphin

- 噴気孔 / *blowhole*
- 背びれ / *dorsal fin*
- 尾 / *tail*
- 口 / *mouth*
- 胸びれ / *pectoral fin*
- 目 / *eye*
- 尾びれ / *caudal fin*

海棲哺乳動物の例
examples of marine mammals

- アザラシ（海豹） / *seal*
- アシカ（海驢） / *sea lion*
- セイウチ（海象） / *walrus*
- セミクジラ（背美鯨） / *northern right whale*

哺乳動物 | MAMMALS

イッカク（一角）
narwhal

イルカ（海豚）
dolphin

ネズミイルカ（鼠海豚）
porpoise

ザトウクジラ（座頭鯨）
humpback whale

シロイルカ（白海豚）／シロクジラ（白鯨）
beluga whale

シャチ（鯱）
killer whale

マッコウクジラ（抹香鯨）
sperm whale

動物界

人体 | HUMAN BODY

多くの動物の体と同じく、人間の体も左右対称、つまり多くの部位が対になっています。実際、人体の左半分と右半分は対称的です。すべての体が同じ型でできているとはいえ、まったく同じ物は2つとありません。体型、身長、人体のプロポーションは人によってずいぶんと異なります。

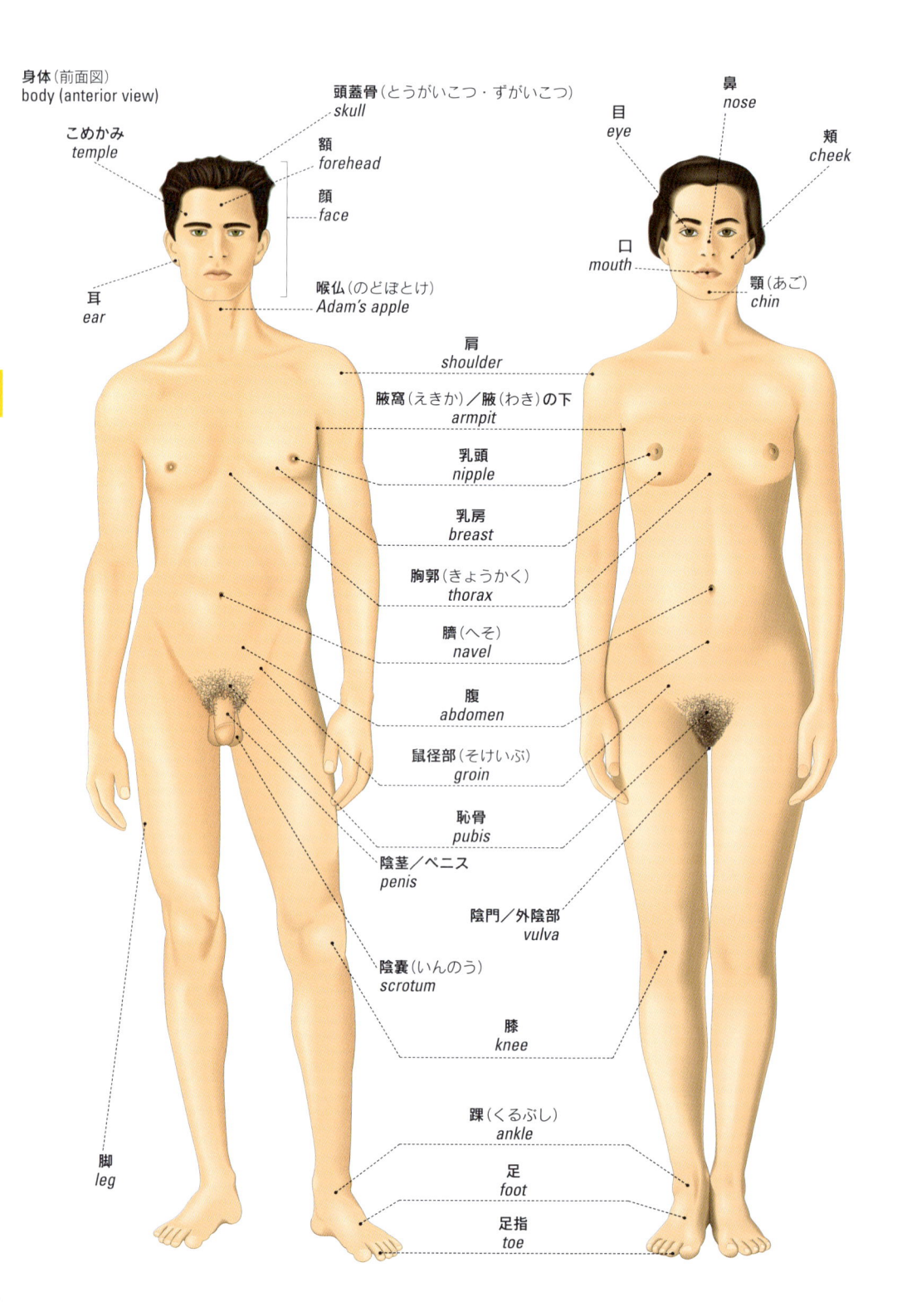

身体(前面図)
body (anterior view)

- こめかみ / temple
- 頭蓋骨(とうがいこつ・ずがいこつ) / skull
- 額 / forehead
- 顔 / face
- 耳 / ear
- 喉仏(のどぼとけ) / Adam's apple
- 鼻 / nose
- 目 / eye
- 頬 / cheek
- 口 / mouth
- 顎(あご) / chin
- 肩 / shoulder
- 腋窩(えきか)／腋(わき)の下 / armpit
- 乳頭 / nipple
- 乳房 / breast
- 胸郭(きょうかく) / thorax
- 臍(へそ) / navel
- 腹 / abdomen
- 鼠径部(そけいぶ) / groin
- 恥骨 / pubis
- 陰茎／ペニス / penis
- 陰門／外陰部 / vulva
- 陰嚢(いんのう) / scrotum
- 膝 / knee
- 踝(くるぶし) / ankle
- 足 / foot
- 足指 / toe
- 脚 / leg

人間

人体 | HUMAN BODY

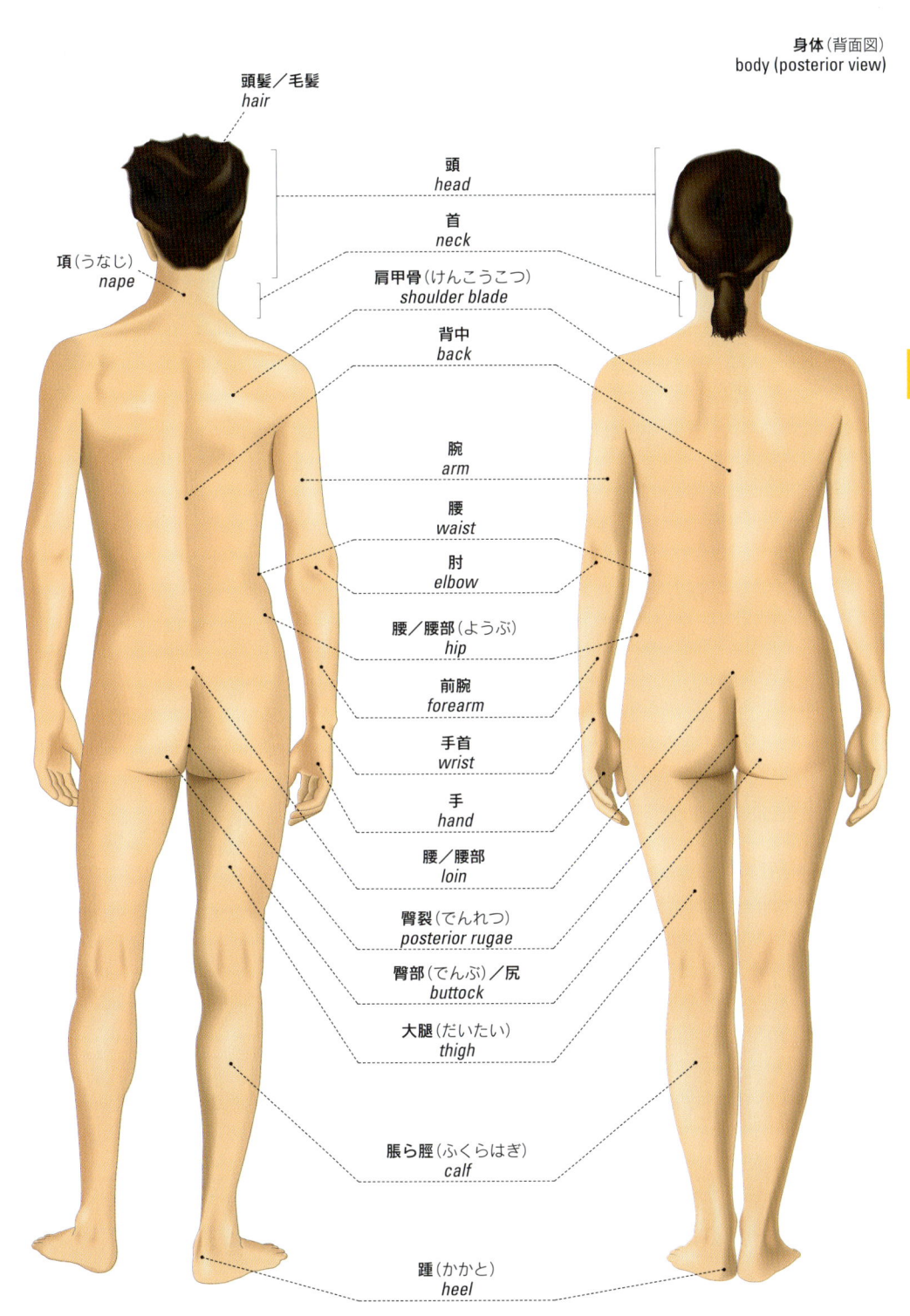

身体（背面図）
body (posterior view)

頭髪／毛髪
hair

頭
head

首
neck

項（うなじ）
nape

肩甲骨（けんこうこつ）
shoulder blade

背中
back

腕
arm

腰
waist

肘
elbow

腰／腰部（ようぶ）
hip

前腕
forearm

手首
wrist

手
hand

腰／腰部
loin

臀裂（でんれつ）
posterior rugae

臀部（でんぶ）／尻
buttock

大腿（だいたい）
thigh

脹ら脛（ふくらはぎ）
calf

踵（かかと）
heel

人間

91

骨格 | SKELETON

骨格は体の骨組みです。体を形づくっている２０６の骨は私たちの器官を支え、保護してくれています。例えば頭蓋骨は脳を保護しています。骨は短いか、長いか、平らかの３つに分類できます。骨の大部分は、関節によって骨同士が結合されています。筋肉が骨を動かしてくれるので、人間は立ち続けたりも、動いたりもできるのです。

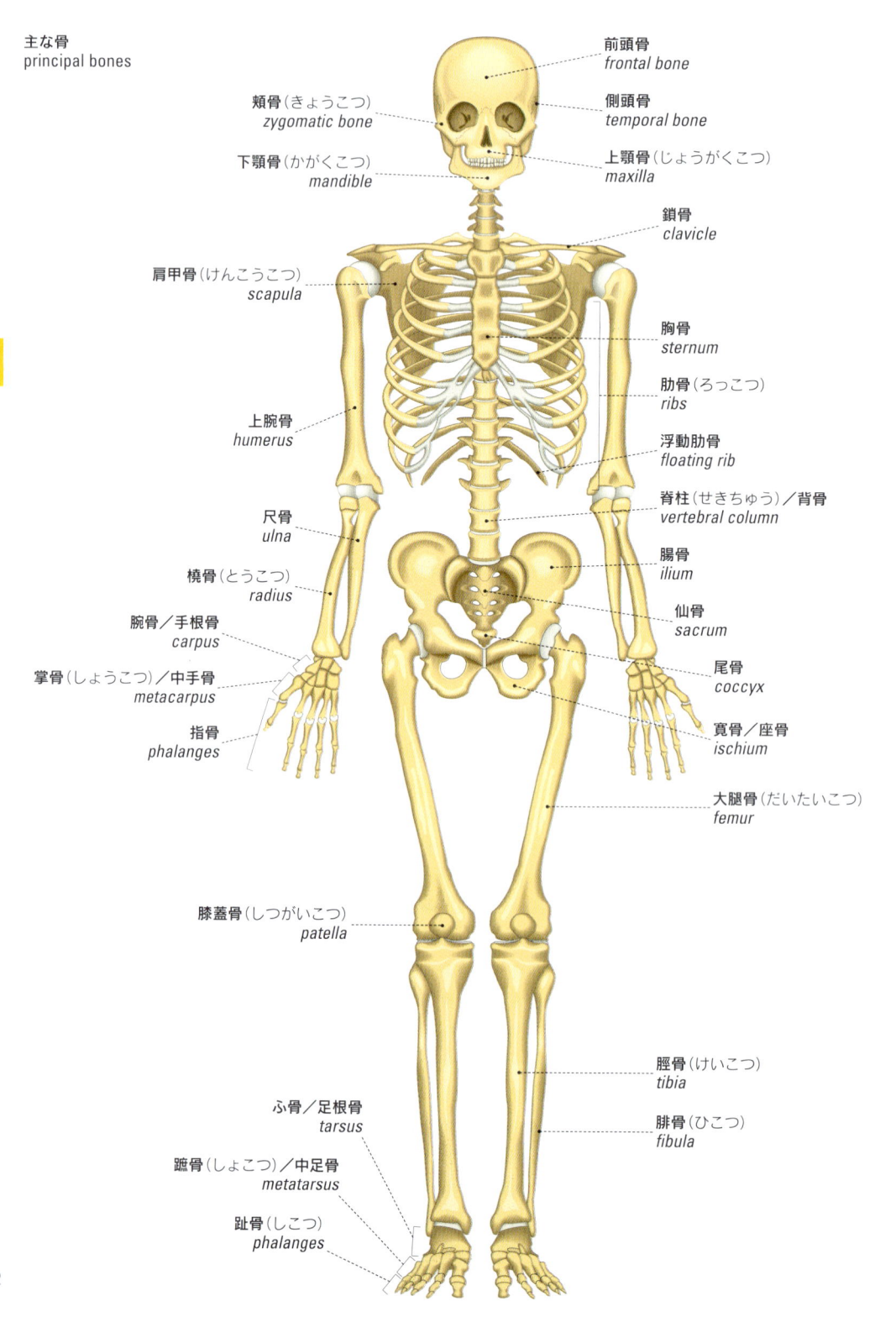

主な骨 / principal bones

- 頬骨（きょうこつ） / zygomatic bone
- 下顎骨（かがくこつ） / mandible
- 肩甲骨（けんこうこつ） / scapula
- 上腕骨 / humerus
- 尺骨 / ulna
- 橈骨（とうこつ） / radius
- 腕骨／手根骨 / carpus
- 掌骨（しょうこつ）／中手骨 / metacarpus
- 指骨 / phalanges
- 膝蓋骨（しつがいこつ） / patella
- ふ骨／足根骨 / tarsus
- 蹠骨（しょこつ）／中足骨 / metatarsus
- 趾骨（しこつ） / phalanges
- 前頭骨 / frontal bone
- 側頭骨 / temporal bone
- 上顎骨（じょうがくこつ） / maxilla
- 鎖骨 / clavicle
- 胸骨 / sternum
- 肋骨（ろっこつ） / ribs
- 浮動肋骨 / floating rib
- 脊柱（せきちゅう）／背骨 / vertebral column
- 腸骨 / ilium
- 仙骨 / sacrum
- 尾骨 / coccyx
- 寛骨／座骨 / ischium
- 大腿骨（だいたいこつ） / femur
- 脛骨（けいこつ） / tibia
- 腓骨（ひこつ） / fibula

人間

骨格 | SKELETON

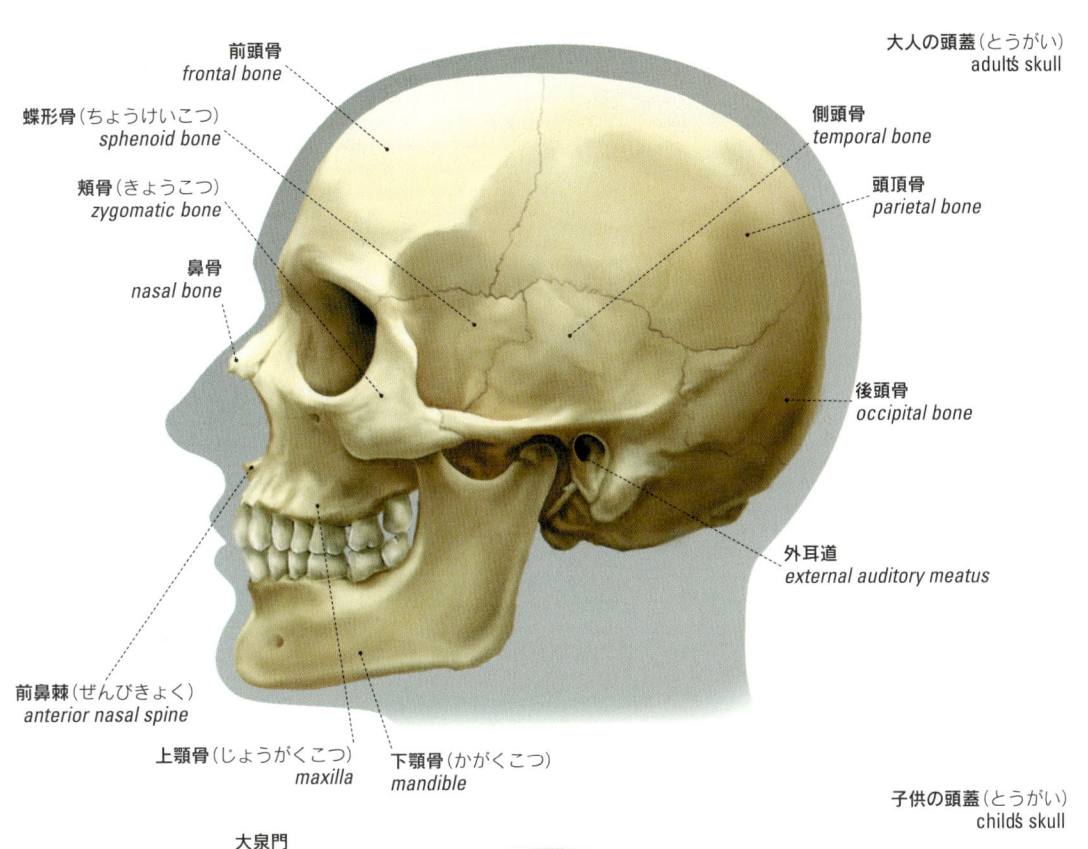

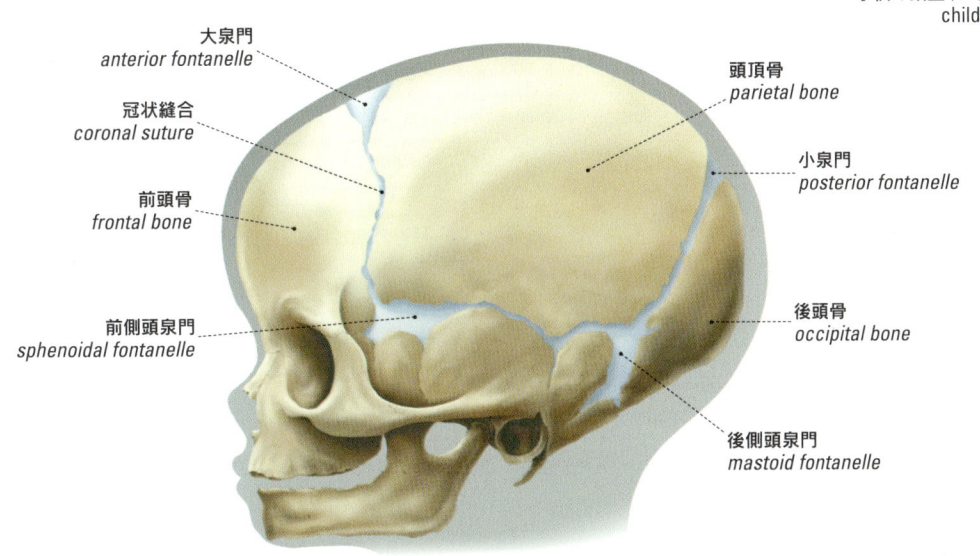

大人の頭蓋（とうがい）
adult's skull

前頭骨
frontal bone

蝶形骨（ちょうけいこつ）
sphenoid bone

頬骨（きょうこつ）
zygomatic bone

鼻骨
nasal bone

側頭骨
temporal bone

頭頂骨
parietal bone

後頭骨
occipital bone

外耳道
external auditory meatus

前鼻棘（ぜんびきょく）
anterior nasal spine

上顎骨（じょうがくこつ）
maxilla

下顎骨（かがくこつ）
mandible

子供の頭蓋（とうがい）
child's skull

大泉門
anterior fontanelle

冠状縫合
coronal suture

前頭骨
frontal bone

前側頭泉門
sphenoidal fontanelle

頭頂骨
parietal bone

小泉門
posterior fontanelle

後頭骨
occipital bone

後側頭泉門
mastoid fontanelle

骨の種類
types of bones

短骨
short bone

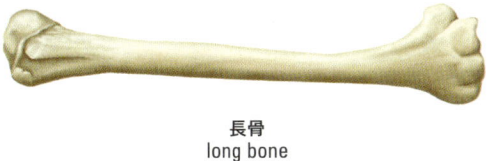

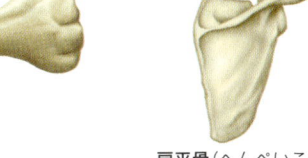

長骨
long bone

扁平骨（へんぺいこつ）
flat bone

歯 | TEETH

顎の骨の中に固く組み込まれて、歯は、消化の最初の段階である、物を噛み砕くのにきわめて重要な役割を果たしています。それぞれの型の歯は、飲み込むのが楽になるように、食べ物を小さな塊に変形させる働きをします。例えば、口の前方にあって、よく切れる切歯は食べ物を切断し、尖った犬歯はそれを切り刻み、大臼歯と小臼歯はそれを砕きます。

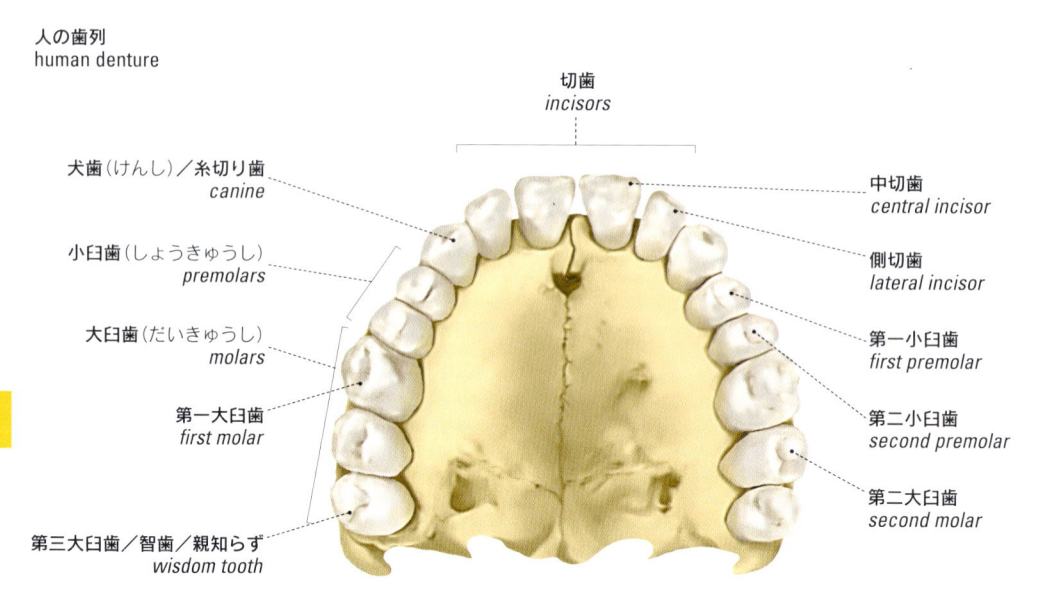

人の歯列 / human denture

- 切歯 / incisors
- 犬歯（けんし）／糸切り歯 / canine
- 小臼歯（しょうきゅうし）/ premolars
- 大臼歯（だいきゅうし）/ molars
- 第一大臼歯 / first molar
- 第三大臼歯／智歯／親知らず / wisdom tooth
- 中切歯 / central incisor
- 側切歯 / lateral incisor
- 第一小臼歯 / first premolar
- 第二小臼歯 / second premolar
- 第二大臼歯 / second molar

大臼歯（だいきゅうし）の断面図 / cross section of a molar

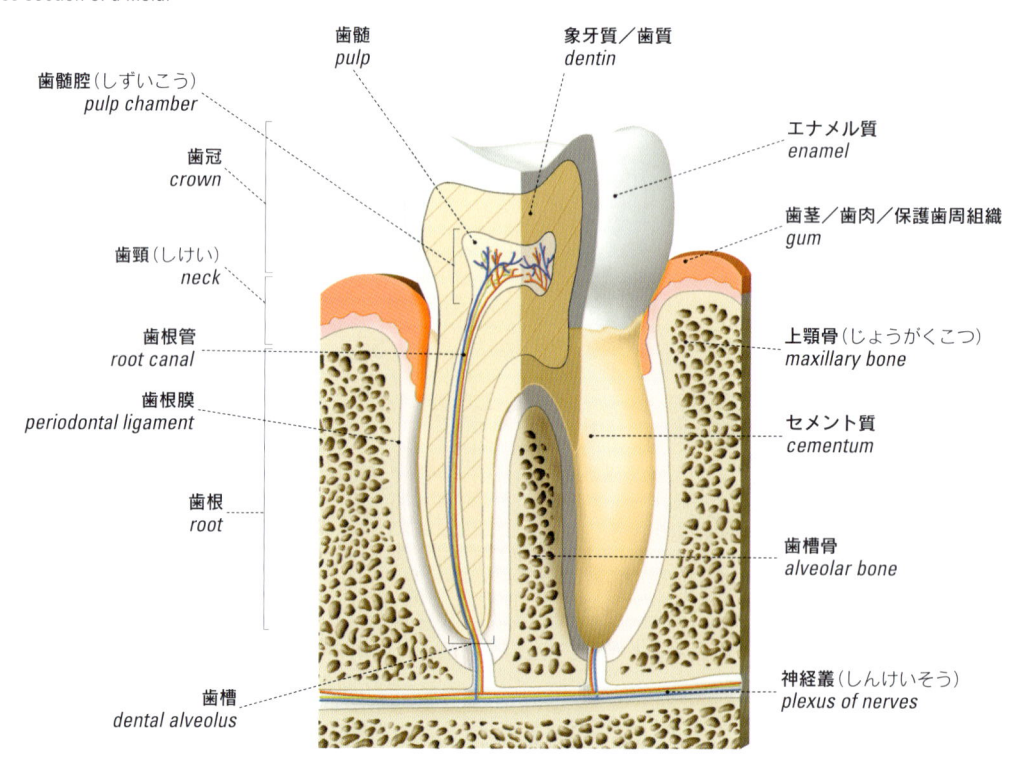

- 歯髄 / pulp
- 象牙質／歯質 / dentin
- 歯髄腔（しずいこう）/ pulp chamber
- エナメル質 / enamel
- 歯冠 / crown
- 歯茎／歯肉／保護歯周組織 / gum
- 歯頸（しけい）/ neck
- 歯根管 / root canal
- 上顎骨（じょうがくこつ）/ maxillary bone
- 歯根膜 / periodontal ligament
- セメント質 / cementum
- 歯根 / root
- 歯槽骨 / alveolar bone
- 歯槽 / dental alveolus
- 神経叢（しんけいそう）/ plexus of nerves

人間

筋肉 | MUSCLES

筋肉がなければ体は骨と器官から成る動かない塊にすぎません。私たちのあらゆる動きは体全体を張り巡らす筋肉によって作り出されます。筋肉は脳からの命令を受けて収縮し、骨を持ち上げ、体を動かします。ほほえんだりする際に行動を起こす筋肉のように、骨には作用せずに皮膚に作用する筋肉もあります。

主要な筋肉
principal muscles

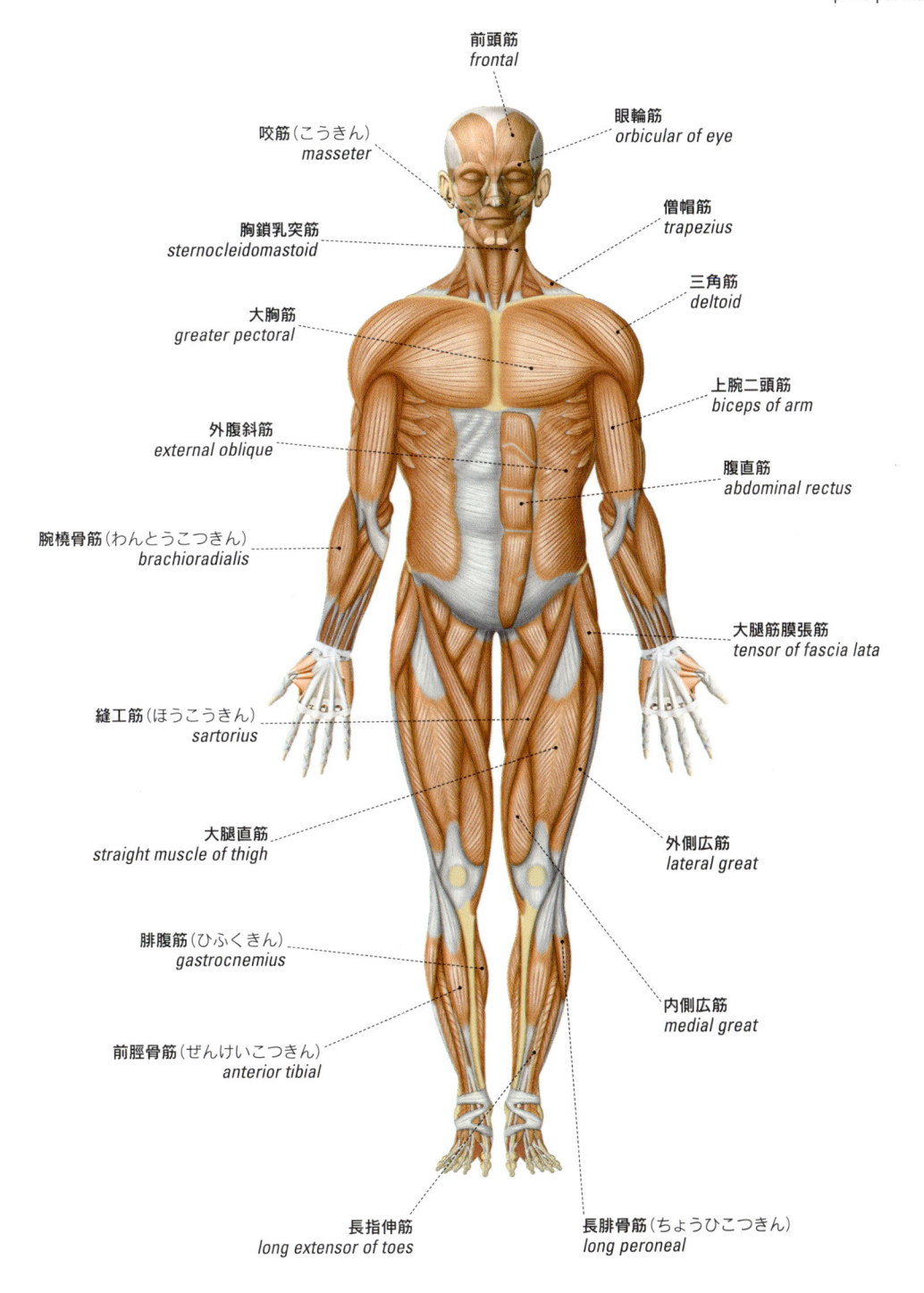

- 前頭筋 / frontal
- 咬筋（こうきん）/ masseter
- 眼輪筋 / orbicular of eye
- 胸鎖乳突筋 / sternocleidomastoid
- 僧帽筋 / trapezius
- 大胸筋 / greater pectoral
- 三角筋 / deltoid
- 外腹斜筋 / external oblique
- 上腕二頭筋 / biceps of arm
- 腕橈骨筋（わんとうこつきん）/ brachioradialis
- 腹直筋 / abdominal rectus
- 大腿筋膜張筋 / tensor of fascia lata
- 縫工筋（ほうこうきん）/ sartorius
- 大腿直筋 / straight muscle of thigh
- 外側広筋 / lateral great
- 腓腹筋（ひふくきん）/ gastrocnemius
- 内側広筋 / medial great
- 前脛骨筋（ぜんけいこつきん）/ anterior tibial
- 長指伸筋 / long extensor of toes
- 長腓骨筋（ちょうひこつきん）/ long peroneal

人間

解剖学 | ANATOMY

人体にはおよそ10の組織、言い換えれば器官があります。すべての組織が独自の役割を持ってはいても、いくつかは、体がうまく機能するように助け合わなければなりません。例えば、呼吸器の肺が大量の酸素を作り、循環器の血管がそれを体の全細胞に送り込むといった具合です。

消化器系
DIGESTIVE SYSTEM

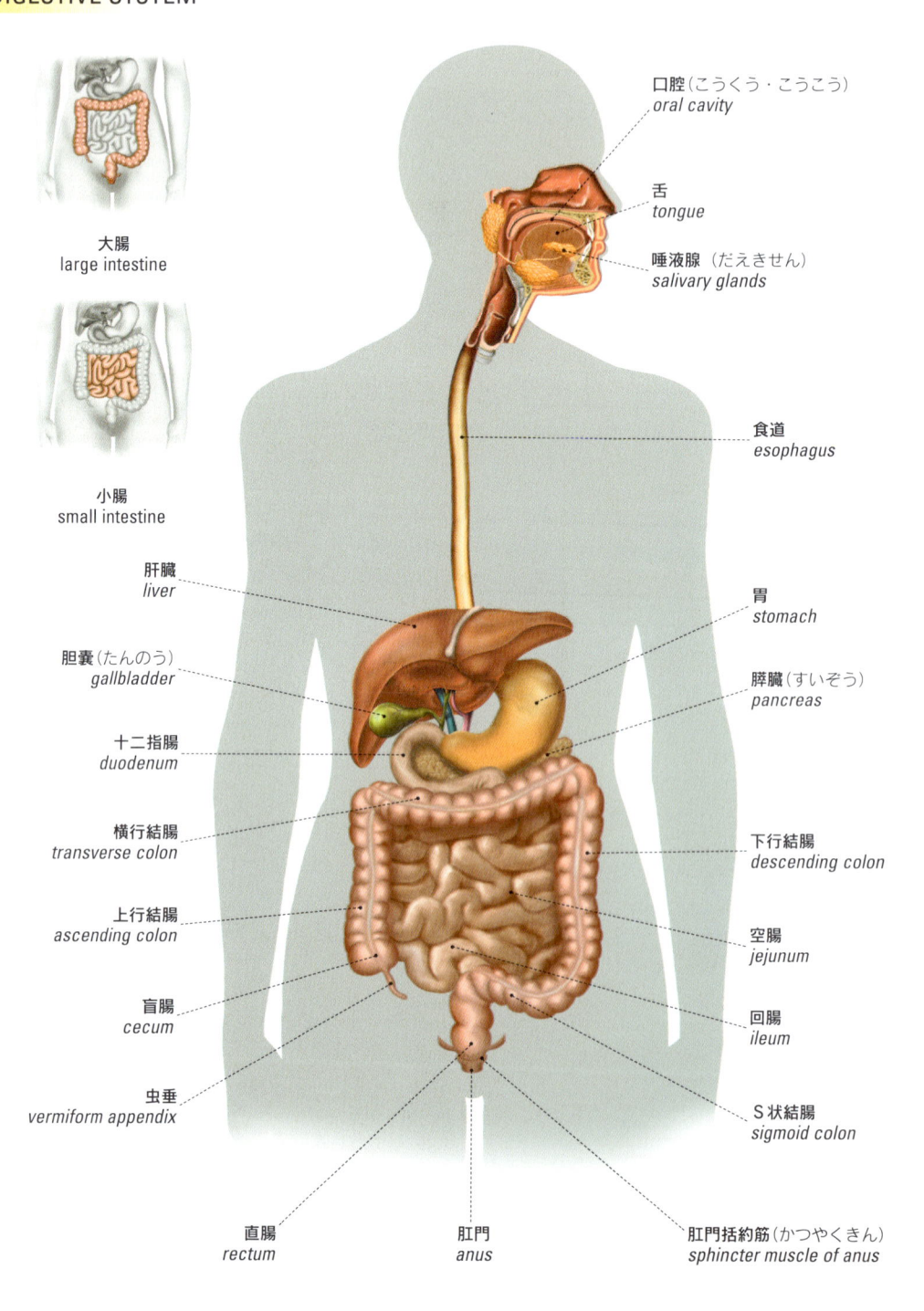

大腸
large intestine

小腸
small intestine

口腔（こうくう・こうこう）
oral cavity

舌
tongue

唾液腺（だえきせん）
salivary glands

食道
esophagus

肝臓
liver

胃
stomach

胆嚢（たんのう）
gallbladder

膵臓（すいぞう）
pancreas

十二指腸
duodenum

横行結腸
transverse colon

下行結腸
descending colon

上行結腸
ascending colon

空腸
jejunum

盲腸
cecum

回腸
ileum

虫垂
vermiform appendix

S状結腸
sigmoid colon

直腸
rectum

肛門
anus

肛門括約筋（かつやくきん）
sphincter muscle of anus

人間

96

解剖学 | ANATOMY

呼吸器系
RESPIRATORY SYSTEM

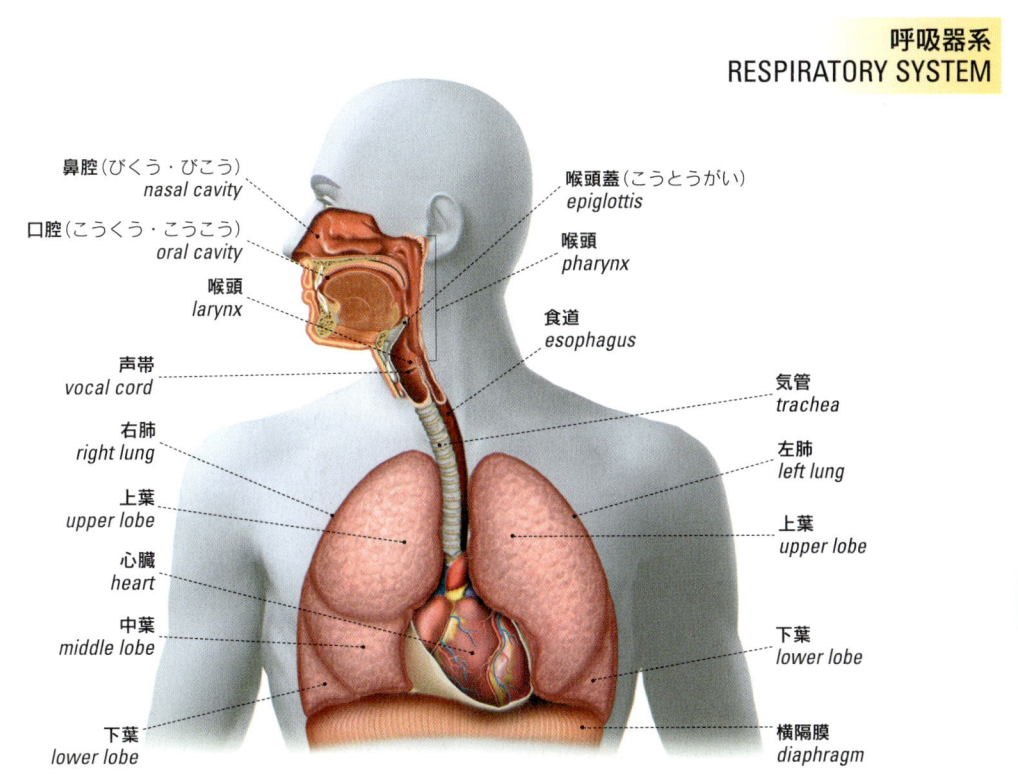

- 鼻腔（びくう・びこう） nasal cavity
- 口腔（こうくう・こうこう） oral cavity
- 喉頭 larynx
- 声帯 vocal cord
- 右肺 right lung
- 上葉 upper lobe
- 心臓 heart
- 中葉 middle lobe
- 下葉 lower lobe
- 喉頭蓋（こうとうがい） epiglottis
- 喉頭 pharynx
- 食道 esophagus
- 気管 trachea
- 左肺 left lung
- 上葉 upper lobe
- 下葉 lower lobe
- 横隔膜 diaphragm

神経系
NERVOUS SYSTEM

中枢神経系
central nervous system

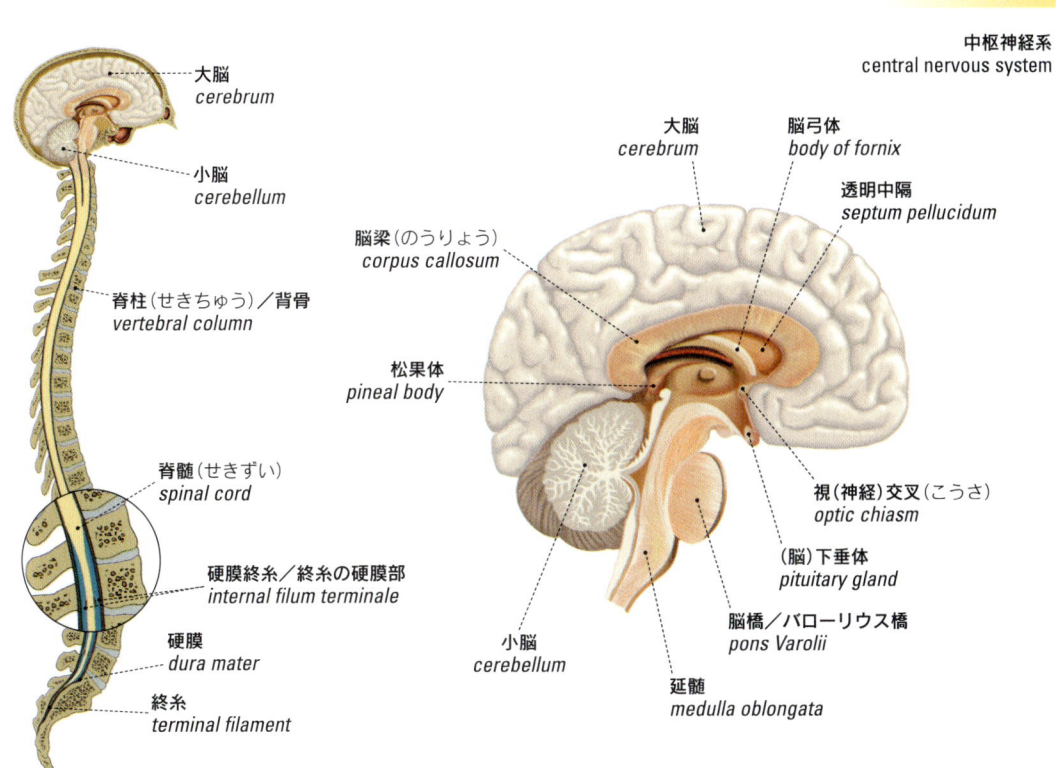

- 大脳 cerebrum
- 小脳 cerebellum
- 脊柱（せきちゅう）／背骨 vertebral column
- 脊髄（せきずい） spinal cord
- 硬膜終糸／終糸の硬膜部 internal filum terminale
- 硬膜 dura mater
- 終糸 terminal filament
- 大脳 cerebrum
- 脳梁（のうりょう） corpus callosum
- 松果体 pineal body
- 小脳 cerebellum
- 脳弓体 body of fornix
- 透明中隔 septum pellucidum
- 視（神経）交叉（こうさ） optic chiasm
- （脳）下垂体 pituitary gland
- 脳橋／バローリウス橋 pons Varolii
- 延髄 medulla oblongata

人間

解剖学 | ANATOMY

循環器系
CIRCULATORY SYSTEM

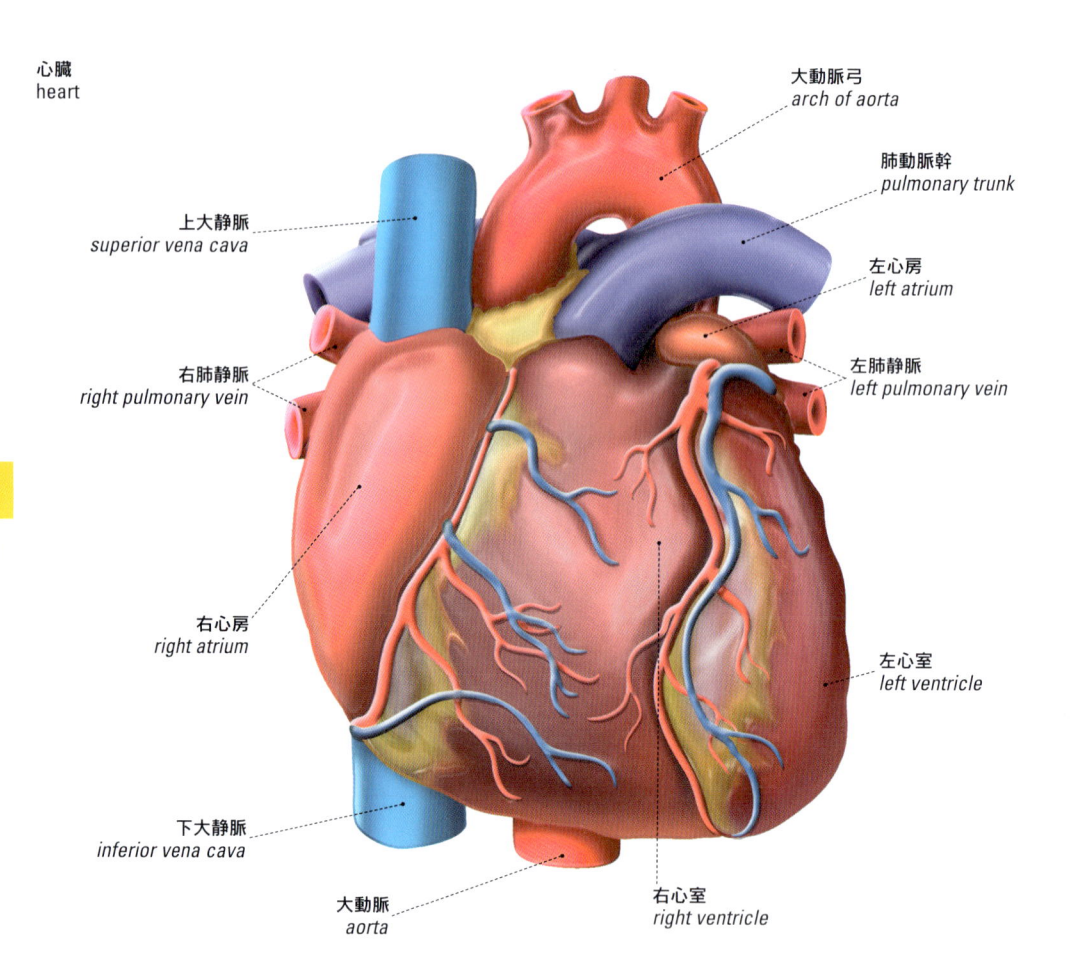

心臓
heart

大動脈弓
arch of aorta

肺動脈幹
pulmonary trunk

上大静脈
superior vena cava

左心房
left atrium

右肺静脈
right pulmonary vein

左肺静脈
left pulmonary vein

右心房
right atrium

左心室
left ventricle

下大静脈
inferior vena cava

大動脈
aorta

右心室
right ventricle

血液の組成
composition of the blood

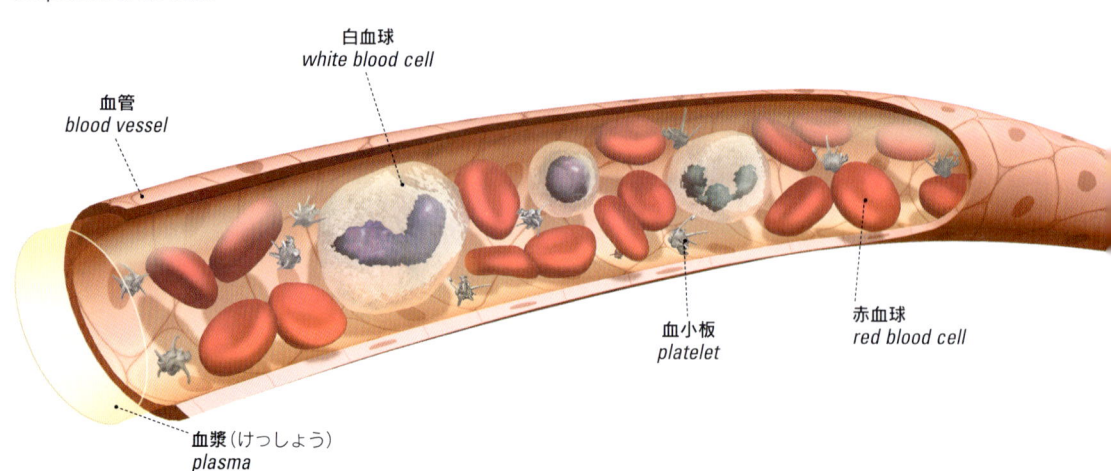

白血球
white blood cell

血管
blood vessel

血小板
platelet

赤血球
red blood cell

血漿(けっしょう)
plasma

解剖学 | ANATOMY

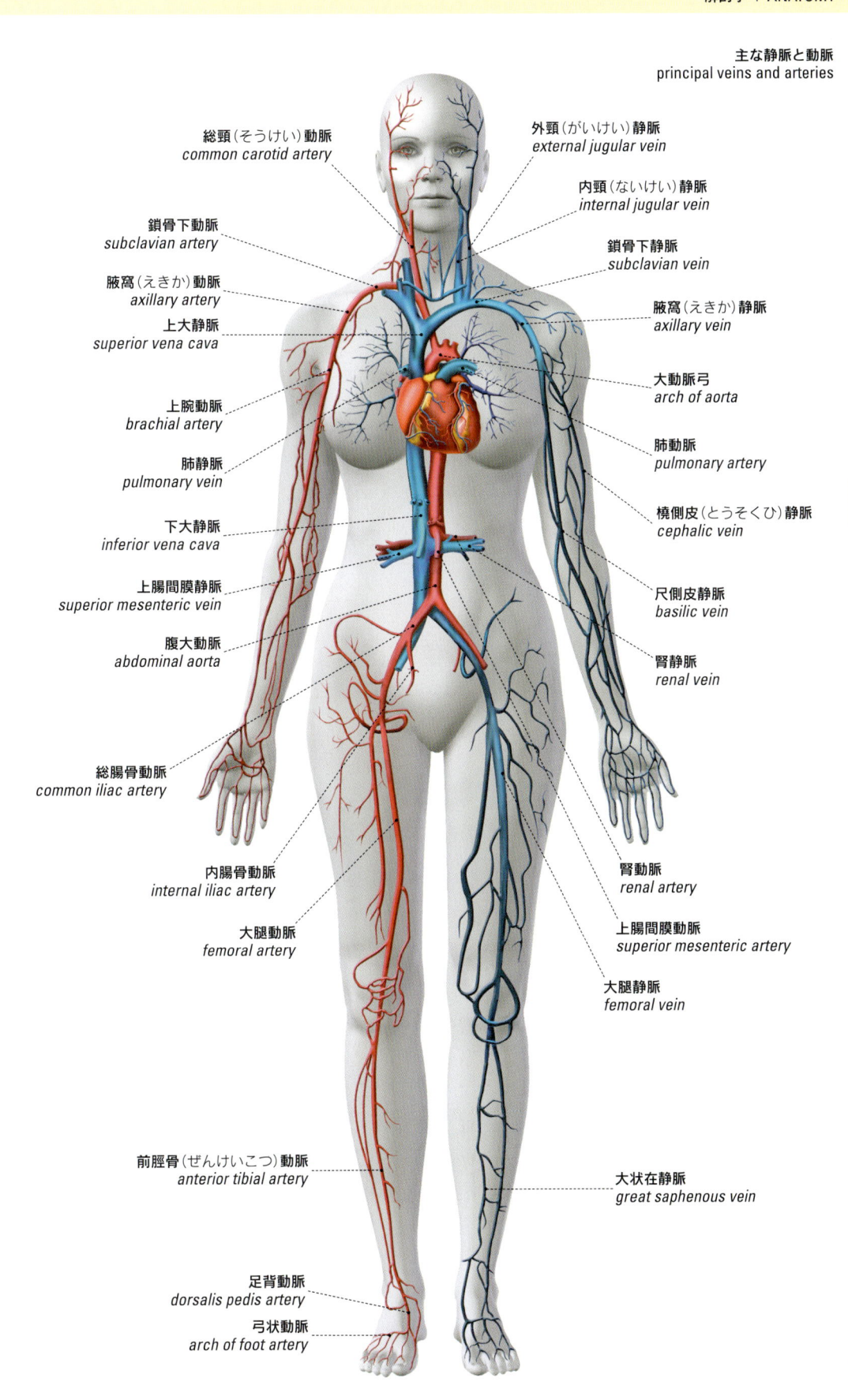

主な静脈と動脈
principal veins and arteries

- 総頸（そうけい）動脈 common carotid artery
- 外頸（がいけい）静脈 external jugular vein
- 内頸（ないけい）静脈 internal jugular vein
- 鎖骨下動脈 subclavian artery
- 鎖骨下静脈 subclavian vein
- 腋窩（えきか）動脈 axillary artery
- 腋窩（えきか）静脈 axillary vein
- 上大静脈 superior vena cava
- 大動脈弓 arch of aorta
- 上腕動脈 brachial artery
- 肺動脈 pulmonary artery
- 肺静脈 pulmonary vein
- 橈側皮（とうそくひ）静脈 cephalic vein
- 下大静脈 inferior vena cava
- 尺側皮静脈 basilic vein
- 上腸間膜静脈 superior mesenteric vein
- 腎静脈 renal vein
- 腹大動脈 abdominal aorta
- 総腸骨動脈 common iliac artery
- 内腸骨動脈 internal iliac artery
- 腎動脈 renal artery
- 大腿動脈 femoral artery
- 上腸間膜動脈 superior mesenteric artery
- 大腿静脈 femoral vein
- 前脛骨（ぜんけいこつ）動脈 anterior tibial artery
- 大伏在静脈 great saphenous vein
- 足背動脈 dorsalis pedis artery
- 弓状動脈 arch of foot artery

人間

感覚器官 | SENSE ORGANS

五感は身の回りで起こっていることを人間に知らせてくれます。感覚器官は特殊な細胞からできていて、感覚受容器が情報を集め、それを神経器官に伝え、ついで脳に送ります。脳は、音、像、においといった感覚信号を解釈し、身の回りの世界に反応します。

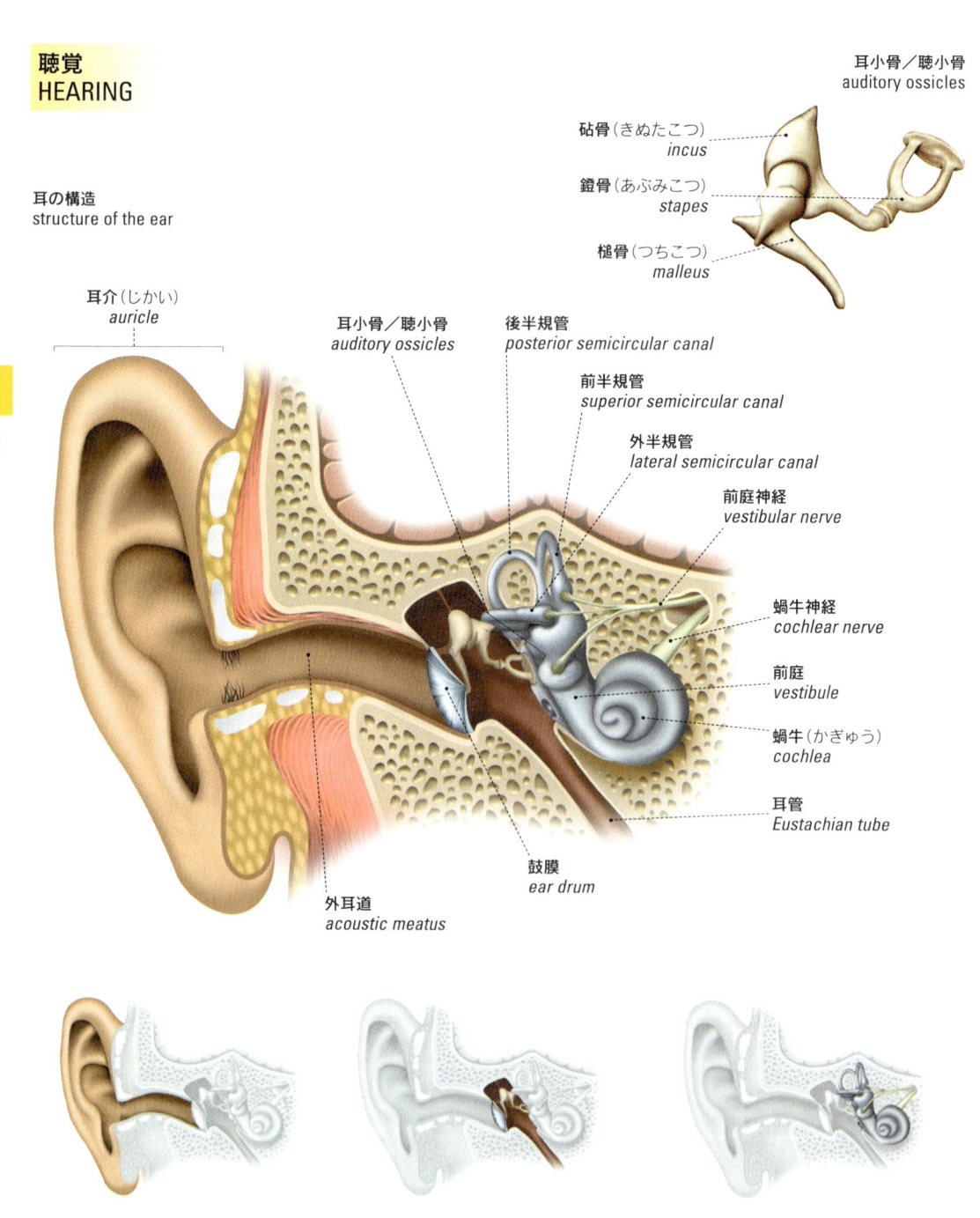

聴覚
HEARING

耳小骨／聴小骨
auditory ossicles

砧骨（きぬたこつ）
incus

鐙骨（あぶみこつ）
stapes

槌骨（つちこつ）
malleus

耳の構造
structure of the ear

耳介（じかい）
auricle

耳小骨／聴小骨
auditory ossicles

後半規管
posterior semicircular canal

前半規管
superior semicircular canal

外半規管
lateral semicircular canal

前庭神経
vestibular nerve

蝸牛神経
cochlear nerve

前庭
vestibule

蝸牛（かぎゅう）
cochlea

耳管
Eustachian tube

鼓膜
ear drum

外耳道
acoustic meatus

外耳
external ear

中耳
middle ear

内耳
internal ear

感覚器官 | SENSE ORGANS

触覚
TOUCH

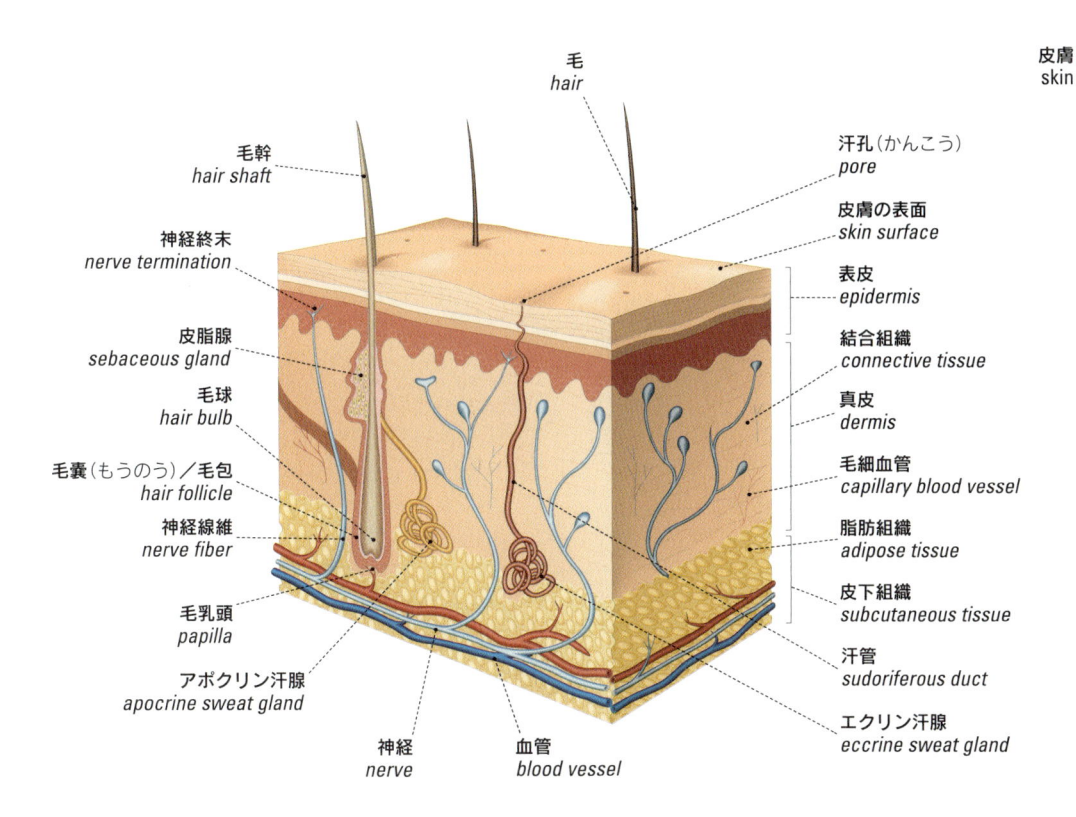

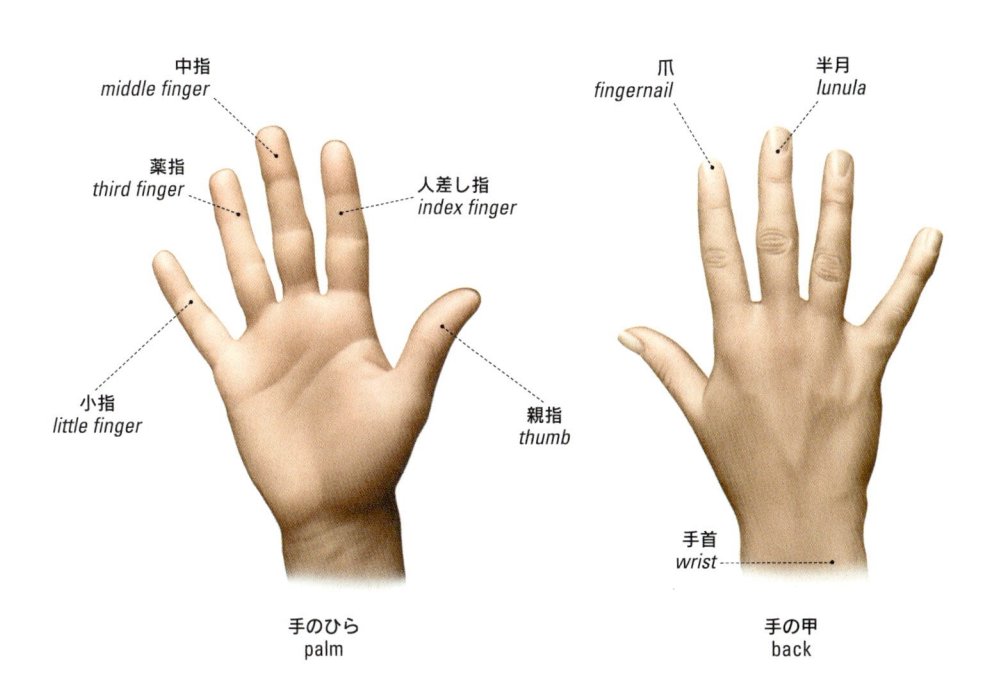

皮膚 / skin

- 毛幹 / hair shaft
- 毛 / hair
- 汗孔(かんこう) / pore
- 皮膚の表面 / skin surface
- 神経終末 / nerve termination
- 表皮 / epidermis
- 皮脂腺 / sebaceous gland
- 結合組織 / connective tissue
- 毛球 / hair bulb
- 真皮 / dermis
- 毛嚢(もうのう)／毛包 / hair follicle
- 毛細血管 / capillary blood vessel
- 神経線維 / nerve fiber
- 脂肪組織 / adipose tissue
- 皮下組織 / subcutaneous tissue
- 毛乳頭 / papilla
- 汗管 / sudoriferous duct
- アポクリン汗腺 / apocrine sweat gland
- 神経 / nerve
- 血管 / blood vessel
- エクリン汗腺 / eccrine sweat gland

手 / hand

- 中指 / middle finger
- 爪 / fingernail
- 半月 / lunula
- 薬指 / third finger
- 人差し指 / index finger
- 小指 / little finger
- 親指 / thumb
- 手首 / wrist
- 手のひら / palm
- 手の甲 / back

感覚器官 | SENSE ORGANS

視覚
SIGHT

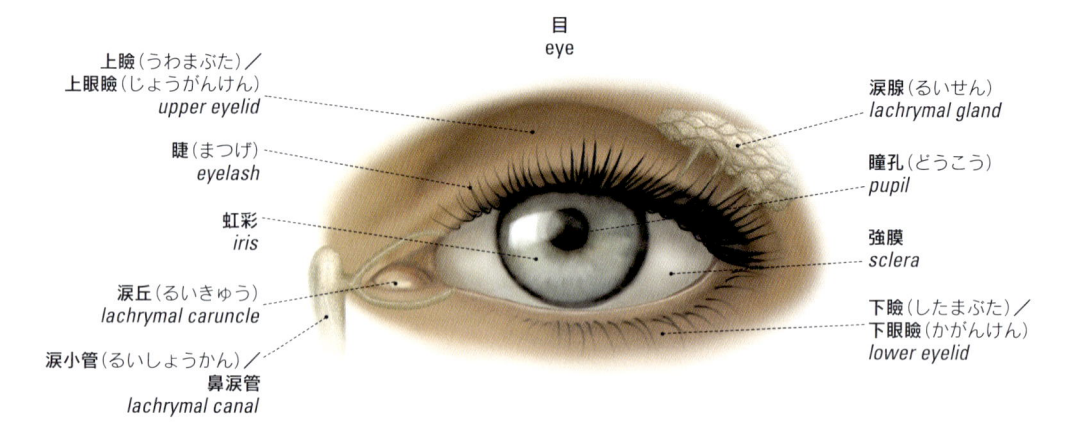

目 / eye

- 上瞼（うわまぶた）／上眼瞼（じょうがんけん） / upper eyelid
- 睫（まつげ） / eyelash
- 虹彩 / iris
- 涙丘（るいきゅう） / lachrymal caruncle
- 涙小管（るいしょうかん）／鼻涙管 / lachrymal canal
- 涙腺（るいせん） / lachrymal gland
- 瞳孔（どうこう） / pupil
- 強膜 / sclera
- 下瞼（したまぶた）／下眼瞼（かがんけん） / lower eyelid

嗅覚（きゅうかく）と味覚
SMELL AND TASTE

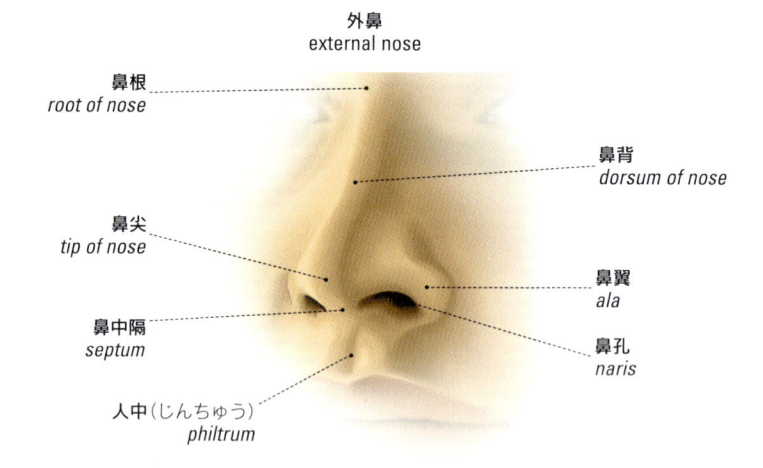

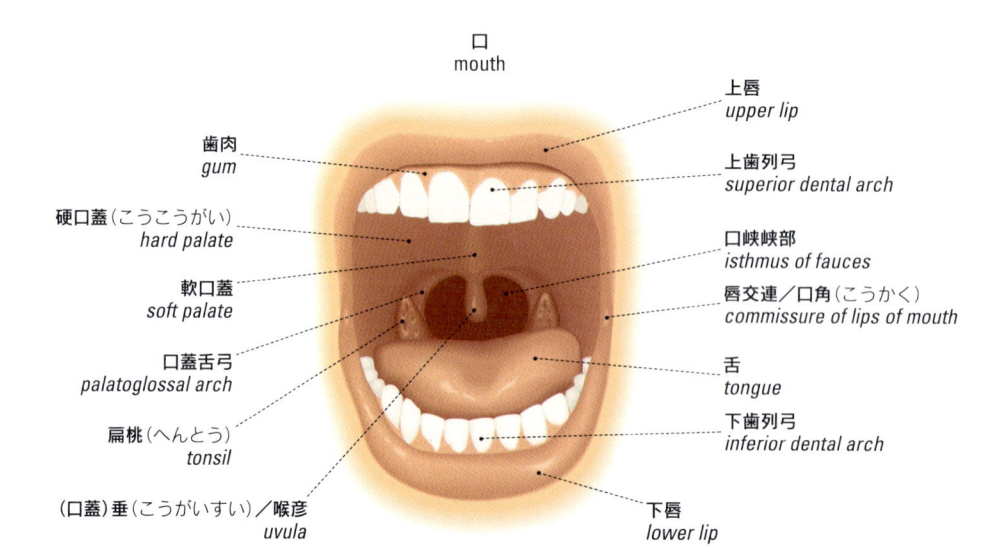

外鼻 / external nose

- 鼻根 / root of nose
- 鼻尖 / tip of nose
- 鼻中隔 / septum
- 人中（じんちゅう） / philtrum
- 鼻背 / dorsum of nose
- 鼻翼 / ala
- 鼻孔 / naris

口 / mouth

- 歯肉 / gum
- 硬口蓋（こうこうがい） / hard palate
- 軟口蓋 / soft palate
- 口蓋舌弓 / palatoglossal arch
- 扁桃（へんとう） / tonsil
- （口蓋）垂（こうがいすい）／喉彦 / uvula
- 上唇 / upper lip
- 上歯列弓 / superior dental arch
- 口峡部 / isthmus of fauces
- 唇交連／口角（こうかく） / commissure of lips of mouth
- 舌 / tongue
- 下歯列弓 / inferior dental arch
- 下唇 / lower lip

野菜 | VEGETABLES

野菜とは、栄養を摂取するための食用植物の集まりで、植物の食べられる部分によって、例えば、ピーマンは果菜、ホウレンソウは葉菜、アスパラガスは茎菜といったように分類されます。食事の付け合わせとしても、主菜としても、野菜は世界中ほぼ至る所で人間の食べ物の一部となっています。

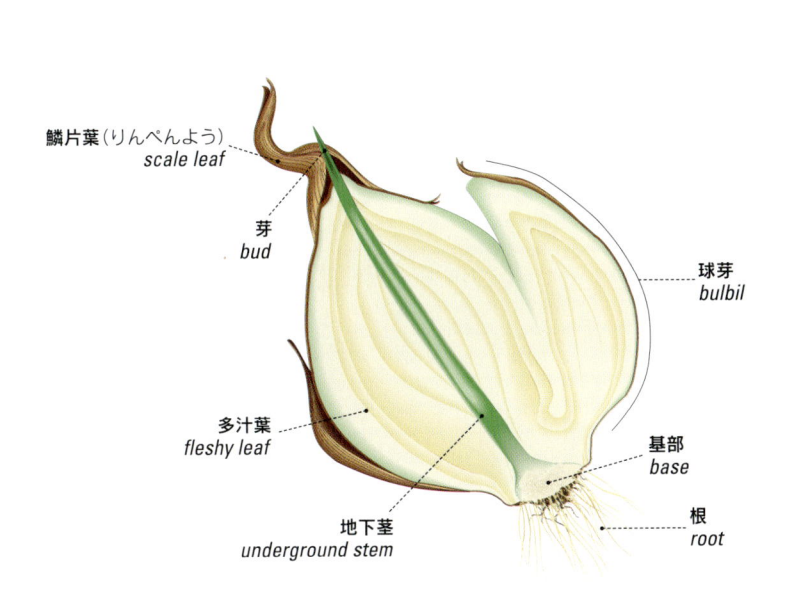

ネギ類
BULB VEGETABLES

球根の断面図
section of a bulb

鱗片葉（りんぺんよう）
scale leaf

芽
bud

球芽
bulbil

多汁葉
fleshy leaf

基部
base

地下茎
underground stem

根
root

ネギの例
EXAMPLES OF BULB VEGETABLES

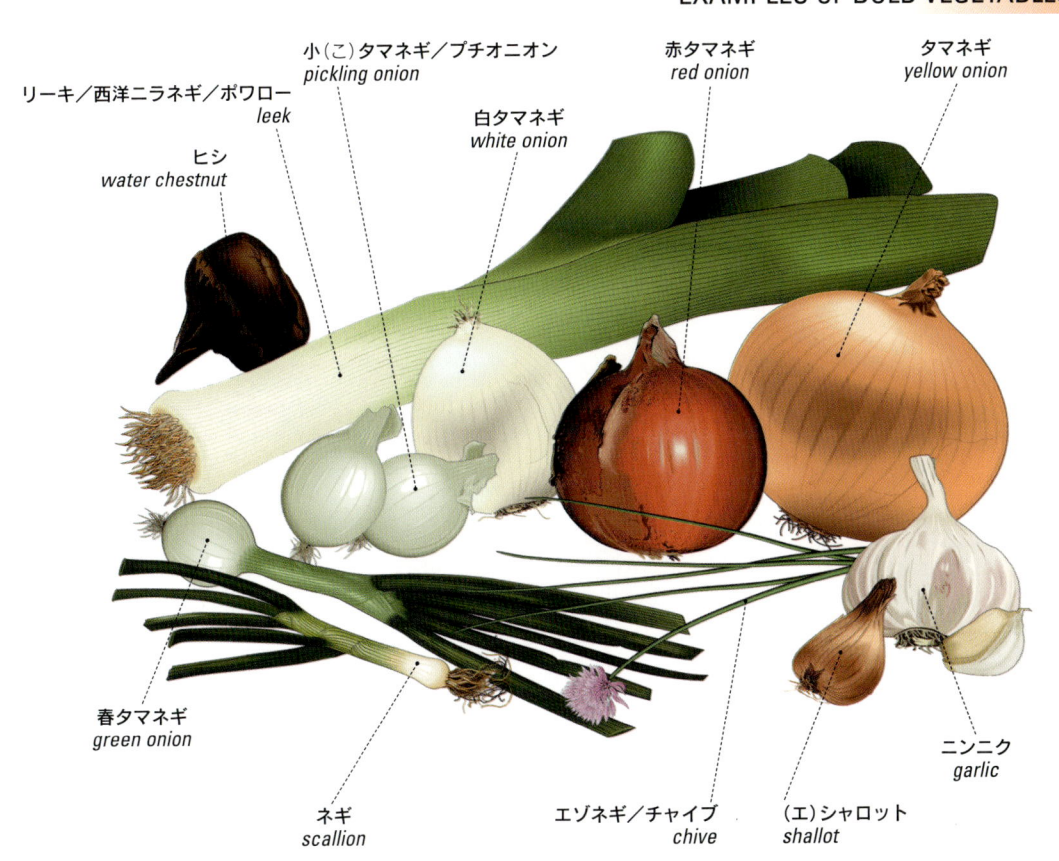

リーキ／西洋ニラネギ／ポワロー
leek

小（こ）タマネギ／プチオニオン
pickling onion

赤タマネギ
red onion

タマネギ
yellow onion

白タマネギ
white onion

ヒシ
water chestnut

春タマネギ
green onion

ネギ
scallion

エゾネギ／チャイブ
chive

（エ）シャロット
shallot

ニンニク
garlic

食べ物

野菜 | VEGETABLES

イモ類
TUBER VEGETABLES

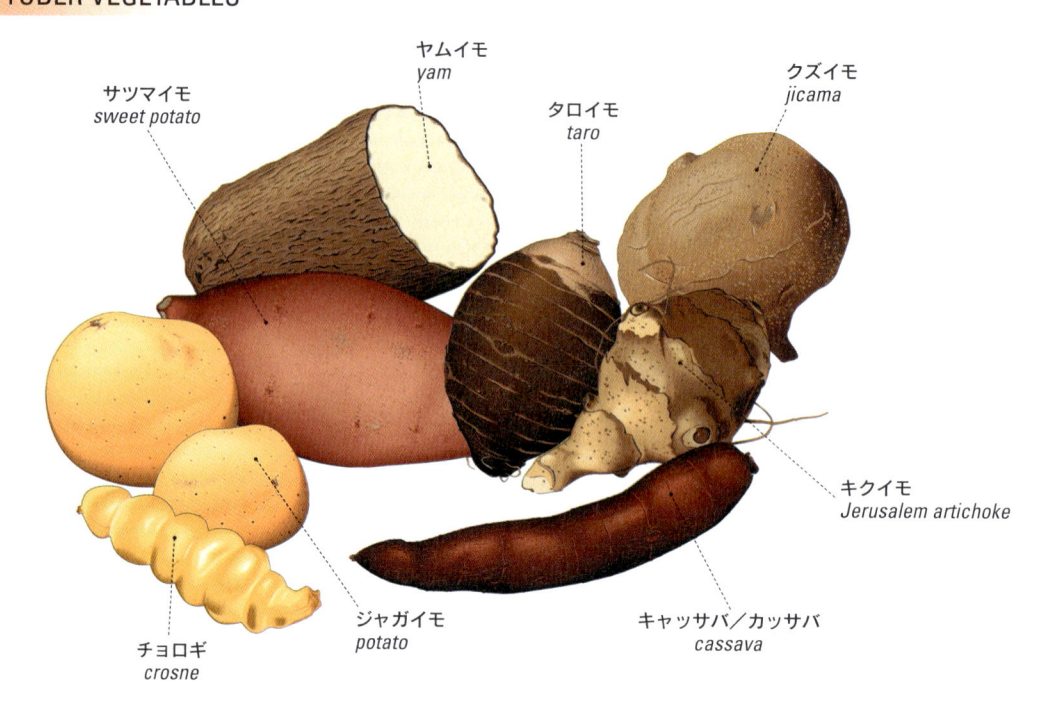

- サツマイモ / sweet potato
- ヤムイモ / yam
- タロイモ / taro
- クズイモ / jicama
- キクイモ / Jerusalem artichoke
- チョロギ / crosne
- ジャガイモ / potato
- キャッサバ／カッサバ / cassava

根菜類
ROOT VEGETABLES

- パースニップ／アメリカボウフウ（防風） / parsnip
- カブカンラン（蕪甘藍）／スウェーデンカブ / rutabaga
- サトイモ／マランガ / malanga
- セルリアク／コンヨウセロリ／コンセロリ / celeriac
- ビート／ビーツ / beet
- ハツカダイコン / radish
- 黒ダイコン / black radish
- ダイコン / daikon
- ゴボウ / burdock
- カブ / turnip
- ニンジン / carrot
- ワサビダイコン／ホースラディッシュ / horseradish
- バラモンジン／西洋ゴボウ / salsify
- キクゴボウ / black salsify

食べ物

野菜 | VEGETABLES

茎菜類
STALK VEGETABLES

- フダンソウ / Swiss chard
- タケノコ / bamboo shoot
- ウイキョウ／フェンネル / fennel
- コールラビ / kohlrabi
- セロリ / celery
- ダイオウ／ルバーブ / rhubarb
- アスパラガス / asparagus
- ゼンマイ / fiddlehead fern
- カルドン / cardoon

花菜類
INFLORESCENT VEGETABLES

- カリフラワー / cauliflower
- ブロッコリ / broccoli
- 中国ブロッコリ／カイラン / Gai-lohn
- アーティチョーク／朝鮮アザミ / artichoke
- ブロッコリカブ / broccoli rabe

食べ物

野菜 | VEGETABLES

葉菜類
LEAF VEGETABLES

- キャベツ / green cabbage
- 赤キャベツ / red cabbage
- 白キャベツ / white cabbage
- サボイキャベツ／チリメンキャベツ / savoy cabbage
- 白菜 / pe-tsai
- チコリ / Belgian endive
- チンゲンサイ / pak-choi
- ロメインレタス / romaine lettuce
- ハマナ / sea kale
- コラード / collards
- ハゴロモカンラン(羽衣) / curled kale
- エンダイブ / curled endive
- キクヂシャ / escarole
- 赤チコリ／ラディッキョ / radicchio
- ケール／ハボタン / ornamental kale
- アイスバーグレタス / iceberg lettuce
- サニーレタス / leaf lettuce
- セルタス / celtuce
- ブドウの葉 / grape leaf
- コショウソウ(胡椒草)／カイワレダイコン / garden cress
- スイバ／スカンポ / garden sorrel
- スベリヒユ / purslane
- クレソン / watercress
- タンポポ / dandelion
- コーンサラダ／マーシュ／ノヂシャ / corn salad
- メキャベツ / Brussels sprouts
- バターヘッドレタス／サラダ菜 / butterhead lettuce
- イラクサ / nettle
- ホウレンソウ / spinach
- キバナスズシロ／ルッコラ／ロケット / arugula

食べ物

106

野菜 | VEGETABLES

果菜類
FRUIT VEGETABLES

ナタウリ
straightneck squash

ヘチマカボチャ
crookneck squash

西洋カボチャ／クリカボチャ
autumn squash

カボチャ
pumpkin

ハヤトウリ
chayote

エイコーンスクワッシュ／
ドングリカボチャ
acorn squash

ペポカボチャ
summer squash

ソウメンカボチャ／キンシウリ
spaghetti squash

（スクワッシュ）パティパン
pattypan squash

ナス
eggplant

トウガン
wax gourd

ピーマン
green sweet pepper

アボカド
avocado

トマト
tomato

オクラ
okra

赤パプリカ
red sweet pepper

トウガラシ
hot pepper

チェリートマト
currant tomato

黄パプリカ
yellow sweet pepper

オリーブ
olive

オオブドウホオズキ
tomatillo

種なしキュウリ
seedless cucumber

キュウリ
cucumber

ニガウリ
bitter melon

ズッキーニ
zucchini

ガーキン
gherkin

食べ物

107

豆類 | LEGUMES

豆類には約１３，０００種類の植物が含まれ、一大グループを形成しています。これらすべての植物は、きわめて栄養価の高い種をたくさん包んだ、さやの形をした実によって区別されます。レンズマメ、ソラマメ、ピーナッツなどは豆類のほんの数例にすぎません。豆類は、南アメリカの多くの国々で、はるか昔から主食のように考えられています。

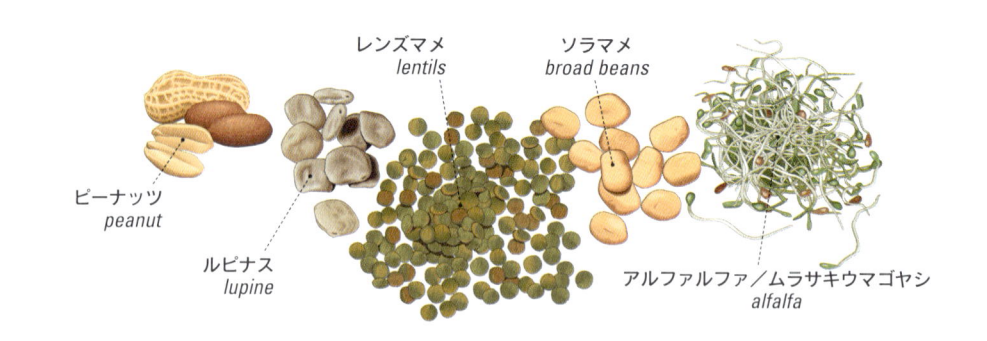

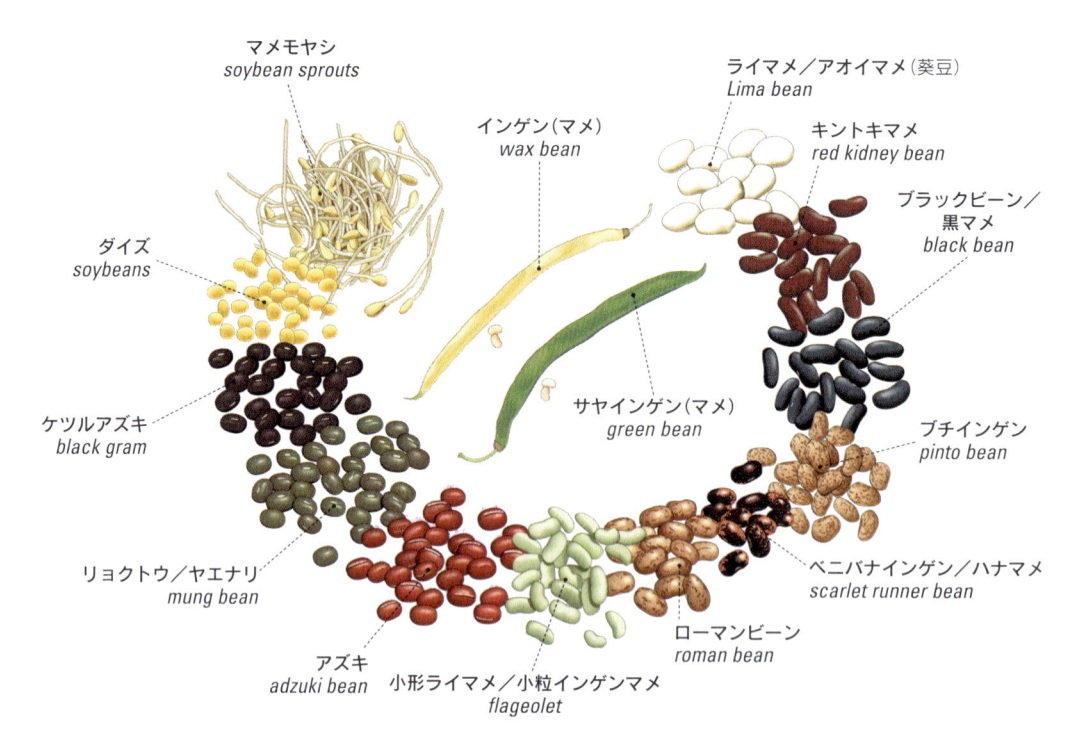

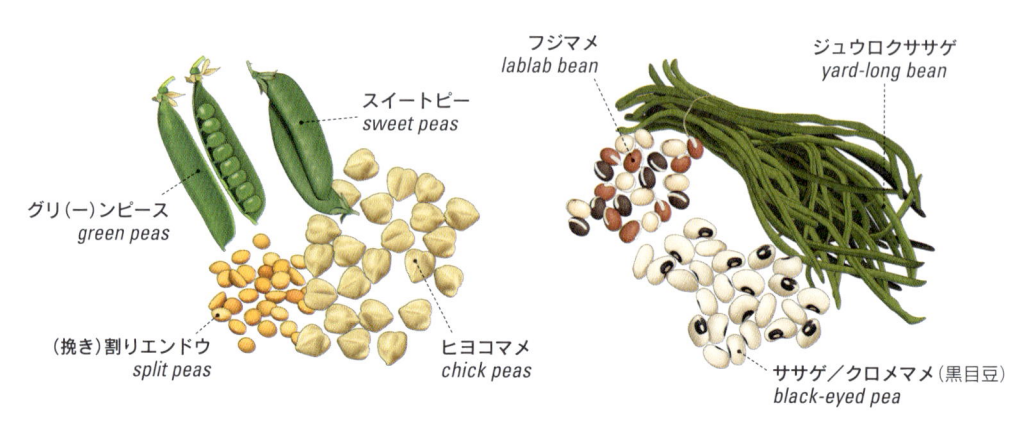

- ピーナッツ peanut
- レンズマメ lentils
- ソラマメ broad beans
- ルピナス lupine
- アルファルファ／ムラサキウマゴヤシ alfalfa
- マメモヤシ soybean sprouts
- インゲン（マメ） wax bean
- ライマメ／アオイマメ（葵豆） Lima bean
- キントキマメ red kidney bean
- ブラックビーン／黒マメ black bean
- ダイズ soybeans
- サヤインゲン（マメ） green bean
- プチインゲン pinto bean
- ケツルアズキ black gram
- ベニバナインゲン／ハナマメ scarlet runner bean
- リョクトウ／ヤエナリ mung bean
- ローマンビーン roman bean
- アズキ adzuki bean
- 小形ライマメ／小粒インゲンマメ flageolet
- スイートピー sweet peas
- フジマメ lablab bean
- ジュウロクササゲ yard-long bean
- グリ（ー）ンピース green peas
- （挽き）割りエンドウ split peas
- ヒヨコマメ chick peas
- ササゲ／クロメマメ（黒目豆） black-eyed pea

食べ物

果物 | FRUITS

果物は、植物学的な意味では、植物の小さな胚、つまり種を含んだ器官と言うことができます。例えば、オリーブ、クルミの実、キュウリは、翼果のカエデのように食べられない物をすべて除けば、果物です。果物はリンゴやサクランボのように甘い食べ物で、ふだんは軽食やデザートとして食べられます。

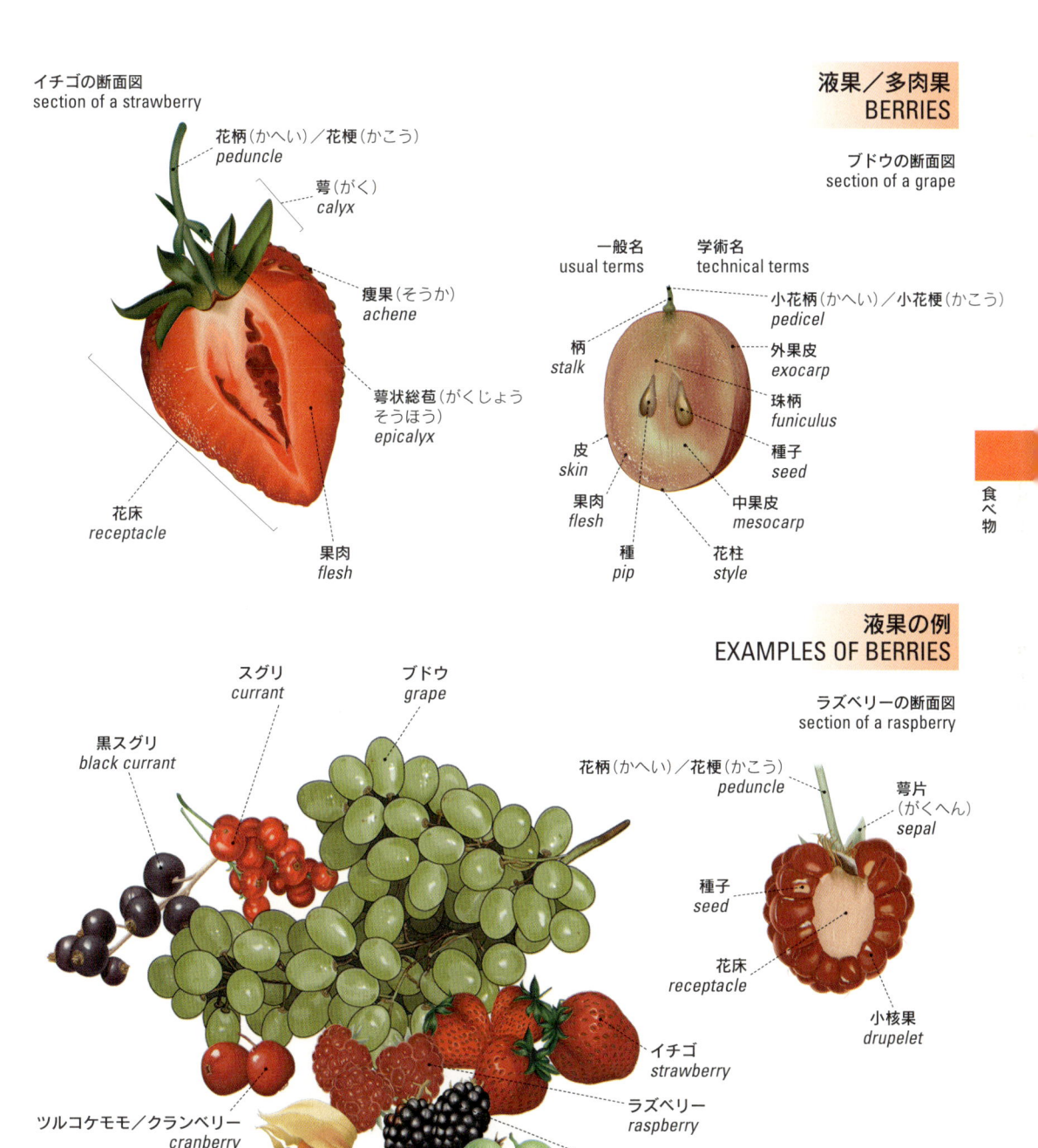

イチゴの断面図 / section of a strawberry

- 花柄（かへい）／花梗（かこう） peduncle
- 萼（がく） calyx
- 瘦果（そうか） achene
- 萼状総苞（がくじょうそうほう） epicalyx
- 花床 receptacle
- 果肉 flesh

液果／多肉果 BERRIES

ブドウの断面図 / section of a grape

一般名 usual terms / 学術名 technical terms

- 小花柄（かへい）／小花梗（かこう） pedicel
- 柄 stalk / 外果皮 exocarp
- 珠柄 funiculus
- 皮 skin / 種子 seed
- 果肉 flesh / 中果皮 mesocarp
- 種 pip / 花柱 style

食べ物

液果の例 EXAMPLES OF BERRIES

ラズベリーの断面図 / section of a raspberry

- 花柄（かへい）／花梗（かこう） peduncle
- 萼片（がくへん） sepal
- 種子 seed
- 花床 receptacle
- 小核果 drupelet

- スグリ currant
- ブドウ grape
- 黒スグリ black currant
- イチゴ strawberry
- ツルコケモモ／クランベリー cranberry
- ラズベリー raspberry
- 黒イチゴ blackberry
- ホオズキ alkekengi
- グ(ー)ズベリー gooseberry
- コケモモ bilberry
- 赤コケモモ red whortleberry
- ブルーベリー blueberry

果物 | FRUITS

石果
STONE FRUITS

モモの断面図
section of a peach

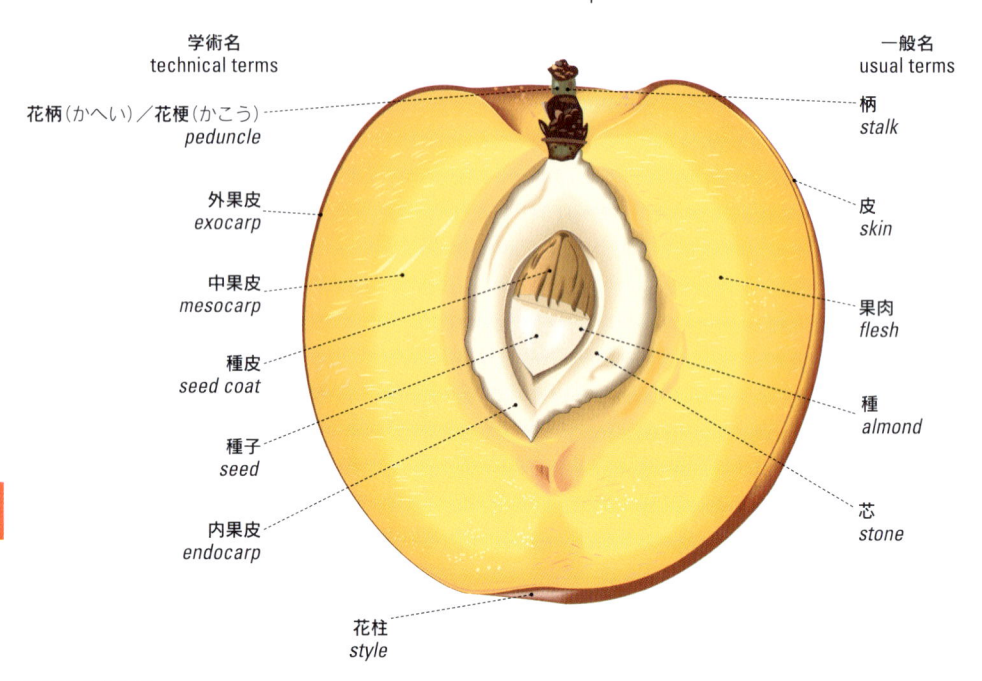

学術名
technical terms

花柄（かへい）／花梗（かこう）
peduncle

外果皮
exocarp

中果皮
mesocarp

種皮
seed coat

種子
seed

内果皮
endocarp

花柱
style

一般名
usual terms

柄
stalk

皮
skin

果肉
flesh

種
almond

芯
stone

石果の例
EXAMPLES OF STONE FRUITS

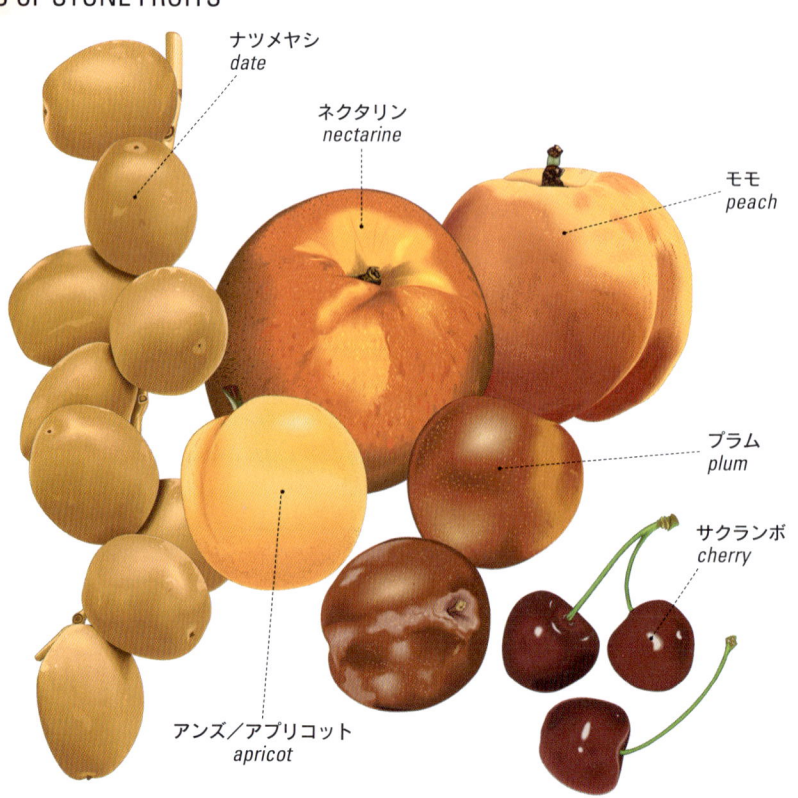

ナツメヤシ
date

ネクタリン
nectarine

モモ
peach

プラム
plum

サクランボ
cherry

アンズ／アプリコット
apricot

果物 | FRUITS

ナシ状果
POME FRUITS

リンゴの断面図
section of an apple

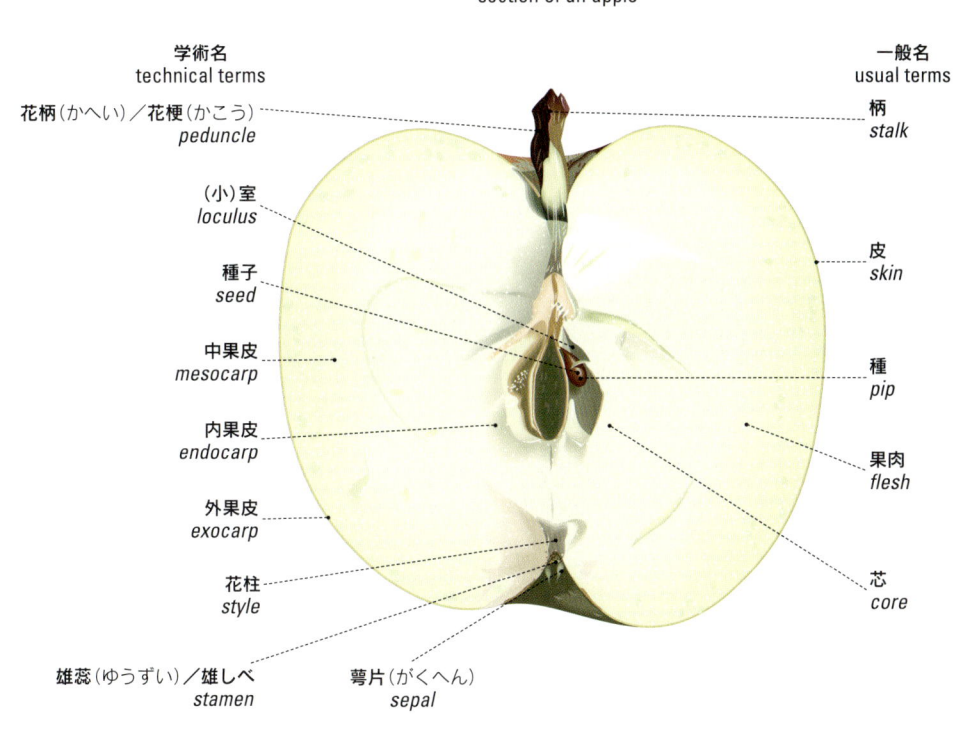

学術名
technical terms

花柄(かへい)／花梗(かこう)
peduncle

(小)室
loculus

種子
seed

中果皮
mesocarp

内果皮
endocarp

外果皮
exocarp

花柱
style

雄蕊(ゆうずい)／雄しべ
stamen

萼片(がくへん)
sepal

一般名
usual terms

柄
stalk

皮
skin

種
pip

果肉
flesh

芯
core

食べ物

ナシ状果の例
EXAMPLES OF POME FRUITS

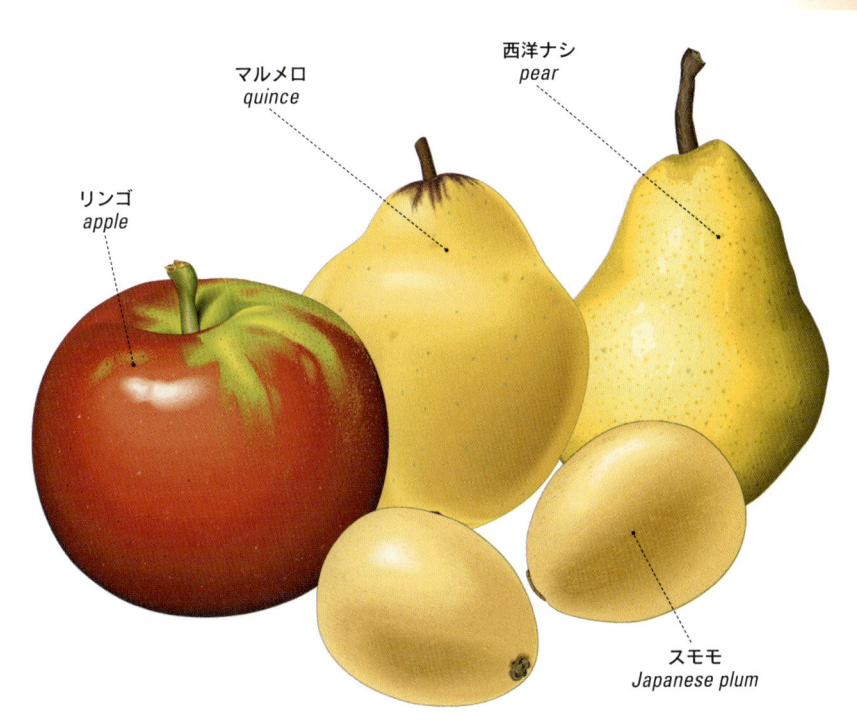

マルメロ
quince

西洋ナシ
pear

リンゴ
apple

スモモ
Japanese plum

111

果物 | FRUITS

柑橘(かんきつ)果物
CITRUS FRUITS

オレンジの断面図
section of an orange

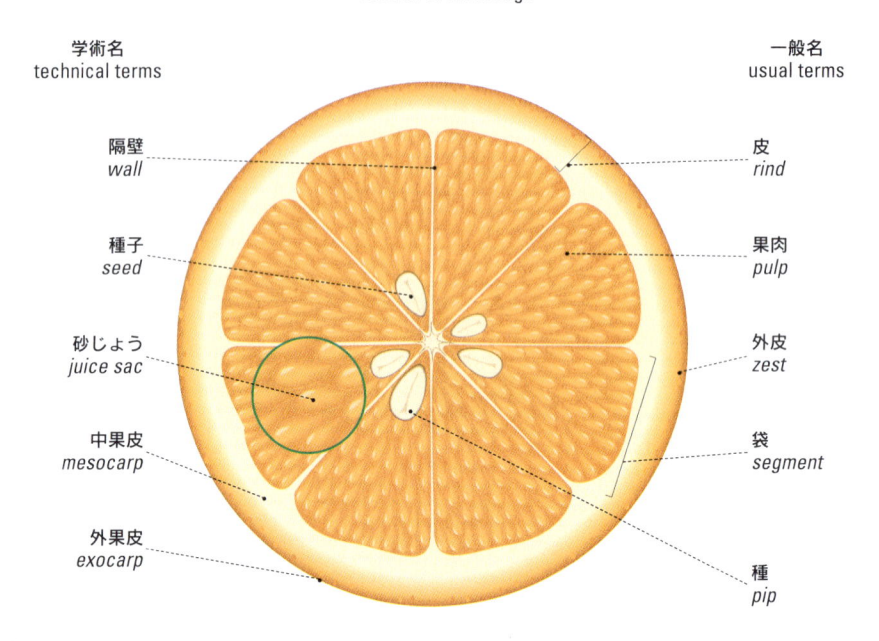

学術名　　　　　　　　　　　　　　　　　　　　　　　　一般名
technical terms　　　　　　　　　　　　　　　　　　　usual terms

隔壁　　　　　　　　　　　　　　　　　　　　　　　　　皮
wall　　　　　　　　　　　　　　　　　　　　　　　　rind

種子　　　　　　　　　　　　　　　　　　　　　　　　果肉
seed　　　　　　　　　　　　　　　　　　　　　　　　pulp

砂じょう　　　　　　　　　　　　　　　　　　　　　　外皮
juice sac　　　　　　　　　　　　　　　　　　　　　zest

中果皮　　　　　　　　　　　　　　　　　　　　　　　袋
mesocarp　　　　　　　　　　　　　　　　　　　　　segment

外果皮　　　　　　　　　　　　　　　　　　　　　　　種
exocarp　　　　　　　　　　　　　　　　　　　　　　pip

柑橘果物の例
EXAMPLES OF CITRUS FRUITS

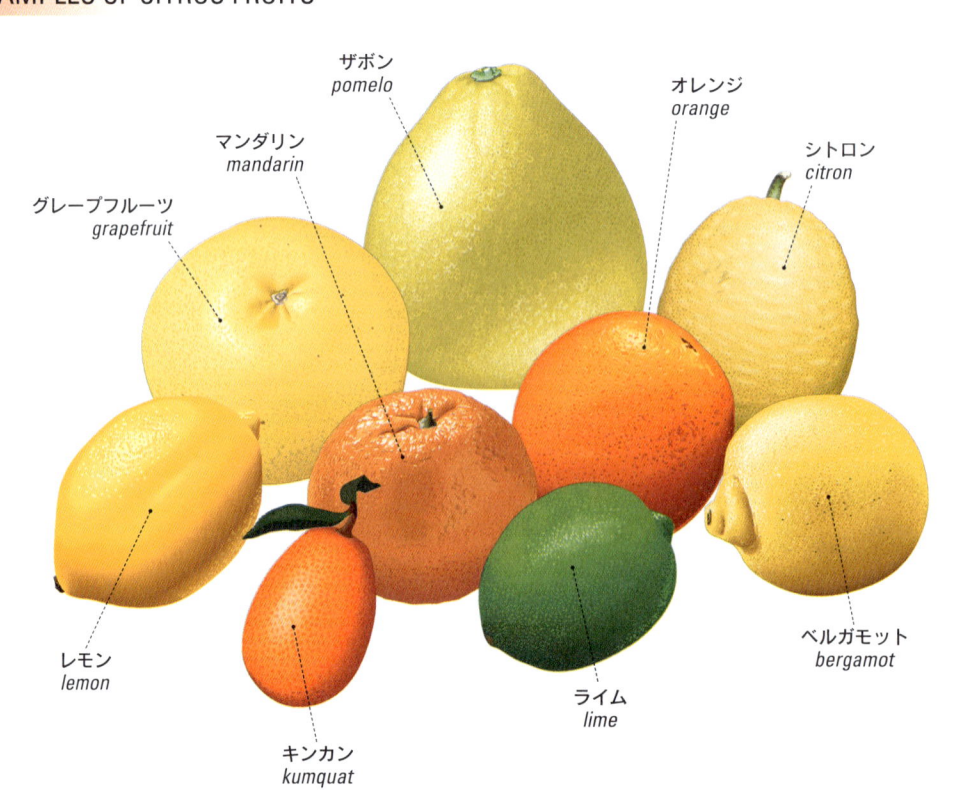

ザボン
pomelo

オレンジ
orange

マンダリン
mandarin

シトロン
citron

グレープフルーツ
grapefruit

レモン
lemon

キンカン
kumquat

ライム
lime

ベルガモット
bergamot

果物 | FRUITS

メロン類
MELONS

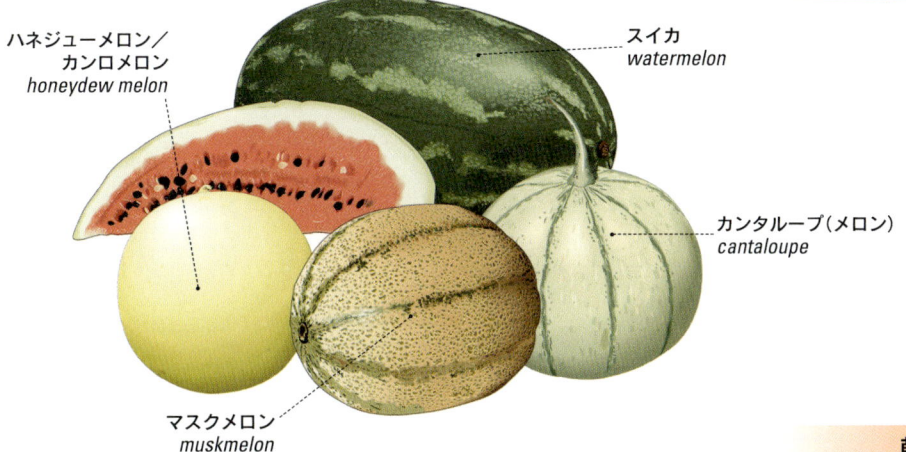

ハネジューメロン／
カンロメロン
honeydew melon

スイカ
watermelon

カンタループ（メロン）
cantaloupe

マスクメロン
muskmelon

乾果
DRY FRUITS

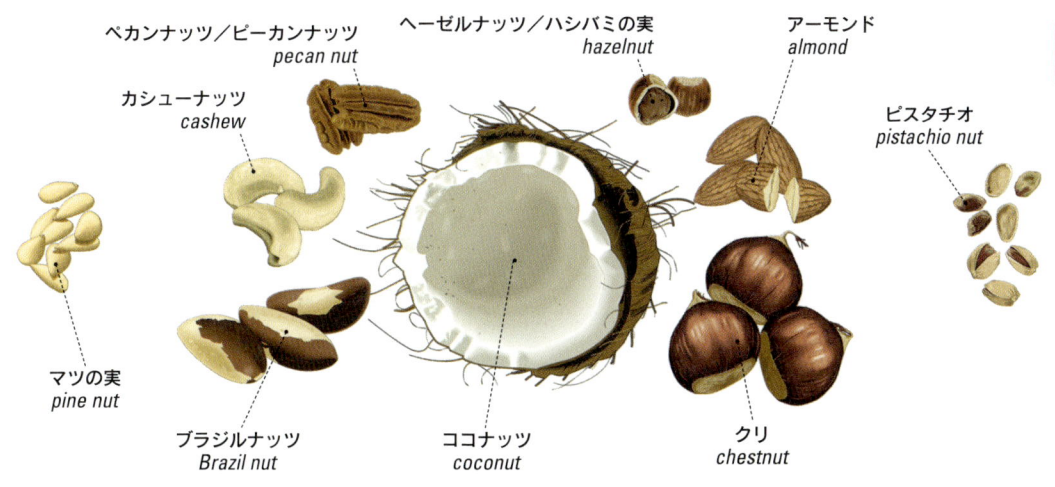

ペカンナッツ／ピーカンナッツ
pecan nut

ヘーゼルナッツ／ハシバミの実
hazelnut

アーモンド
almond

カシューナッツ
cashew

ピスタチオ
pistachio nut

食べ物

マツの実
pine nut

ブラジルナッツ
Brazil nut

ココナッツ
coconut

クリ
chestnut

熱帯果物／トロピカルフルーツ
TROPICAL FRUITS

パイナップル
pineapple

パパイヤ
papaya

マンゴー
mango

ザクロ
pomegranate

キーウィ（フルーツ）
kiwi

ライチ
litchi

スターフルーツ／カランボー
ラ／ゴレンシの実／ヨウトウ
carambola

バナナ
banana

パッションフルーツ
passion fruit

イチジク
fig

113

さまざまな食品 | MISCELLANEOUS FOODS

食事に出る食べ物は、食事をする地域、時間帯によって変わります。食べ物の大部分は果物、野菜、穀物製品、乳製品といった大きなグループのどれかに属します。体はそれぞれの食べ物からさまざまな栄養分を取るので、健康であるためには偏らない食事をすることが大事です。

穀物[シリアル]食品
CEREAL PRODUCTS

雑穀パン
multigrain bread

白パン
white bread

ベーグル
bagel

クロワッサン
croissant

フランスパン／バゲット
baguette

チャパティ
Indian chapati bread

米
rice

パスタ
pasta

ピタパン
pita bread

トルティーヤ／トルティージャ
tortilla

卵と乳製品
EGGS AND DAIRY PRODUCTS

ヨーグルト
yogurt

バター
butter

ウズラの卵
quail egg

鶏卵(けいらん)
hen egg

牛乳パック
milk carton

アイスクリーム
ice cream

チーズ
cheese

食べ物

さまざまな食品 | MISCELLANEOUS FOODS

食事
MEALS

ペパローニ
pepperoni

サラダ
salad

七面鳥
turkey

魚
fish

加熱ハム／調理ハム
cooked ham

ステーキ
steak

シチュー
stew

ピザ（パイ）／ピッツァ
pizza

フルーツジュース
fruit juice

スパゲッティ
spaghetti

サンドウィッチ
sandwich

ケーキ
cake

パイ
pie

クッキー／ビスケット
cookies

小瓶類
small jars

食べ物

115

衣類 | CLOTHING

衣服は体を温めたり、覆ったり、飾ったり、保護したりするのに役立ちます。私たちの服装は、性別、時代、年齢、気候といった多くの要素に大きく左右されます。先進国では服飾産業が盛んで、季節ごとに新しい衣類を買う楽しみがあります。

男性用衣類
MEN'S CLOTHING

シャツ
shirt

襟
collar

襟先
collar point

胸ポケット
breast pocket

ボタン付き前開き
buttoned placket

前身(頃)(まえみごろ)
front

ボタン
button

袖口／カフス
cuff

裾
shirttail

ネクタイ
necktie

小剣／従端
rear apron

中接(なかつぎ)
neck end

小剣通し
loop

大剣／主端
front apron

裏地
lining

ベルト
belt

ベルト通し
belt loop

パンチ穴
punch hole

タング
tongue

バックル
buckle

サスペンダー／ズボン吊り
suspenders

弾性帯
elastic webbing

調節スライド／バックル
adjustment slide

革の端／ボタン留め
leather end

ボタン穴
button loop

ズボン／パンツ
pants

ウエストバンド留め
waistband extension

ウエストバンド／ウエスマン
waistband

ベルト通し
belt loop

前ポケット
front top pocket

タック[ナイフ]プリーツ
knife pleat

ファスナー隠し／比翼／前立て
fly

折り目
crease

折り返し
cuff

サスペンダー・クリップ
suspender clip

ボー・タイ／蝶ネクタイ
bow tie

衣類 | CLOTHING

フード
hood

フロッグ
frog

ウインドブレーカー
windbreaker

ダブル・ジャケット
double-breasted jacket

トグル・ボタン
toggle fastening

ダッフル・コート
duffle coat

スナップ（ファスナー）
snap fastener

レインコート
raincoat

ゴム入りウエストバンド
elastic waistband

ブルゾン
jacket

シングル・ジャケット
single-breasted jacket

衣類と身の回り品

男性用下着
MEN'S UNDERWEAR

ブリーフ
briefs

ウエストゴム
waistband

前立て
fly

ランニングシャツ
athletic shirt

ゴム入りレッグ・ホール
elasticized leg opening

股(布)／クロッチ
crotch

トランクス
boxer shorts

ズボン下
drawers

117

衣類 | CLOTHING

女性用衣類
WOMEN'S CLOTHING

ケープ
cape

スーツ
suit

ジャケット
jacket

スカート
skirt

ピー・ジャケット／ピー・コート
pea jacket

ポロ・ドレス／ポロ・ワンピース
polo dress

ポンチョ
poncho

プリンセス・ドレス／プリンセス型ワンピース
princess dress

クラシック・ブラウス
classic blouse

スキー・パンツ
ski pants

セミ・タイト・スカート
straight skirt

サロン／腰巻きスカート
sarong

プリーツ・スカート
pleated skirt

衣類と身の回り品

衣類｜CLOTHING

パジャマ
pajamas

オーバーコート
overcoat

バスローブ
bathrobe

キュロット
culottes

靴下／ホーザリー
hose

ショート・ソックス
short sock

ソックス
sock

ストッキング
stocking

パンティー・ストッキング
panty hose

衣類と身の回り品

女性用下着
WOMEN'S UNDERWEAR

肩（吊り）紐／ショルダー・ストラップ
shoulder strap

カップ
cup

カップ台
midriff band

ブラジャー
bra

ハーフ・スリップ／ペチコート
half-slip

ボディ(ー)・スーツ
body suit

ブリーフ(ス)
briefs

119

衣類 | CLOTHING

セーター
SWEATERS

Vネック・カーディガン
V-neck cardigan

ハンガー・ループ
hanger loop

Vネック
V-neck

ゴム編みカフス
ribbing

玉縁(たまぶち)ポケット／
箱ポケット
welt pocket

ボタン
button

タートルネック
turtleneck

ボタン付き前開き
buttoned placket

ポロ・シャツ
knit shirt

クルー・ネック・セーター
crew neck sweater

ニット・ベスト
sweater vest

カーディガン
cardigan

衣類 | CLOTHING

子供服
CHILDREN'S CLOTHING

Tシャツ・ドレス
T-shirt dress

ジャンプスーツ
jumpsuit

ジーンズ
jeans

ショート・パンツ
shorts

オーバーオール／サロペット
high-back overalls

調整可能な肩紐(ひも)
adjustable strap

胸当て
bib

前立て
fly

パジャマ
pajamas

おくるみ／ドレスオール
bunting bag

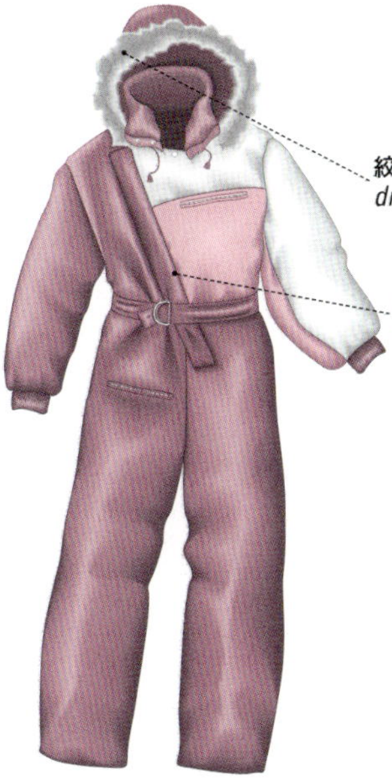

絞り紐(ひも)付きフード
drawstring hood

比翼式打ち合わせ[打ち合い]
fly front closing

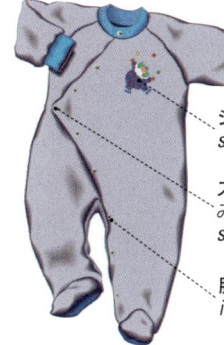

カバーオール
sleepers

シルク・スクリーン・プリント
screen print

スナップ付き前身(頃)(まえみごろ)
snap-fastening front

股下スナップ・ボタン
inside-leg snap-fastening

スノースーツ
snowsuit

ロンパース
rompers

衣類と身の回り品

衣類 | CLOTHING

スポーツウエア
SPORTSWEAR

タンク・トップ
tank top

水着
swimsuit

トレーナー
sweat shirt

フード付きトレーナー／スウェット・パーカー
hooded sweat shirt

ボクサー・ショーツ[パンツ]
boxer shorts

水泳パンツ
swimming trunks

スウェット[トレーニング]パンツ
sweat pants

アノラック
anorak

スパッツ
footless tights

レッグ・ウォーマー
leg-warmer

レオタード
leotard

ズボン／パンツ
pants

ランニング・シューズ
running shoe

舌革／べろ
tongue

紐穴／鳩目／アイレット
eyelet

靴紐（ひも）
shoelace

飾り穴
punch hole

ミッド・ソール
middle sole

踵（かかと）
heel

スタッド
stud

エア・ユニット[クッション]
air unit

紐先金具／タグ
tag

本底／外底／表底／アウトソール
outsole

身の回り品 | PERSONAL ARTICLES

多くの小物は実に実用的にできています。例えば、つばの大きな帽子は太陽の直射から頭を守り、1対の手袋やミトンは寒さから手を守ってくれます。さらにはベルトとハンドバッグが似合うと服装に調和が生まれます。このような小物の中にはさらに毎日の体の手入れに役立つ物もあります。

紳士（用）手袋
MEN'S GLOVES

手袋の甲側
back of a glove

手袋の手のひら側
palm of a glove

手袋の指
glove finger

親指
thumb

平（ひら）
palm

ミトン
mitten

半返し縫い／飾りステッチ
stitching

スナップ・ボタン
snap fastener

運転用手袋
driving glove

婦人（用）手袋
WOMEN'S GLOVES

ショーティ
short glove

手首丈グラブ
wrist-length glove

ゴーントリット
gauntlet

イブニング・グラブ
evening glove

ミット／指なしアーム・ロング
mitt

ゴーントリット
gauntlet

衣類と身の回り品

身の回り品 | PERSONAL ARTICLES

かぶり物
HEADGEAR

フェルト帽／中折れ
felt hat

- 蝶結び／ボー — *bow*
- ハットバンド／帽子のリボン／まき — *hatband*
- 縁取り — *binding*
- クラウン — *crown*
- ブリム／つば — *brim*

ハンティング・キャップ／狩猟帽
hunting cap
- 耳隠し／耳覆い — *ear flap*
- つば／ひさし — *peak*

ダービー・ハット／山高帽
derby

シルク・ハット
top hat

キャスケット／鳥打ち帽
cap

パナマ帽
panama

カートウィール
cartwheel hat

トーク
toque

雨用帽子
gob hat
- クラウン — *crown*
- ブリム／つば — *brim*

バラクラバ帽／目出し帽／ノルウェー帽
balaclava

ストッキング・キャップ／ニット帽
stocking cap

ベレー帽
beret

身の回り品 | PERSONAL ARTICLES

靴
SHOES

靴の各部
parts of a shoe

- 裏当て／ライニング／インナー / lining
- 舌革／べろ / tongue
- カフ／バックステー / cuff
- 靴紐(ひも) / shoelace
- ヒール・グリップ / heel grip
- 爪(先)革／甲革／バンプ / vamp
- 月形芯／外側カウンター / outside counter
- ステッチ / stitch
- 飾り穴 / punch hole
- 踵(かかと) / heel
- 腰革前部 / nose of the quarter
- 紐先金具 / tag
- 甲当て／前革 / eyelet tab
- 紐穴／鳩目／アイレット / eyelet
- 本底／外底／表底／アウトソール / outsole
- 爪先の飾り革 / perforated toe cap

衣類と身の回り品

パンプス / pump

バレリーナ［バレー］シューズ / ballerina

スニーカー / tennis shoe

サイ・ブーツ／ロング・ブーツ / thigh-boot

サンダル / sandal

ローファー / loafer

エスパドリーユ / espadrille

つっかけ / clog

モカシン / moccasin

125

身の回り品 | PERSONAL ARTICLES

革製品
LEATHER GOODS

アタッシュ・ケース
attaché case

仕切り
divider

留め金
clasp

アコーディオン式書類入れ
expandable file pouch

ポケット
pocket

蝶番(ちょうつがい)
hinge

ペン・ホルダー
pen holder

裏地／裏当て／裏打ち
lining

フレーム
frame

取っ手／握り
handle

ダイヤル・ロック
combination lock

襠(まち)付きの折り鞄
bottom-fold portfolio

格納式取っ手[握り]
retractable handle

外ポケット
exterior pocket

ブリーフケース
briefcase

タブ／べろ
tab

キー・ロック
key lock

襠(まち)
gusset

ライティング・ケース／ノートファイル
writing case

小銭入れ
coin purse

クラッチ・バッグ／抱え鞄[バッグ]
underarm portfolio

がま口／小銭入れ
purse

キー・ケース
key case

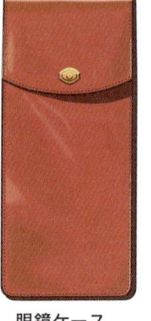

眼鏡ケース
eyeglasses case

二つ折り札入れ
wallet

身の回り品 | PERSONAL ARTICLES

手荷物とハンドバッグ
LUGGAGE AND HANDBAGS

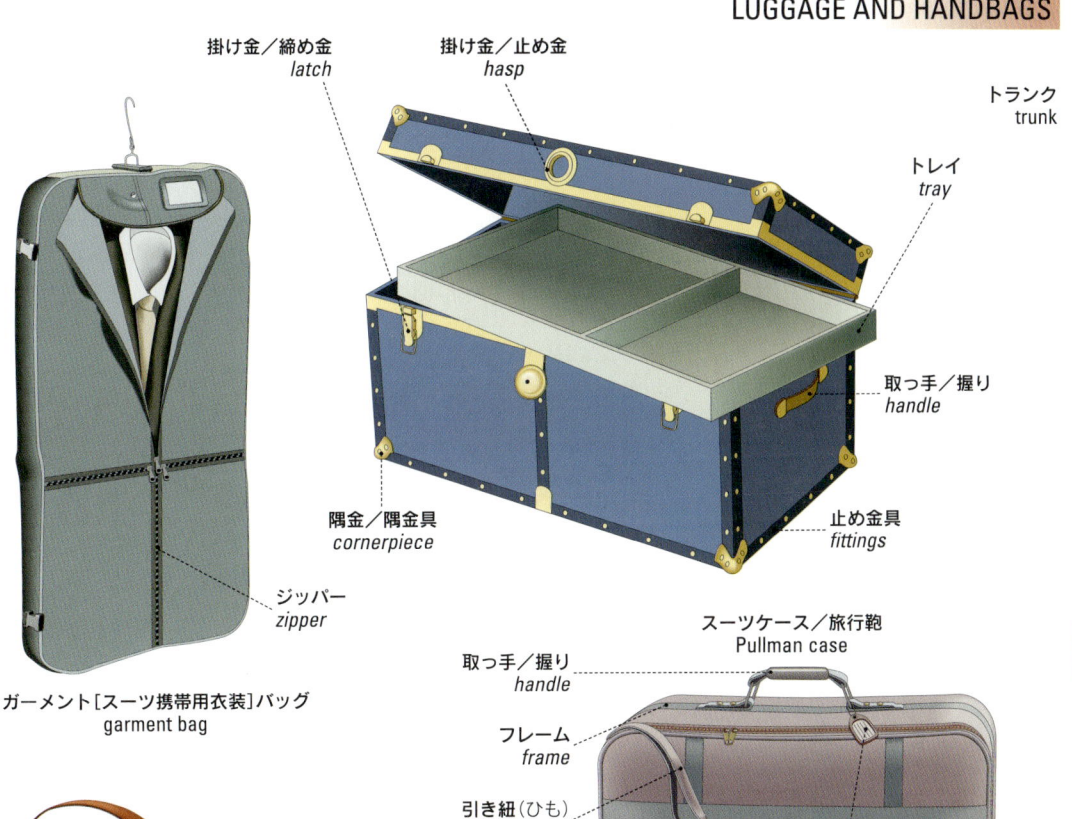

掛け金／締め金　latch

掛け金／止め金　hasp

トランク　trunk

トレイ　tray

取っ手／握り　handle

隅金／隅金具　cornerpiece

止め金具　fittings

ジッパー　zipper

ガーメント[スーツ携帯用衣装]バッグ
garment bag

スーツケース／旅行鞄
Pullman case

取っ手／握り　handle

フレーム　frame

引き紐（ひも）　pull strap

バックル　buckle

肩紐（ひも）　shoulder strap

ショルダー・バッグ
shoulder bag

キャスター　wheel

当て布　trim

名札　identification tag

ショッピング・バッグ／買い物袋
carrier bag

鳩目　eyelet

絞り紐（ひも）　drawstring

前ポケット　front pocket

ドロースリング・バッグ
drawstring bag

メンズ・バッグ／
男性用ショルダー・バッグ
men's bag

ドロースリング・バッグ
drawstring bag

衣類と身の回り品

身の回り品 | PERSONAL ARTICLES

眼鏡
EYEGLASSES

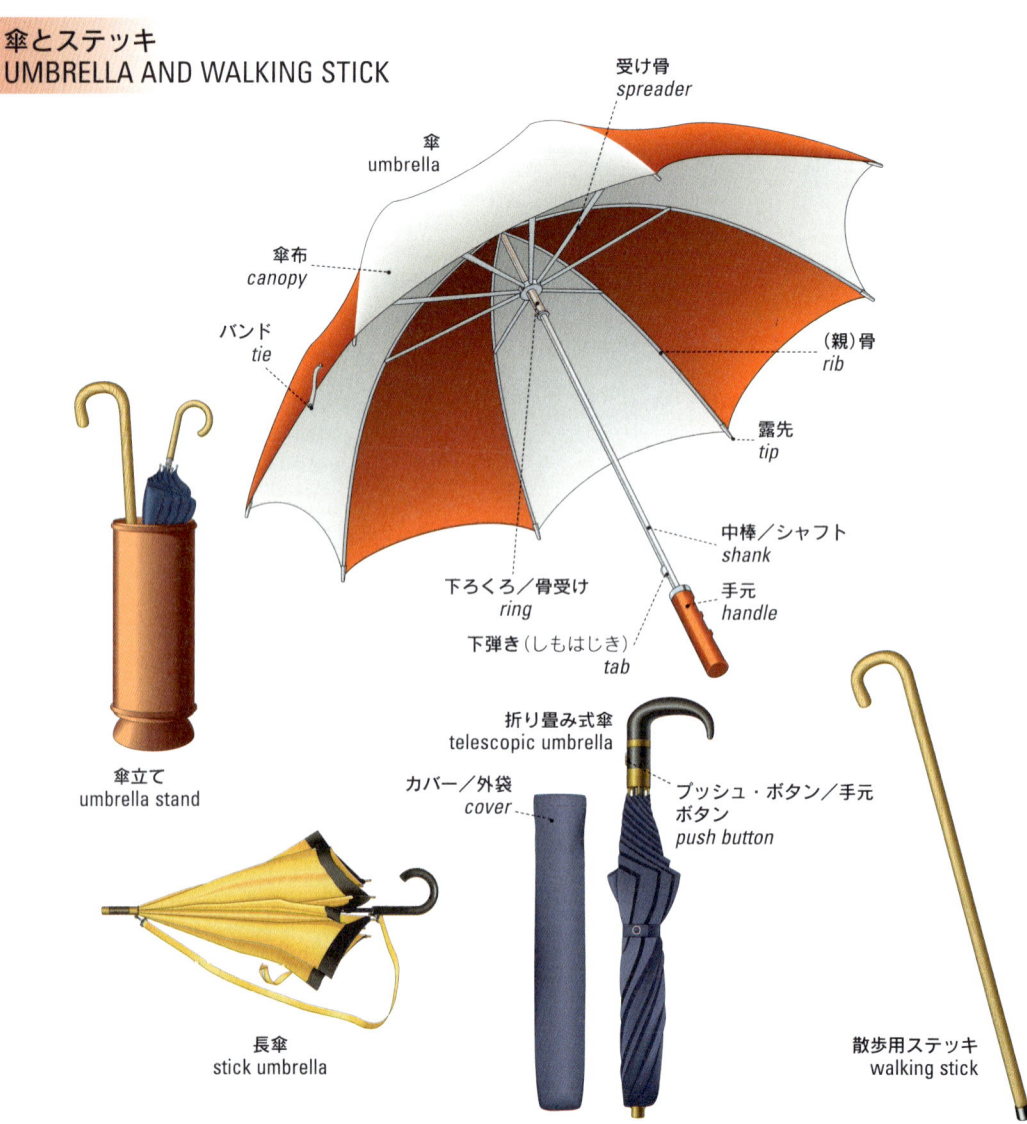

眼鏡の各部
eyeglasses parts

- ブリッジ / bridge
- 眼鏡レンズ / glass lens
- 山（わたり）/ bar
- テンプル / temple
- ベンド / bend
- リム／縁 / rim
- 耳当て／モダン／先セル / earpiece
- パッド・アーム / pad arm

ハーフ・グラス／読書用眼鏡
half-glasses

サングラス
sunglasses

モノクル／片眼鏡
monocle

傘とステッキ
UMBRELLA AND WALKING STICK

- 受け骨 / spreader
- 傘 / umbrella
- 傘布 / canopy
- バンド / tie
- （親）骨 / rib
- 露先 / tip
- 中棒／シャフト / shank
- 下ろくろ／骨受け / ring
- 手元 / handle
- 下弾き（しもはじき）/ tab

傘立て
umbrella stand

折り畳み式傘
telescopic umbrella

カバー／外袋
cover

プッシュ・ボタン／手元ボタン
push button

長傘
stick umbrella

散歩用ステッキ
walking stick

身の回り品 | PERSONAL ARTICLES

宝飾品 / JEWELRY

- フープ・イヤリング / hoop earrings
- バンド（型）リング / band ring 
- ピアス・イヤリング / pierced earrings 
- ロケット / locket
- ブローチ / brooch 
- ロープ・ネックレス / rope
- チャーム・ブレスレット / charm bracelet
- バングル／腕輪 / bangle 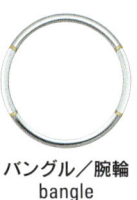
- マチネ・レングス・ネックレス / matinee-length necklace 
- ペンダント / pendant
- シグネット・リング／印環 / signet ring 

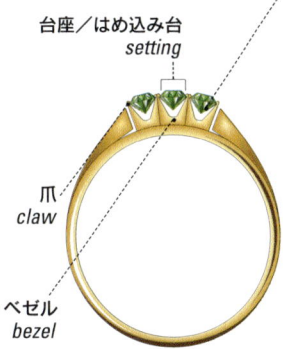

指輪の各部 / parts of a ring
- 石 / stone
- 台座／はめ込み台 / setting
- 爪 / claw
- ベゼル / bezel

準貴石 / semiprecious stones
- アメシスト／アメジスト / amethyst 
- ラピス・ラズリ / lapis lazuli 
- アクアマリン / aquamarine 
- トパーズ / topaz 
- トルマリン / tourmaline 
- オパール / opal 
- トルコ石 / turquoise 
- ガーネット / garnet 

貴石 / precious stones
- エメラルド / emerald 
- サファイア / sapphire 
- ダイヤモンド / diamond 
- ルビー / ruby 

衣類と身の回り品

身の回り品 | PERSONAL ARTICLES

整髪
HAIRDRESSING

フラット・バック・ブラシ／
クッション・ブラシ
flat-back brush

回転ブラシ／ロール・ブラシ
round brush

ベント・ブラシ／スケルトン・ブラシ
vent brush

テール・コーム
tail comb

バーバー・コーム
barber comb

アフロ・ピック
Afro pick

ウェーブ・クリップ
wave clip

バリカン
clippers

ボビー・ピン／ヘア・ピン／
アメリカ・ピン
bobby pin

カール・アイロン／ヘアー・アイロン／
電気鏝（ごて）
curling iron

回転コード
swivel cord

押さえレバー
clamp lever

グリップ／取っ手
handle

温度表示器
heat ready indicator

電源スイッチ
on-off switch

押さえ
clamp

電源表示灯
on-off indicator

スタンド／台
stand

バレル／胴部
barrel

クール・チップ
cool tip

バレッタ
barrette

身の回り品 | PERSONAL ARTICLES

ヘア・ドライヤー
hair dryer

（送風）ファン内蔵部
fan housing

本体
barrel

吸い込み口グリル
air-inlet grille

吹き出し口グリル
air-outlet grille

風量切り替えスイッチ
speed selector switch

温度切り替えスイッチ
heat selector switch

電源スイッチ
on-off switch

取っ手
handle

フード／口先ノズル
air concentrator

フック
hang-up ring

電気コード／電源コード
power supply cord

髭（ひげ）剃り | SHAVING

衣類と身の回り品

アフター・シェーブ・ローション
after shave

毛
bristle

シェービング・カップ
shaving mug

スクリーン
screen

際（きわ）剃り刃／トリマー
trimmer

剃り角度設定つまみ
closeness setting

本体／ハウジング
housing

シェービング・ブラシ
shaving brush

シェービング・フォーム
shaving foam

充電灯／チャージ・ライト［ランプ］
charging light

ヘッド
head

電源スイッチ
on-off switch

継ぎ環
collar

持ち手／ハンドル
handle

充電残量表示ランプ
charge indicator

(替え刃)インジェクター
blade injector

電気かみそり
electric razor

両刃かみそり
double-edged razor

使い捨てかみそり
disposable razor

131

身の回り品 | PERSONAL ARTICLES

全身の手入れ／ボディー・ケア
BODY CARE

爪磨き／爪やすり／エメリー・ボード
emery boards

オー・ド・トワレ
eau de toilette

爪切り鋏（ばさみ）
nail scissors

持ち手／レバー
lever

折り畳み式爪やすり
folding nail file

爪磨き
nail cleaner

爪切り
nail clippers

刃
jaw

化粧石鹸（せっけん）
toilet soap

ヘア・コンディショナー
hair conditioner

シャンプー
shampoo

へちまスポンジ[たわし]
vegetable sponge

デオドラント／制汗剤／脱臭剤
deodorant

(手袋型)洗顔[浴用]タオル
washcloth

洗顔[浴用]タオル
washcloth

マッサージ・グローブ
massage glove

背中洗い用[長柄]ボディー・ブラシ
back brush

大型バス・タオル
bath sheet

バス・タオル
bath towel

海綿
natural sponge

衣類と身の回り品

身の回り品 | PERSONAL ARTICLES

歯磨き
DENTAL CARE

歯ブラシ
toothbrush

毛／刷毛（はけ）
bristle

列
row

スティミュレーター・チップ
stimulator tip

持ち手／柄
handle

頭部
head

練り歯磨き／歯磨き剤
toothpaste

口内洗浄剤［液］
mouthwash

デンタル・フロス／糸楊枝
dental floss

化粧／メーキャップ
MAKEUP

頬（ほお）紅
powder blusher

リキッド・ファンデーション
liquid foundation

パウダー・パフ
powder puff

（アイ）ブロウ・ブラシとアイ・ラッシュ・コーム
brow brush and lash comb

リキッド・アイライナー
liquid eyeliner

アイシャドー
eyeshadow

口紅
lipstick

固形パウダー
pressed powder

リキッド・マスカラ
liquid mascara

衣類と身の回り品

133

家屋の外観 | EXTERIOR OF A HOUSE

外装資材、屋根が平らであるか切り妻であるか、車庫があるかないか、何階建てであるかは、家の外観を決定づける要素です。一方では家を取り囲む土地もまた重要な要素で、小さな花壇、菜園、プール、物置をつくるためのスペースが十分にあるかどうかが問題です。

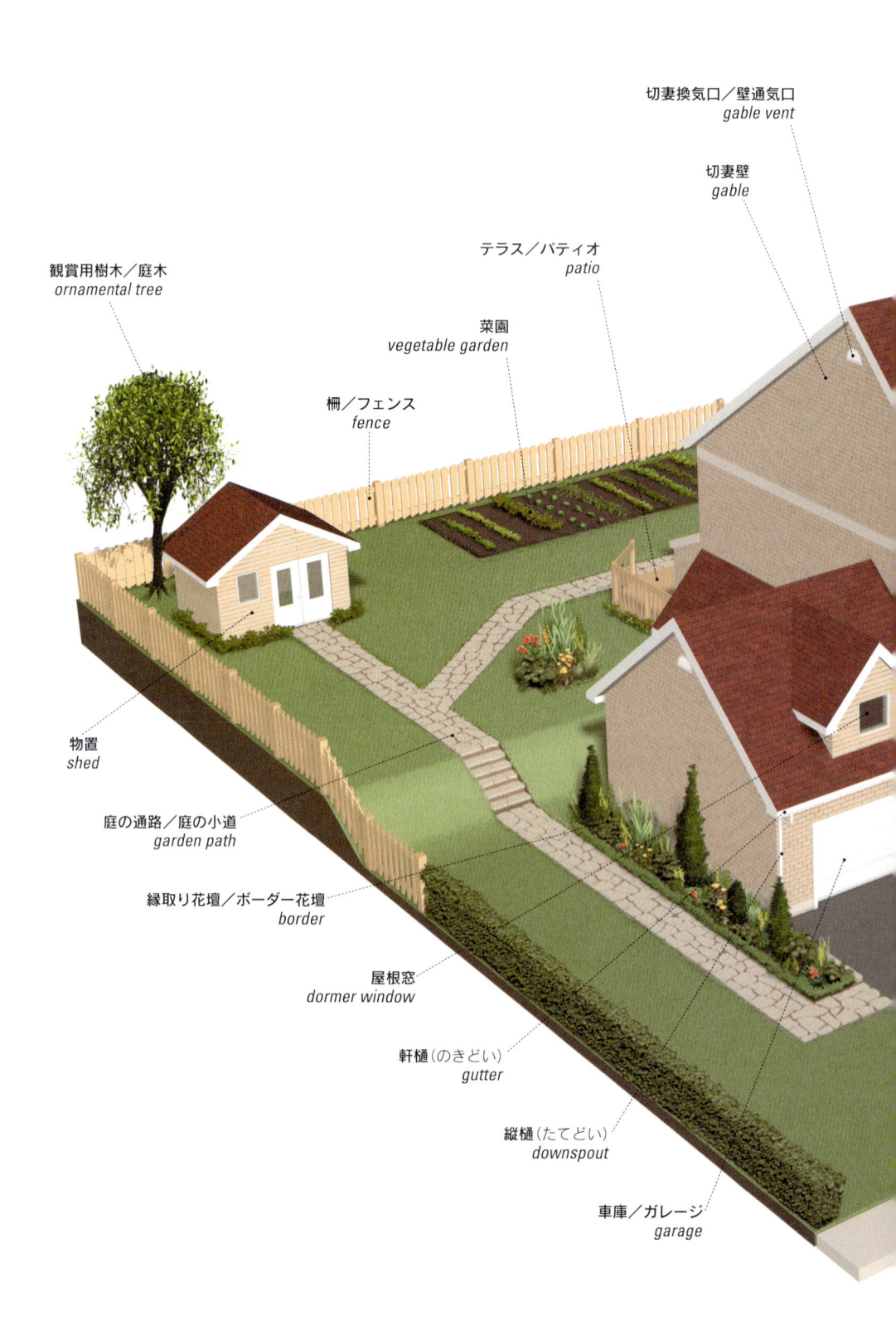

- 切妻換気口／壁通気口 *gable vent*
- 切妻壁 *gable*
- テラス／パティオ *patio*
- 観賞用樹木／庭木 *ornamental tree*
- 菜園 *vegetable garden*
- 柵／フェンス *fence*
- 物置 *shed*
- 庭の通路／庭の小道 *garden path*
- 縁取り花壇／ボーダー花壇 *border*
- 屋根窓 *dormer window*
- 軒樋（のきどい） *gutter*
- 縦樋（たてどい） *downspout*
- 車庫／ガレージ *garage*

家

家屋の外観 | EXTERIOR OF A HOUSE

据え置き式プール
above ground swimming pool

埋設式プール
in-ground swimming pool

フィルター／浄化槽
filter

ステップ／階段
steps

飛び込み台
diving board

避雷針
lightning rod

煙突
chimney

屋根
roof

軒蛇腹
cornice

天窓／明かり取り
skylight

階段
steps

敷地平面図
site plan

家

生け垣
hedge

芝生
lawn

地下窓
basement window

花壇
flower bed

歩道
sidewalk

ポーチ
porch

私有車道
driveway

家屋の構成要素 | ELEMENTS OF A HOUSE

造りが木、煉瓦、わらのどれであっても、どの家も屋根と壁の基本的な要素からできています。壁には人が出入りする外扉がつくられ、窓のように開いている物は、光や新鮮な空気が入り込むように設計されています。現代の家屋にはさまざまな形のドアや窓が数多く付いています。

ドア
DOOR

- 軒蛇腹(のきじゃばら) cornice
- まぐさ header
- パネル／鏡板 panel
- 脇柱／側柱／抱き jamb
- 手先框(かまち) shutting stile
- 中パネル middle panel
- 錠(前) lock
- 吊元框(つりもとかまち) hanging stile
- ドアの握り[取っ手]／ドアノブ doorknob
- 蝶番(ちょうつがい) hinge
- 敷居 threshold

錠(前) lock

- 錠(前) lock
- 鍵座／長座 escutcheon
- デッド[本締め]ボルト dead bolt
- フェースプレート／フロント板／錠面 faceplate
- ラッチ[空締め]ボルト latch bolt
- 丸座 rose
- ドアの握り[取っ手]／ドアノブ doorknob

ドアの例 examples of doors

- 引き戸 sliding door
- 開き戸 conventional door
- 折り畳み式ドア folding door
- アコーディオン・ドア sliding folding door

家屋の構成要素 | ELEMENTS OF A HOUSE

窓
WINDOW

- 組子／桟(さん) muntin
- 上框(かまち) top rail of sash
- 枠／額縁 casing
- 鎧(よろい)戸 jalousie
- 開き窓(枠) casement
- 縦框 hanging stile
- 窓枠 sash frame
- フック hook
- 蝶番(ちょうつがい) hinge
- 雨戸 shutter
- 窓ガラス pane

窓の例 / examples of windows

- フランス窓 / French window
- 両開き窓 / casement window 
- 鎧(よろい)窓 / louvered window 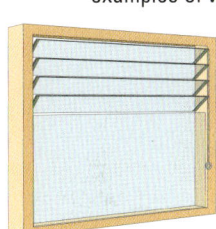
- 水平回転窓 / horizontal pivoting window 
- 上げ下げ窓／サッシ窓 / sash window 
- 垂直回転窓 / vertical pivoting window 
- 引き違い窓 / sliding window 
- アコーディオン窓 / sliding folding window 

家

主な部屋 | MAIN ROOMS

部屋はふつう家の中で同じ階にあるか、あるいはいくつかの階に振り分けられているかのどちらかです。現代社会においては、家庭の需要と予算に応じて部屋の数は家によってまちまちです。ほとんどの家に台所、食堂、応接間、風呂などがあります。

立面図 / ELEVATION

- 中二階 / mezzanine floor
- 二階 / second floor
- 一階 / first floor
- 地階 / basement

一階 / FIRST FLOOR

- ガラス屋根 / glassed roof
- テラス・ドア / patio door
- 台所 / kitchen
- ダイニング・キッチン／食事コーナー / dinette
- 食料戸棚／食器戸棚 / pantry
- ダイニング・ルーム／食堂 / dining room
- 居間 / sitting room
- 洗濯室 / laundry room
- 暖炉 / fireplace
- トイレ／洗面所 / toilet
- 応接間／居間 / living room
- 手すり / guard
- 玄関ホール / entrance hall
- 階段 / stairs
- 玄関 / main entrance
- クロゼット／収納室 / closet
- 玄関広間 / hall
- 階段 / steps

家

主な部屋 | MAIN ROOMS

二階 / SECOND FLOOR

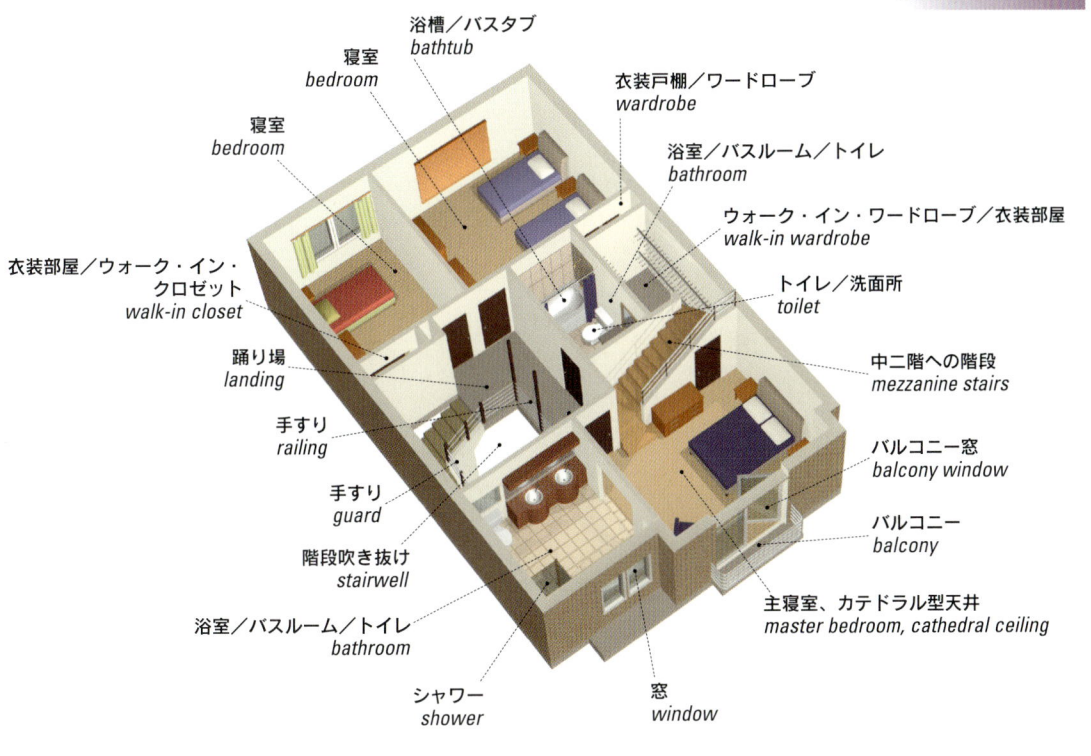

- 浴槽／バスタブ — bathtub
- 寝室 — bedroom
- 衣装戸棚／ワードローブ — wardrobe
- 浴室／バスルーム／トイレ — bathroom
- 寝室 — bedroom
- ウォーク・イン・ワードローブ／衣装部屋 — walk-in wardrobe
- 衣装部屋／ウォーク・イン・クロゼット — walk-in closet
- トイレ／洗面所 — toilet
- 踊り場 — landing
- 中二階への階段 — mezzanine stairs
- 手すり — railing
- 手すり — guard
- バルコニー窓 — balcony window
- 階段吹き抜け — stairwell
- バルコニー — balcony
- 浴室／バスルーム／トイレ — bathroom
- 主寝室、カテドラル型天井 — master bedroom, cathedral ceiling
- シャワー — shower
- 窓 — window

中二階 / MEZZANINE FLOOR

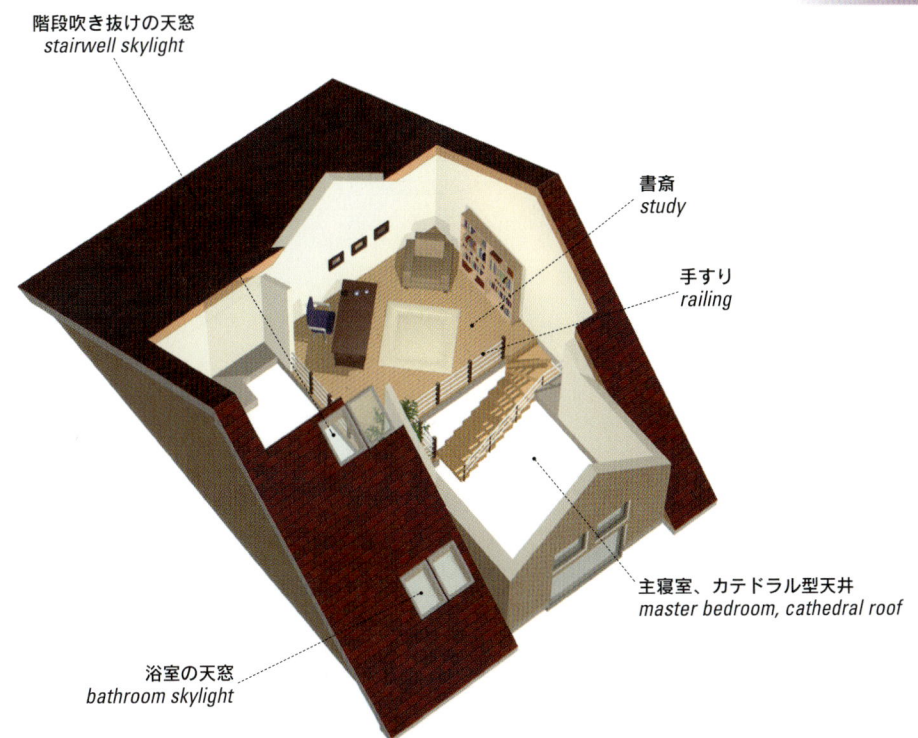

- 階段吹き抜けの天窓 — stairwell skylight
- 書斎 — study
- 手すり — railing
- 主寝室、カテドラル型天井 — master bedroom, cathedral roof
- 浴室の天窓 — bathroom skylight

家

139

家具調度 | HOUSE FURNITURE

家具調度とは家やマンションの中の家具の集まりです。家具は、座ったり、横になったり、物を片付けたりするのに役立ち、文化や時代を反映する物ですから、生活スタイルに合わせて選ぶ必要があります。例えば、遊牧民は余計な家具は持たないようにしています。その一方で発展途上国では、最低限必要な家具調度さえ持てない貧しい人々がたくさんいます。

椅子、背もたれ椅子、肘掛け椅子
SEATS, SIDE CHAIRS, AND ARMCHAIRS

背もたれ椅子の各部
parts of a side chair

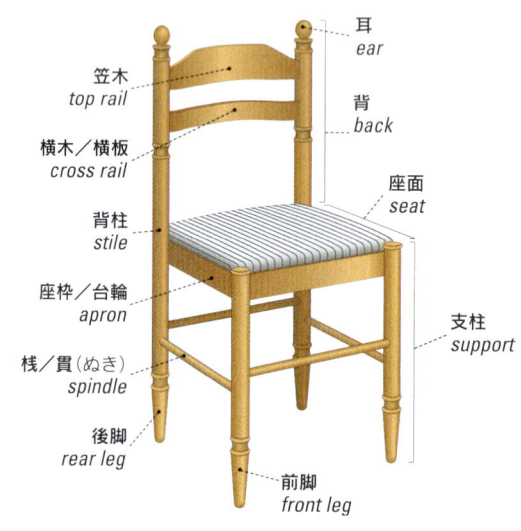

- 耳 ear
- 笠木 top rail
- 背 back
- 横木／横板 cross rail
- 座面 seat
- 背柱 stile
- 座枠／台輪 apron
- 支柱 support
- 桟／貫（ぬき）spindle
- 後脚 rear leg
- 前脚 front leg

ロッキング・チェア／揺り椅子
rocking chair

フットスツール／足（載せ）台
footstool

バー・スツール
bar stool

肘掛け椅子
armchair

ビーン・バッグ(チェア)
bean bag chair

クラブ・チェア
club chair

ラブ・チェア[シート]
love seat

オットマン(チェア)
ottoman

ベンチ
bench

ソファー／長椅子
sofa

折り畳み椅子
folding chair

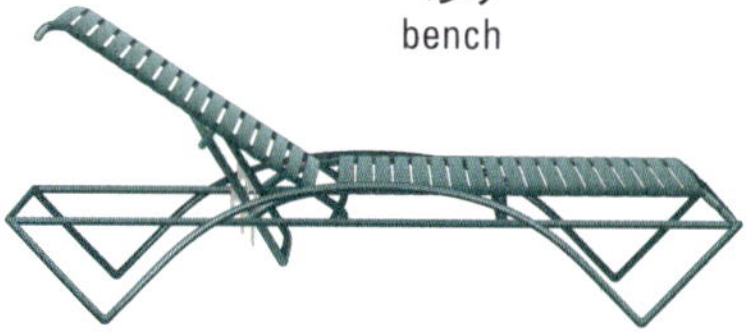

デッキ・チェア
chaise longue

家具調度 | HOUSE FURNITURE

収納家具
STORAGE FURNITURE

大型衣装だんす
armoire

縁飾り
cornice

装飾帯／帯状装飾
frieze

中枠／中方立て（なかほだて）
center post

錠（前）
lock

枠框
frame stile

蝶番（ちょうつがい）
hinge

脚
foot

台座／持ち送り台
bracket base

ドレッサー／鏡台
dresser

西洋だんす
chiffonier

幼児用家具
CHILDREN'S FURNITURE

おむつ替え用テーブル
changing table

ベビー・チェア
high chair

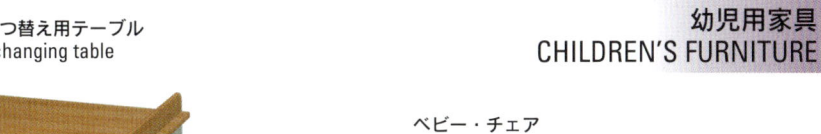

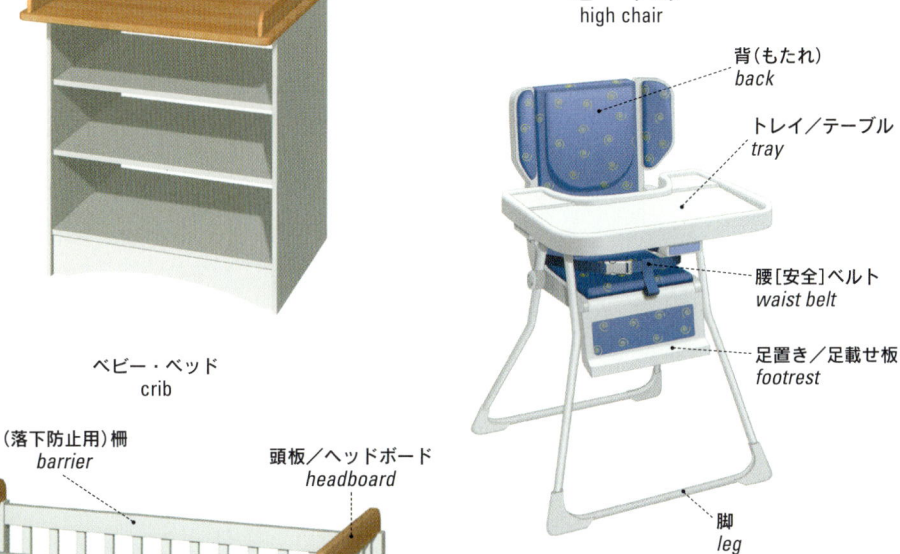

背（もたれ）
back

トレイ／テーブル
tray

腰[安全]ベルト
waist belt

足置き／足載せ板
footrest

脚
leg

ベビー・ベッド
crib

（落下防止用）柵
barrier

頭板／ヘッドボード
headboard

羽根板
slat

マットレス
mattress

引き出し
drawer

キャスター
caster

補助椅子／ブースター・シート
booster seat

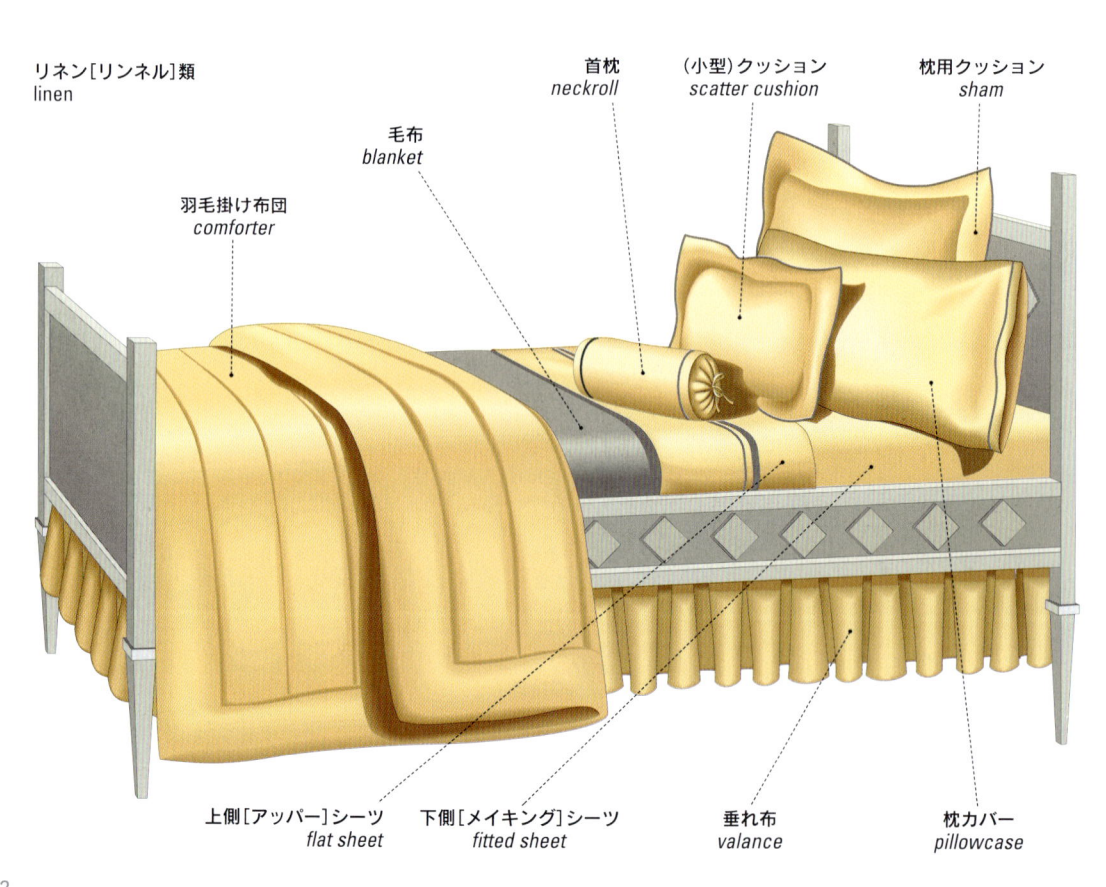

家具調度 | HOUSE FURNITURE

ベッド／寝台
BED

各部
parts

- 足板／止め板／フットボード — footboard
- ゴム・バンド — elastic
- マットレス・カバー — mattress cover
- マットレス — mattress
- 長枕 — bolster
- 頭板／ヘッドボード — headboard
- 枕カバー — pillow protector
- 取っ手 — handle
- ちょうちんばね／ボックス[コイル]スプリング — box spring
- 枕 — pillow
- 脚 — leg

リネン[リンネル]類
linen

- 羽毛掛け布団 — comforter
- 毛布 — blanket
- 首枕 — neckroll
- （小型)クッション — scatter cushion
- 枕用クッション — sham
- 上側[アッパー]シーツ — flat sheet
- 下側[メイキング]シーツ — fitted sheet
- 垂れ布 — valance
- 枕カバー — pillowcase

142

台所 | KITCHEN

台所は、食事コーナーであれ広い部屋であれ、食事の用意をする場所です。現代の台所には、冷蔵庫、レンジ、あらゆる種類の小さな家電製品、さまざまな家庭用品などが備え付けられています。今では料理を作る人は、食事の準備をしたり、食べ物をすばやく、効率的に焼いたりするのに、便利な道具を自由にいろいろと使っています。

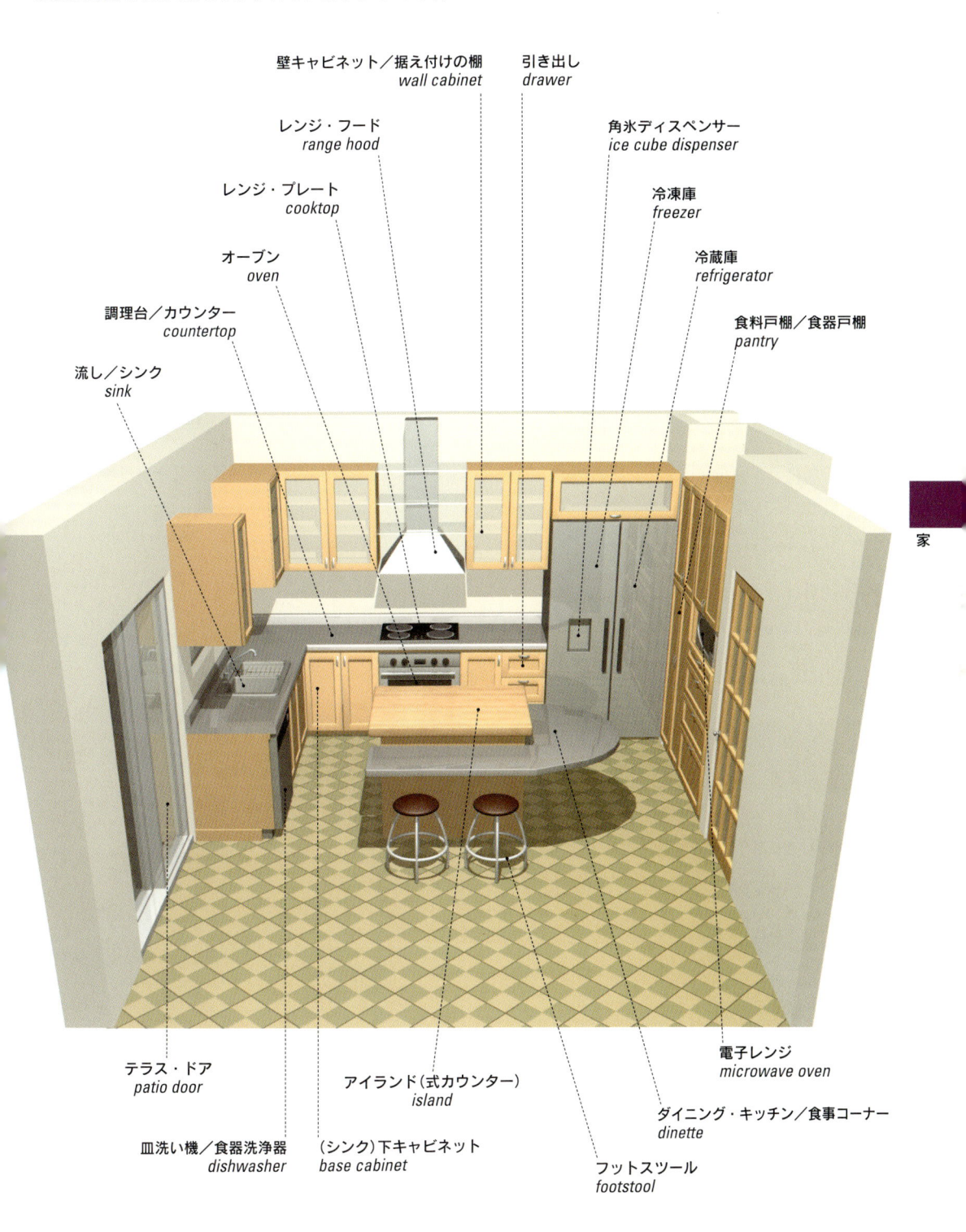

- 壁キャビネット／据え付けの棚 wall cabinet
- 引き出し drawer
- レンジ・フード range hood
- 角氷ディスペンサー ice cube dispenser
- レンジ・プレート cooktop
- 冷凍庫 freezer
- オーブン oven
- 冷蔵庫 refrigerator
- 調理台／カウンター countertop
- 食料戸棚／食器戸棚 pantry
- 流し／シンク sink
- テラス・ドア patio door
- アイランド（式カウンター）island
- 電子レンジ microwave oven
- 皿洗い機／食器洗浄器 dishwasher
- （シンク）下キャビネット base cabinet
- フットスツール footstool
- ダイニング・キッチン／食事コーナー dinette

家

台所 | KITCHEN

ガラス器
GLASSWARE

タンブラー／グラス
tumbler; glass

ブルゴーニュ・グラス／赤ワイン用グラス
burgundy glass

白ワイン用グラス
white wine glass

スパークリング・ワイン・グラス
sparkling wine glass

シャンパン・グラス
champagne flute

水差し／デカンタ（ー）／
デキャンタ（ー）／カラ（ッ）フェ
decanter

小デカンタ（ー）
small decanter

ビア・マグ／ビール・ジョッキ
beer mug

食器
DINNERWARE

カップ
cup

デミタス
demitasse

バター皿
butter dish

砂糖入れ／シュガー・ポット
sugar bowl

コーヒー・マグ
coffee mug

ラムカン皿／ココット皿
ramekin

クリーム入れ／クリーマー
creamer

塩入れ
salt shaker

胡椒（こしょう）入れ
pepper shaker

グレービー（ソース）入れ
gravy boat

台所 | KITCHEN

スープ・ボウル
soup bowl

スープ皿／深皿
rim soup bowl

ディナー皿
dinner plate

サラダ皿
salad plate

パン皿
bread and butter plate

サラダ取り皿
salad dish

大皿
platter

サラダ・ボウル
salad bowl

魚皿
fish platter

野菜ボウル
vegetable bowl

水差し／ピッチャー
water pitcher

ティーポット
teapot

スープ・チューリン／スープ鉢
soup tureen

家

145

台所 | KITCHEN

銀器
SILVERWARE

バター・ナイフ
butter knife

切っ先
tip

峰
back

柄
handle

刃(先)
cutting edge

腹
side

ナイフ
knife

ステーキ・ナイフ
steak knife

チーズ・ナイフ
cheese knife

歯
tine

溝
slot

首
neck

フォーク
fork

先
point

フォンデュ・フォーク
fondue fork

スプーン
spoon

腹
inside

スープ・スプーン
soup spoon

コーヒー・スプーン
coffee spoon

ティースプーン
teaspoon

台所 | KITCHEN

台所用品
KITCHEN UTENSILS

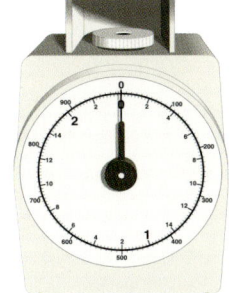

上皿秤
kitchen scale

レモン搾り器
citrus juicer

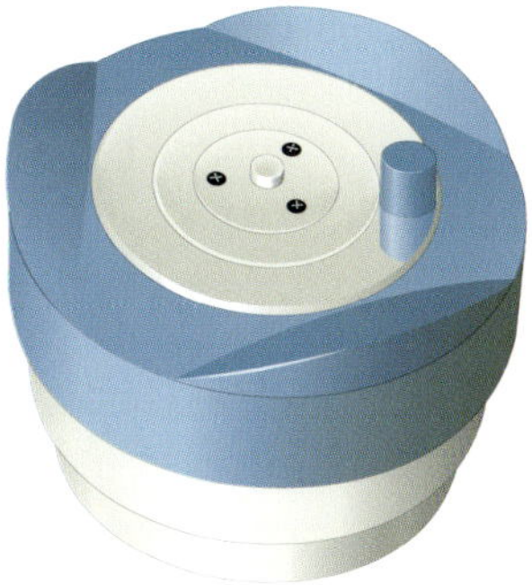

サラダ用水切り(器)／サラダ・スピナー
salad spinner

水切りボウル／コランダー
colander

下ろし金
grater

芯抜き[取り]器
apple corer

皮むき器／ピーラー
peeler

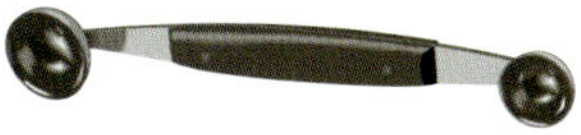

メロンくり抜き器
melon baller

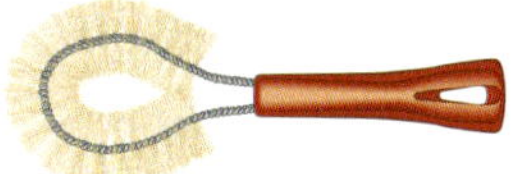

野菜ブラシ
vegetable brush

缶切り
can opener

レバー式コルク抜き
lever corkscrew

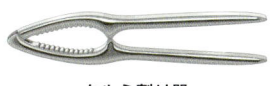

クルミ割り器
nutcracker

栓抜き
bottle opener

家

台所 | KITCHEN

マフィン型
muffin pan

漏斗（じょうご）
funnel

計量カップ
measuring cup

クッキー型
cookie cutters

計量スプーン
measuring spoons

（ミキシング）ボウル
mixing bowls

卵泡立て器
egg beater

スポイト
baster

泡立て器／ホイッパー
whisk

麺（めん）棒／伸（の）し棒
rolling pin

ジャガ芋つぶし器／マッシャー
potato masher

料理包丁
cook's knife

トング
tongs

へら／スパチュラ
spatula

玉杓子／レードル
ladle

アイスクリームすくい［スクープ］
ice cream scoop

台所 | KITCHEN

調理器具
COOKING UTENSILS

深型両手鍋／深鍋
stock pot

二重鍋／湯煎(ゆせん)鍋
double boiler

ソースパン
saucepan

フライ・パン
frying pan

ソテー・パン
sauté pan

ロースト鍋
roasting pans

蓋(ふた)
lid

中華鍋セット
wok set

油切り
rack

中華鍋
wok

火口(ほくち)
burner ring

フォンデュ鍋
fondue pot

スタンド
stand

バーナー
burner

フォンデュ・セット
fondue set

蒸し器用かご
steamer basket

安全弁
safety valve

圧力調節器
pressure regulator

圧力鍋
pressure cooker

家

149

台所 | KITCHEN

家電製品
DOMESTIC APPLIANCES

フード・プロセッサー
food processor

ブレンダー／ミキサー／ジューサー
blender

プッシャー
pusher

蓋（ふた）
cap

フィード・チューブ
feed tube

容器／コンテナー／ミキサー・ボトル
container

蓋（ふた）
lid

刃／カッター／ナイフ
blade

切り刃
cutting blade

容器
bowl

スピード調節つまみ
speed selector

モーター内蔵部
motor unit

モーター内蔵部
motor unit

（スピード調節）ボタン
push button

回転軸
spindle

モーター内蔵部
motor unit

攪拌（かくはん）器取り付け部
blending attachment

ハンド・ブレンダー／ハンディ（ー）・フード・プロセッサー
hand blender

電気ナイフ
electric knife

ハンド・ミキサー
hand mixer

缶切り
can opener

ワッフル焼き器
waffle iron

台所 | KITCHEN

ドリップ式コーヒー・メーカー
automatic drip coffee maker

蓋（ふた）
lid

水容器
reservoir

水位
water level

表示灯
signal lamp

電源スイッチ
on-off switch

フィルター・バスケット［ホルダー］
basket

コーヒー・ポット
carafe

保温ヒーター［トレイ］
warming plate

レモン搾り器
citrus juicer

トースター
toaster

ガイド
bread guide

パン投入口
slot

レバー
lever

取っ手
handle

温度［焼き色］調節つまみ
temperature control

やかん
kettle

深揚げ鍋
deep fryer

ラクレット・グリル
raclette with grill

ホット・プレート／グリドル
griddle

家

151

台所 | KITCHEN

冷蔵庫
refrigerator

冷凍室／冷凍庫
freezer compartment

製氷皿
ice cube tray

ドア・ストッパー
door stop

冷凍室ドア
freezer door

扉パッキン／（ドア）ガスケット
magnetic gasket

取っ手
handle

サーモスタット制御ノブ／自動温度調節器
thermostat control

スイッチ
switch

卵立て
egg tray

バター室
butter compartment

乳製品室
dairy compartment

冷蔵室ドア
storage door

フリー棚
door shelf

ガード・レール
guard rail

チルド・ケース
meat keeper

棚（板）
shelf

フック取り付け板
shelf channel

野菜保存室
crisper

ガラス・カバー
glass cover

冷蔵室
refrigerator compartment

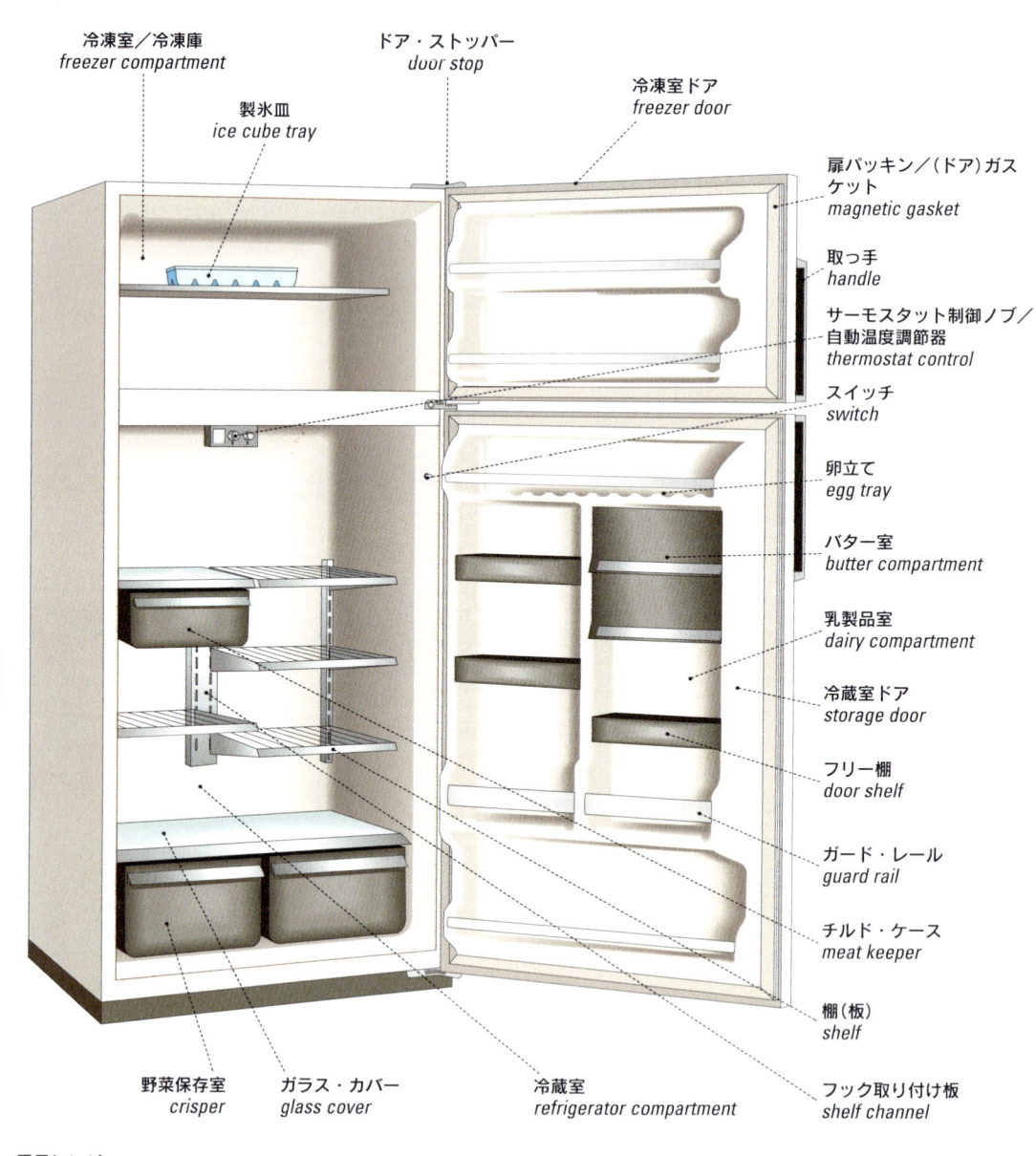

電子レンジ
microwave oven

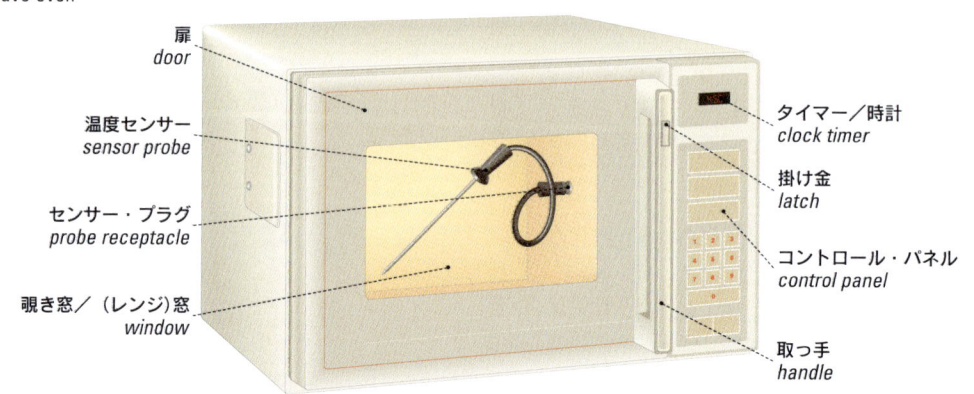

扉
door

温度センサー
sensor probe

センサー・プラグ
probe receptacle

覗き窓／（レンジ）窓
window

タイマー／時計
clock timer

掛け金
latch

コントロール・パネル
control panel

取っ手
handle

台所 | KITCHEN

電気レンジ
electric range

オーブン調節つまみ
oven control knob

タイマー／時計
clock timer

表示灯
signal lamp

飾り板／汚れ除(よ)け
backguard

調節つまみ
control knob

補助コンセント
timed outlet

コントロール・パネル
control panel

レンジ上面
cooktop

ヒーター
surface element

レンジ上面の縁
cooktop edge

取っ手
handle

グリル／焼き網
rack

オーブン
oven

覗き窓／(レンジ)窓
window

引き出し
drawer

家

レンジ・フード
range hood

フィルター
filter

ガス・レンジ
gas range

ヒーター
surface element

火口(ほくち)／バーナー
burner

蓋(ふた)
lid

火力調節つまみ
burner control knobs

火口格子
grate

汁受け皿
drip bowl

取っ手
handle

レンジ上面
cooktop

覗き窓／(レンジ)窓
window

コントロール・パネル／操作盤
control panel

座金／ワッシャー
trim ring

グリル／焼き網
rack

オーブン
oven

扉
door

引き出し
drawer

153

浴室／バスルーム | BATHROOM

入浴は昔からある習慣です。しかし、水道から水が出る最初の風呂が出現したのは１９世紀になってからでした。現代の西洋の家では、風呂にはトイレ、洗面台、シャワー、浴槽が付いています。大きいか小さいか、簡素か豪華かとは無関係に、風呂は何よりもまず衛生を考えて作られた場所です。

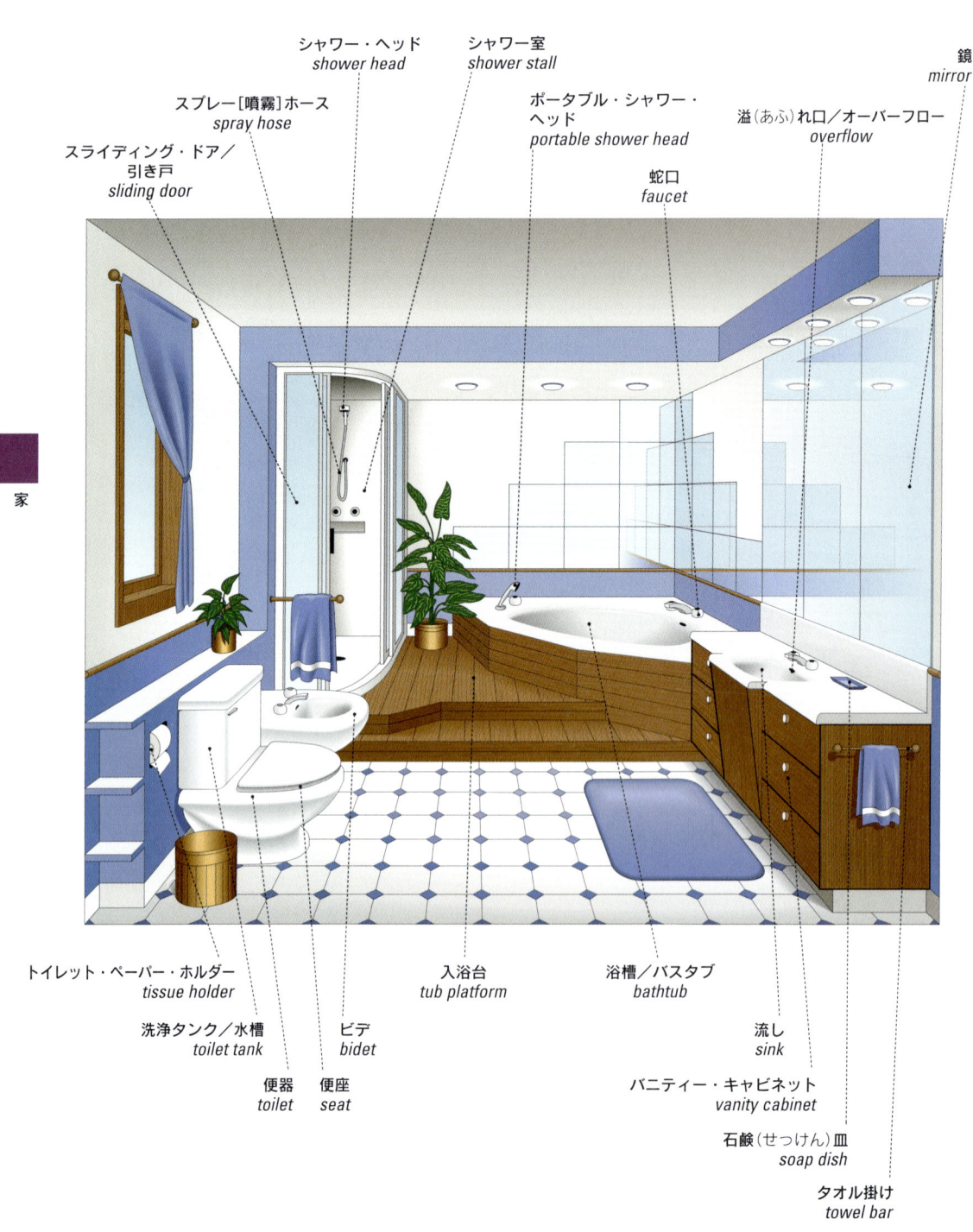

- シャワー・ヘッド / shower head
- シャワー室 / shower stall
- スプレー[噴霧]ホース / spray hose
- ポータブル・シャワー・ヘッド / portable shower head
- 鏡 / mirror
- スライディング・ドア／引き戸 / sliding door
- 蛇口 / faucet
- 溢(あふ)れ口／オーバーフロー / overflow
- トイレット・ペーパー・ホルダー / tissue holder
- 入浴台 / tub platform
- 浴槽／バスタブ / bathtub
- 洗浄タンク／水槽 / toilet tank
- ビデ / bidet
- 流し / sink
- 便器 / toilet
- 便座 / seat
- バニティー・キャビネット / vanity cabinet
- 石鹸(せっけん)皿 / soap dish
- タオル掛け / towel bar

家

照明と暖房 | LIGHTING AND HEATING

光と温度の具合は住居の快適さを左右します。照明器具といろいろな電灯があると、部屋に合った照明ができます。暖炉のような直接暖房であれ、ある1箇所からすべての部屋に熱を供給するセントラル・ヒーティングのような間接暖房であれ、暖房装置は温度を快適に保たなければなりません。

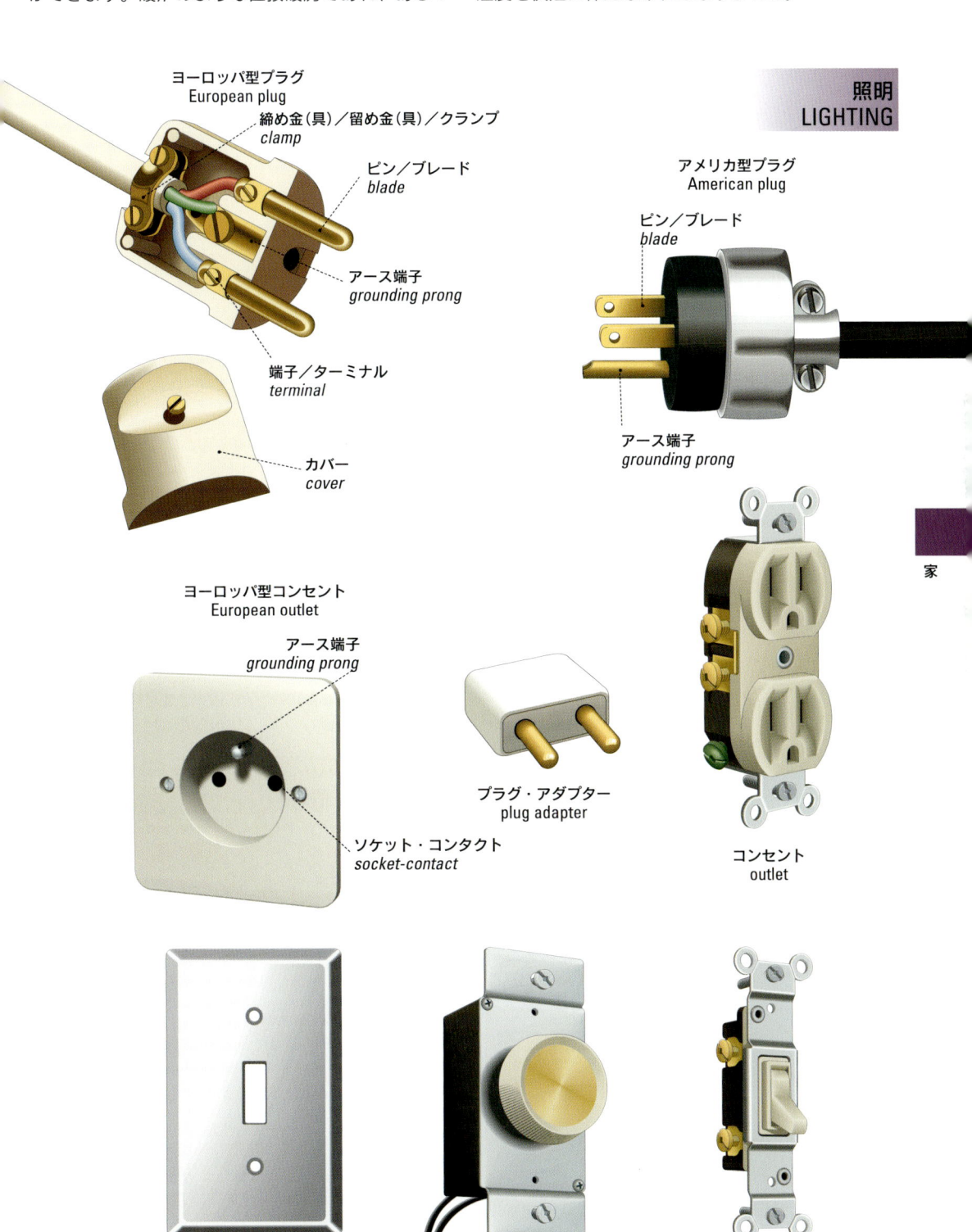

照明
LIGHTING

ヨーロッパ型プラグ
European plug

締め金(具)／留め金(具)／クランプ
clamp

ピン／ブレード
blade

アース端子
grounding prong

端子／ターミナル
terminal

カバー
cover

アメリカ型プラグ
American plug

ピン／ブレード
blade

アース端子
grounding prong

ヨーロッパ型コンセント
European outlet

アース端子
grounding prong

プラグ・アダプター
plug adapter

ソケット・コンタクト
socket-contact

コンセント
outlet

スイッチ・プレート[板]
switch plate

調光スイッチ
dimmer switch

スイッチ
switch

家

155

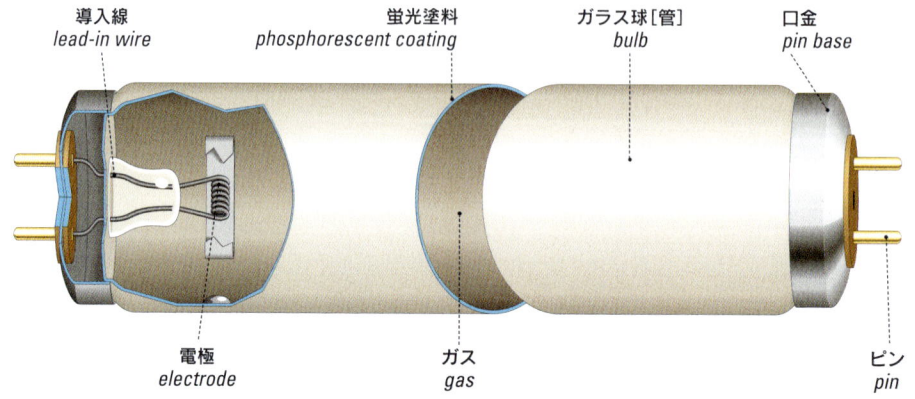

照明と暖房 | LIGHTING AND HEATING

白熱電球
incandescent lamp

- フィラメント / filament
- 不活性ガス / inert gas
- 導入線 / lead-in wire
- 口金 / base

省エネ電球
energy-saving bulb

- 外球 / bulb
- 蛍光管／発光管 / fluorescent tube
- 蛍光管固定クリップ / tube retention clip
- 取り付け台 / mounting plate
- 電子安定器 / electronic ballast
- ケース / housing
- 口金 / base

電球 / bulb

ねじ込み口金 / screw base

差し込み口金 / bayonet base

ランプ・ソケット / lamp socket

蛍光管／発光管
fluorescent tube

- 導入線 / lead-in wire
- 蛍光塗料 / phosphorescent coating
- ガラス球[管] / bulb
- 口金 / pin base
- 電極 / electrode
- ガス / gas
- ピン / pin

家

照明と暖房 | LIGHTING AND HEATING

照明器具
LIGHTS

アーム・ライト[ランプ]
adjustable lamp

アーム
arm

電源スイッチ
on-off switch

笠／シェード
shade

ばね
spring

調節クランプ
adjustable clamp

変圧器
transformer

スポットライト
spot

可動照明
track lighting

シャンデリア
chandelier

吊り下げ灯／ペンダント（ライト）
hanging pendant

天井灯／シーリング・ライト
ceiling fitting

フロア・スタンド[ランプ]
floor lamp

台
base

街灯／ポール・ライト
post lantern

クリップ式スポットライト
clamp spotlight

デスク・ランプ
desk lamp

笠／シェード
shade

台
stand

テーブル・ランプ
table lamp

家

157

照明と暖房 | LIGHTING AND HEATING

暖房
HEATING

暖炉
fireplace

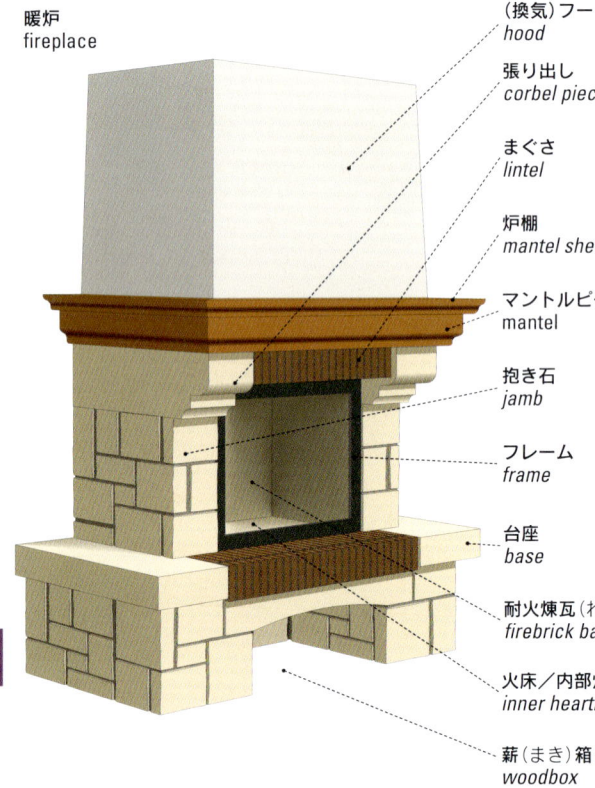

（換気）フード
hood

張り出し
corbel piece

まぐさ
lintel

炉棚
mantel shelf

マントルピース
mantel

抱き石
jamb

フレーム
frame

台座
base

耐火煉瓦（れんが）の背壁
firebrick back

火床／内部炉床
inner hearth

薪（まき）箱
woodbox

暖炉用鉄器具
fire irons

薪（まき）運び台
log carrier

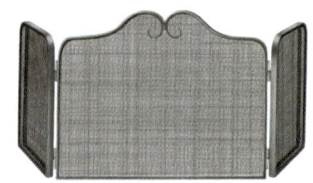

火除（よ）け／火の粉止め（衝立（ついたて））
fireplace screen

火掻（か）き棒
poker

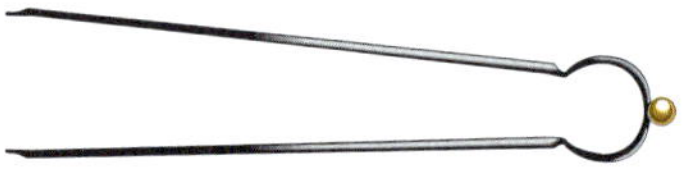

火箸（ひばし）
log tongs

帚（ほうき）
broom

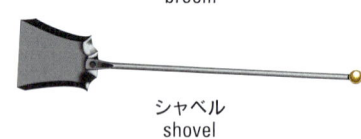

シャベル
shovel

放射［輻射式］暖房器
radiant heater

ファン・ヒーター／温風器
fan heater

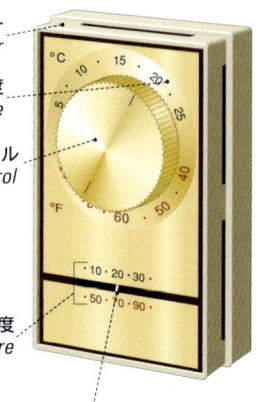

足元温風ヒーター／対流式電気暖房器
electric baseboard radiator

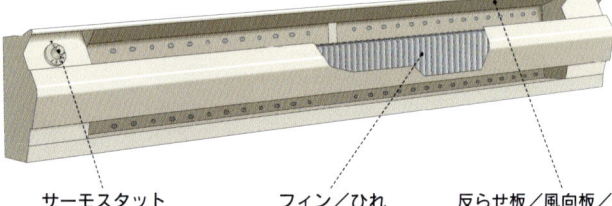

サーモスタット
thermostat

フィン／ひれ
fin

反らせ板／風向板／ディフレクター
deflector

室内サーモスタット
room thermostat

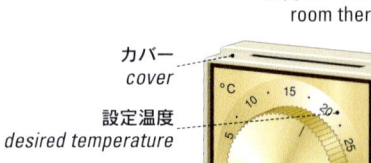

カバー
cover

設定温度
desired temperature

温度調節ダイヤル
temperature control

実際温度
actual temperature

指針／ポインター
pointer

家

家事用品と家電製品 | HOUSEHOLD EQUIPMENT AND APPLIANCES

家事は電気が発明されるまで人力に頼らざるをえず、掃除をするにも、洗濯をするにも、すべて人間の手を使っていました。初期のあらゆる家電製品は電気を熱に変える物で、その最初の家電製品が電気アイロンでした。電気を動きに変える電動モーターの出現で、洗濯機や乾燥機などの家電製品は新しい世代を迎えることになりました。

台所用スポンジ
scouring pad

キッチン・タオル
kitchen towel

注ぎ口
pouring spout

取っ手
handle

バケツ
pail

ブラシ
brush

スチーム・アイロン
steam iron

モップ
mop

ハンド掃除機
hand vacuum cleaner

蓋（ふた）
lid

取っ手
handle

シリンダー・タイプの電気掃除機
cylinder vacuum cleaner

スティック・タイプ電気掃除機
upright vacuum cleaner

ごみ箱
refuse container

ちり取り
dustpan

帚（ほうき）
broom

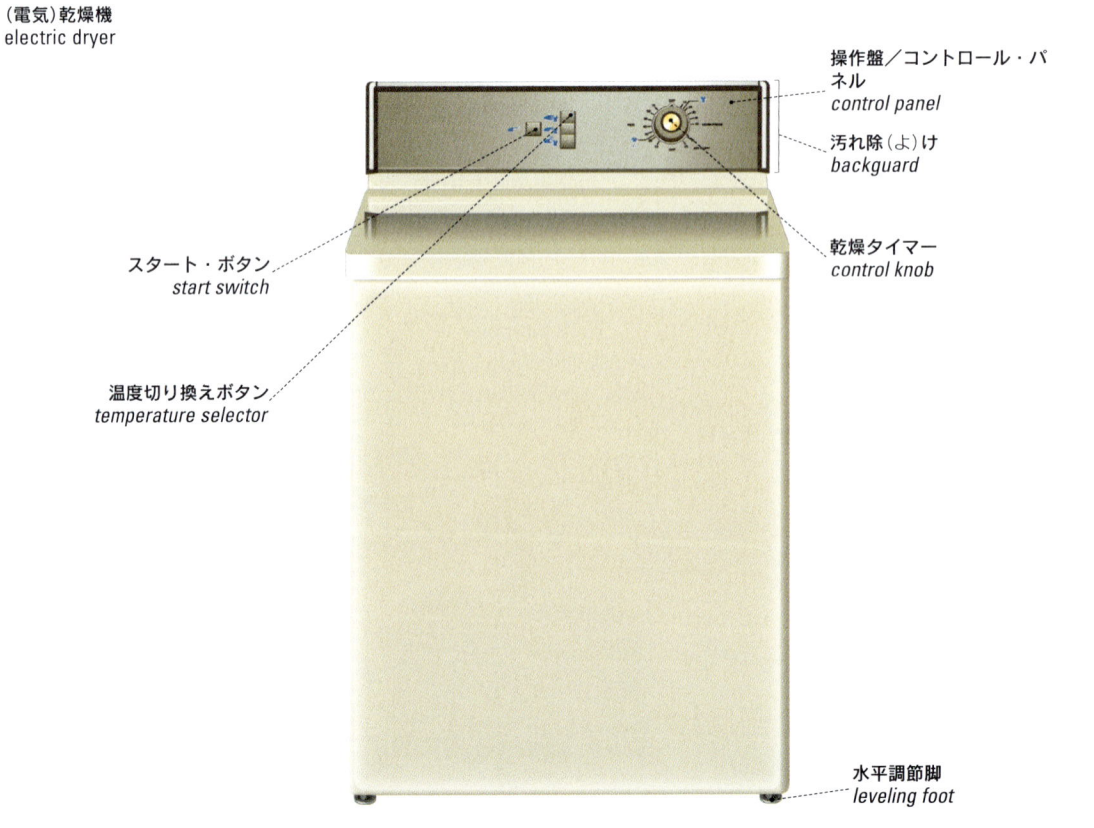

家事用品と家電製品 | HOUSEHOLD EQUIPMENT AND APPLIANCES

（電気）洗濯機
washer

温度切り換えボタン
temperature selector

汚れ除（よ）け
backguard

洗濯タイマー
control knob

操作盤／コントロール・パネル
control panel

蓋（ふた）
lid

水位切り換えボタン
water-level selector

水平調節脚
leveling foot

（電気）乾燥機
electric dryer

操作盤／コントロール・パネル
control panel

汚れ除（よ）け
backguard

スタート・ボタン
start switch

乾燥タイマー
control knob

温度切り換えボタン
temperature selector

水平調節脚
leveling foot

日曜大工 | DO-IT-YOURSELF

部屋を塗装したり、ヒューズを取り替えたり、水が漏れる蛇口を修理したりするのに、プロの手を借りる必要はありません。器用な人なら誰でもこのような手作業をこなして、日曜大工に専念できます。大工仕事が好きな人でも、適切な資材、よい方法、よい道具を選べば仕事が楽になります。

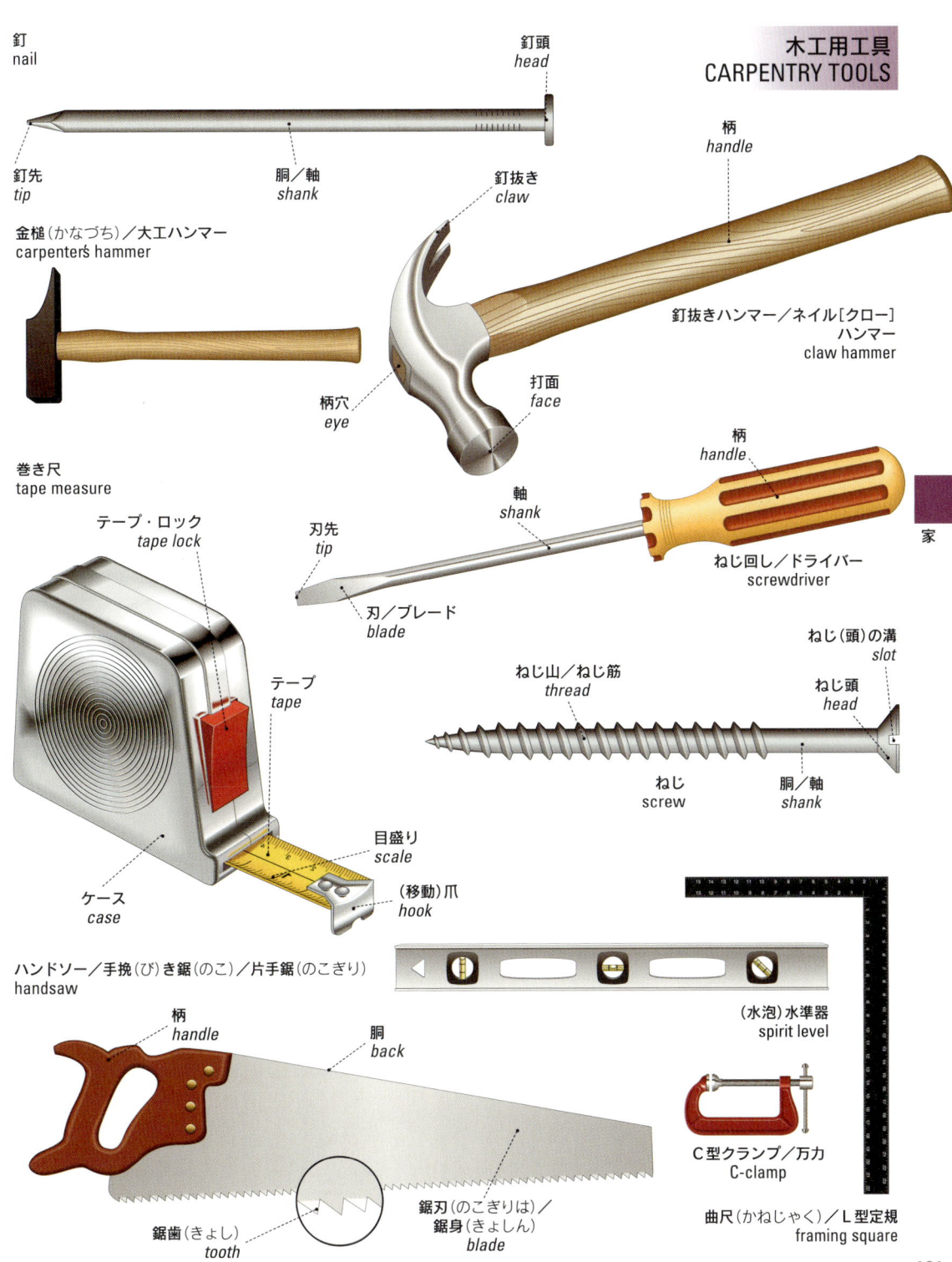

木工用工具
CARPENTRY TOOLS

釘 nail
釘頭 head
柄 handle
釘先 tip
胴／軸 shank
釘抜き claw
金槌（かなづち）／大工ハンマー carpenter's hammer
柄穴 eye
打面 face
釘抜きハンマー／ネイル［クロー］ハンマー claw hammer

巻き尺 tape measure
テープ・ロック tape lock
刃先 tip
柄 handle
軸 shank
テープ tape
刃／ブレード blade
ねじ回し／ドライバー screwdriver

ねじ（頭）の溝 slot
ねじ山／ねじ筋 thread
ねじ頭 head
ねじ screw
胴／軸 shank

目盛り scale
ケース case
（移動）爪 hook

ハンドソー／手挽（び）き鋸（のこ）／片手鋸（のこぎり） handsaw
柄 handle
胴 back
鋸歯（きょし） tooth
鋸刃（のこぎりは）／鋸身（きょしん） blade

（水泡）水準器 spirit level
C型クランプ／万力 C-clamp
曲尺（かねじゃく）／L型定規 framing square

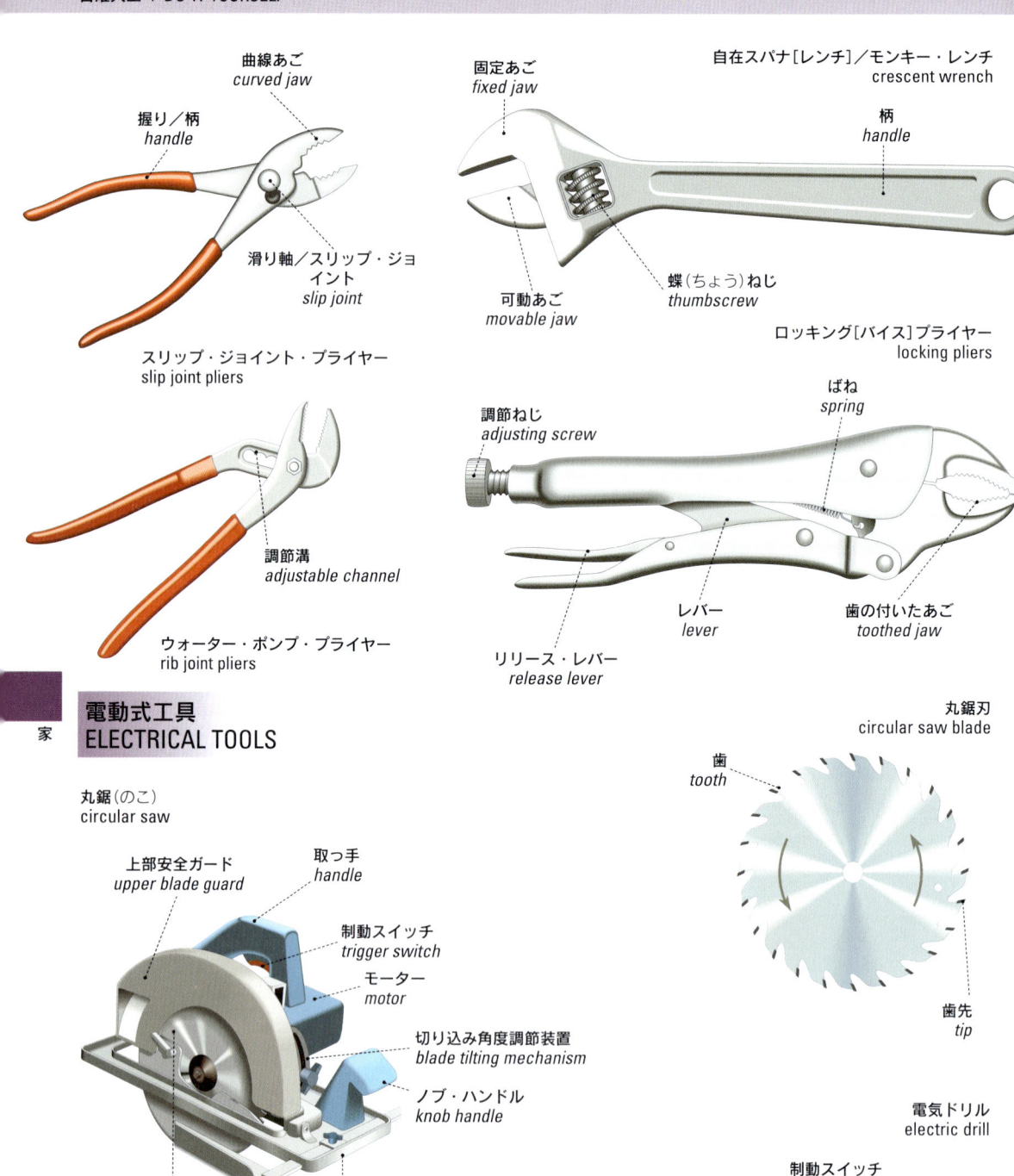

日曜大工 | DO-IT-YOURSELF

曲線あご curved jaw
握り／柄 handle
滑り軸／スリップ・ジョイント slip joint
スリップ・ジョイント・プライヤー slip joint pliers

固定あご fixed jaw
可動あご movable jaw
蝶（ちょう）ねじ thumbscrew
自在スパナ［レンチ］／モンキー・レンチ crescent wrench
柄 handle

調節溝 adjustable channel
ウォーター・ポンプ・プライヤー rib joint pliers

調節ねじ adjusting screw
ばね spring
ロッキング［バイス］プライヤー locking pliers
レバー lever
リリース・レバー release lever
歯の付いたあご toothed jaw

電動式工具
ELECTRICAL TOOLS

丸鋸（のこ） circular saw

上部安全ガード upper blade guard
取っ手 handle
制動スイッチ trigger switch
モーター motor
切り込み角度調節装置 blade tilting mechanism
ノブ・ハンドル knob handle
定盤／ベース（プレート） base plate
鋸刃（のこぎりは）／鋸身（きょしん） blade

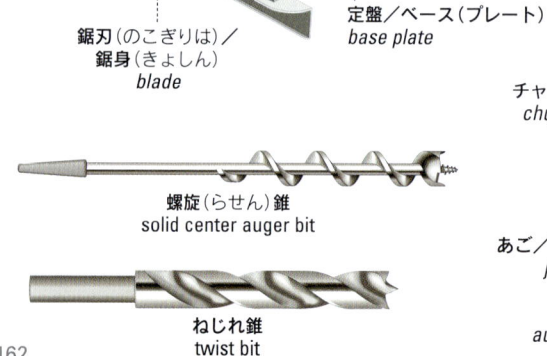

螺旋（らせん）錐 solid center auger bit
ねじれ錐 twist bit

丸鋸刃 circular saw blade
歯 tooth
歯先 tip

電気ドリル electric drill
ケース housing
制動スイッチ trigger switch
ピストル型グリップ pistol grip handle
チャック chuck
あご／くわえ部 jaw
ケーブル・スリーブ cable sleeve
補助ハンドル auxiliary handle
（電気）ケーブル cable

日曜大工 | DO-IT-YOURSELF

塗装
PAINTING UPKEEP

ローラー刷毛（はけ）とトレイ
paint roller and tray

柄／ハンドル
handle

ローラー・フレーム
roller frame

ローラー・カバー
roller cover

柄
handle

はばき金
ferrule

剛毛
bristles

刷毛（はけ）／ブラシ
brush

刻み付きナット
knurled bolt

刃
blade

柄
handle

きさげ／スクレイパー
scraper

足場付きはしご
platform ladder

延長［継ぎ足し、繰り出し］はしご
extension ladder

横桟
rung

滑車
pulley

支柱／縦材
side rail

固定装置／縮梯防止装置
locking device

脚立（きゃたつ）
stepladder

巻き上げロープ
hoisting rope

滑り止め付き石付き
antislip shoe

家

園芸／ガーデニング | GARDENING

観賞用庭園や菜園を耕したり、家庭で庭いじりをしたりする趣味の園芸は、ますます人気が高まっています。園芸家の好み、使える空間の広さ、周囲の状況に応じて、庭の外観も異なってきます。栽培植物に詳しくて、適切な園芸道具を選べば、土地をじょうずに活用することができます。

手押し車／猫車
wheelbarrow

ハンドル
handle

トレイ
tray

共柄熊手／小型草かき
small hand cultivator

移植鏝（ごて）
trowel

剪定（せんてい）[植木]鋏（ばさみ）
pruning shears

レッグ／脚
leg

ホイール／車輪
wheel

草取り／除草器
weeder

（生け垣用の）刈り込み鋏
hedge shears

ハンド・スプレー／
トリガー・スプレー
sprayer

園芸用手袋
gardening gloves

シャベル／スコップ
shovel

芝切り／芝縁刈り
lawn edger

人力散布機
spreader

園芸／ガーデニング | GARDENING

動力式芝刈り機
power mower

速度調節つまみ
speed control

ハンドル
handle

イグニッション・キー
ignition key

安全ハンドル
safety handle

集草箱
grassbox

スターター
starter

モーター
motor

燃料注入口キャップ
filler cap

スプレー・ノズル
spray nozzle

ホース車
hose trolley

如雨露（じょうろ）
watering can

熊手／集草レーキ
lawn rake

熊手／レーキ
rake

堆肥箱
compost bin

家

165

実験器具 | LABORATORY EQUIPMENT

実験室での実験の性格によって、科学者は特殊な器具を使い分けます。例えば微生物学者は顕微鏡を使ってシャーレの中で培養された微生物を観察し、化学者はその生成物を、ビーカー、三角フラスコ、ピペットなど、さまざまな目盛り付き容器の中で混ぜたりします。

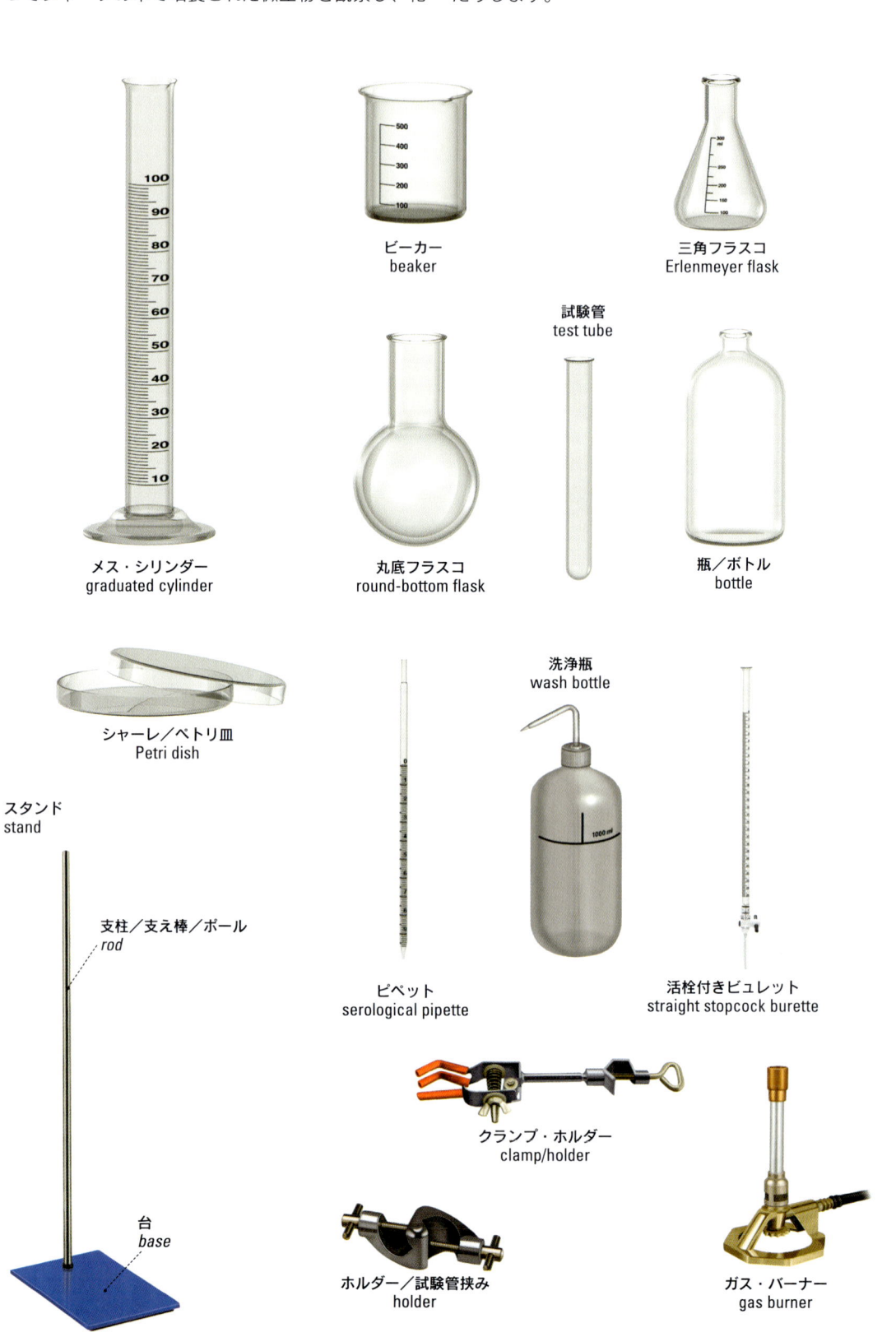

ビーカー
beaker

三角フラスコ
Erlenmeyer flask

試験管
test tube

メス・シリンダー
graduated cylinder

丸底フラスコ
round-bottom flask

瓶／ボトル
bottle

シャーレ／ペトリ皿
Petri dish

洗浄瓶
wash bottle

スタンド
stand

支柱／支え棒／ボール
rod

ピペット
serological pipette

活栓付きビュレット
straight stopcock burette

クランプ・ホルダー
clamp/holder

台
base

ホルダー／試験管挟み
holder

ガス・バーナー
gas burner

科学

実験器具 | LABORATORY EQUIPMENT

ルーペと顕微鏡
MAGNIFYING GLASS AND MICROSCOPES

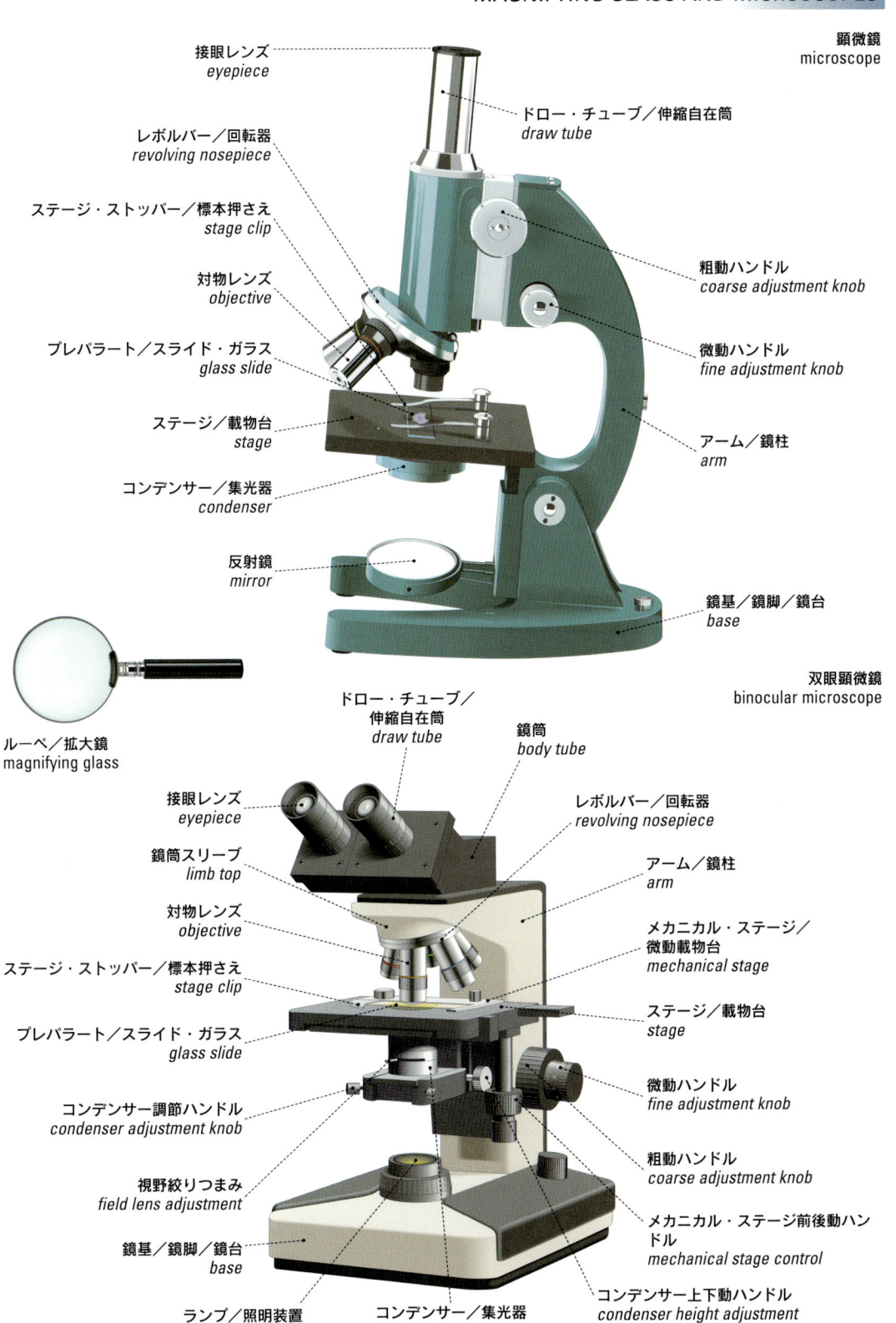

顕微鏡
microscope

接眼レンズ
eyepiece

ドロー・チューブ／伸縮自在筒
draw tube

レボルバー／回転器
revolving nosepiece

ステージ・ストッパー／標本押さえ
stage clip

粗動ハンドル
coarse adjustment knob

対物レンズ
objective

微動ハンドル
fine adjustment knob

プレパラート／スライド・ガラス
glass slide

ステージ／載物台
stage

アーム／鏡柱
arm

コンデンサー／集光器
condenser

反射鏡
mirror

鏡基／鏡脚／鏡台
base

ルーペ／拡大鏡
magnifying glass

双眼顕微鏡
binocular microscope

ドロー・チューブ／伸縮自在筒
draw tube

鏡筒
body tube

接眼レンズ
eyepiece

レボルバー／回転器
revolving nosepiece

鏡筒スリーブ
limb top

アーム／鏡柱
arm

対物レンズ
objective

メカニカル・ステージ／微動載物台
mechanical stage

ステージ・ストッパー／標本押さえ
stage clip

ステージ／載物台
stage

プレパラート／スライド・ガラス
glass slide

微動ハンドル
fine adjustment knob

コンデンサー調節ハンドル
condenser adjustment knob

粗動ハンドル
coarse adjustment knob

視野絞りつまみ
field lens adjustment

メカニカル・ステージ前後動ハンドル
mechanical stage control

鏡基／鏡脚／鏡台
base

ランプ／照明装置
lamp

コンデンサー／集光器
condenser

コンデンサー上下動ハンドル
condenser height adjustment

科学

167

計測機器 | MEASURING DEVICES

人間は太古の昔からさまざまなものを計測する機器を開発してきました。例えば、時間の経過を測定する最初の器具は日時計で、少なくとも３，０００年間は日付を刻み続けています。物理、化学、数学のような精密科学においては、さまざまな測定結果が正確であるか否かはとても重要です。そのために数え切れないほどの特殊な器具が考案されてきました。

時間測定
MEASURE OF TIME

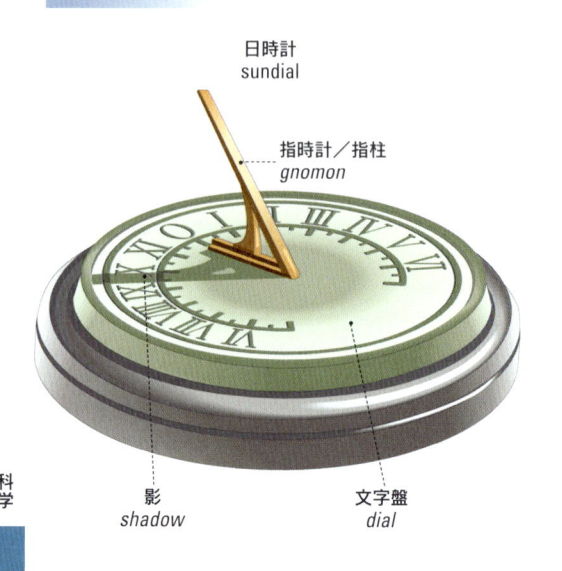

日時計
sundial

指時計／指柱
gnomon

影
shadow

文字盤
dial

ストップウォッチ
stopwatch

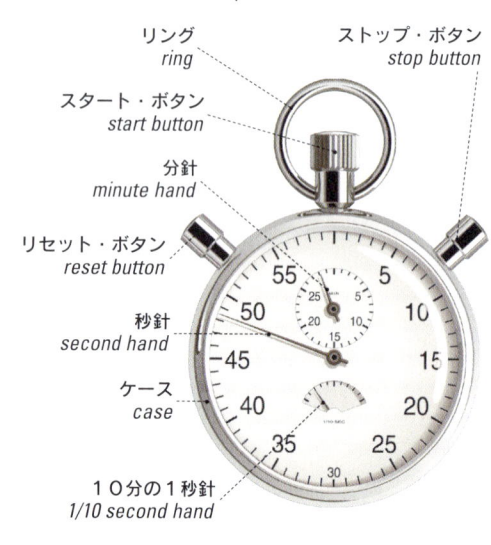

リング
ring

ストップ・ボタン
stop button

スタート・ボタン
start button

分針
minute hand

リセット・ボタン
reset button

秒針
second hand

ケース
case

１０分の１秒針
1/10 second hand

デジタル時計
digital watch

液晶ディスプレイ
liquid-crystal display

アナログ時計
analog watch

文字盤
dial

竜頭(りゅうず)
crown

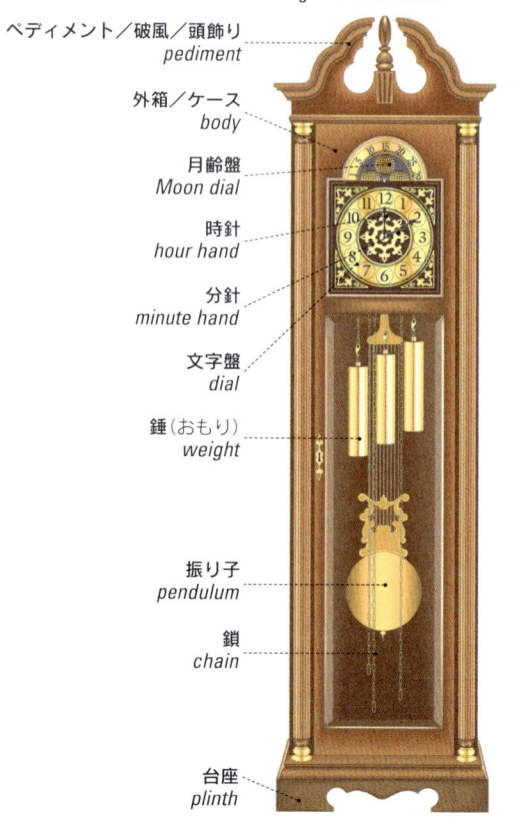

バンド
strap

グランドファーザー・クロック／箱時計
grandfather clock

ペディメント／破風／頭飾り
pediment

外箱／ケース
body

月齢盤
Moon dial

時針
hour hand

分針
minute hand

文字盤
dial

錘(おもり)
weight

振り子
pendulum

鎖
chain

台座
plinth

科学

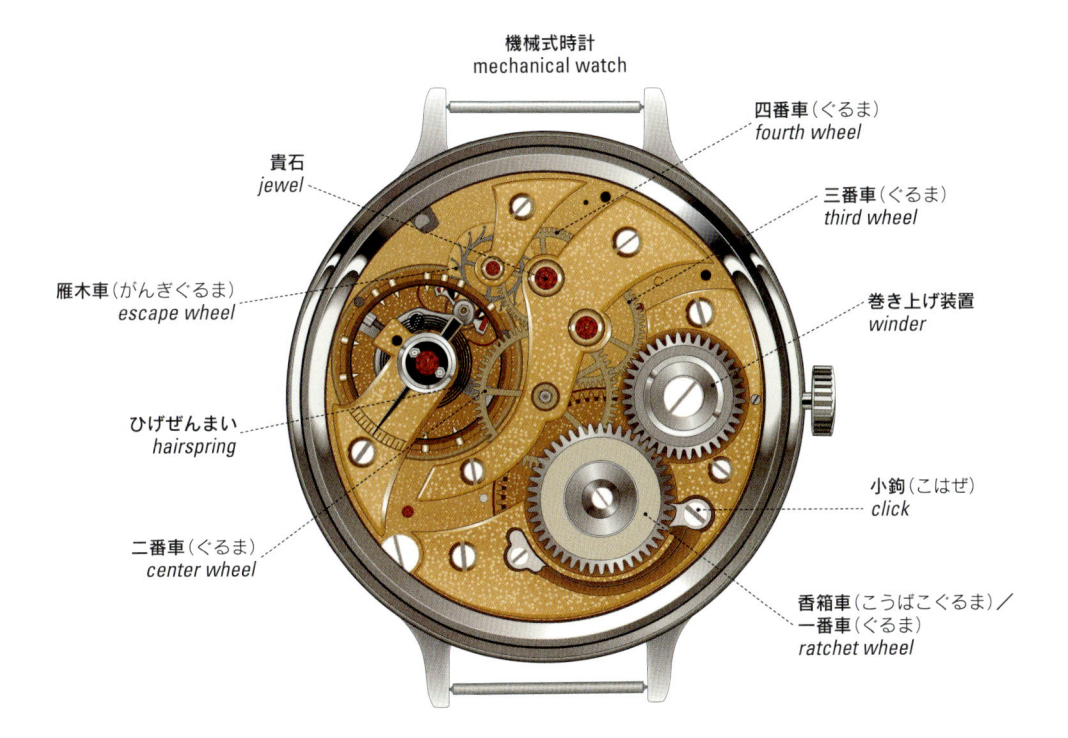

計測機器 | MEASURING DEVICES

機械式時計
mechanical watch

四番車（ぐるま）
fourth wheel

三番車（ぐるま）
third wheel

貴石
jewel

巻き上げ装置
winder

雁木車（がんぎぐるま）
escape wheel

ひげぜんまい
hairspring

小鉤（こはぜ）
click

二番車（ぐるま）
center wheel

香箱車（こうばこぐるま）／
一番車（ぐるま）
ratchet wheel

温度測定
MEASURE OF TEMPERATURE

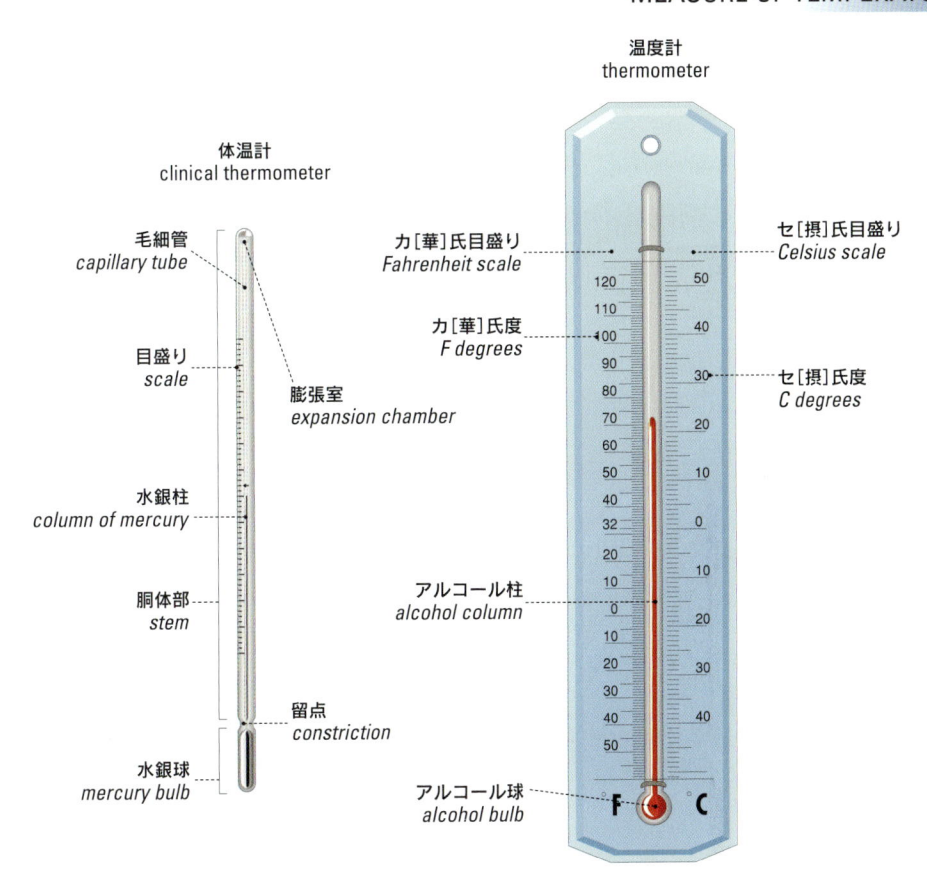

温度計
thermometer

体温計
clinical thermometer

毛細管
capillary tube

カ[華]氏目盛り
Fahrenheit scale

セ[摂]氏目盛り
Celsius scale

カ[華]氏度
F degrees

目盛り
scale

膨張室
expansion chamber

セ[摂]氏度
C degrees

水銀柱
column of mercury

胴体部
stem

アルコール柱
alcohol column

留点
constriction

水銀球
mercury bulb

アルコール球
alcohol bulb

計測機器 | MEASURING DEVICES

重量測定
MEASURE OF WEIGHT

竿秤（さおばかり）／棹秤（さおばかり）
steelyard

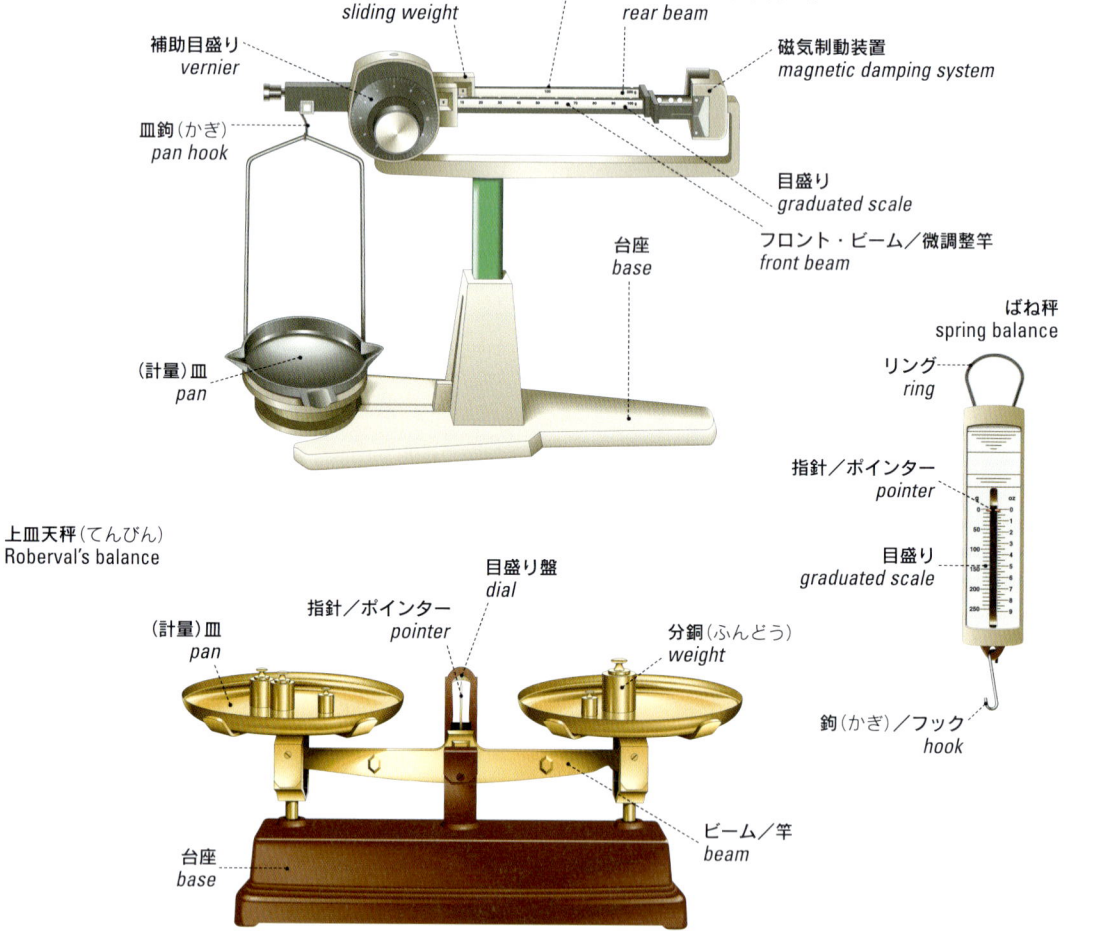

刻み目／ノッチ
notch

送り錘（おもり）
sliding weight

リア・ビーム／粗調整棹
rear beam

補助目盛り
vernier

磁気制動装置
magnetic damping system

皿鉤（かぎ）
pan hook

目盛り
graduated scale

フロント・ビーム／微調整竿
front beam

台座
base

（計量）皿
pan

ばね秤
spring balance

リング
ring

上皿天秤（てんびん）
Roberval's balance

指針／ポインター
pointer

目盛り盤
dial

目盛り
graduated scale

（計量）皿
pan

指針／ポインター
pointer

分銅（ふんどう）
weight

鉤（かぎ）／フック
hook

ビーム／竿
beam

台座
base

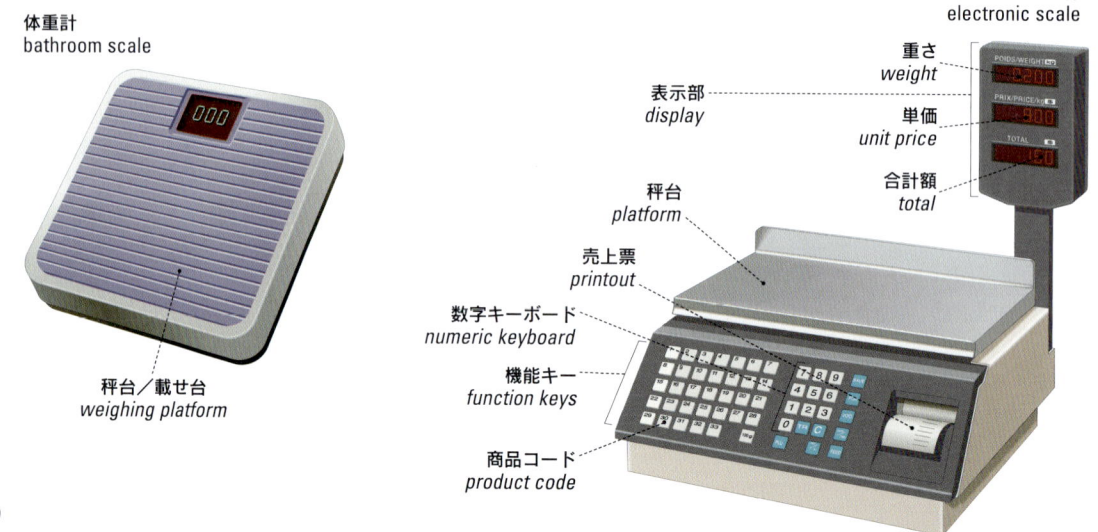

体重計
bathroom scale

電子秤
electronic scale

重さ
weight

表示部
display

単価
unit price

合計額
total

秤台
platform

売上票
printout

数字キーボード
numeric keyboard

機能キー
function keys

秤台／載せ台
weighing platform

商品コード
product code

幾何学 | GEOMETRY

幾何学は点、線、円や正方形などの平面、さらには球や立方体などの立体を研究する数学の一部門です。それは2次元と3次元のあらゆる形を測定するための巧妙な方法を教えてくれます。幾何学は平面や空間の物体を研究することで、工学や建築といった数多くの分野の中心的存在になっています。

幾何学的な形
GEOMETRICAL SHAPES

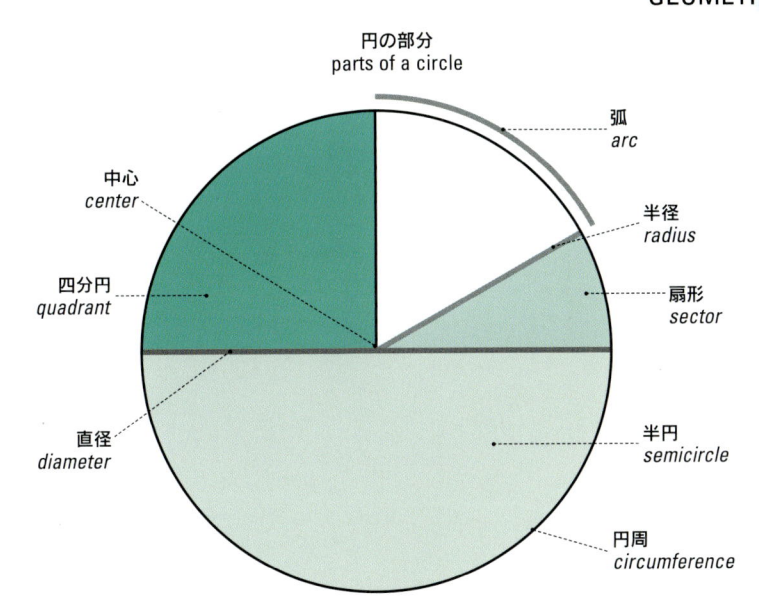

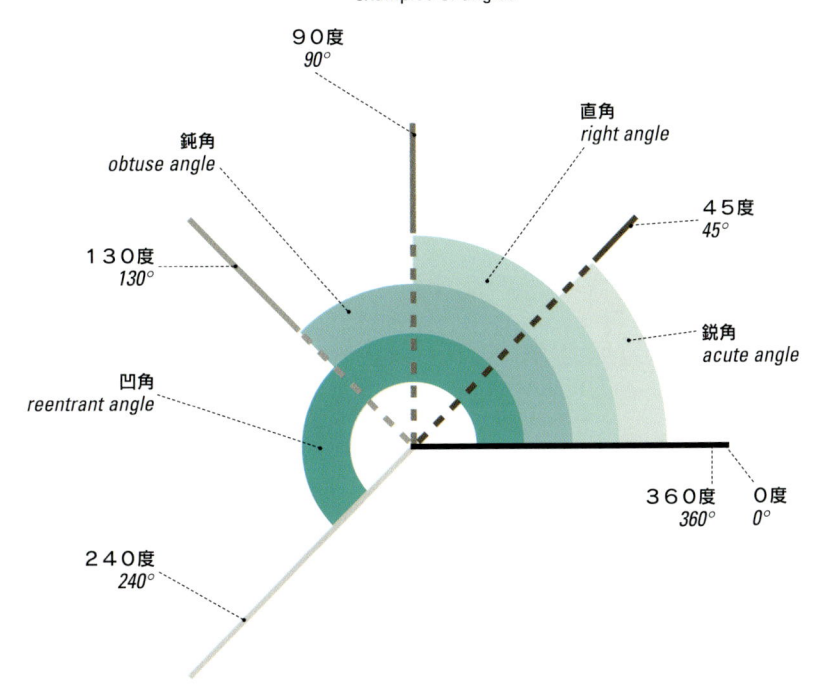

円の部分
parts of a circle

- 弧 / arc
- 中心 / center
- 半径 / radius
- 四分円 / quadrant
- 扇形 / sector
- 直径 / diameter
- 半円 / semicircle
- 円周 / circumference

角度の例
examples of angles

- 90度 / 90°
- 直角 / right angle
- 鈍角 / obtuse angle
- 45度 / 45°
- 130度 / 130°
- 鋭角 / acute angle
- 凹角 / reentrant angle
- 360度 / 360°
- 0度 / 0°
- 240度 / 240°

科学

幾何学 | GEOMETRY

多角形
polygons

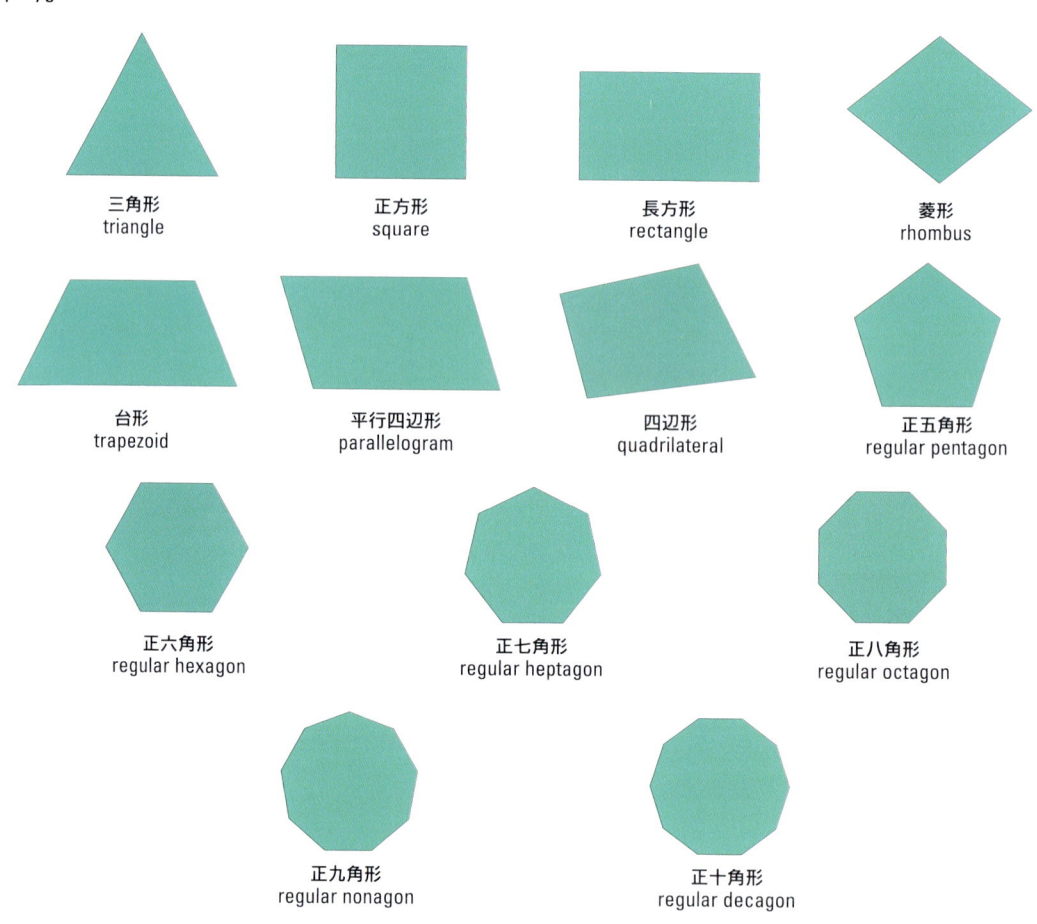

| 三角形 triangle | 正方形 square | 長方形 rectangle | 菱形 rhombus |

| 台形 trapezoid | 平行四辺形 parallelogram | 四辺形 quadrilateral | 正五角形 regular pentagon |

| 正六角形 regular hexagon | 正七角形 regular heptagon | 正八角形 regular octagon |

| 正九角形 regular nonagon | 正十角形 regular decagon |

立体
solids

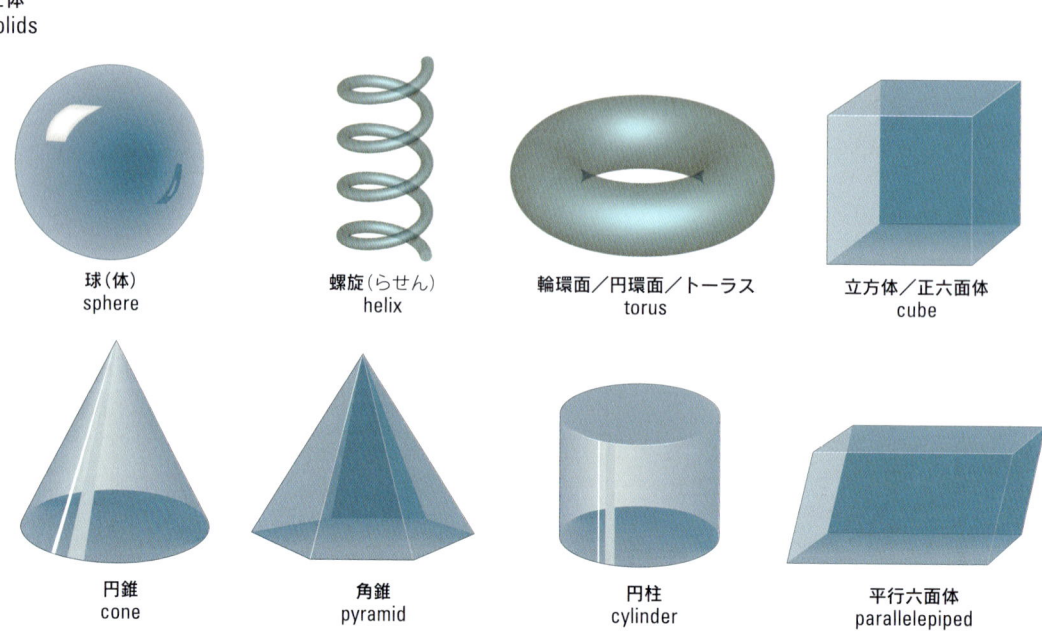

| 球（体） sphere | 螺旋（らせん） helix | 輪環面／円環面／トーラス torus | 立方体／正六面体 cube |

| 円錐 cone | 角錐 pyramid | 円柱 cylinder | 平行六面体 parallelepiped |

太陽エネルギー | SOLAR ENERGY

天気が良くても悪くても、地球は太陽から膨大な量のエネルギーを毎日受け取っています。地球上での生活に不可欠な太陽エネルギーは、とりわけ水や住居の内部を温めるための特殊な太陽（熱）集熱器によって部分的に集められます。尽きることがなく、汚染とは無縁の、このような形のエネルギーは、太陽電池によって電気にも変換されます。

太陽電池の仕組み
SOLAR-CELL SYSTEM

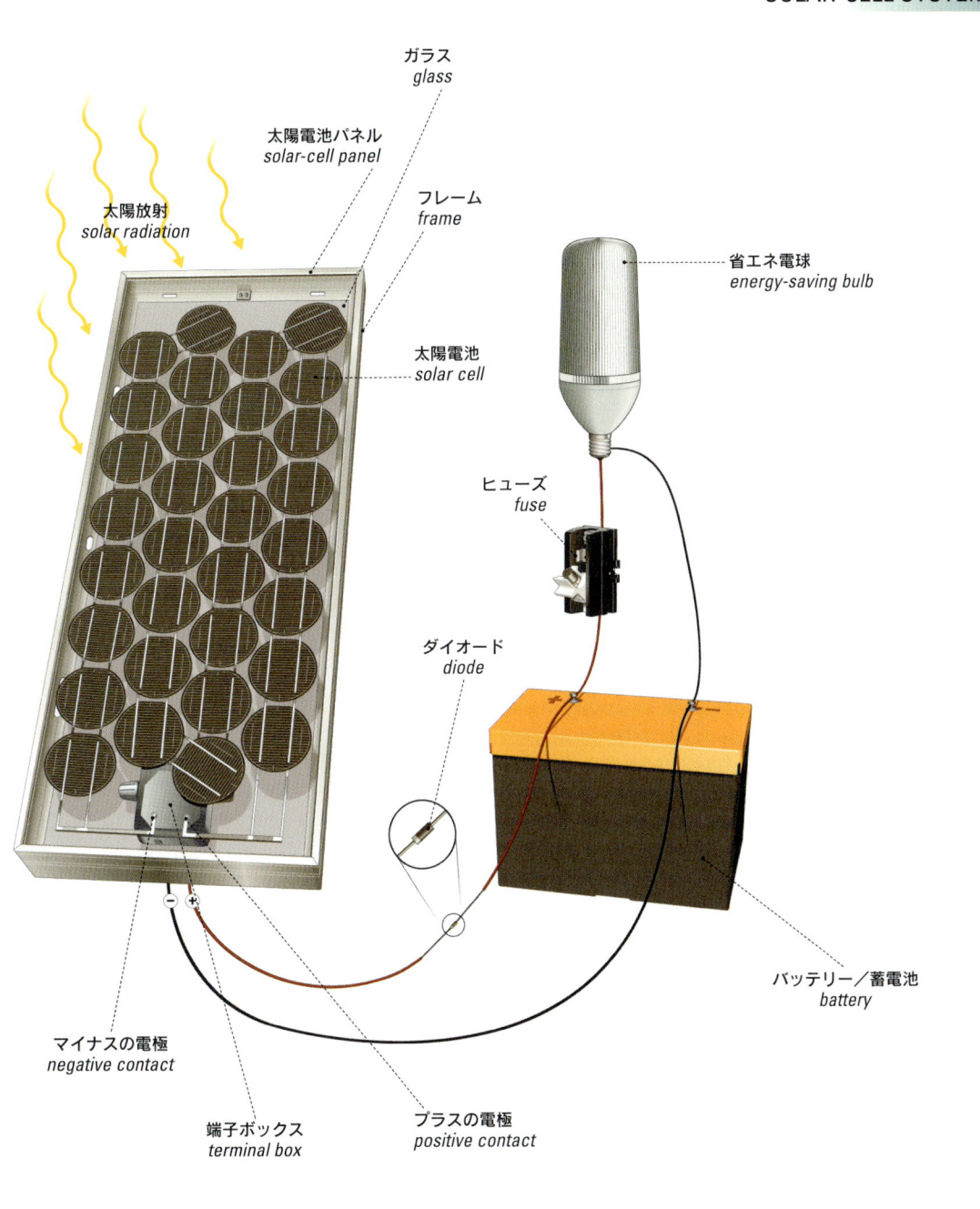

- ガラス / glass
- 太陽電池パネル / solar-cell panel
- フレーム / frame
- 太陽放射 / solar radiation
- 省エネ電球 / energy-saving bulb
- 太陽電池 / solar cell
- ヒューズ / fuse
- ダイオード / diode
- バッテリー／蓄電池 / battery
- マイナスの電極 / negative contact
- 端子ボックス / terminal box
- プラスの電極 / positive contact

エネルギー

水力電気 | HYDROELECTRICITY

運動する物すべてがそうであるように、水流もエネルギーを持っています。水力発電所はこのエネルギーを電気に変換しながらじょうずに利用しています。水は次にタービンを回転させる発電所に送られ、今度は電流を作り出す発電装置を動かします。

水力発電所
HYDROELECTRIC COMPLEX

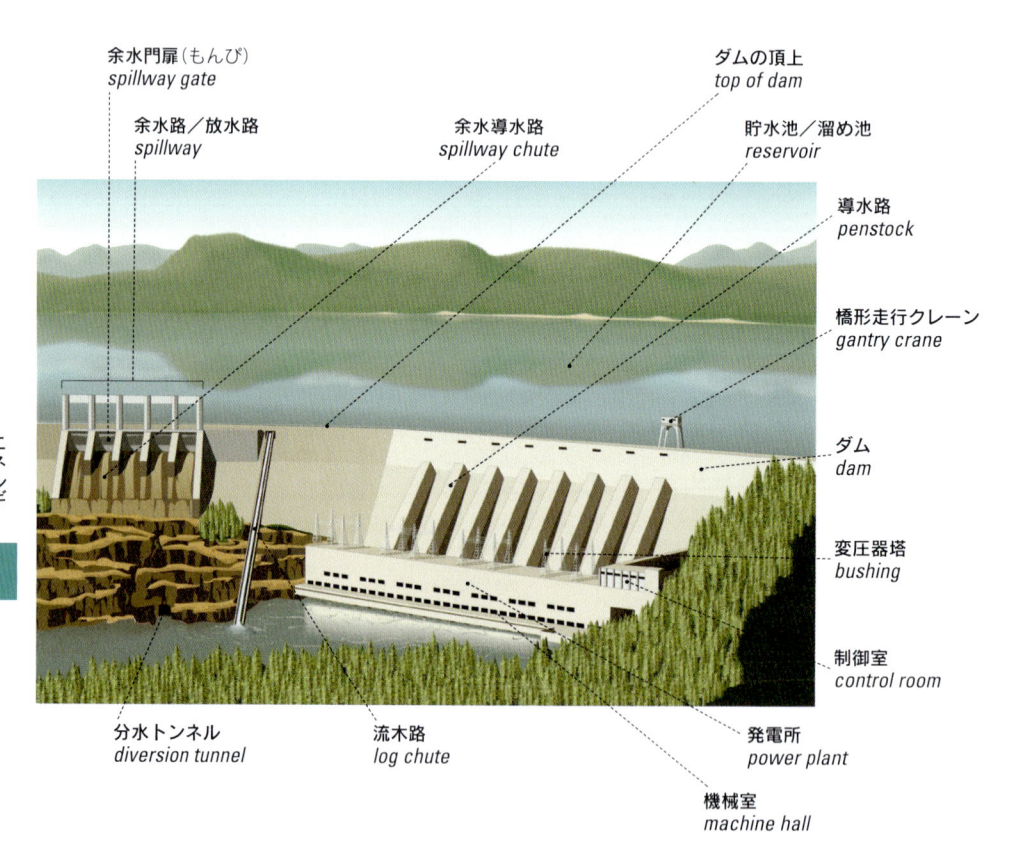

- 余水門扉（もんぴ） spillway gate
- 余水路／放水路 spillway
- 余水導水路 spillway chute
- ダムの頂上 top of dam
- 貯水池／溜め池 reservoir
- 導水路 penstock
- 橋形走行クレーン gantry crane
- ダム dam
- 変圧器塔 bushing
- 制御室 control room
- 分水トンネル diversion tunnel
- 流木路 log chute
- 発電所 power plant
- 機械室 machine hall

エネルギー

ダムの例
examples of dams

- 表面遮水壁型ダム embankment dam
- 重力（式）ダム gravity dam 
- アーチ・ダム arch dam 
- バットレス［挟壁］ダム buttress dam

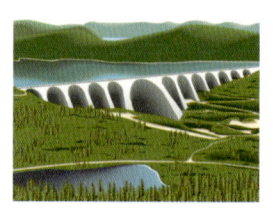

水力電気 | HYDROELECTRICITY

水力発電所の断面図
cross section of a hydroelectric power plant

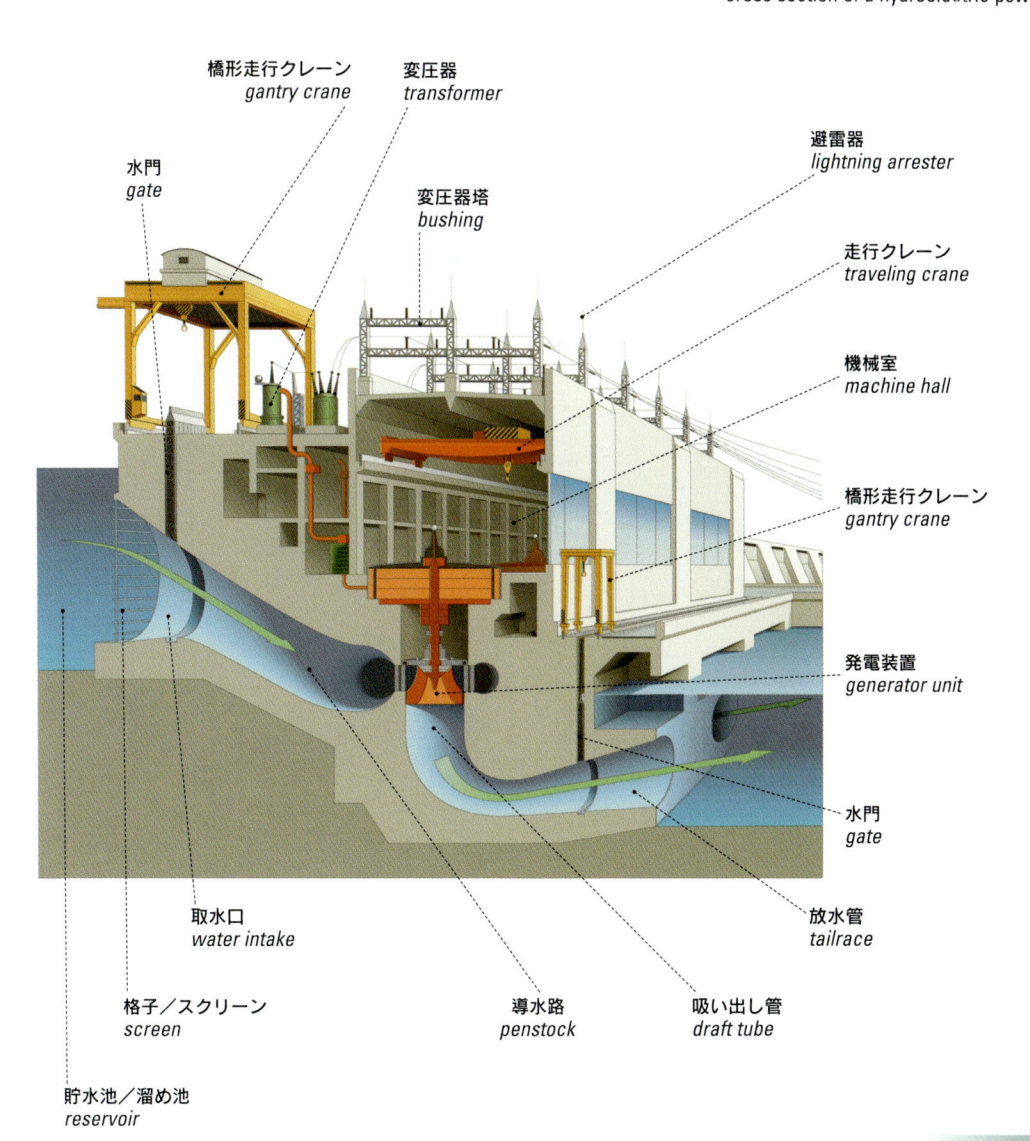

- 橋形走行クレーン gantry crane
- 変圧器 transformer
- 避雷器 lightning arrester
- 水門 gate
- 変圧器塔 bushing
- 走行クレーン traveling crane
- 機械室 machine hall
- 橋形走行クレーン gantry crane
- 発電装置 generator unit
- 水門 gate
- 取水口 water intake
- 放水管 tailrace
- 格子／スクリーン screen
- 導水路 penstock
- 吸い出し管 draft tube
- 貯水池／溜め池 reservoir

エネルギー

電気回路
ELECTRIC CIRCUIT

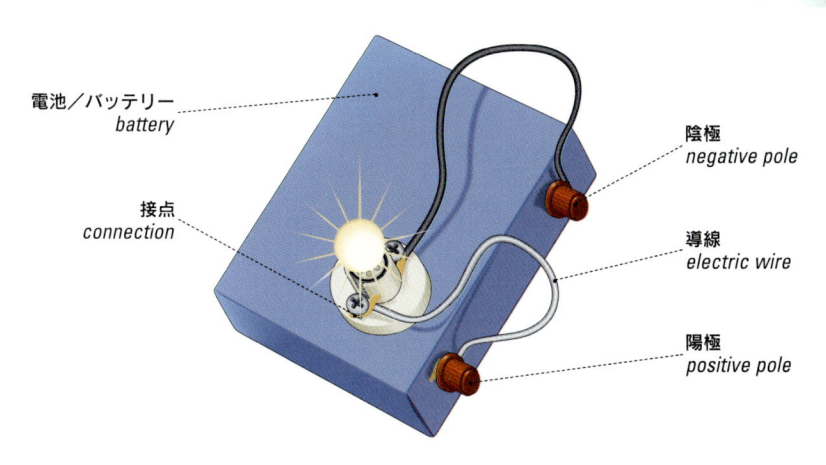

- 電池／バッテリー battery
- 陰極 negative pole
- 接点 connection
- 導線 electric wire
- 陽極 positive pole

水力電気 | HYDROELECTRICITY

電気発生の過程
STEPS IN PRODUCTION OF ELECTRICITY

発電機電圧でのエネルギー伝達
energy transmission at the generator voltage

送電網へのエネルギーの統合
energy integration to the transmission network

水の備蓄
supply of water

電圧上昇／昇圧
voltage increase

高圧送電
high-tension electricity transmission

電圧降下／降圧
voltage decrease

消費者への送電
transmission to consumers

圧力水
water under pressure

発電機による電気発生
production of electricity by the generator

機械作業の電気への変換
transformation of mechanical work into electricity

回転運動のローターへの伝送
transmission of the rotative movement to the rotor

タービンの回転
rotation of the turbine

タービンからの排水
turbined water draining

エネルギー

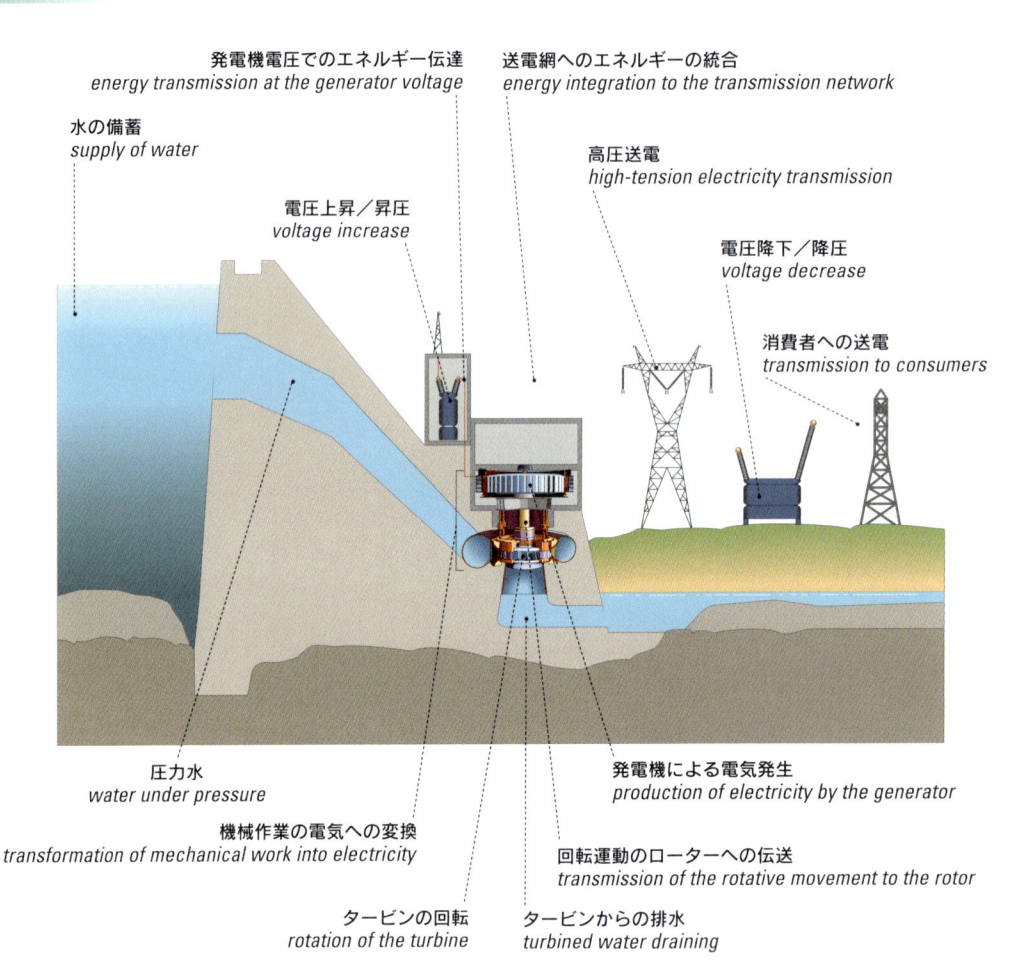

送電
ELECTRICITY TRANSMISSION

架空（送）電線
overhead connection

中圧配電線
medium-tension distribution line

絶縁器／碍子（がいし）
insulator

避雷器
lightning arrester

ヒューズ
fuse

変圧器／トランス
transformer

ブレーカー／安全器
fuse cutout

ヒューズ・ホルダー
fuse holder

低圧配電線
low-tension distribution line

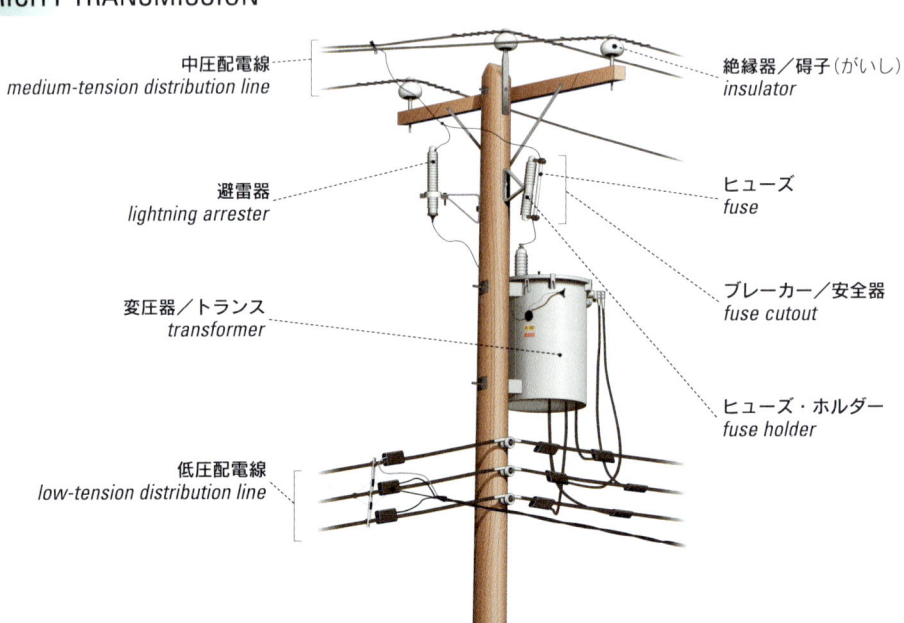

核エネルギー | NUCLEAR ENERGY

原子力エネルギーは原子核の分裂によって生み出されます。原子核が2つに分裂すると、例えばウランの原子核は、原子力発電所で電気に変換できる膨大な量のエネルギーを放出します。発電所は、危険な放射性物質が外部に漏れるのを防ぐために、安全装置を備えています。

原子力発電所
NUCLEAR GENERATING STATION

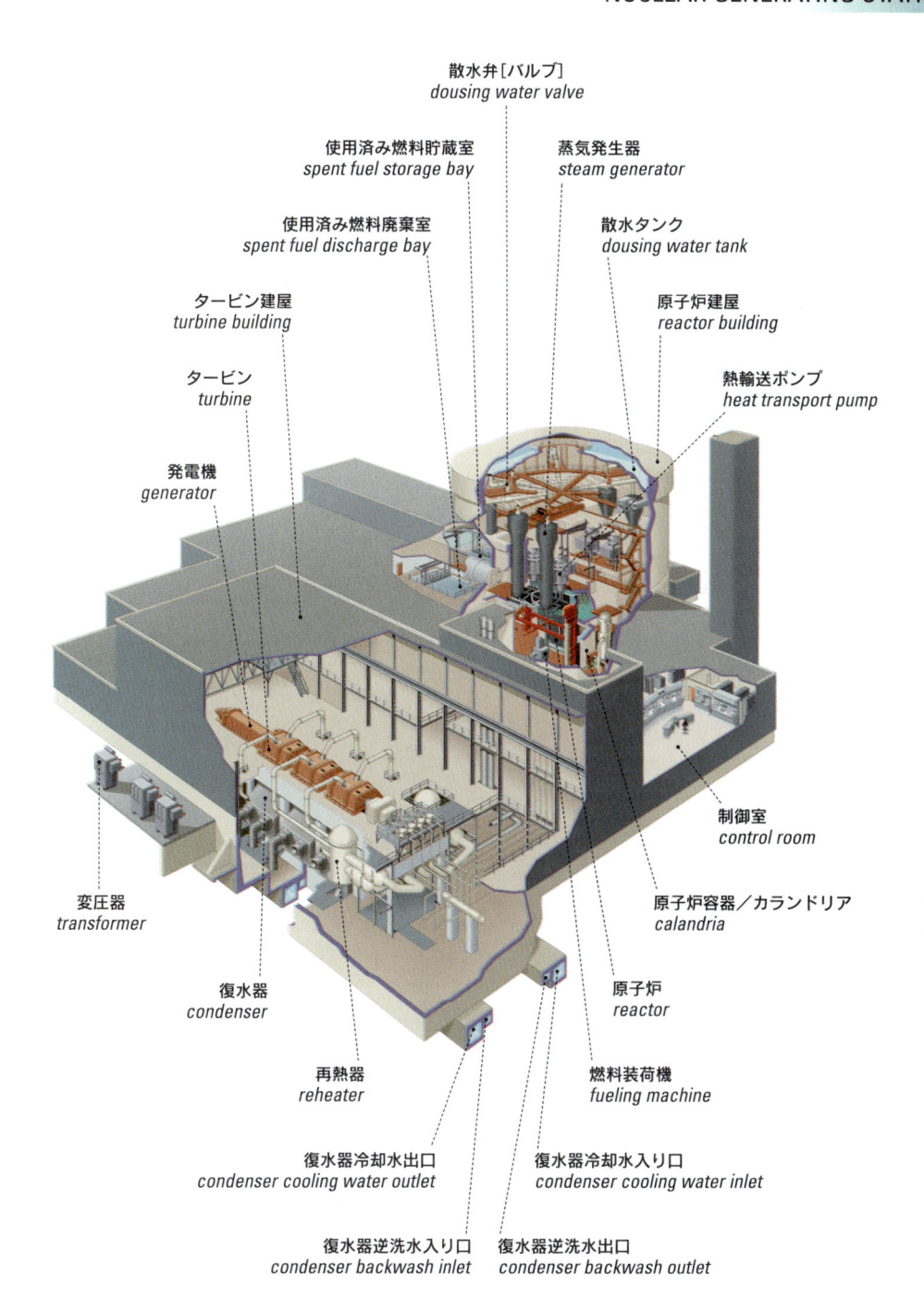

- 散水弁[バルブ] / dousing water valve
- 使用済み燃料貯蔵室 / spent fuel storage bay
- 蒸気発生器 / steam generator
- 使用済み燃料廃棄室 / spent fuel discharge bay
- 散水タンク / dousing water tank
- タービン建屋 / turbine building
- 原子炉建屋 / reactor building
- タービン / turbine
- 熱輸送ポンプ / heat transport pump
- 発電機 / generator
- 制御室 / control room
- 変圧器 / transformer
- 原子炉容器／カランドリア / calandria
- 復水器 / condenser
- 原子炉 / reactor
- 再熱器 / reheater
- 燃料装荷機 / fueling machine
- 復水器冷却水出口 / condenser cooling water outlet
- 復水器冷却水入り口 / condenser cooling water inlet
- 復水器逆洗水入り口 / condenser backwash inlet
- 復水器逆洗水出口 / condenser backwash outlet

エネルギー

核エネルギー | NUCLEAR ENERGY

核エネルギーによる電気発生
PRODUCTION OF ELECTRICITY FROM NUCLEAR ENERGY

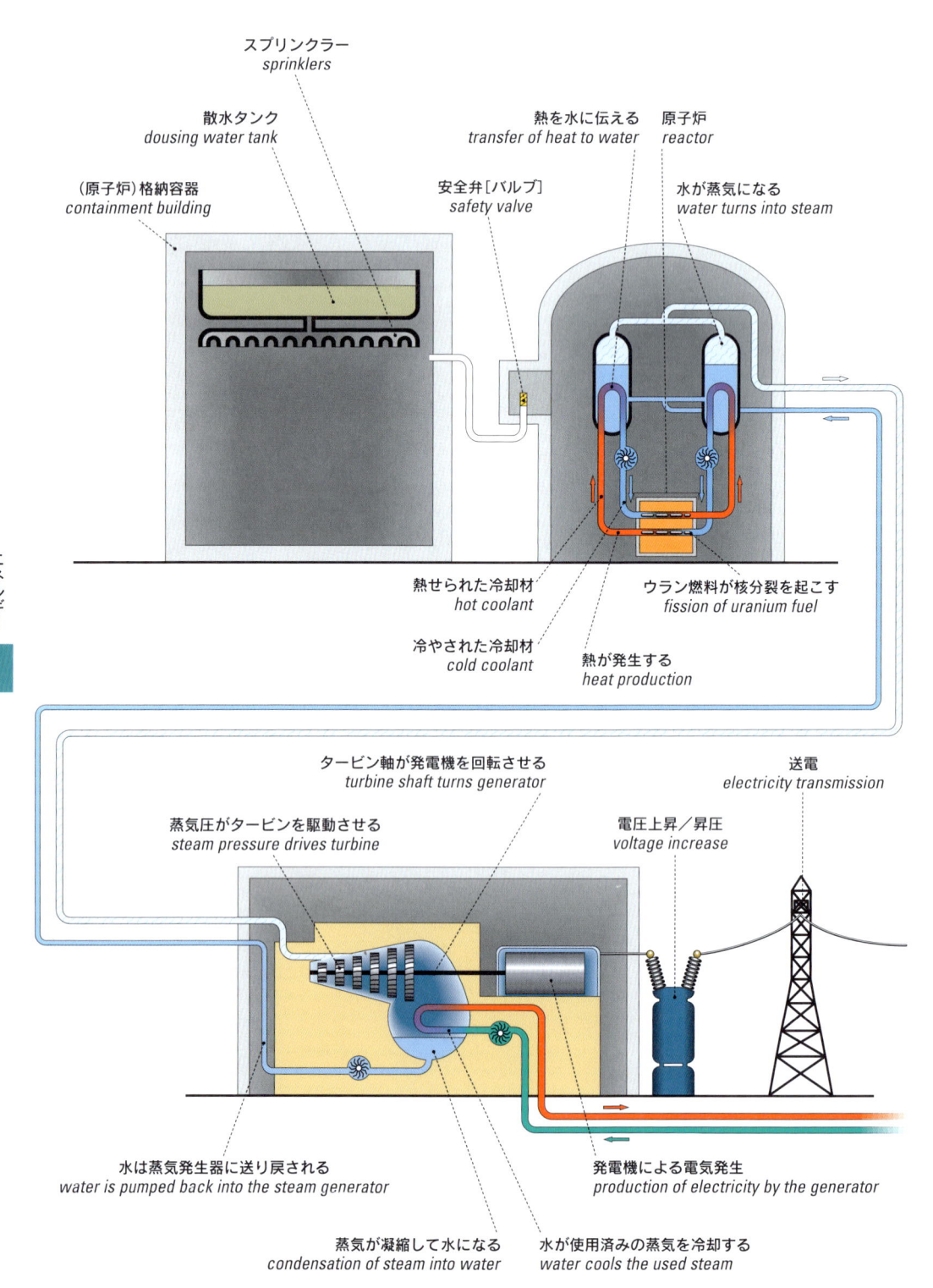

スプリンクラー
sprinklers

散水タンク
dousing water tank

熱を水に伝える
transfer of heat to water

原子炉
reactor

(原子炉)格納容器
containment building

安全弁[バルブ]
safety valve

水が蒸気になる
water turns into steam

熱せられた冷却材
hot coolant

ウラン燃料が核分裂を起こす
fission of uranium fuel

冷やされた冷却材
cold coolant

熱が発生する
heat production

タービン軸が発電機を回転させる
turbine shaft turns generator

送電
electricity transmission

蒸気圧がタービンを駆動させる
steam pressure drives turbine

電圧上昇／昇圧
voltage increase

水は蒸気発生器に送り戻される
water is pumped back into the steam generator

発電機による電気発生
production of electricity by the generator

蒸気が凝縮して水になる
condensation of steam into water

水が使用済みの蒸気を冷却する
water cools the used steam

エネルギー

風力エネルギー | WIND ENERGY

モーターが発明される以前には、風力エネルギーは、船を進め、粉をひき、水を揚げるための風車を回すのに利用されていました。人間は1世紀以上前から、この自然の力を風車を使って電気エネルギーに変換できるようになりました。羽根は、風の効果で回転しながら、電気を生み出すモーターを動かします。

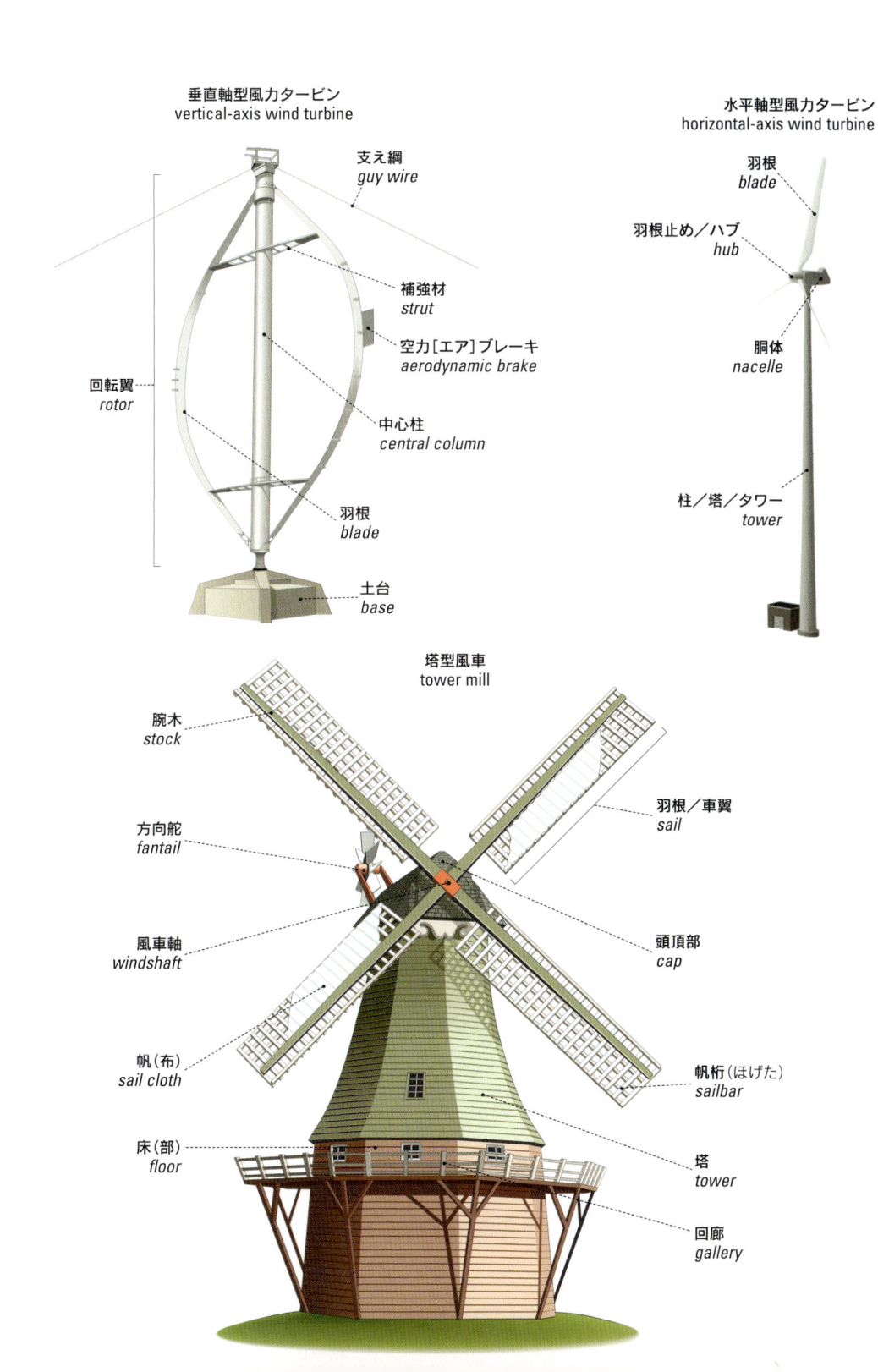

垂直軸型風力タービン
vertical-axis wind turbine

- 支え綱 / guy wire
- 補強材 / strut
- 空力[エア]ブレーキ / aerodynamic brake
- 中心柱 / central column
- 回転翼 / rotor
- 羽根 / blade
- 土台 / base

水平軸型風力タービン
horizontal-axis wind turbine

- 羽根 / blade
- 羽根止め／ハブ / hub
- 胴体 / nacelle
- 柱／塔／タワー / tower

塔型風車
tower mill

- 腕木 / stock
- 方向舵 / fantail
- 風車軸 / windshaft
- 帆（布）/ sail cloth
- 床（部）/ floor
- 羽根／車翼 / sail
- 頭頂部 / cap
- 帆桁（ほげた）/ sailbar
- 塔 / tower
- 回廊 / gallery

エネルギー

179

化石エネルギー | FOSSIL ENERGY

石油、石炭、天然ガスは、もともと何百万年も前に生きていた生物が一部化石化した物です。このような燃えやすい化石は地球の下層土中に少量ですが見つかります。原油を精製すると５００以上の石油製品ができます。中でも貴重なガソリンは、モーターの中でエンジン用燃料として使われます。石油を黒い黄金と呼んだりするのはそのためです。

石油 OIL

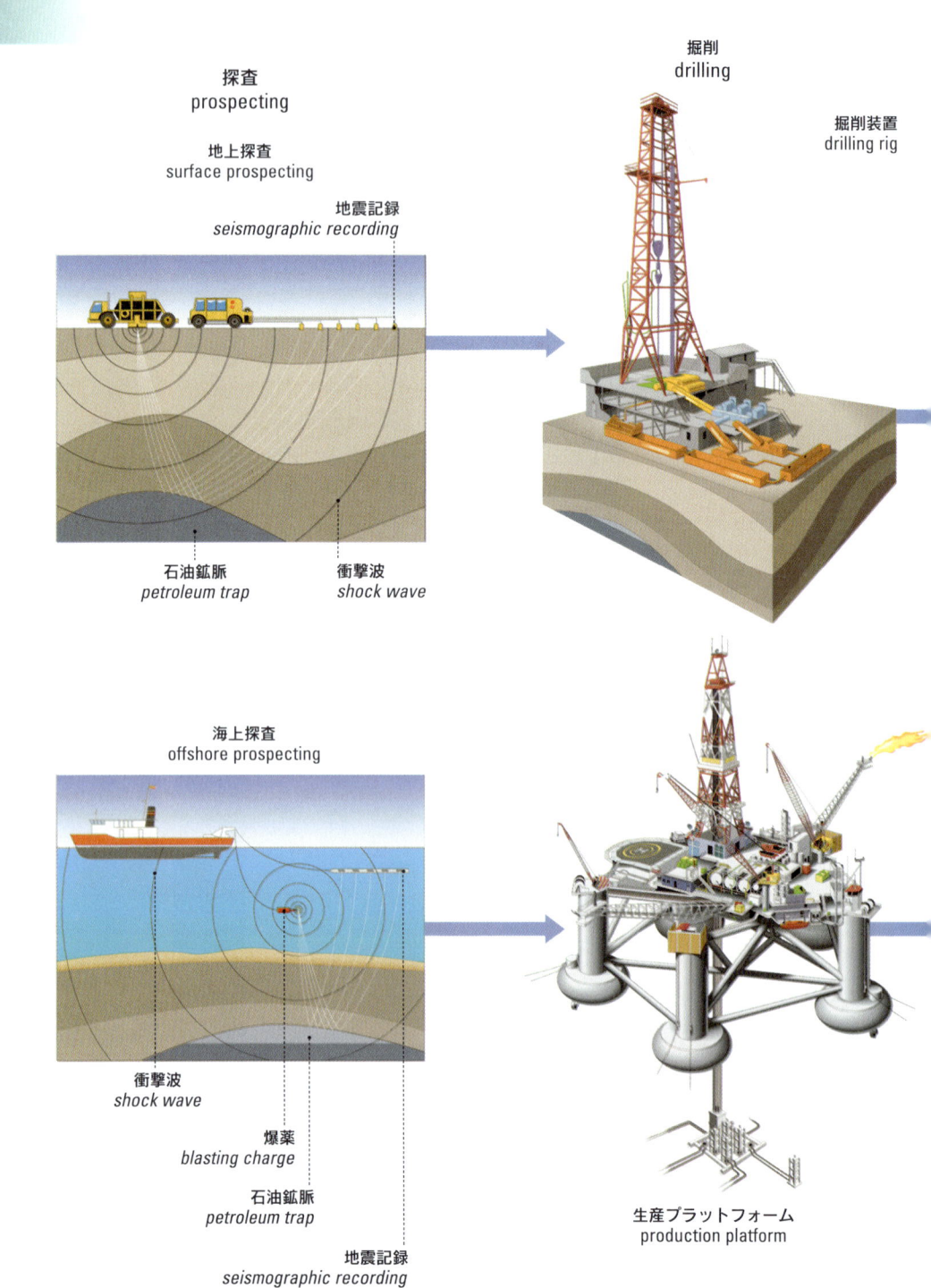

探査
prospecting

地上探査
surface prospecting

地震記録
seismographic recording

石油鉱脈
petroleum trap

衝撃波
shock wave

掘削
drilling

掘削装置
drilling rig

海上探査
offshore prospecting

衝撃波
shock wave

爆薬
blasting charge

石油鉱脈
petroleum trap

地震記録
seismographic recording

生産プラットフォーム
production platform

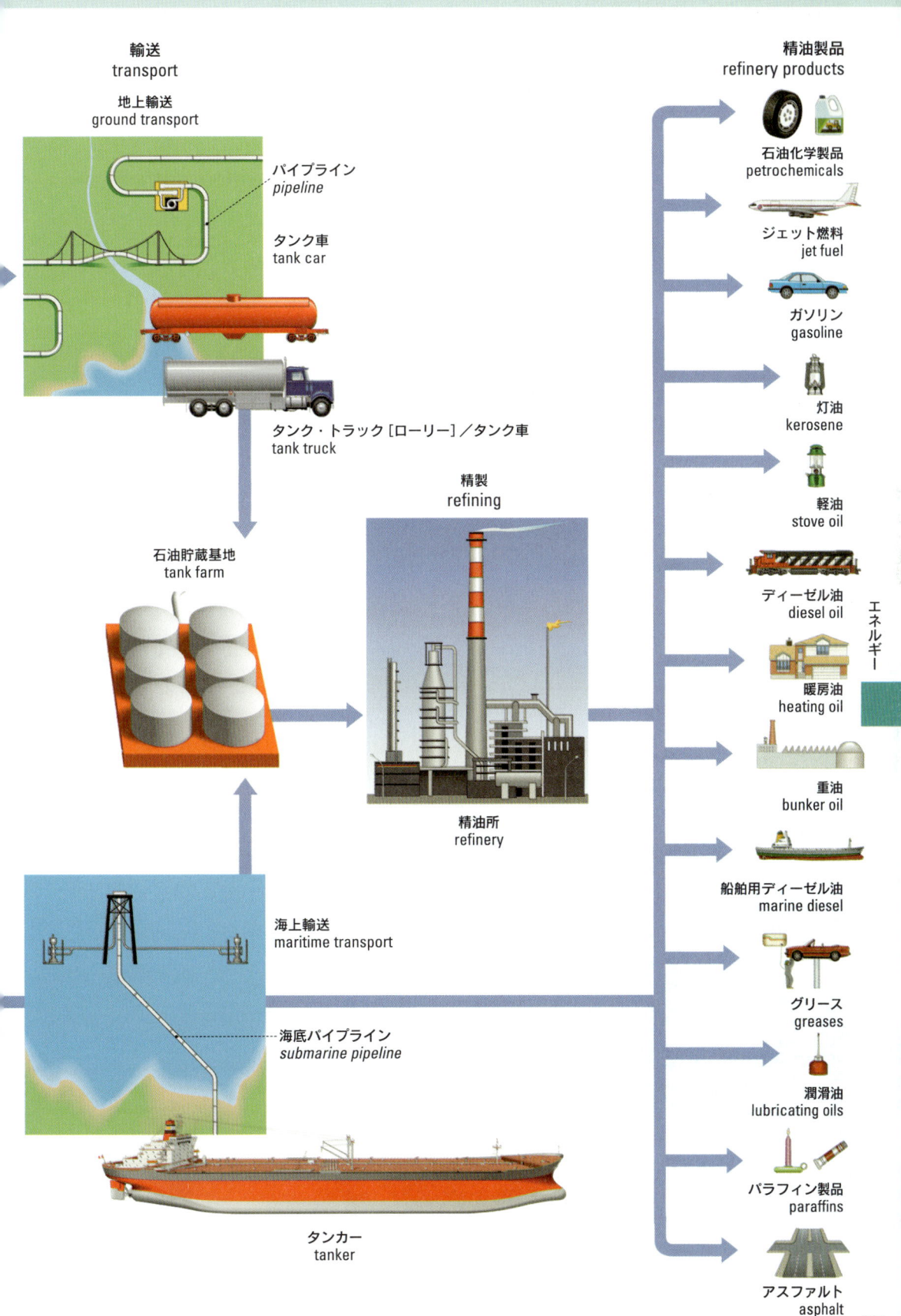

化石エネルギー | FOSSIL ENERGY

輸送
transport

地上輸送
ground transport

パイプライン
pipeline

タンク車
tank car

タンク・トラック［ローリー］／タンク車
tank truck

石油貯蔵基地
tank farm

精製
refining

精油所
refinery

海上輸送
maritime transport

海底パイプライン
submarine pipeline

タンカー
tanker

精油製品
refinery products

石油化学製品
petrochemicals

ジェット燃料
jet fuel

ガソリン
gasoline

灯油
kerosene

軽油
stove oil

ディーゼル油
diesel oil

暖房油
heating oil

重油
bunker oil

船舶用ディーゼル油
marine diesel

グリース
greases

潤滑油
lubricating oils

パラフィン製品
paraffins

アスファルト
asphalt

エネルギー

181

道路輸送 | ROAD TRANSPORT

車輪が発明されて、自転車や車が登場し、人はますます遠い距離を、ますます速く移動できるようになりました。19世紀に最初のモデルがつくられて以来、車は絶えず進歩して、大衆の身近な乗り物になりました。今日、何百万という車が道路を走るようになって、道路網がますます整備されるようになりました。

道路網
ROAD SYSTEM

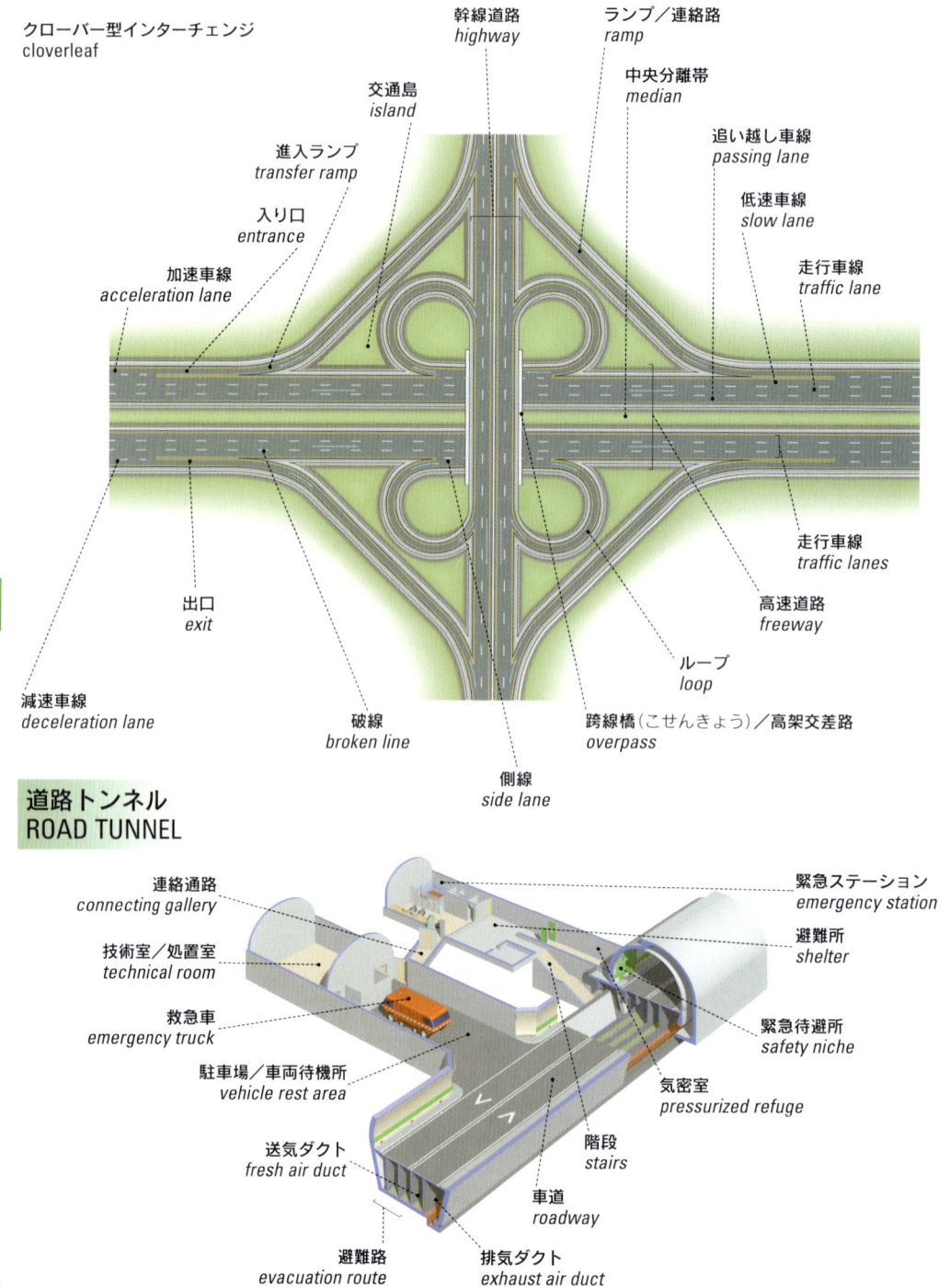

- クローバー型インターチェンジ cloverleaf
- 幹線道路 highway
- ランプ／連絡路 ramp
- 交通島 island
- 中央分離帯 median
- 進入ランプ transfer ramp
- 追い越し車線 passing lane
- 入り口 entrance
- 低速車線 slow lane
- 加速車線 acceleration lane
- 走行車線 traffic lane
- 出口 exit
- 走行車線 traffic lanes
- 高速道路 freeway
- 減速車線 deceleration lane
- ループ loop
- 破線 broken line
- 跨線橋（こせんきょう）／高架交差路 overpass
- 側線 side lane

道路トンネル
ROAD TUNNEL

- 連絡通路 connecting gallery
- 緊急ステーション emergency station
- 技術室／処置室 technical room
- 避難所 shelter
- 救急車 emergency truck
- 緊急待避所 safety niche
- 駐車場／車両待機所 vehicle rest area
- 気密室 pressurized refuge
- 送気ダクト fresh air duct
- 階段 stairs
- 車道 roadway
- 避難路 evacuation route
- 排気ダクト exhaust air duct

輸送と重機

道路輸送 | ROAD TRANSPORT

固定橋
FIXED BRIDGES

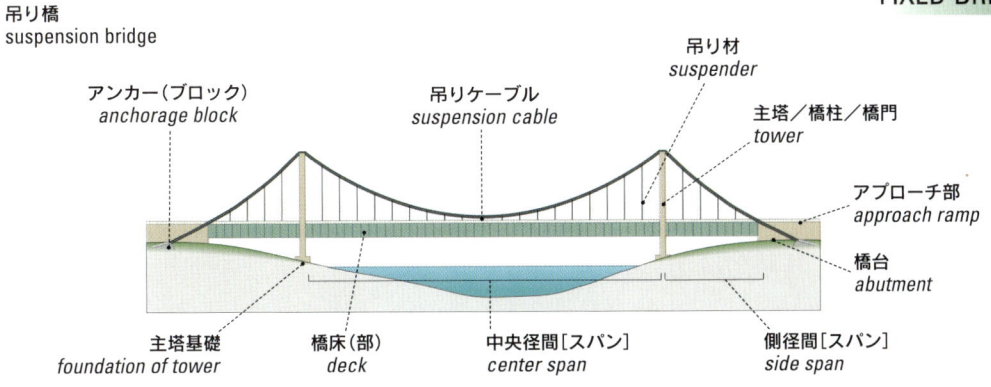

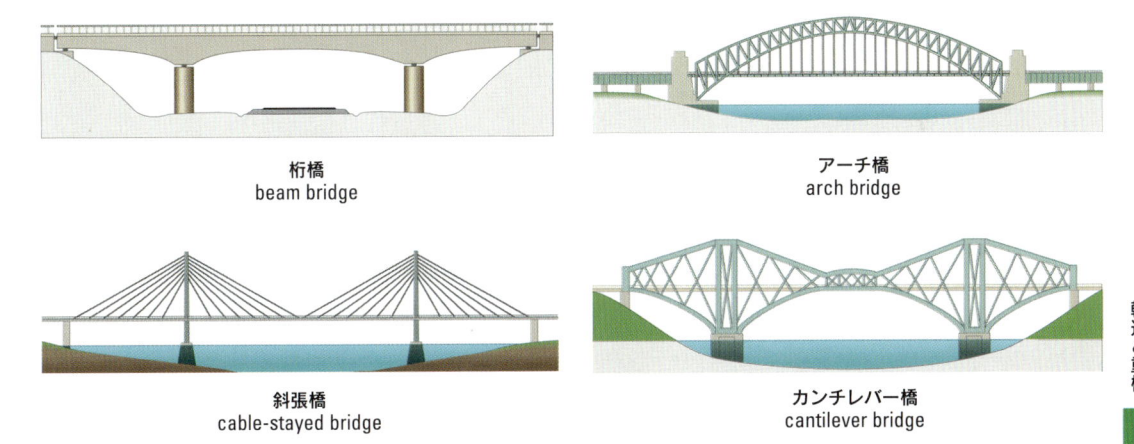

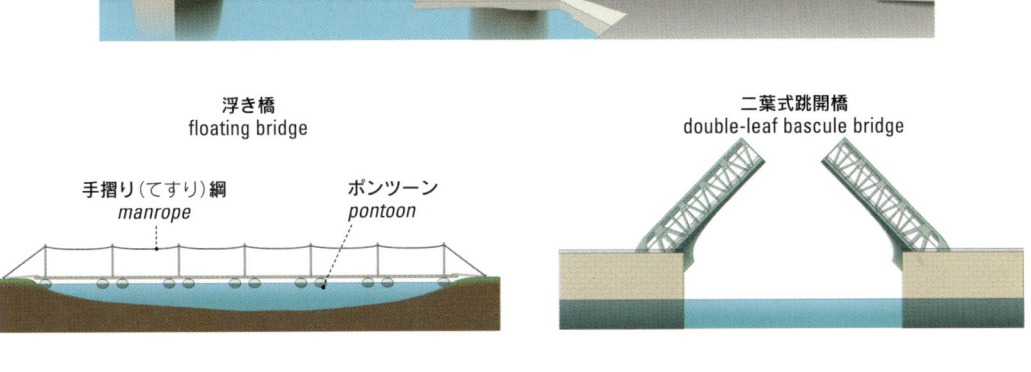

吊り橋
suspension bridge

- アンカー（ブロック） anchorage block
- 吊りケーブル suspension cable
- 吊り材 suspender
- 主塔／橋柱／橋門 tower
- アプローチ部 approach ramp
- 橋台 abutment
- 主塔基礎 foundation of tower
- 橋床（部） deck
- 中央径間[スパン] center span
- 側径間[スパン] side span

桁橋
beam bridge

アーチ橋
arch bridge

斜張橋
cable-stayed bridge

カンチレバー橋
cantilever bridge

可動橋
MOVABLE BRIDGES

旋回橋
swing bridge

- 回転台 turntable

浮き橋
floating bridge

- 手摺り（てすり）綱 manrope
- ポンツーン pontoon

二葉式跳開橋
double-leaf bascule bridge

輸送と重機

183

道路輸送 | ROAD TRANSPORT

自動車
AUTOMOBILE

車体
body

フロント・ガラス［ウインドー］
windshield

ワイパー
windshield wiper

アウター［ドア］ミラー
outside mirror

ウォッシャー・ノズル
washer nozzle

フロント・ガード
cowl

ボンネット／
（エンジン）フード
hood

グリル
grille

バンパー・モール
bumper molding

ヘッドライト／前照灯
headlight

フロント（バンパー）スポイラー
front fascia

フェンダー
fender

輸送と重機

184

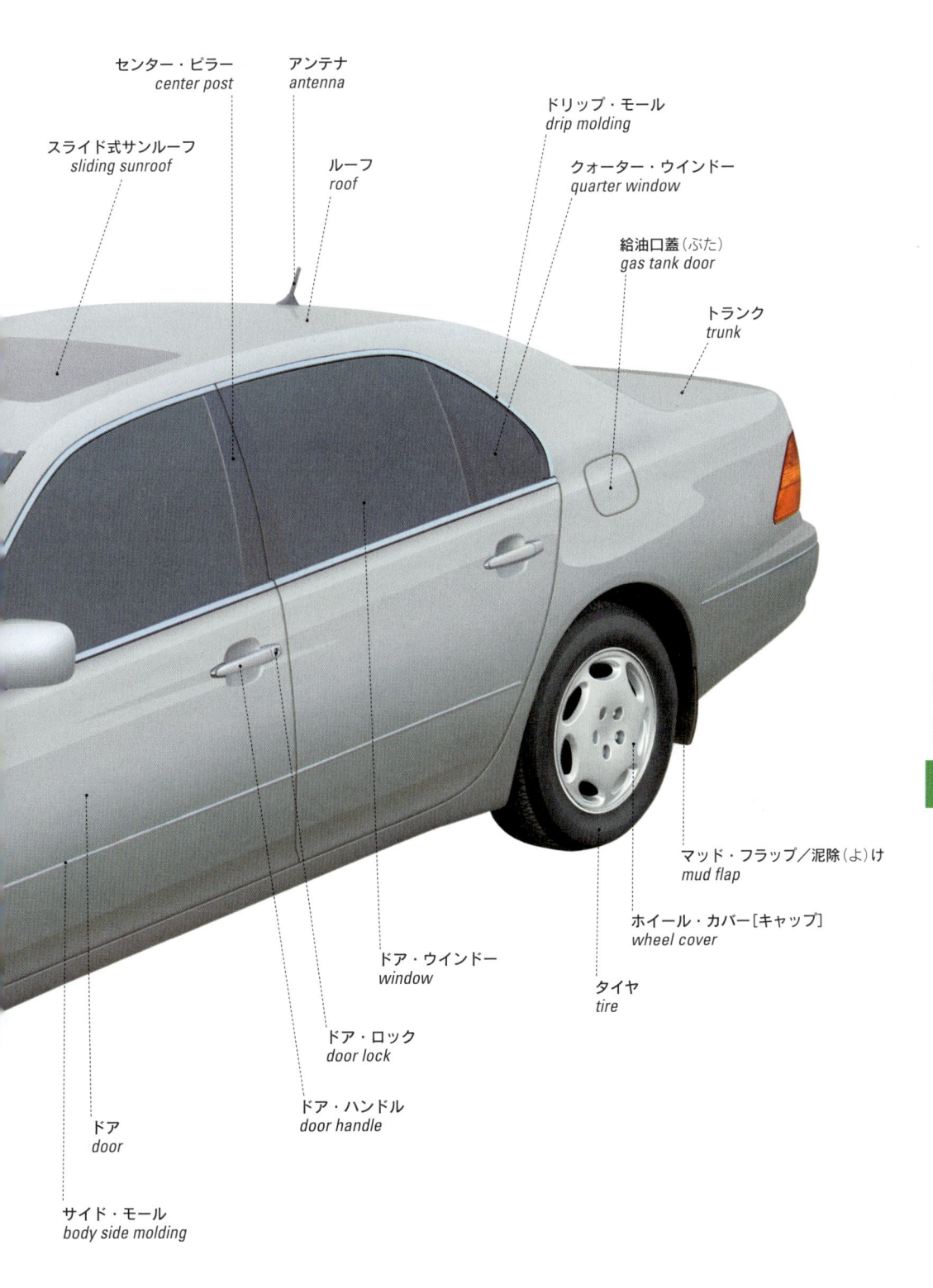

道路輸送 | ROAD TRANSPORT

センター・ピラー
center post

アンテナ
antenna

ドリップ・モール
drip molding

スライド式サンルーフ
sliding sunroof

ルーフ
roof

クォーター・ウインドー
quarter window

給油口蓋（ぶた）
gas tank door

トランク
trunk

マッド・フラップ／泥除（よ）け
mud flap

ホイール・カバー［キャップ］
wheel cover

ドア・ウインドー
window

タイヤ
tire

ドア・ロック
door lock

ドア・ハンドル
door handle

ドア
door

サイド・モール
body side molding

輸送と重機

185

道路輸送 | ROAD TRANSPORT

車体の例
examples of bodies

スポーツ・カー
sports car

超小型車／マイクロ・コンパクト・カー
micro compact car

ハッチバック
hatchback

クーペ／ツー・ドア・セダン
two-door sedan

コンバーチブル／オープン・カー
convertible

フォー・ドア・セダン
four-door sedan

ステーション・ワゴン
station wagon

ミニバン
minivan

ワゴン車／オフ・ロード車
sport-utility vehicle

ピックアップ・トラック／
荷台付き小型トラック
pickup truck

リムジン
limousine

輸送と重機

186

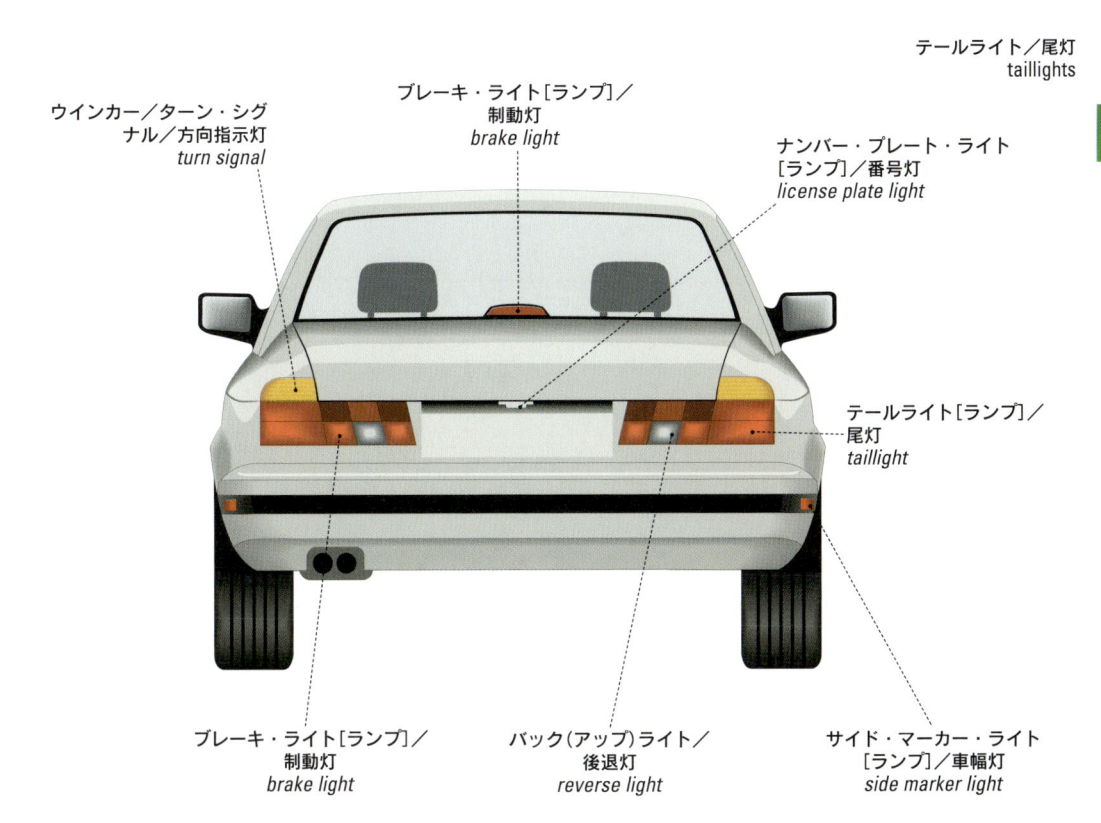

道路輸送 | ROAD TRANSPORT

ハイ・ビーム
high beam

ヘッドライト[ランプ]／前照灯
headlights

ロー・ビーム
low beam

ウインカー／ターン・シグナル／方向指示灯
turn signal

フォッグ・ライト[ランプ]／霧灯
fog light

サイド・マーカー・ライト[ランプ]／車幅灯
side marker light

テールライト／尾灯
taillights

ウインカー／ターン・シグナル／方向指示灯
turn signal

ブレーキ・ライト[ランプ]／制動灯
brake light

ナンバー・プレート・ライト[ランプ]／番号灯
license plate light

テールライト[ランプ]／尾灯
taillight

ブレーキ・ライト[ランプ]／制動灯
brake light

バック（アップ）ライト／後退灯
reverse light

サイド・マーカー・ライト[ランプ]／車幅灯
side marker light

輸送と重機

187

道路輸送 | ROAD TRANSPORT

ダッシュボード／計器板
dashboard

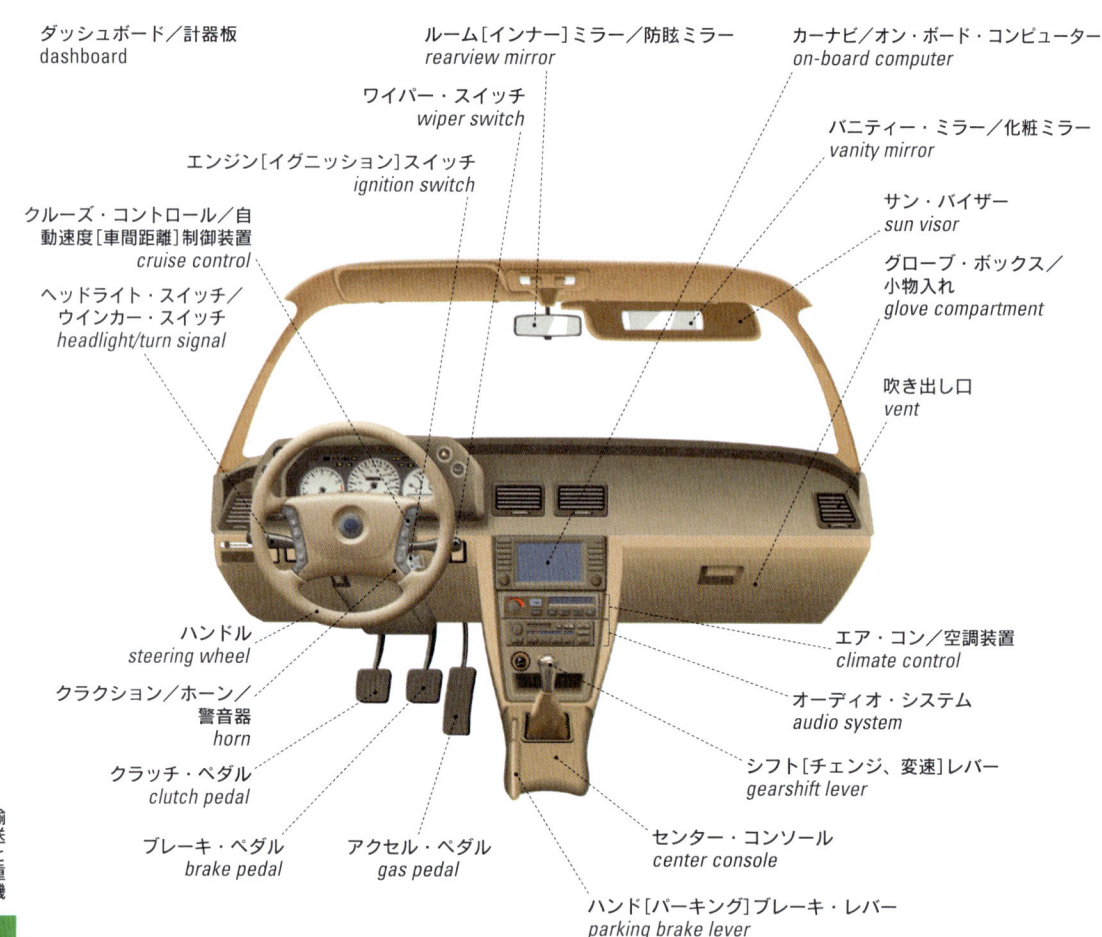

ルーム［インナー］ミラー／防眩ミラー
rearview mirror

カーナビ／オン・ボード・コンピューター
on-board computer

ワイパー・スイッチ
wiper switch

バニティー・ミラー／化粧ミラー
vanity mirror

エンジン［イグニッション］スイッチ
ignition switch

サン・バイザー
sun visor

クルーズ・コントロール／自動速度［車間距離］制御装置
cruise control

グローブ・ボックス／小物入れ
glove compartment

ヘッドライト・スイッチ／ウインカー・スイッチ
headlight/turn signal

吹き出し口
vent

ハンドル
steering wheel

エア・コン／空調装置
climate control

クラクション／ホーン／警音器
horn

オーディオ・システム
audio system

クラッチ・ペダル
clutch pedal

シフト［チェンジ、変速］レバー
gearshift lever

ブレーキ・ペダル
brake pedal

アクセル・ペダル
gas pedal

センター・コンソール
center console

ハンド［パーキング］ブレーキ・レバー
parking brake lever

計器盤
instrument panel

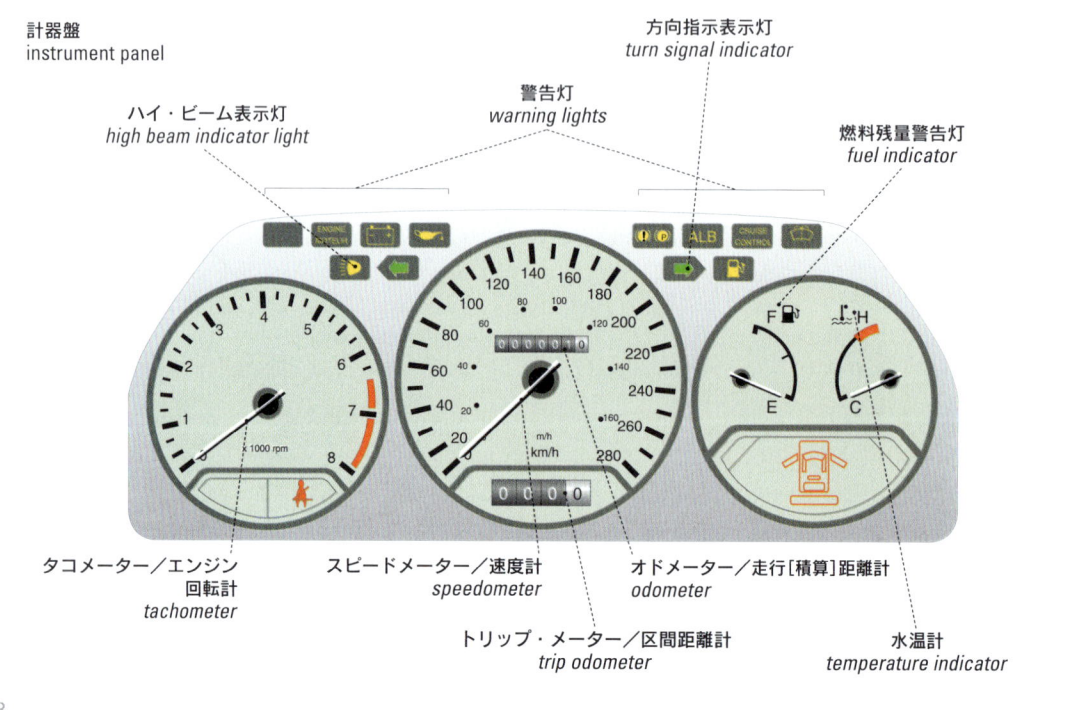

方向指示表示灯
turn signal indicator

ハイ・ビーム表示灯
high beam indicator light

警告灯
warning lights

燃料残量警告灯
fuel indicator

タコメーター／エンジン回転計
tachometer

スピードメーター／速度計
speedometer

オドメーター／走行［積算］距離計
odometer

トリップ・メーター／区間距離計
trip odometer

水温計
temperature indicator

188

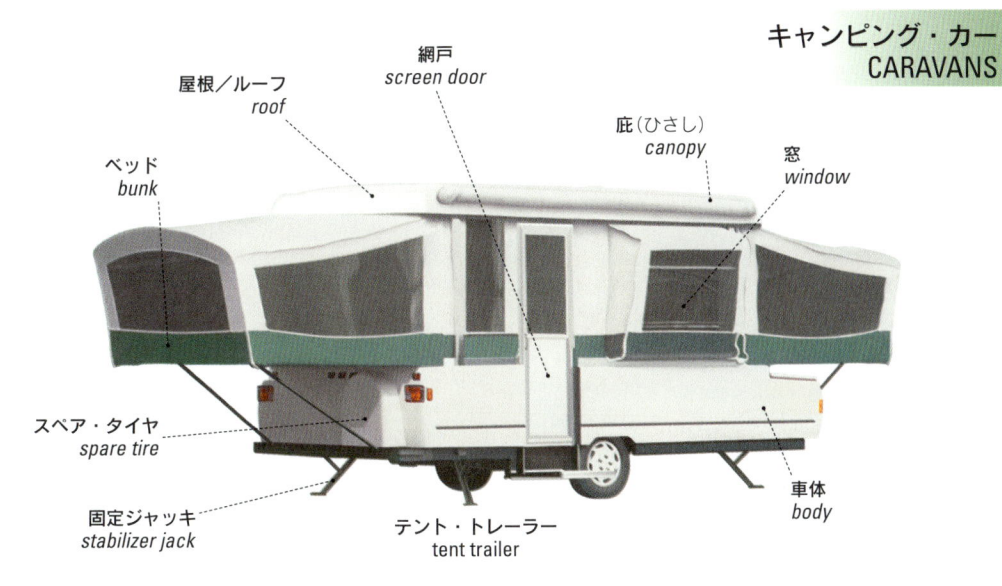

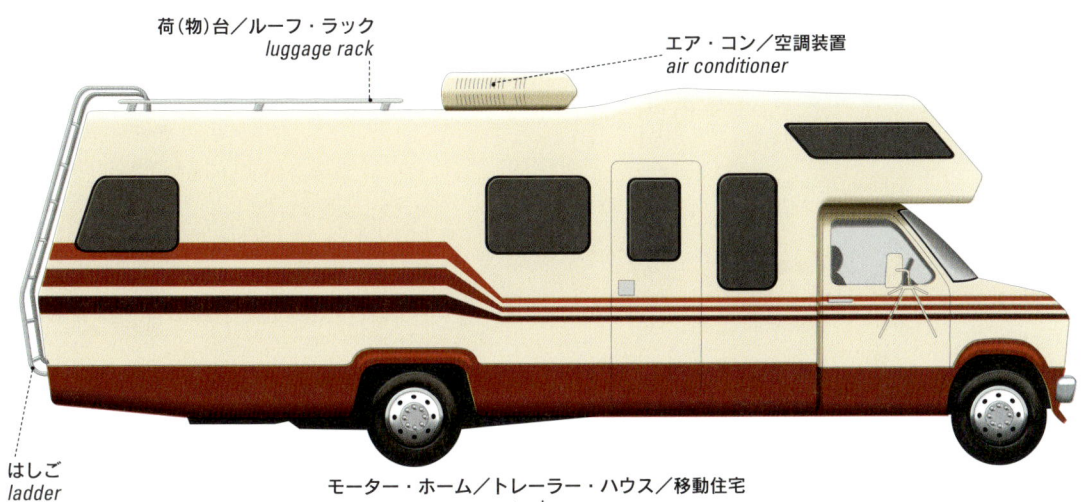

道路輸送 | ROAD TRANSPORT

キャンピング・カー
CARAVANS

- 屋根／ルーフ roof
- 網戸 screen door
- 庇（ひさし） canopy
- 窓 window
- ベッド bunk
- スペア・タイヤ spare tire
- 固定ジャッキ stabilizer jack
- テント・トレーラー tent trailer
- 車体 body

- 荷（物）台／ルーフ・ラック luggage rack
- エア・コン／空調装置 air conditioner
- はしご ladder
- モーター・ホーム／トレーラー・ハウス／移動住宅 motor home

輸送と重機

トレーラー trailer

189

道路輸送 | ROAD TRANSPORT

バス
BUSES

輸送と重機

スクール・バス
school bus

二階建てバス
double-deck bus

市内バス
city bus

小型［マイクロ］バス
minibus

長距離バス
coach

連結［連接］バス
articulated bus

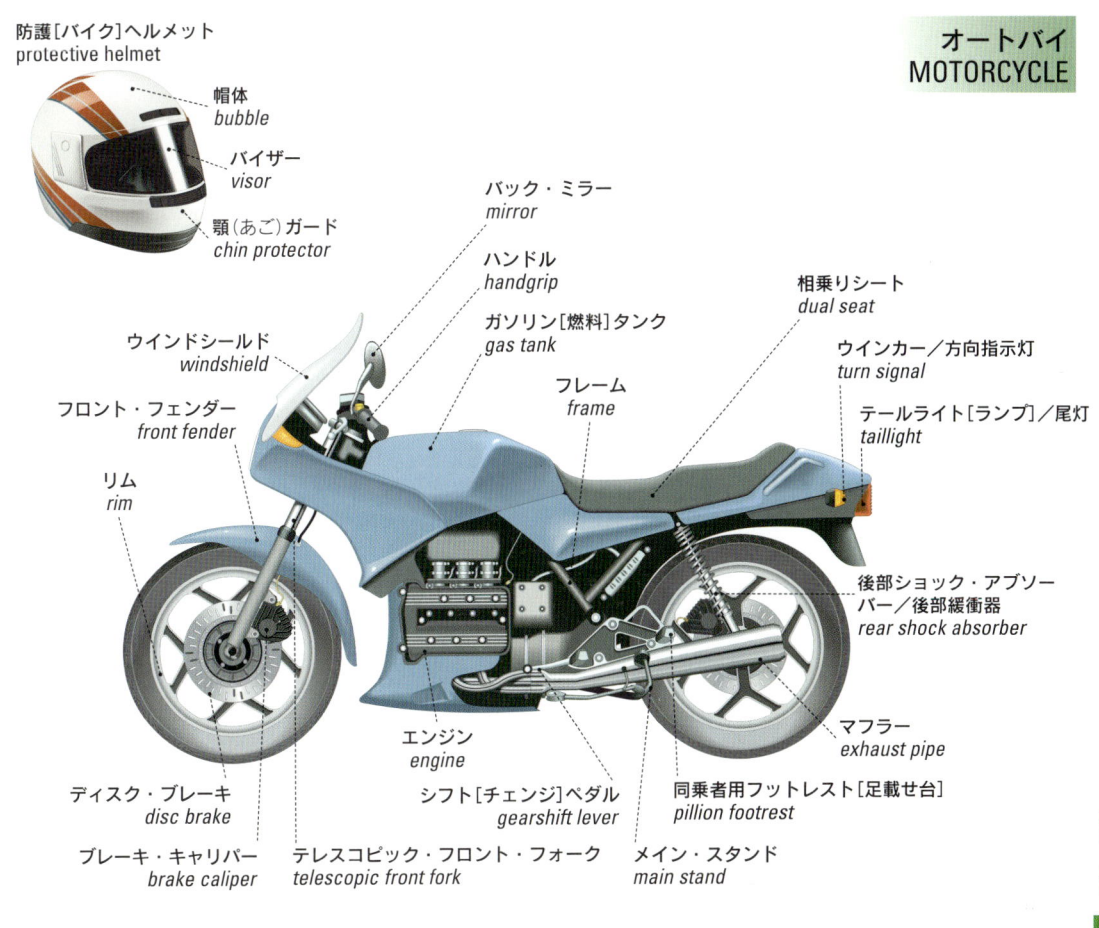

道路輸送 | ROAD TRANSPORT

オートバイ
MOTORCYCLE

防護[バイク]ヘルメット
protective helmet

帽体
bubble

バイザー
visor

顎(あご)ガード
chin protector

バック・ミラー
mirror

ハンドル
handgrip

ガソリン[燃料]タンク
gas tank

相乗りシート
dual seat

ウインドシールド
windshield

フレーム
frame

ウインカー／方向指示灯
turn signal

フロント・フェンダー
front fender

テールライト[ランプ]／尾灯
taillight

リム
rim

後部ショック・アブソーバー／後部緩衝器
rear shock absorber

マフラー
exhaust pipe

エンジン
engine

ディスク・ブレーキ
disc brake

シフト[チェンジ]ペダル
gearshift lever

同乗者用フットレスト[足載せ台]
pillion footrest

ブレーキ・キャリパー
brake caliper

テレスコピック・フロント・フォーク
telescopic front fork

メイン・スタンド
main stand

オートバイの例
examples of motorcycles

オフ・ロード・バイク
off-road motorcycle

モーペッド
moped

エプロン
apron

バック・ミラー
mirror

シート
seat

荷台
luggage rack

ツーリング・バイク
touring motorcycle

床板／フロアボード
floorboard

スクーター
motor scooter

191

道路輸送 | ROAD TRANSPORT

トラック運送
TRUCKING

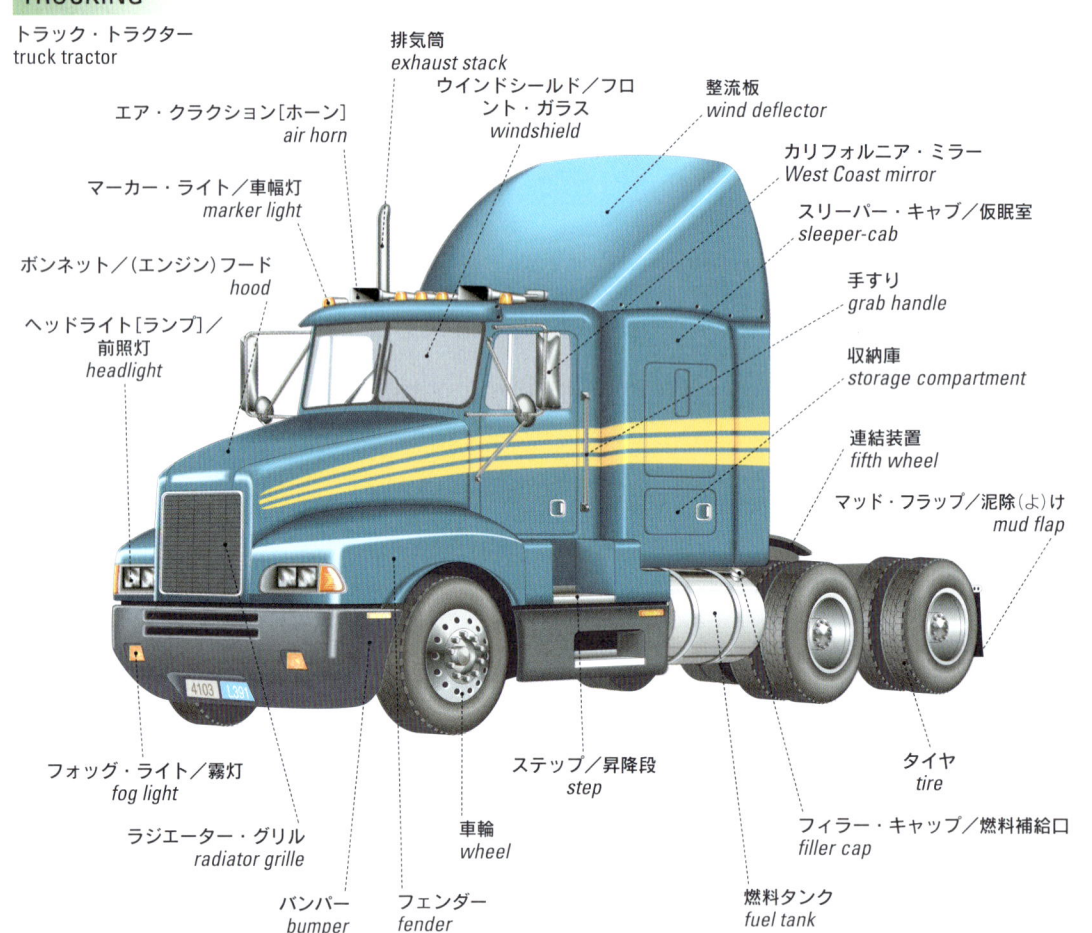

- トラック・トラクター truck tractor
- 排気筒 exhaust stack
- ウインドシールド／フロント・ガラス windshield
- 整流板 wind deflector
- エア・クラクション［ホーン］ air horn
- カリフォルニア・ミラー West Coast mirror
- マーカー・ライト／車幅灯 marker light
- スリーパー・キャブ／仮眠室 sleeper-cab
- ボンネット／（エンジン）フード hood
- 手すり grab handle
- ヘッドライト［ランプ］／前照灯 headlight
- 収納庫 storage compartment
- 連結装置 fifth wheel
- マッド・フラップ／泥除(よ)け mud flap
- フォッグ・ライト／霧灯 fog light
- ステップ／昇降段 step
- タイヤ tire
- ラジエーター・グリル radiator grille
- 車輪 wheel
- フィラー・キャップ／燃料補給口 filler cap
- バンパー bumper
- フェンダー fender
- 燃料タンク fuel tank

トラックの例
examples of trucks

- バキューム・カー cesspit emptier
- ダンプ・トラック［カー］ dump truck
- 着脱式の車体 detachable body
- トラック・トラクター truck tractor
- セミトレーラー semitrailer

輸送と重機

道路輸送 | ROAD TRANSPORT

レッカー車
tow truck

ブーム／レッカー・クレーン
boom

ウィンチ／巻き上げ機
winch

ケーブル
cable

フック
hook

牽引（けんいん）装置
towing device

ウィンチ操作ハンドル
winch controls

リフト［起伏］シリンダー
elevating cylinder

収集トラック
collection truck

タンク・トラック［ローリー］／タンク車
tank truck

除雪車
snowblower

コンクリート・ミキサー・トラック
concrete mixer truck

バン型トラック
van straight truck

タンデム・トレーラー
tandem tractor trailer

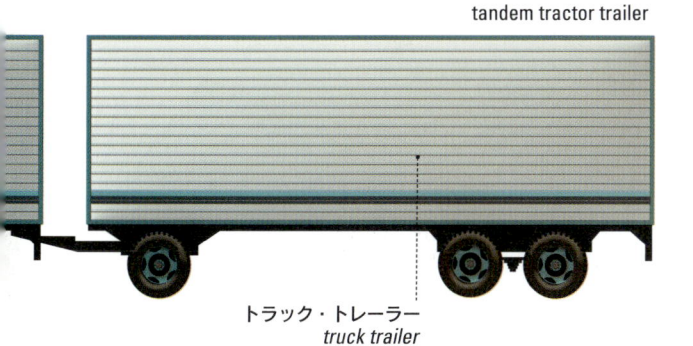

道路清掃車
street sweeper

トラック・トレーラー
truck trailer

輸送と重機

193

道路輸送 | ROAD TRANSPORT

自転車
BICYCLE

サドル／シート
seat

空気入れ／タイヤ・ポンプ
tire pump

サドル支柱
seat post

荷(物)台／キャリア
carrier

後ろブレーキ
rear brake

発電器
generator

反射器
reflector

尾灯／テールライト［ランプ］
rear light

泥除(よ)け
fender

後ろディレーラー［変速機］
rear derailleur

チェーン
drive chain

前ディレーラー［変速機］
front derailleur

ペダル
pedal

トウ・クリップ
toe clip

付属品
accessories

自転車用チャイルドシート
child carrier

防護［サイクル］ヘルメット
protective helmet

ロック
lock

サドルバッグ
bicycle bag

輸送と重機

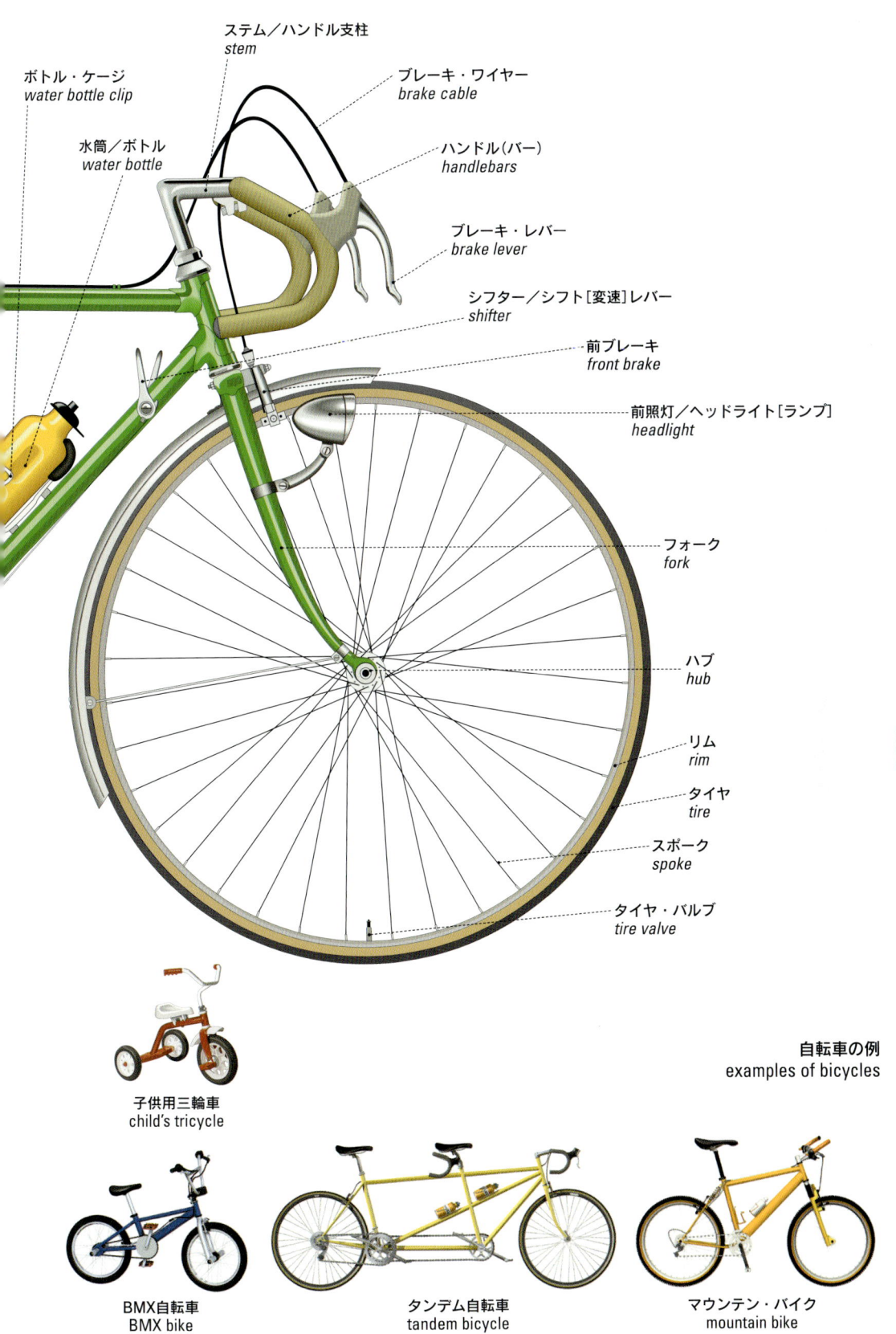

道路輸送 | ROAD TRANSPORT

ボトル・ケージ
water bottle clip

水筒／ボトル
water bottle

ステム／ハンドル支柱
stem

ブレーキ・ワイヤー
brake cable

ハンドル（バー）
handlebars

ブレーキ・レバー
brake lever

シフター／シフト[変速]レバー
shifter

前ブレーキ
front brake

前照灯／ヘッドライト[ランプ]
headlight

フォーク
fork

ハブ
hub

リム
rim

タイヤ
tire

スポーク
spoke

タイヤ・バルブ
tire valve

輸送と重機

自転車の例
examples of bicycles

子供用三輪車
child's tricycle

BMX自転車
BMX bike

タンデム自転車
tandem bicycle

マウンテン・バイク
mountain bike

195

鉄道輸送 | RAIL TRANSPORT

19世紀には鉄道は最高の輸送手段でした。今日でも、車や飛行機よりも列車での移動を好む旅行者がたくさんいます。ますます高性能になって、例えばフランス新幹線（ＴＧＶ）は時速３００ｋｍ以上のスピードでヨーロッパを走り、アジアでも新幹線が走っています。都市部においてはむしろ、鉄道輸送では地下鉄や電車が優勢です。

旅客列車
PASSENGER TRAIN

ディーゼル電気機関車
diesel-electric locomotive

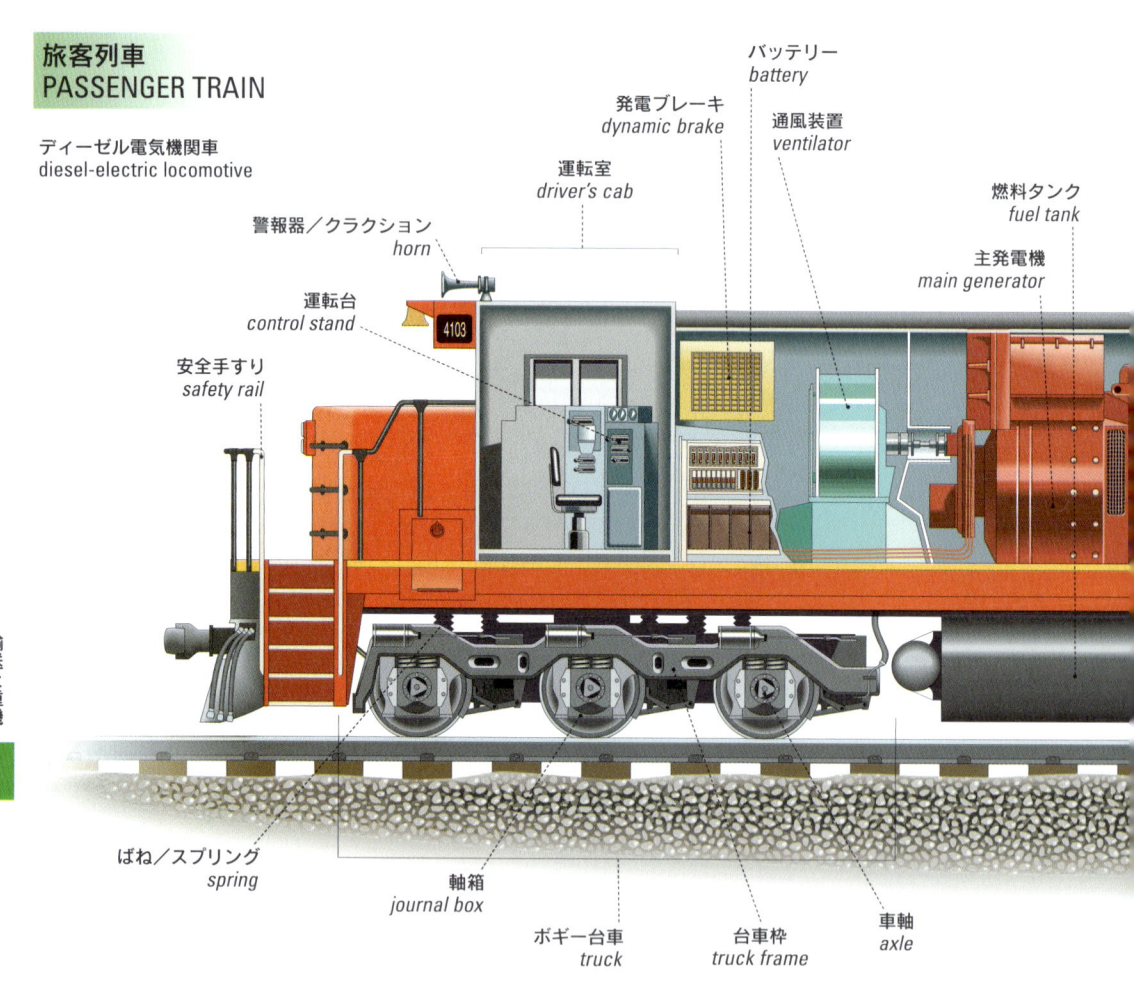

バッテリー
battery

発電ブレーキ
dynamic brake

通風装置
ventilator

運転室
driver's cab

燃料タンク
fuel tank

警報器／クラクション
horn

主発電機
main generator

運転台
control stand

安全手すり
safety rail

ばね／スプリング
spring

軸箱
journal box

ボギー台車
truck

台車枠
truck frame

車軸
axle

貨車の例
examples of freight cars

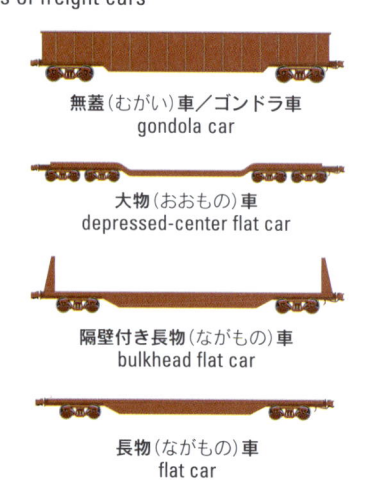

無蓋（むがい）車／ゴンドラ車
gondola car

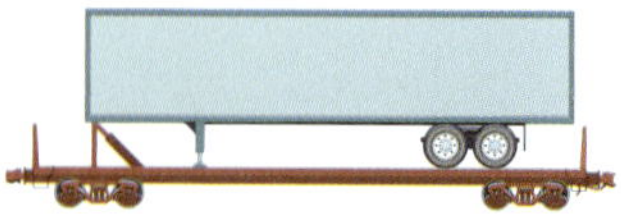

一貫輸送車
intermodal car

大物（おおもの）車
depressed-center flat car

冷蔵車
refrigerator car

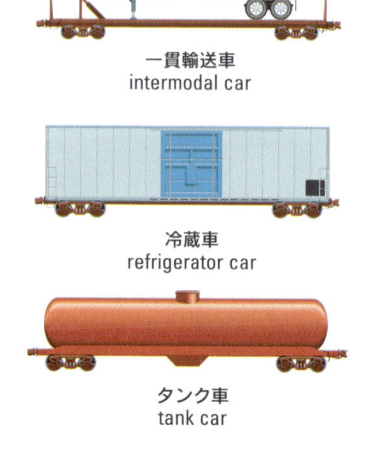

隔壁付き長物（ながもの）車
bulkhead flat car

タンク車
tank car

長物（ながもの）車
flat car

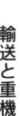

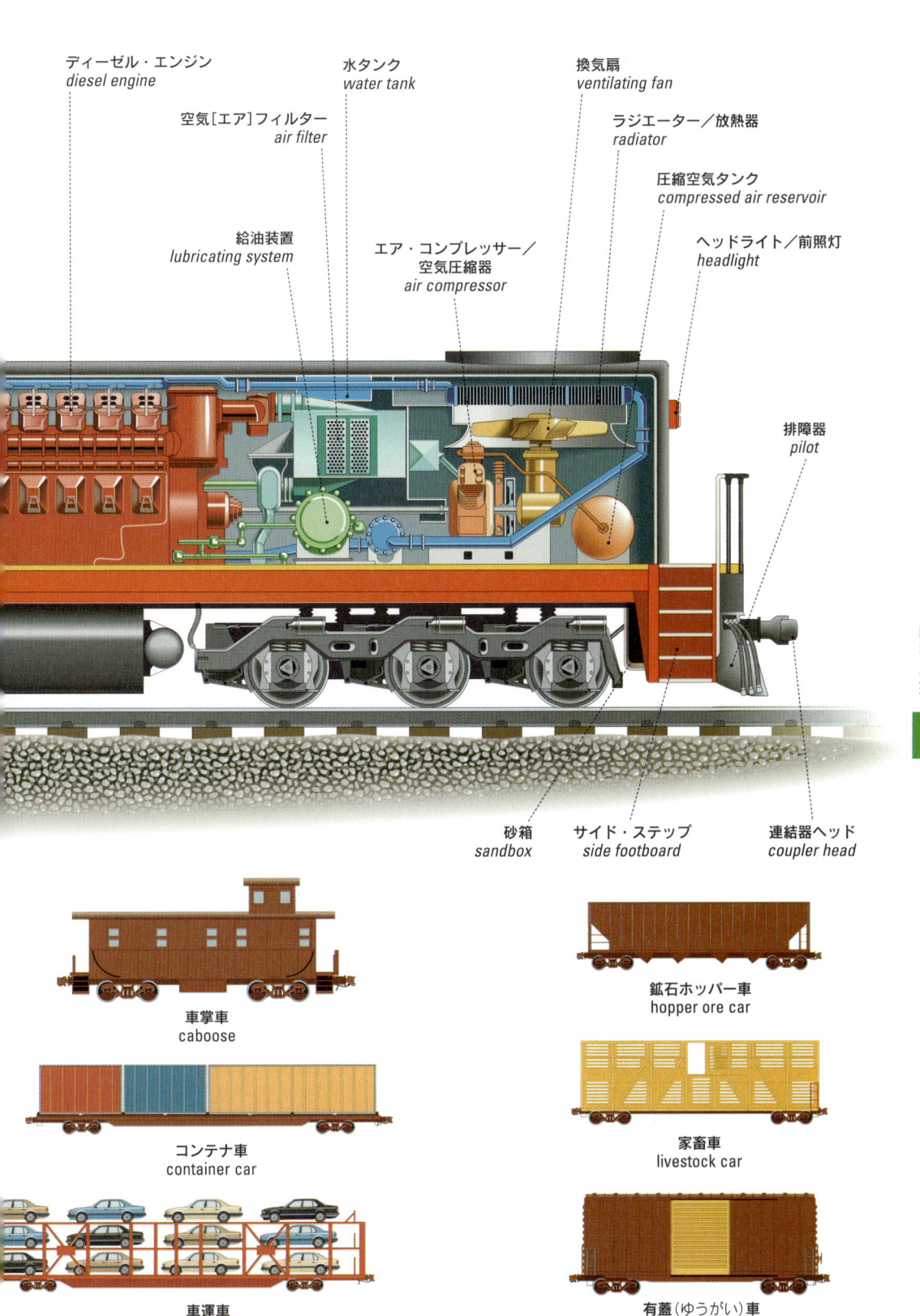

鉄道輸送 | RAIL TRANSPORT

ディーゼル・エンジン
diesel engine

水タンク
water tank

換気扇
ventilating fan

空気[エア]フィルター
air filter

ラジエーター／放熱器
radiator

圧縮空気タンク
compressed air reservoir

給油装置
lubricating system

エア・コンプレッサー／空気圧縮器
air compressor

ヘッドライト／前照灯
headlight

排障器
pilot

砂箱
sandbox

サイド・ステップ
side footboard

連結器ヘッド
coupler head

車掌車
caboose

鉱石ホッパー車
hopper ore car

コンテナ車
container car

家畜車
livestock car

車運車
automobile car

有蓋(ゆうがい)車
box car

輸送と重機

鉄道輸送 | RAIL TRANSPORT

高速列車
high-speed train

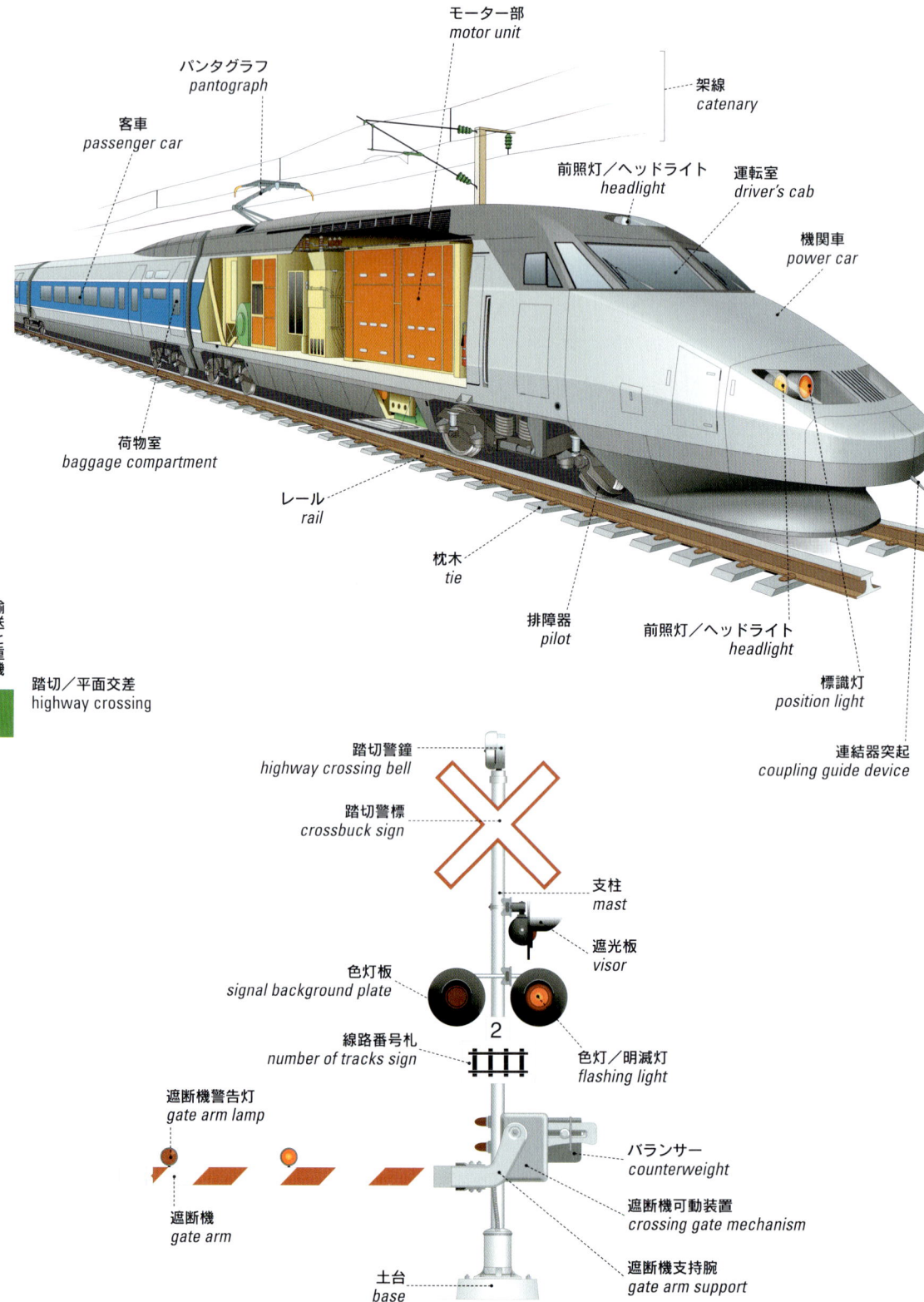

モーター部
motor unit

パンタグラフ
pantograph

架線
catenary

客車
passenger car

前照灯／ヘッドライト
headlight

運転室
driver's cab

機関車
power car

荷物室
baggage compartment

レール
rail

枕木
tie

排障器
pilot

前照灯／ヘッドライト
headlight

標識灯
position light

連結器突起
coupling guide device

輸送と重機

踏切／平面交差
highway crossing

踏切警鐘
highway crossing bell

踏切警標
crossbuck sign

支柱
mast

遮光板
visor

色灯板
signal background plate

線路番号札
number of tracks sign

色灯／明滅灯
flashing light

遮断機警告灯
gate arm lamp

バランサー
counterweight

遮断機可動装置
crossing gate mechanism

遮断機
gate arm

土台
base

遮断機支持腕
gate arm support

198

鉄道輸送 | RAIL TRANSPORT

地下鉄
SUBWAY

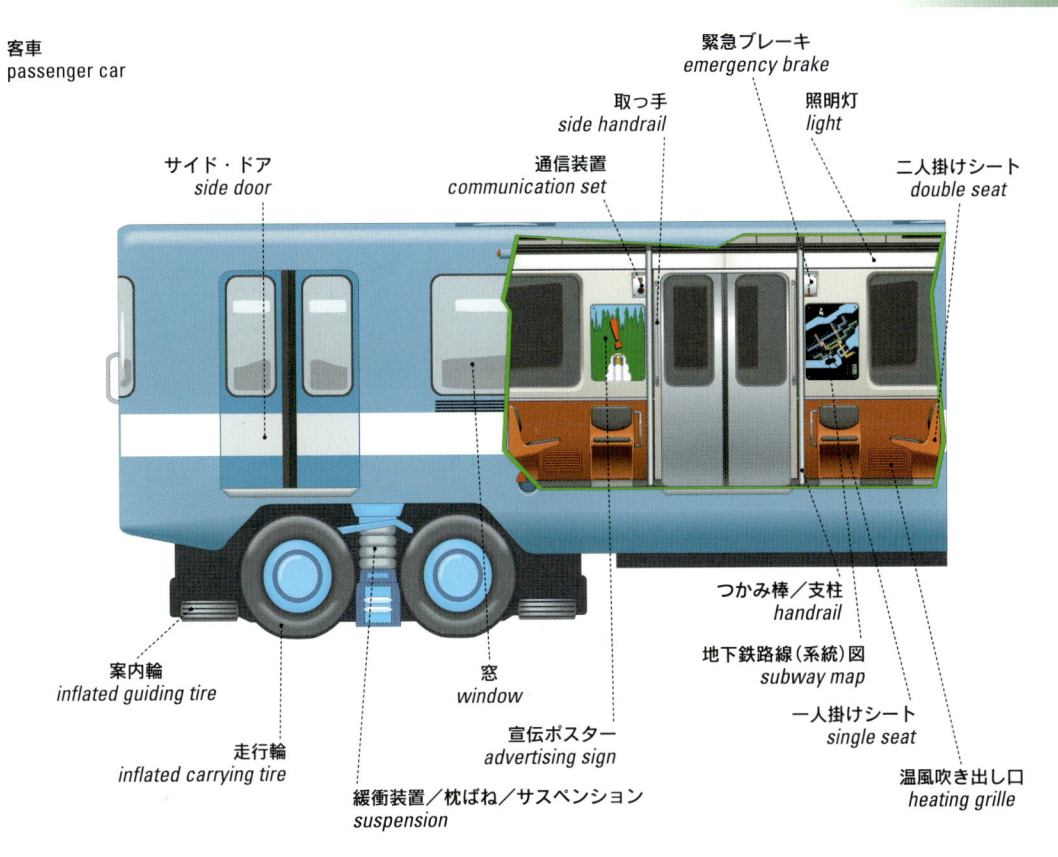

客車 / passenger car

- サイド・ドア / side door
- 取っ手 / side handrail
- 緊急ブレーキ / emergency brake
- 照明灯 / light
- 通信装置 / communication set
- 二人掛けシート / double seat
- 案内輪 / inflated guiding tire
- 走行輪 / inflated carrying tire
- 緩衝装置／枕ばね／サスペンション / suspension
- 窓 / window
- 宣伝ポスター / advertising sign
- つかみ棒／支柱 / handrail
- 地下鉄路線（系統）図 / subway map
- 一人掛けシート / single seat
- 温風吹き出し口 / heating grille

地下鉄車両 / subway train

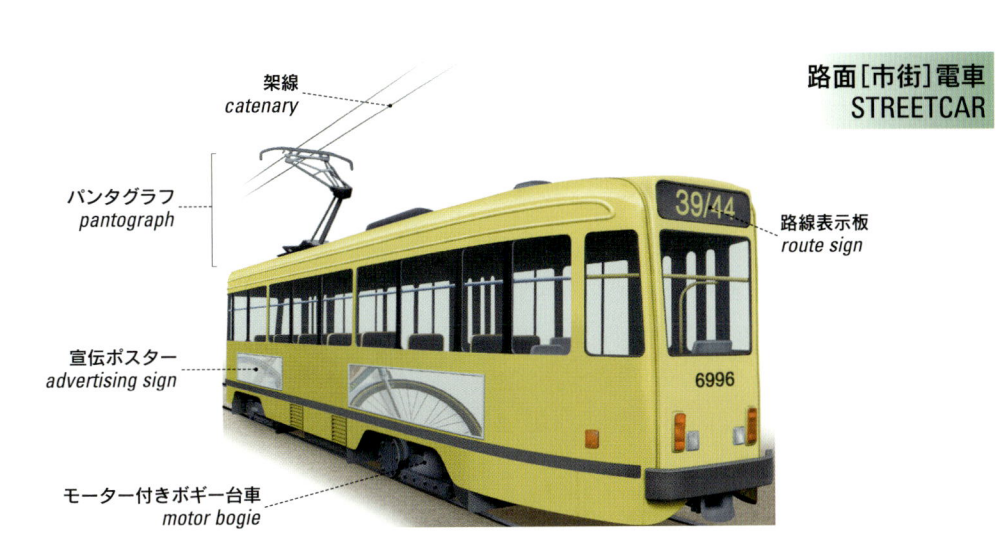

- 動力車 / motor car
- 付随車 / trailer car
- 動力車 / motor car

路面[市街]電車
STREETCAR

- 架線 / catenary
- パンタグラフ / pantograph
- 路線表示板 / route sign
- 宣伝ポスター / advertising sign
- モーター付きボギー台車 / motor bogie

輸送と重機

199

海上輸送 | MARITIME TRANSPORT

ロバやラクダに頼っていた頃から、小舟は最も古い輸送手段でした。見知らぬ国同士の地上交易は不便が多く、14世紀頃から高性能の大型帆船による交易へと移って行きました。19世紀になって、風力に頼ることをやめて、大型蒸気船が重要な位置を占めるようになりました。今日では、主に商品を安く運ぶ際に海路が利用されています。

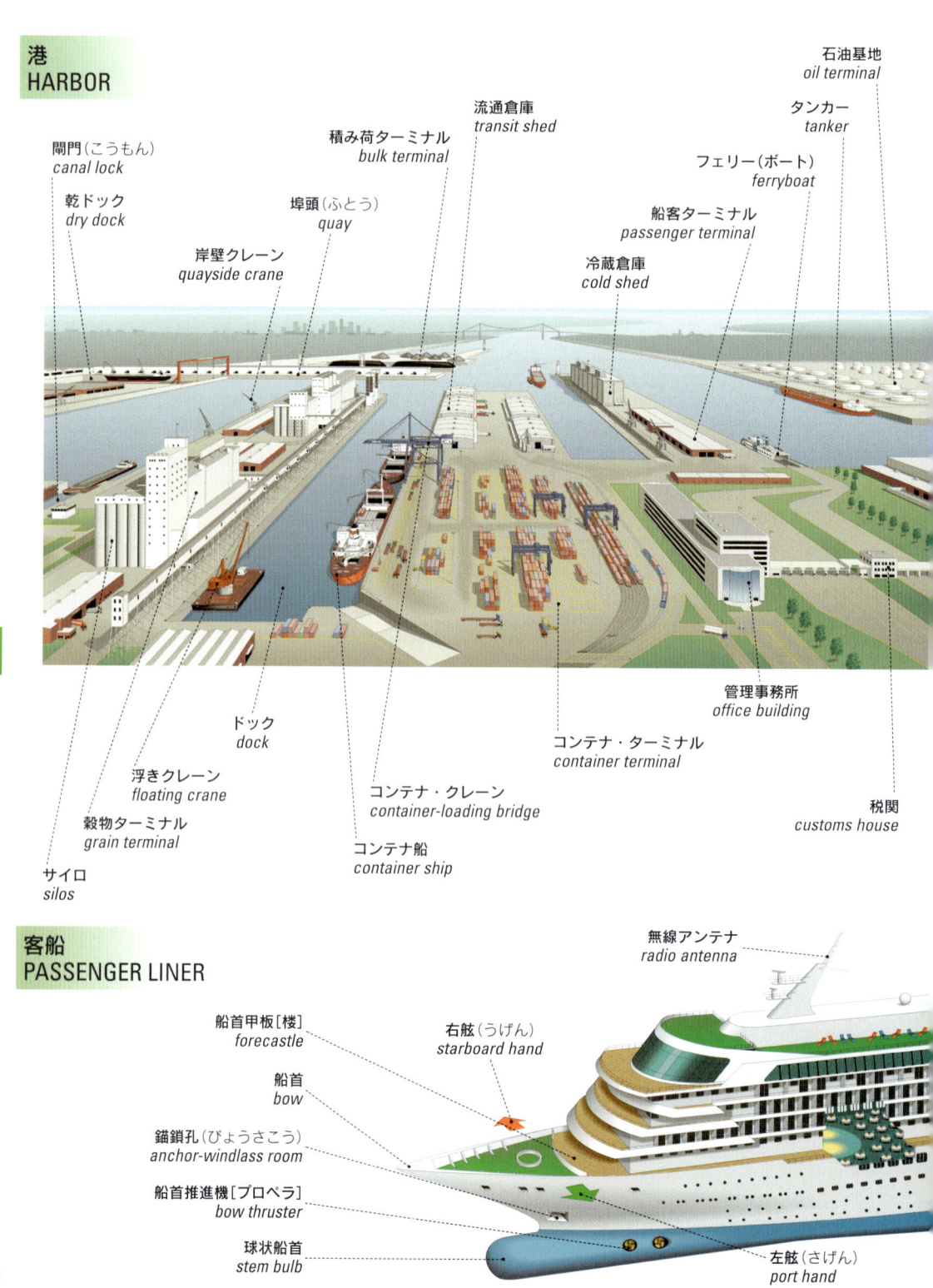

港 HARBOR

- 閘門(こうもん) canal lock
- 乾ドック dry dock
- 岸壁クレーン quayside crane
- 積み荷ターミナル bulk terminal
- 埠頭(ふとう) quay
- 流通倉庫 transit shed
- 冷蔵倉庫 cold shed
- 石油基地 oil terminal
- タンカー tanker
- フェリー(ボート) ferryboat
- 船客ターミナル passenger terminal
- ドック dock
- 浮きクレーン floating crane
- 穀物ターミナル grain terminal
- サイロ silos
- コンテナ・クレーン container-loading bridge
- コンテナ船 container ship
- 管理事務所 office building
- コンテナ・ターミナル container terminal
- 税関 customs house

客船 PASSENGER LINER

- 船首甲板[楼] forecastle
- 船首 bow
- 錨鎖孔(びょうさこう) anchor-windlass room
- 船首推進機[プロペラ] bow thruster
- 球状船首 stem bulb
- 無線アンテナ radio antenna
- 右舷(うげん) starboard hand
- 左舷(さげん) port hand

輸送と重機

海上輸送 | MARITIME TRANSPORT

4本マスト・バーク（型帆船）
FOUR-MASTED BARK

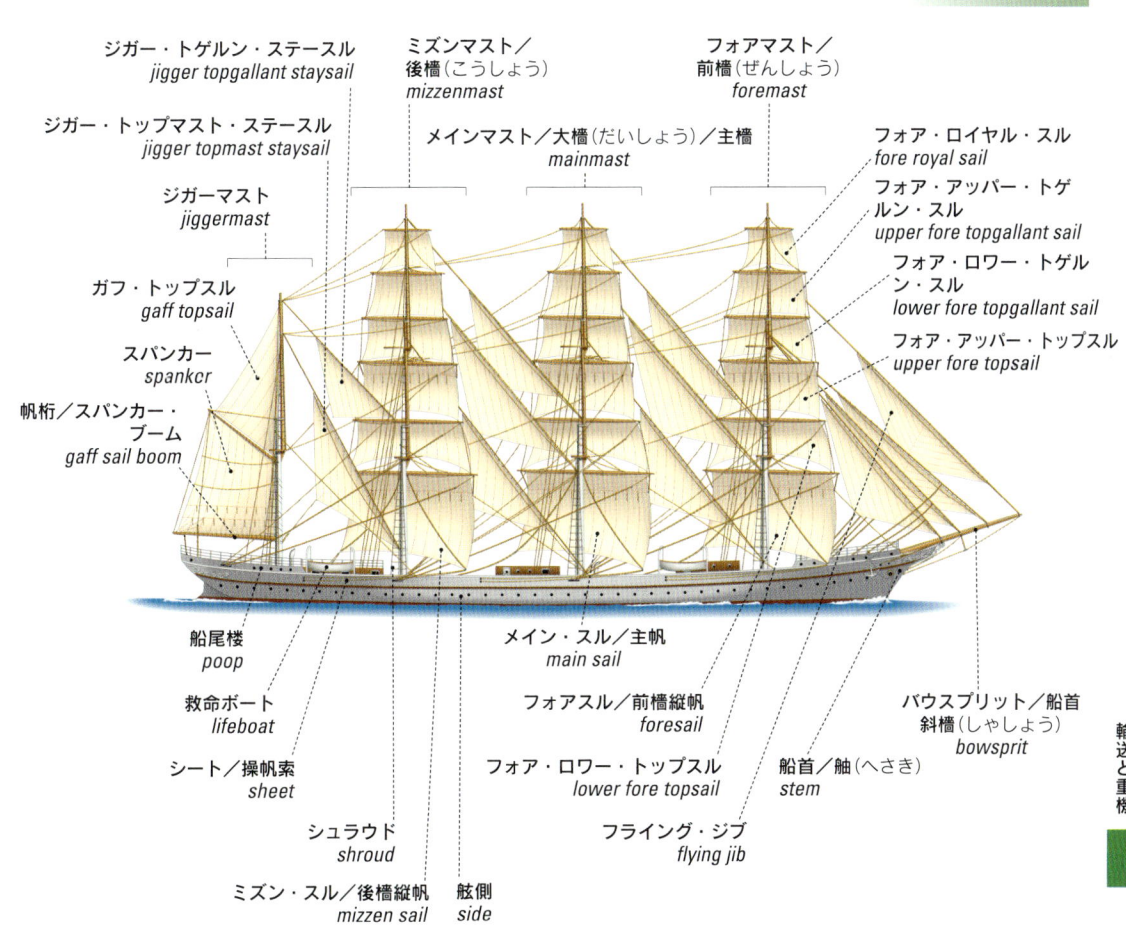

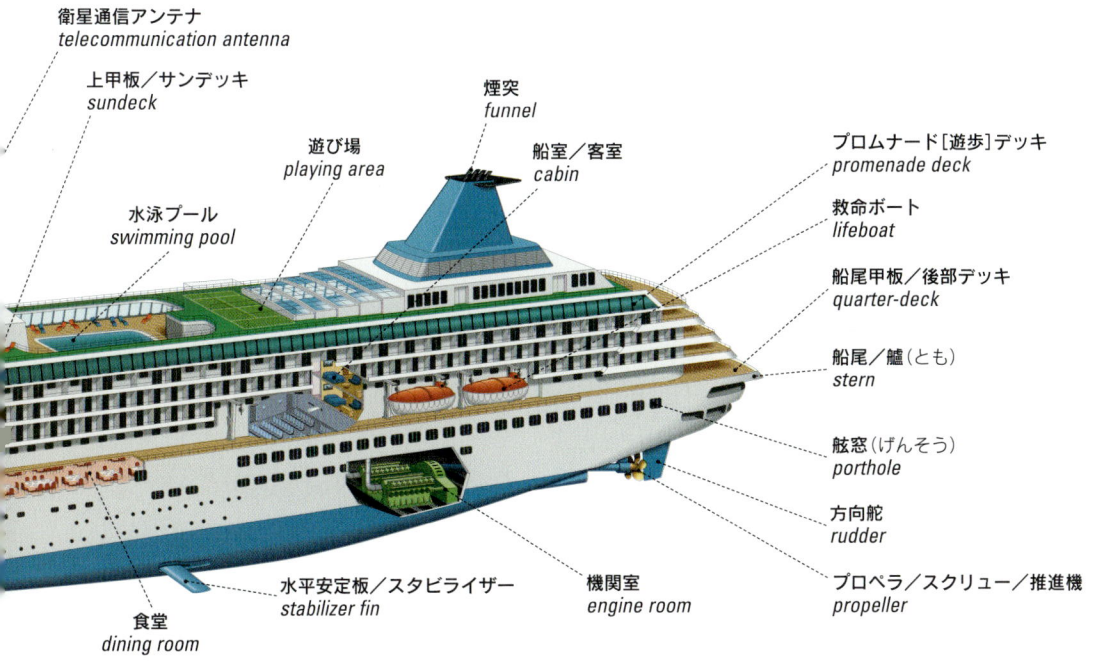

- ジガー・トゲルン・ステースル / jigger topgallant staysail
- ジガー・トップマスト・ステースル / jigger topmast staysail
- ジガーマスト / jiggermast
- ガフ・トップスル / gaff topsail
- スパンカー / spanker
- 帆桁／スパンカー・ブーム / gaff sail boom
- ミズンマスト／後檣（こうしょう）/ mizzenmast
- メインマスト／大檣（だいしょう）／主檣 / mainmast
- フォアマスト／前檣（ぜんしょう）/ foremast
- フォア・ロイヤル・スル / fore royal sail
- フォア・アッパー・トゲルン・スル / upper fore topgallant sail
- フォア・ロワー・トゲルン・スル / lower fore topgallant sail
- フォア・アッパー・トップスル / upper fore topsail
- 船尾楼 / poop
- 救命ボート / lifeboat
- シート／操帆索 / sheet
- シュラウド / shroud
- ミズン・スル／後檣縦帆 / mizzen sail
- 舷側 / side
- メイン・スル／主帆 / main sail
- フォアスル／前檣縦帆 / foresail
- フォア・ロワー・トップスル / lower fore topsail
- フライング・ジブ / flying jib
- 船首／舳（へさき）/ stem
- バウスプリット／船首斜檣（しゃしょう）/ bowsprit

輸送と重機

- 衛星通信アンテナ / telecommunication antenna
- 上甲板／サンデッキ / sundeck
- 水泳プール / swimming pool
- 遊び場 / playing area
- 煙突 / funnel
- 船室／客室 / cabin
- プロムナード［遊歩］デッキ / promenade deck
- 救命ボート / lifeboat
- 船尾甲板／後部デッキ / quarter-deck
- 船尾／艫（とも）/ stern
- 舷窓（げんそう）/ porthole
- 方向舵 / rudder
- プロペラ／スクリュー／推進機 / propeller
- 食堂 / dining room
- 水平安定板／スタビライザー / stabilizer fin
- 機関室 / engine room

201

海上輸送 | MARITIME TRANSPORT

ボートと船の例
EXAMPLES OF BOATS AND SHIPS

小型モーターボート
runabout

モーター・ヨット
motor yacht

ハウスボート
houseboat

タグボート／引き船
tug

ホバークラフト
hovercraft

水中翼船
hydrofoil boat

フェリー（ボート）
ferry boat

砕氷船
ice breaker

トロール船
trawler

輸送と重機

航空輸送 | AIR TRANSPORT

ヘリコプターや飛行機が登場する以前は、長旅をするときの唯一の手段は汽車か船でした。1950年代にはジェット機が、長距離で、速い空の旅を可能にし、航空交通に革命をもたらしました。飛行機が近づけないような場所でも離着陸ができるため、ヘリコプターは特に救助活動で役に立っています。

ヘリコプター
HELICOPTER

- ドライブ・シャフト／駆動軸 / drive shaft
- ローター・ハブ / rotor hub
- 排気筒 / exhaust pipe
- 位置灯 / position light
- 垂直尾翼[安定板] / fin
- 反トルク・ローター / anti-torque tail rotor
- ローター（ブレード）／回転翼 / rotor blade
- スリーブ / sleeve
- 尾そり / tail skid
- ローター・ヘッド / rotor head
- 水平尾翼[安定板] / horizontal stabilizer
- コックピット／操縦室 / flight deck
- テール・ブーム／尾部支柱 / tail boom
- 荷物室 / baggage compartment
- 空気取り入れ口 / air inlet
- 燃料タンク / fuel tank
- アンテナ / antenna
- キャビン／客室 / cabin
- 操縦桿（かん） / control stick
- そり / skid
- 昇降ステップ / boarding step
- 着陸舷窓 / landing window
- 着陸灯 / landing light

輸送と重機

ヘリコプターの例 / examples of helicopters

- 戦術輸送ヘリコプター / tactical transport helicopter
- 救急ヘリコプター / ambulance helicopter
- 消防ヘリコプター / water bomber helicopter

航空輸送 | AIR TRANSPORT

空港
AIRPORT

高速誘導路
high-speed exit taxiway

管制室
control tower cab

管制塔
control tower

進入道路
access road

滑走路
taxiway

迂回誘導路
by-pass taxiway

誘導路
taxiway

走行エリア
apron

操縦区域
maneuvering area

サービス道路
service road

空港地上支援機材／空港特殊車両
ground airport equipment

車輪止め
wheel chock

ケータリング車
catering vehicle

整備トラック
aircraft maintenance truck

トウ・バー／牽引(けんいん)棒
tow bar

航空輸送 | AIR TRANSPORT

旅客ターミナル
passenger terminal

整備格納庫
maintenance hangar

搭乗橋
boarding walkway

駐機場
parking area

サテライト・ターミナル
radial passenger loading area

可動式搭乗橋
telescopic corridor

サービス・エリア
service area

誘導路線
taxiway line

給油車／燃料補給車
jet refueler

牽引(けんいん)トラクター
tow tractor

ベルト・ローダー車
baggage conveyor

荷物トレーラー
baggage trailer

タグ車
tow tractor

コンテナ・パレット・ドーリー
container/pallet loader

輸送と重機

航空輸送 | AIR TRANSPORT

飛行機
AIRPLANE

翼形状の例
examples of wing shapes

テーパー翼
tapered wing

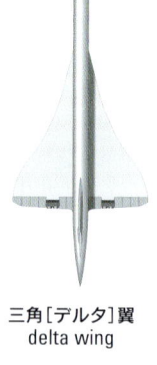

三角［デルタ］翼
delta wing

可変翼
variable geometry wing

直線翼
straight wing

後退翼
swept-back wing

補助翼／エルロン
aileron

後縁
trailing edge

後縁フラップ
trailing edge flap

抵抗板／スポイラー
spoiler

長距離［大型］ジェット機
long-range jet

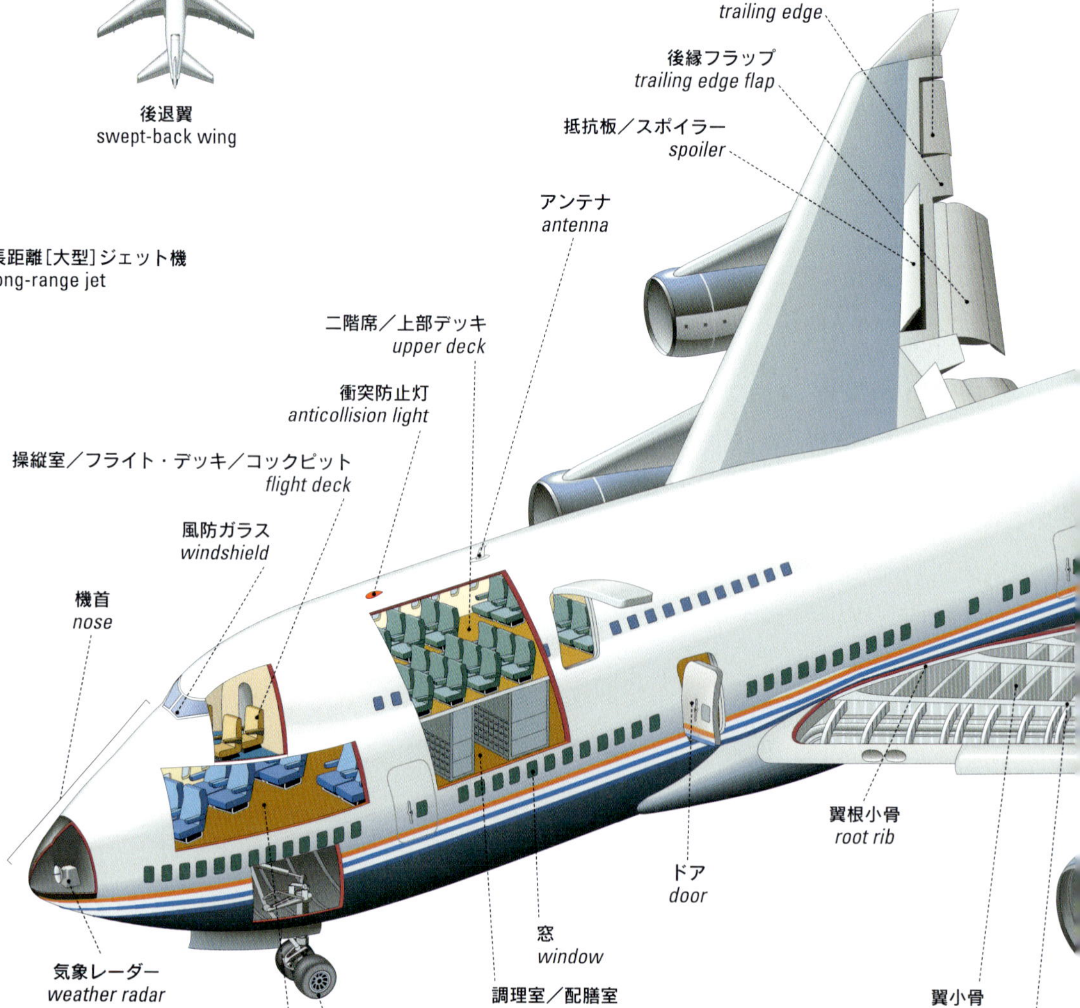

アンテナ
antenna

二階席／上部デッキ
upper deck

衝突防止灯
anticollision light

操縦室／フライト・デッキ／コックピット
flight deck

風防ガラス
windshield

機首
nose

翼根小骨
root rib

ドア
door

窓
window

気象レーダー
weather radar

調理室／配膳室
galley

翼小骨
wing rib

ファースト・クラス客室
first-class cabin

首陸輪／前輪
nose landing gear

翼桁
spar

輸送と重機

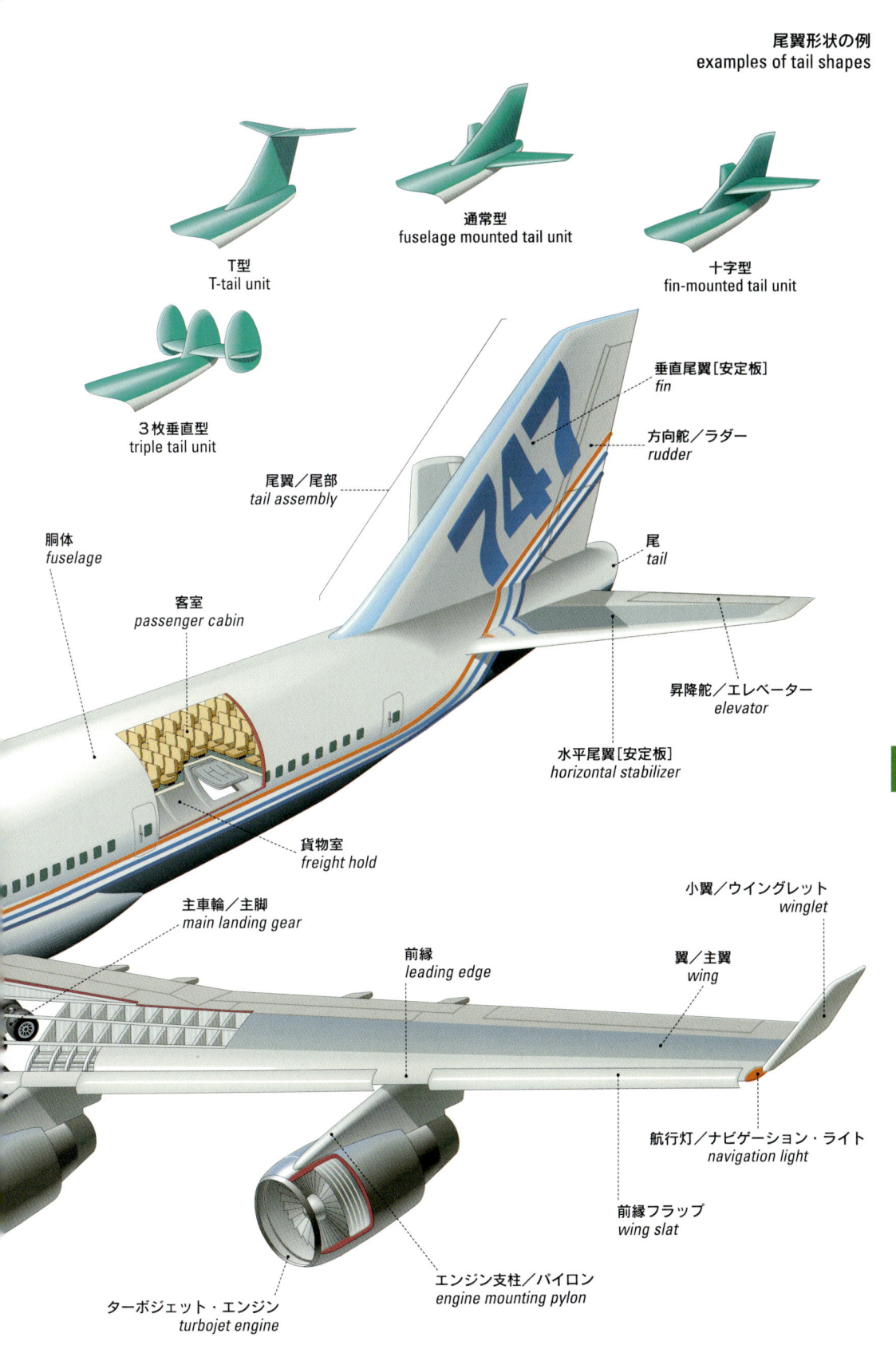

航空輸送 | AIR TRANSPORT

尾翼形状の例
examples of tail shapes

T型
T-tail unit

通常型
fuselage mounted tail unit

十字型
fin-mounted tail unit

3枚垂直型
triple tail unit

- 垂直尾翼［安定板］ / fin
- 方向舵／ラダー / rudder
- 尾翼／尾部 / tail assembly
- 尾 / tail
- 昇降舵／エレベーター / elevator
- 水平尾翼［安定板］ / horizontal stabilizer
- 胴体 / fuselage
- 客室 / passenger cabin
- 貨物室 / freight hold
- 主車輪／主脚 / main landing gear
- 小翼／ウイングレット / winglet
- 前縁 / leading edge
- 翼／主翼 / wing
- 航行灯／ナビゲーション・ライト / navigation light
- 前縁フラップ / wing slat
- エンジン支柱／パイロン / engine mounting pylon
- ターボジェット・エンジン / turbojet engine

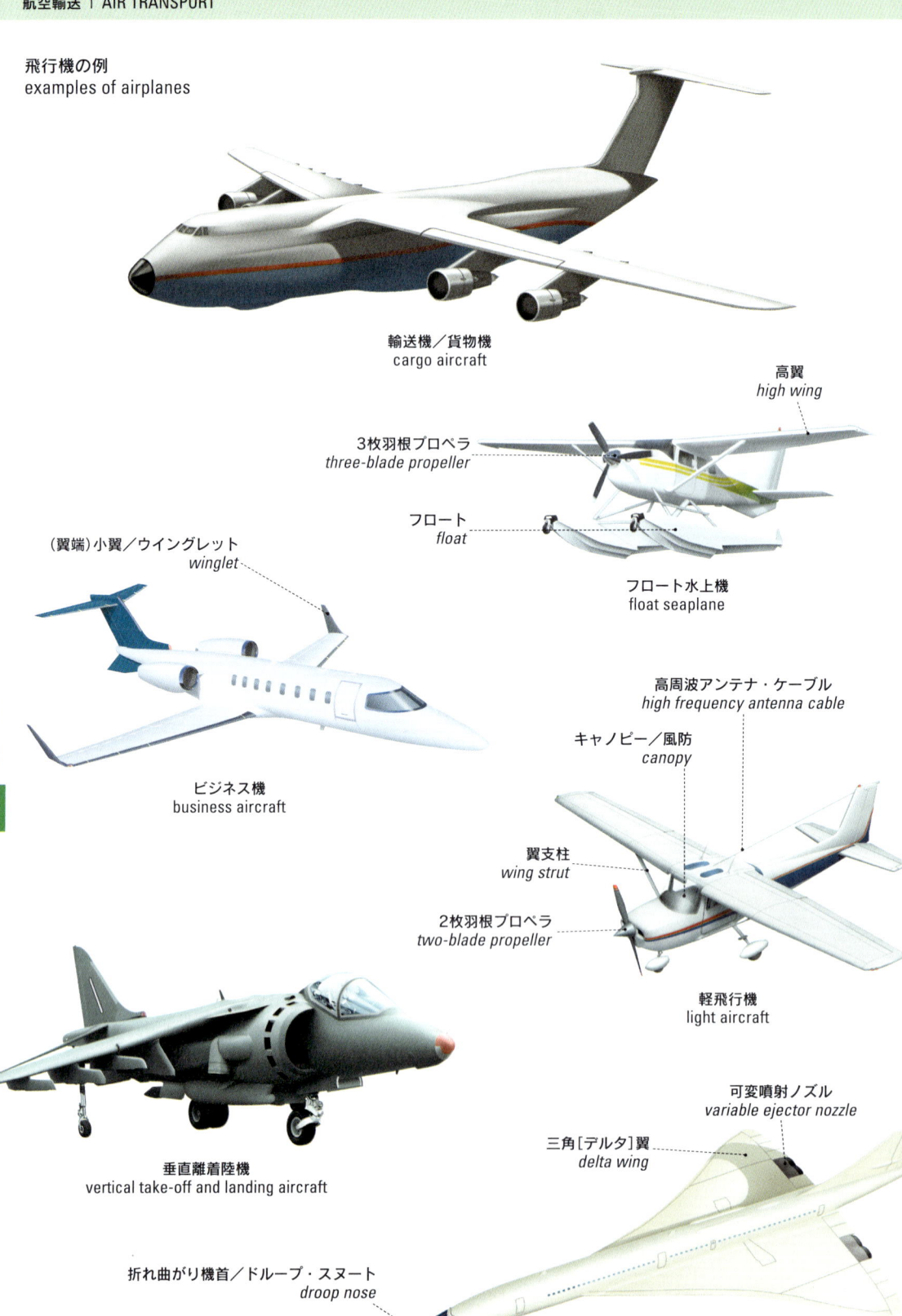

航空輸送 | AIR TRANSPORT

飛行機の例
examples of airplanes

輸送機／貨物機
cargo aircraft

高翼
high wing

3枚羽根プロペラ
three-blade propeller

フロート
float

フロート水上機
float seaplane

(翼端)小翼／ウイングレット
winglet

高周波アンテナ・ケーブル
high frequency antenna cable

キャノピー／風防
canopy

ビジネス機
business aircraft

翼支柱
wing strut

2枚羽根プロペラ
two-blade propeller

軽飛行機
light aircraft

可変噴射ノズル
variable ejector nozzle

三角[デルタ]翼
delta wing

垂直離着陸機
vertical take-off and landing aircraft

折れ曲がり機首／ドループ・スヌート
droop nose

超音速ジェット機
supersonic jetliner

輸送と重機

208

重機 | HEAVY MACHINERY

重機は自動車を除く車両のグループを形成しています。このように何でもこなす車両が道路や高速道路を縦横に走ることはまずありませんが、建設現場、採石場、鉱山などでは活躍しています。大型トラックは、時にはキャタピラーを付けて起伏のある土地を難なく前進したり、強力なエンジンを備えているので、地面を掘ったり、積み荷を動かしたりできます。

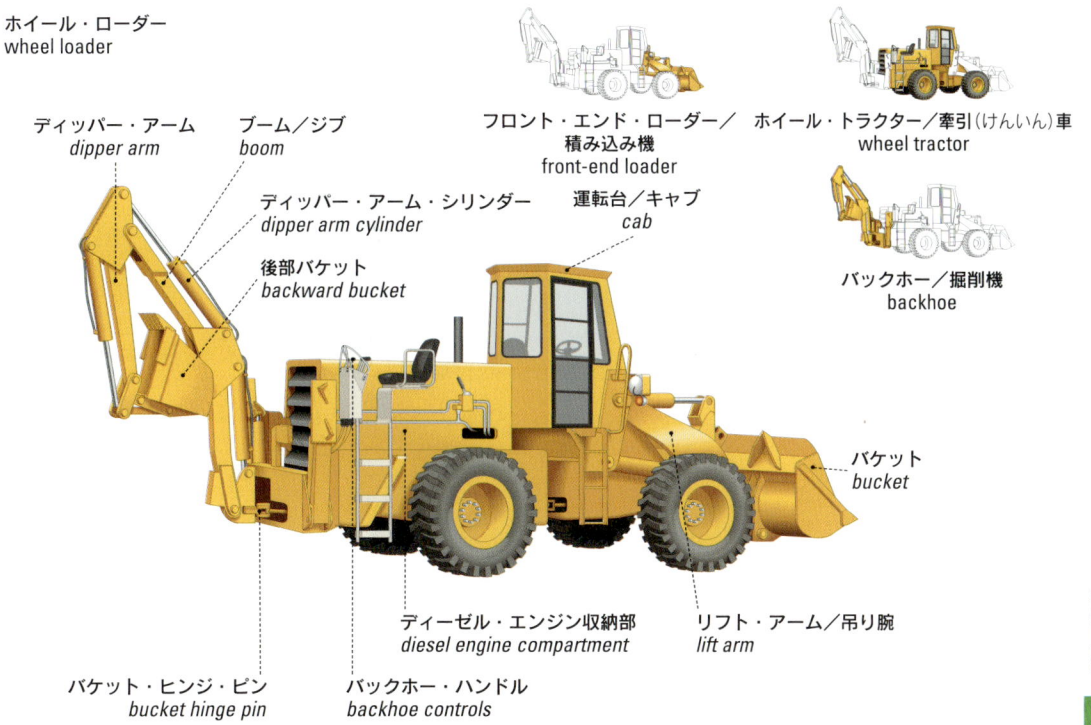

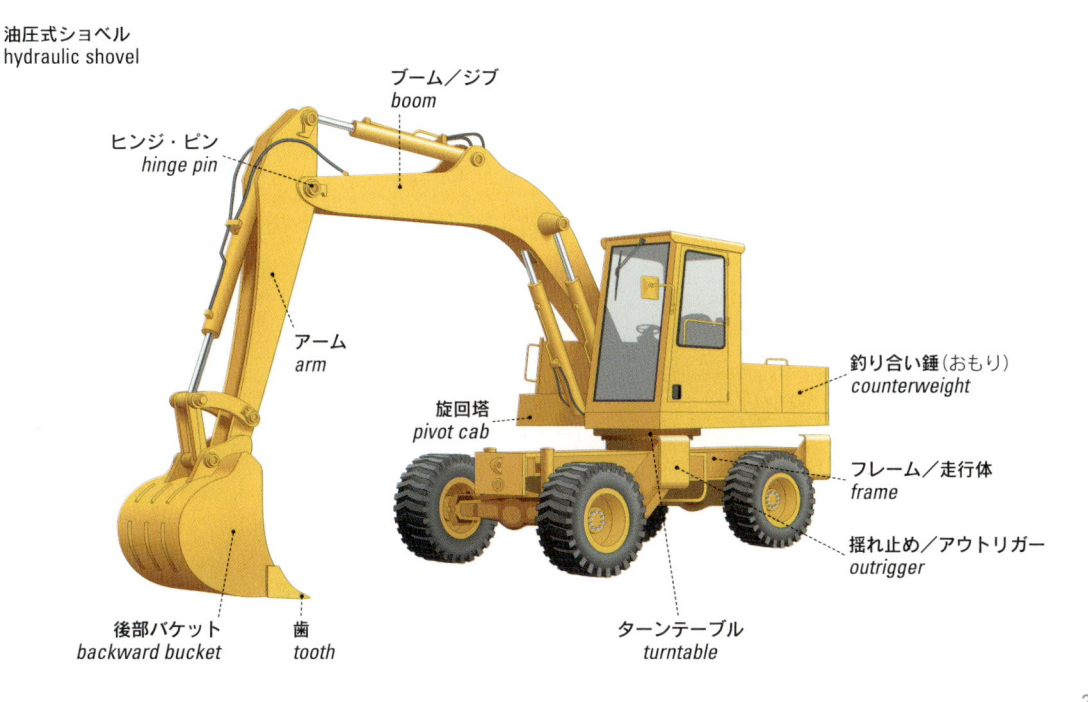

ホイール・ローダー
wheel loader

ディッパー・アーム
dipper arm

ブーム／ジブ
boom

ディッパー・アーム・シリンダー
dipper arm cylinder

後部バケット
backward bucket

フロント・エンド・ローダー／積み込み機
front-end loader

運転台／キャブ
cab

ホイール・トラクター／牽引(けんいん)車
wheel tractor

バックホー／掘削機
backhoe

バケット
bucket

ディーゼル・エンジン収納部
diesel engine compartment

リフト・アーム／吊り腕
lift arm

バケット・ヒンジ・ピン
bucket hinge pin

バックホー・ハンドル
backhoe controls

油圧式ショベル
hydraulic shovel

ヒンジ・ピン
hinge pin

ブーム／ジブ
boom

アーム
arm

旋回塔
pivot cab

釣り合い錘(おもり)
counterweight

フレーム／走行体
frame

揺れ止め／アウトリガー
outrigger

後部バケット
backward bucket

歯
tooth

ターンテーブル
turntable

輸送と重機

重機 | HEAVY MACHINERY

ブルドーザー
bulldozer

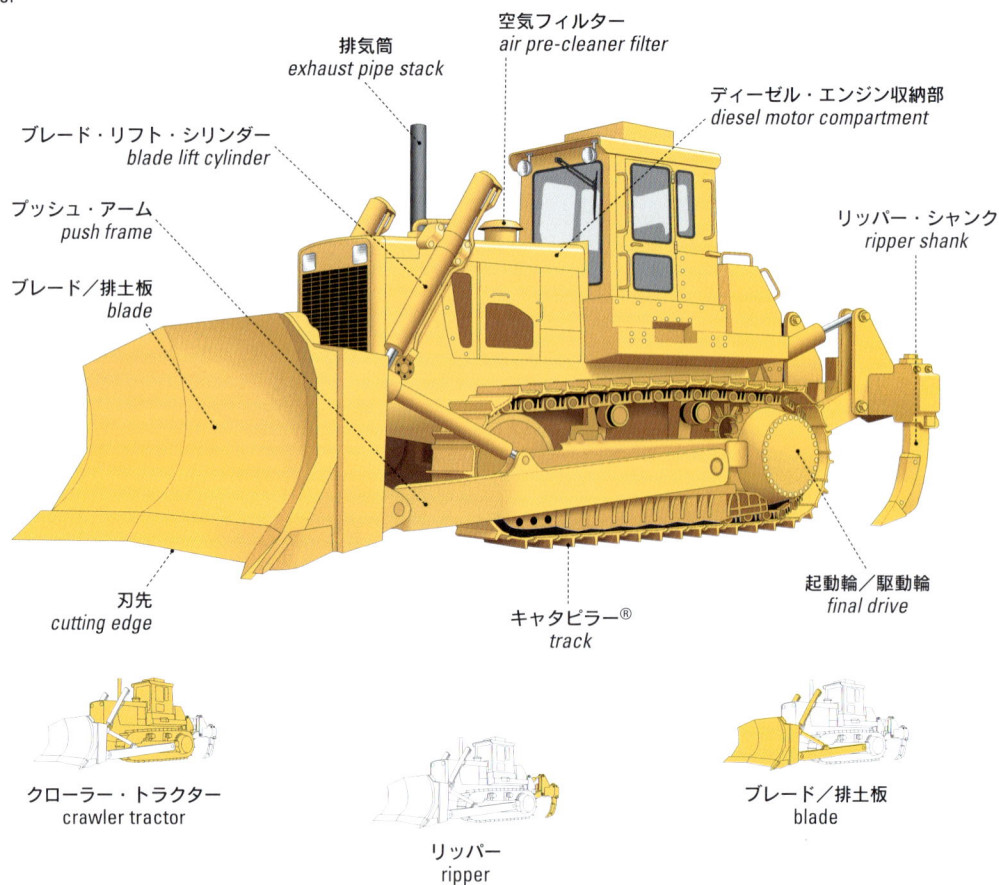

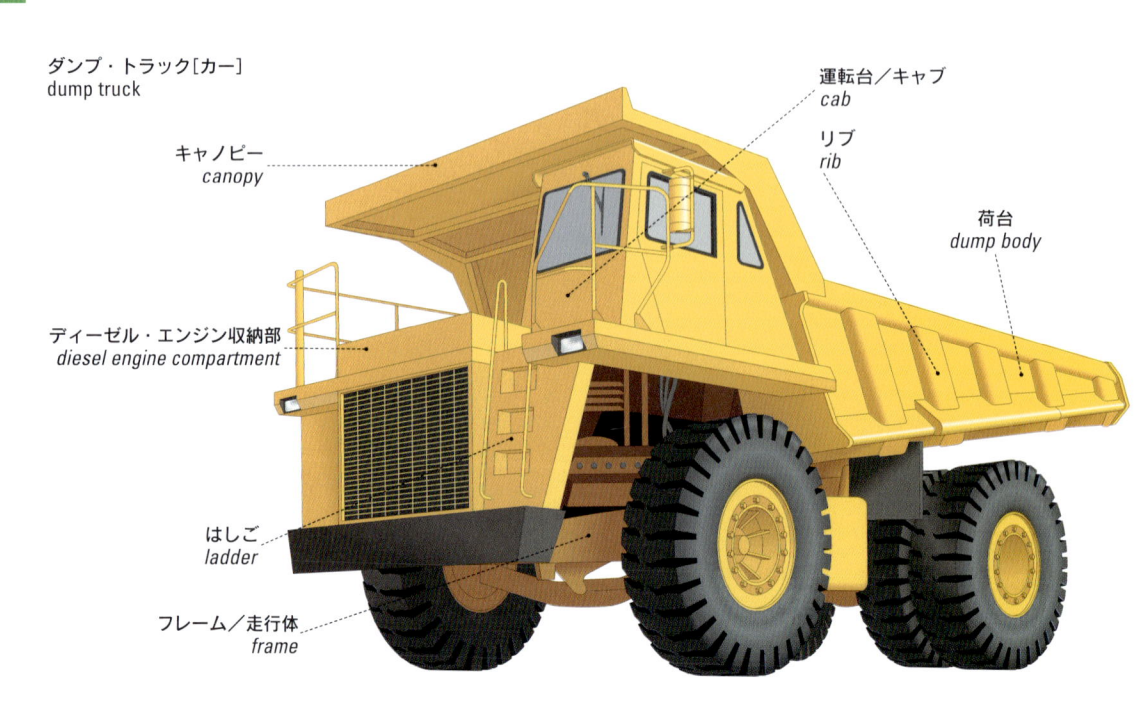

排気筒
exhaust pipe stack

空気フィルター
air pre-cleaner filter

ディーゼル・エンジン収納部
diesel motor compartment

ブレード・リフト・シリンダー
blade lift cylinder

プッシュ・アーム
push frame

リッパー・シャンク
ripper shank

ブレード／排土板
blade

刃先
cutting edge

キャタピラー®
track

起動輪／駆動輪
final drive

クローラー・トラクター
crawler tractor

リッパー
ripper

ブレード／排土板
blade

輸送と重機

ダンプ・トラック[カー]
dump truck

運転台／キャブ
cab

リブ
rib

キャノピー
canopy

荷台
dump body

ディーゼル・エンジン収納部
diesel engine compartment

はしご
ladder

フレーム／走行体
frame

美術 | FINE ARTS

今日では、美術と言えばグラフィック・アートと造形芸術を指します。人類の歴史が始まって以来、人間は自分の感情や識別した世界を、とりわけ絵画や彫刻といった技法で表現しています。画家や彫刻家はさまざまな材料や技術を自由に使うことができ、その使い方で自己の作品に独自のスタイルを確立することができます。

絵画と線画
PAINTING AND DRAWING

カラー・サークル／色彩円／色相環
color circle

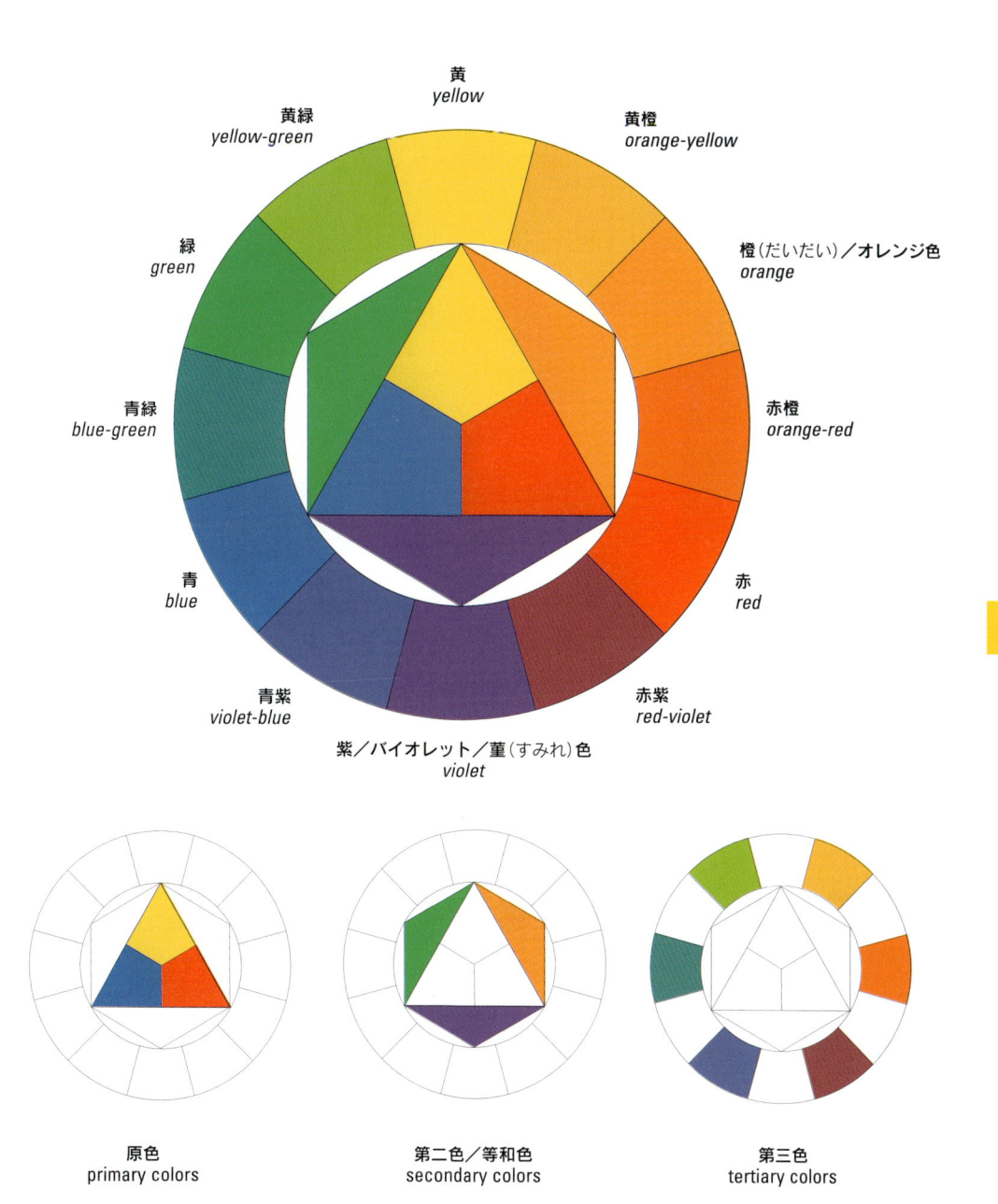

黄
yellow

黄緑
yellow-green

黄橙
orange-yellow

緑
green

橙（だいだい）／オレンジ色
orange

青緑
blue-green

赤橙
orange-red

青
blue

赤
red

青紫
violet-blue

赤紫
red-violet

紫／バイオレット／菫（すみれ）色
violet

原色
primary colors

第二色／等和色
secondary colors

第三色
tertiary colors

芸術

211

美術 | FINE ARTS

絵画用画材
drawing supplies

ハード[ドライ]パステル
dry pastel

フェルト・ペン
felt tip pen

木炭
charcoal

オイル[油性]パステル
oil pastel

ワックス・クレヨン
wax crayons

色鉛筆
colored pencils

絵画用画材
painting supplies

絵筆／丸筆
brush

水彩絵の具[グワッシュ]ケーキ
watercolor/gouache cakes

ペインティング・ナイフ
painting knife

油絵の具
oil paint

扇形筆
fan brush

水彩絵の具[グワッシュ]チューブ
watercolor/gouache tube

芸術

美術 | FINE ARTS

木彫
WOOD CARVING

工程
steps

彫刻具の例
examples of tools

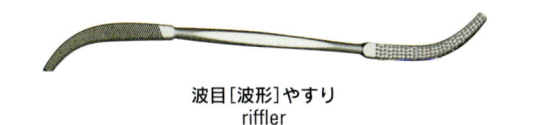

波目[波形]やすり
riffler

下絵
drawing

(切り出し)ナイフ
knife

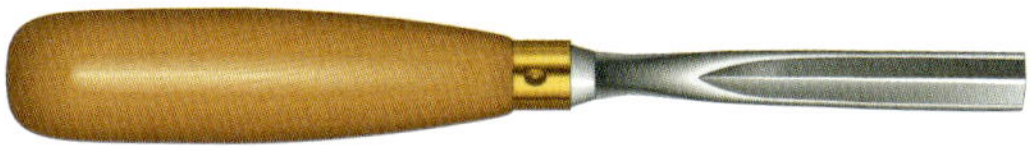

彫刻刀／ビュラン
block cutter

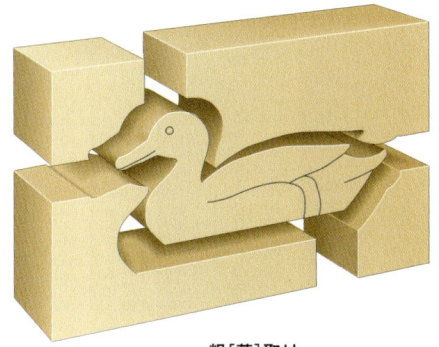

粗[荒]取り
roughing out

薄(刃)のみ
firmer chisel

彫刻／粗[荒]彫り
carving

石目[鬼目]やすり
rasp

仕上げ／完成
finishing

芸術

213

工芸 | CRAFTS

裁縫と編み物は昔からありました。つい最近まで手仕事は女性の仕事でした。衣服がまだ手製だった頃には、裁縫と編み物は実用に即したものでした。現代社会においては、この技巧を要する作業は、指の器用な人たちが熱中する趣味の要素をますます帯びてきました。

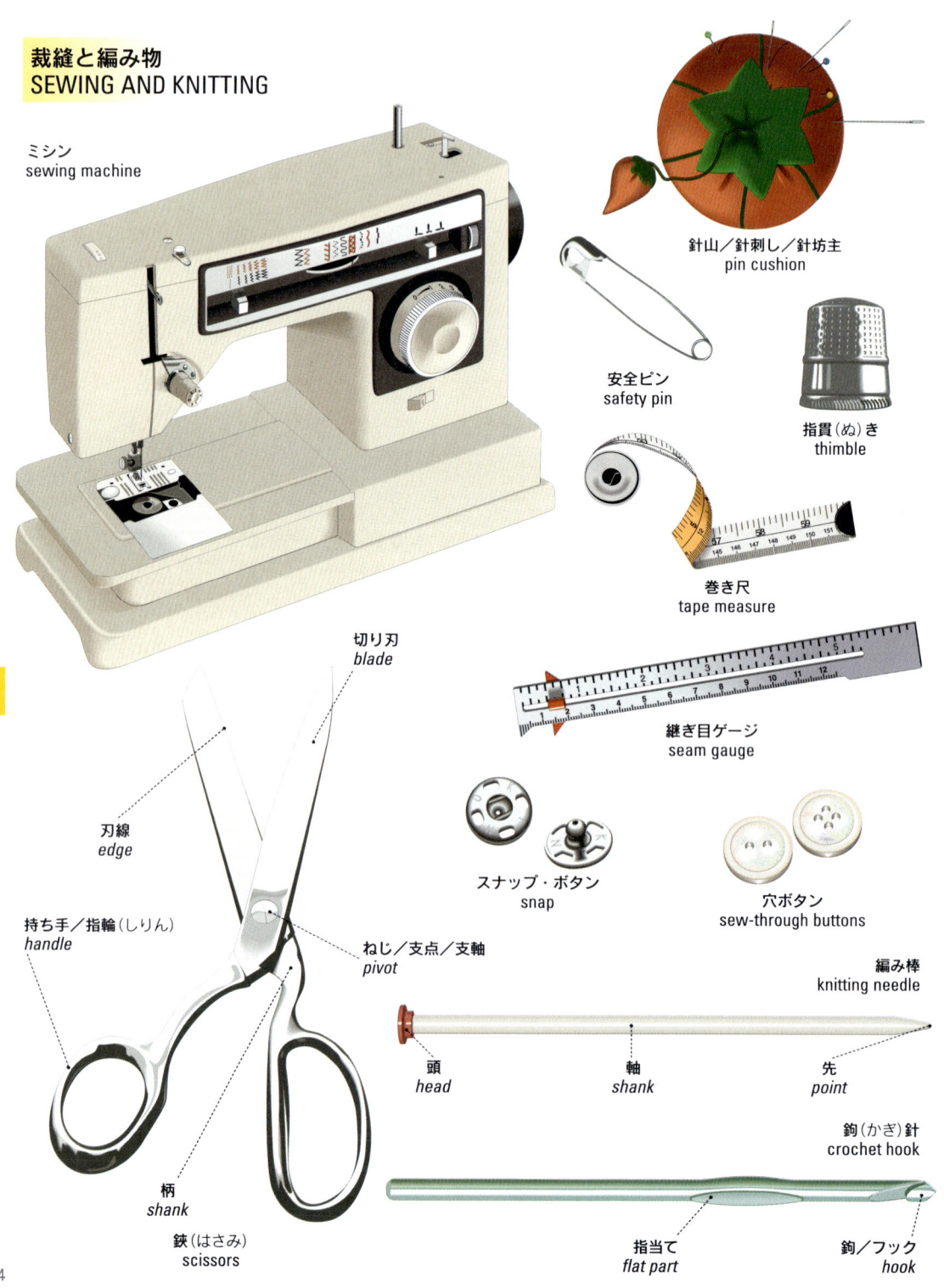

裁縫と編み物
SEWING AND KNITTING

ミシン
sewing machine

針山／針刺し／針坊主
pin cushion

安全ピン
safety pin

指貫（ぬ）き
thimble

巻き尺
tape measure

継ぎ目ゲージ
seam gauge

スナップ・ボタン
snap

穴ボタン
sew-through buttons

切り刃
blade

刃線
edge

持ち手／指輪（しりん）
handle

ねじ／支点／支軸
pivot

柄
shank

鋏（はさみ）
scissors

編み棒
knitting needle

頭
head

軸
shank

先
point

鉤（かぎ）針
crochet hook

指当て
flat part

鉤／フック
hook

家屋 | HOUSES

世界中の人々は身近な材料で自分のための避難所を造っています。このように伝統的な家屋は、鉄板、泥、石、木の枝、わら、芝生、氷結した雪などでできています。その土地の住まいのスタイルが典型的ではあっても、洋の東西を問わず現代の住まいの多くが似通っています。

伝統的な家屋
TRADITIONAL HOUSES

イグルー
igloo

イズバ／丸太小屋
isba

ユルト／パオ／ゲル
yurt

土小屋
hut

ウィグワム
wigwam

藁葺き（わらぶき）小屋
hut

ティピ（ー）
tepee

梁（りょう）
beam

はしご
ladder

杭上住居／高床(式)住居
pile dwelling

アドービ[アドビー]ハウス
adobe house

建築

家屋 | HOUSES

都市住宅
CITY HOUSES

棟割り住宅
semidetached cottage

平屋住宅
one-story house

二階建て住宅
two-story house

連棟住宅
town houses

高層アパート
high-rise apartment

共同住宅
condominiums

建築

建築物の作品 | ARCHITECTURAL WORKS

建築様式の違いを比較し、時代を反映する数多くの傑作に驚異の目を見張りながら、私たちは世界史をたどることができます。城塞の主塔のように実用第一であっても、神の方向に向かってそびえ立つ大聖堂の鐘楼のように象徴的であっても、建造物のあらゆる要素は用途に応じた機能を考慮に入れています。

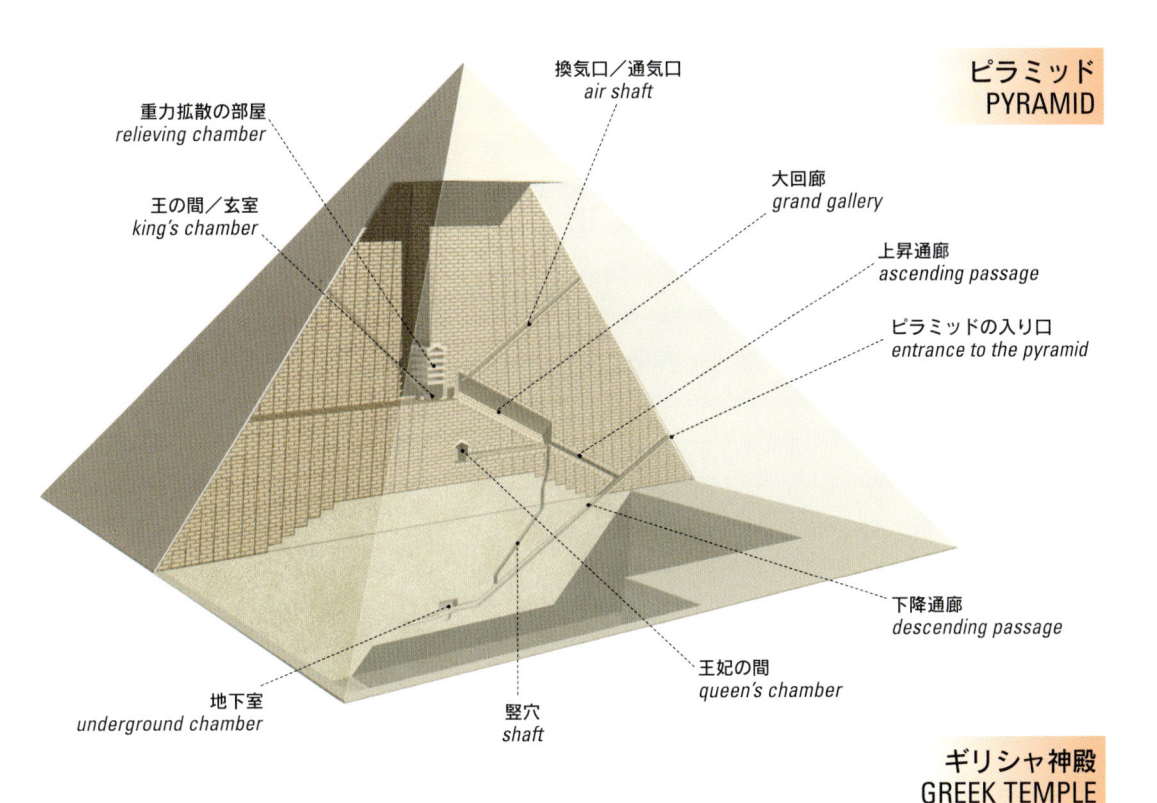

ピラミッド / PYRAMID

- 換気口／通気口 / air shaft
- 重力拡散の部屋 / relieving chamber
- 王の間／玄室 / king's chamber
- 大回廊 / grand gallery
- 上昇通廊 / ascending passage
- ピラミッドの入り口 / entrance to the pyramid
- 下降通廊 / descending passage
- 王妃の間 / queen's chamber
- 地下室 / underground chamber
- 竪穴 / shaft

ギリシャ神殿 / GREEK TEMPLE

- ティンパヌム／三角小間（こま） / tympanum
- アクロテリア／露盤／屋根飾り / acroterion
- アンテフィックス／瓦端飾り / antefix
- ペディメント／（三角）破風（はふ） / pediment
- 梁（はり）／木材 / timber
- 瓦（かわら） / tile
- レーキング［斜めの］コーニス／登り蛇腹 / sloping cornice
- コーニス／頂冠帯 / cornice
- フリーズ／中間帯 / frieze
- アーキトレーブ／台輪 / architrave
- コラム／柱身／円柱 / column
- クレピドーマ／基壇 / crepidoma
- エンタブラチュア／水平材 / entablature
- ナオス／セラ／ケルラ／神室／内室 / naos
- プロナオス／前室／前房／前廊 / pronaos
- （傾）斜路 / ramp
- （鉄）格子 / grille

建築

建築物の作品 | ARCHITECTURAL WORKS

古代ローマの住宅
ROMAN HOUSE

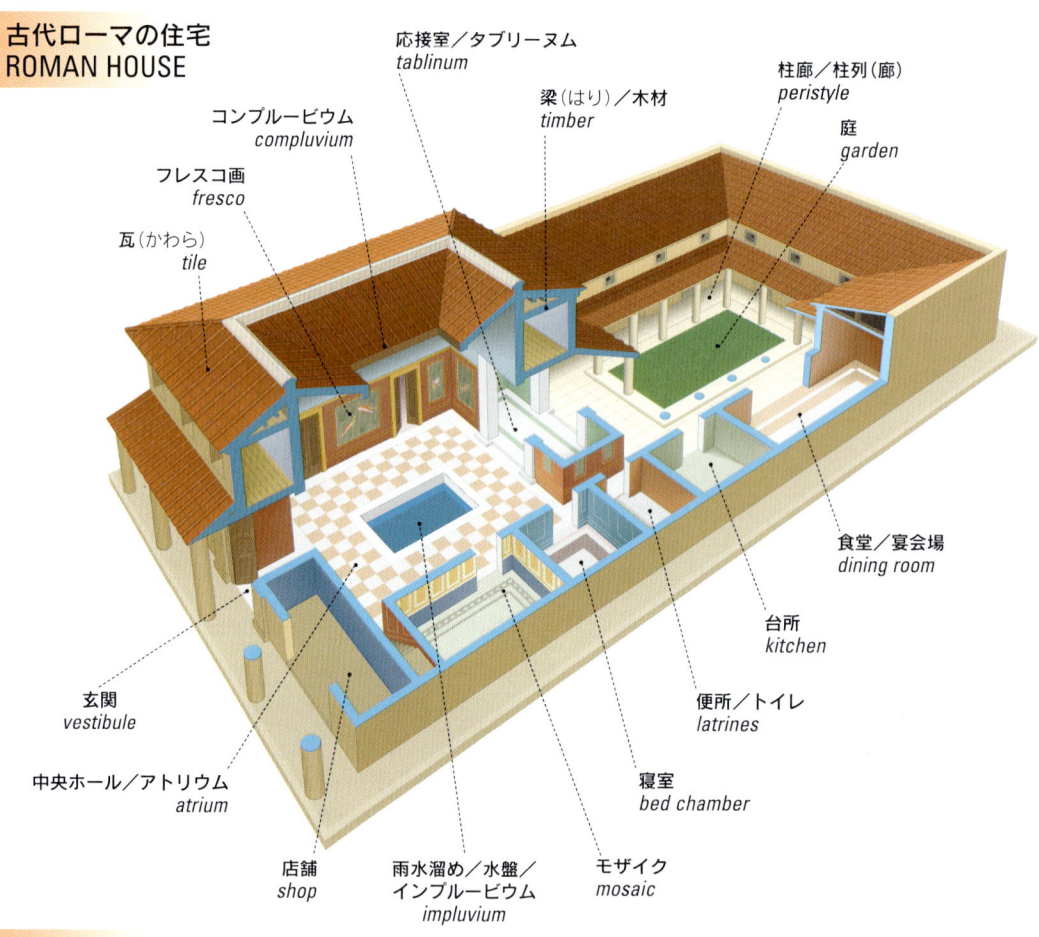

- コンプルービウム / compluvium
- 応接室／タブリーヌム / tablinum
- 梁（はり）／木材 / timber
- 柱廊／柱列（廊） / peristyle
- フレスコ画 / fresco
- 庭 / garden
- 瓦（かわら） / tile
- 食堂／宴会場 / dining room
- 台所 / kitchen
- 便所／トイレ / latrines
- 玄関 / vestibule
- 寝室 / bed chamber
- 中央ホール／アトリウム / atrium
- 店舗 / shop
- 雨水溜め／水盤／インプルービウム / impluvium
- モザイク / mosaic

古代ローマの円形競技場
ROMAN AMPHITHEATER

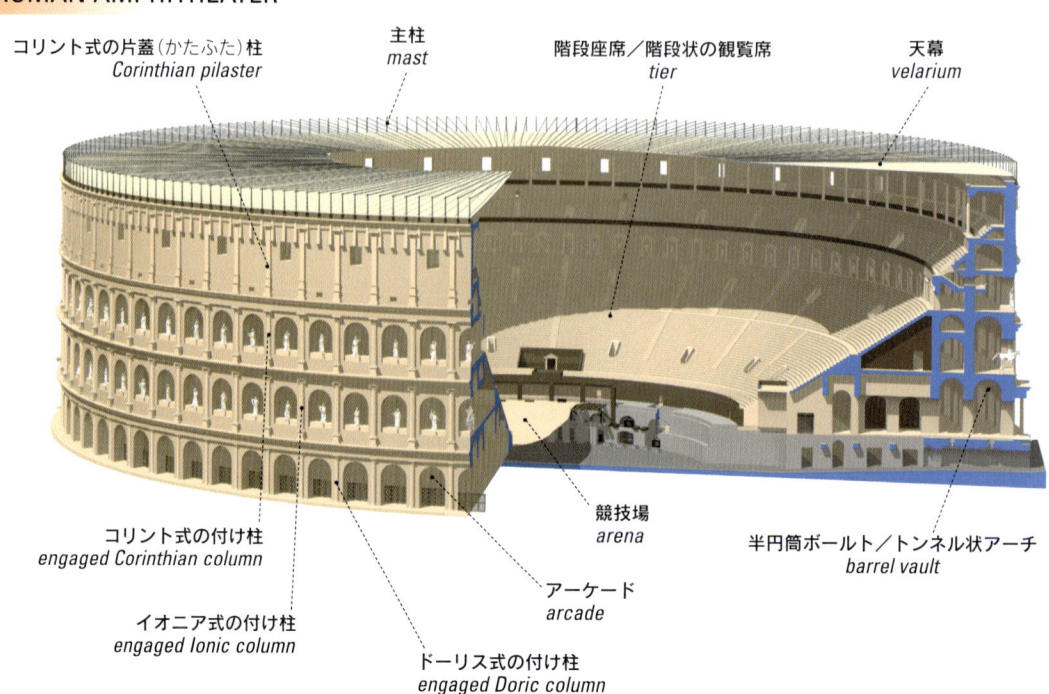

- コリント式の片蓋（かたふた）柱 / Corinthian pilaster
- 主柱 / mast
- 階段座席／階段状の観覧席 / tier
- 天幕 / velarium
- コリント式の付け柱 / engaged Corinthian column
- イオニア式の付け柱 / engaged Ionic column
- ドーリス式の付け柱 / engaged Doric column
- 競技場 / arena
- アーケード / arcade
- 半円筒ボールト／トンネル状アーチ / barrel vault

建築物の作品 | ARCHITECTURAL WORKS

モスク / MOSQUE

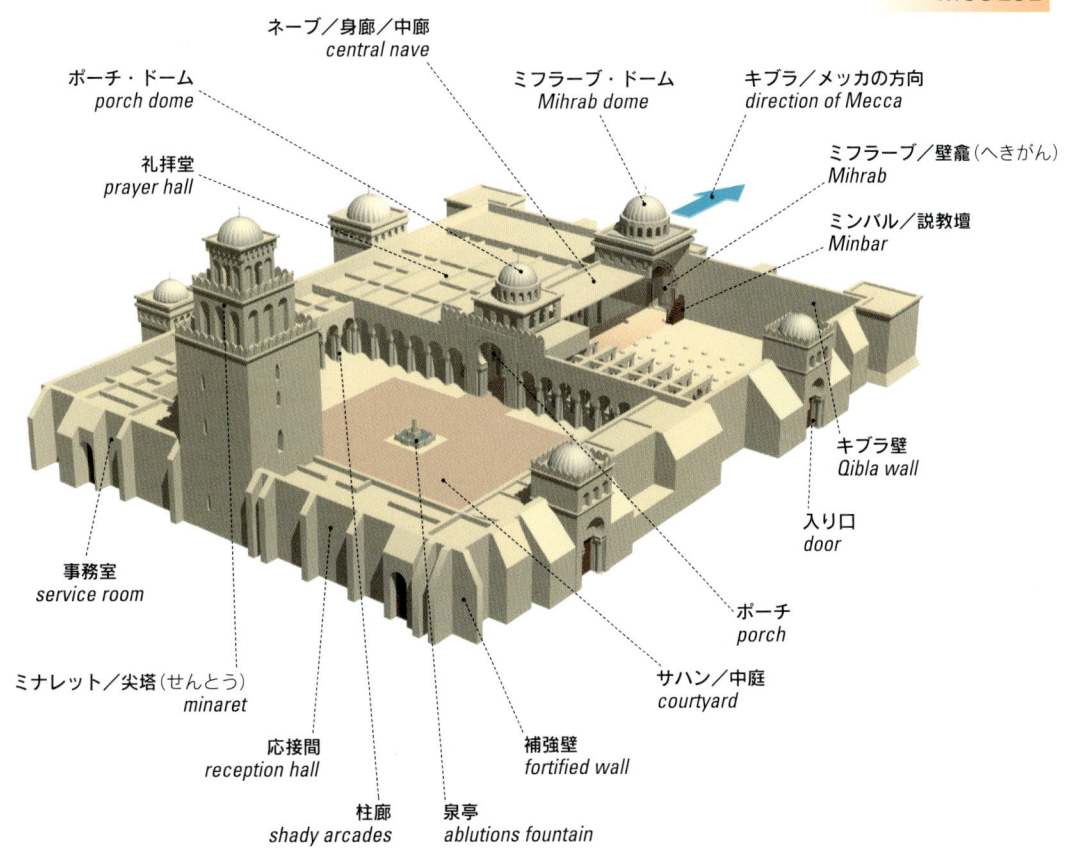

- ポーチ・ドーム / porch dome
- ネーブ／身廊／中廊 / central nave
- ミフラーブ・ドーム / Mihrab dome
- キブラ／メッカの方向 / direction of Mecca
- 礼拝堂 / prayer hall
- ミフラーブ／壁龕（へきがん） / Mihrab
- ミンバル／説教壇 / Minbar
- キブラ壁 / Qibla wall
- 入り口 / door
- 事務室 / service room
- ポーチ / porch
- サハン／中庭 / courtyard
- ミナレット／尖塔（せんとう） / minaret
- 応接間 / reception hall
- 柱廊 / shady arcades
- 泉亭 / ablutions fountain
- 補強壁 / fortified wall

アステカ神殿 / AZTEC TEMPLE

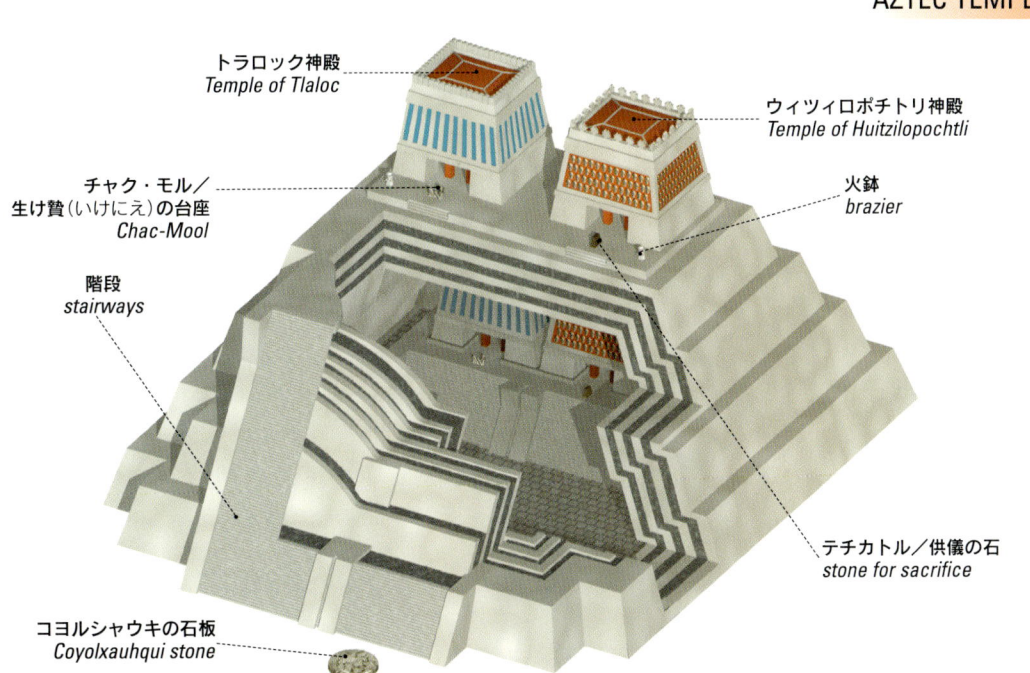

- トラロック神殿 / Temple of Tlaloc
- ウィツィロポチトリ神殿 / Temple of Huitzilopochtli
- チャク・モル／生け贄（いけにえ）の台座 / Chac-Mool
- 火鉢 / brazier
- 階段 / stairways
- テチカトル／供儀の石 / stone for sacrifice
- コヨルシャウキの石板 / Coyolxauhqui stone

建築

建築物の作品 | ARCHITECTURAL WORKS

城
CASTLE

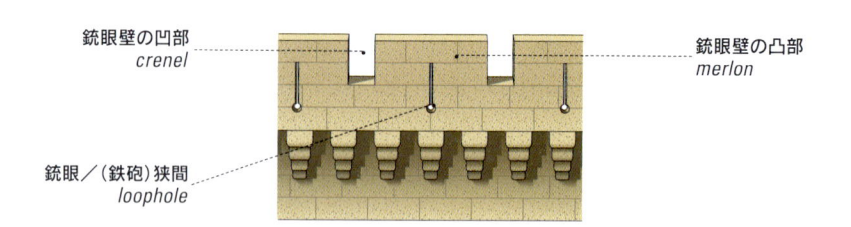

石落とし／刎(は)ね出し[突き出し]狭間(はざま)
machicolation

銃眼壁の凹部 crenel
銃眼壁の凸部 merlon
銃眼／(鉄砲)狭間 loophole

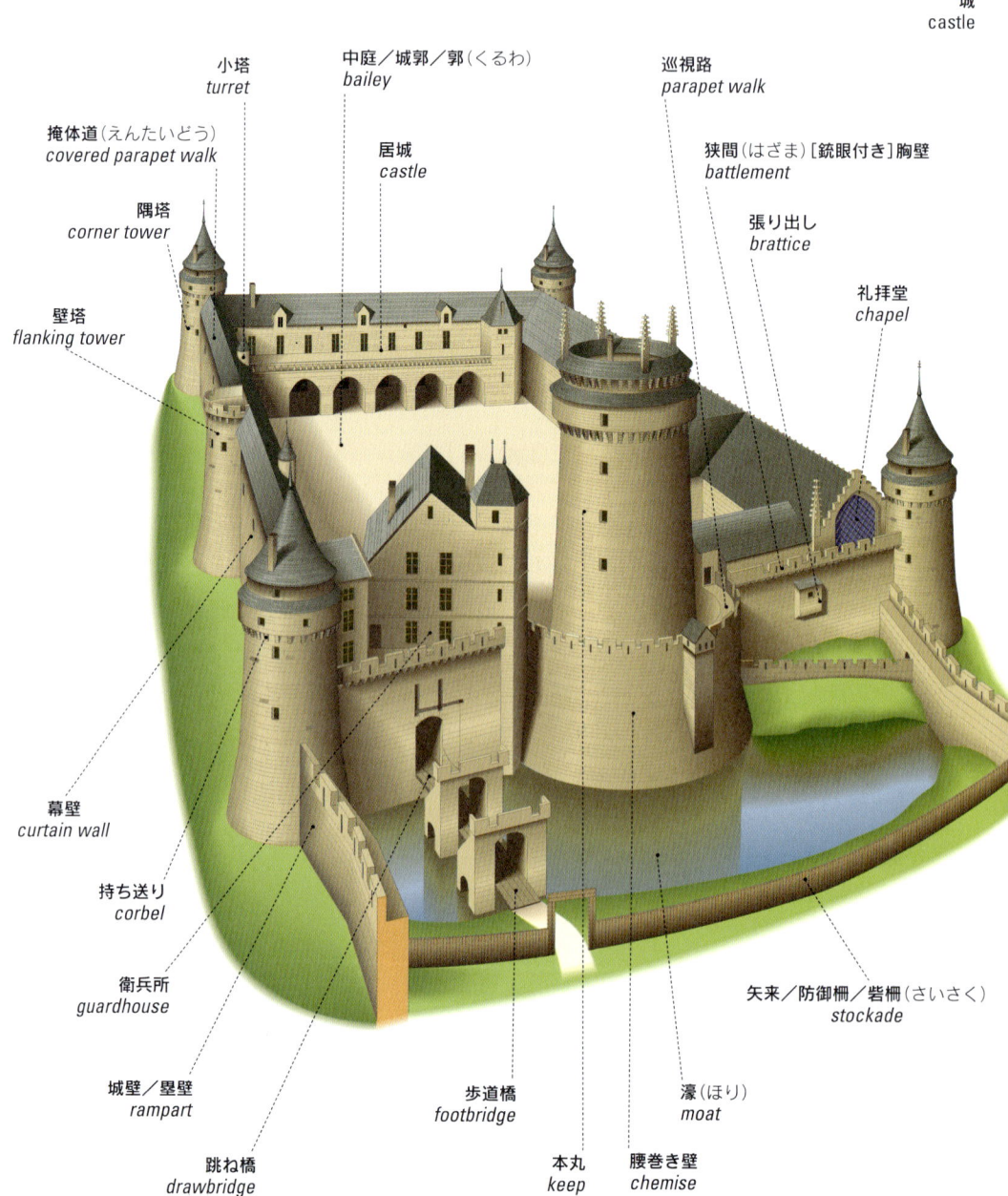

城 castle

小塔 turret
中庭／城郭／郭(くるわ) bailey
巡視路 parapet walk
掩体道(えんたいどう) covered parapet walk
居城 castle
狭間(はざま)[銃眼付き]胸壁 battlement
隅塔 corner tower
張り出し brattice
礼拝堂 chapel
壁塔 flanking tower
幕壁 curtain wall
持ち送り corbel
衛兵所 guardhouse
矢来／防御柵／砦柵(さいさく) stockade
城壁／塁壁 rampart
歩道橋 footbridge
濠(ほり) moat
本丸 keep
腰巻き壁 chemise
跳ね橋 drawbridge

建築

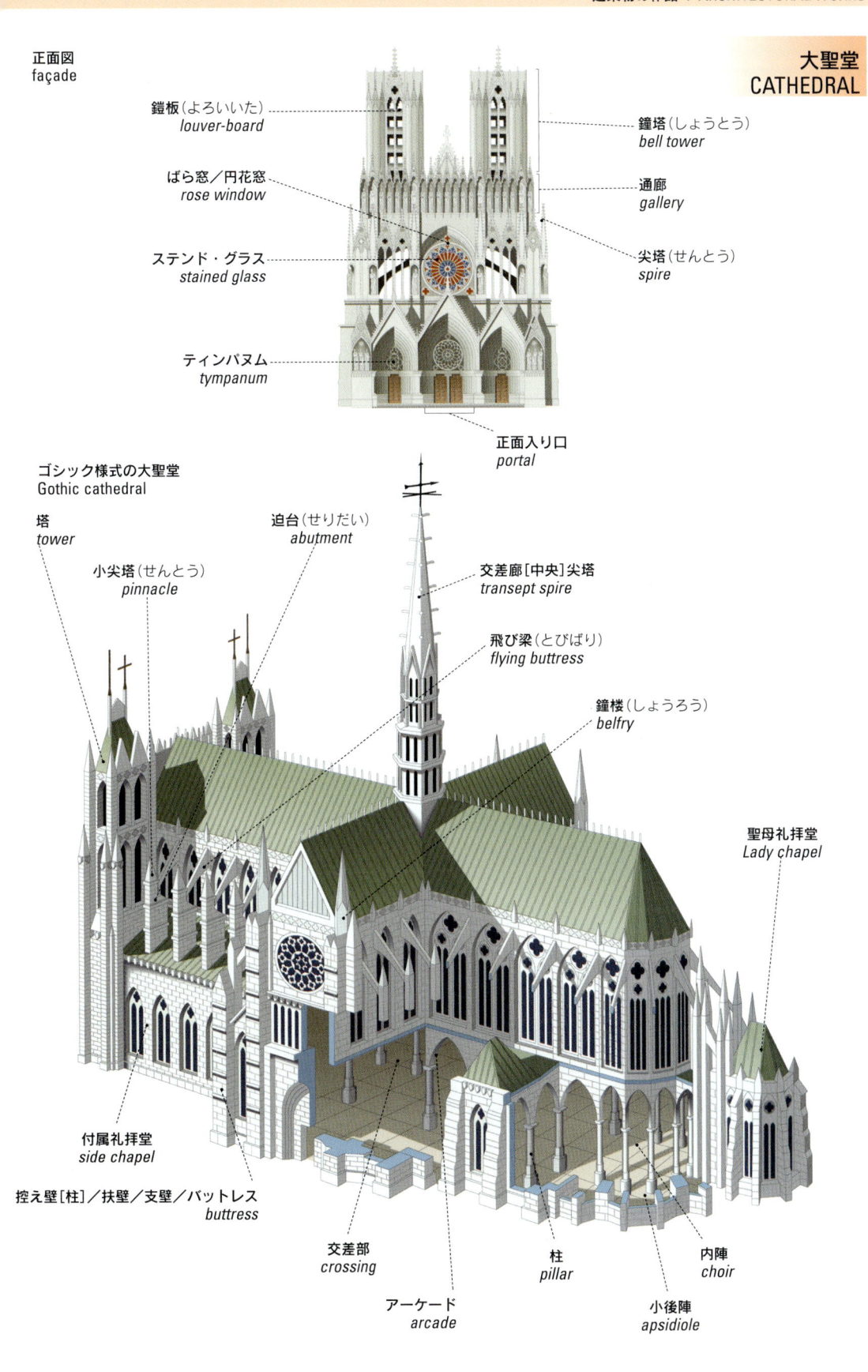

建築物の作品 | ARCHITECTURAL WORKS

大聖堂
CATHEDRAL

正面図
façade

鎧板（よろいいた）
louver-board

ばら窓／円花窓
rose window

ステンド・グラス
stained glass

ティンパヌム
tympanum

鐘塔（しょうとう）
bell tower

通廊
gallery

尖塔（せんとう）
spire

正面入り口
portal

ゴシック様式の大聖堂
Gothic cathedral

塔
tower

小尖塔（せんとう）
pinnacle

迫台（せりだい）
abutment

交差廊[中央]尖塔
transept spire

飛び梁（とびばり）
flying buttress

鐘楼（しょうろう）
belfry

聖母礼拝堂
Lady chapel

付属礼拝堂
side chapel

控え壁[柱]／扶壁／支壁／バットレス
buttress

交差部
crossing

アーケード
arcade

柱
pillar

内陣
choir

小後陣
apsidiole

建築

221

楽譜記号 | MUSICAL NOTATION

曲を演奏するのに必要な要素は、楽譜記号を使って五線譜上にすべて書き写されています。そのため音、長さ、高さを表す指示記号を数多く記した総譜は、演奏のための大事な道具と言うことができます。この共通の言語のお陰で、音楽家たちは言葉の壁を感じることなく一様に、数多くの楽曲を理解し、演奏できるのです。

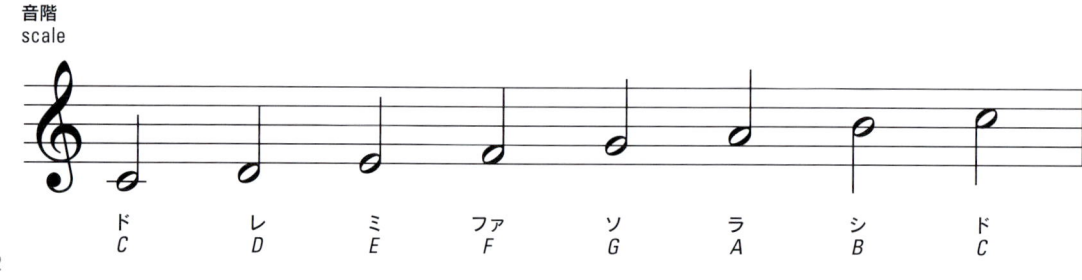

譜表 / staff
線間／間（かん） / space
線 / line
加線 / ledger line

音部記号 / clefs
ト音記号 / G clef
ヘ音記号 / F clef
ハ音記号 / C clef

拍子記号 / time signatures
2分の2拍子 / two-two time
4分の3拍子 / three-four time
4分の4拍子 / four-four time
縦線 / bar line
繰り返し記号 / repeat mark

音程 / intervals
1度 / unison
2度 / second
3度 / third
4度 / fourth
5度 / fifth
6度 / sixth
7度 / seventh
8度／オクターブ / octave

音階 / scale
ド / C　レ / D　ミ / E　ファ / F　ソ / G　ラ / A　シ / B　ド / C

楽譜記号 | MUSICAL NOTATION

休符 rest symbols

- 全休符 whole rest
- 2分休符 half rest
- 4分休符 quarter rest
- 8分休符 eighth rest
- 16分休符 sixteenth rest
- 32分休符 thirty-second rest
- 64分休符 sixty-fourth rest

装飾音 ornaments

- アッポジャトゥーラ／前打音／倚音（いおん） appoggiatura
- トリル／シェーク／顫音（せんおん） trill
- ターン／回音 turn
- モルデント／漣音（れんおん） mordent

音符 note symbols

- 全音符 whole note
- 2分音符 half note
- 4分音符 quarter note
- 8分音符 eighth note
- 16分音符 sixteenth note
- 32分音符 thirty-second note
- 64分音符 sixty-fourth note

臨時記号 accidentals

- 調号 key signature
- フラット／変記号 flat
- シャープ／嬰（えい）記号 sharp
- ナチュラル／本位記号 natural
- ダブル・シャープ／重嬰（じゅうえい）記号 double sharp
- ダブル・フラット／重変記号 double flat

その他の記号 other signs

- 和音 chord
- アクセント記号 accent mark
- タイ tie
- アルペッジョ arpeggio
- フェルマータ／延長記号／延音［延声］記号 pause

音楽

楽器 | MUSICAL INSTRUMENTS

あらゆる文明において、人類は演奏するのにさまざまな形の物を使いました。今日では、伝統的な物から電子的な物まで、あらゆる種類の音楽に合った数多くの楽器があります。このような楽器は弦楽器、管楽器、打楽器の3大グループに分けることができますが、鍵盤楽器といった別の基準によるグループ分けもできます。

伝統[民族]楽器
TRADITIONAL MUSICAL INSTRUMENTS

アコーディオン
accordion

トレブル[高音]レジスター
treble register

低音(域)用指盤[ボタン部]
bass keyboard

(空気)ボタン
button

高音(域)用鍵盤
treble keyboard

バス[低音]レジスター
bass register

鍵(けん)／キー
key

蛇腹
bellows

飾り板／グリル
grille

バグパイプ
bagpipes

ハーモニカ
harmonica

ドローン・パイプ
drone pipe

パンの笛／パンパイプ
panpipe

吹き込み管／ブローパイプ
blow pipe

空気袋／(パイプ)バッグ
windbag

指管／チャンター
chanter

バンジョー
banjo

楽器 | MUSICAL INSTRUMENTS

トーキング・ドラム
talking drum

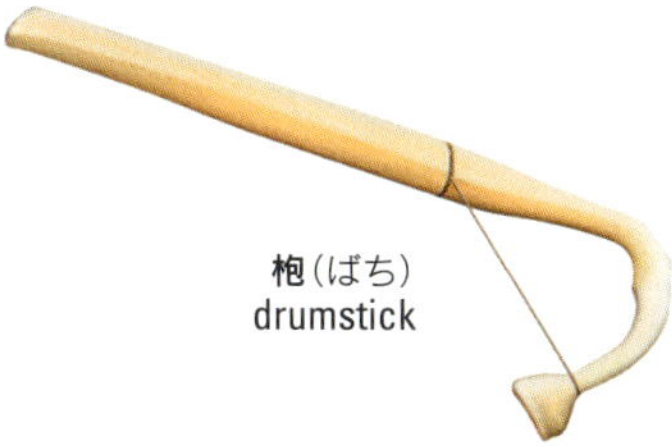

枹（ばち）
drumstick

ジェンベ／ジャンベ／ジンベ
djembe

マンドリン
mandolin

チター
zither

ピック／爪
plectrum

バラライカ
balalaika

リラ
lyre

コーラ
kora

音楽

225

楽器 | MUSICAL INSTRUMENTS

鍵盤楽器
KEYBOARD INSTRUMENTS

アップライト[竪(たて)型]ピアノ / upright piano

- 弦押さえ / pressure bar
- ハンマー・レール / hammer rail
- マフラー・フェルト / muffler felt
- ハンマー / hammer
- チューニング・ピン / tuning pin
- ピン板 / pin block
- 本体／ボディー / case
- 鍵(けん)／キー / key
- 鍵盤台 / keybed
- ペダル・レール / pedal rod
- 長駒(ながごま) / treble bridge
- 弦 / strings
- 鍵盤 / keyboard
- シフト[ソフト]ペダル / soft pedal
- マフラー・ペダル／弱音[消音]ペダル / muffler pedal
- ダンパー[ラウド]ペダル / damper pedal
- 短駒(たんごま) / bass bridge
- 鉄骨 / metal frame
- 響板／共鳴板 / soundboard

コンサート・グランド / concert grand

ハープシコード／チェンバロ／クラブサン / harpsichord

オルガン / organ

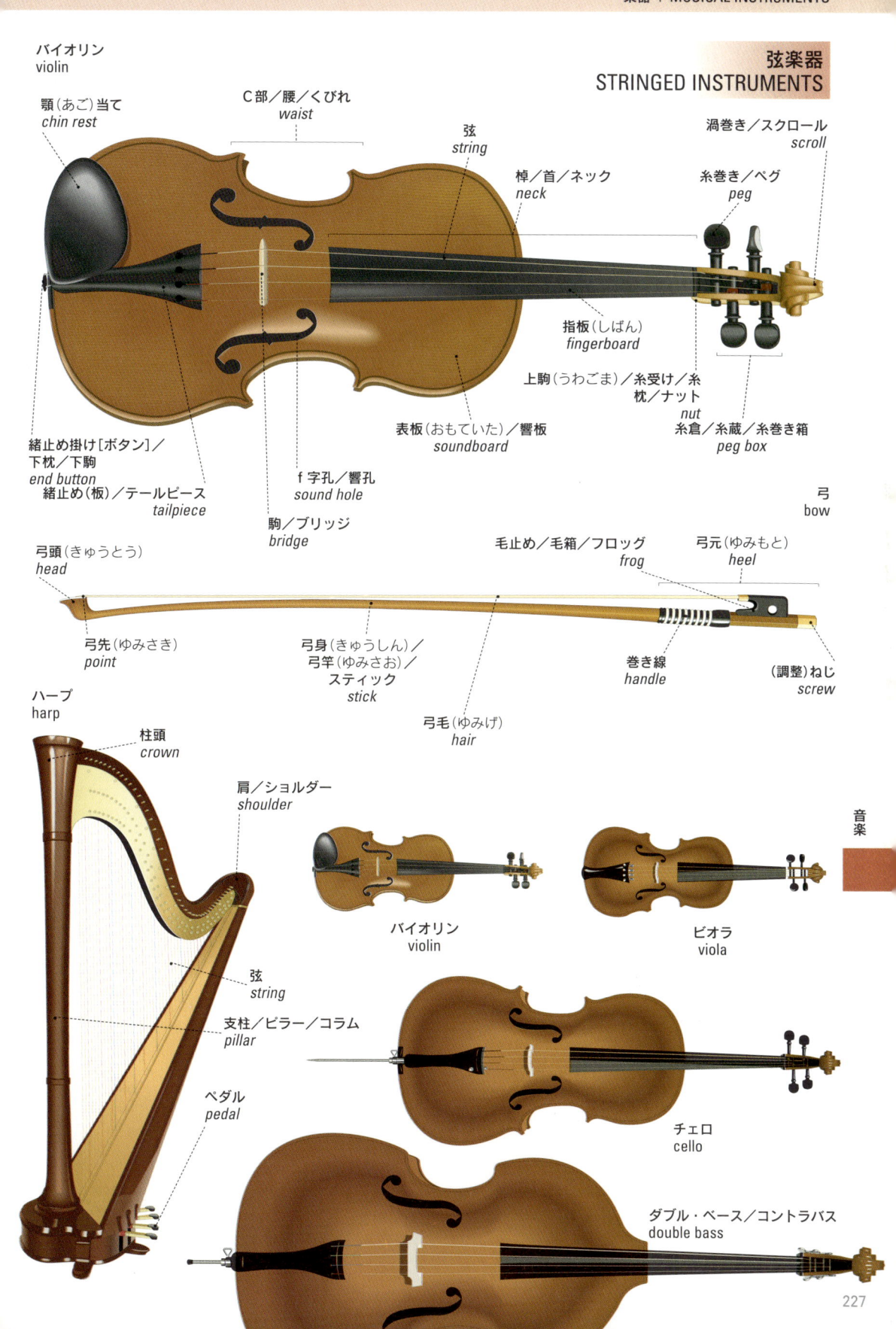

楽器 | MUSICAL INSTRUMENTS

弦楽器
STRINGED INSTRUMENTS

バイオリン / violin

- 顎(あご)当て / chin rest
- C部／腰／くびれ / waist
- 弦 / string
- 棹／首／ネック / neck
- 渦巻き／スクロール / scroll
- 糸巻き／ペグ / peg
- 指板(しばん) / fingerboard
- 上駒(うわごま)／糸受け／糸枕／ナット / nut
- 糸倉／糸蔵／糸巻き箱 / peg box
- 緒止め掛け[ボタン]／下枕／下駒 / end button
- 緒止め(板)／テールピース / tailpiece
- 表板(おもていた)／響板 / soundboard
- f字孔／響孔 / sound hole
- 駒／ブリッジ / bridge

弓 / bow

- 弓頭(きゅうとう) / head
- 弓先(ゆみさき) / point
- 弓身(きゅうしん)／弓竿(ゆみさお)／スティック / stick
- 毛止め／毛箱／フロッグ / frog
- 弓元(ゆみもと) / heel
- 巻き線 / handle
- (調整)ねじ / screw
- 弓毛(ゆみげ) / hair

ハープ / harp

- 柱頭 / crown
- 肩／ショルダー / shoulder
- 弦 / string
- 支柱／ピラー／コラム / pillar
- ペダル / pedal

バイオリン / violin

ビオラ / viola

チェロ / cello

ダブル・ベース／コントラバス / double bass

音楽

227

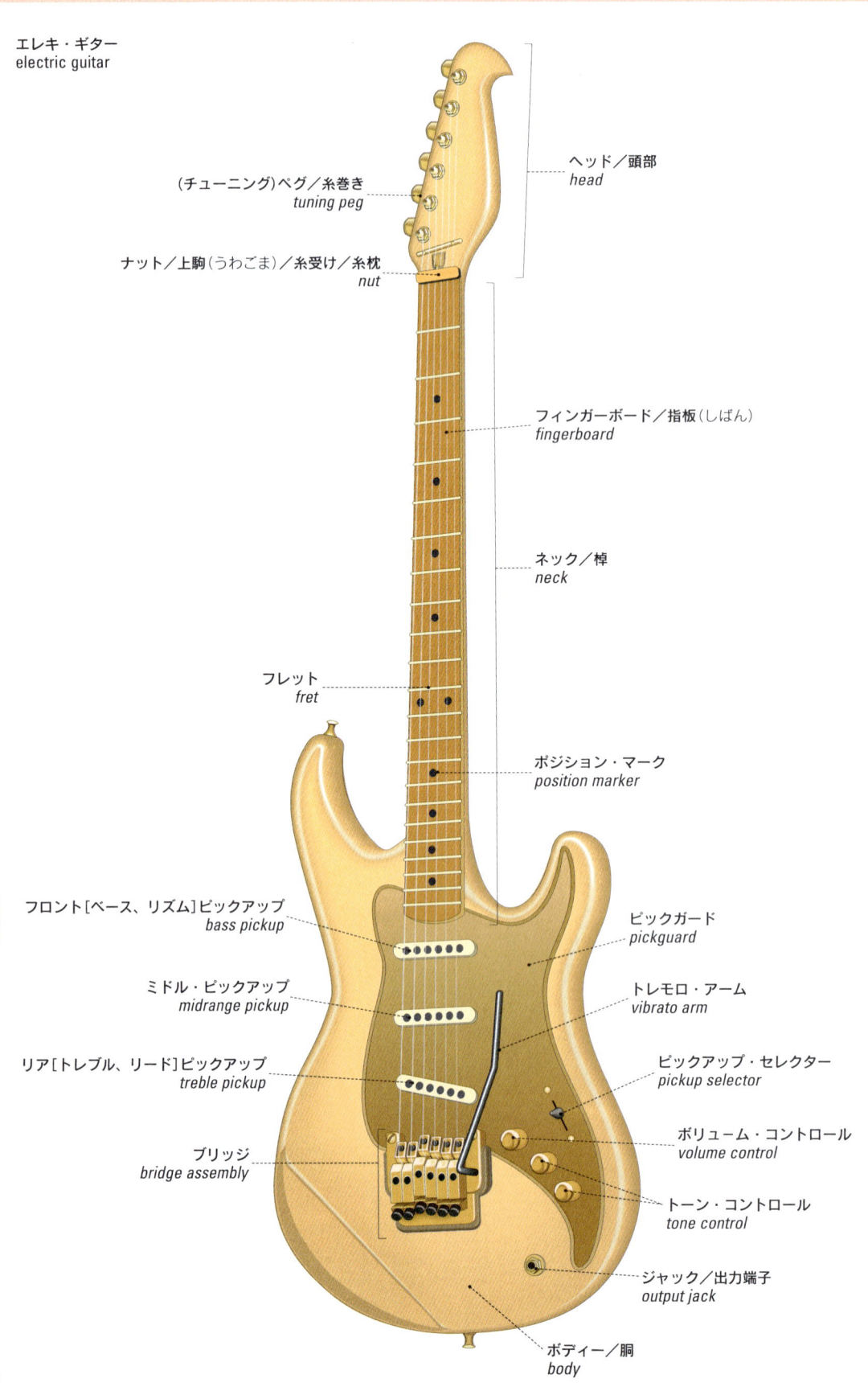

楽器 | MUSICAL INSTRUMENTS

エレキ・ギター
electric guitar

（チューニング）ペグ／糸巻き
tuning peg

ナット／上駒（うわごま）／糸受け／糸枕
nut

ヘッド／頭部
head

フィンガーボード／指板（しばん）
fingerboard

ネック／棹
neck

フレット
fret

ポジション・マーク
position marker

フロント［ベース、リズム］ピックアップ
bass pickup

ミドル・ピックアップ
midrange pickup

リア［トレブル、リード］ピックアップ
treble pickup

ブリッジ
bridge assembly

ピックガード
pickguard

トレモロ・アーム
vibrato arm

ピックアップ・セレクター
pickup selector

ボリューム・コントロール
volume control

トーン・コントロール
tone control

ジャック／出力端子
output jack

ボディー／胴
body

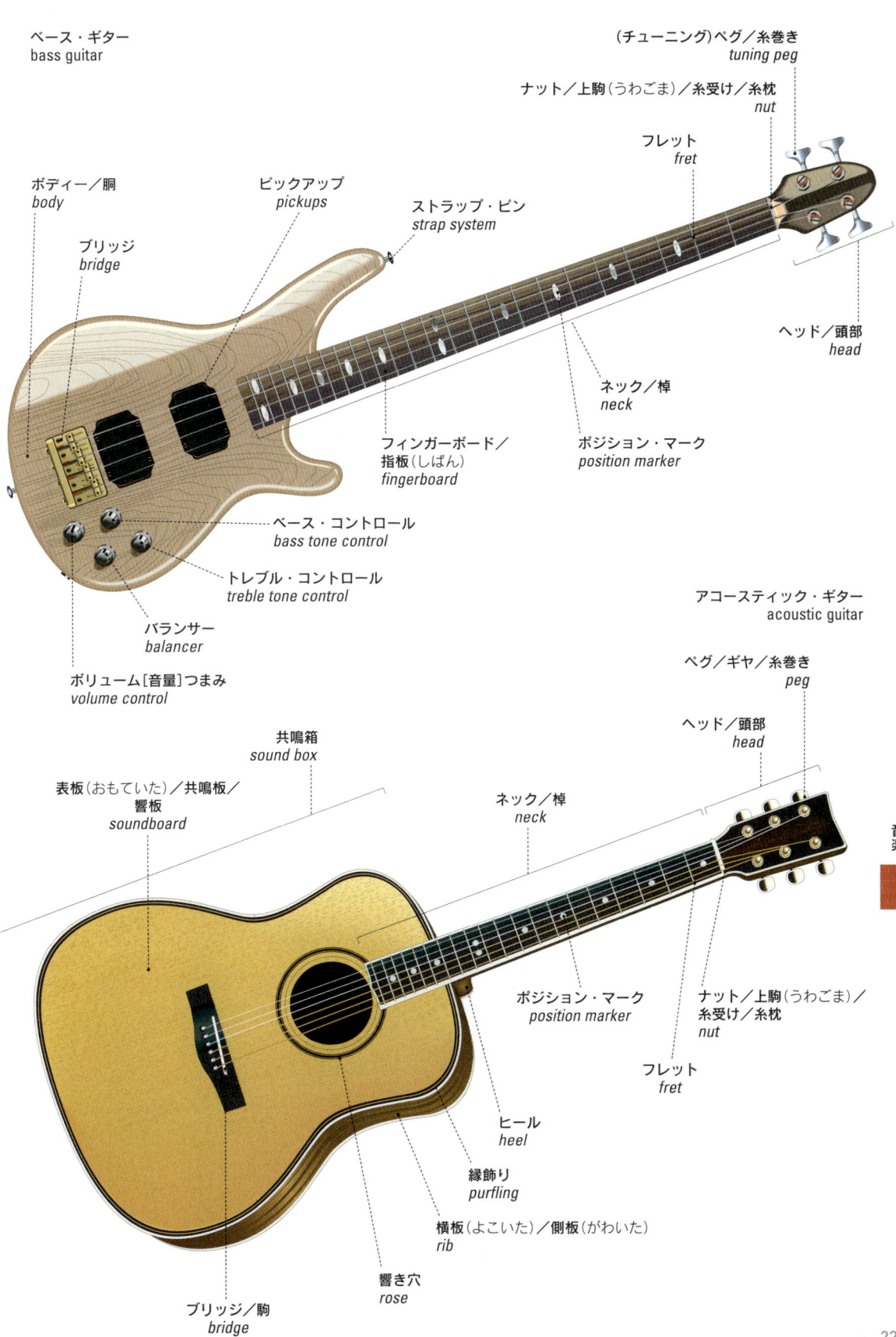

楽器 | MUSICAL INSTRUMENTS

ベース・ギター
bass guitar

ボディー／胴
body

ピックアップ
pickups

ストラップ・ピン
strap system

（チューニング）ペグ／糸巻き
tuning peg

ナット／上駒（うわごま）／糸受け／糸枕
nut

フレット
fret

ブリッジ
bridge

ネック／棹
neck

ヘッド／頭部
head

フィンガーボード／指板（しばん）
fingerboard

ポジション・マーク
position marker

ベース・コントロール
bass tone control

トレブル・コントロール
treble tone control

バランサー
balancer

ボリューム［音量］つまみ
volume control

共鳴箱
sound box

アコースティック・ギター
acoustic guitar

ペグ／ギヤ／糸巻き
peg

ヘッド／頭部
head

表板（おもていた）／共鳴板／響板
soundboard

ネック／棹
neck

ポジション・マーク
position marker

ナット／上駒（うわごま）／糸受け／糸枕
nut

フレット
fret

ヒール
heel

縁飾り
purfling

横板（よこいた）／側板（がわいた）
rib

響き穴
rose

ブリッジ／駒
bridge

音楽

楽器 | MUSICAL INSTRUMENTS

管楽器
WIND INSTRUMENTS

トランペット
trumpet

ピストン・バルブ／バルブ・ボタン
finger button

小指掛け／第2トリガー
little finger hook

ベル
bell

マウス・パイプ／吹き込み管
mouthpipe

指掛け（リング）／第3トリガー
ring

マウスピース・レシーバー
mouthpiece receiver

マウスピース／吹き口／歌口
mouthpiece

第1抜き差し管
first valve slide

主管抜き差し管／チューニング・スライド
tuning slide

親指掛け／第1トリガー
thumb hook

第3抜き差し管
third valve slide

ウォーター・キー／唾（つば）抜き
water key

バルブ
valve

バルブ・ケース［ケーシング］
valve casing

第2抜き差し管
second valve slide

コルネット
cornet

ビューグル
bugle

ミュート／弱音器
mute

トロンボーン
trombone

フレンチ・ホルン／ダブル・ホルン
French horn

サクソルン／ユーフォニウム
saxhorn

チューバ
tuba

230

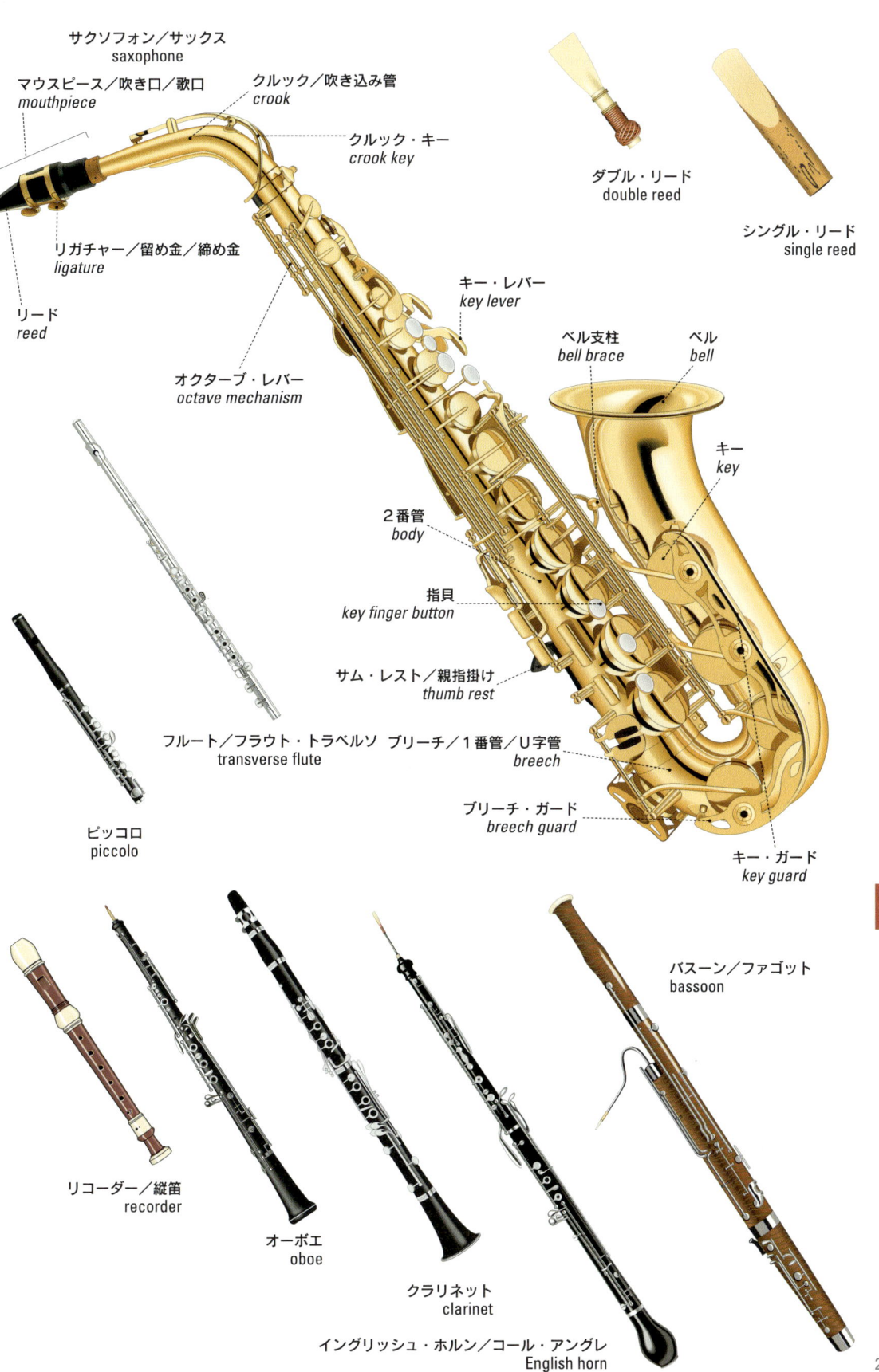

楽器 | **MUSICAL INSTRUMENTS**

サクソフォン／サックス
saxophone

マウスピース／吹き口／歌口
mouthpiece

クルック／吹き込み管
crook

クルック・キー
crook key

ダブル・リード
double reed

シングル・リード
single reed

リガチャー／留め金／締め金
ligature

リード
reed

キー・レバー
key lever

ベル支柱
bell brace

ベル
bell

オクターブ・レバー
octave mechanism

キー
key

２番管
body

指貝
key finger button

サム・レスト／親指掛け
thumb rest

フルート／フラウト・トラベルソ
transverse flute

ブリーチ／１番管／U字管
breech

ブリーチ・ガード
breech guard

ピッコロ
piccolo

キー・ガード
key guard

音楽

バスーン／ファゴット
bassoon

リコーダー／縦笛
recorder

オーボエ
oboe

クラリネット
clarinet

イングリッシュ・ホルン／コール・アングレ
English horn

231

楽器 | MUSICAL INSTRUMENTS

打楽器
PERCUSSION INSTRUMENTS

- ドラムス／ドラム・セット drums
- シンバル cymbal
- ハイ・ハット・シンバル high-hat cymbal
- トップ／打面 batter head
- スネア・ドラム／小太鼓 snare drum
- バス・ドラム bass drum
- 三脚 tripod stand
- タム・タム tom-tom
- フロア・タム／テナー・ドラム tenor drum
- ビーター／マレット mallet
- ペダル pedal
- ばち／スティック sticks
- ワイヤー・ブラシ wire brush
- ばち／マレット mallets
- ビーター／打棒 metal rod
- トライアングル triangle
- 橇（そり）の鈴／スレイ・ベル sleigh bells
- 釣り鐘状の鈴 set of bells
- カスタネット castanets
- シストルム sistrum
- ティンパニ／ケトル・ドラム kettledrum
- ボンゴ bongos
- ジングル jingle
- タンバリン tambourine
- シロフォン／ザイロフォン／木琴 xylophone

楽器 | MUSICAL INSTRUMENTS

電子楽器
ELECTRONIC INSTRUMENTS

シンセサイザー
synthesizer

システム・ボタン
system buttons

ボリューム・コントロール
volume control

データ・エントリー・ダイヤル
fine data entry control

ディスク・ドライブ
disk drive

機能表示窓［画面］／
液晶ディスプレイ
function display

シーケンサー・コントロール
sequencer control

データ・エントリー・スライダー
fast data entry control

プログラム・セレクター
program selector

音声編集ボタン
voice edit buttons

モジュレーション・ホイール
modulation wheel

キーボード／鍵盤
keyboard

ピッチ・ホイール
pitch wheel

ウインド・シンセサイザー・コントローラー
wind synthesizer controller

マウスピース
mouthpiece

電子ドラム・パッド
electronic drum pad

キー／鍵（けん）
keys

電子ピアノ
electronic piano

譜面台［立て］
music stand

リズム設定ボタン／リズム・セレクター
rhythm selector

音量調節つまみ／ボリューム・コントロール
volume control

テンポ調節つまみ／
テンポ・コントロール
tempo control

電源スイッチ
power switch

ヘッドホン端子
headphone jack

音色（選択）ボタン
voice selector

シフト［ソフト］ペダル
soft pedal

ダンパー［ラウド］ペダル
damper pedal

音楽

233

交響[管弦]楽団 | SYMPHONY ORCHESTRA

オーケストラは一緒に演奏する音楽家の集まりです。集まった楽器の数や種類によって様々なタイプの合奏団があります。管弦楽団あるいは交響楽団は、１００から１５０の楽器を弦楽器、木管楽器、金管楽器、打楽器といった４つの部門に分けた、最も規模の大きい合奏団と言うことができます。楽器の奏者は全員、指揮者の下で演奏します。

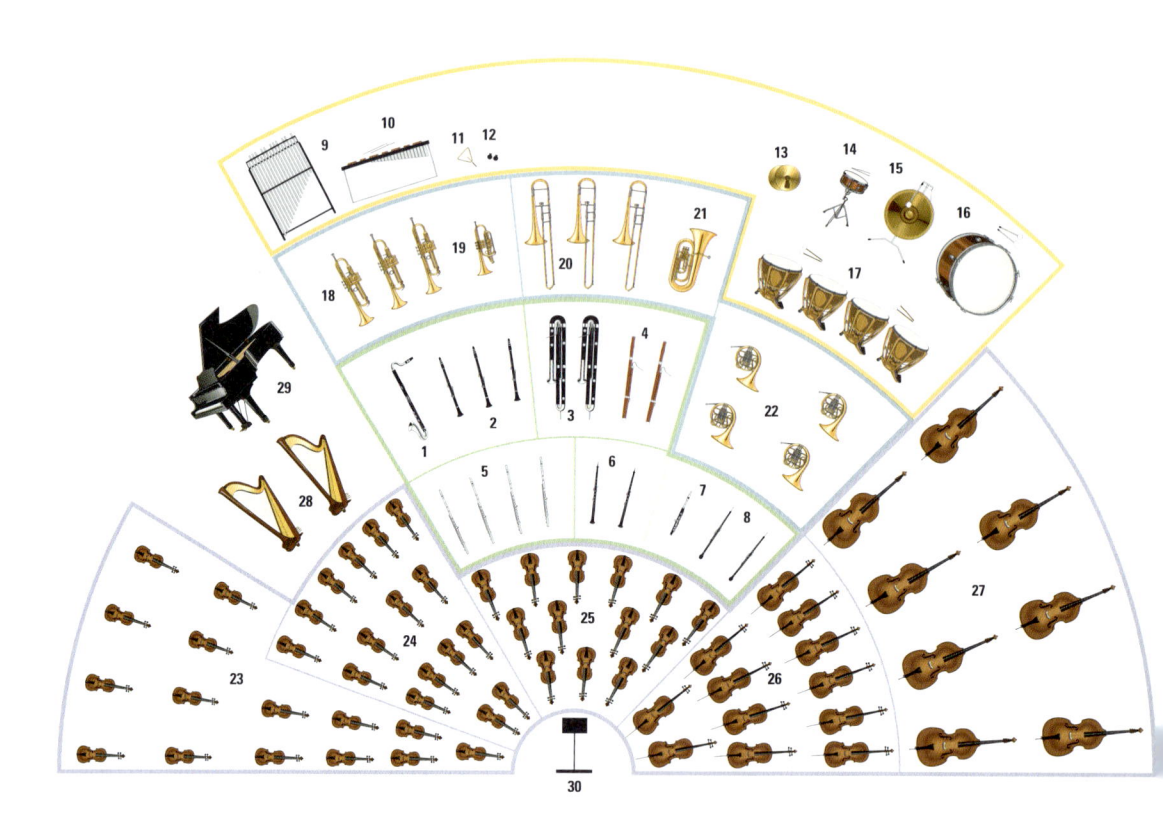

木管楽器の仲間／木管楽器群
woodwind family

1. バス・クラリネット / bass clarinet
2. クラリネット / clarinets
3. コントラバスーン[ファゴット] / contrabassoons
4. バスーン／ファゴット / bassoons
5. フルート / flutes
6. オーボエ / oboes
7. ピッコロ / piccolo
8. イングリッシュ・ホルン／コール・アングレ / English horns

打楽器
percussion instruments

9. チャイム／組み鐘 / tubular bells
10. シロフォン／木琴 / xylophone
11. トライアングル / triangle
12. カスタネット / castanets
13. シンバル / cymbals
14. スネア・ドラム／小太鼓 / snare drum
15. どら／ゴング / gong
16. バス・ドラム／大太鼓 / bass drum
17. ティンパニ / timpani

金管楽器の仲間／金管楽器群
brass family

18. トランペット / trumpets
19. コルネット / cornet
20. トロンボーン / trombones
21. チューバ / tuba
22. フレンチ・ホルン／ダブル・ホルン / French horns

バイオリンの仲間／弦楽器群
violin family

23. 第１バイオリン / first violins
24. 第２バイオリン / second violins
25. ビオラ / violas
26. チェロ / cellos
27. ダブル・ベース／コントラバス / double basses

28. ハープ / harps
29. ピアノ / piano
30. 指揮台 / conductor's podium

音楽

写真 | PHOTOGRAPHY

器械を使って写真を撮るときには、物体から出た光は感光性のフィルム上に像を結びます。光によって一度感光すると、フィルムは現像され、ネガとなります。ネガから白い印画紙上に投影されて、撮影された場面の像が忠実に浮かび上がります。今日ではさまざまなカメラが出回っていますが、ごく最新の物としてはデジタル・カメラが有名です。

一眼レフ・カメラ
single-lens reflex (SLR) camera

フィルム巻き戻しボタン
film rewind knob

アクセサリー・シュー
accessory shoe

表示パネル
control panel

ホット・シュー接点／ストロボ接点／X接点
hot-shoe contact

機能選択ダイヤル
command control dial

フィルム巻き上げモード・ボタン
film advance mode

フィルム感度設定ボタン
film speed

露出モード・ボタン
exposure mode

レンズ・キャップ
lens cap

リモコン端末
remote control terminal

ズーム・レンズ
zoom lens

フォーカス・モード切替ボタン
focus mode selector

カメラ・ボディー[本体]
camera body

シャッター・レリーズ・ボタン
shutter release button

(対物)レンズ
objective lens

カメラ用アクセサリー[付属品]
photographic accessories

ストロボ／フラッシュ
electronic flash

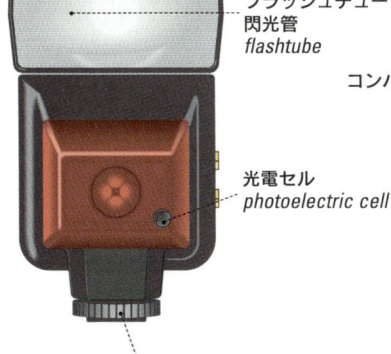

フラッシュチューブ／閃光管
flashtube

コンパクト・フラッシュ・メモリー・カード
compact flash memory card

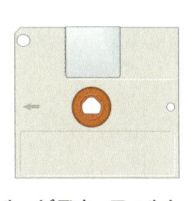

スチ(ー)ル・ビデオ・フィルム・ディスク
still video film disk

光電セル
photoelectric cell

取り付け脚
mounting foot

カートリッジ・フィルム
cartridge film

フィルム・ディスク
film disk

通信

写真 | PHOTOGRAPHY

スチ(ー)ル・カメラの例
examples of still cameras

ポケット・カメラ
pocket camera

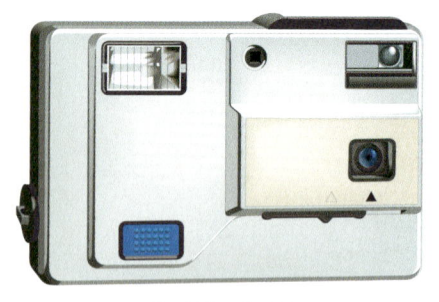

ディスク・カメラ
disk camera

ポラロイド®・カメラ
Polaroid® camera

レンジファインダー・カメラ
rangefinder

水中カメラ
underwater camera

デジタル・カメラ
digital camera

使い捨てカメラ／レンズ付きフィルム
disposable camera

ビュー・カメラ
view camera

ラジオ | RADIO

ラジオは遠く離れた場所で起きた重要な出来事を実況中継します。ラジオ放送では、司会者の声がマイクを通して電気信号に変換され、この信号はさらにラジオ放送局によってラジオ電波に変換されます。ラジオ受信機が最終的にこの電波を受信し、音に変えるのです。

ラジオ（スタジオとコントロール・ルーム）
radio (studio and control room)

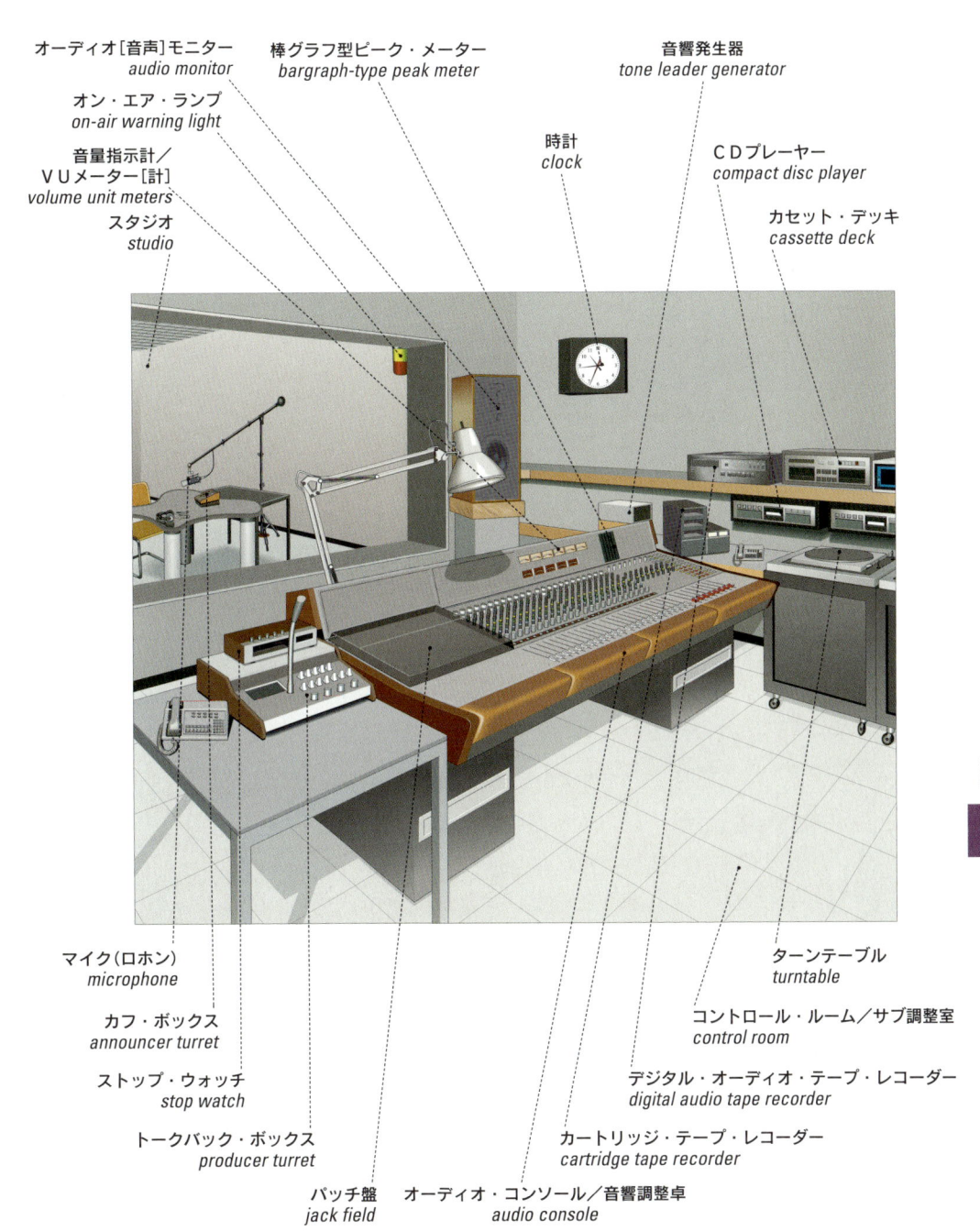

- オーディオ[音声]モニター / audio monitor
- 棒グラフ型ピーク・メーター / bargraph-type peak meter
- 音響発生器 / tone leader generator
- オン・エア・ランプ / on-air warning light
- 時計 / clock
- ＣＤプレーヤー / compact disc player
- 音量指示計／ＶＵメーター[計] / volume unit meters
- カセット・デッキ / cassette deck
- スタジオ / studio
- マイク（ロホン） / microphone
- ターンテーブル / turntable
- カフ・ボックス / announcer turret
- コントロール・ルーム／サブ調整室 / control room
- ストップ・ウォッチ / stop watch
- デジタル・オーディオ・テープ・レコーダー / digital audio tape recorder
- トークバック・ボックス / producer turret
- カートリッジ・テープ・レコーダー / cartridge tape recorder
- パッチ盤 / jack field
- オーディオ・コンソール／音響調整卓 / audio console

通信

テレビ | TELEVISION

テレビ・スタジオのカメラとマイクによって像と音が電気信号に変換されます。この信号はさらにテレビ放送局によってラジオ電波に変換されます。テレビ放送は、衛星か地下ケーブルで、あるいは直接、テレビ受像機に伝えられます。この受信機は、カセット・ビデオ・デッキやＤＶＤビデオ・プレーヤーから来る信号も受信することができます。

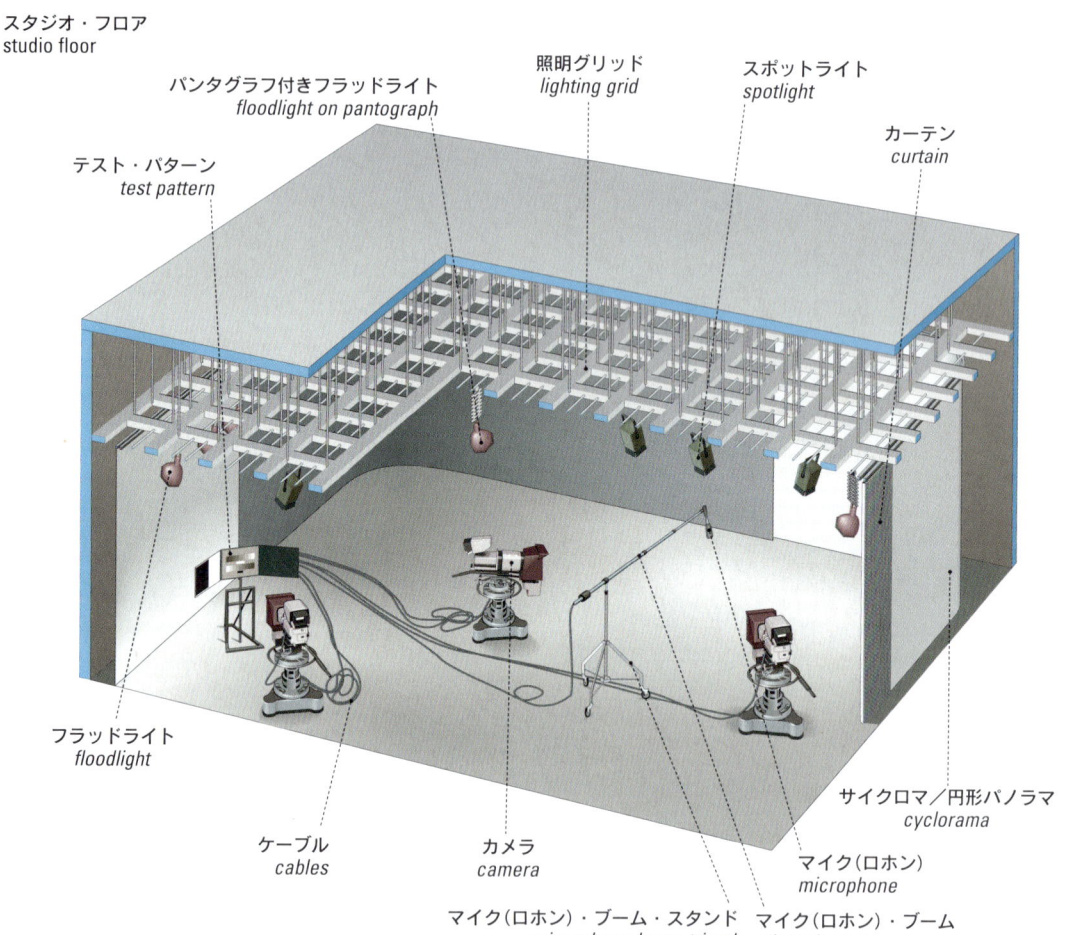

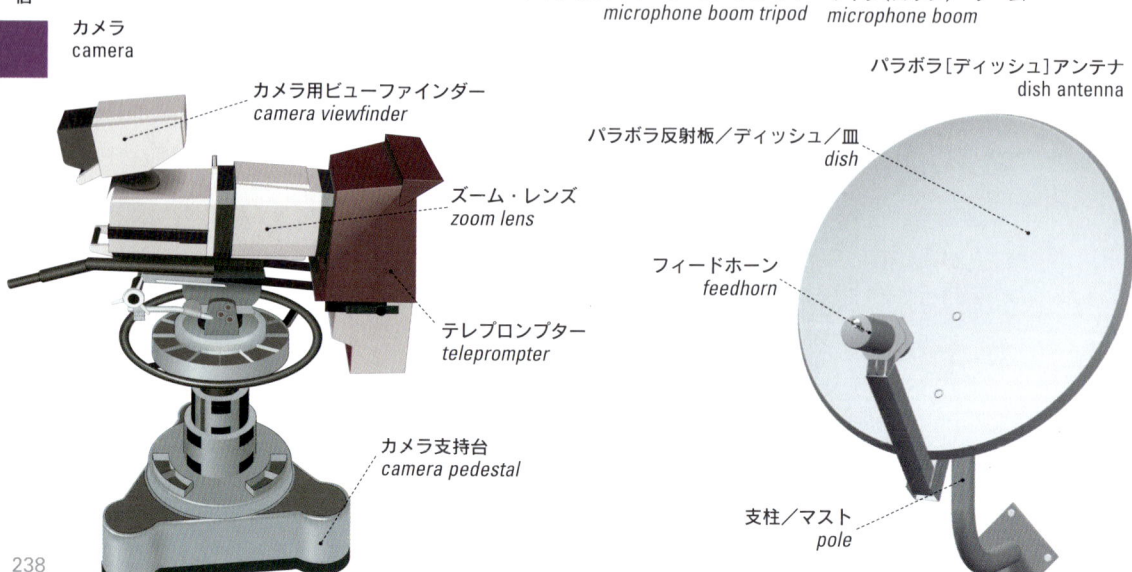

- スタジオ・フロア / studio floor
- パンタグラフ付きフラッドライト / floodlight on pantograph
- 照明グリッド / lighting grid
- スポットライト / spotlight
- カーテン / curtain
- テスト・パターン / test pattern
- フラッドライト / floodlight
- サイクロマ／円形パノラマ / cyclorama
- ケーブル / cables
- カメラ / camera
- マイク（ロホン）・ブーム・スタンド / microphone boom tripod
- マイク（ロホン）・ブーム / microphone boom
- マイク（ロホン） / microphone

通信

- カメラ / camera
- カメラ用ビューファインダー / camera viewfinder
- ズーム・レンズ / zoom lens
- テレプロンプター / teleprompter
- カメラ支持台 / camera pedestal
- パラボラ［ディッシュ］アンテナ / dish antenna
- パラボラ反射板／ディッシュ／皿 / dish
- フィードホーン / feedhorn
- 支柱／マスト / pole

テレビ | TELEVISION

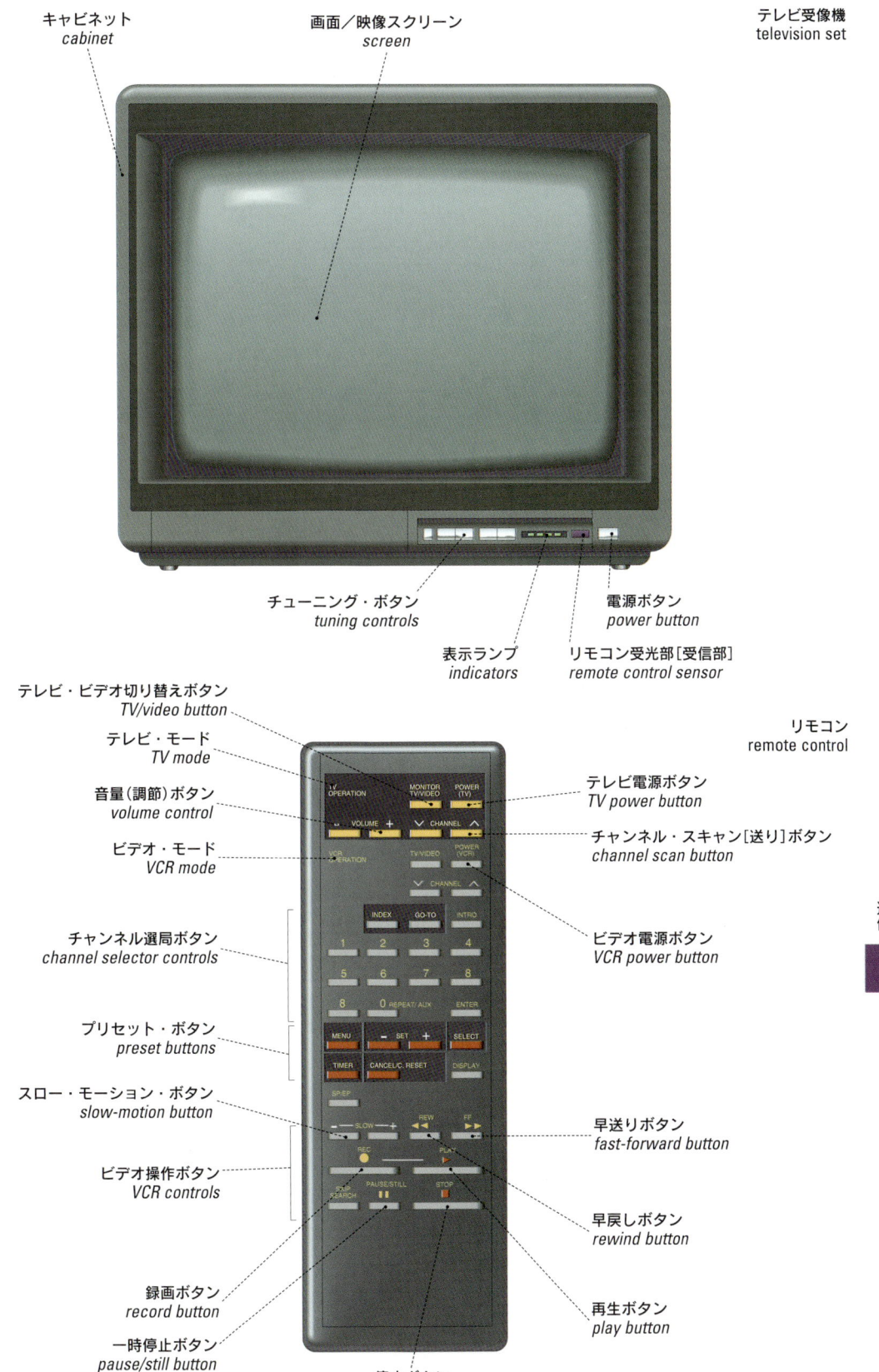

キャビネット
cabinet

画面／映像スクリーン
screen

テレビ受像機
television set

チューニング・ボタン
tuning controls

表示ランプ
indicators

電源ボタン
power button

リモコン受光部［受信部］
remote control sensor

テレビ・ビデオ切り替えボタン
TV/video button

テレビ・モード
TV mode

音量（調節）ボタン
volume control

ビデオ・モード
VCR mode

チャンネル選局ボタン
channel selector controls

プリセット・ボタン
preset buttons

スロー・モーション・ボタン
slow-motion button

ビデオ操作ボタン
VCR controls

録画ボタン
record button

一時停止ボタン
pause/still button

停止ボタン
stop button

テレビ電源ボタン
TV power button

チャンネル・スキャン［送り］ボタン
channel scan button

ビデオ電源ボタン
VCR power button

早送りボタン
fast-forward button

早戻しボタン
rewind button

再生ボタン
play button

リモコン
remote control

通信

239

テレビ | TELEVISION

ビデオ（カセット）・レコーダー
videocassette recorder (VCR)

ビデオカセット
videocassette

録画テープ
recording tape

カセット収納部［挿入口］
cassette compartment

データ表示窓［画面］
data display

電源ボタン
power button

リール
reel

カセット取り出しボタン
cassette eject switch

操作ボタン
controls

録画ボタン
record button

プリセット・ボタン
preset buttons

DVDプレーヤー
DVD player

電源ボタン
power button

表示窓［画面］
display

ディスク・トレー
disc tray

DVD／デジタル多用途ディスク
digital versatile disc (DVD)

アナログ・ビデオ・カメラ
analog camcorder

アイカップ
eyecup

録画編集ボタン
edit search button

電子ビューファインダー
electronic viewfinder

電源・機能スイッチ
power/functions switch

ビデオテープ操作ボタン
videotape operation controls

ズーム・レンズ
zoom lens

表示パネル
display panel

ナイト［夜間撮影］モード切り換えスイッチ
nightshot switch

マイク（ロホン）
microphone

フォーカス・スイッチ［つまみ］
focus selector

ズーム・ダイヤル
near/far dial

通信

240

音声再生装置 | SOUND REPRODUCING SYSTEM

20世紀の技術革新はめざましく、曲を録音し、ますます忠実に再現することが可能になりました。音楽が大好きなアマチュアは、今ではさまざまな音楽装置を自由に使っています。好きなカセットやＣＤを聴くためには、私たちは個別に異なった装置を選んだり、ステレオ・コンポを買ったりします。塩化ビニール製の古いレコードを聴くためにレコード・プレーヤーを持っている人もいます。

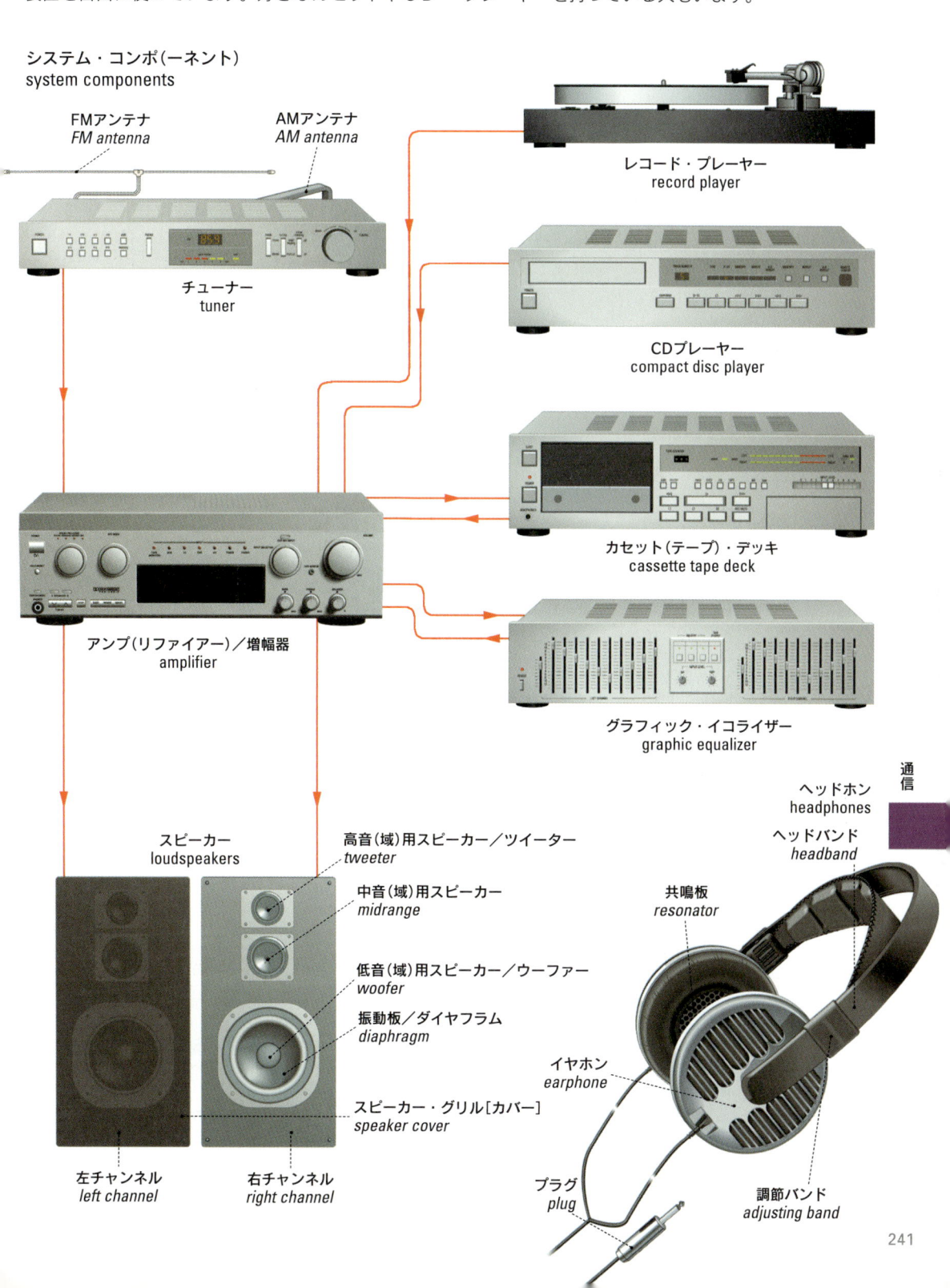

システム・コンポ（ーネント）
system components

FMアンテナ
FM antenna

AMアンテナ
AM antenna

チューナー
tuner

レコード・プレーヤー
record player

CDプレーヤー
compact disc player

カセット（テープ）・デッキ
cassette tape deck

アンプ（リファイアー）／増幅器
amplifier

グラフィック・イコライザー
graphic equalizer

スピーカー
loudspeakers

高音（域）用スピーカー／ツイーター
tweeter

中音（域）用スピーカー
midrange

低音（域）用スピーカー／ウーファー
woofer

振動板／ダイヤフラム
diaphragm

スピーカー・グリル［カバー］
speaker cover

左チャンネル
left channel

右チャンネル
right channel

ヘッドホン
headphones

ヘッドバンド
headband

共鳴板
resonator

イヤホン
earphone

プラグ
plug

調節バンド
adjusting band

ポータブル音響機器 | PORTABLE SOUND SYSTEMS

電子素子が小型化するにつれて、今後は歩きながら音楽が聴けるようになります。例えば、ポータブルＣＤプレーヤーのような装置は、ミニ・ステレオ・セットとも言うべき物ですが、独自の機能を持っています。また、レーザー・ラジカセは、カセット、ＣＤに録音された曲やラジオ放送を聴くことができます。

ポータブルCDラジカセ
portable CD radio cassette recorder

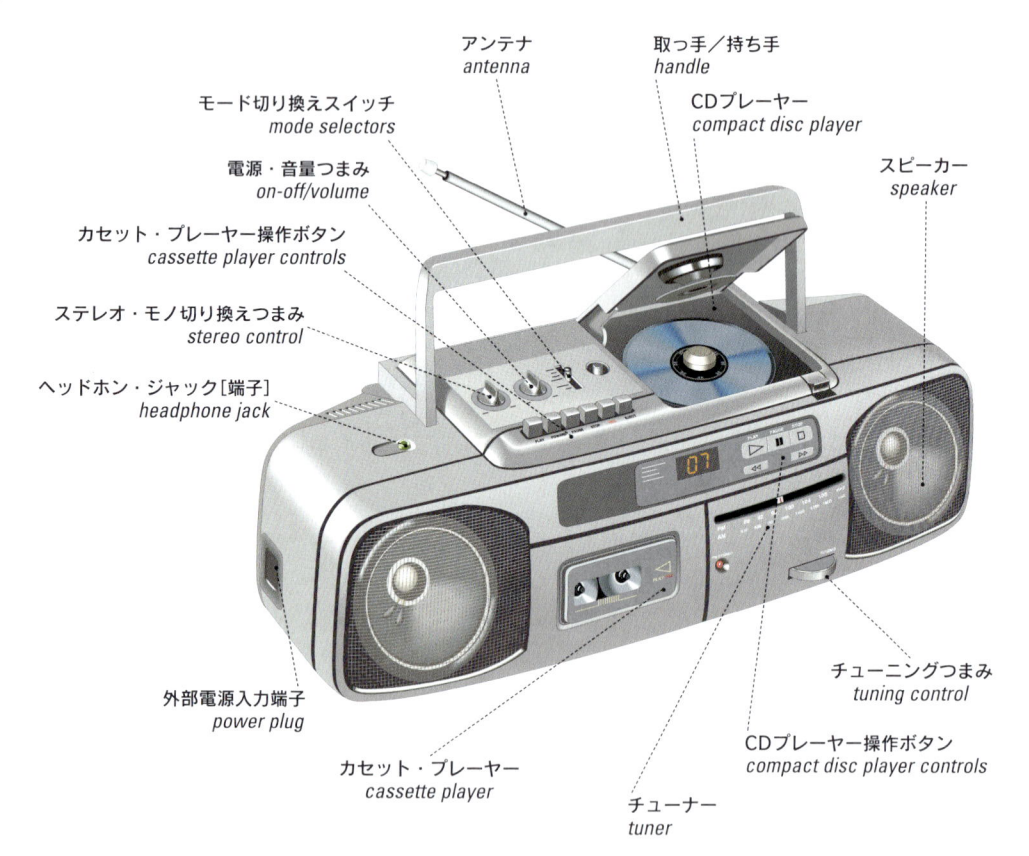

アンテナ
antenna

取っ手／持ち手
handle

モード切り換えスイッチ
mode selectors

ＣＤプレーヤー
compact disc player

電源・音量つまみ
on-off/volume

スピーカー
speaker

カセット・プレーヤー操作ボタン
cassette player controls

ステレオ・モノ切り換えつまみ
stereo control

ヘッドホン・ジャック[端子]
headphone jack

外部電源入力端子
power plug

チューニングつまみ
tuning control

カセット・プレーヤー
cassette player

ＣＤプレーヤー操作ボタン
compact disc player controls

チューナー
tuner

周波数表示窓[画面]
frequency display

伸縮式アンテナ
telescoping antenna

取っ手／持ち手
handle

チューニングつまみ
tuning control

高音調節つまみ
treble tone control

低音調節つまみ
bass tone control

音量(調節)つまみ
volume control

ポータブル・ラジオ
portable radio

タイマー付きラジオ
clock radio

通信

ポータブル音響機器 | PORTABLE SOUND SYSTEMS

CD／コンパクト・ディスク
compact disc

インナー・ミラー・バンド／製品番号領域
technical identification band

記録領域［エリア］／読み出し面
pressed area

リード・イン領域［エリア］
reading start

ポータブルCDプレーヤー
portable compact disc player

表示窓［画面］／ディスプレイ
display

イヤホン
earphones

ポータブル・デジタル・オーディオ・プレーヤー
portable digital audio player

カセット（テープ）
cassette

巻き取りリール
take-up reel

ケース
housing

録音テープ／磁気テープ
recording tape

ガイド・ローラー
guide roller

テープ・ガイド
tape-guide

再生ヘッド用窓
playing window

ポータブル・ラジカセ
personal radio cassette player

ヘッドバンド
headband

ヘッドホン・プラグ
headphone plug

コード
cable

音量（調節）つまみ
volume control

電源ボタン
on-off button

チューニングつまみ
tuning dial

巻き戻しボタン
rewind button

チューナー
tuner

再生ボタン
play button

ヘッドホン
headphones

早送りボタン
fast-forward button

オート・リバース・ボタン
auto-reverse button

カセット・プレーヤー
cassette player

通信

243

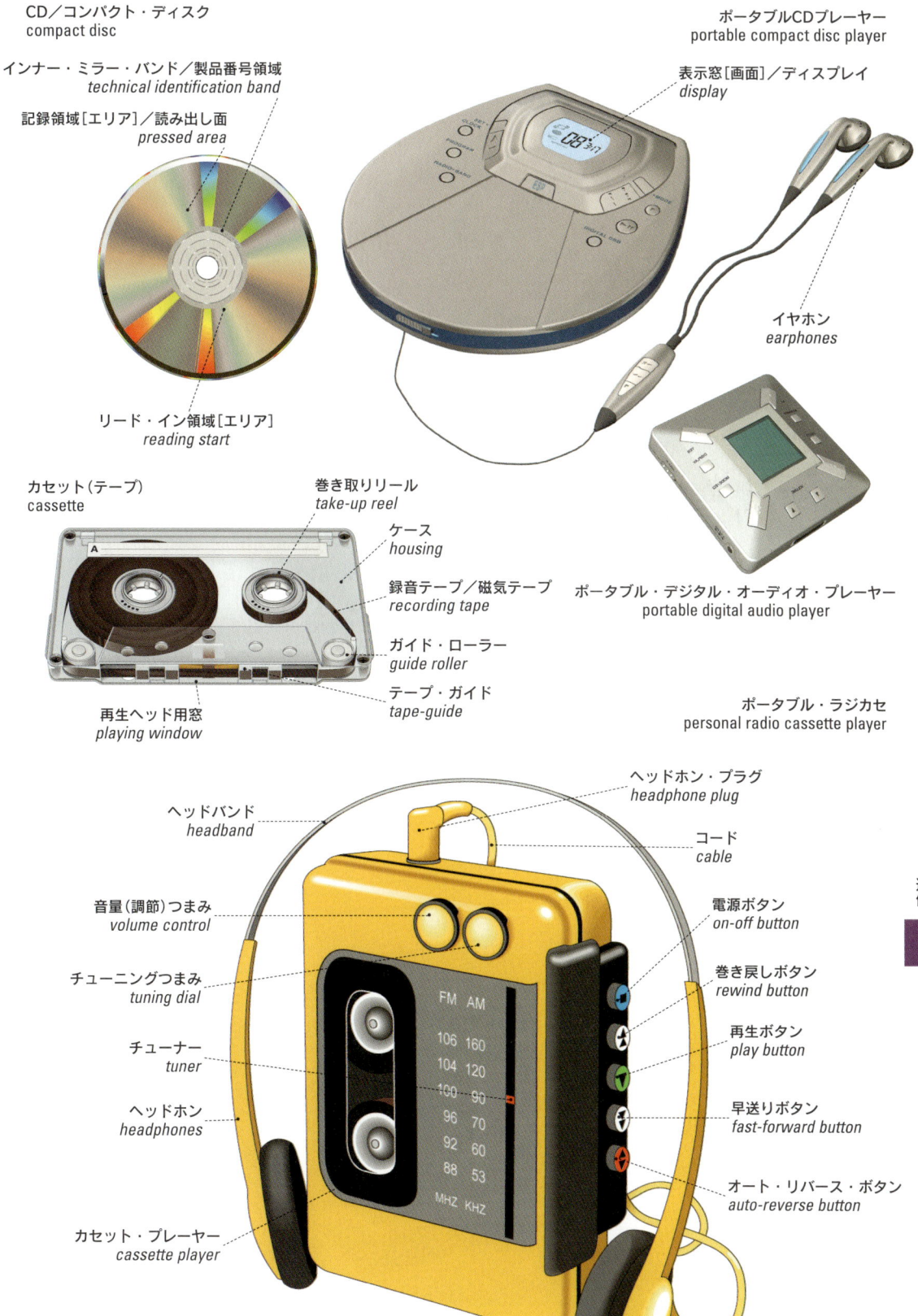

電話通信 | COMMUNICATION BY TELEPHONE

携帯であれコードレスであれ、電話は、テレビやラジオと同様に、今後とも遠距離通信の最も重要な手段の一つであり続けるはずです。今では、何千キロと離れた二人の話し相手が会話をし、インターネット上の文書により連絡を取り合い、ファックスで書類を送受信するのが可能になっています。このような情報のやり取りは、とりわけ通信衛星を通してますます迅速にできるようになっています。

電話機
telephone set

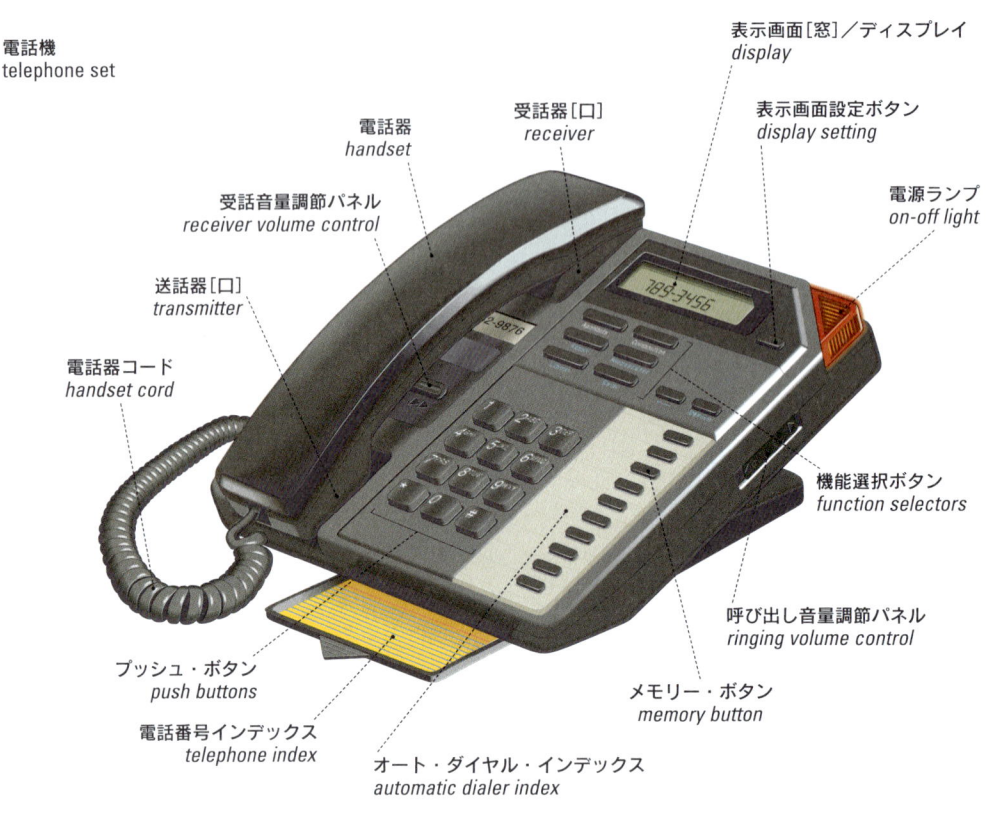

電話器
handset

受話器[口]
receiver

表示画面[窓]／ディスプレイ
display

表示画面設定ボタン
display setting

受話音量調節パネル
receiver volume control

電源ランプ
on-off light

送話器[口]
transmitter

電話器コード
handset cord

機能選択ボタン
function selectors

呼び出し音量調節パネル
ringing volume control

プッシュ・ボタン
push buttons

メモリー・ボタン
memory button

電話番号インデックス
telephone index

オート・ダイヤル・インデックス
automatic dialer index

留守番電話機
telephone answering machine

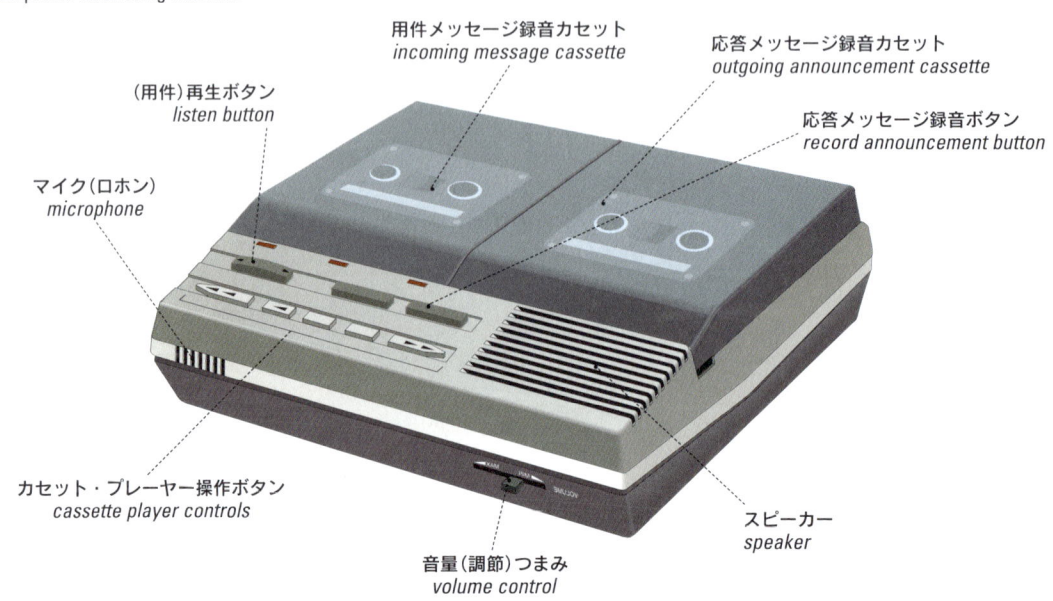

用件メッセージ録音カセット
incoming message cassette

応答メッセージ録音カセット
outgoing announcement cassette

（用件）再生ボタン
listen button

応答メッセージ録音ボタン
record announcement button

マイク(ロホン)
microphone

カセット・プレーヤー操作ボタン
cassette player controls

スピーカー
speaker

音量（調節）つまみ
volume control

通信

電話通信 | COMMUNICATION BY TELEPHONE

公衆電話機
pay phone

硬貨投入[挿入]口
coin slot

表示窓[画面]／ディスプレイ
display

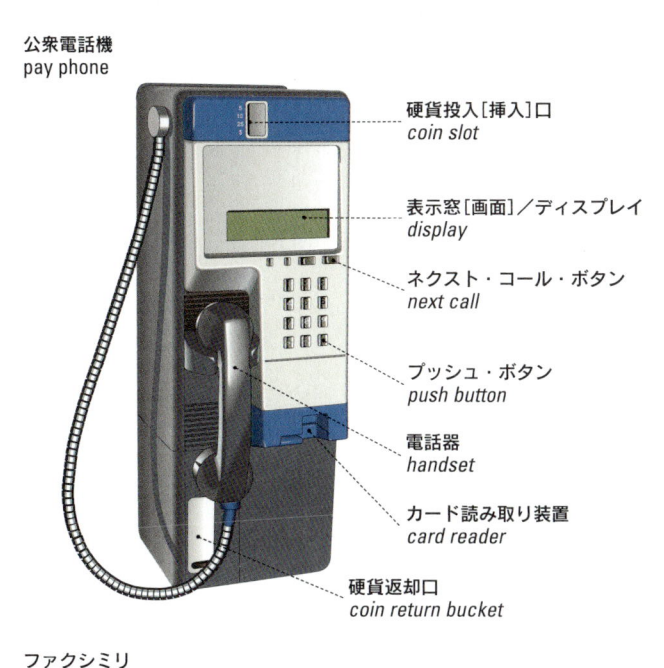

ネクスト・コール・ボタン
next call

プッシュ・ボタン
push button

電話器
handset

カード読み取り装置
card reader

硬貨返却口
coin return bucket

プッシュ式電話機／プッシュ・ボタン電話機
push-button telephone

コードレス電話機
cordless telephone

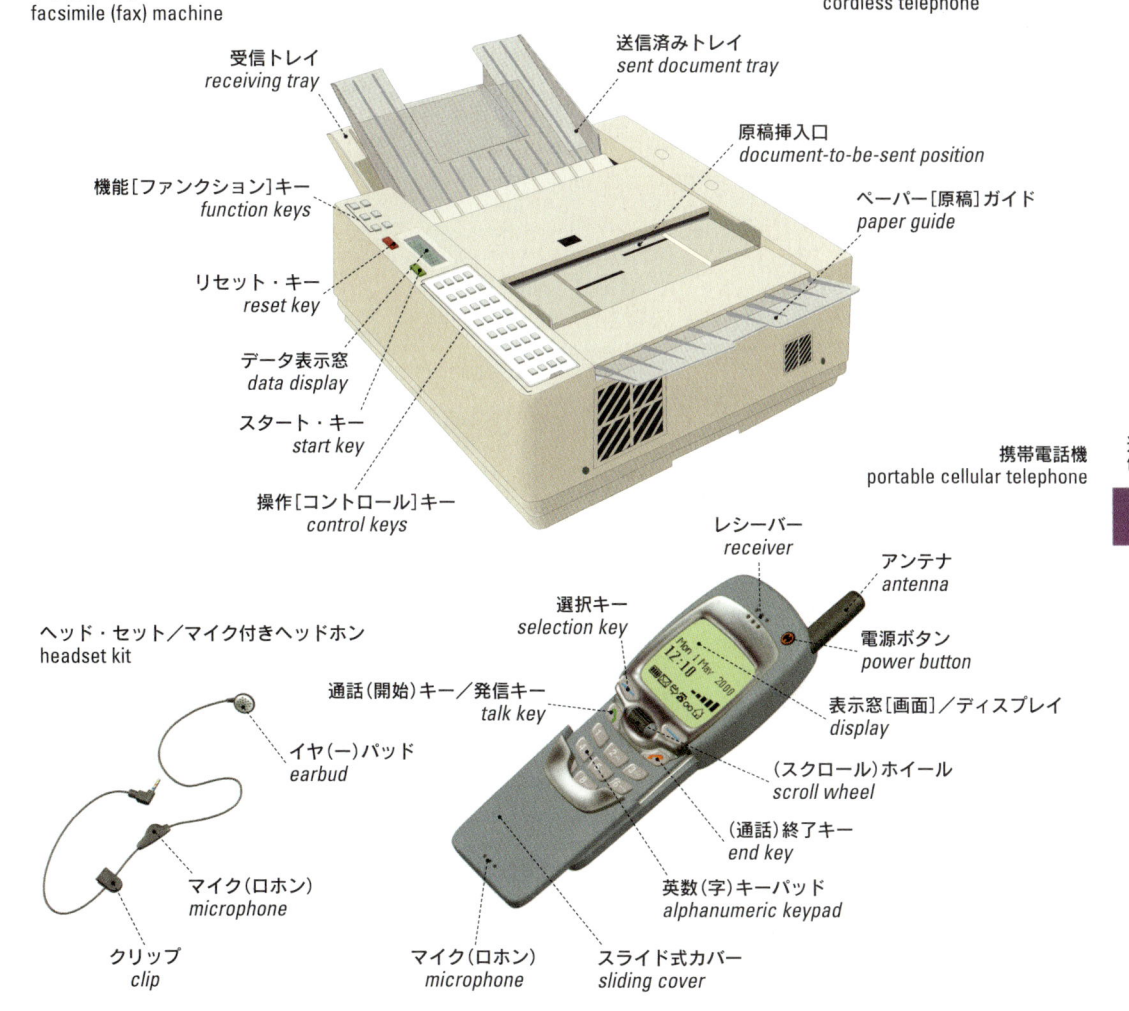

ファクシミリ
facsimile (fax) machine

受信トレイ
receiving tray

送信済みトレイ
sent document tray

原稿挿入口
document-to-be-sent position

ペーパー[原稿]ガイド
paper guide

機能[ファンクション]キー
function keys

リセット・キー
reset key

データ表示窓
data display

スタート・キー
start key

操作[コントロール]キー
control keys

携帯電話機
portable cellular telephone

通信

ヘッド・セット／マイク付きヘッドホン
headset kit

レシーバー
receiver

アンテナ
antenna

選択キー
selection key

電源ボタン
power button

通話(開始)キー／発信キー
talk key

表示窓[画面]／ディスプレイ
display

イヤ(ー)パッド
earbud

(スクロール)ホイール
scroll wheel

(通話)終了キー
end key

マイク(ロホン)
microphone

英数(字)キーパッド
alphanumeric keypad

クリップ
clip

マイク(ロホン)
microphone

スライド式カバー
sliding cover

245

パーソナル・コンピューター／パソコン | PERSONAL COMPUTER

コンピューターは、コード化された情報を驚くべき速さで変換したり、保存したり、伝えたりする電子機器です。パソコンは、マウス、キーボード、モニター、プリンターといった周辺装置と、それらを接続する本体から成り立っています。目に見える所でも見えない所でも、コンピューターは今では至る所で活躍しています。

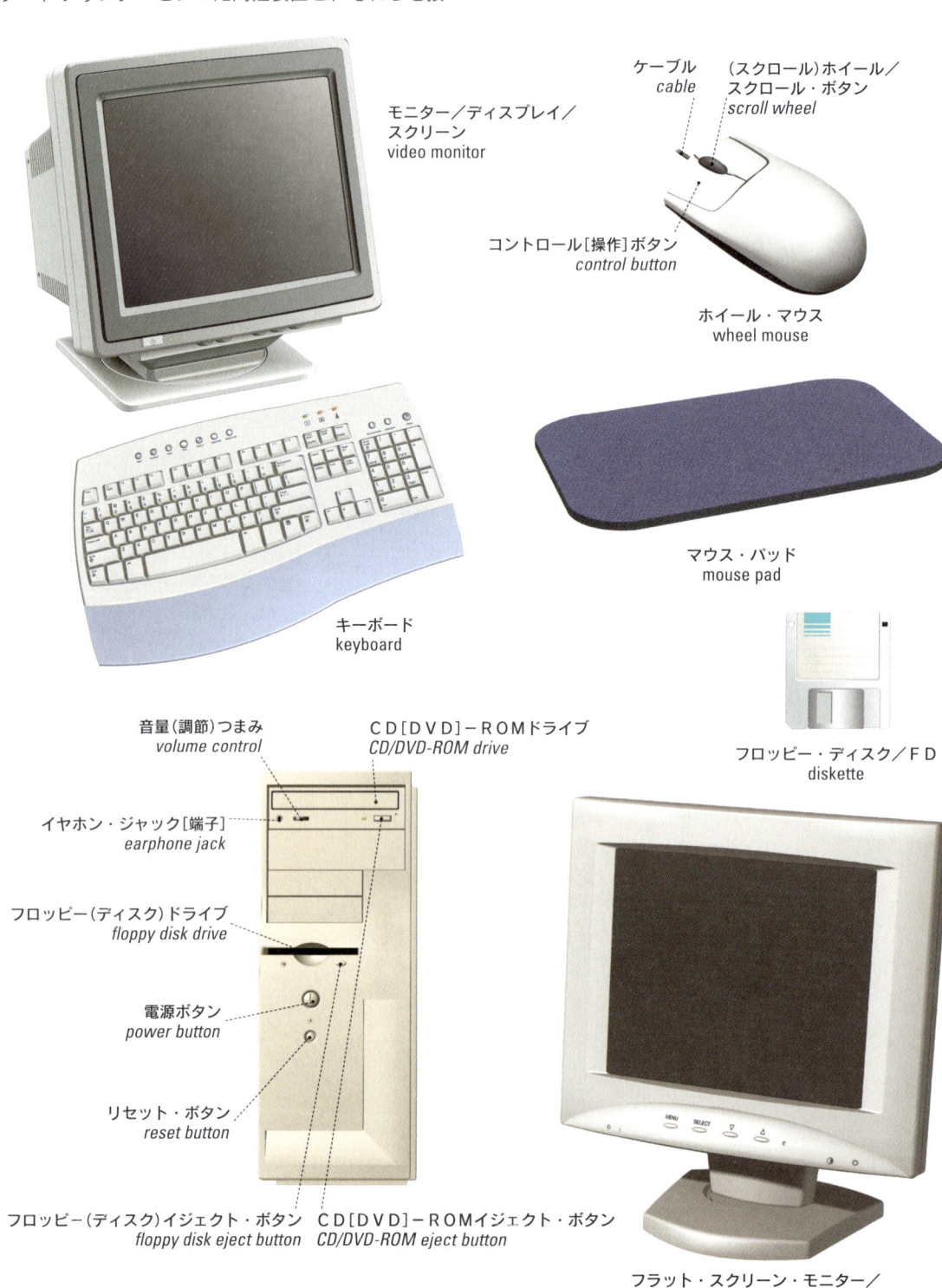

モニター／ディスプレイ／スクリーン
video monitor

ケーブル
cable

（スクロール）ホイール／スクロール・ボタン
scroll wheel

コントロール［操作］ボタン
control button

ホイール・マウス
wheel mouse

キーボード
keyboard

マウス・パッド
mouse pad

音量（調節）つまみ
volume control

CD［DVD］－ROMドライブ
CD/DVD-ROM drive

フロッピー・ディスク／FD
diskette

イヤホン・ジャック［端子］
earphone jack

フロッピー（ディスク）ドライブ
floppy disk drive

電源ボタン
power button

リセット・ボタン
reset button

フロッピー（ディスク）イジェクト・ボタン
floppy disk eject button

CD［DVD］－ROMイジェクト・ボタン
CD/DVD-ROM eject button

タワー・ケース
tower case

フラット・スクリーン・モニター／平面型ディスプレイ
flat screen monitor

通信

パーソナル・コンピューター／パソコン | PERSONAL COMPUTER

トナー・カートリッジ
toner cartridge

光学式スキャナー
optical scanner

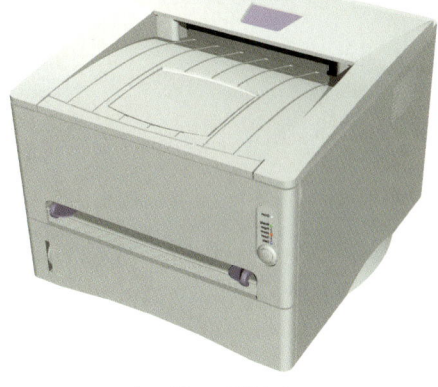

レーザー・プリンター
laser printer

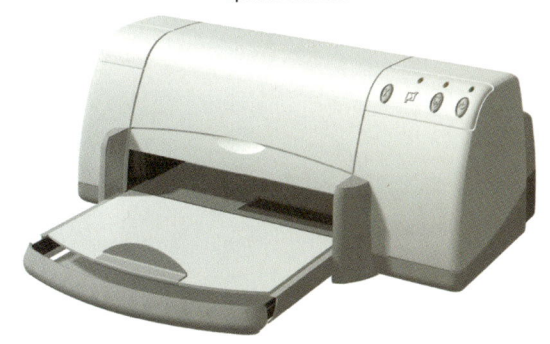

インクジェット・プリンター
inkjet printer

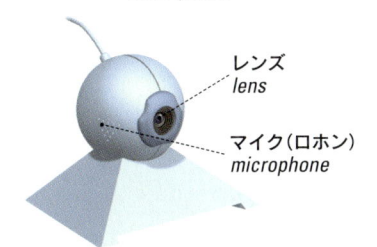

レンズ
lens

マイク（ロホン）
microphone

ウェブカメラ／ウェブカム
Webcam

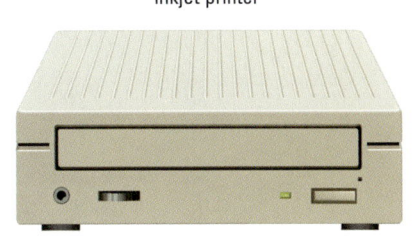

ＣＤ－ＲＯＭプレーヤー
CD/ROM player

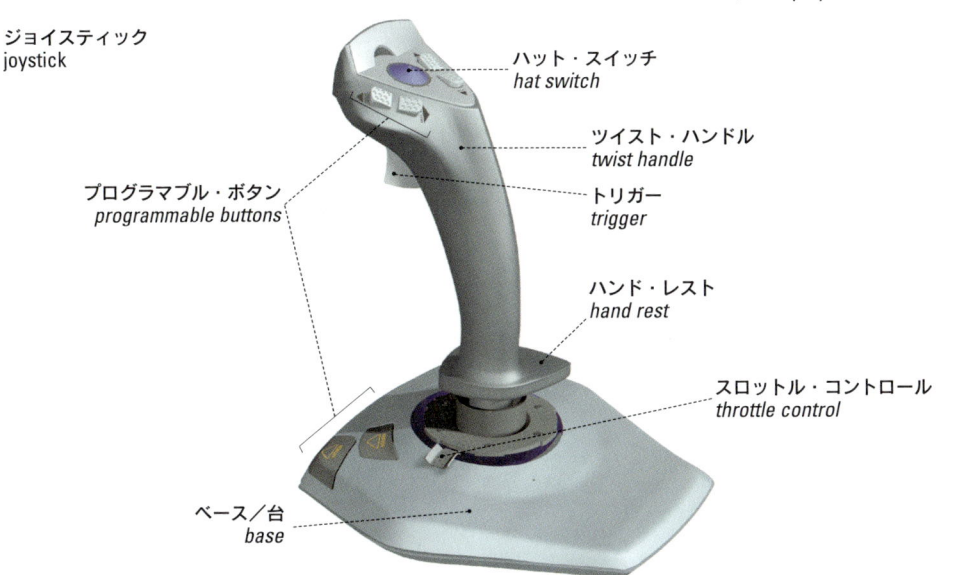

ジョイスティック
joystick

ハット・スイッチ
hat switch

ツイスト・ハンドル
twist handle

トリガー
trigger

プログラマブル・ボタン
programmable buttons

ハンド・レスト
hand rest

スロットル・コントロール
throttle control

ベース／台
base

通信

インターネット | INTERNET

インターネットとは、メディアの世界に大革命をもたらした世界規模のコミュニケーション・システムと言うことができます。これは電話回線やケーブルで相互に接続された情報ネットワークの総体で、同一の言語で、世界中で情報伝達が可能です。1991年にアメリカで始まり、WWWは何百万という世界中のコンピューターとユーザーを結び付け、通信と情報交換を容易にしてくれています。

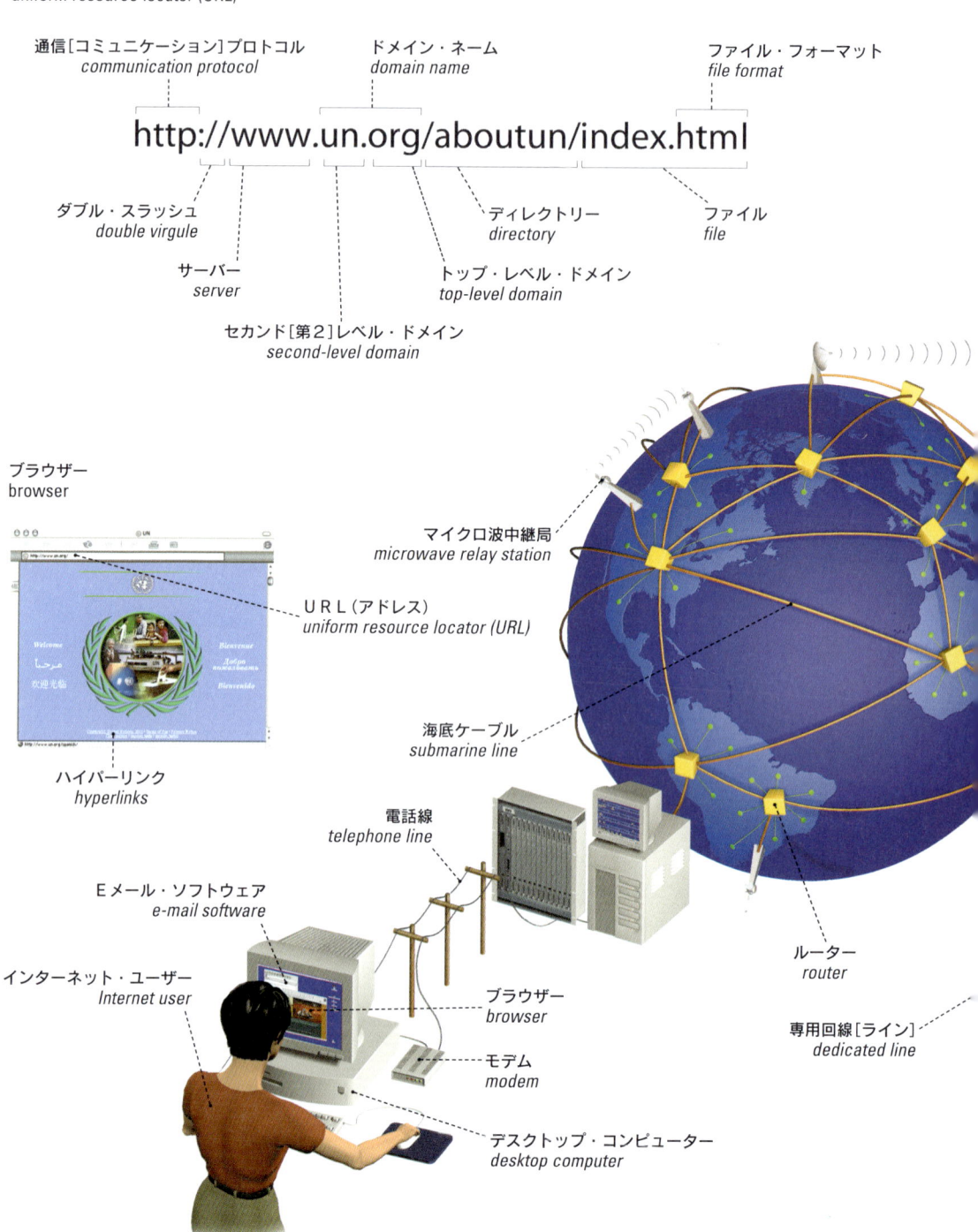

URL（アドレス）
uniform resource locator (URL)

通信[コミュニケーション]プロトコル
communication protocol

ドメイン・ネーム
domain name

ファイル・フォーマット
file format

http://www.un.org/aboutun/index.html

ダブル・スラッシュ
double virgule

サーバー
server

ディレクトリー
directory

ファイル
file

トップ・レベル・ドメイン
top-level domain

セカンド[第2]レベル・ドメイン
second-level domain

ブラウザー
browser

URL（アドレス）
uniform resource locator (URL)

マイクロ波中継局
microwave relay station

ハイパーリンク
hyperlinks

海底ケーブル
submarine line

電話線
telephone line

Eメール・ソフトウェア
e-mail software

ブラウザー
browser

ルーター
router

インターネット・ユーザー
Internet user

モデム
modem

専用回線[ライン]
dedicated line

デスクトップ・コンピューター
desktop computer

通信

インターネット | INTERNET

インターネットの利用
Internet uses

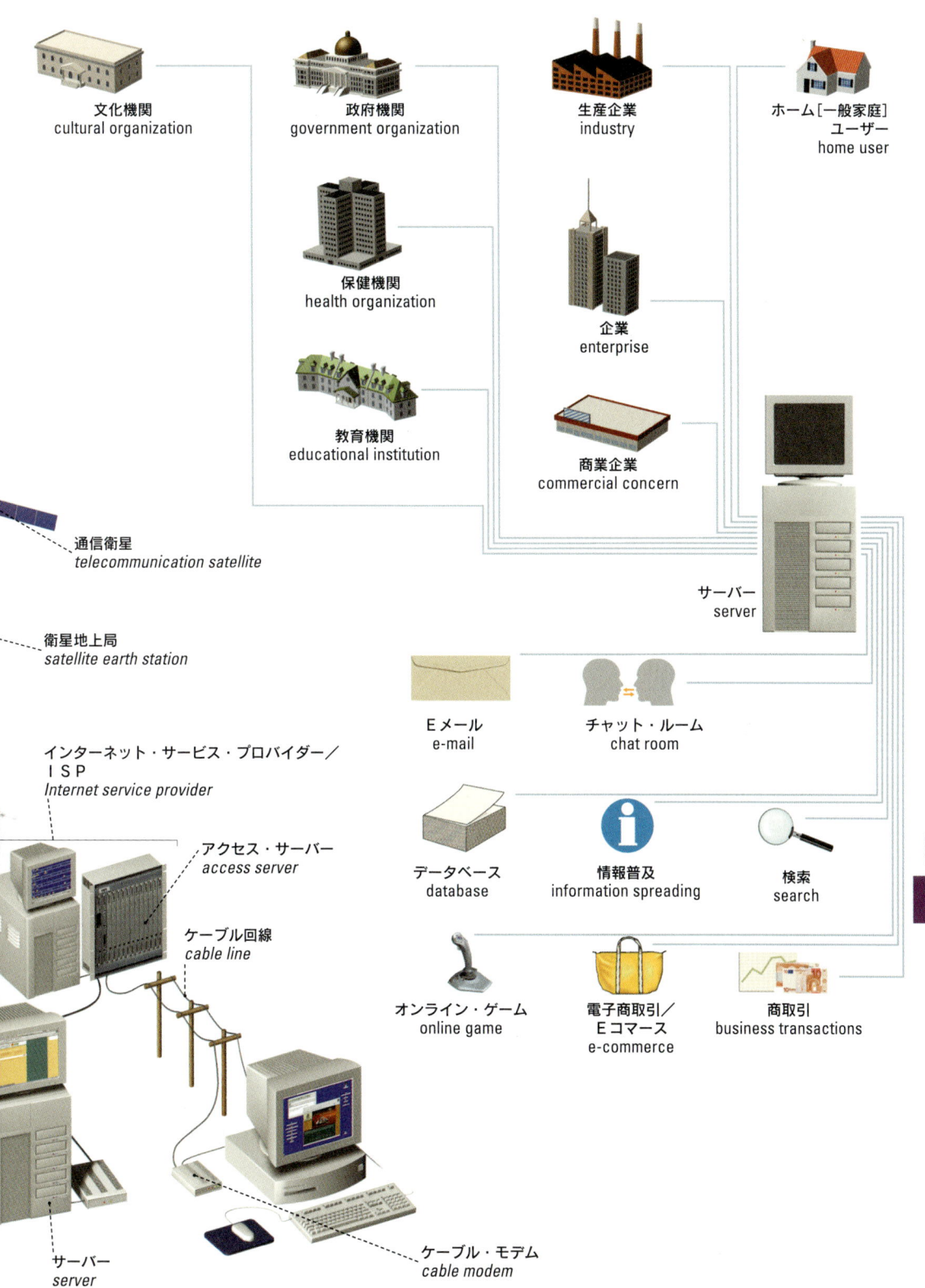

文化機関
cultural organization

政府機関
government organization

生産企業
industry

ホーム[一般家庭]ユーザー
home user

保健機関
health organization

企業
enterprise

教育機関
educational institution

商業企業
commercial concern

通信衛星
telecommunication satellite

サーバー
server

衛星地上局
satellite earth station

Eメール
e-mail

チャット・ルーム
chat room

インターネット・サービス・プロバイダー／ＩＳＰ
Internet service provider

データベース
database

情報普及
information spreading

検索
search

通信

アクセス・サーバー
access server

ケーブル回線
cable line

オンライン・ゲーム
online game

電子商取引／Eコマース
e-commerce

商取引
business transactions

サーバー
server

ケーブル・モデム
cable modem

249

中心街 | DOWNTOWN

街とは多くの住民が集まった人口密集地域のことです。住民の大部分が住宅街に住み、街を取り巻く工業地区で働いたり、中心街の大きなオフィス・ビルで勤務したりしています。街の中心地は市役所、大学、美術館といったさまざまな施設のあるビジネス街にもなり、あらゆる種類のサービスを提供しています。

- 大聖堂 cathedral
- コンベンション・センター convention center
- オフィス・タワー office tower
- 広場 square
- 公園 park
- 鉄道駅 railroad station
- 中央分離帯 median strip
- プラネタリウム planetarium
- 鉄道線路 railroad track
- 高速道路 freeway
- 通り／街路 street
- 配送傾斜路 delivery ramp
- 安全地帯 traffic island
- ブルバード／大通り boulevard

中心街 | CITY CENTRE

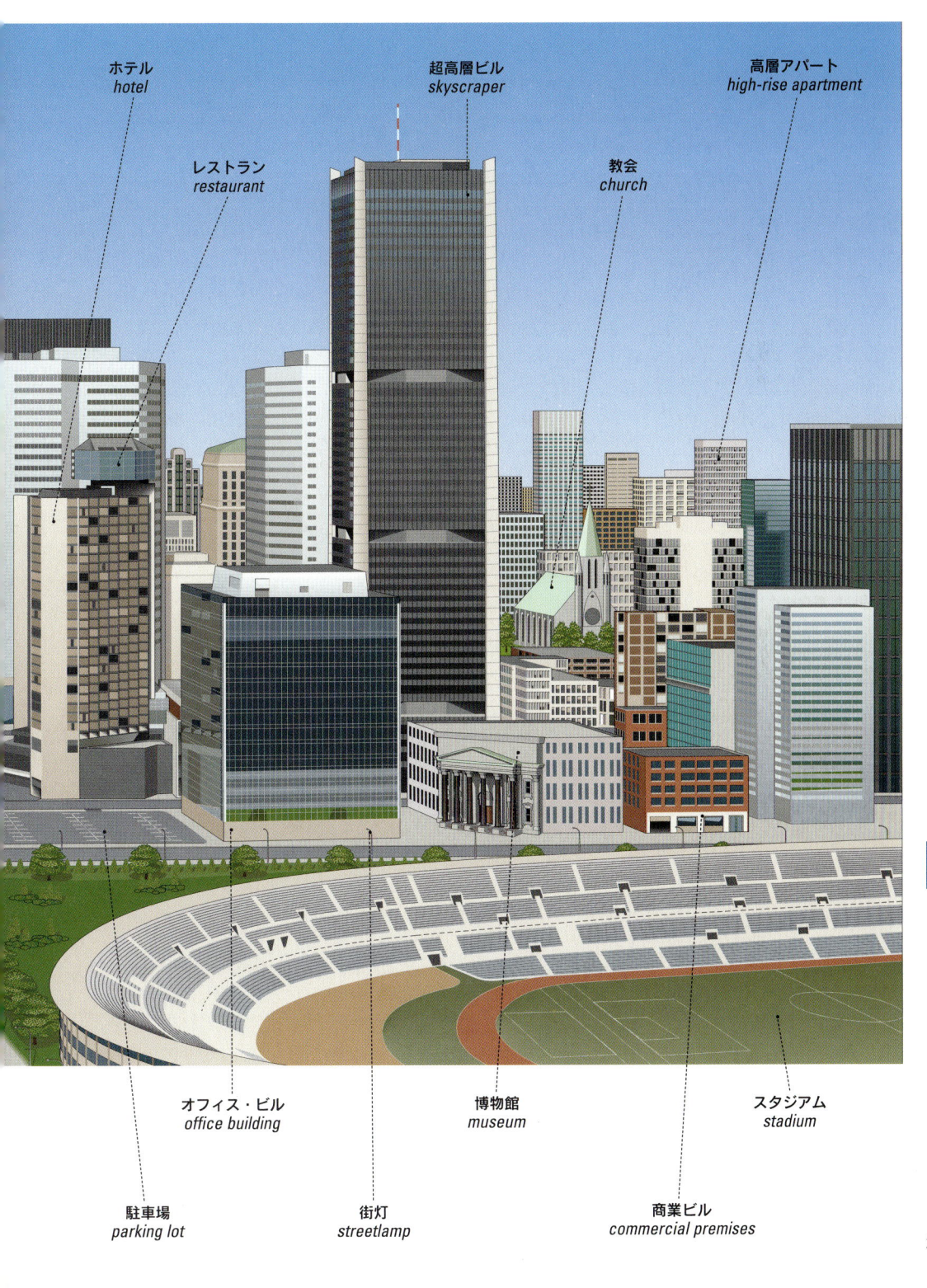

ホテル / hotel

レストラン / restaurant

超高層ビル / skyscraper

教会 / church

高層アパート / high-rise apartment

駐車場 / parking lot

オフィス・ビル / office building

街灯 / streetlamp

博物館 / museum

商業ビル / commercial premises

スタジアム / stadium

ターミナルと駅 | TERMINAL AND STATIONS

街によっては列車、地下鉄、飛行機といった乗り物が止まるために特別に設けられた場所があります。旅客ターミナルが街の外部にあるのがふつうとすれば、地下鉄の駅はどのような都市においても市の中心部にあります。列車が出発し、到着する駅は街の景観の一部になっています。

旅客ターミナル
PASSENGER TERMINAL

- 荷物預かりカウンター / baggage check-in counter
- チケット・カウンター / ticket counter
- 手荷物受取所 / baggage claim area
- ホテル予約デスク[カウンター] / hotel reservation desk
- 自動改札ドア / automatically controlled door
- ロビー / lobby
- シャトル列車 / railroad shuttle service
- 駐車場 / parking lot
- 案内カウンター / information counter
- 電車ホーム / platform
- ベルト・コンベヤー / conveyor belt

タラップ車／パッセンジャー・ステップ車
mobile passenger stairs

タラップ／パッセンジャー・ステップ
universal step

ターミナルと駅 | TERMINAL AND STATIONS

旅客搭乗橋
passenger transfer vehicle

手荷物検査（場）
security check

送迎デッキ
observation deck

出国審査（場）
passport control

発着案内板
flight information board

出発ロビー
boarding room

旅客搭乗橋
passenger transfer vehicle

荷物発送所
freight expedition

荷物受取所
freight reception

税関（検査場）
customs control

免税店
duty-free shop

旅客駅
PASSENGER STATION

線路／軌道
track

手押し車／手荷物カート
baggage cart

改札係
ticket collector

事務室
office

旅客列車
passenger train

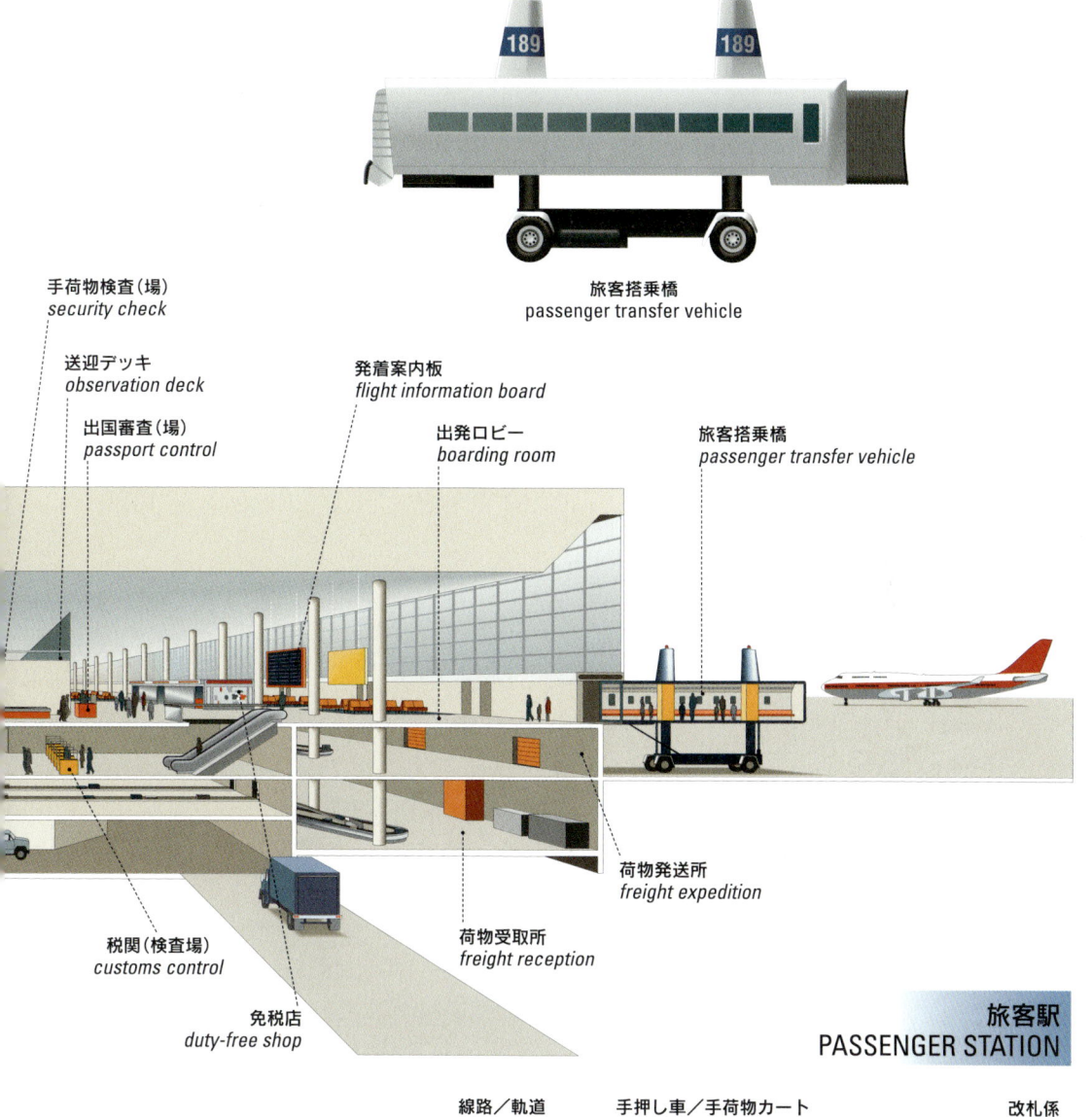

小荷物取扱所
parcels office

手荷物室［一時預かり所］
baggage room

旅客ホーム
passenger platform

（列車）時刻表
schedules

社会

253

ターミナルと駅 | TERMINAL AND STATIONS

地下鉄駅
SUBWAY STATION

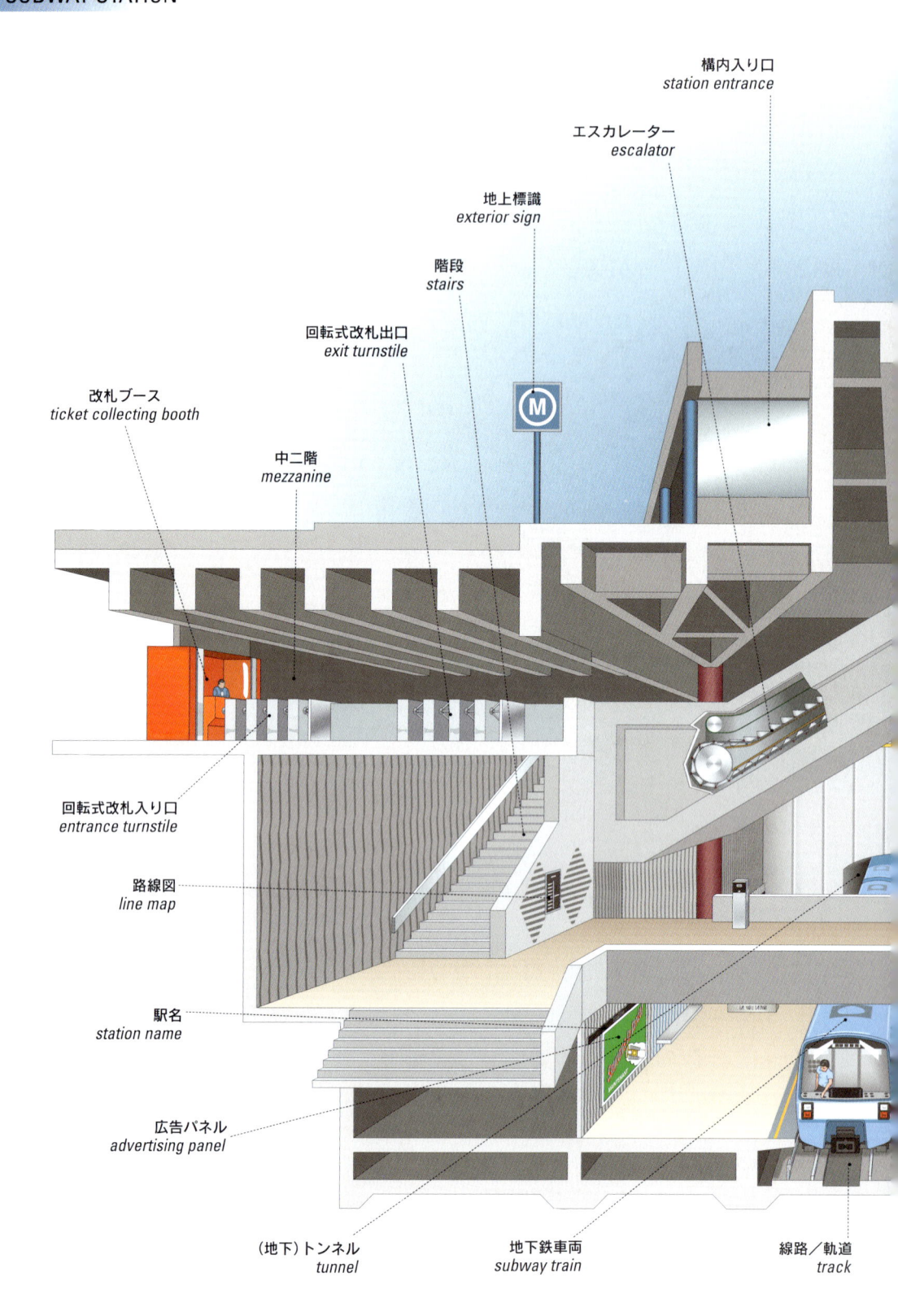

構内入り口
station entrance

エスカレーター
escalator

地上標識
exterior sign

階段
stairs

回転式改札出口
exit turnstile

改札ブース
ticket collecting booth

中二階
mezzanine

回転式改札入り口
entrance turnstile

路線図
line map

駅名
station name

広告パネル
advertising panel

（地下）トンネル
tunnel

地下鉄車両
subway train

線路／軌道
track

ターミナルと駅 | TERMINAL AND STATIONS

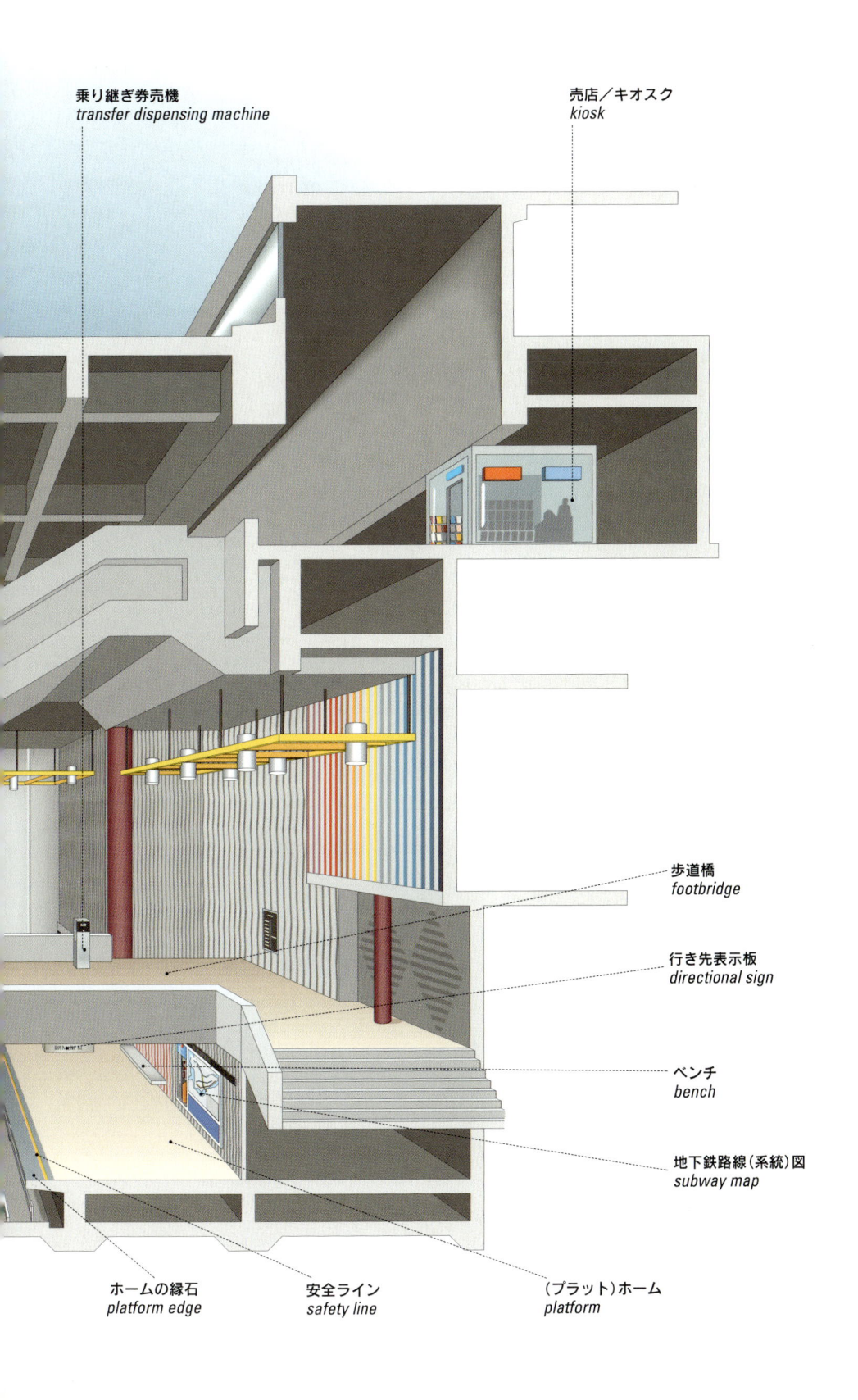

乗り継ぎ券売機
transfer dispensing machine

売店／キオスク
kiosk

歩道橋
footbridge

行き先表示板
directional sign

ベンチ
bench

地下鉄路線（系統）図
subway map

ホームの縁石
platform edge

安全ライン
safety line

（プラット）ホーム
platform

社会

商業サービス | COMMERCIAL SERVICES

どのような街にもサービスを提供する施設がたくさんあります。いくつか例を挙げれば、スーパーマーケット、いろいろな店が入っているショッピング・センター、レストラン、ガソリン・スタンドなどで、どれもが顧客に特別なサービスを提供しています。そこでは、食べ物、衣服、調理済み食品、ガソリンなど、あらゆる消費財を手に入れることができます。

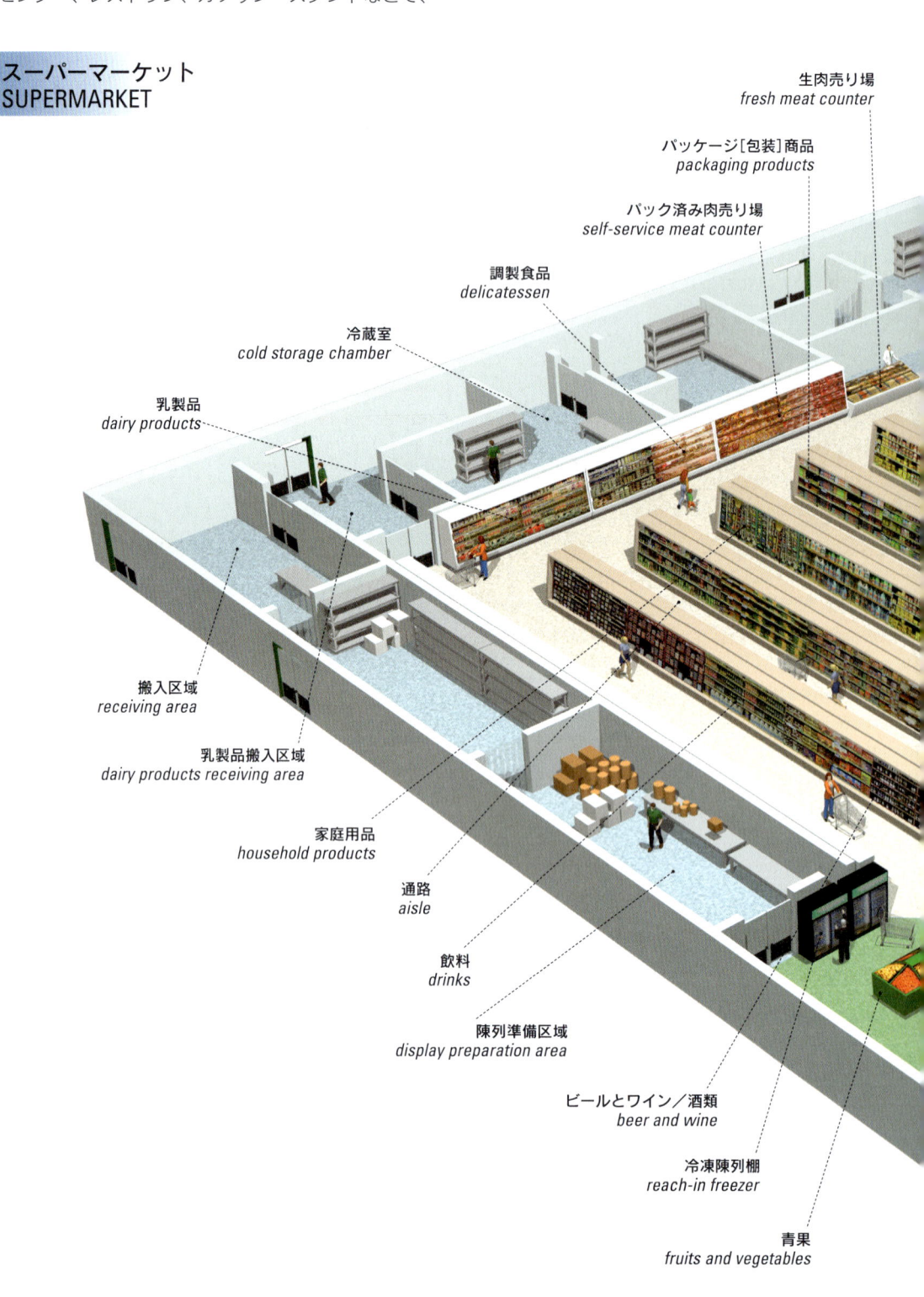

スーパーマーケット
SUPERMARKET

生肉売り場
fresh meat counter

パッケージ[包装]商品
packaging products

パック済み肉売り場
self-service meat counter

調製食品
delicatessen

冷蔵室
cold storage chamber

乳製品
dairy products

搬入区域
receiving area

乳製品搬入区域
dairy products receiving area

家庭用品
household products

通路
aisle

飲料
drinks

陳列準備区域
display preparation area

ビールとワイン／酒類
beer and wine

冷凍陳列棚
reach-in freezer

青果
fruits and vegetables

社会

商業サービス | COMMERCIAL SERVICES

レジ／精算所
checkout

レジスター
cash register

光学スキャナー
optical scanner

電子決済端末
electronic payment terminal

食料品袋
grocery bags

レジ係
cashier

袋詰め係
bagger

冷蔵室
cold storage chamber

魚介類
seafood

商品陳列棚
gondola

インスタント食品
convenience food

チーズ売り場
cheese counter

冷凍食品保存庫
frozen food storage

冷凍食品
frozen foods

パン売り場／ベーカリー
bakery

総菜
prepared foods

レジ／精算所
checkouts

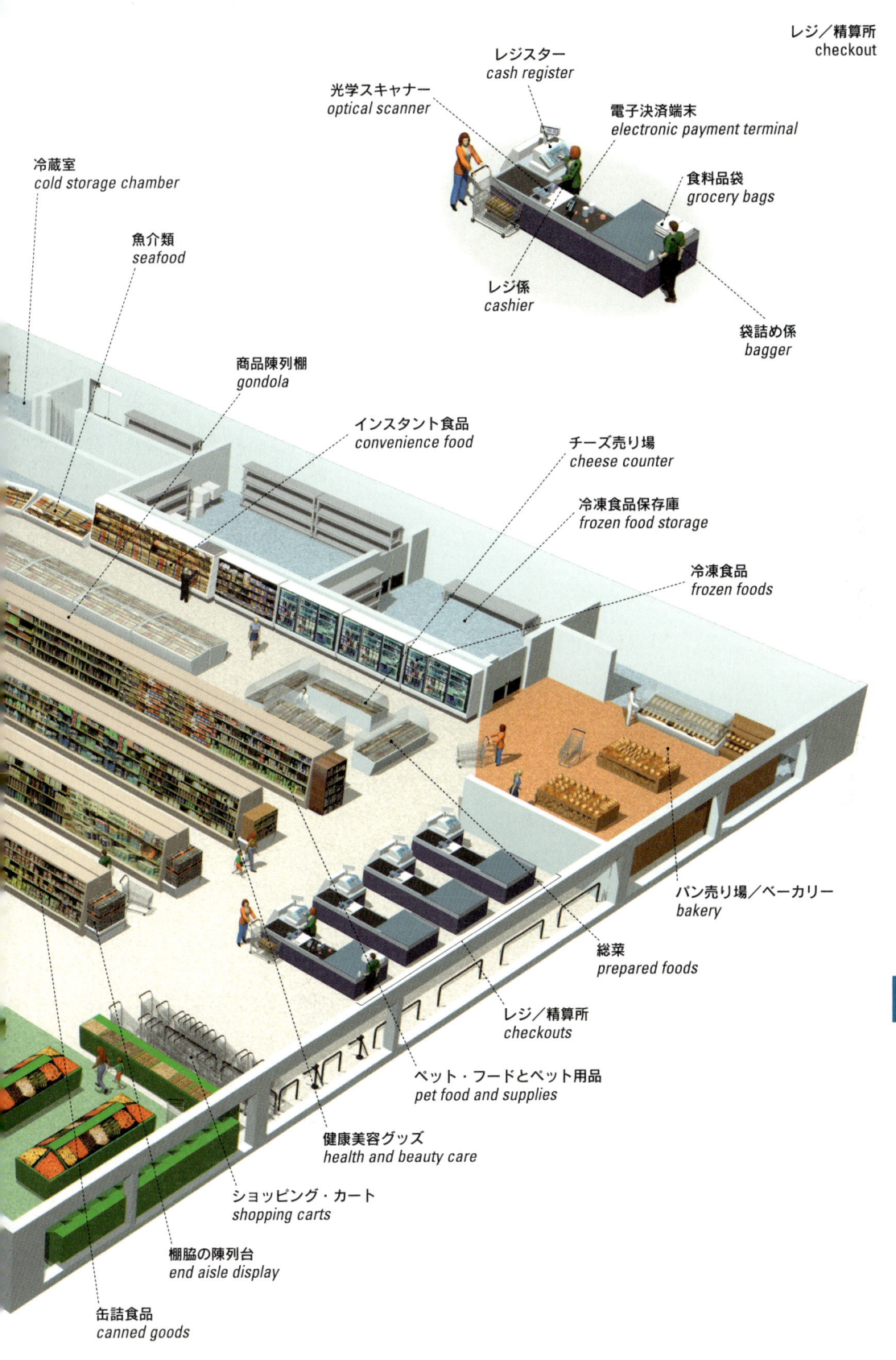

ペット・フードとペット用品
pet food and supplies

健康美容グッズ
health and beauty care

ショッピング・カート
shopping carts

棚脇の陳列台
end aisle display

缶詰食品
canned goods

社会

257

商業サービス | COMMERCIAL SERVICES

ショッピング・センター
SHOPPING CENTER

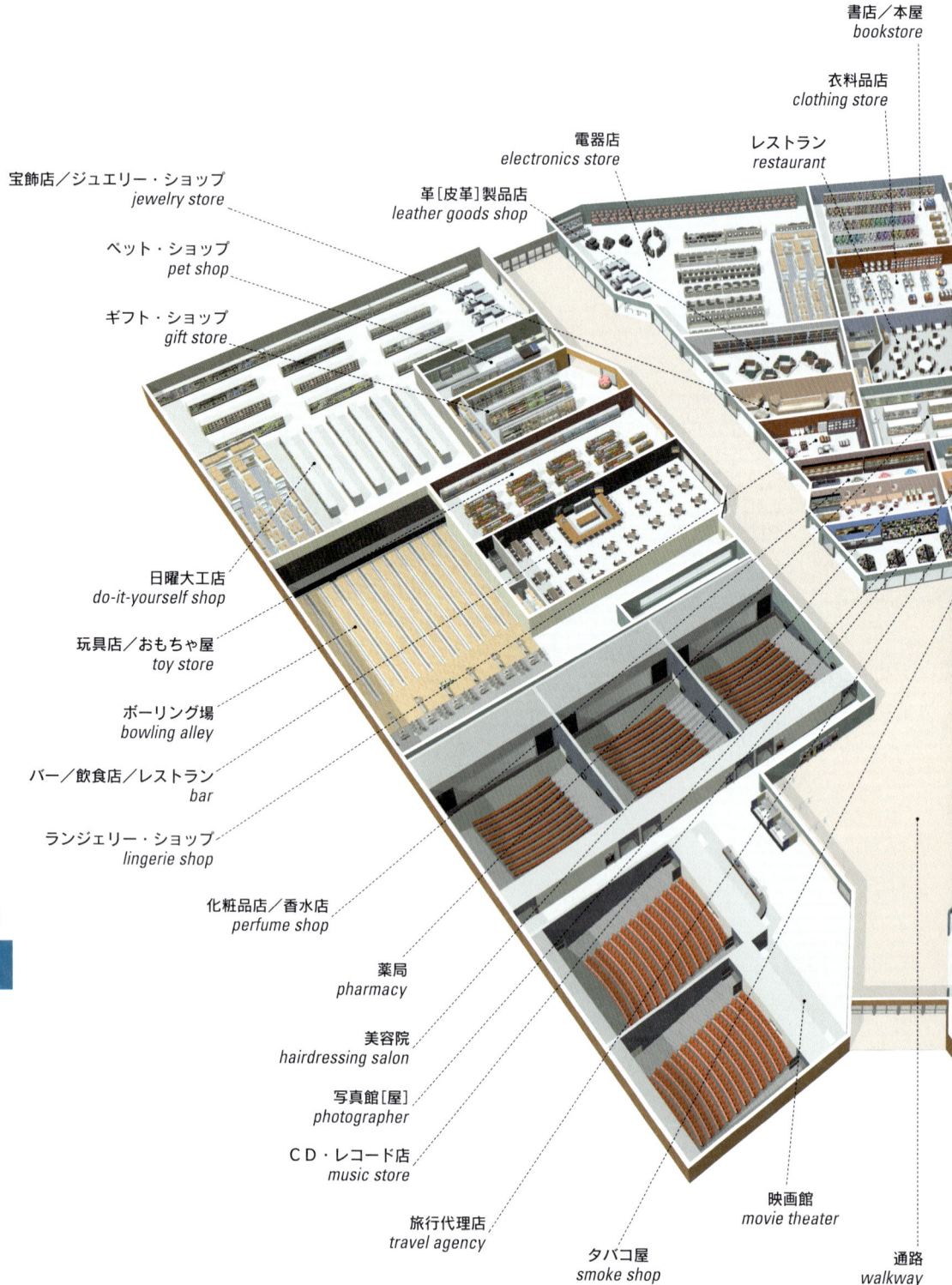

書店／本屋
bookstore

衣料品店
clothing store

電器店
electronics store

レストラン
restaurant

宝飾店／ジュエリー・ショップ
jewelry store

革[皮革]製品店
leather goods shop

ペット・ショップ
pet shop

ギフト・ショップ
gift store

日曜大工店
do-it-yourself shop

玩具店／おもちゃ屋
toy store

ボーリング場
bowling alley

バー／飲食店／レストラン
bar

ランジェリー・ショップ
lingerie shop

化粧品店／香水店
perfume shop

薬局
pharmacy

美容院
hairdressing salon

写真館[屋]
photographer

ＣＤ・レコード店
music store

旅行代理店
travel agency

タバコ屋
smoke shop

映画館
movie theater

通路
walkway

社会

258

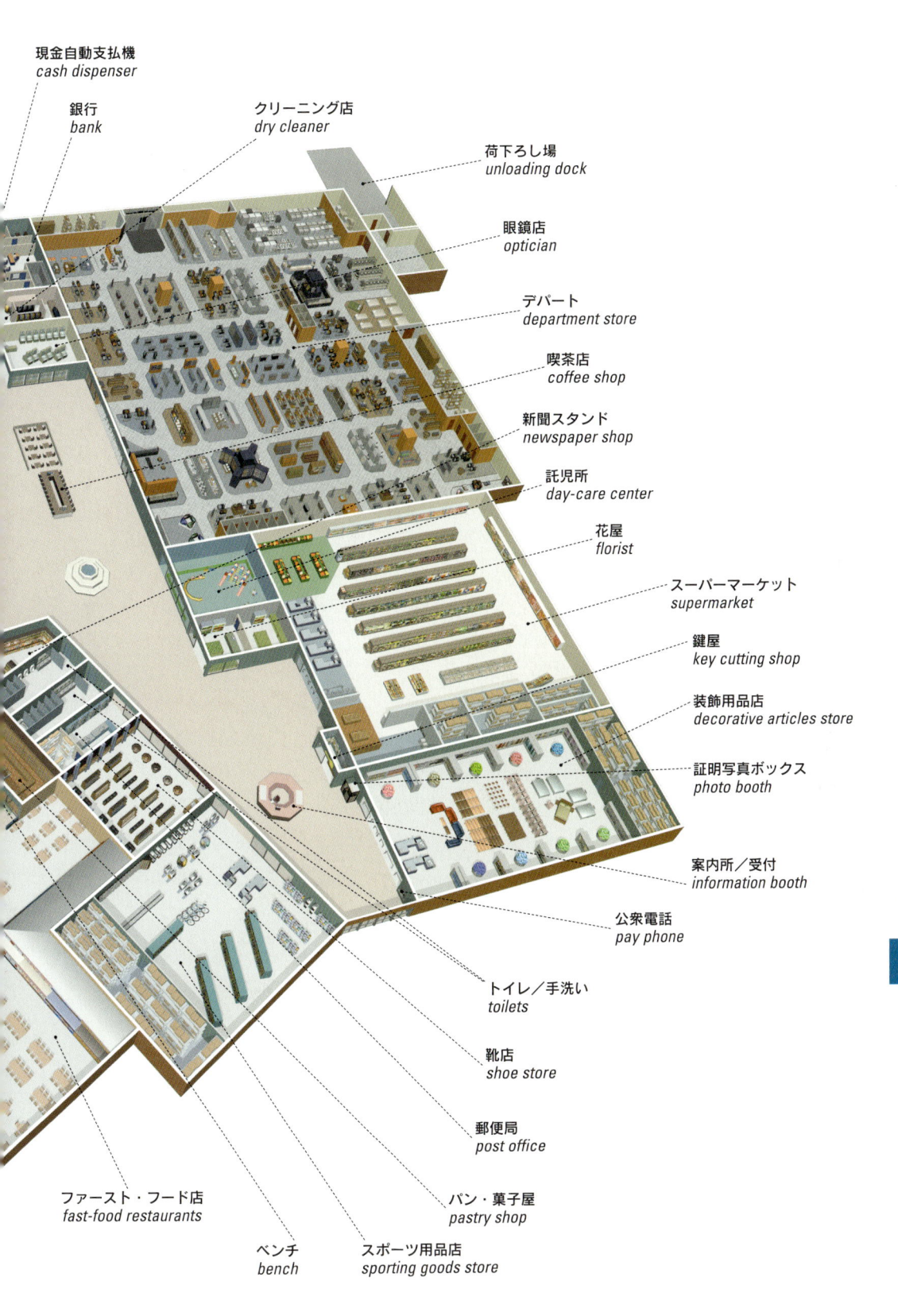

商業サービス | COMMERCIAL SERVICES

- 現金自動支払機 / cash dispenser
- 銀行 / bank
- クリーニング店 / dry cleaner
- 荷下ろし場 / unloading dock
- 眼鏡店 / optician
- デパート / department store
- 喫茶店 / coffee shop
- 新聞スタンド / newspaper shop
- 託児所 / day-care center
- 花屋 / florist
- スーパーマーケット / supermarket
- 鍵屋 / key cutting shop
- 装飾用品店 / decorative articles store
- 証明写真ボックス / photo booth
- 案内所／受付 / information booth
- 公衆電話 / pay phone
- トイレ／手洗い / toilets
- 靴店 / shoe store
- 郵便局 / post office
- ファースト・フード店 / fast-food restaurants
- パン・菓子屋 / pastry shop
- ベンチ / bench
- スポーツ用品店 / sporting goods store

社会

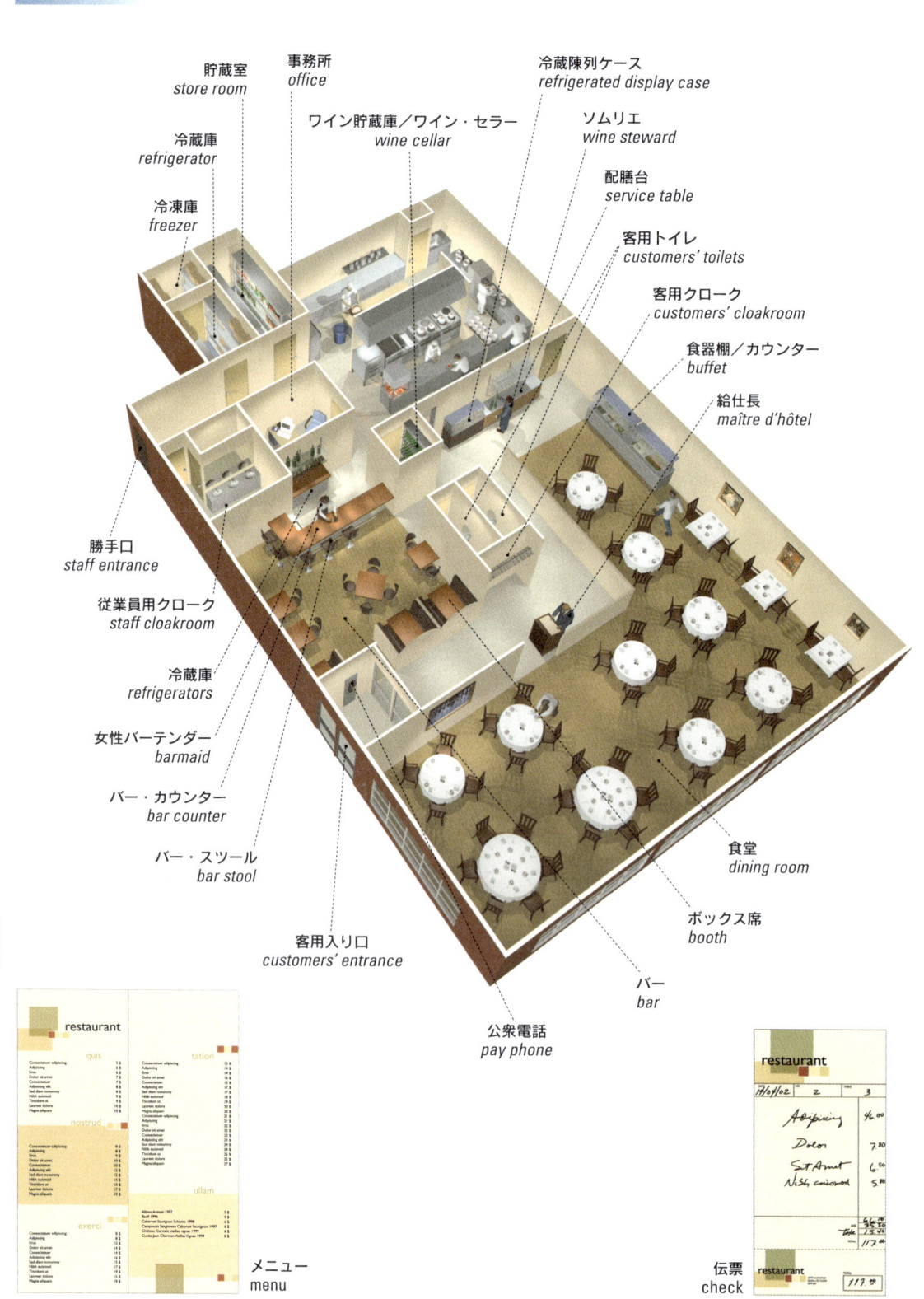

商業サービス | COMMERCIAL SERVICES

レストラン
RESTAURANT

- 貯蔵室 / store room
- 事務所 / office
- 冷蔵陳列ケース / refrigerated display case
- ワイン貯蔵庫／ワイン・セラー / wine cellar
- ソムリエ / wine steward
- 冷蔵庫 / refrigerator
- 配膳台 / service table
- 冷凍庫 / freezer
- 客用トイレ / customers' toilets
- 客用クローク / customers' cloakroom
- 食器棚／カウンター / buffet
- 給仕長 / maître d'hôtel
- 勝手口 / staff entrance
- 従業員用クローク / staff cloakroom
- 冷蔵庫 / refrigerators
- 女性バーテンダー / barmaid
- バー・カウンター / bar counter
- バー・スツール / bar stool
- 食堂 / dining room
- ボックス席 / booth
- 客用入り口 / customers' entrance
- バー / bar
- 公衆電話 / pay phone
- メニュー / menu
- 伝票 / check

社会

商業サービス | COMMERCIAL SERVICES

ガソリン・スタンド
SERVICE STATION

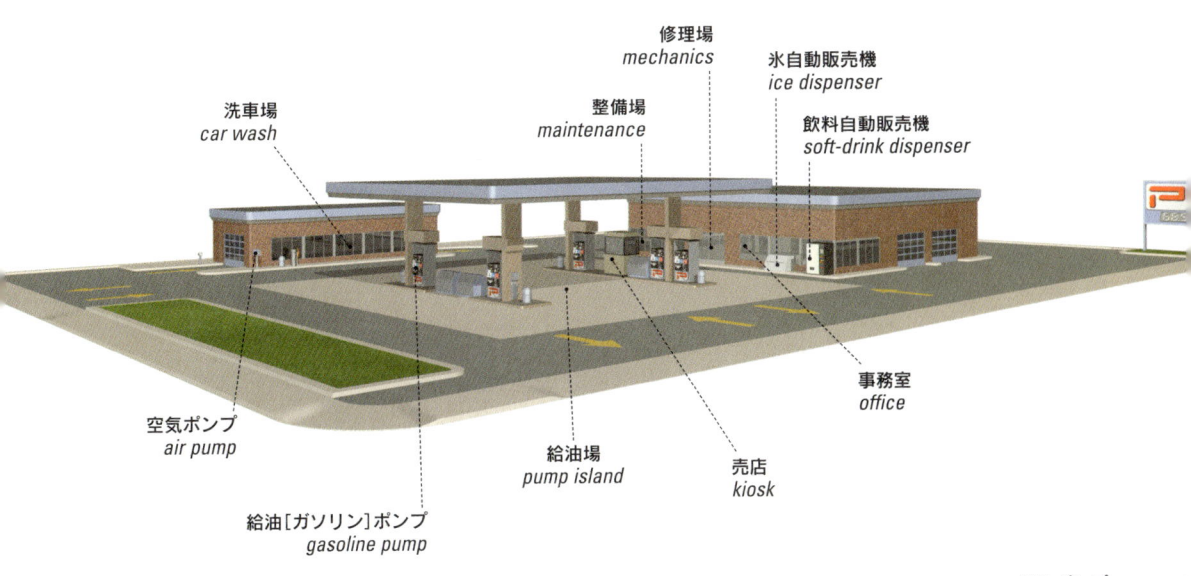

- 洗車場 / car wash
- 修理場 / mechanics
- 整備場 / maintenance
- 氷自動販売機 / ice dispenser
- 飲料自動販売機 / soft-drink dispenser
- 空気ポンプ / air pump
- 事務室 / office
- 給油場 / pump island
- 売店 / kiosk
- 給油[ガソリン]ポンプ / gasoline pump

給油ポンプ / gasoline pump

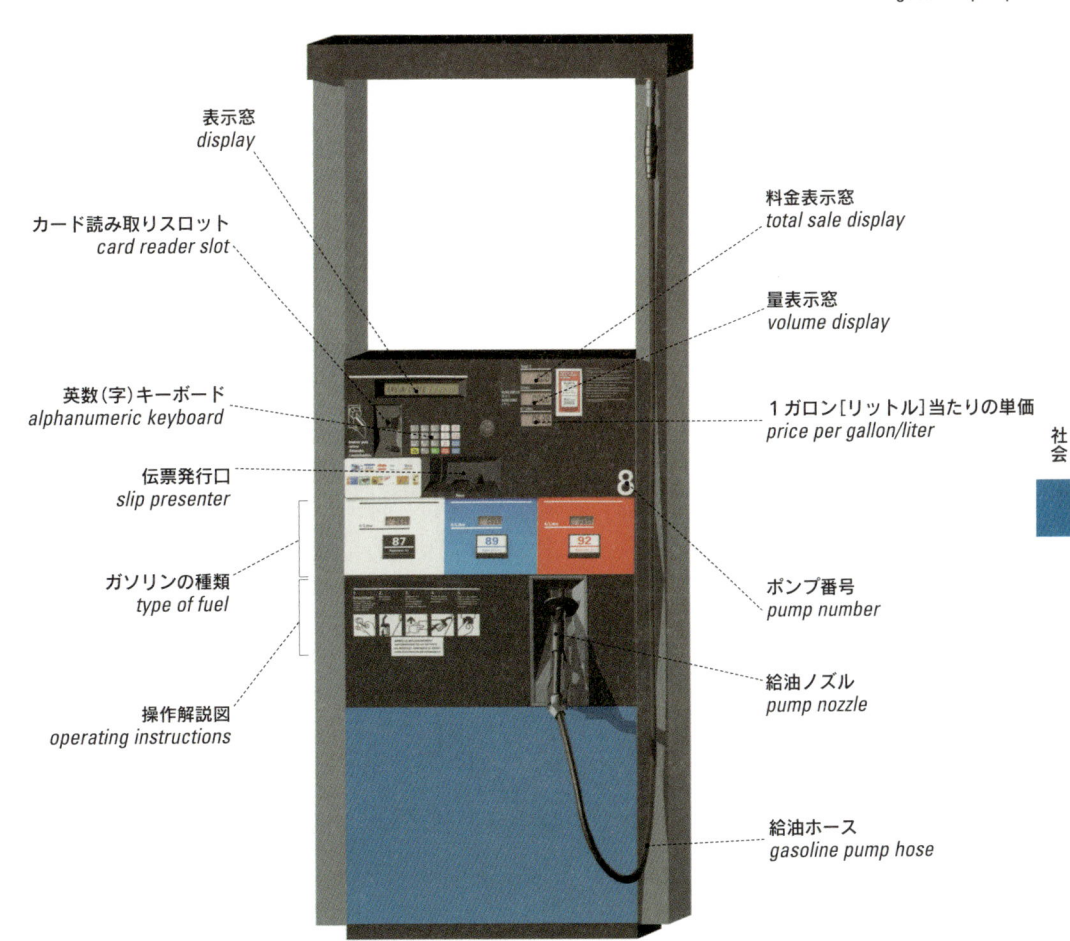

- 表示窓 / display
- カード読み取りスロット / card reader slot
- 英数(字)キーボード / alphanumeric keyboard
- 伝票発行口 / slip presenter
- ガソリンの種類 / type of fuel
- 操作解説図 / operating instructions
- 料金表示窓 / total sale display
- 量表示窓 / volume display
- 1ガロン[リットル]当たりの単価 / price per gallon/liter
- ポンプ番号 / pump number
- 給油ノズル / pump nozzle
- 給油ホース / gasoline pump hose

安全 | SAFETY

火事に敢然と立ち向かい、負傷者を助けるだけではなく、消防士はあらゆる手段で私たちの安全を保証してくれます。道路上で事故があっても、洪水があっても、最初に現場に駆け付けてくれるのは消防士です。警察官も私たちの安全を守ってくれます。法律の番人たちは秩序を徹底させる以外にも、公共の場で未然に事故を防ぐために、監視しながら犯罪を予防しています。

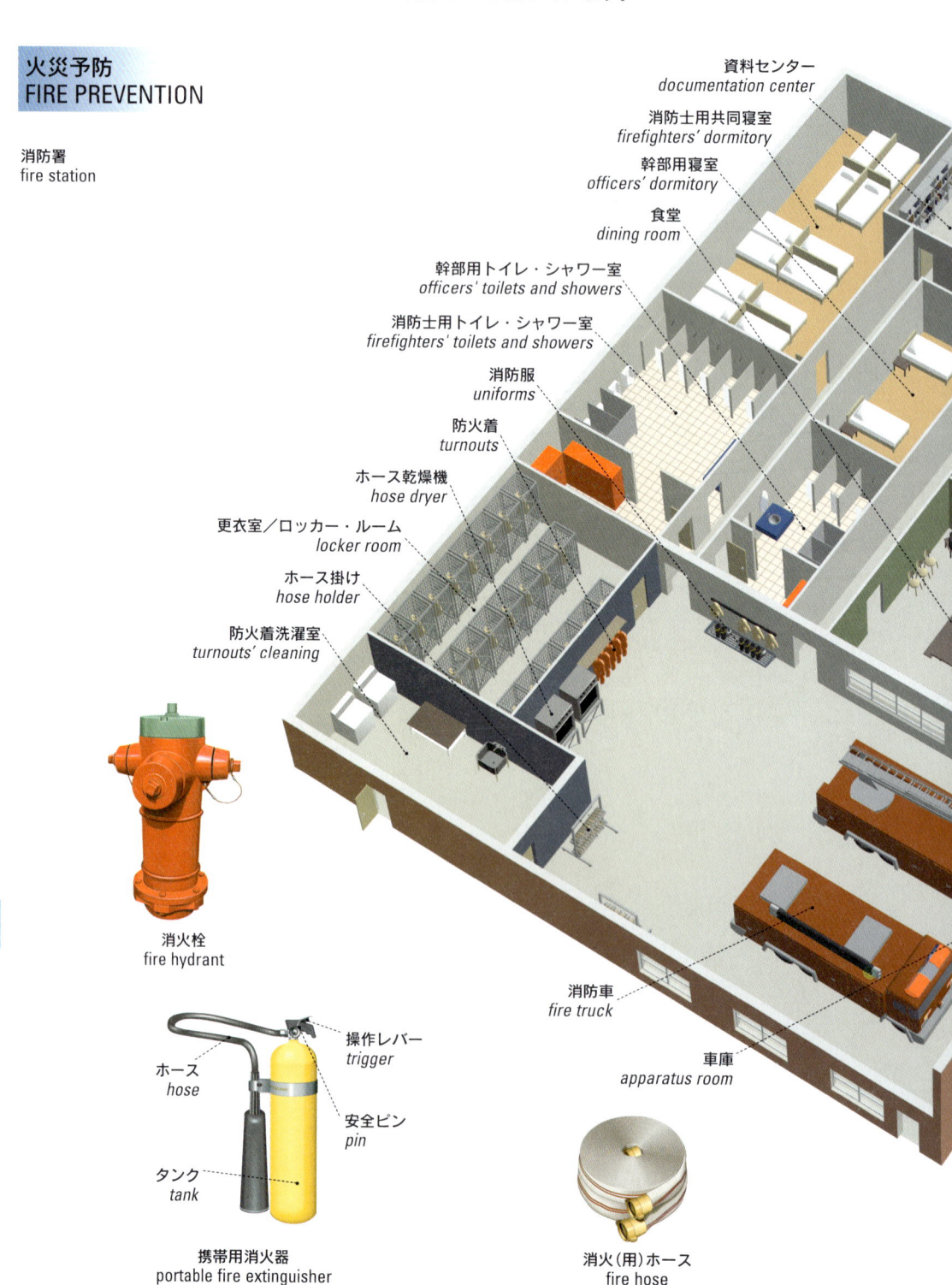

火災予防
FIRE PREVENTION

消防署
fire station

資料センター
documentation center

消防士用共同寝室
firefighters' dormitory

幹部用寝室
officers' dormitory

食堂
dining room

幹部用トイレ・シャワー室
officers' toilets and showers

消防士用トイレ・シャワー室
firefighters' toilets and showers

消防服
uniforms

防火着
turnouts

ホース乾燥機
hose dryer

更衣室／ロッカー・ルーム
locker room

ホース掛け
hose holder

防火着洗濯室
turnouts' cleaning

消火栓
fire hydrant

操作レバー
trigger

ホース
hose

安全ピン
pin

タンク
tank

携帯用消火器
portable fire extinguisher

消防車
fire truck

車庫
apparatus room

消火(用)ホース
fire hose

社会

安全 | SAFETY

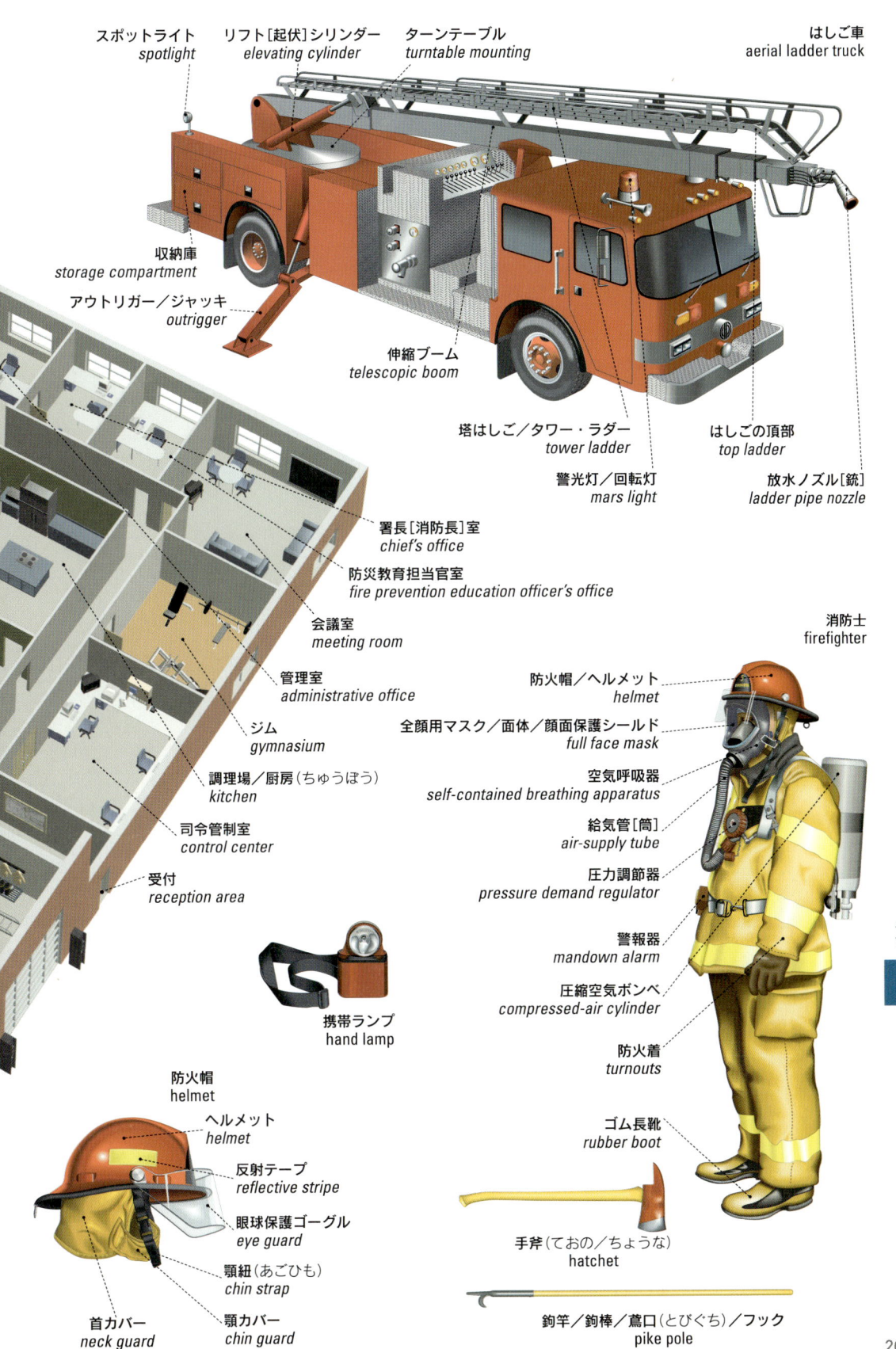

はしご車 / aerial ladder truck

- スポットライト / spotlight
- リフト[起伏]シリンダー / elevating cylinder
- ターンテーブル / turntable mounting
- 収納庫 / storage compartment
- アウトリガー／ジャッキ / outrigger
- 伸縮ブーム / telescopic boom
- 塔はしご／タワー・ラダー / tower ladder
- 警光灯／回転灯 / mars light
- はしごの頂部 / top ladder
- 放水ノズル[銃] / ladder pipe nozzle

建物

- 署長[消防長]室 / chief's office
- 防災教育担当官室 / fire prevention education officer's office
- 会議室 / meeting room
- 管理室 / administrative office
- ジム / gymnasium
- 調理場／厨房（ちゅうぼう）/ kitchen
- 司令管制室 / control center
- 受付 / reception area

携帯ランプ / hand lamp

消防士 / firefighter

- 防火帽／ヘルメット / helmet
- 全顔用マスク／面体／顔面保護シールド / full face mask
- 空気呼吸器 / self-contained breathing apparatus
- 給気管[筒] / air-supply tube
- 圧力調節器 / pressure demand regulator
- 警報器 / mandown alarm
- 圧縮空気ボンベ / compressed-air cylinder
- 防火着 / turnouts
- ゴム長靴 / rubber boot
- 手斧（ておの／ちょうな）/ hatchet
- 鉤竿／鉤棒／鳶口（とびぐち）／フック / pike pole

防火帽 / helmet

- ヘルメット / helmet
- 反射テープ / reflective stripe
- 眼球保護ゴーグル / eye guard
- 顎紐（あごひも）/ chin strap
- 顎カバー / chin guard
- 首カバー / neck guard

社会

263

犯罪防止
CRIME PREVENTION

警察署
police station

取り調べ室／聴取室
interrogation room

ガレージ／車庫
garage

未成年者房
juvenile cell

男子房
men's cell

女子房
women's cell

収容者用シャワー室
prisoners' shower

鑑識課
identification section

司令室／管制室
control room

署員休憩室
staff lounge

署員用クローク［ロッカー・ルーム］
staff cloakroom

署員用トイレ
staff toilet

署長室
chief officer's office

報告書作成室
report writing room

苦情相談窓口［室］
complaints office

副署長室
junior officer's office

待合室
waiting room

装備
equipment

案内所／受付
information desk

管理事務所
administrative office

安全 | SAFETY

社会

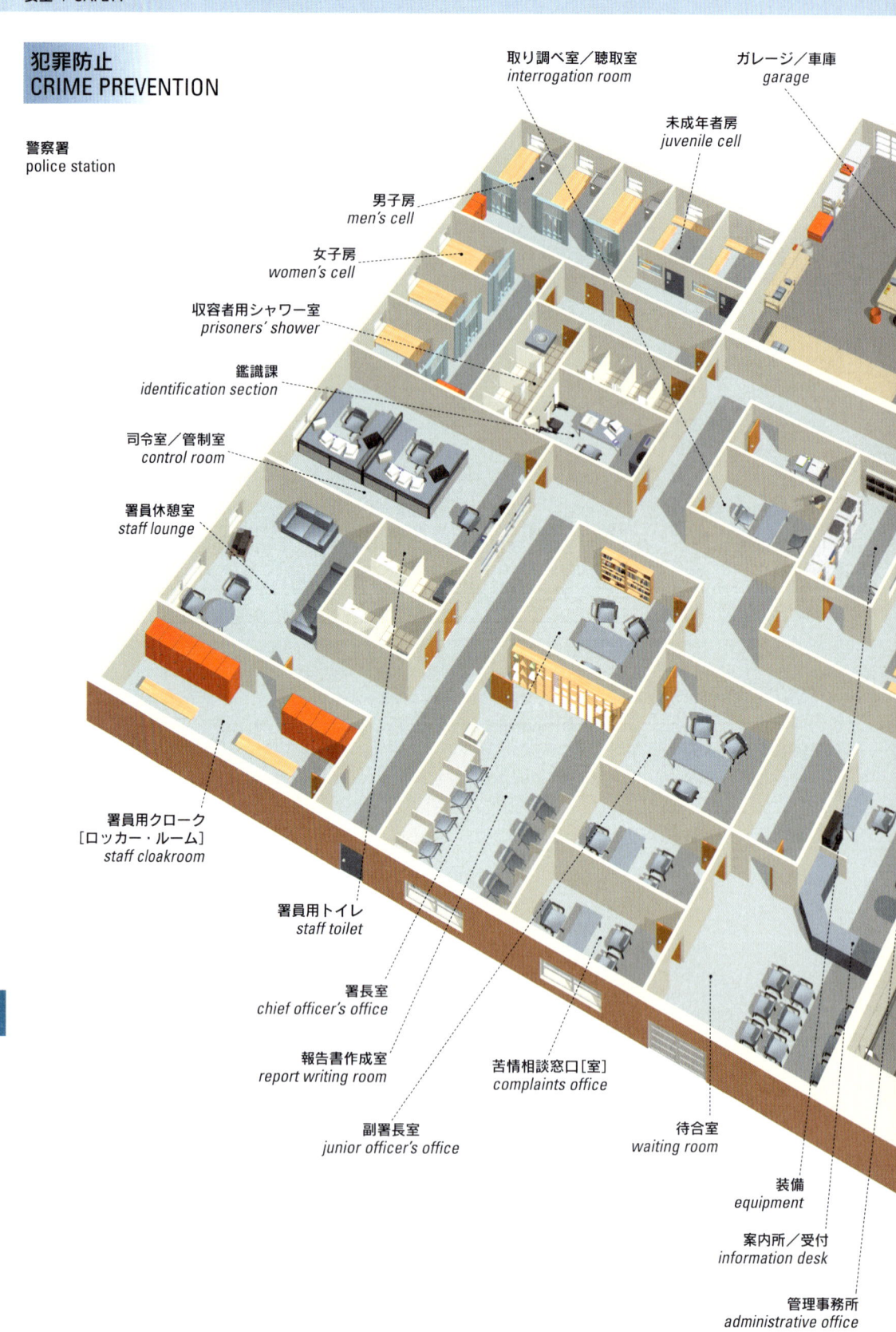

安全 | SAFETY

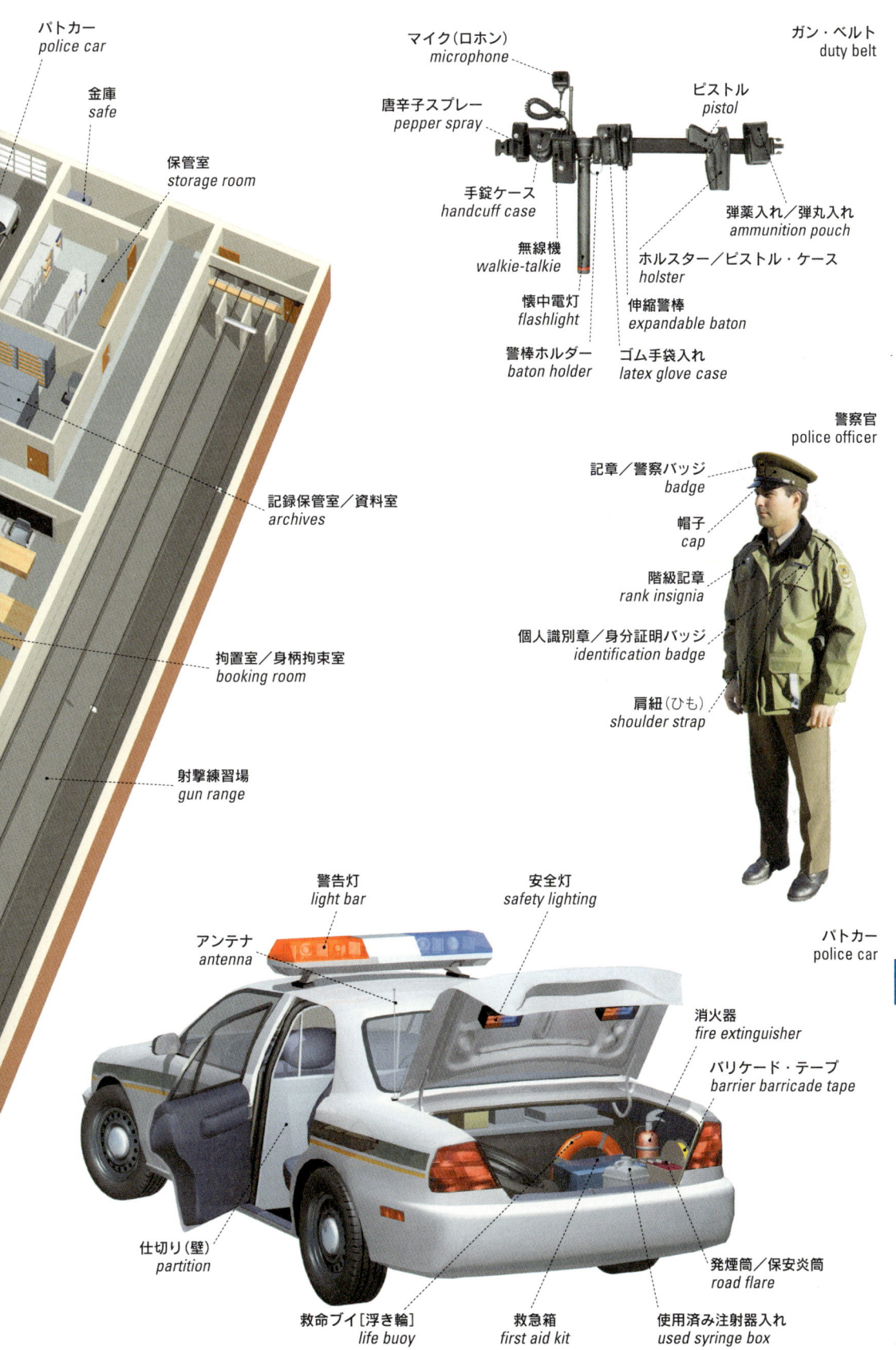

- パトカー police car
- 金庫 safe
- 保管室 storage room
- 記録保管室／資料室 archives
- 拘置室／身柄拘束室 booking room
- 射撃練習場 gun range

- マイク（ロホン） microphone
- 唐辛子スプレー pepper spray
- 手錠ケース handcuff case
- 無線機 walkie-talkie
- 懐中電灯 flashlight
- 警棒ホルダー baton holder

- ガン・ベルト duty belt
- ピストル pistol
- 弾薬入れ／弾丸入れ ammunition pouch
- ホルスター／ピストル・ケース holster
- 伸縮警棒 expandable baton
- ゴム手袋入れ latex glove case

- 警察官 police officer
- 記章／警察バッジ badge
- 帽子 cap
- 階級記章 rank insignia
- 個人識別章／身分証明バッジ identification badge
- 肩紐（ひも） shoulder strap

- 警告灯 light bar
- 安全灯 safety lighting
- アンテナ antenna
- パトカー police car
- 消火器 fire extinguisher
- バリケード・テープ barrier barricade tape
- 仕切り（壁） partition
- 救命ブイ［浮き輪］ life buoy
- 救急箱 first aid kit
- 発煙筒／保安炎筒 road flare
- 使用済み注射器入れ used syringe box

社会

健康 | HEALTH

大衆に医療サービスを施す施設の中では、最も多様なサービスを提供できる病院が一番充実しています。大都市では医療施設は大医療センターになり、あらゆる科の専門家が昼夜を問わず病人や負傷者に質の高い治療を行っています。

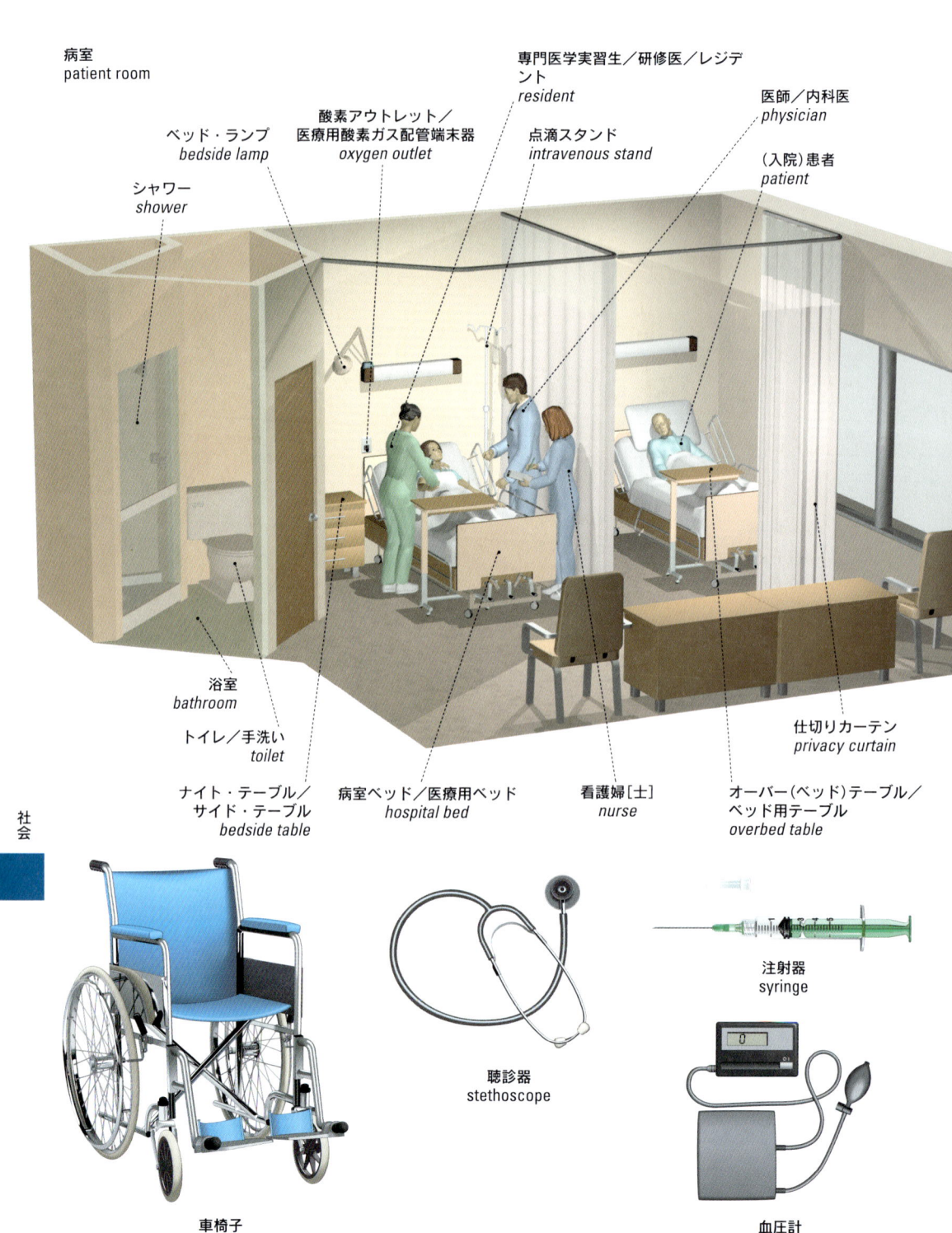

病室
patient room

ベッド・ランプ
bedside lamp

シャワー
shower

酸素アウトレット／医療用酸素ガス配管端末器
oxygen outlet

専門医学実習生／研修医／レジデント
resident

点滴スタンド
intravenous stand

医師／内科医
physician

(入院)患者
patient

浴室
bathroom

トイレ／手洗い
toilet

ナイト・テーブル／サイド・テーブル
bedside table

病室ベッド／医療用ベッド
hospital bed

看護婦[士]
nurse

オーバー(ベッド)テーブル／ベッド用テーブル
overbed table

仕切りカーテン
privacy curtain

車椅子
wheelchair

聴診器
stethoscope

注射器
syringe

血圧計
blood pressure monitor

社会

健康 | HEALTH

救急車
ambulance

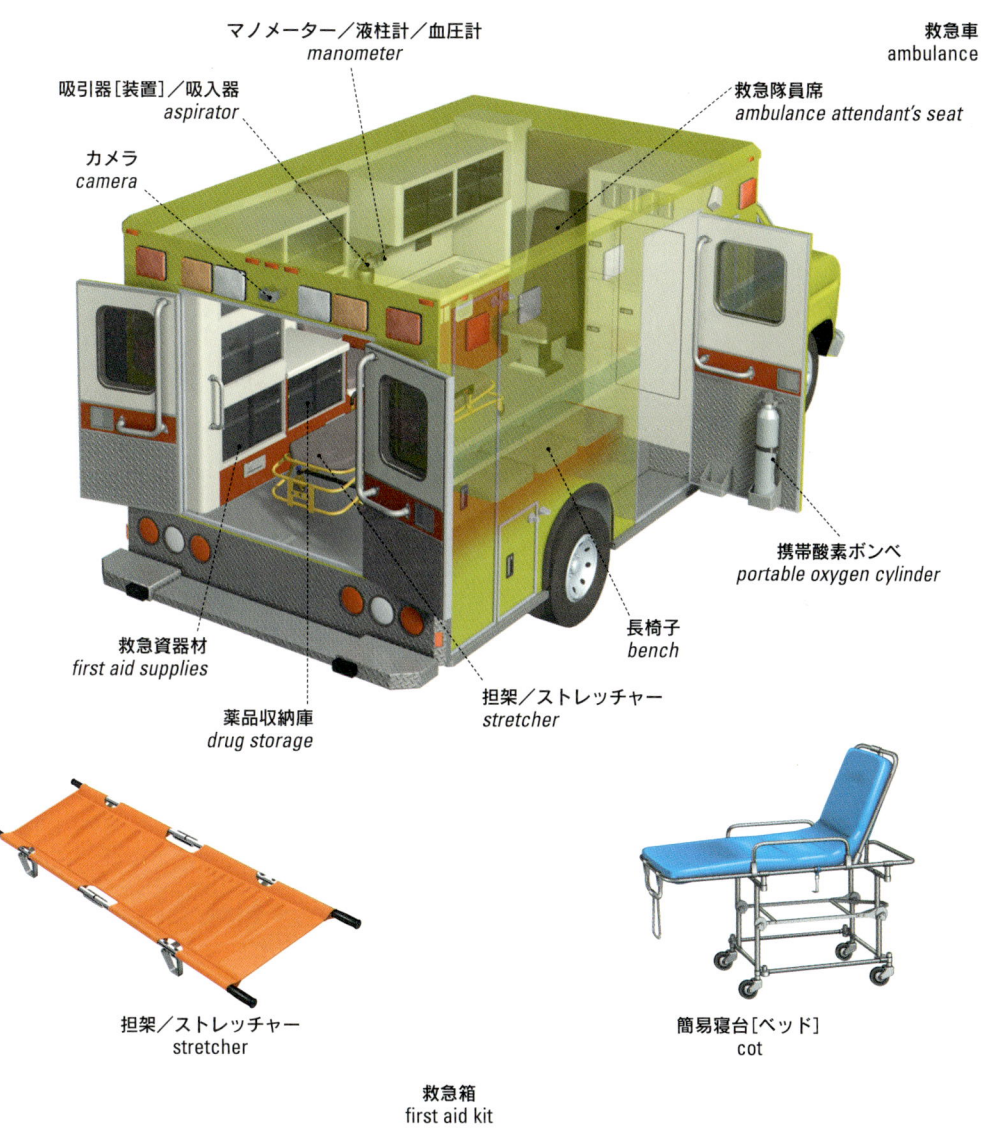

- マノメーター／液柱計／血圧計 manometer
- 吸引器[装置]／吸入器 aspirator
- カメラ camera
- 救急隊員席 ambulance attendant's seat
- 携帯酸素ボンベ portable oxygen cylinder
- 長椅子 bench
- 担架／ストレッチャー stretcher
- 薬品収納庫 drug storage
- 救急資器材 first aid supplies

担架／ストレッチャー
stretcher

簡易寝台[ベッド]
cot

救急箱
first aid kit

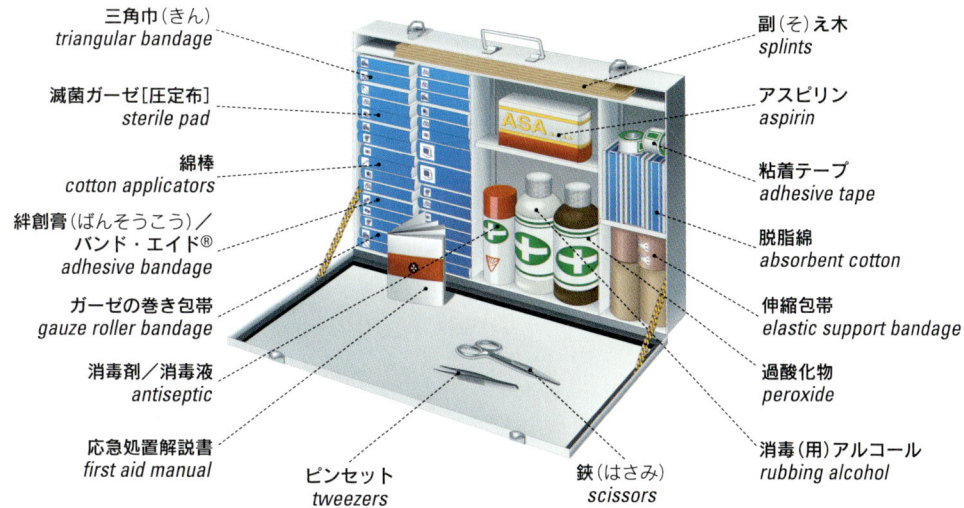

- 三角巾(きん) triangular bandage
- 滅菌ガーゼ[圧定布] sterile pad
- 綿棒 cotton applicators
- 絆創膏(ばんそうこう)／バンド・エイド® adhesive bandage
- ガーゼの巻き包帯 gauze roller bandage
- 消毒剤／消毒液 antiseptic
- 応急処置解説書 first aid manual
- ピンセット tweezers
- 鋏(はさみ) scissors
- 副(そ)え木 splints
- アスピリン aspirin
- 粘着テープ adhesive tape
- 脱脂綿 absorbent cotton
- 伸縮包帯 elastic support bandage
- 過酸化物 peroxide
- 消毒(用)アルコール rubbing alcohol

社会

267

教育 | EDUCATION

どの先進国でも教育はある決められた年齢まで義務化されています。初等教育は4歳から7歳くらいの間で始まり、一般的にはお金が掛かりません。子供たちは学校で読み、書き、計算を学ぶだけではなく、知的にも、肉体的にも、道徳的にも成長します。それでも発展途上国では、財源不足のために、きちんとした教育が受けられない子供たちがたくさんいます。

学校
SCHOOL

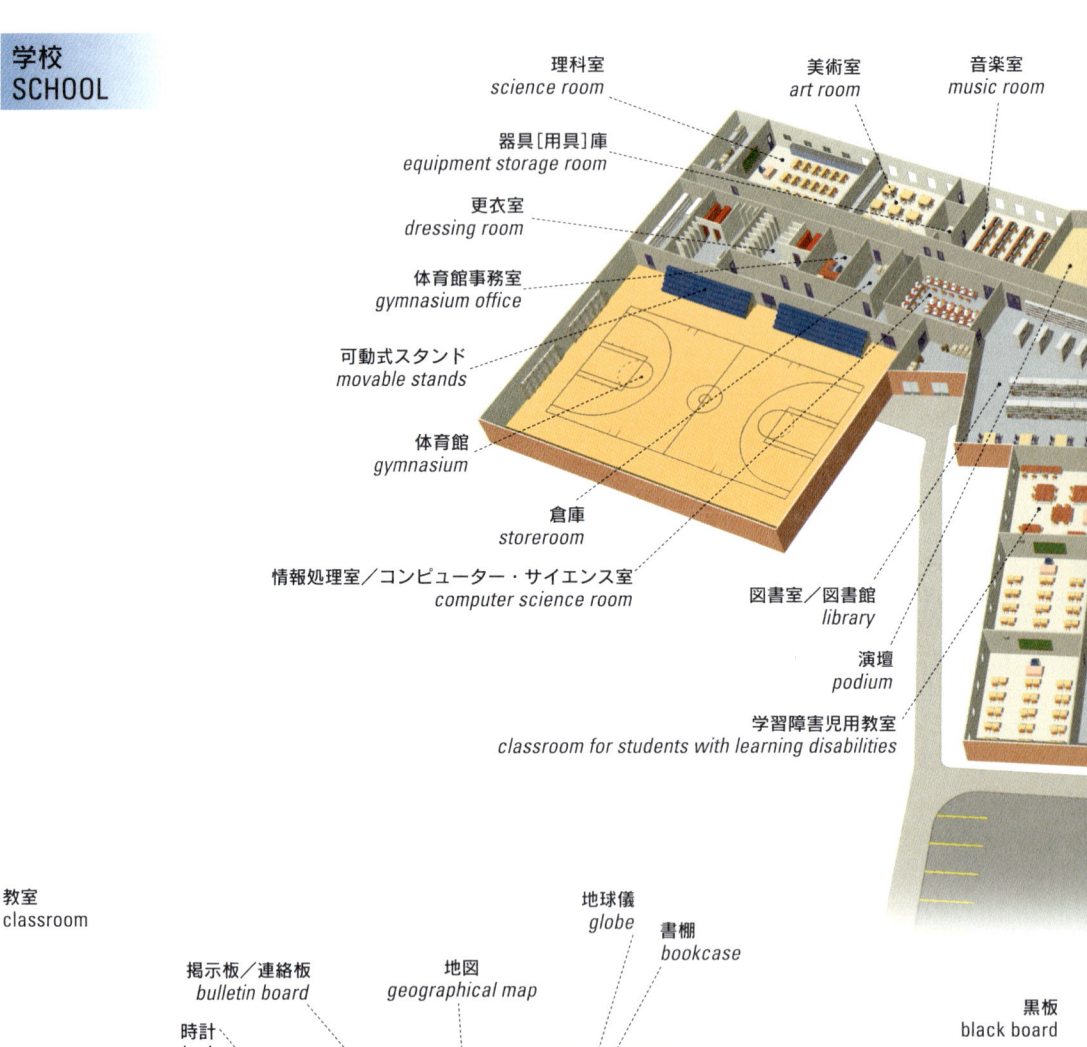

- 理科室 / science room
- 美術室 / art room
- 音楽室 / music room
- 器具[用具]庫 / equipment storage room
- 更衣室 / dressing room
- 体育館事務室 / gymnasium office
- 可動式スタンド / movable stands
- 体育館 / gymnasium
- 倉庫 / storeroom
- 情報処理室／コンピューター・サイエンス室 / computer science room
- 図書室／図書館 / library
- 演壇 / podium
- 学習障害児用教室 / classroom for students with learning disabilities

教室
classroom

- 掲示板／連絡板 / bulletin board
- 地図 / geographical map
- 地球儀 / globe
- 書棚 / bookcase
- 黒板 / black board
- 時計 / clock
- 教師 / teacher
- 黒板 / blackboard
- 肘掛け椅子 / armchair
- テレビ受像機 / television set
- 教卓／教師用机 / teacher's desk
- 生徒(用)机 / student's desk
- 生徒 / student
- 椅子 / armless chair
- コンピューター / computer

社会

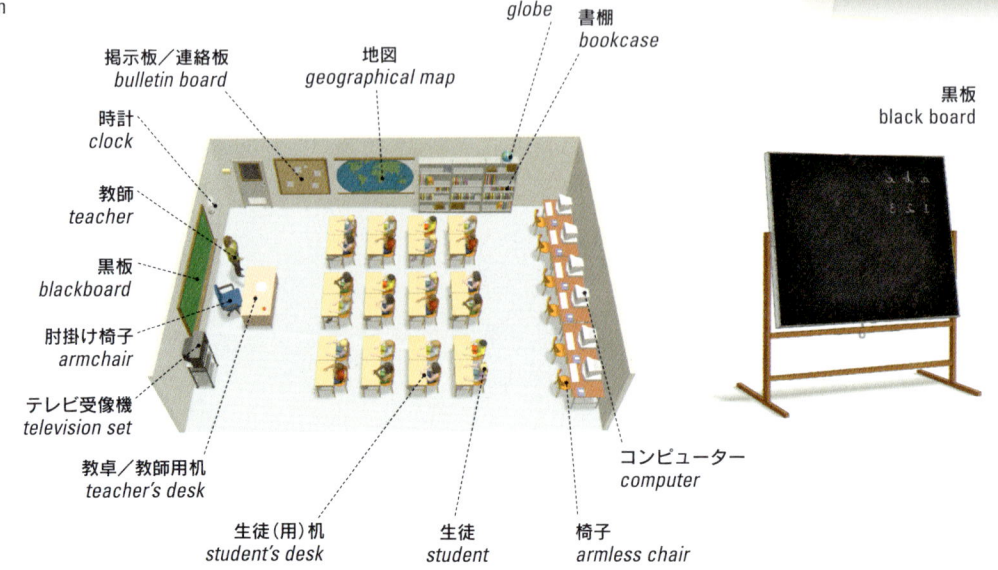

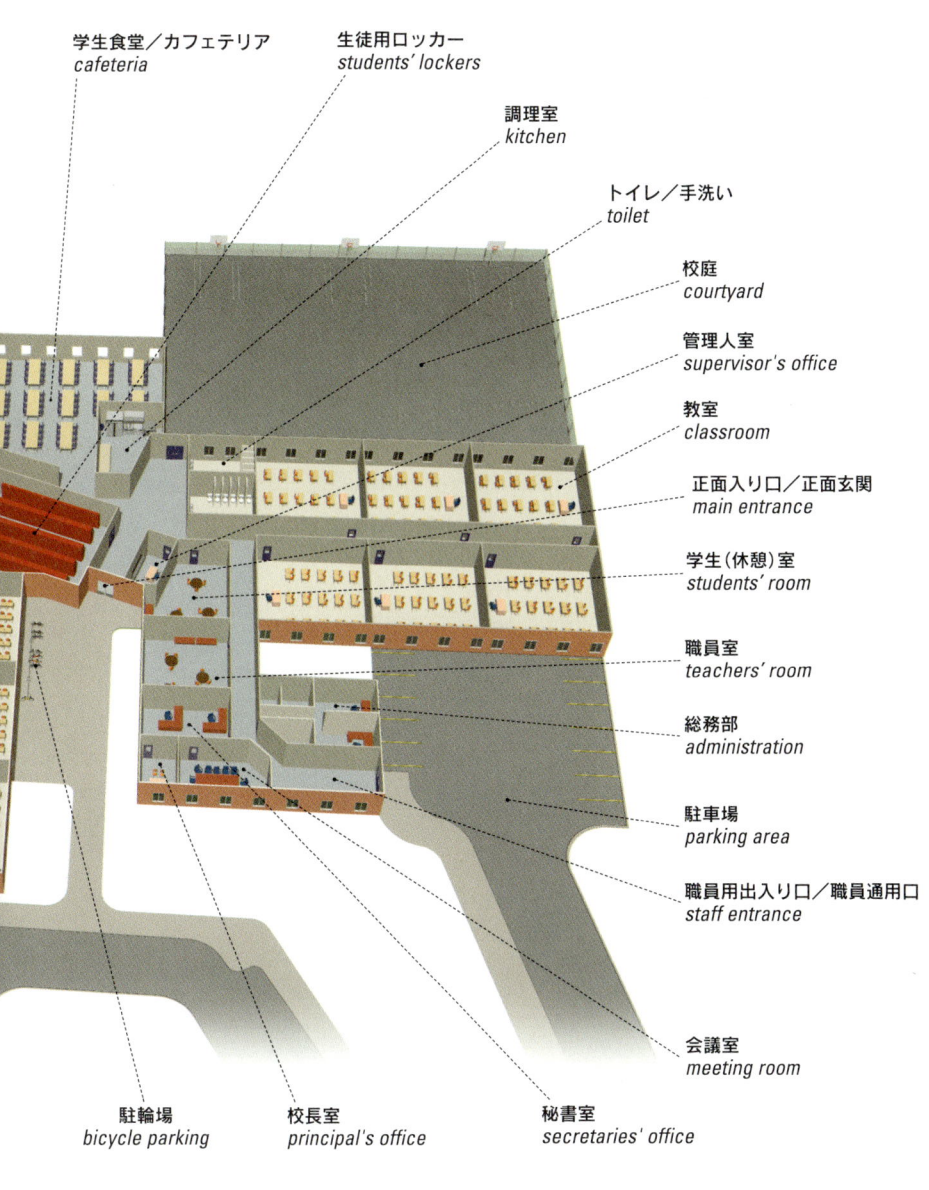

教育 | EDUCATION

学生食堂／カフェテリア
cafeteria

生徒用ロッカー
students' lockers

調理室
kitchen

トイレ／手洗い
toilet

校庭
courtyard

管理人室
supervisor's office

教室
classroom

正面入り口／正面玄関
main entrance

学生（休憩）室
students' room

職員室
teachers' room

総務部
administration

駐車場
parking area

職員用出入り口／職員通用口
staff entrance

会議室
meeting room

駐輪場
bicycle parking

校長室
principal's office

秘書室
secretaries' office

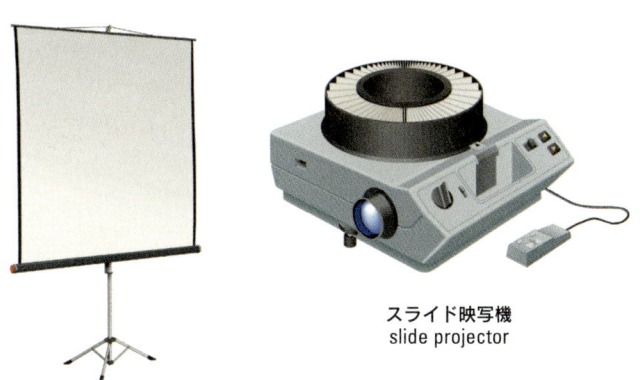

社会

映写ヘッド
projection head

ミラー／鏡
mirror

光学レンズ
optical lens

光学ステージ
optical stage

映写スクリーン
projection screen

スライド映写機
slide projector

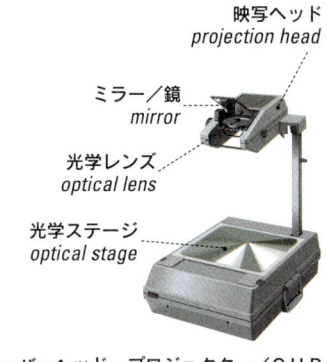

オーバーヘッド・プロジェクター／ＯＨＰ
overhead projector

教育 | EDUCATION

学校用文房具
school supplies

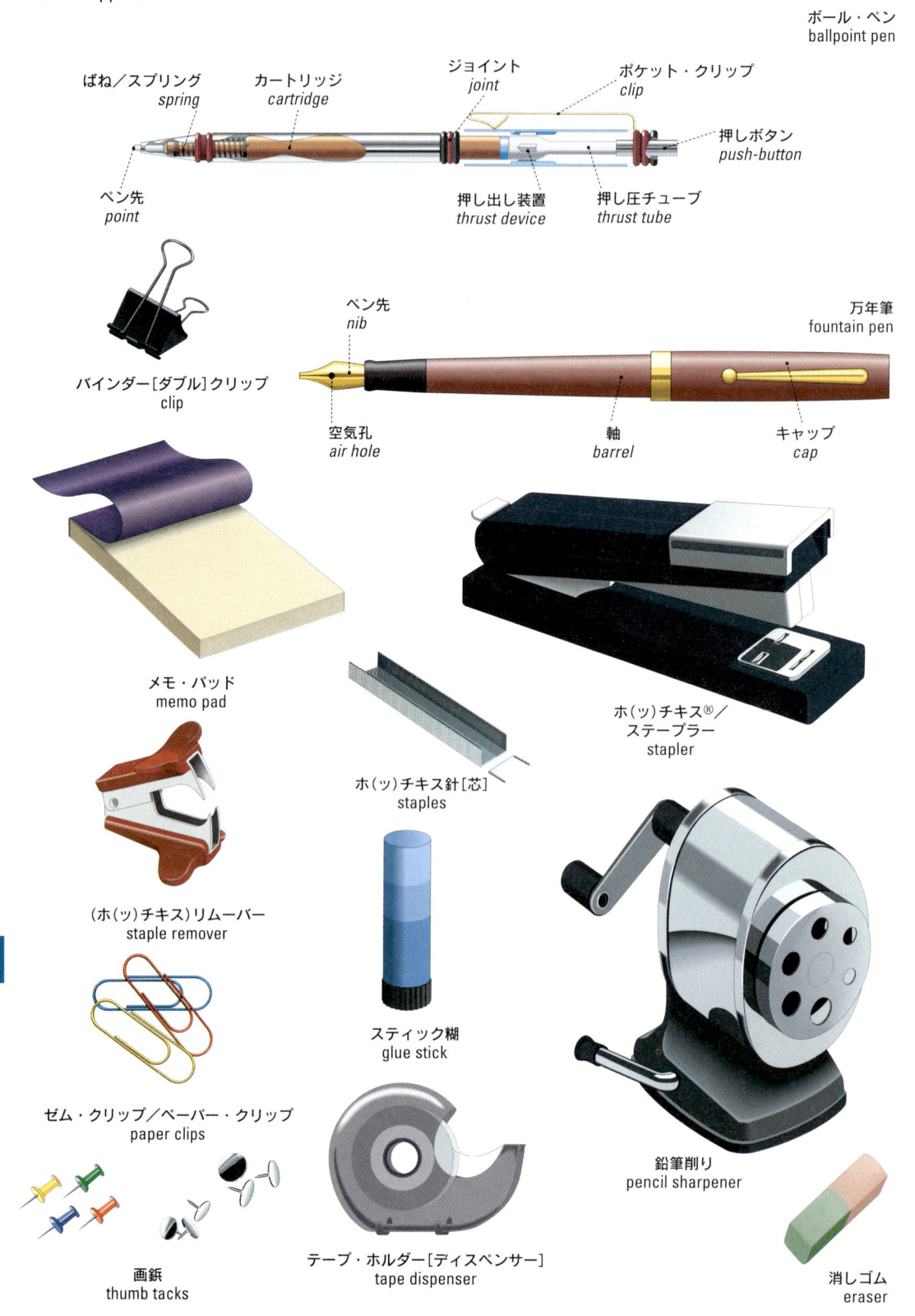

ボール・ペン / ballpoint pen

- ばね／スプリング / spring
- カートリッジ / cartridge
- ジョイント / joint
- ポケット・クリップ / clip
- 押しボタン / push-button
- ペン先 / point
- 押し出し装置 / thrust device
- 押し圧チューブ / thrust tube

バインダー［ダブル］クリップ / clip

万年筆 / fountain pen
- ペン先 / nib
- 空気孔 / air hole
- 軸 / barrel
- キャップ / cap

メモ・パッド / memo pad

ホ(ッ)チキス®／ステープラー / stapler

ホ(ッ)チキス針［芯］ / staples

(ホ(ッ)チキス)リムーバー / staple remover

スティック糊 / glue stick

ゼム・クリップ／ペーパー・クリップ / paper clips

画鋲 / thumb tacks

テープ・ホルダー［ディスペンサー］ / tape dispenser

鉛筆削り / pencil sharpener

消しゴム / eraser

教育 | EDUCATION

目盛り
scale

定規
ruler

分度器
protractor

直角定規／三角定規
framing square

シャープ・ペンシル®
mechanical pencil

鉛筆型消しゴム
eraser holder

マーカー
marker

鉛筆
pencil

蛍光ペン
highlighter pen

鉛筆型紙巻き消しゴム
stick holder

ノート／帳面
notebook

リング・ファイル［バインダー］
ring binder

スパイラル［スプリング］ノート
spiral binder

ルーズ・リーフ
loose-leaf paper

肩掛けかばん／ランドセル
satchel

社会

娯楽 | ENTERTAINMENT

映画の撮影スタジオで働く人たちから、楽しみで映画を見に行く人たちまで、映画に夢中になっている人はたくさんいます。すべての映画ファンにとって第七芸術と言われる映画は、単なる娯楽で、動きのある像を撮影し、それを映写するだけの手段ではありません。私たちは映画を通して椅子に快適に座ったままで大きな感動を得ることができます。

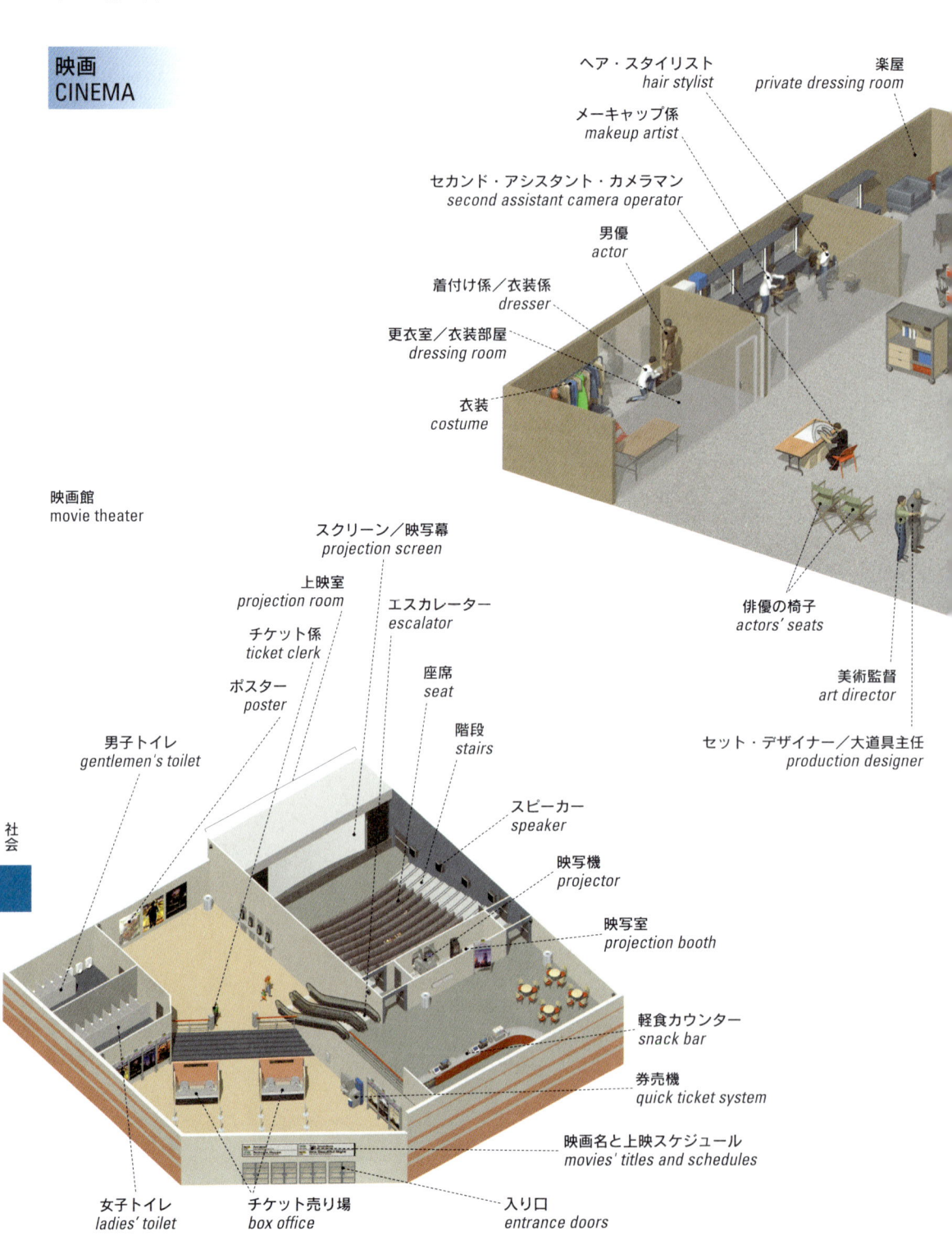

映画
CINEMA

- ヘア・スタイリスト / hair stylist
- 楽屋 / private dressing room
- メーキャップ係 / makeup artist
- セカンド・アシスタント・カメラマン / second assistant camera operator
- 男優 / actor
- 着付け係／衣装係 / dresser
- 更衣室／衣装部屋 / dressing room
- 衣装 / costume
- 映画館 / movie theater
- スクリーン／映写幕 / projection screen
- 上映室 / projection room
- エスカレーター / escalator
- チケット係 / ticket clerk
- 俳優の椅子 / actors' seats
- ポスター / poster
- 座席 / seat
- 美術監督 / art director
- 男子トイレ / gentlemen's toilet
- 階段 / stairs
- セット・デザイナー／大道具主任 / production designer
- スピーカー / speaker
- 映写機 / projector
- 映写室 / projection booth
- 軽食カウンター / snack bar
- 券売機 / quick ticket system
- 映画名と上映スケジュール / movies' titles and schedules
- 女子トイレ / ladies' toilet
- チケット売り場 / box office
- 入口 / entrance doors

社会

娯楽 | ENTERTAINMENT

映画（撮影）セット
movie set

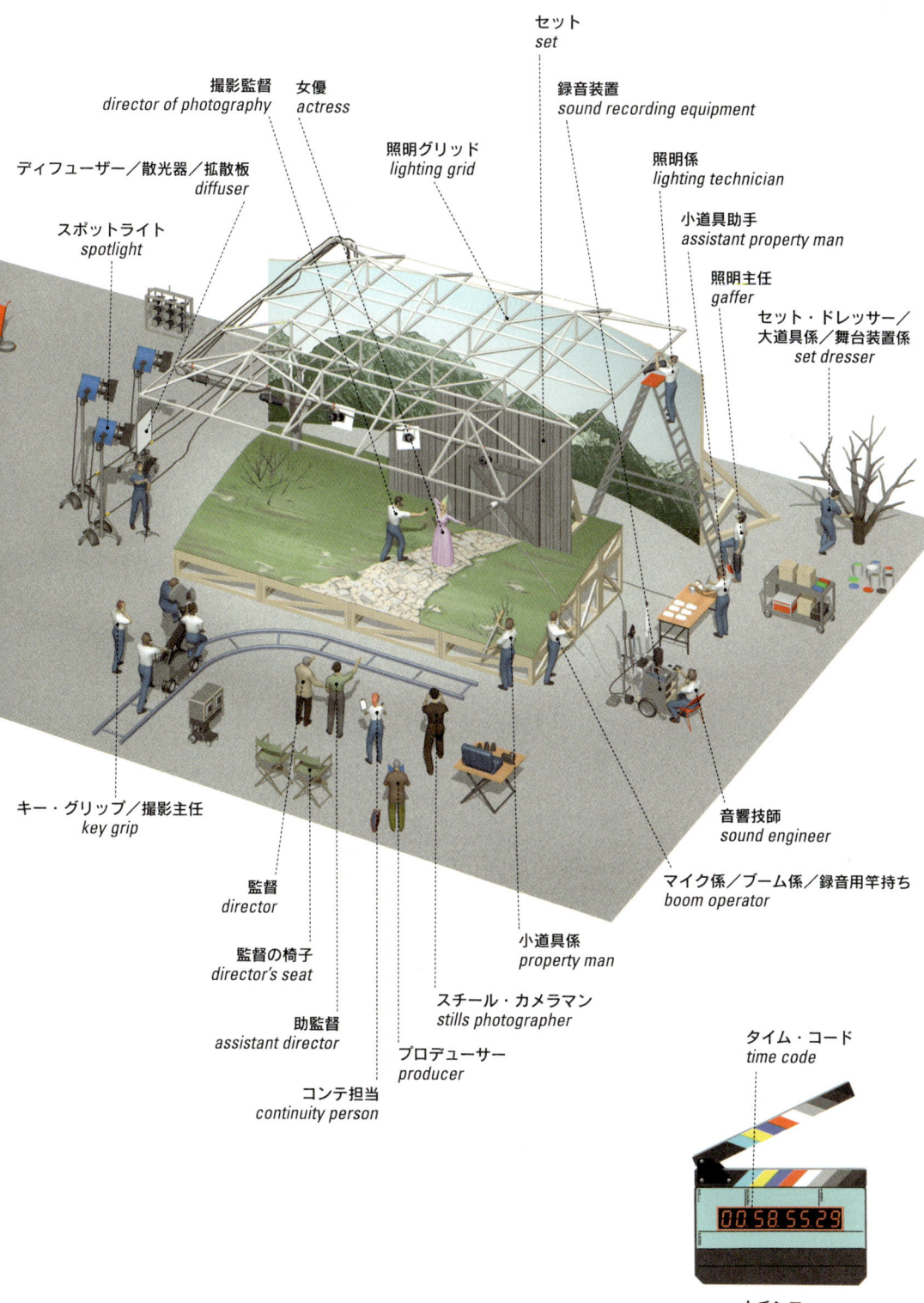

撮影監督
director of photography

女優
actress

セット
set

録音装置
sound recording equipment

照明グリッド
lighting grid

照明係
lighting technician

ディフューザー／散光器／拡散板
diffuser

小道具助手
assistant property man

スポットライト
spotlight

照明主任
gaffer

セット・ドレッサー／
大道具係／舞台装置係
set dresser

キー・グリップ／撮影主任
key grip

音響技師
sound engineer

マイク係／ブーム係／録音用竿持ち
boom operator

監督
director

監督の椅子
director's seat

小道具係
property man

助監督
assistant director

スチール・カメラマン
stills photographer

タイム・コード
time code

プロデューサー
producer

コンテ担当
continuity person

カチンコ
clapper/the slate

体操 | GYMNASTICS

体操で重要なのは、いかに完璧な動きをするかということです。芸術性を競う体操では敏捷性、力強さ、柔軟性が要求されます。女子特有のリズムを競う体操では、さらに振り付けのセンスも必要です。トランポリンを使った体操では、空中で複雑でアクロバット的な演技をこなさなければなりません。

器械体操
GYMNASTICS

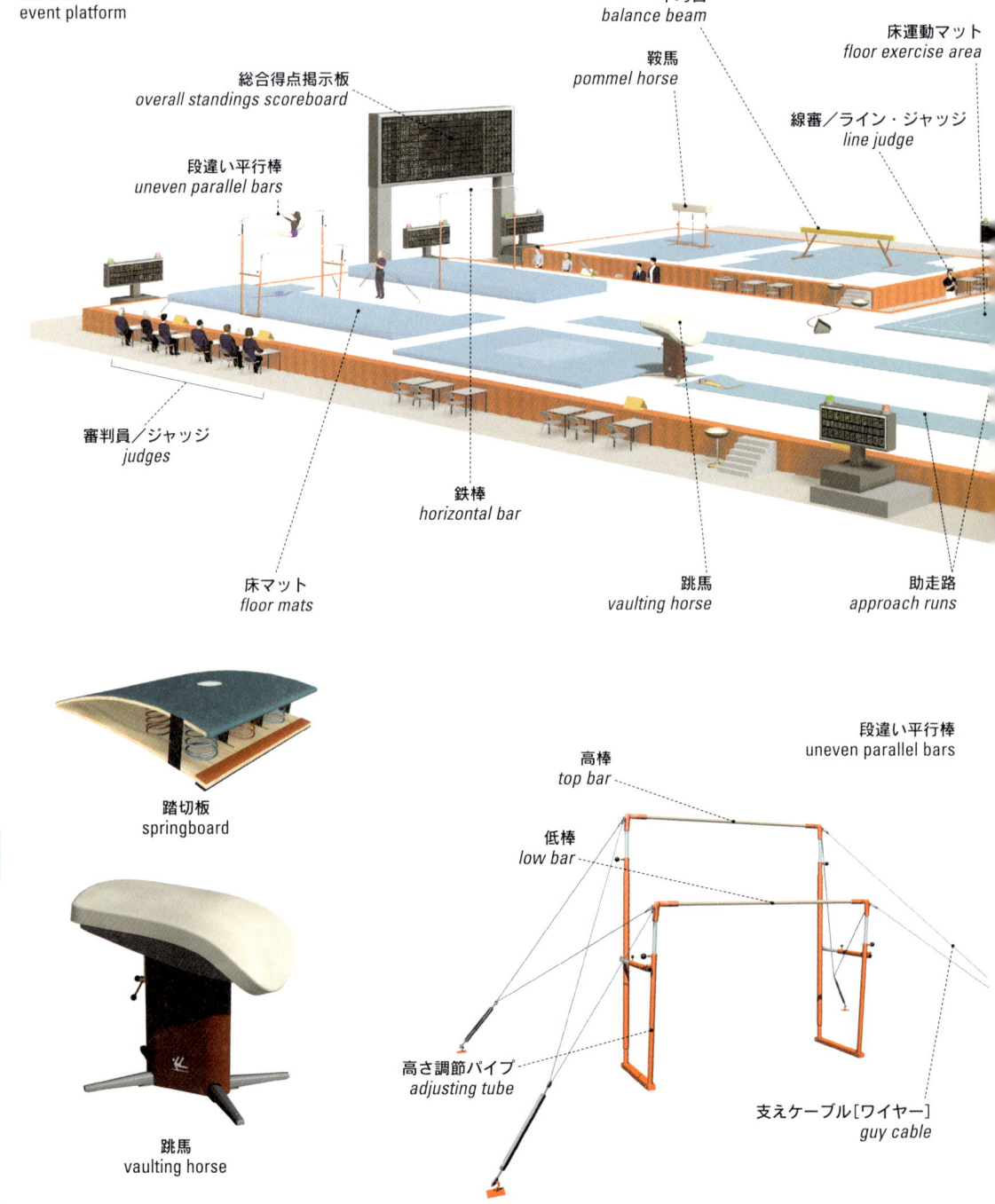

- 演技台 event platform
- 総合得点掲示板 overall standings scoreboard
- 平均台 balance beam
- 鞍馬 pommel horse
- 床運動マット floor exercise area
- 段違い平行棒 uneven parallel bars
- 線審／ライン・ジャッジ line judge
- 審判員／ジャッジ judges
- 鉄棒 horizontal bar
- 床マット floor mats
- 跳馬 vaulting horse
- 助走路 approach runs
- 踏切板 springboard
- 跳馬 vaulting horse
- 段違い平行棒 uneven parallel bars
- 高棒 top bar
- 低棒 low bar
- 高さ調節パイプ adjusting tube
- 支えケーブル［ワイヤー］ guy cable

スポーツ

274

体操 | GYMNASTICS

平均台
balance beam

支柱
upright

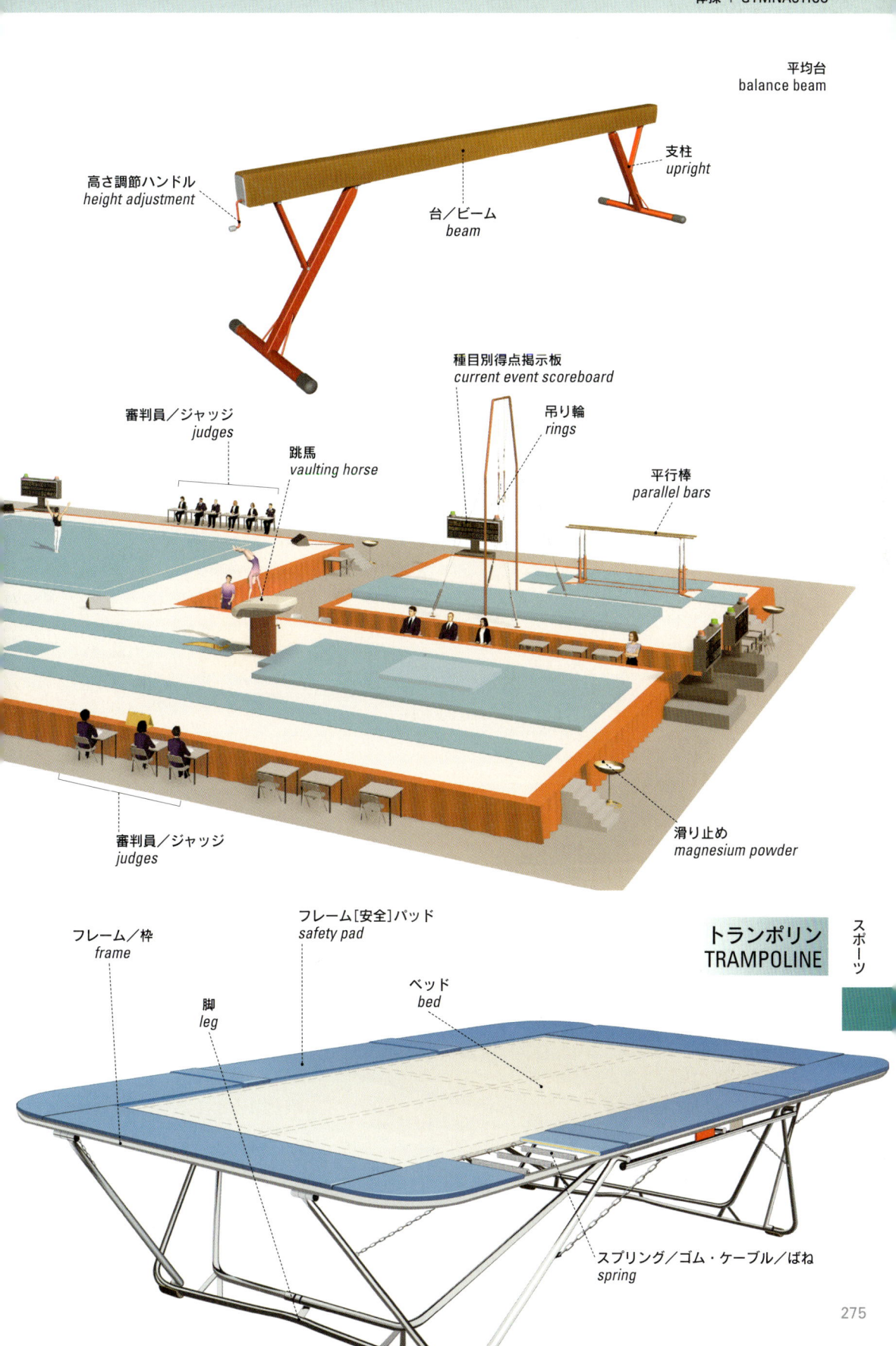

高さ調節ハンドル
height adjustment

台／ビーム
beam

種目別得点掲示板
current event scoreboard

吊り輪
rings

審判員／ジャッジ
judges

跳馬
vaulting horse

平行棒
parallel bars

審判員／ジャッジ
judges

滑り止め
magnesium powder

フレーム／枠
frame

フレーム［安全］パッド
safety pad

トランポリン
TRAMPOLINE

スポーツ

脚
leg

ベッド
bed

スプリング／ゴム・ケーブル／ばね
spring

275

水泳 | SWIMMING

水泳選手の主な目的は、最小限の努力でいかに速く水中を進むかということです。そのためには集中的で、一貫したトレーニングを積まなければなりません。選手はふつうクロール、平泳ぎ、バタフライ、背泳ぎの4泳法の中で得意な泳法を一つ持っています。

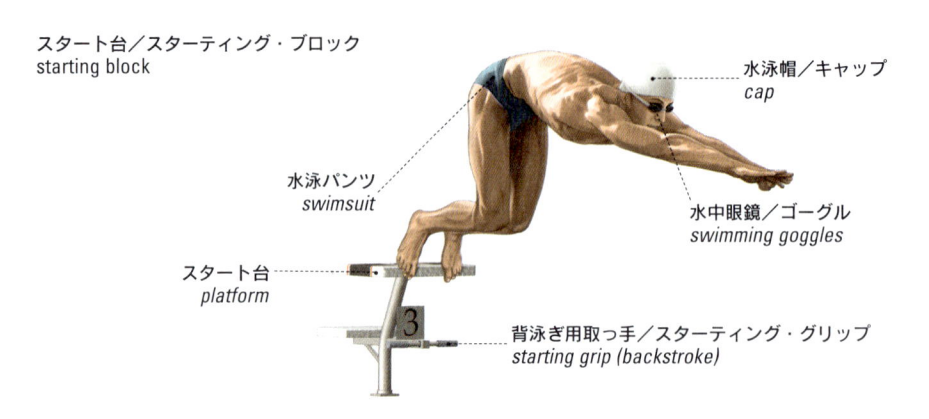

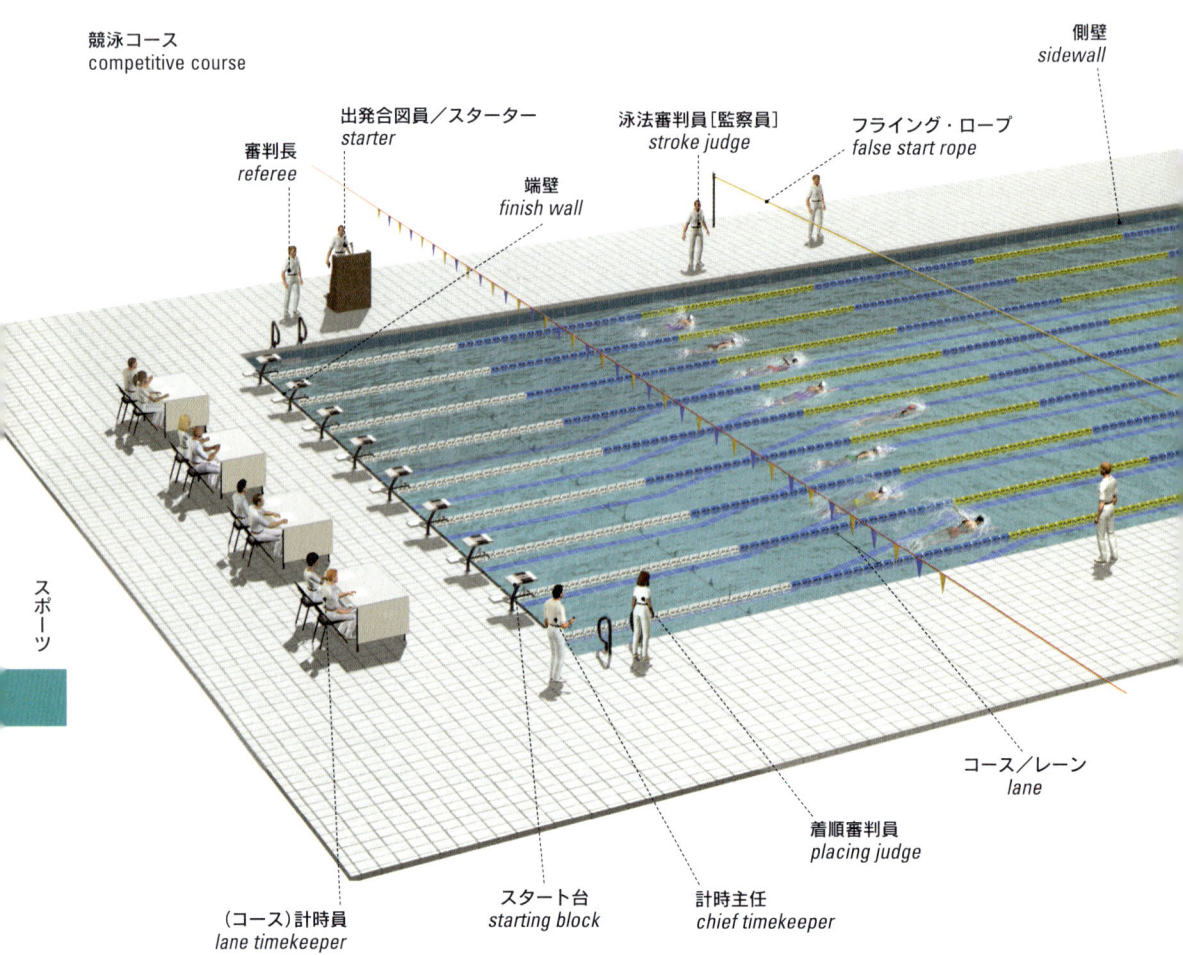

スタート台／スターティング・ブロック
starting block

水泳帽／キャップ
cap

水泳パンツ
swimsuit

水中眼鏡／ゴーグル
swimming goggles

スタート台
platform

背泳ぎ用取っ手／スターティング・グリップ
starting grip (backstroke)

競泳コース
competitive course

側壁
sidewall

出発合図員／スターター
starter

泳法審判員［監察員］
stroke judge

フライング・ロープ
false start rope

審判長
referee

端壁
finish wall

コース／レーン
lane

着順審判員
placing judge

（コース）計時員
lane timekeeper

スタート台
starting block

計時主任
chief timekeeper

スポーツ

水泳 | SWIMMING

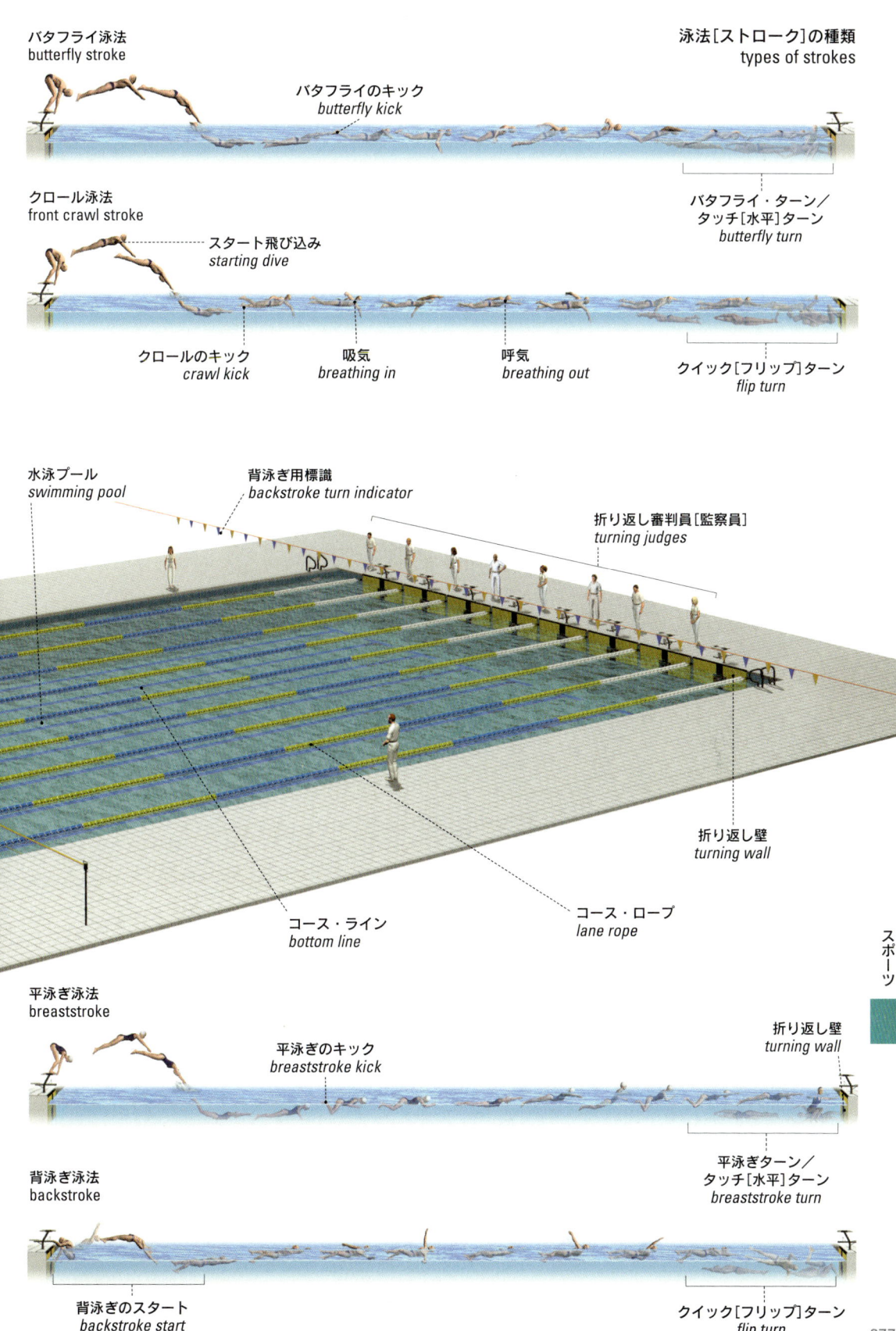

泳法[ストローク]の種類
types of strokes

バタフライ泳法
butterfly stroke

バタフライのキック
butterfly kick

バタフライ・ターン／
タッチ[水平]ターン
butterfly turn

クロール泳法
front crawl stroke

スタート飛び込み
starting dive

クロールのキック
crawl kick

吸気
breathing in

呼気
breathing out

クイック[フリップ]ターン
flip turn

水泳プール
swimming pool

背泳ぎ用標識
backstroke turn indicator

折り返し審判員[監察員]
turning judges

折り返し壁
turning wall

コース・ライン
bottom line

コース・ロープ
lane rope

スポーツ

平泳ぎ泳法
breaststroke

平泳ぎのキック
breaststroke kick

折り返し壁
turning wall

平泳ぎターン／
タッチ[水平]ターン
breaststroke turn

背泳ぎ泳法
backstroke

背泳ぎのスタート
backstroke start

クイック[フリップ]ターン
flip turn

海上スポーツ | NAUTICAL SPORTS

水上スポーツの中でも、ボートのような競技では多くの選手が参加し、フィニッシュ・ラインを通過するためにみんなで力を合わせて一つにならなければなりません。サーフィン、カヌー・カヤック、ウインドサーフィンでは、選手が一人ですべてをこなさなければなりません。スピードを競うこのようなスポーツでは、すばやい反応と秀でた平衡感覚が必要です。

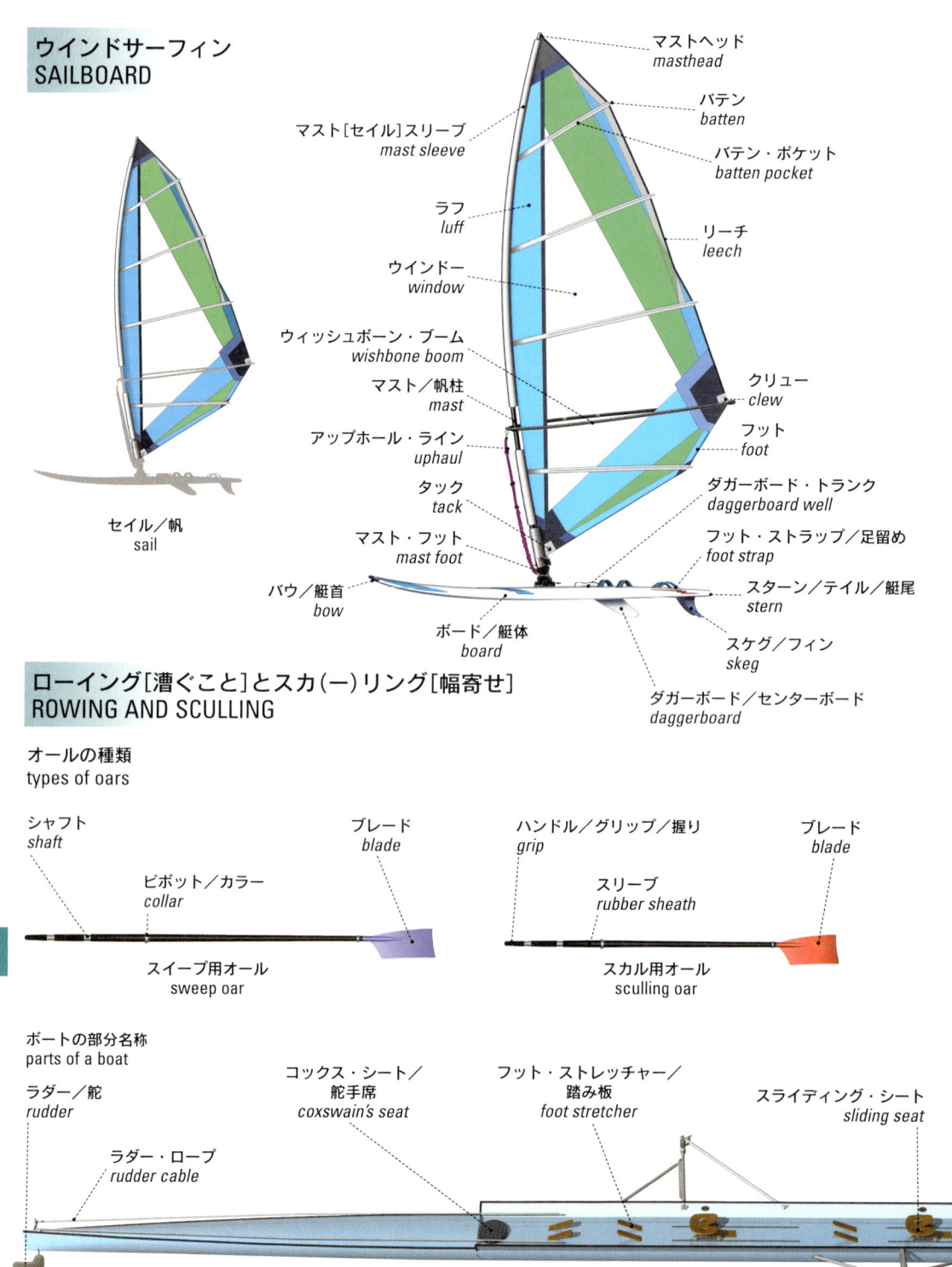

ウインドサーフィン
SAILBOARD

- マストヘッド / masthead
- バテン / batten
- バテン・ポケット / batten pocket
- マスト[セイル]スリーブ / mast sleeve
- ラフ / luff
- リーチ / leech
- ウインドー / window
- ウィッシュボーン・ブーム / wishbone boom
- クリュー / clew
- マスト／帆柱 / mast
- フット / foot
- アップホール・ライン / uphaul
- ダガーボード・トランク / daggerboard well
- タック / tack
- フット・ストラップ／足留め / foot strap
- マスト・フット / mast foot
- スターン／テイル／艇尾 / stern
- バウ／艇首 / bow
- スケグ／フィン / skeg
- ボード／艇体 / board
- ダガーボード／センターボード / daggerboard
- セイル／帆 / sail

ローイング[漕ぐこと]とスカ(ー)リング[幅寄せ]
ROWING AND SCULLING

オールの種類 / types of oars

- シャフト / shaft
- ブレード / blade
- ハンドル／グリップ／握り / grip
- ブレード / blade
- ピボット／カラー / collar
- スリーブ / rubber sheath
- スイープ用オール / sweep oar
- スカル用オール / sculling oar

ボートの部分名称 / parts of a boat

- ラダー／舵 / rudder
- コックス・シート／舵手席 / coxswain's seat
- フット・ストレッチャー／踏み板 / foot stretcher
- スライディング・シート / sliding seat
- ラダー・ロープ / rudder cable

海上スポーツ | NAUTICAL SPORTS

カヌー・カヤック
CANOE-KAYAK

激流
whitewater

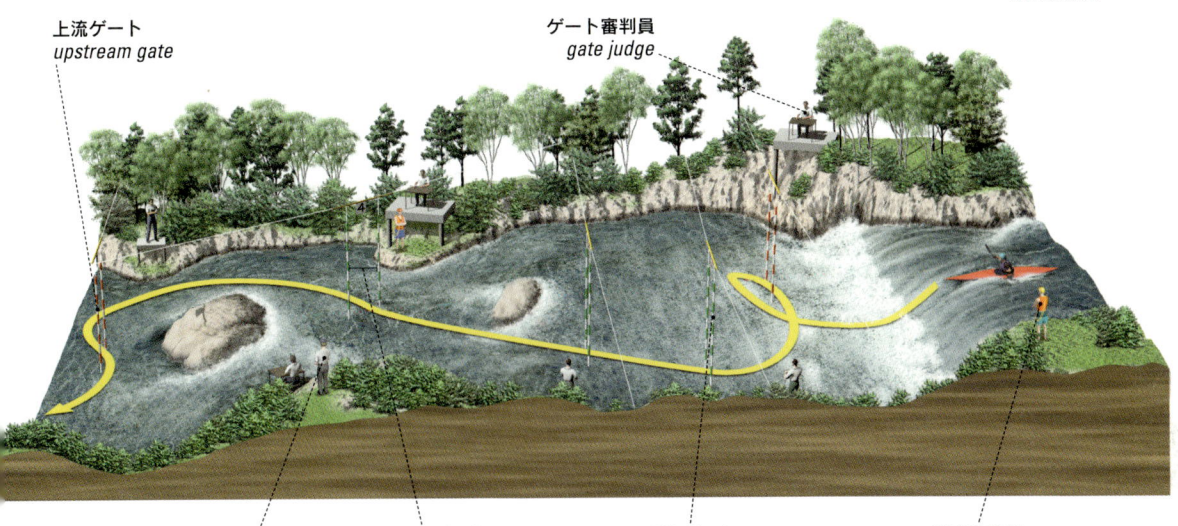

上流ゲート
upstream gate

ゲート審判員
gate judge

主審
chief judge

コース・ゲート
course gate

下流ゲート
downstream gate

安全監察員
safety officer

カヌー
canoe

シングル(ブレード)パドル
single-bladed paddle

スプレー・スカート
spray skirt

カヤック
kayak

ダブル(ブレード)パドル
double-bladed paddle

オールロック
oarlock

アウトリガー
outrigger

スキューバ・ダイビング
SCUBA DIVING

スキューバ・ダイバー
scuba diver

フード
hood

マスク
mask

スノーケル/シュノーケル
snorkel

空気ホース
air hose

BC/バランシング・ベスト/浮力調節具
buoyancy compensator

コンソール・ゲージ/計器コンソール
information console

スキューバ・タンク/圧縮空気タンク
compressed-air cylinder

オクトパス/予備レギュレーター
emergency regulator

ダイビング・グローブ
diving glove

フィン/足びれ
fin

ウェット・スーツ
wet suit

ブーツ
boot

バウ・ボール
bow ball

スポーツ

279

乗馬スポーツ | EQUESTRIAN SPORTS

競馬では、ほかのすべての馬術競技と同様に、人と馬が一つのチームを作ります。決勝線を一番で通過するためには、人と馬の息が完璧に合わなければなりません。走っている間にあらゆる判断をするのは騎手で、馬を操るために主に両脚と両手を使います。

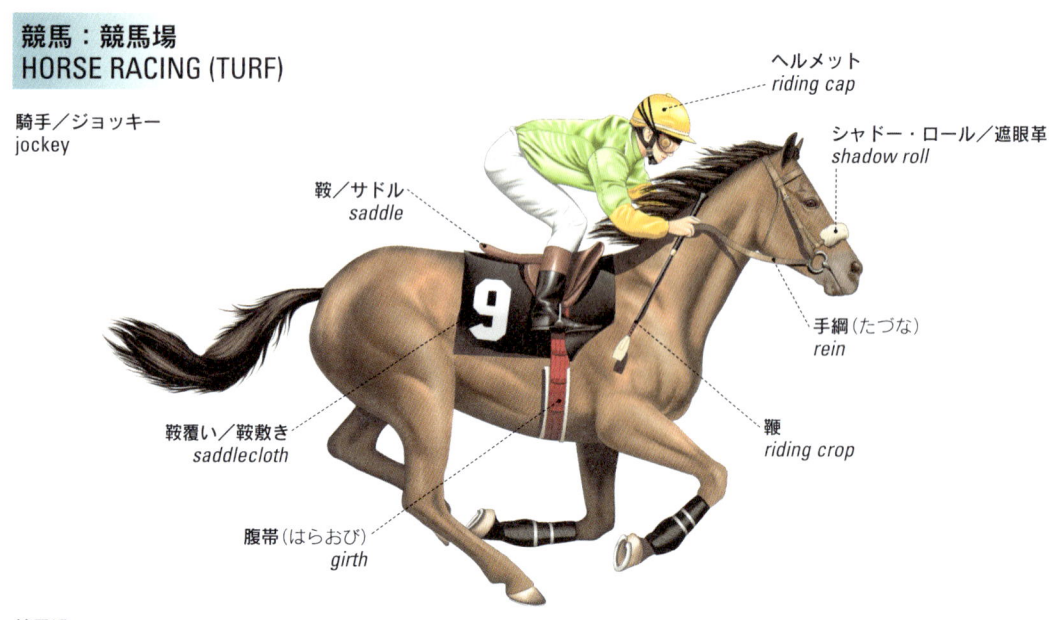

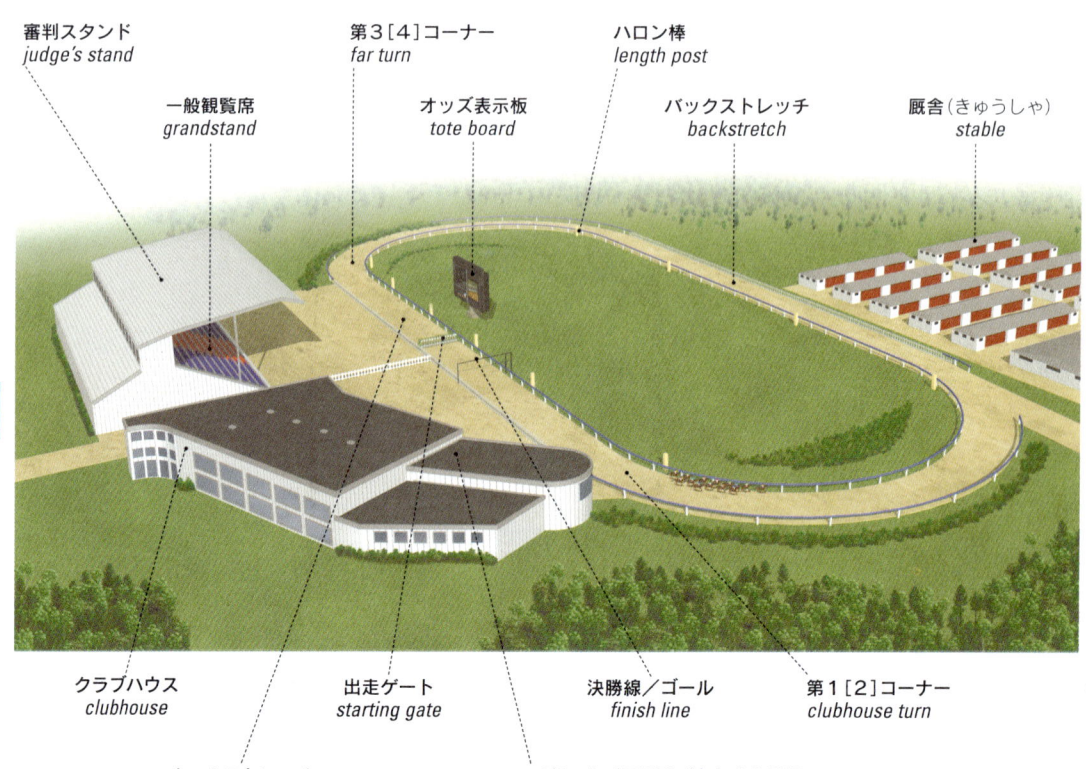

競馬：競馬場
HORSE RACING (TURF)

- 騎手／ジョッキー / jockey
- ヘルメット / riding cap
- シャドー・ロール／遮眼革 / shadow roll
- 鞍／サドル / saddle
- 手綱（たづな）/ rein
- 鞍覆い／鞍敷き / saddlecloth
- 鞭 / riding crop
- 腹帯（はらおび）/ girth

競馬場 / racetrack

- 審判スタンド / judge's stand
- 第3［4］コーナー / far turn
- ハロン棒 / length post
- 一般観覧席 / grandstand
- オッズ表示板 / tote board
- バックストレッチ / backstretch
- 厩舎（きゅうしゃ）/ stable
- クラブハウス / clubhouse
- 出走ゲート / starting gate
- 決勝線／ゴール / finish line
- 第1［2］コーナー / clubhouse turn
- ホームストレッチ / homestretch
- パドック／下見所／曳（ひ）き馬場 / paddock

正確さを競うスポーツ | PRECISION AND ACCURACY SPORTS

名前から分かるように、このスポーツでは無駄な動きを完璧に抑え、極度に集中しなければなりません。実際、矢を射たり、石を滑らせたり、ボールを投げ出したり、小さなボールを打ったりするとき、きわめて正確に動作をこなす必要があります。目的はただ一つ、しばしば遠くから、きわめて正確に標的をねらうことです。

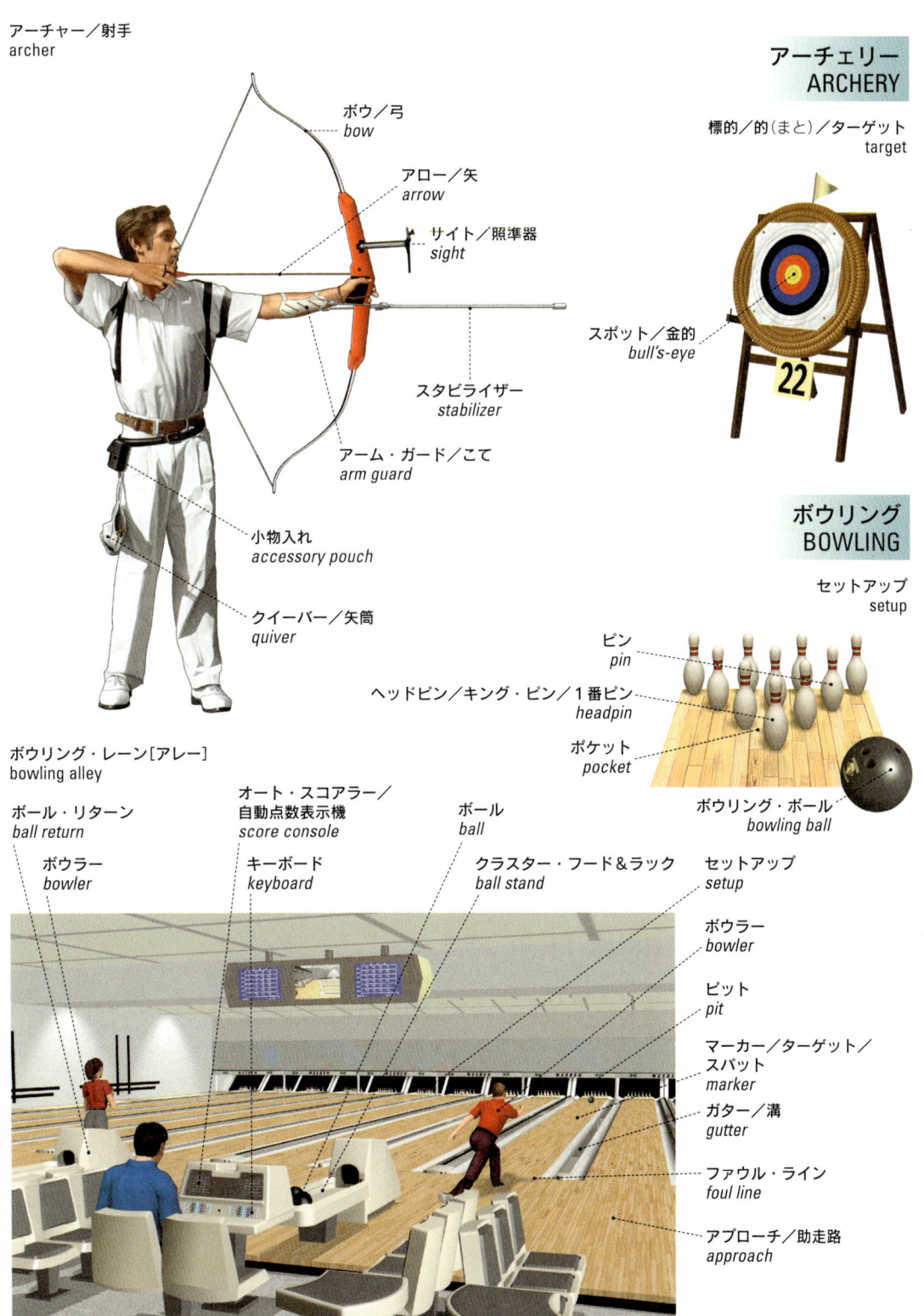

アーチャー／射手
archer

ボウ／弓
bow

アロー／矢
arrow

サイト／照準器
sight

スタビライザー
stabilizer

アーム・ガード／こて
arm guard

小物入れ
accessory pouch

クイーバー／矢筒
quiver

アーチェリー ARCHERY

標的／的(まと)／ターゲット
target

スポット／金的
bull's-eye

ボウリング BOWLING

セットアップ
setup

ピン
pin

ヘッドピン／キング・ピン／1番ピン
headpin

ポケット
pocket

ボウリング・ボール
bowling ball

ボウリング・レーン［アレー］
bowling alley

ボール・リターン
ball return

ボウラー
bowler

オート・スコアラー／自動点数表示機
score console

キーボード
keyboard

ボール
ball

クラスター・フード＆ラック
ball stand

セットアップ
setup

ボウラー
bowler

ピット
pit

マーカー／ターゲット／スパット
marker

ガター／溝
gutter

ファウル・ライン
foul line

アプローチ／助走路
approach

スポーツ

281

正確さを競うスポーツ | PRECISION AND ACCURACY SPORTS

ゴルフ
GOLF

コース
course

- グリーン / green
- ホール / hole
- カート道路 / cart path
- クラブハウス / clubhouse
- フェアウェイ / fairway
- 練習［パッティング］グリーン / practice green
- 池 / pond
- 駐車場 / parking
- 木立 / trees
- サンド・バンカー / sand bunker
- ラフ / rough
- ティー・グラウンド / teeing ground
- ウォーター・ハザード / water hazard

ゴルフ道具と小物
golf equipment and accessories

- グリップ / grip
- シャフト / shaft
- フェース / face
- ヘッド / head
- パター / putter
- アイアン / iron
- ウッド / wood

ゴルフ・ボール
golf ball

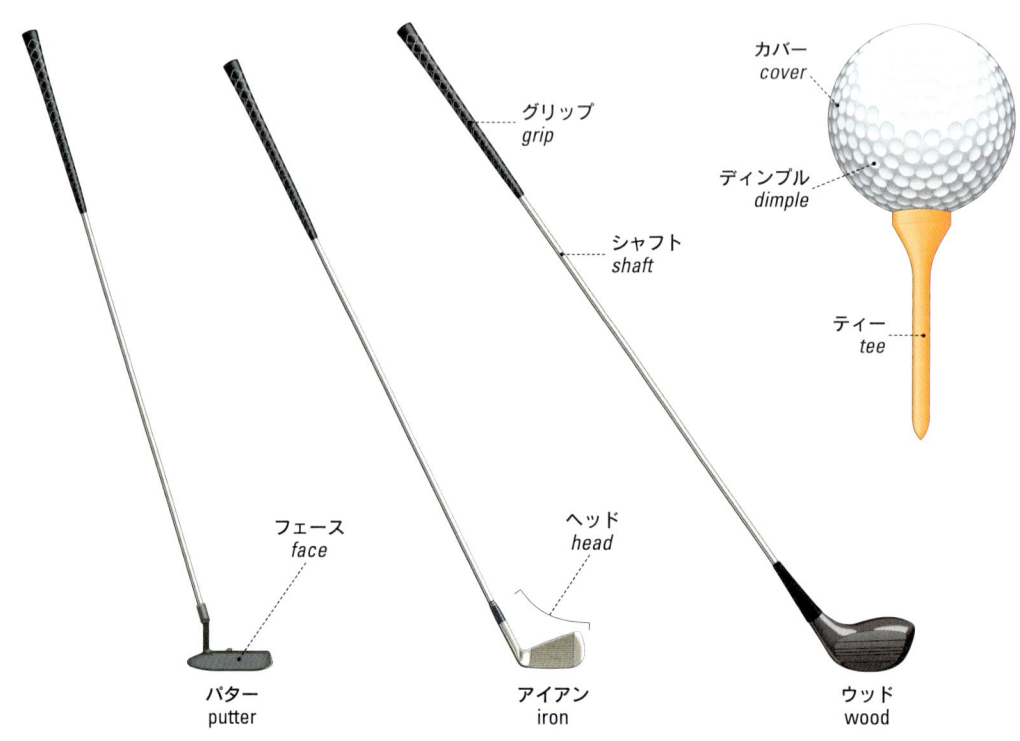

- カバー / cover
- ディンプル / dimple
- ティー / tee

スポーツ

282

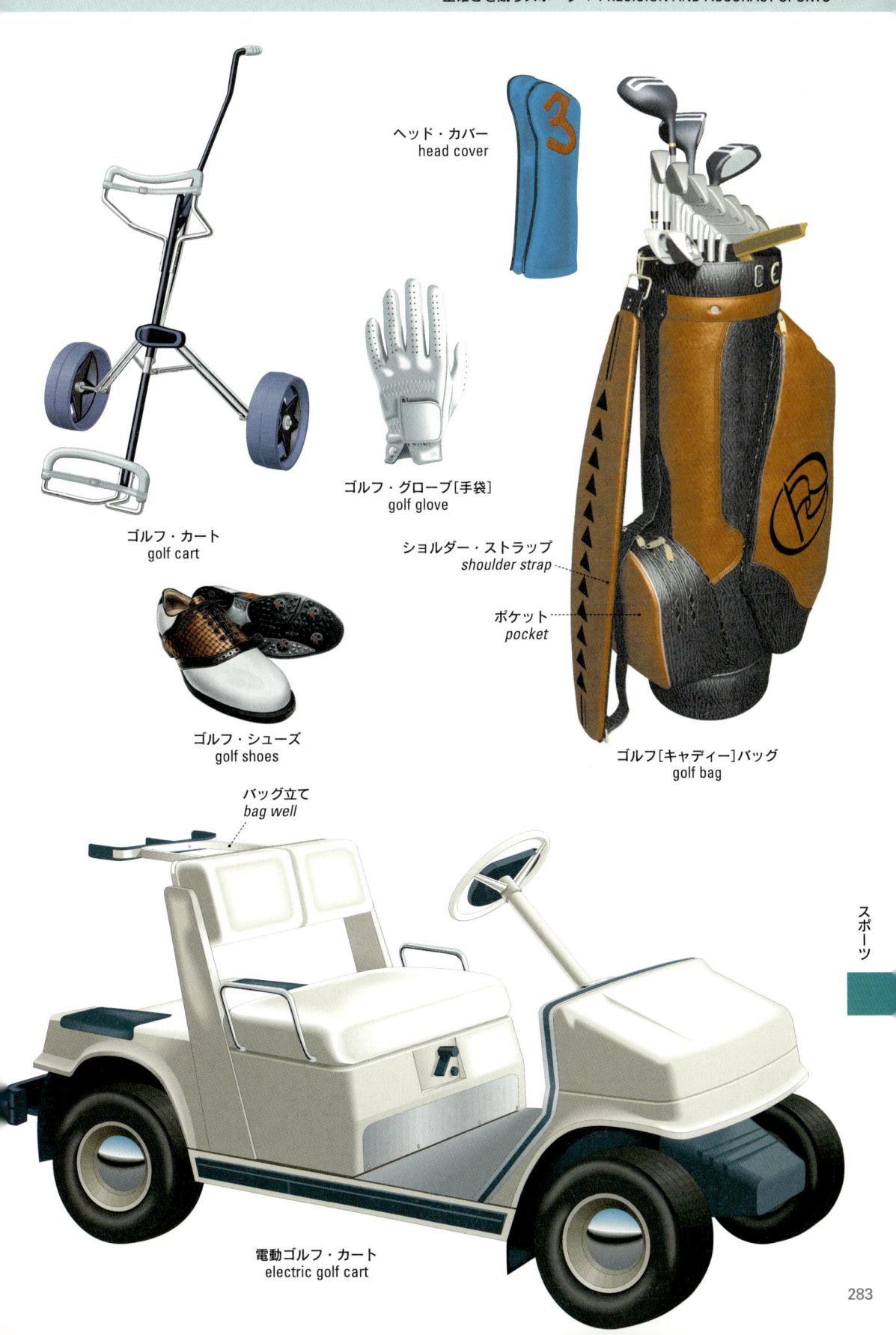

正確さを競うスポーツ | PRECISION AND ACCURACY SPORTS

ヘッド・カバー
head cover

ゴルフ・グローブ[手袋]
golf glove

ゴルフ・カート
golf cart

ゴルフ・シューズ
golf shoes

ショルダー・ストラップ
shoulder strap

ポケット
pocket

ゴルフ[キャディー]バッグ
golf bag

バッグ立て
bag well

電動ゴルフ・カート
electric golf cart

スポーツ

283

ウインター・スポーツ | WINTER SPORTS

スケート・リンク、凍ったトラック、雪の積もった斜面で行われるウインター・スポーツは、車を使わない、世界中で最もスピードの出るスポーツということになります。一人であれチームであれ、娯楽であれ競技であれ、スキー、スケート、スノーシュー、リュージュといったスポーツはどれも特別な装備を必要とします。

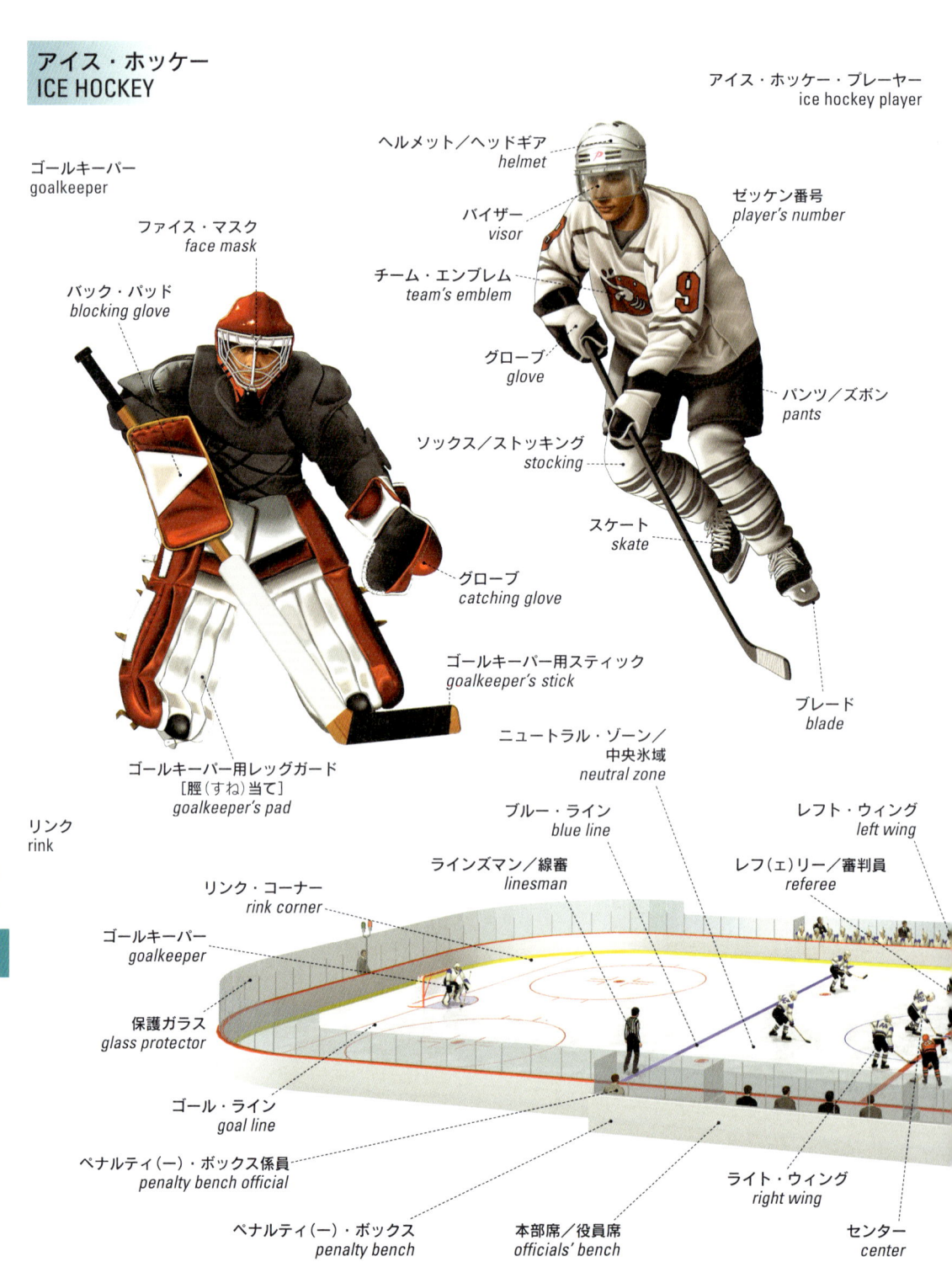

アイス・ホッケー
ICE HOCKEY

- ゴールキーパー / goalkeeper
- ファイス・マスク / face mask
- バック・パッド / blocking glove
- ヘルメット／ヘッドギア / helmet
- バイザー / visor
- チーム・エンブレム / team's emblem
- グローブ / glove
- ソックス／ストッキング / stocking
- スケート / skate
- グローブ / catching glove
- ゴールキーパー用スティック / goalkeeper's stick
- ゴールキーパー用レッグガード［脛（すね）当て］/ goalkeeper's pad
- アイス・ホッケー・プレーヤー / ice hockey player
- ゼッケン番号 / player's number
- パンツ／ズボン / pants
- ブレード / blade
- ニュートラル・ゾーン／中央氷域 / neutral zone
- ブルー・ライン / blue line
- ラインズマン／線審 / linesman
- レフ(ェ)リー／審判員 / referee
- レフト・ウィング / left wing
- リンク / rink
- リンク・コーナー / rink corner
- ゴールキーパー / goalkeeper
- 保護ガラス / glass protector
- ゴール・ライン / goal line
- ペナルティ(一)・ボックス係員 / penalty bench official
- ペナルティ(一)・ボックス / penalty bench
- 本部席／役員席 / officials' bench
- ライト・ウィング / right wing
- センター / center

スポーツ

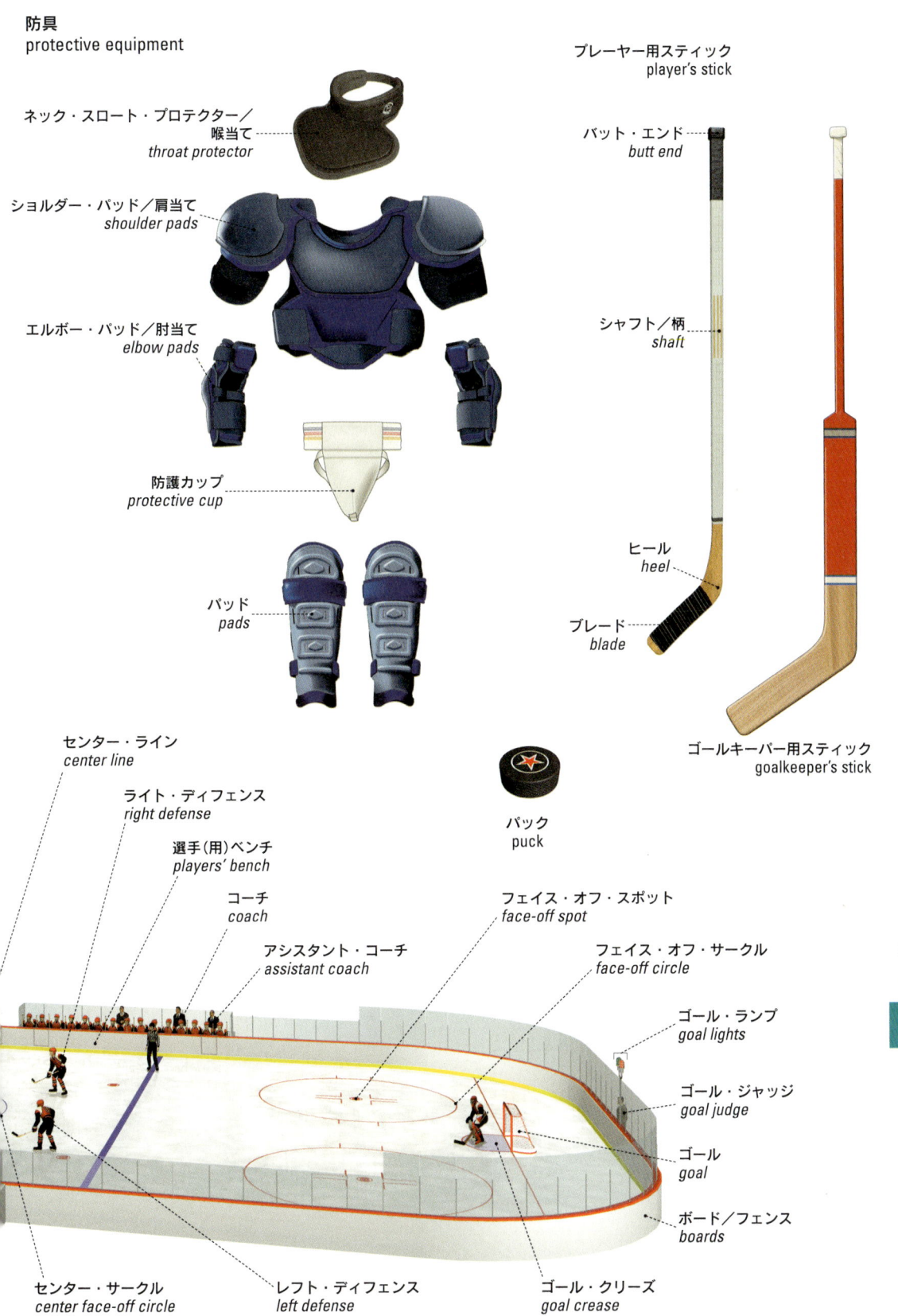

ウインター・スポーツ | WINTER SPORTS

防具
protective equipment

- ネック・スロート・プロテクター／喉当て
  throat protector
- ショルダー・パッド／肩当て
  shoulder pads
- エルボー・パッド／肘当て
  elbow pads
- 防護カップ
  protective cup
- パッド
  pads

プレーヤー用スティック
player's stick

- バット・エンド
  butt end
- シャフト／柄
  shaft
- ヒール
  heel
- ブレード
  blade

ゴールキーパー用スティック
goalkeeper's stick

パック
puck

- センター・ライン
  center line
- ライト・ディフェンス
  right defense
- 選手(用)ベンチ
  players' bench
- コーチ
  coach
- アシスタント・コーチ
  assistant coach
- フェイス・オフ・スポット
  face-off spot
- フェイス・オフ・サークル
  face-off circle
- ゴール・ランプ
  goal lights
- ゴール・ジャッジ
  goal judge
- ゴール
  goal
- ボード／フェンス
  boards
- センター・サークル
  center face-off circle
- レフト・ディフェンス
  left defense
- ゴール・クリーズ
  goal crease

スポーツ

285

ウインター・スポーツ | WINTER SPORTS

スケート
SKATING

アイス・ホッケー・スケート靴
hockey skate

アキレス腱ガード
tendon guard

ブーツ
boot

先芯
toe box

ブレード／刃
blade

ポイント
point

スピード・スケート靴
speed skate

フィギュア・スケート靴
figure skate

裏当て／ライニング／インナー
lining

ホック
hook

舌革／べろ
tongue

バックステー
backstay

エッジ・カバー／ブレード・カバー
skate guard

ブーツ
boot

紐(ひも)
lace

ヒール／踵(かかと)
heel

紐穴／鳩目／アイレット
eyelet

ソール／底
sole

支柱
stanchion

エッジ
edge

ブレード／刃
blade

トウ・ピック
toe pick

スポーツ

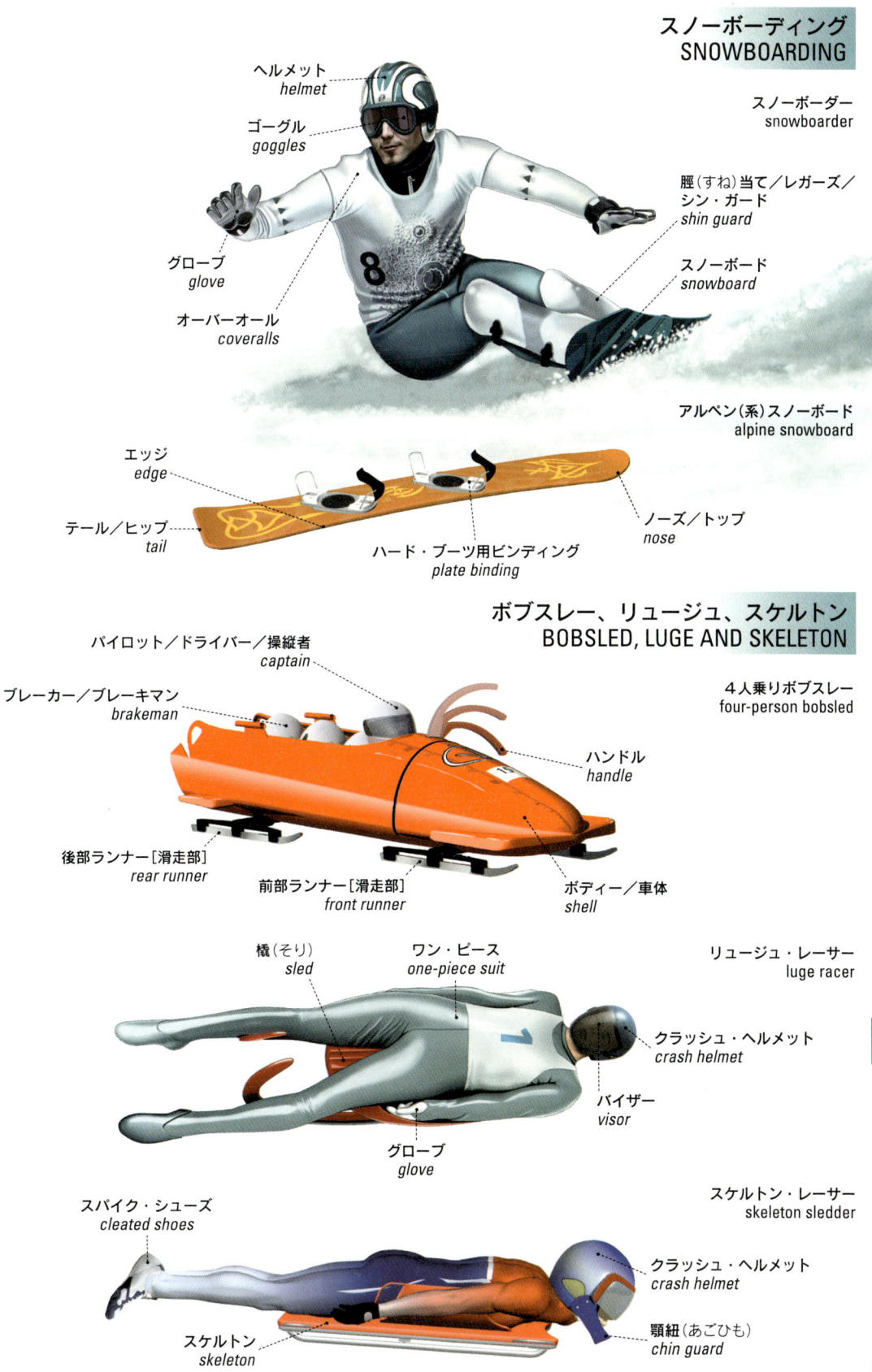

ウインター・スポーツ | WINTER SPORTS

スノーボーディング
SNOWBOARDING

- ヘルメット / helmet
- ゴーグル / goggles
- グローブ / glove
- オーバーオール / coveralls
- スノーボーダー / snowboarder
- 脛(すね)当て／レガーズ／シン・ガード / shin guard
- スノーボード / snowboard

アルペン(系)スノーボード / alpine snowboard

- エッジ / edge
- テール／ヒップ / tail
- ハード・ブーツ用ビンディング / plate binding
- ノーズ／トップ / nose

ボブスレー、リュージュ、スケルトン
BOBSLED, LUGE AND SKELETON

- パイロット／ドライバー／操縦者 / captain
- ブレーカー／ブレーキマン / brakeman
- 4人乗りボブスレー / four-person bobsled
- ハンドル / handle
- 後部ランナー[滑走部] / rear runner
- 前部ランナー[滑走部] / front runner
- ボディー／車体 / shell

- 橇(そり) / sled
- ワン・ピース / one-piece suit
- グローブ / glove
- リュージュ・レーサー / luge racer
- クラッシュ・ヘルメット / crash helmet
- バイザー / visor

- スパイク・シューズ / cleated shoes
- スケルトン / skeleton
- スケルトン・レーサー / skeleton sledder
- クラッシュ・ヘルメット / crash helmet
- 顎紐(あごひも) / chin guard

スポーツ

287

ウインター・スポーツ | WINTER SPORTS

スノーシュー／かんじき
SNOWSHOES

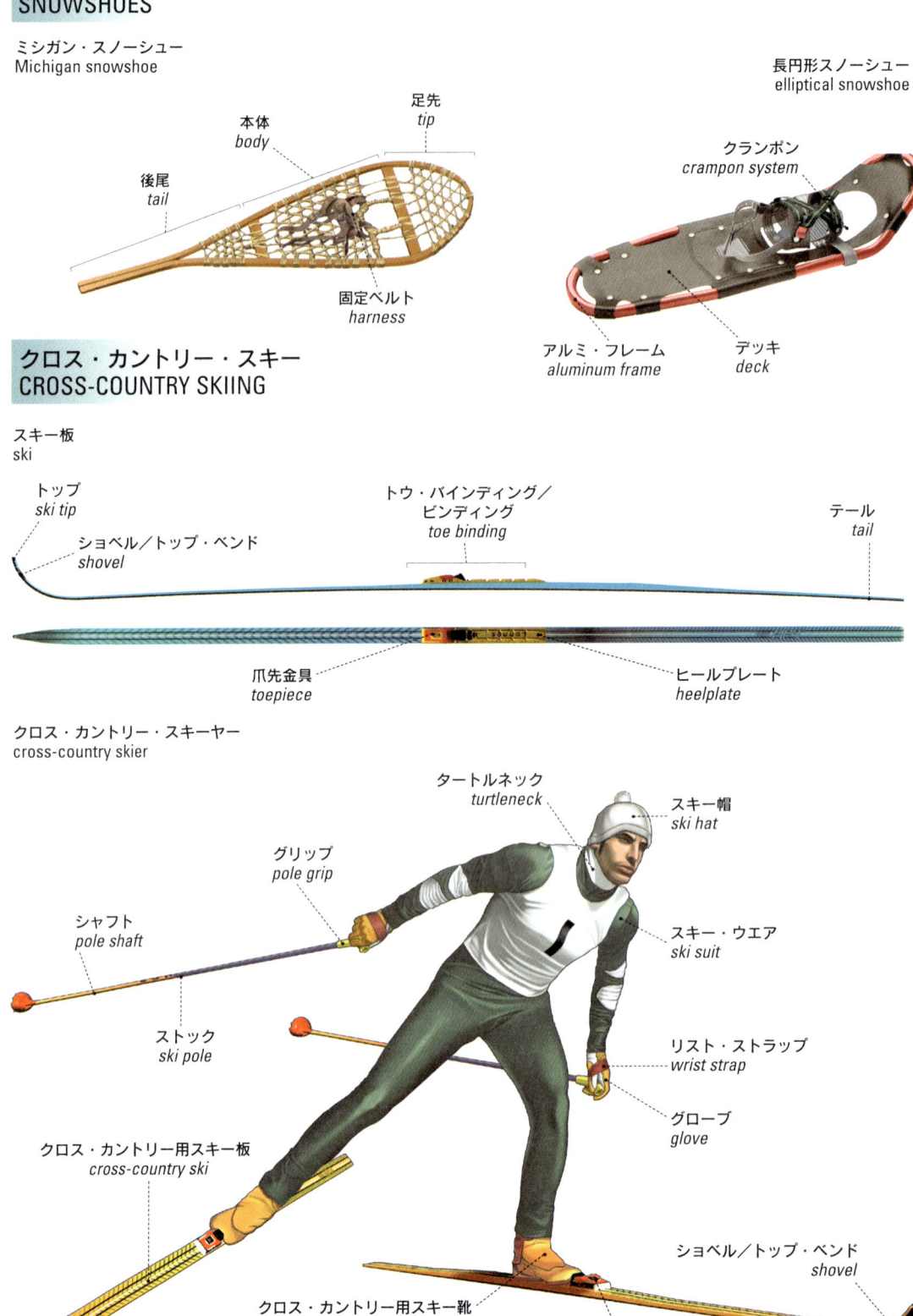

ミシガン・スノーシュー
Michigan snowshoe

- 本体 / body
- 足先 / tip
- 後尾 / tail
- 固定ベルト / harness

長円形スノーシュー
elliptical snowshoe

- クランポン / crampon system
- アルミ・フレーム / aluminum frame
- デッキ / deck

クロス・カントリー・スキー
CROSS-COUNTRY SKIING

スキー板 / ski

- トップ / ski tip
- ショベル／トップ・ベンド / shovel
- トウ・バインディング／バインディング / toe binding
- テール / tail
- 爪先金具 / toepiece
- ヒールプレート / heelplate

クロス・カントリー・スキーヤー
cross-country skier

- タートルネック / turtleneck
- スキー帽 / ski hat
- グリップ / pole grip
- シャフト / pole shaft
- スキー・ウエア / ski suit
- ストック / ski pole
- リスト・ストラップ / wrist strap
- グローブ / glove
- クロス・カントリー用スキー板 / cross-country ski
- ショベル／トップ・ベンド / shovel
- クロス・カントリー用スキー靴 / boot
- バインディング／ビンディング / binding

スポーツ

ウインター・スポーツ | WINTER SPORTS

アルペン・スキー
ALPINE SKIING

セーフティー・バインディング／ビンディング／締め具
safety binding

ベース・プレート
base plate

リリース[解放]レバー
manual release

スキー・ブレーキ／ブレーキ・レバー
brake arm

ブレーキ・ペダル
brake pedal

摩擦防止パッド
antifriction pad

ヒールピース／靴踵(かかと)締め具
heelpiece

トウピース／靴先締め具
toepiece

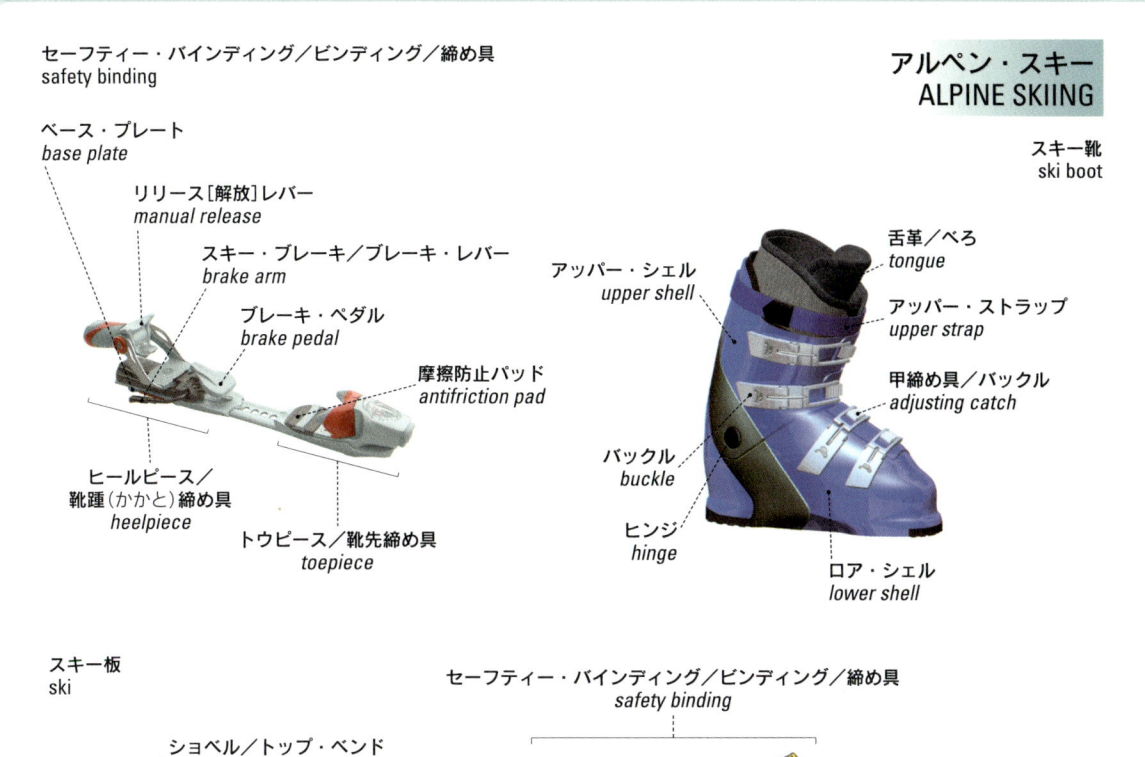

スキー靴
ski boot

舌革／べろ
tongue

アッパー・シェル
upper shell

アッパー・ストラップ
upper strap

甲締め具／バックル
adjusting catch

バックル
buckle

ヒンジ
hinge

ロア・シェル
lower shell

スキー板
ski

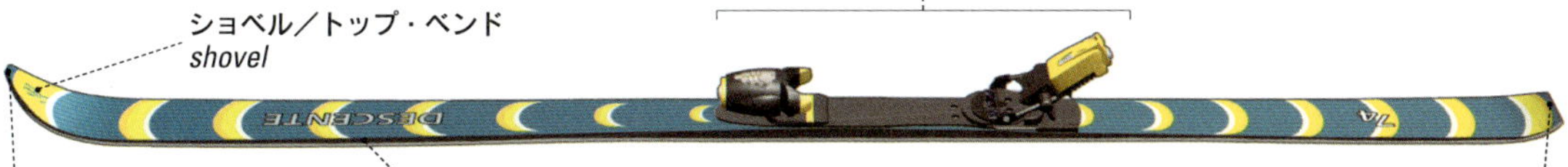

セーフティー・バインディング／ビンディング／締め具
safety binding

ショベル／トップ・ベンド
shovel

トップ
tip

エッジ
edge

テール
tail

アルペン・スキーヤー
alpine skier

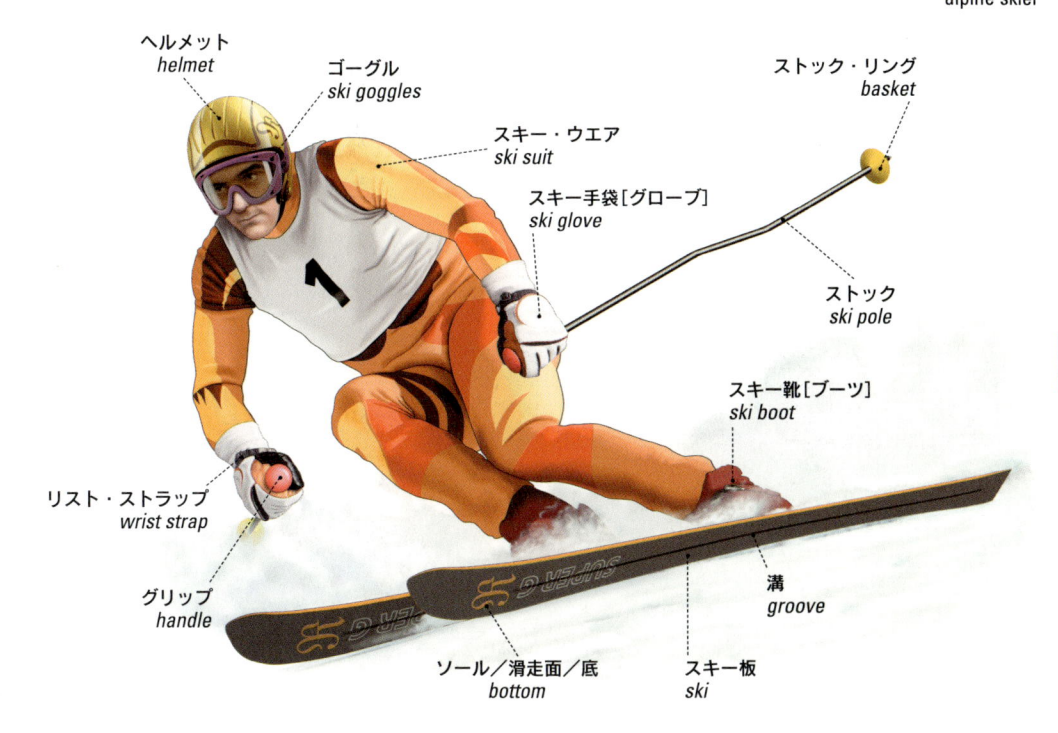

ヘルメット
helmet

ゴーグル
ski goggles

スキー・ウエア
ski suit

スキー手袋[グローブ]
ski glove

ストック・リング
basket

ストック
ski pole

スキー靴[ブーツ]
ski boot

リスト・ストラップ
wrist strap

グリップ
handle

ソール／滑走面／底
bottom

スキー板
ski

溝
groove

スポーツ

289

球技 | BALL SPORTS

球技は本質的にチーム対抗で行われます。野球、クリケット、（フィールド）ホッケー、サッカー、バスケットボール、バレーボールでは、プレーヤーはルールを守りながら、相手の作戦の裏をかいて、ボールをできるだけ頻繁に狙った所に送り出すようにします。

野球
BASEBALL

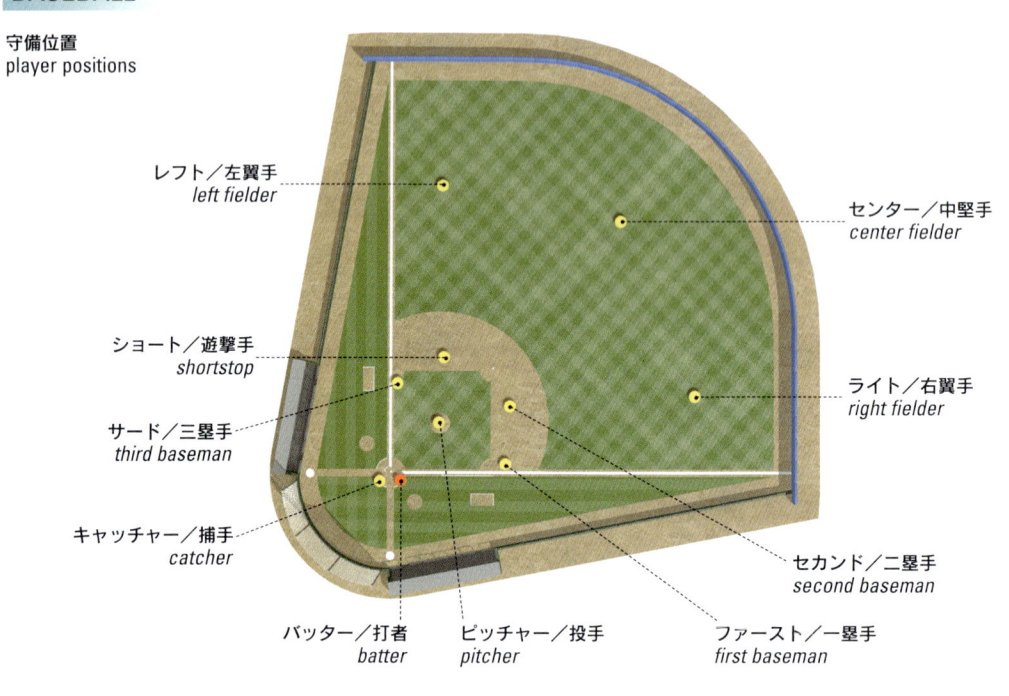

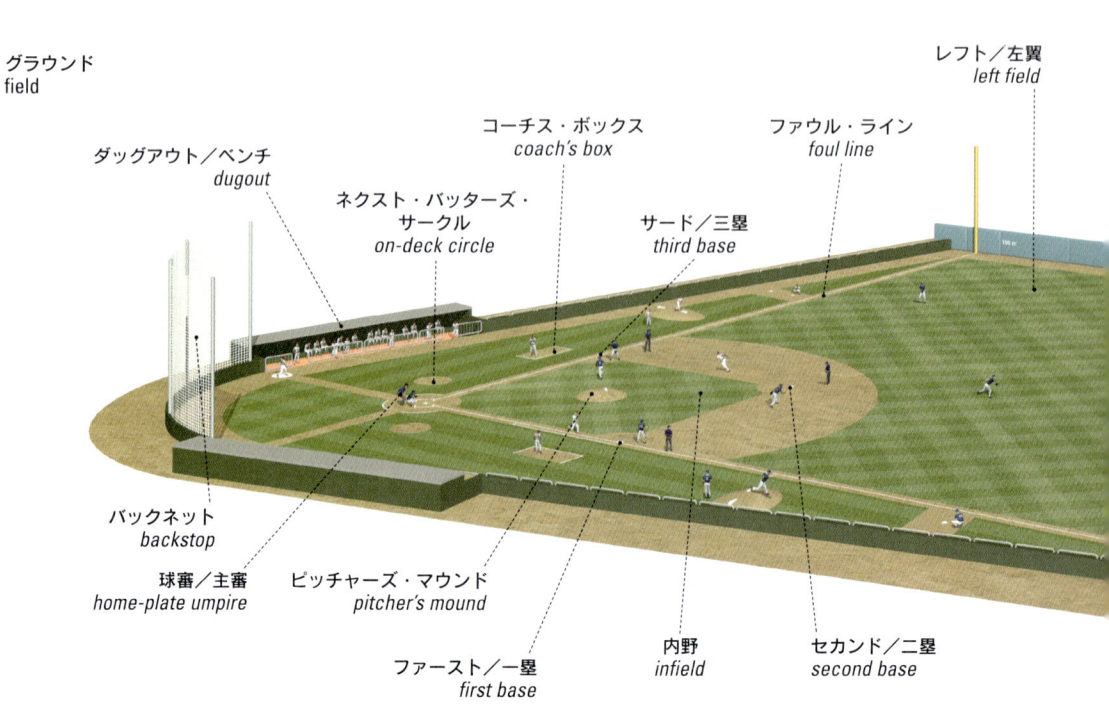

守備位置
player positions

- レフト／左翼手 *left fielder*
- センター／中堅手 *center fielder*
- ショート／遊撃手 *shortstop*
- サード／三塁手 *third baseman*
- ライト／右翼手 *right fielder*
- キャッチャー／捕手 *catcher*
- セカンド／二塁手 *second baseman*
- バッター／打者 *batter*
- ピッチャー／投手 *pitcher*
- ファースト／一塁手 *first baseman*

- グラウンド *field*
- レフト／左翼 *left field*
- ダッグアウト／ベンチ *dugout*
- コーチス・ボックス *coach's box*
- ファウル・ライン *foul line*
- ネクスト・バッターズ・サークル *on-deck circle*
- サード／三塁 *third base*
- バックネット *backstop*
- 球審／主審 *home-plate umpire*
- ピッチャーズ・マウンド *pitcher's mound*
- ファースト／一塁 *first base*
- 内野 *infield*
- セカンド／二塁 *second base*

スポーツ

球技 | BALL SPORTS

野球ボール
baseball

バット
bat

打者[バッター]用ヘルメット
batter's helmet

バッター／打者
batter

ユニフォーム／チーム・シャツ
team shirt

キャッチャー／捕手
catcher

マスク
mask

バッティング・グローブ／
打撃用手袋
batting glove

アンダーシャツ
undershirt

フレーム
frame

スロート・ガード／喉当て
throat protector

キャッチャー・ミット
catcher's glove

ズボン／パンツ
pants

チェスト・プロテクター／
胸当て
chest protector

ストッキング／
スターラップ・ソックス
stirrup sock

スパイク・シューズ
spiked shoe

レガーズ／レッグ・ガード
leg guard

ニー・パッド／膝当て
knee pad

(内)野手用グローブ
fielder's glove

トウ・ガード
toe guard

網
web

外野フェンス
outfield fence

ストラップ
strap

センター／中堅
center field

親指
thumb

ファウル・ポール
foul line post

指
finger

手のひら
palm

踵(かかと)
heel

警告(表示地)帯
warning track

紐(ひも)
lace

スポーツ

グリップ／握り
handle

バット
bat

ライト／右翼
right field

グリップ・エンド
knob

打球面
hitting area

291

球技 | BALL SPORTS

クリケット
CRICKET

クリケッター／バッツマン
cricket player (batsman)

ヘルメット
helmet

フェイス・マスク
face mask

バット
bat

グローブ
glove

レガーズ／レッグ・ガード／脛（すね）当て
pad

クリケット・シューズ
cricket shoe

スパイク
stud

ウィケット
wicket

ベイル／横木
bail

スタンプ
stump

バット
bat

グリップ
handle

柳材
willow

クリケット・ボール
cricket ball

ピッチ
pitch

ウィケットキーパー
wicketkeeper

バッツマン／打者
batsman

ポッピング・クリース／打者線
popping crease

ボウリング・クリース／投手線
bowling crease

投球
delivery

ボウラー／投手
bowler

アンパイア／審判員
umpire

リターン・クリース
return crease

ウィケット
wicket

スポーツ

フィールド
field

アンパイア／審判員
umpire

サイト・スクリーン
screen

ウィケットキーパー
wicketkeeper

ピッチ
pitch

ボウラー／投手
bowler

アンパイア／審判員／主審
umpire

292

球技 | BALL SPORTS

（フィールド）ホッケー
FIELD HOCKEY

フィールド・プレーヤー
field player

ユニフォーム／チーム・シャツ
team shirt

ショート・パンツ
shorts

シン・ガード／脛（すね）当て
shin guard

シューズ
shoe

スティック
stick

ホッケー・ボール
hockey ball

スティック
stick

グリップ
handle

テープ
tape

ヘッド
blade

グラウンド
playing field

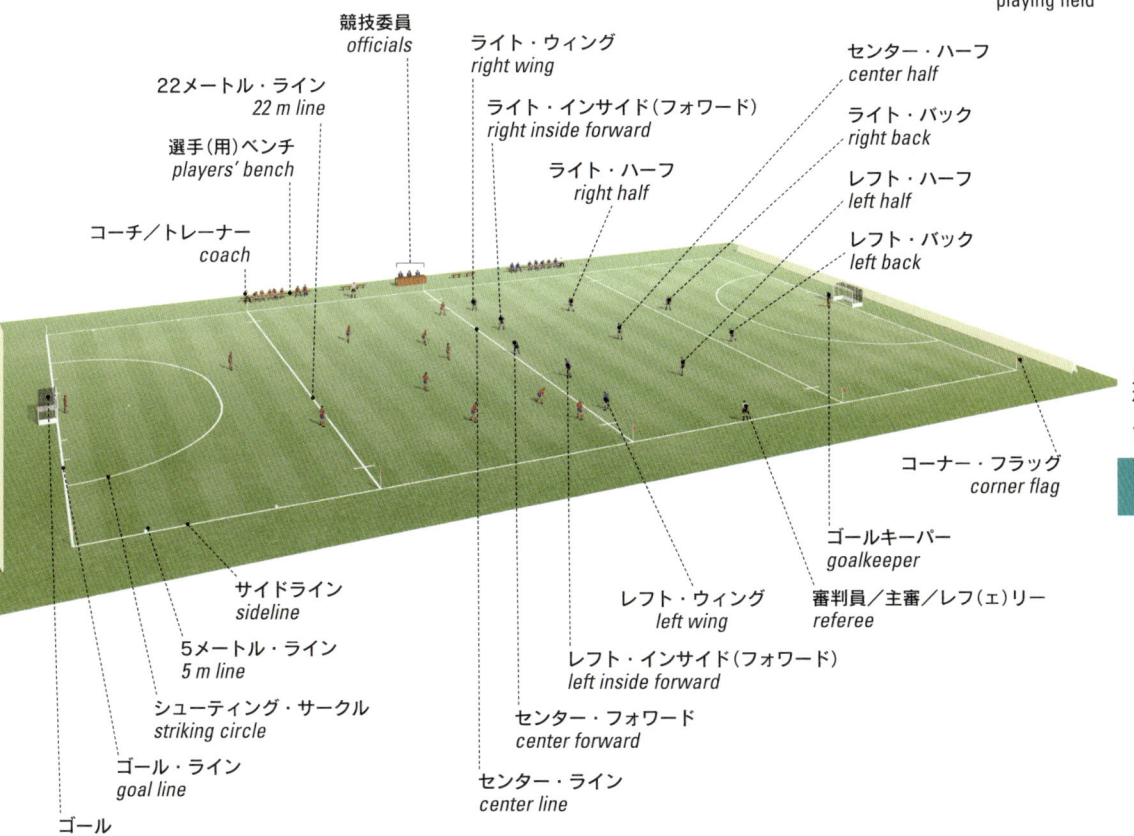

競技委員
officials

22メートル・ライン
22 m line

選手（用）ベンチ
players' bench

コーチ／トレーナー
coach

ライト・ウィング
right wing

ライト・インサイド（フォワード）
right inside forward

ライト・ハーフ
right half

センター・ハーフ
center half

ライト・バック
right back

レフト・ハーフ
left half

レフト・バック
left back

コーナー・フラッグ
corner flag

ゴールキーパー
goalkeeper

審判員／主審／レフ（ェ）リー
referee

レフト・ウィング
left wing

レフト・インサイド（フォワード）
left inside forward

センター・フォワード
center forward

センター・ライン
center line

サイドライン
sideline

5メートル・ライン
5 m line

シューティング・サークル
striking circle

ゴール・ライン
goal line

ゴール
goal

スポーツ

293

球技 | BALL SPORTS

バスケットボール
BASKETBALL

ポジション
player positions

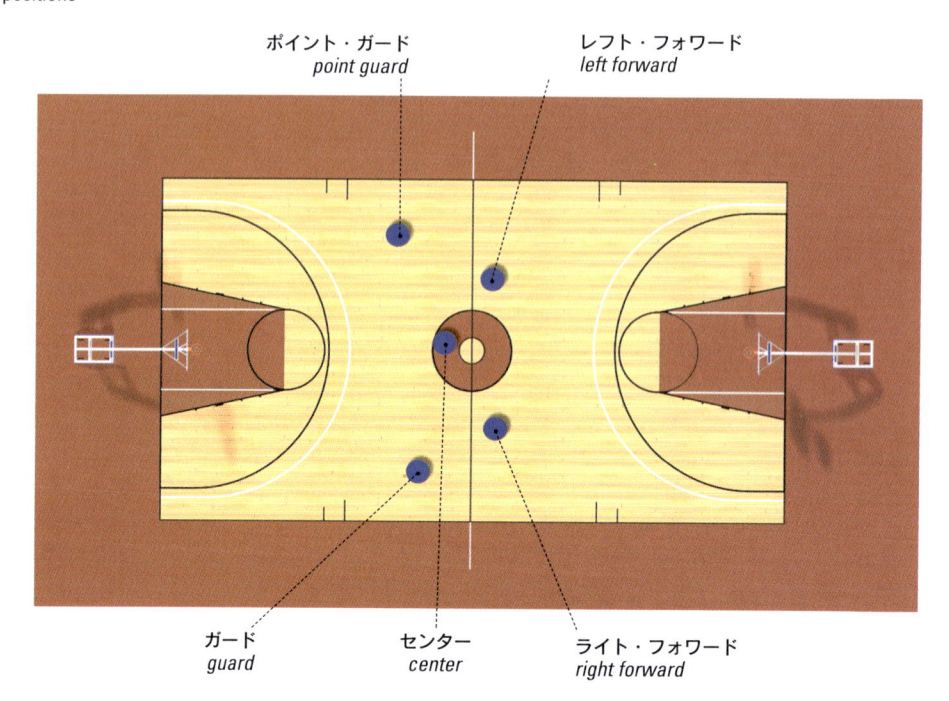

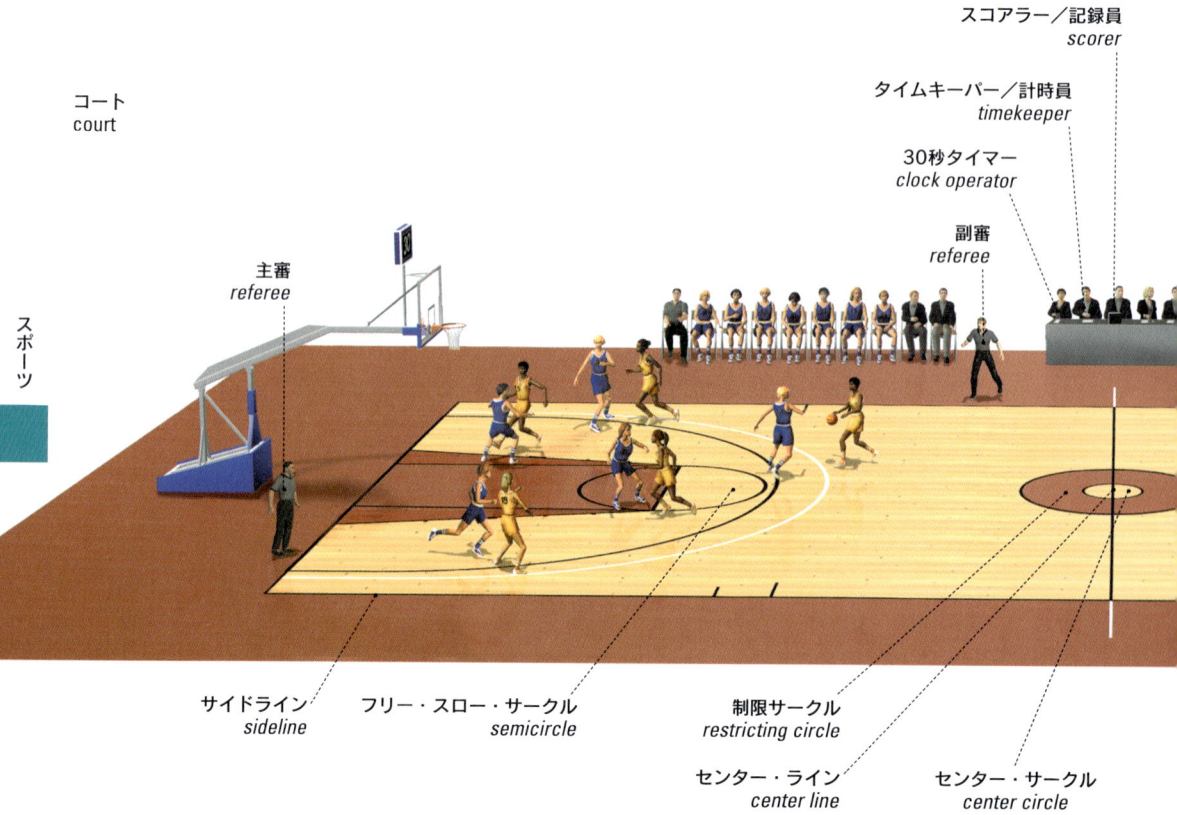

ポイント・ガード
point guard

レフト・フォワード
left forward

ガード
guard

センター
center

ライト・フォワード
right forward

コート
court

主審
referee

副審
referee

30秒タイマー
clock operator

タイムキーパー／計時員
timekeeper

スコアラー／記録員
scorer

サイドライン
sideline

フリー・スロー・サークル
semicircle

制限サークル
restricting circle

センター・ライン
center line

センター・サークル
center circle

スポーツ

球技 | BALL SPORTS

バスケットボーラー
basketball player

バックストップ
backstop

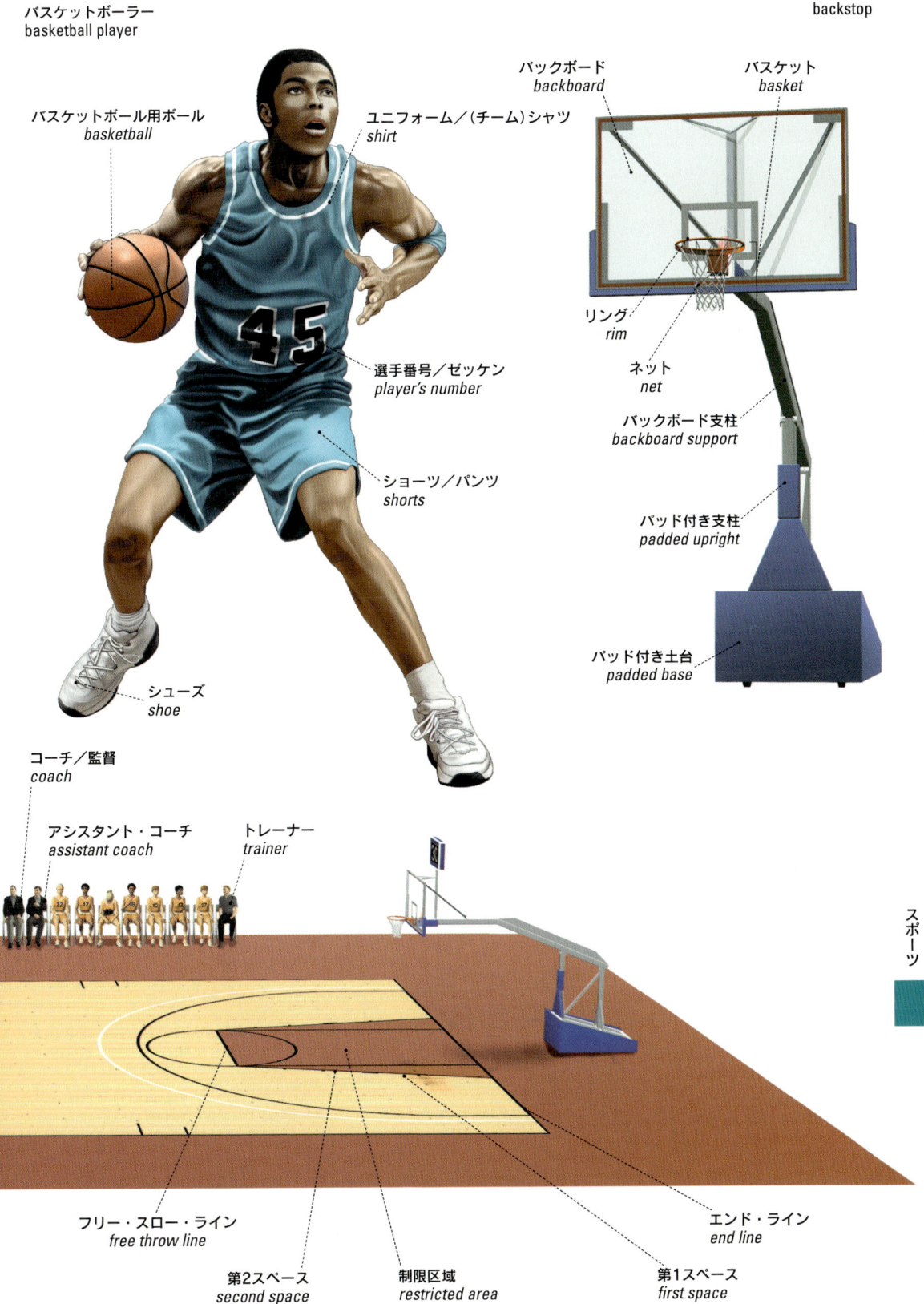

バスケットボール用ボール
basketball

ユニフォーム／(チーム)シャツ
shirt

バックボード
backboard

バスケット
basket

選手番号／ゼッケン
player's number

リング
rim

ネット
net

バックボード支柱
backboard support

ショーツ／パンツ
shorts

パッド付き支柱
padded upright

シューズ
shoe

パッド付き土台
padded base

コーチ／監督
coach

アシスタント・コーチ
assistant coach

トレーナー
trainer

フリー・スロー・ライン
free throw line

第2スペース
second space

制限区域
restricted area

第1スペース
first space

エンド・ライン
end line

スポーツ

球技 | BALL SPORTS

アメリカン・フットボール／アメフト
AMERICAN FOOTBALL

スクリメージ（ディフェンス）
scrimmage (defense)

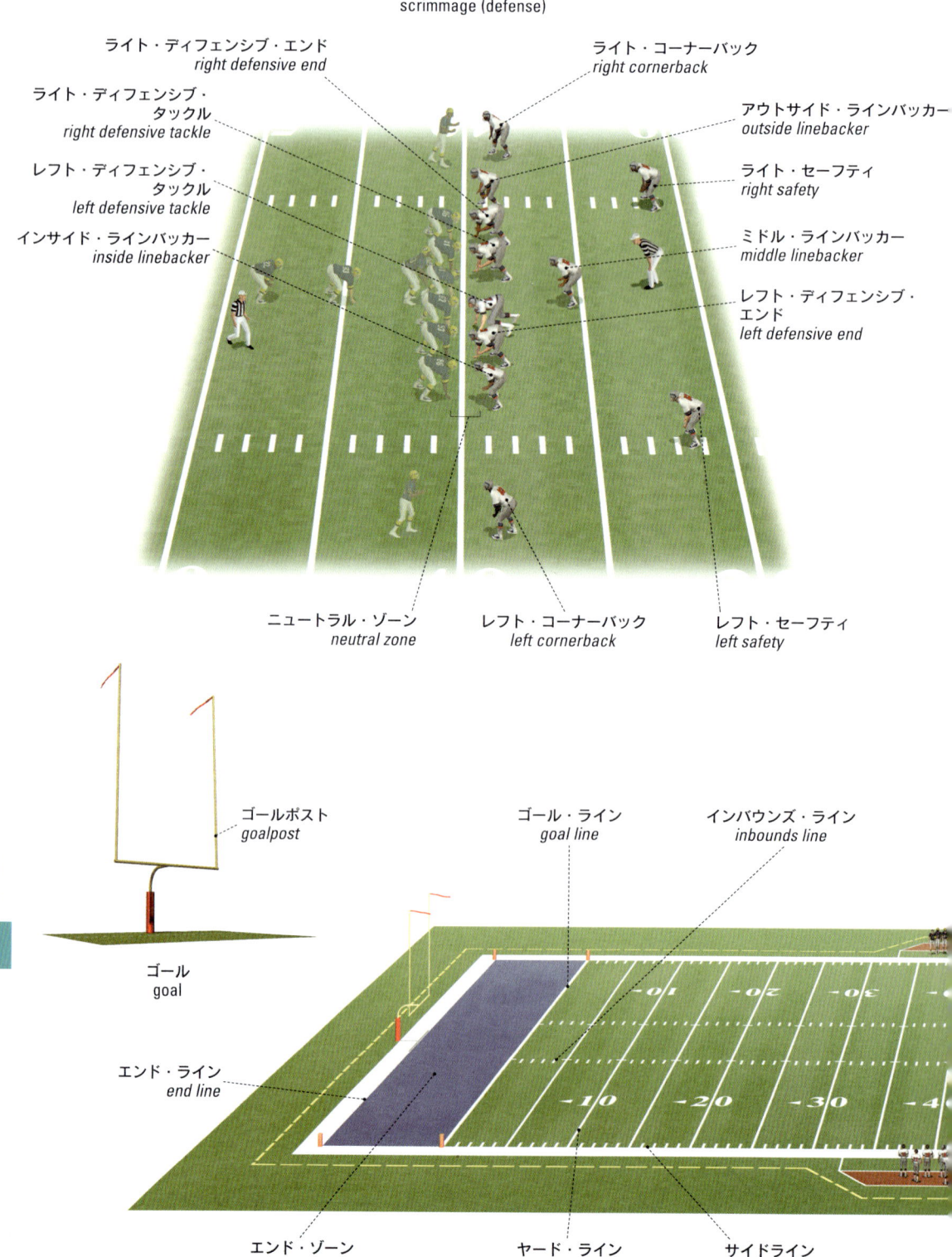

ライト・ディフェンシブ・エンド
right defensive end

ライト・ディフェンシブ・タックル
right defensive tackle

レフト・ディフェンシブ・タックル
left defensive tackle

インサイド・ラインバッカー
inside linebacker

ライト・コーナーバック
right cornerback

アウトサイド・ラインバッカー
outside linebacker

ライト・セーフティ
right safety

ミドル・ラインバッカー
middle linebacker

レフト・ディフェンシブ・エンド
left defensive end

ニュートラル・ゾーン
neutral zone

レフト・コーナーバック
left cornerback

レフト・セーフティ
left safety

ゴールポスト
goalpost

ゴール
goal

エンド・ライン
end line

ゴール・ライン
goal line

インバウンズ・ライン
inbounds line

エンド・ゾーン
end zone

ヤード・ライン
yard line

サイドライン
sideline

スポーツ

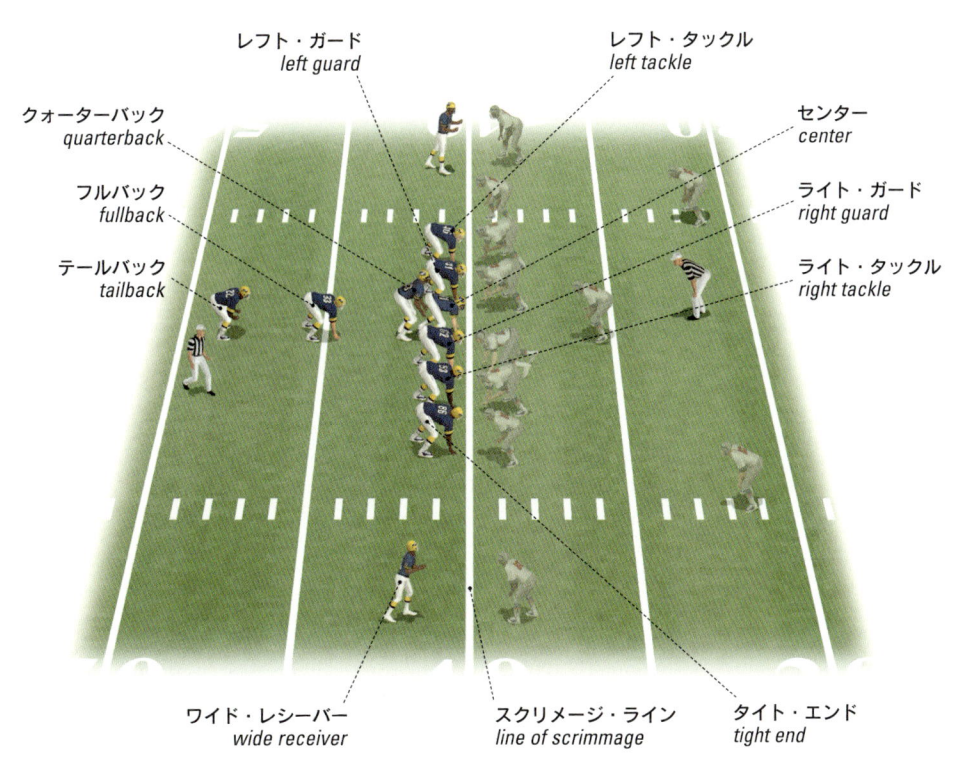

球技 | BALL SPORTS

スクリメージ（オフェンス）
scrimmage (offense)

レフト・ガード
left guard

レフト・タックル
left tackle

クォーターバック
quarterback

センター
center

フルバック
fullback

ライト・ガード
right guard

テールバック
tailback

ライト・タックル
right tackle

ワイド・レシーバー
wide receiver

スクリメージ・ライン
line of scrimmage

タイト・エンド
tight end

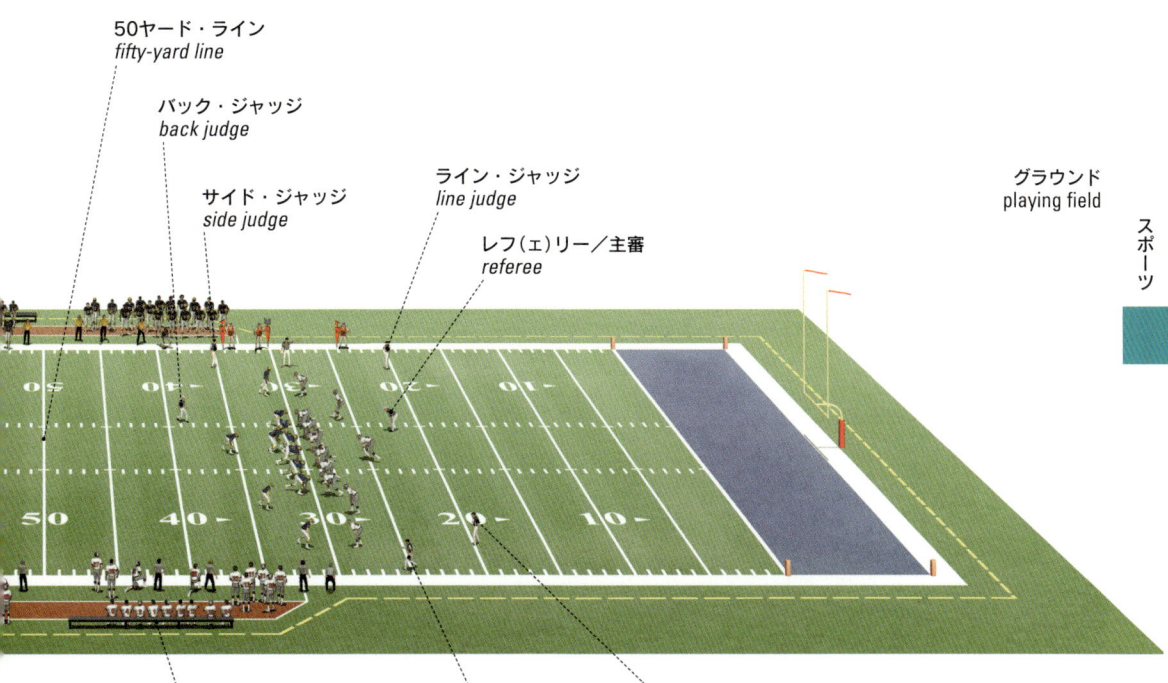

50ヤード・ライン
fifty-yard line

バック・ジャッジ
back judge

サイド・ジャッジ
side judge

ライン・ジャッジ
line judge

レフ(ェ)リー／主審
referee

グラウンド
playing field

スポーツ

選手(用)ベンチ
players' bench

アンパイア／副審
umpire

ヘッド・ラインズマン
head linesman

297

球技 | BALL SPORTS

フットボーラー
football player

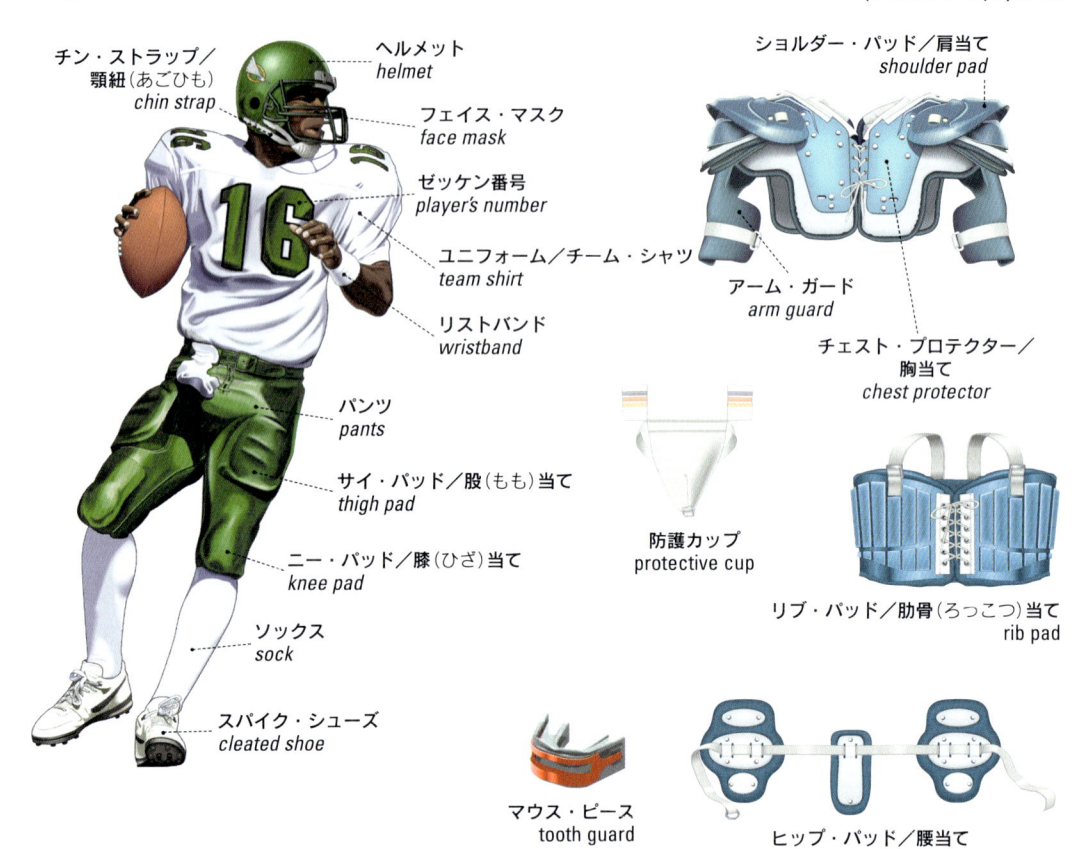

チン・ストラップ／
顎紐（あごひも）
chin strap

ヘルメット
helmet

フェイス・マスク
face mask

ゼッケン番号
player's number

ユニフォーム／チーム・シャツ
team shirt

リストバンド
wristband

パンツ
pants

サイ・パッド／股（もも）当て
thigh pad

ニー・パッド／膝（ひざ）当て
knee pad

ソックス
sock

スパイク・シューズ
cleated shoe

フットボール用ボール
football

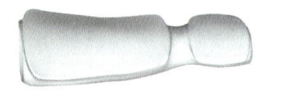

マウス・ピース
tooth guard

フォアアーム・パッド／前腕当て
forearm pad

防具
protective equipment

ショルダー・パッド／肩当て
shoulder pad

アーム・ガード
arm guard

チェスト・プロテクター／
胸当て
chest protector

防護カップ
protective cup

リブ・パッド／肋骨（ろっこつ）当て
rib pad

ヒップ・パッド／腰当て
hip pad

ネック・ロール
neck pad

エルボー・パッド／肘（ひじ）当て
elbow pad

カナディアン・フットボール
CANADIAN FOOTBALL

グラウンド
playing field

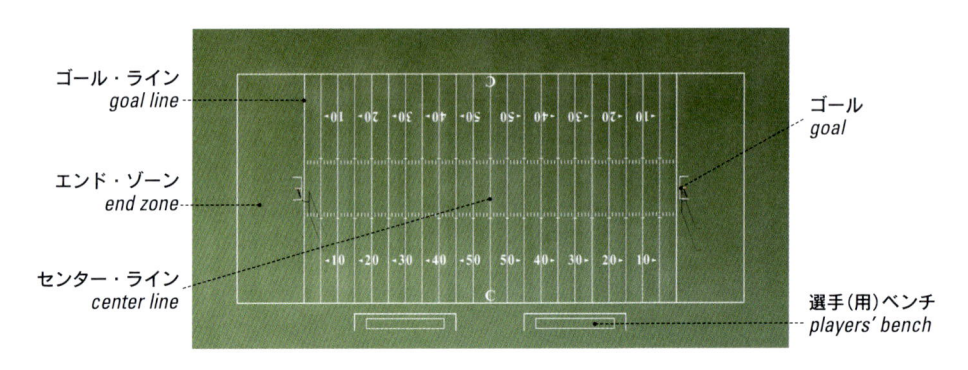

ゴール・ライン
goal line

エンド・ゾーン
end zone

センター・ライン
center line

ゴール
goal

選手（用）ベンチ
players' bench

298

球技 | BALL SPORTS

バレーボール
VOLLEYBALL

コート
court

スコアラー／記録員
scorer

アンパイア／副審
umpire

レフト・バック
left back

レフト・アタッカー
left attacker

エンド・ライン
end line

リベロ
libero

選手(用)ベンチ
players' bench

フリー・ゾーン
clear space

サイドライン
sideline

バック・ゾーン
back zone

センター・バック
center back

レフ(ェ)リー／主審
referee

ラインズマン／線審
linesman

アタック・ライン
attack line

ネット
net

ライト・バック
right back

ライト・アタッカー
right attacker

アタック・ゾーン
attack zone

センター・アタッカー
center attacker

バレーボール用ボール
volleyball

ビーチ・バレー（ボール）
BEACH VOLLEYBALL

コート
court

ビーチ・バレー用ボール
beach volleyball

スコアラー／記録員
scorer

フリー・ゾーン
free zone

副審
second referee

主審
first referee

選手椅子
players' chairs

線審
line judge

砂
sand

ライン
line

ネット
net

スポーツ

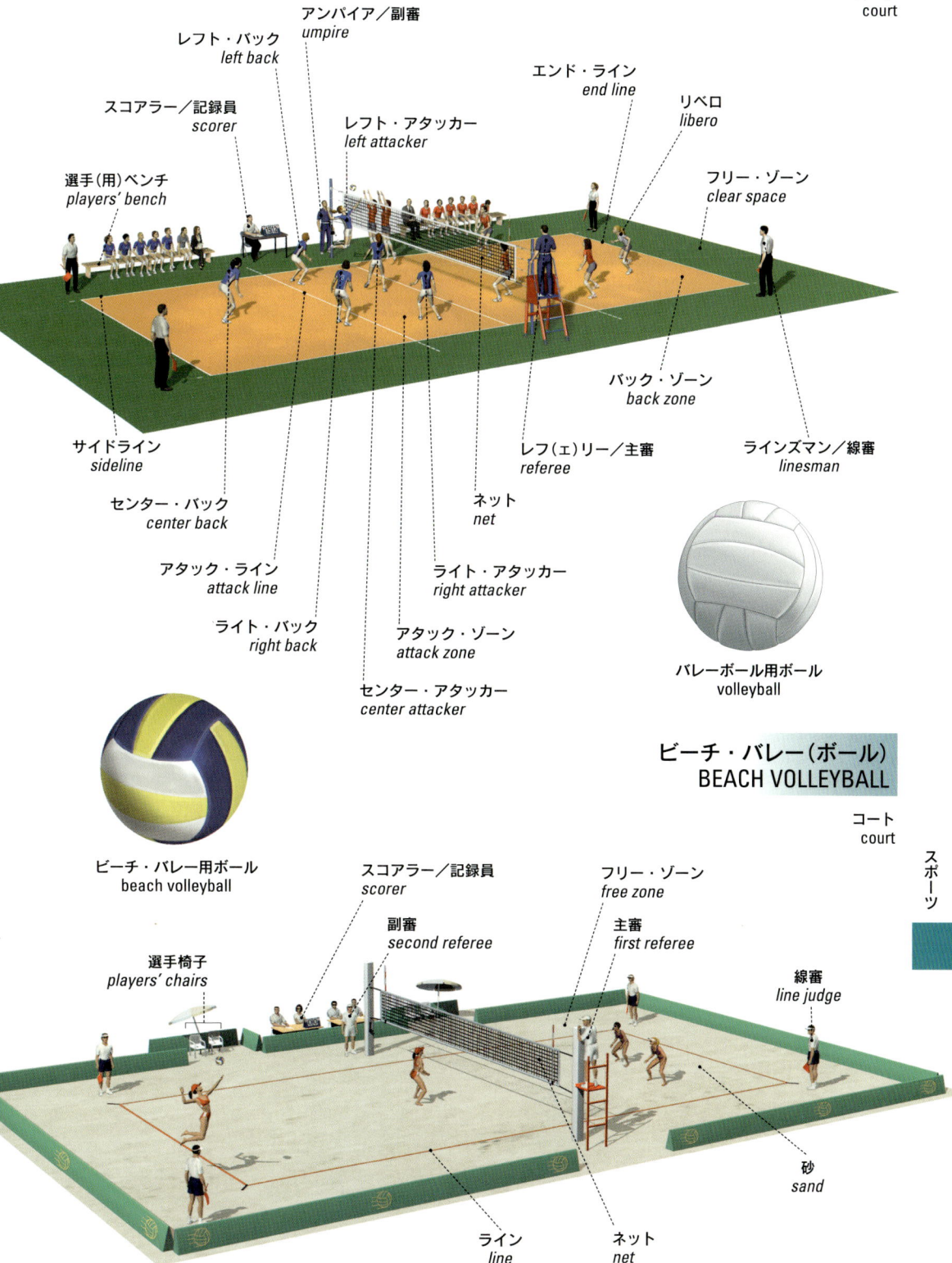

299

球技 | BALL SPORTS

サッカー
SOCCER

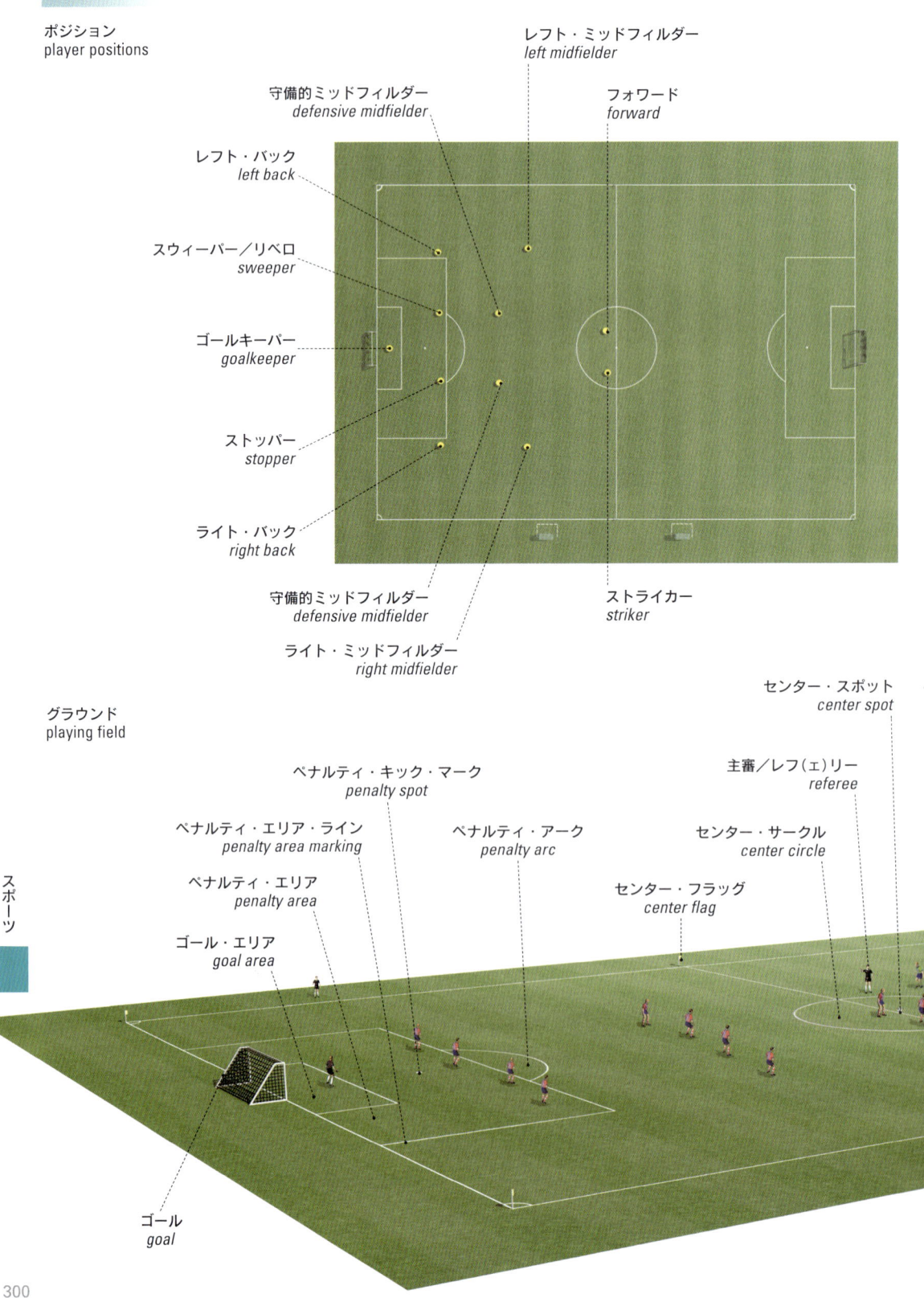

ポジション
player positions

守備的ミッドフィルダー
defensive midfielder

レフト・ミッドフィルダー
left midfielder

フォワード
forward

レフト・バック
left back

スウィーパー／リベロ
sweeper

ゴールキーパー
goalkeeper

ストッパー
stopper

ライト・バック
right back

守備的ミッドフィルダー
defensive midfielder

ストライカー
striker

ライト・ミッドフィルダー
right midfielder

グラウンド
playing field

ペナルティ・キック・マーク
penalty spot

センター・スポット
center spot

ペナルティ・エリア・ライン
penalty area marking

ペナルティ・アーク
penalty arc

主審／レフ(ェ)リー
referee

ペナルティ・エリア
penalty area

センター・サークル
center circle

ゴール・エリア
goal area

センター・フラッグ
center flag

スポーツ

ゴール
goal

球技 | BALL SPORTS

サッカー・プレーヤー
soccer player

ゴールキーパー・グローブ
goalkeeper's gloves

ユニフォーム／チーム・シャツ
team shirt

サッカー・シューズ
soccer shoe

ショーツ
shorts

取り替え式スパイク
interchangeable studs

シン・ガード／脛（すね）当て
shin guard

ストッキング
sock

サッカー・ボール
soccer ball

コーナー・フラッグ
corner flag

コーナー・アーク
corner arc

スポーツ

タッチ・ライン
touch line

ハーフウェイ・ライン
halfway line

線審／ラインズマン
linesman

控えベンチ
substitute's bench

301

ラケット・スポーツ | RACKET SPORTS

テニスは世界中どの国でも、1対1か2対2で、クレー・コート、ハード・コート、ローン・コートなどで行われます。プレーヤーはネットに掛からないようにボールを打ち合います。ボールのスピードは時速200キロを超えることもあります。大きなトーナメントには毎年のように多くの観客が押し寄せ、中でもイギリスで開催されるウィンブルドン大会は有名で、最も歴史があります。

テニス
TENNIS

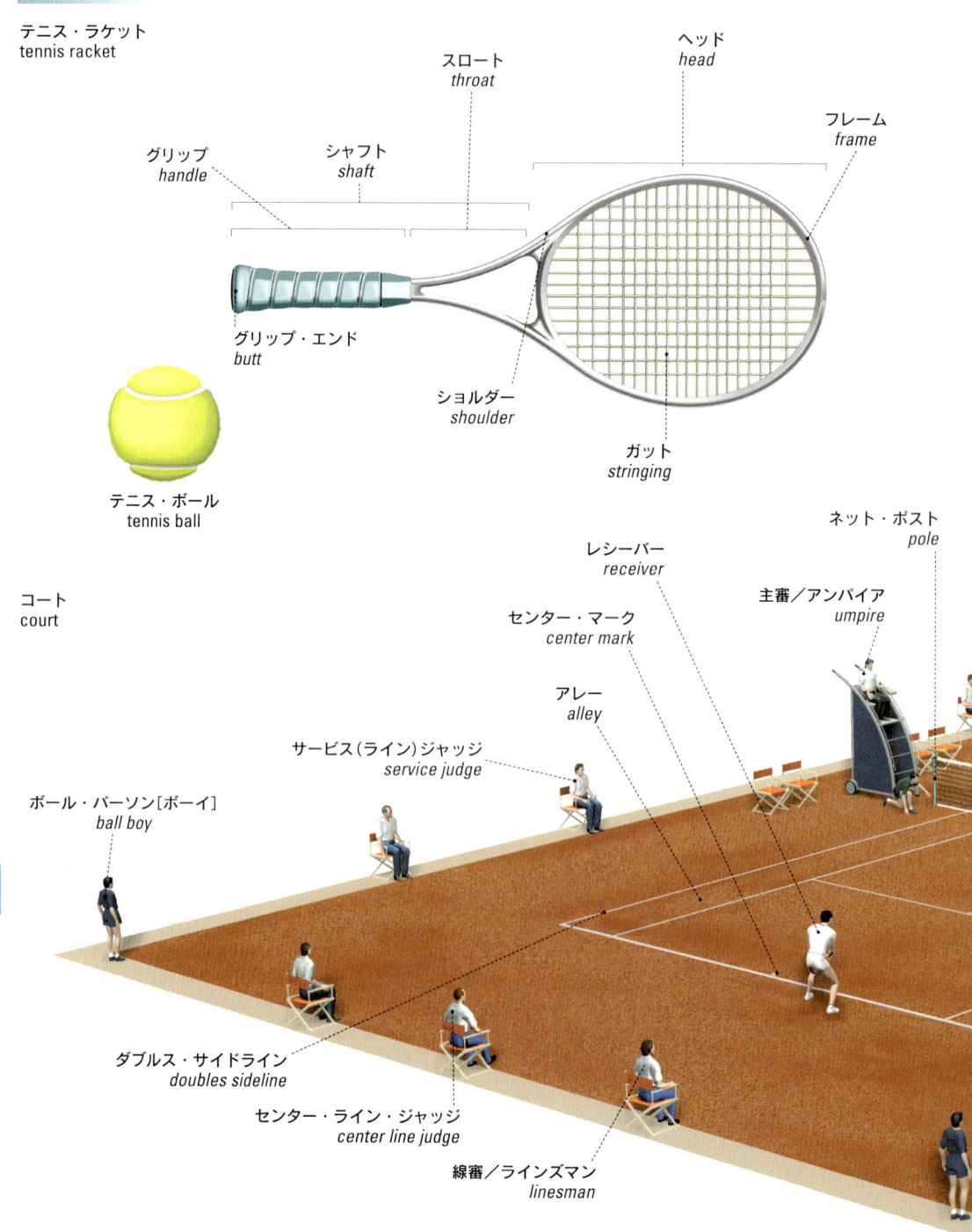

テニス・ラケット
tennis racket

スロート
throat

ヘッド
head

グリップ
handle

シャフト
shaft

フレーム
frame

グリップ・エンド
butt

ショルダー
shoulder

ガット
stringing

テニス・ボール
tennis ball

レシーバー
receiver

ネット・ポスト
pole

コート
court

センター・マーク
center mark

主審／アンパイア
umpire

アレー
alley

サービス（ライン）ジャッジ
service judge

ボール・パーソン［ボーイ］
ball boy

ダブルス・サイドライン
doubles sideline

センター・ライン・ジャッジ
center line judge

線審／ラインズマン
linesman

スポーツ

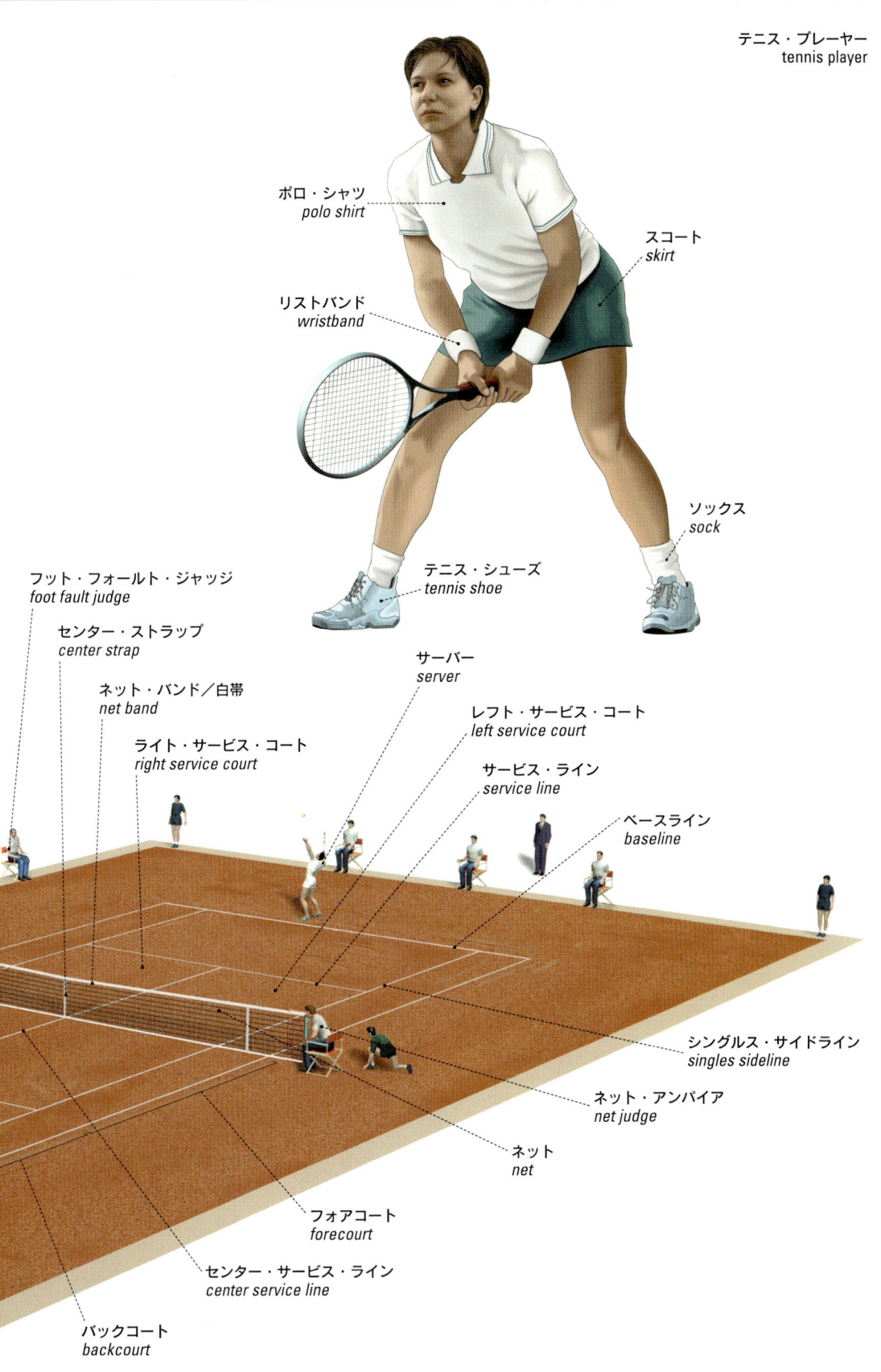

ラケット・スポーツ | RACKET SPORTS

テニス・プレーヤー
tennis player

ポロ・シャツ
polo shirt

スコート
skirt

リストバンド
wristband

ソックス
sock

テニス・シューズ
tennis shoe

フット・フォールト・ジャッジ
foot fault judge

センター・ストラップ
center strap

ネット・バンド／白帯
net band

ライト・サービス・コート
right service court

サーバー
server

レフト・サービス・コート
left service court

サービス・ライン
service line

ベースライン
baseline

シングルス・サイドライン
singles sideline

ネット・アンパイア
net judge

ネット
net

フォアコート
forecourt

センター・サービス・ライン
center service line

バックコート
backcourt

スポーツ

303

格闘技 | COMBAT SPORTS

空手、ボクシング、レスリング、柔道は格闘技で、体重がほぼ同じ二人が手に武器を持たずに戦います。もし肉体的にも心理的にも調子を整えるのが空手家であれば、ボクサーには巧みさ、まれに見る耐久力が要求されます。すべての武術、あるいは攻防の技術を要するその他の格闘技においては、力と動きを完全にコントロールすることも必要です。

ボクシング
BOXING

ボクサー
boxer

ヘッドギア
headgear

グローブ
glove

トランクス
boxing trunks

パンチング・ボール
punching ball

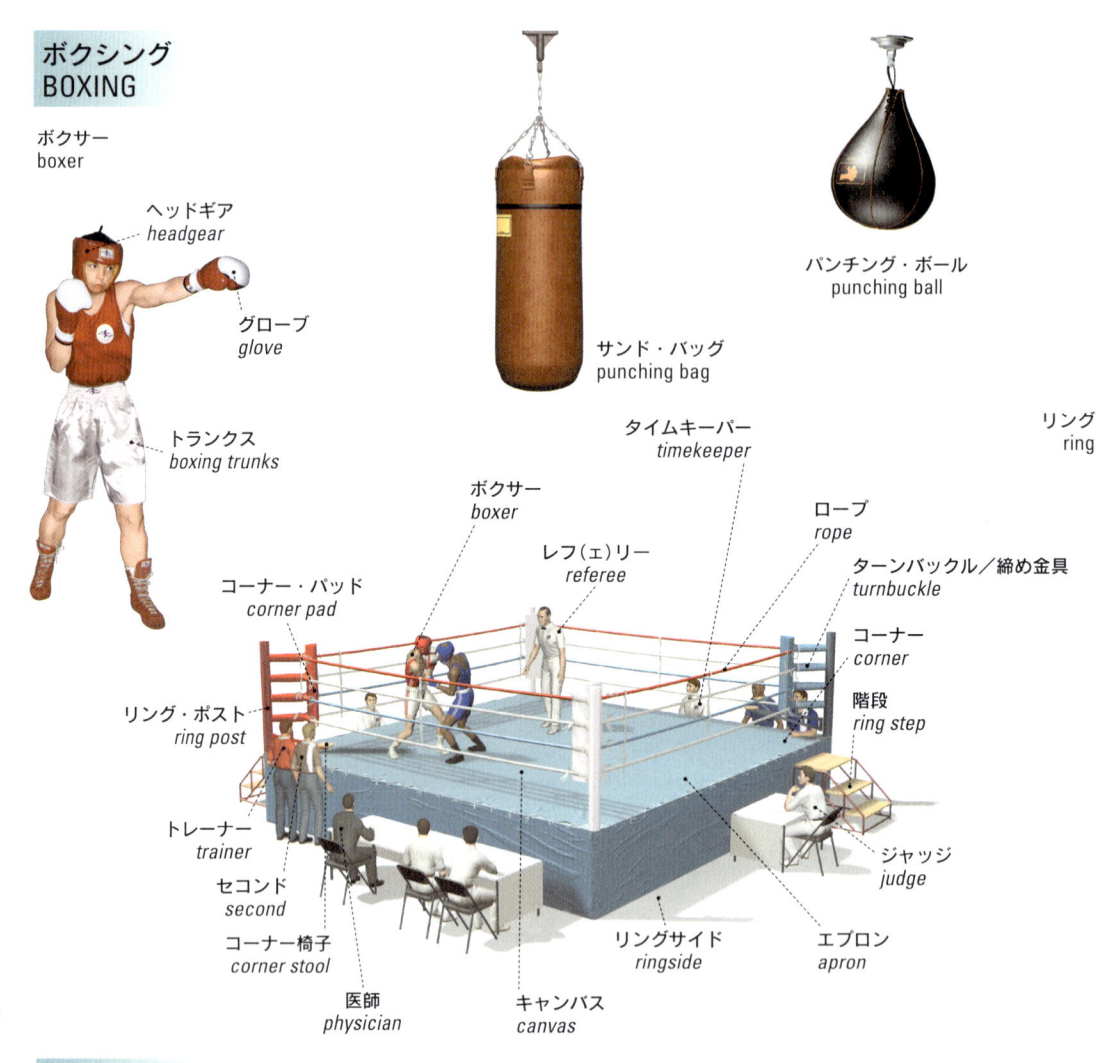

サンド・バッグ
punching bag

コーナー・パッド
corner pad

リング・ポスト
ring post

トレーナー
trainer

セコンド
second

コーナー椅子
corner stool

医師
physician

ボクサー
boxer

レフ(ェ)リー
referee

キャンバス
canvas

タイムキーパー
timekeeper

リングサイド
ringside

リング
ring

ロープ
rope

ターンバックル／締め金具
turnbuckle

コーナー
corner

階段
ring step

ジャッジ
judge

エプロン
apron

レスリング
WRESTLING

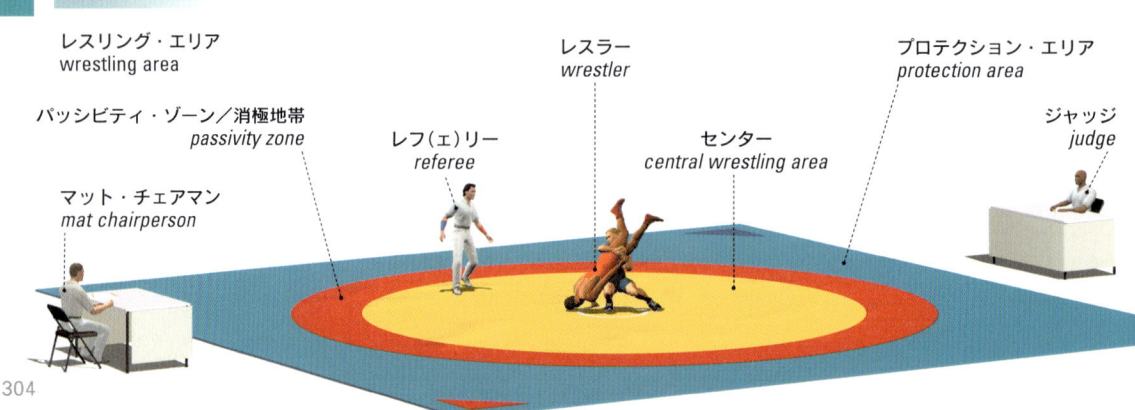

レスリング・エリア
wrestling area

パッシビティ・ゾーン／消極地帯
passivity zone

マット・チェアマン
mat chairperson

レフ(ェ)リー
referee

レスラー
wrestler

センター
central wrestling area

プロテクション・エリア
protection area

ジャッジ
judge

スポーツ

格闘技 | COMBAT SPORTS

競技場
competition area

空手
KARATE

- 監査役 arbitration committee
- 空手家 karate-ka
- 副審 corner judge
- 計時員 timekeeper
- 記録員 scorekeeper
- 主審 referee

- 空手着／空手衣 karate-gi
- 帯 obi
- 空手家 karate-ka
- 畳 mat

柔道
JUDO

- 柔道着／柔道衣 judo-gi
- 上衣／上着 jacket
- 帯 belt
- ズボン／下穿(ば)き／股下 trousers

- 記録係と計時係 scorers and timekeepers
- 得点掲示板 scoreboard
- 医療班 medical team
- 競技者／試合者 contestant
- 場外／安全区域[地帯] safety area
- 試合場 contest area
- 主審 referee
- 副審 judge
- 危険区域[地帯] danger area

スポーツ

305

モーター・スポーツ | MOTOR SPORTS

自動車レースは、閉ざされたさまざまなサーキット上で行われ、高速が出るように設計された特別な車が走り回ります。このような車のドライバーは、ほかのモーター・スポーツのドライバーと同様に、鋼鉄のような神経、危険を避ける反射神経、さらにはレーシング・カーを完璧に操縦する能力を持ち合わせていなければなりません。

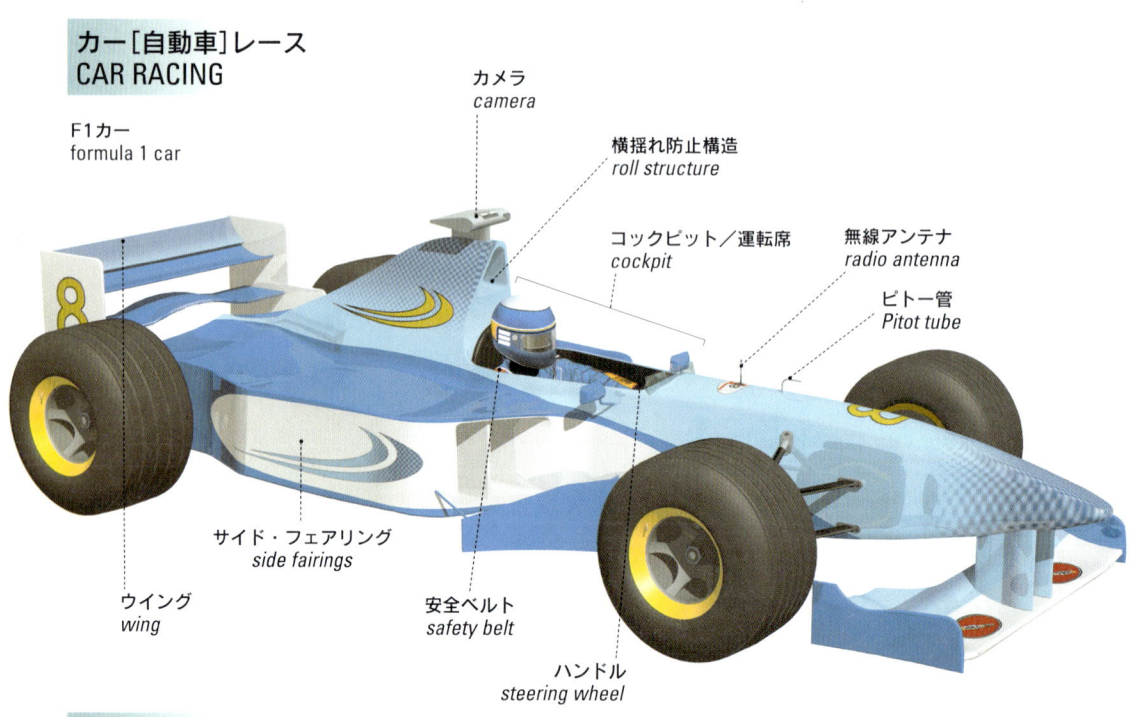

カー[自動車]レース
CAR RACING

F1カー
formula 1 car

カメラ
camera

横揺れ防止構造
roll structure

コックピット／運転席
cockpit

無線アンテナ
radio antenna

ピトー管
Pitot tube

サイド・フェアリング
side fairings

ウイング
wing

安全ベルト
safety belt

ハンドル
steering wheel

オートバイ・レース
MOTORCYCLING

モトクロス・スーパークロス用のオートバイ
motocross and supercross motorcycle

防護服
protective suit

ヘルメット
helmet

グローブ／手袋
glove

ゴーグル／防護眼鏡
protective goggles

ズボン
pants

ハンド・プロテクター[ガード]
hand protector

ブーツ
boot

ナンバー・プレート
number plate

スパイク・タイヤ
nubby tire

フォーク
fork

保護板
protective plate

スポーツ

ローラー・スポーツ | SPORTS ON WHEELS

スケートボードとイン・ラインスケートは、高い反射神経とよい平衡感覚を同時に要求するスポーツです。このスポーツをするプレーヤーは、創造力を使ってアクロバット的な姿勢をつくり、身に付けている技術を巧みに生かしてスピードを出します。

スケートボーダー / skateboarder

インナー・ブーツ / inner boot
イン・ライン・スケート靴／ローラー・ブレード® / in-line skate
アッパー・シェル / upper shell
バックル / adjusting buckle
ブーツ / boot
車軸／心棒 / axle
ヒール・ストップ / heel stop
ウィール／車輪 / wheel
トラック / truck

スケートボード / skateboard
グリップ[デッキ]テープ / grip tape
ウィール／車輪 / wheel

スケーター / skater
ヘルメット / helmet
エルボー・パッド／肘(ひじ)当て / elbow pad
リスト・ガード / wrist guard
ニー・パッド／膝(ひざ)当て / knee pad

ハーフ・パイプ / ramp
ガード・レール / guard rail
プラットフォーム / platform
リップ / coping
バーティカル／ウォール / vertical section
ボトム／フラット / flat

スポーツ

自転車競技 ｜ CYCLING

起伏のある地面上であれトラック上であれ、サイクリストはよい平衡感覚、高い反射神経、大変な忍耐力を持ち合わせていなければなりません。さまざまなスポーツで使われる自転車は、実に多様な目的に使われます。例えば、ロード・レース用自転車はスピードを出すために使われ、クロス・カントリー用自転車はむしろ障害物を乗り越え、難しいトラックを走るために設計されています。

ロード・レース
ROAD RACING

ロード・レース用自転車とサイクリスト
road-racing bicycle and cyclist

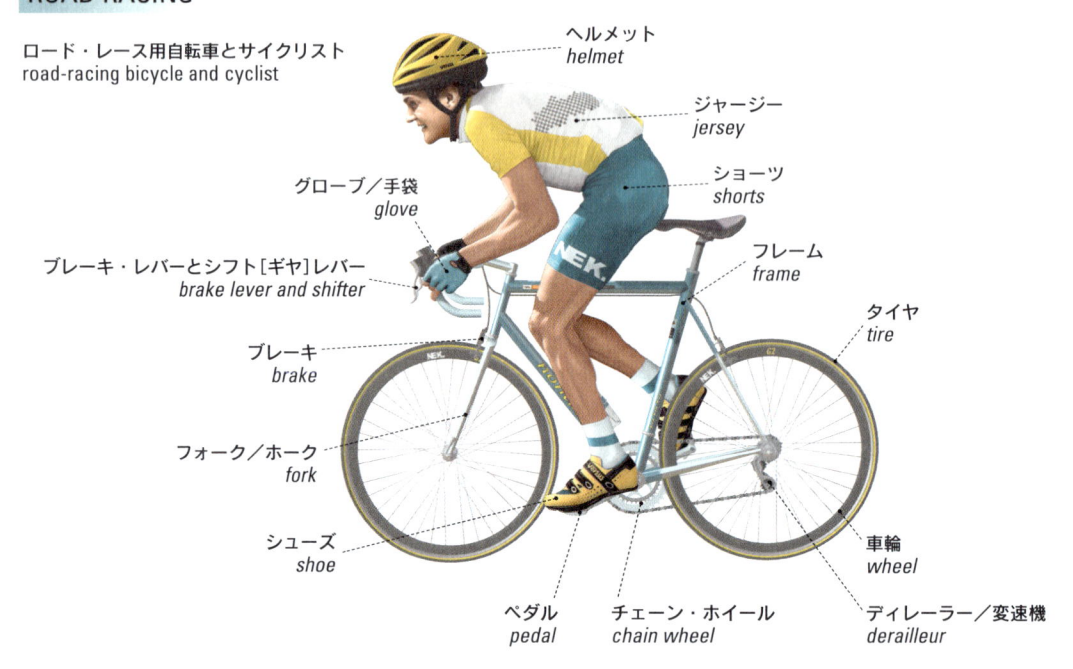

ヘルメット
helmet

ジャージー
jersey

ショーツ
shorts

グローブ／手袋
glove

ブレーキ・レバーとシフト［ギヤ］レバー
brake lever and shifter

フレーム
frame

タイヤ
tire

ブレーキ
brake

フォーク／ホーク
fork

シューズ
shoe

車輪
wheel

ペダル
pedal

チェーン・ホイール
chain wheel

ディレーラー／変速機
derailleur

バイシクル・モトクロス
BMX

バイシクル・モトクロスとサイクリスト
BMX and cyclist

ステップ
foot pegs

ヘルメット
helmet

ハンドルバー
handlebars

グローブ／手袋
glove

シングル・チェーン・ホイール
single chain wheel

ステップ
foot pegs

シングル・スプロケット
single sprocket

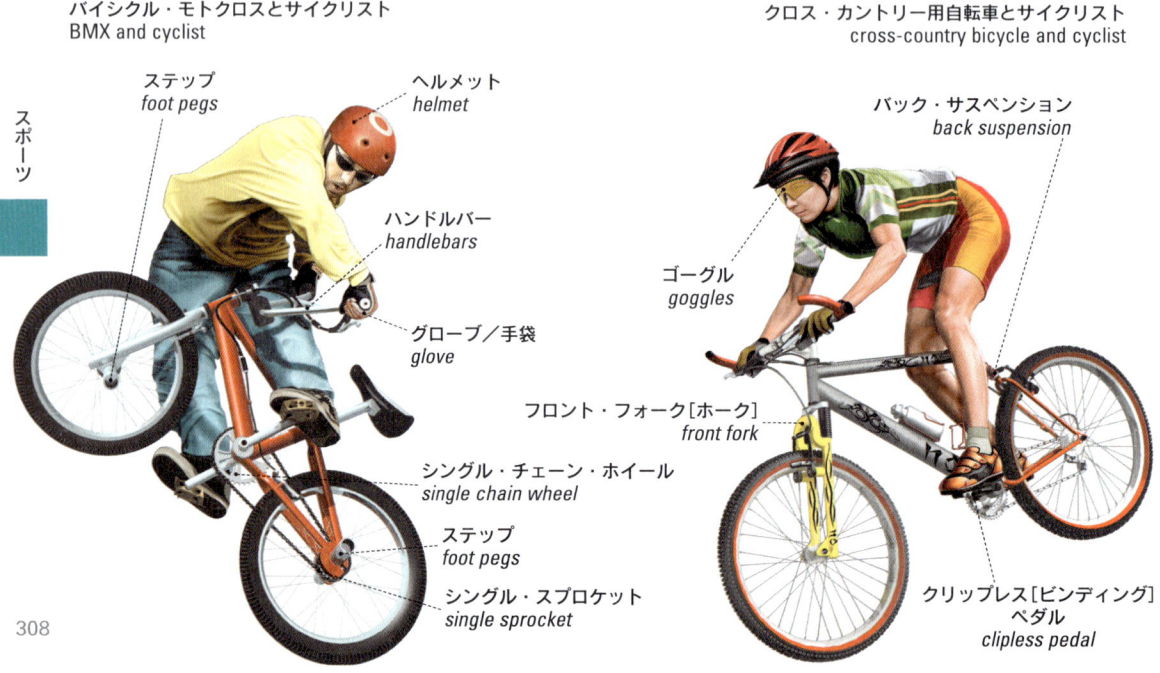

マウンテン・バイキング
MOUNTAIN BIKING

クロス・カントリー用自転車とサイクリスト
cross-country bicycle and cyclist

バック・サスペンション
back suspension

ゴーグル
goggles

フロント・フォーク［ホーク］
front fork

クリップレス［ビンディング］ペダル
clipless pedal

スポーツ

キャンプ | CAMPING

キャンプは、安上がりの旅行をし、野外を楽しむためには理想的な活動です。寝袋と何らかの道具さえあれば十分で、さらにテント、折り畳み式ベッド、マットレスでもあればキャンプはより快適になるはずです。あまりお薦めはできませんが、ちょっと冒険してみれば、踏み固められた小道から外れて、ふだん近づけない場所を探検したりもできます。

テント TENTS

家族用［ロッジ型］テント
family tent

居間 living room
フレーム frame
寝室 bedroom
庇（ひさし）／日除（よ）け window canopy
ロープ／張り網 guy line
メッシュ窓／網戸 screen window
ゴム・ロープ elastic strainer
ループ stake loop
仕切り canvas divider
グラ（ウ）ンド・シート sewn-in floor
壁 wall

家形［ウォール］テント
wall tent

2人用テント
two-person tent

1人用テント
one-person tent

ワゴン・テント
wagon tent

パップ［楔（くさび）形］テント
pup tent

ドーム形テント
dome tent

ポップ・アップ・テント
pop-up tent

レジャーとゲーム

キャンプ | CAMPING

寝袋／シュラ(ー)フ／スリーピング・バッグ
SLEEPING BAGS

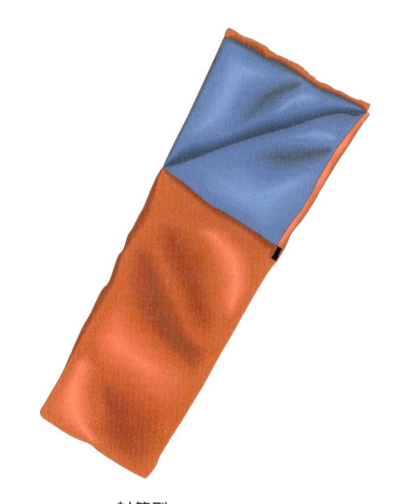

封筒型
rectangular

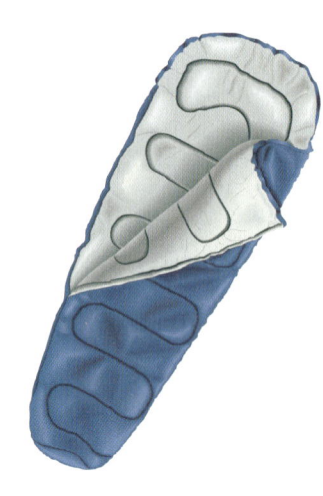

セミ・マミー型
semi-mummy

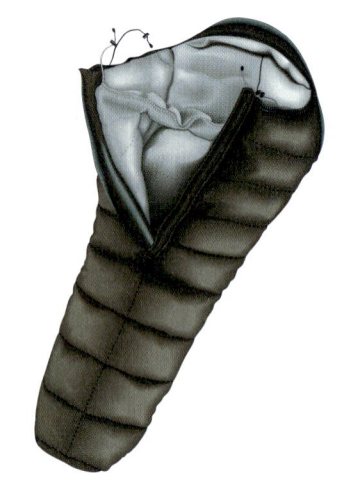

マミー型／人形型
mummy

ベッドとマット(レス)
BED AND MATTRESS

エア・マット(レス)
air mattress

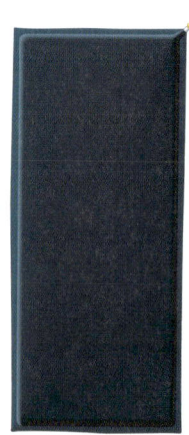

セルフ・インフレーティング・マット(レス)
self-inflating mattress

フォーム・パッド[マット(レス)]
foam pad

空気(入れ)ポンプ
inflator

空気入れ[抜き]ポンプ
inflator-deflator

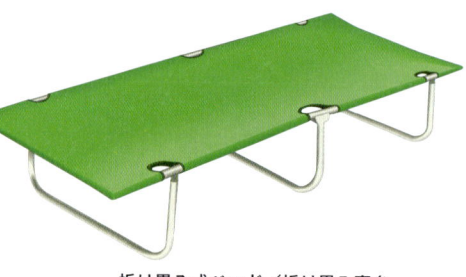

折り畳み式ベッド／折り畳み寝台
folding cot

キャンプ | CAMPING

キャンプ用品
CAMPING EQUIPMENT

スイス・アーミー・ナイフ／軍用ナイフ
Swiss army knife

鋏（はさみ）
scissors

ルーペ／拡大鏡／虫眼鏡
magnifier

スモール[ペン]ブレード／小刃
pen blade

栓抜き
bottle opener

ねじ回し
screwdriver

爪掛け
nail nick

錐（きり）／千枚通し
awl

魚のうろこ落とし
fish scaler

定規
ruler

やすり
file

プラスねじ回し
cross-tip screwdriver

ねじ回し
screwdriver

ラージ・ブレード／大刃
large blade

缶切り
can opener

コルク栓抜き
corkscrew

ボトル
bottle

カップ
cup

ストッパー
stopper

魔法瓶
vacuum bottle

コーヒー・ポット
coffee pot

カップ
cup

皿
plate

柄／取っ手
handle

ソースパン／片手鍋
saucepan

フライ・パン
frying pan

クーラー・ボックス
cooler

水タンク
water carrier

ハリケーン・ランプ
hurricane lamp

水筒
canteen

レジャーとゲーム

311

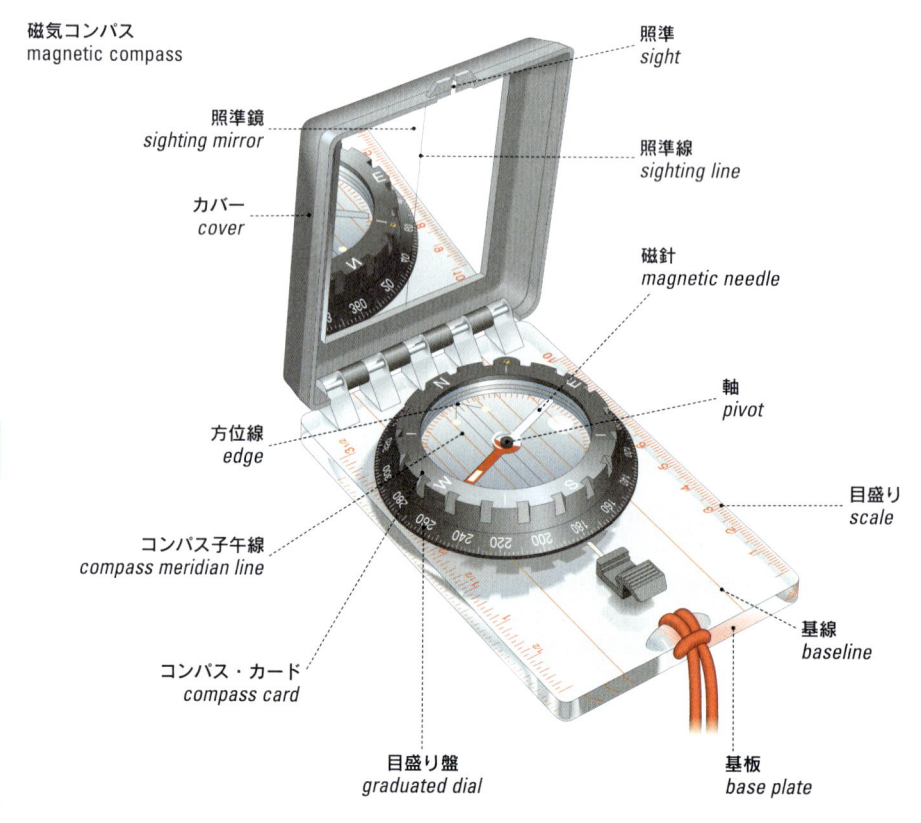

キャンプ | CAMPING

バックパック
backpack

ショルダー・ベルト
shoulder strap

雨蓋（あまぶた）
top flap

バックル／留め金
tightening buckle

サイド・コンプレッション・ベルト
side compression strap

フロント・コンプレッション・ベルト
front compression strap

ベルト・ループ／ベルト通し
strap loop

ウエスト・ベルト
waist belt

ナイフ
knife

鞘（さや）
sheath

革鞘
leather sheath

手斧（ておの・ちょうな）
hatchet

弓鋸（のこ）
bow saw

磁気コンパス
magnetic compass

照準鏡
sighting mirror

カバー
cover

方位線
edge

コンパス子午線
compass meridian line

コンパス・カード
compass card

目盛り盤
graduated dial

照準
sight

照準線
sighting line

磁針
magnetic needle

軸
pivot

目盛り
scale

基線
baseline

基板
base plate

レジャーとゲーム

312

ゲーム | GAMES

さいころはエジプトのずいぶん古い墓で見つかり、チェスは太古の昔までさかのぼります。ボード・ゲームは恐らく遊ぶ楽しみと同じくらい古いものなのでしょう。今日、室内ゲームには、とりわけドミノ、トランプ、バックギャモン、ダーツ、ビデオ・ゲームといった数多くの種類があります。一人でやっても皆でやっても、ふつうの娯楽として熱中してしまいます。

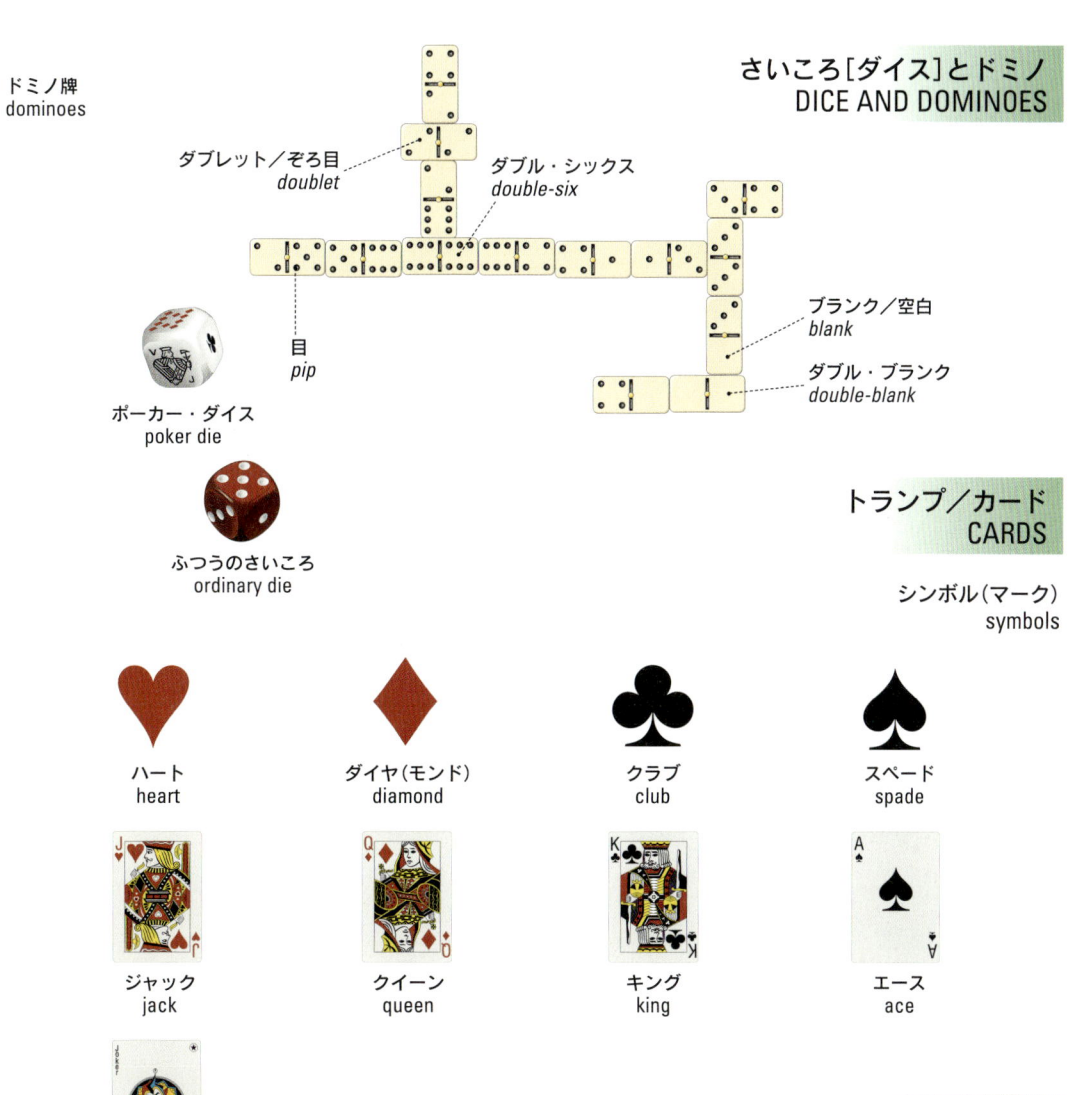

さいころ[ダイス]とドミノ
DICE AND DOMINOES

ドミノ牌
dominoes

ダブレット／ぞろ目
doublet

ダブル・シックス
double-six

目
pip

ブランク／空白
blank

ダブル・ブランク
double-blank

ポーカー・ダイス
poker die

ふつうのさいころ
ordinary die

トランプ／カード
CARDS

シンボル(マーク)
symbols

ハート
heart

ダイヤ(モンド)
diamond

クラブ
club

スペード
spade

ジャック
jack

クイーン
queen

キング
king

エース
ace

ジョーカー
joker

ジグソー・パズル
JIGSAW PUZZLE

ピース
piece

絵(柄)
picture

ボード
board

レジャーとゲーム

ゲーム | GAMES

チェス
CHESS

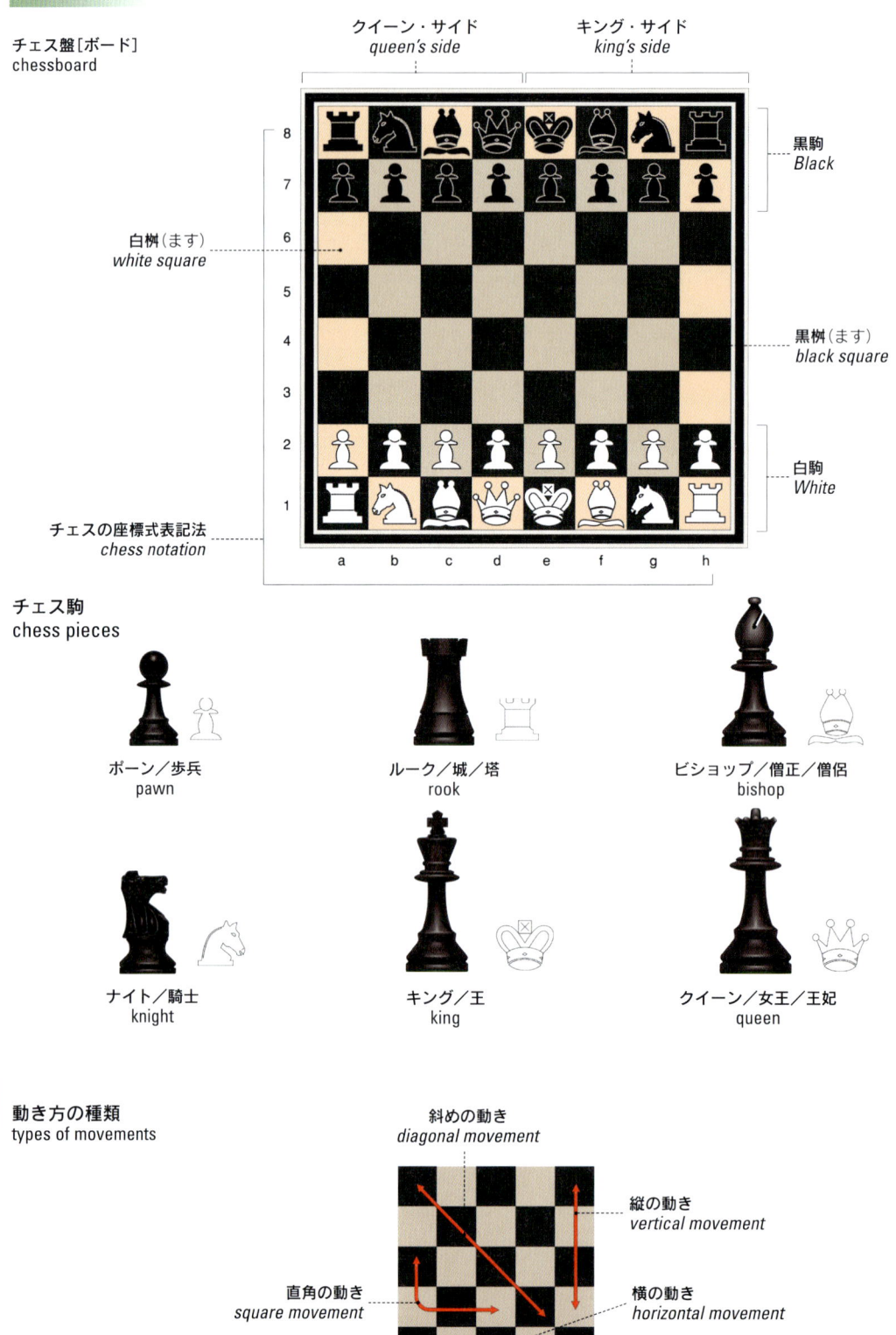

チェス盤［ボード］
chessboard

クイーン・サイド
queen's side

キング・サイド
king's side

黒駒
Black

白桝（ます）
white square

黒桝（ます）
black square

白駒
White

チェスの座標式表記法
chess notation

チェス駒
chess pieces

ポーン／歩兵
pawn

ルーク／城／塔
rook

ビショップ／僧正／僧侶
bishop

ナイト／騎士
knight

キング／王
king

クイーン／女王／王妃
queen

動き方の種類
types of movements

斜めの動き
diagonal movement

縦の動き
vertical movement

直角の動き
square movement

横の動き
horizontal movement

ゲーム | GAMES

バックギャモン／西洋双六
BACKGAMMON

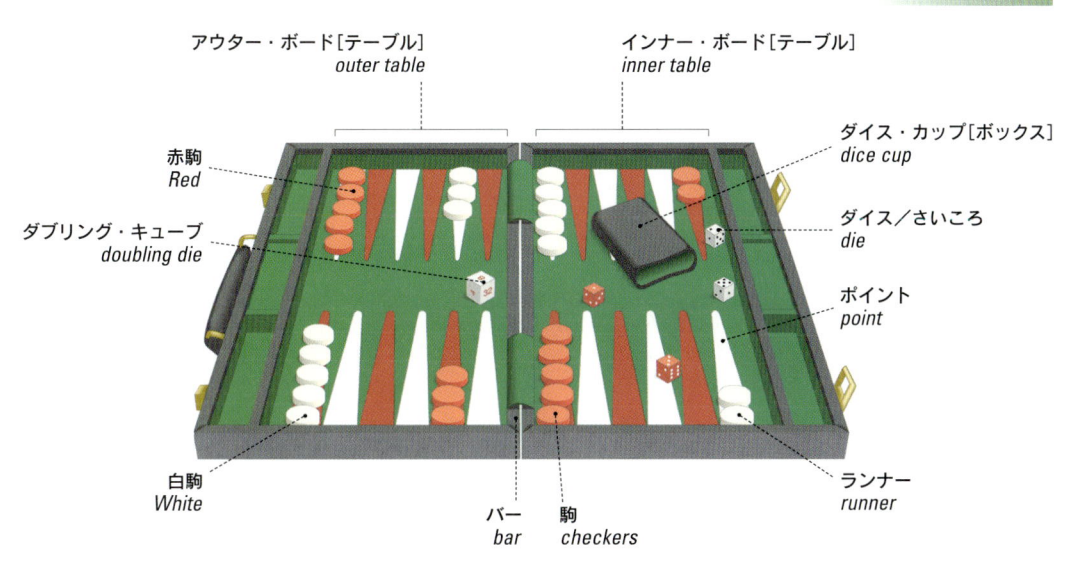

- アウター・ボード［テーブル］ outer table
- インナー・ボード［テーブル］ inner table
- 赤駒 Red
- ダイス・カップ［ボックス］ dice cup
- ダブリング・キューブ doubling die
- ダイス／さいころ die
- ポイント point
- 白駒 White
- バー bar
- 駒 checkers
- ランナー runner

チェッカー／西洋将棋
CHECKERS

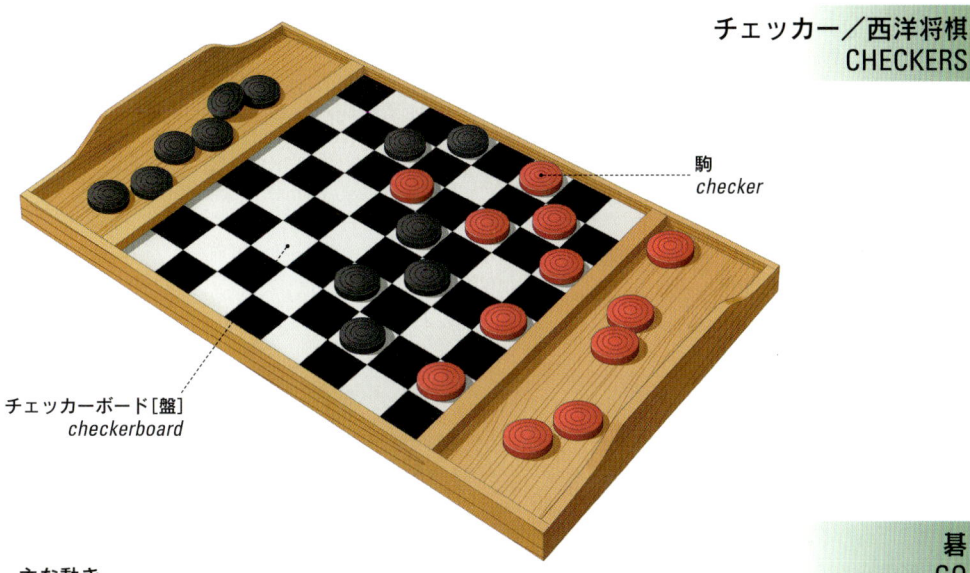

- 駒 checker
- チェッカーボード［盤］ checkerboard

碁
GO

- 主な動き major motions 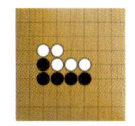
  - ツギ／連絡 connection 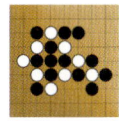
  - 捕獲 capture 
  - ツケ contact
- 碁盤 board
- 星 handicap spot
- 黒石 black stone
- 天元 center
- 白石 white stone

レジャーとゲーム

315

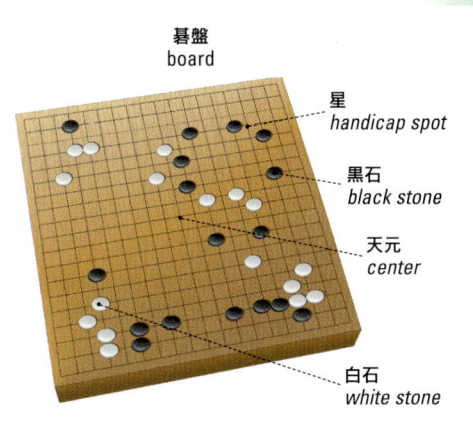

ゲーム | GAMES

ダーツ
DARTS

ダーツボード
dartboard

得点数
segment score number

ダブル・リング
double ring

ダブル［インナー］ブル／
ブルズ・アイ
bull's-eye

トリプル・リング
triple ring

シングル［アウター］ブル
outer bull

コート
playing area

保護板／サラウンド
protective surround

得点板／スコアボード
scoreboard

ダート／投げ矢
dart

シャフト／軸
shaft

ポイント／先端
point

フライト
flight

バレル／胴
barrel

スローイング・ライン
oche

ビデオ・ゲーム
VIDEO ENTERTAINMENT SYSTEM

ゲーム機／ゲーム・コンソール
game console

メモリー・カード・スロット［差込口］
memory card slots

CD・DVDプレーヤー
CD/DVD player

アクション・ボタン［キー］
action buttons

方向ボタン［キー］
directional buttons

コントローラー
controller

ディスプレイ／スクリーン
visual display

コントローラー・ポート
controller ports

リセット・ボタン
reset button

取り出しボタン
eject button

ジョイスティック／操作棒
joysticks

レジャーとゲーム

316

道路標識 | ROAD SIGNS

ふつう主要な道路はすべて道路標識で示されています。これらの標識の多くは世界共通で、これによって運転者は、進路、停止義務など、言葉では分からない道路交通法を理解することができます。そのほか、ある地域に特有の標識もありますが、すべて国際標識から類推がつくはずです。

主な国際道路標識
MAJOR INTERNATIONAL ROAD SIGNS

交差点につき一時停止
stop at intersection

車両進入禁止
no entry

前方優先道路
yield

信号機あり
signal ahead

指定方向外進行禁止
direction to be followed

指定方向外進行禁止
direction to be followed

指定方向外進行禁止
direction to be followed

歩行者通行止め
closed to pedestrians

落石注意／落石の恐れあり
falling rocks

鹿（の飛び出し）に注意
deer crossing

自動二輪車通行止め
closed to motorcycles

大型貨物自動車等通行止め
closed to trucks

スクール・ゾーン／学校あり
school zone

横断歩道
pedestrian crossing

前方道路工事中
roadwork ahead

スリップ注意／滑りやすし
slippery road

象徴／シンボル

道路標識｜ROAD SIGNS

北アメリカの主な道路標識
MAJOR NORTH AMERICAN ROAD SIGNS

交差点につき一時停止
stop at intersection

車両進入禁止
no entry

前方優先道路
yield

自動二輪車通行止め
closed to motorcycles

歩行者通行止め
closed to pedestrians

自転車通行止め
closed to bicycles

Uターン[車両転回]禁止
no U-turn

大型貨物自動車等通行止め
closed to trucks

指定方向外進行禁止
direction to be followed

指定方向外進行禁止
direction to be followed

指定方向外進行禁止
direction to be followed

指定方向外進行禁止
direction to be followed

スクール・ゾーン／学校あり
school zone

横断歩道
pedestrian crossing

スリップ注意／滑りやすし
slippery road

信号機あり
signal ahead

落石注意／落石の恐れあり
falling rocks

前方道路工事中
roadwork ahead

象徴／シンボル

一般的な案内標識 | COMMON SYMBOLS

私たちの身の回りにはあらゆる種類の標識があります。一般的な案内標識は単純なイメージで構成されていて、さまざまな情報が一目で理解できるようになっています。それらは理解が容易で、外国語が分からない人でも、例えば最寄りの病院や情報センターがどこにあるかが分かります。とりわけ伝えたい内容は万人に共通で、言葉の壁などありません。

男子トイレ
men's rest room

女子トイレ
women's rest room

両替所
currency exchange

車椅子乗り入れ可能
wheelchair access

キャンプ可（キャンピング・カーおよびテント）
camping (trailer and tent)

ピクニック地域
picnic area

コーヒー・ショップ／喫茶店
coffee shop

キャンプ可（テント）
camping (tent)

ガソリン・スタンド
service station

消火器
fire extinguisher

キャンプ可
（キャンピング・カー）
camping (trailer)

病院
hospital

公衆電話／電話ボックス
telephone

レストラン
restaurant

薬局
pharmacy

警察
police

救急（室）／救護所
first aid

案内所
information

案内所
information

遺失物取扱所
lost and found articles

車椅子乗り入れ禁止
no wheelchair access

ピクニック禁止
picnics prohibited

キャンプ禁止
camping prohibited

タクシー乗り場
taxi transportation

象徴／シンボル

安全標識 | SAFETY SYMBOLS

安全標識は非常に重要です。それらは厄介な事故に巻き込まれないように、起こりうる危険を警告し、危険物の存在を示し、防護用具の装着を促しています。工事現場にある、頭にヘルメットを被った絵のある標識は、現場で働く人たちに保護帽着用の義務を指示しています。

危険物
DANGEROUS MATERIALS

腐食性物質
corrosive

感電の危険あり
electrical hazard

爆発性物質
explosive

可燃性物質
flammable

放射性物質
radioactive

有毒性物質
poison

保護具
PROTECTION

保護眼鏡着用
eye protection

耳栓着用
ear protection

保護帽着用
head protection

手袋着用
hand protection

長靴着用
foot protection

防塵[防毒]マスク着用
respiratory system protection

日本語索引

あ

アーキトレーブ 217
アーケード 218, 221
アース端子 155
アーチェリー 281
アーチ橋 183
アーチ・ダム 174
アーチャー 281
アーティチョーク 105
アーム 157, 167, 209
アーム・ガード 281, 298
アーム・ライト 157
アーム・ランプ 157
アーモンド 113
アイアン 282
ISP 249
アイカップ 240
アイシャドー 133
アイスクリーム 114
アイスクリームすくい 148
アイスクリーム・スクープ 148
アイスバーグレタス 106
アイス・ホッケー 284
アイス・ホッケー・スケート靴 286
アイス・ホッケー・プレーヤー 284
相乗りシート 191
アイブロウ・ブラシとアイ・ラッシュ・コーム 133
アイランド(式カウンター) 143
アイレット 122, 125, 286
アウター・テーブル 315
アウター・ブル 316
アウター・ボード 315
アウター・ミラー 184
アウト・ウォッシュ・プレーン 29
アウトサイド・ラインバッカー 296
アウトソール 122, 125
アウトリガー 209, 263, 279
青 211
アオイマメ 108
青緑 211
青紫 211
赤 211
アカエイ 64
赤キャベツ 106
赤コケモモ 109
赤駒 315
赤橙 211
赤タマネギ 103
赤チコリ 106
赤パプリカ 107
赤紫 211
明かり取り 135
赤ワイン用グラス 144
亜寒帯気候 34
亜寒帯気候における季節 33
亜寒帯林 40
秋 33
アキレス腱ガード 286
アクアマリン 129
アクション・キー 316
アクション・ボタン 316
アクセサリー・シュー 235
アクセス・サーバー 249
アクセル・ペダル 188
アクセント記号 223
踵 84
アクロテリア 217
上げ下げ窓 137
顎 72, 90
あご 162
顎当て 227

アコースティック・ギター 229
アコーディオン 224
アコーディオン式書類入れ 126
アコーディオン・ドア 136
アコーディオン窓 137
顎ガード 191
顎カバー 263
顎紐 263, 287, 298
アザミ 51
アザラシ 88
足 76, 82, 83, 90
脚 67, 83, 90, 141, 164, 275
アジア 19
足板 142
足置き 141
アシカ 88
足先 288
アジサシ 75
アシスタント・コーチ 285, 295
足台 140
足留め 278
足載せ板 141
足載せ台 140
足の例 73
足場付きはしご 163
足ひれ 279
足指 76, 90
趾 73, 78
アズキ 108
アステカ神殿 219
アスパラガス 105
アスピリン 267
アスファルト 181
遊び場 201
温かい上昇気流 37
アタック・ゾーン 299
アタック・ライン 299
アタッシュ・ケース 126
頭 57, 82, 91, 214
頭板 141, 142
頭飾り 168
圧縮 46
圧縮空気タンク 197, 279
圧縮空気ボンベ 263
アッパー・シーツ 142
アッパー・シェル 289, 307
アッパー・ストラップ 289
アップホール・ライン 278
アップライト・ピアノ 226
アッポジャトゥーラ 223
圧力 176
圧力調節器 149, 263
圧力鍋 149
当て布 142
アドービ・ハウス 215
アドビー・ハウス 215
後膝 84
アトリ 74
アトリウム 218
アナウサギ 77
アナグマ 80
穴かご 214
アナログ時計 168
アナログ・ビデオ・カメラ 240
亜熱帯気候 34
亜熱帯多雨気候 34
アノラック 122
アビシニアン 79
アヒル 75
アフター・シェーブ・ローション 131
鐙骨 100
油絵の具 212
油切り 149, 178
アフリカ 19
アプリコット 110

溢れ口 154
アプローチ 281
アプローチ部 183
アフロ・ピック 130
アボカド 107
アポクリン汗腺 101
アポロ 13
亜北極気候 34
雨覆い 72
アマガエル 66
雨戸 137
天の川 11
雨蓋 312
雨水溜め 218
網 291
網戸 189, 309
編み棒 214
雨 36
アメーバ 56
アメシスト 129
アメジスト 129
アメフト 296
雨用帽子 124
アメリカ型プラグ 155
アメリカクロクマ 81
アメリカ・ピン 130
アメリカボウフウ 104
アメリカワシミミズク 74
アメリカンショートヘア 79
アメリカン・フットボール 296
アメンボ 63
アラいグマ 80
粗取り 213
荒取り 213
粗彫り 213
荒彫り 213
氷霰 36
アリ 63
アリアン4 16
アリエル 7
アリゲーター 69
アルコール球 169
アルコール柱 169
アルファルファ 108
アルプスサラマンダー 66
アルペッジョ 223
アルペン系スノーボード 287
アルペン・スキー 289
アルペン・スキーヤー 289
アルペン・スノーボード 287
アルミニウムのリサイクル用コンテナ 46
アルミ・フレーム 288
アレー 302
アロー 281
アロサウルス 70
泡立て器 148
アンカー(ブロック) 183
アンキロサウルス 71
アンズ 110
安全 262
安全監察員 279
安全器 176
安全区域 305
安全地帯 250, 305
安全手すり 196
安全灯 265
安全パッド 275
安全バルブ 178
安全ハンドル 165
安全標識 320
安全ピン 214, 262
安全ベルト 141, 306
安全ライン 255
アンダーシャツ 291

アンテナ 185, 203, 206, 242, 245, 265
アンテフィックス 217
案内カウンター 252
案内所 259, 264, 319
案内輪 199
鞍馬 274
アンバイア 292, 297, 299, 302
アンプ(リファイアー) 241

い

胃 96
イアベトゥス 7
Eコマース 249
Eメール 249
Eメール・ソフトウェア 248
家 134
家形テント 309
イオ 6
イオニア式の付け柱 218
倚音 223
イオンの尾 10
イグアナ 69
育児嚢 76
育児袋 76
イグニッション・キー 165
イグニッション・スイッチ 188
育房 61
イグルー 215
池 282
生け垣 135
生け贄の台座 219
石 129
医師 266, 304
石落とし 220
遺失物取扱所 319
石目やすり 213
衣装 272
衣装係 272
衣装戸棚 139
衣装部屋 139, 272
移植鏝 164
椅子 140
椅子、背もたれ椅子、肘掛け椅子 140
イズバ 215
イセエビ 58
緯線 20
イタチ 80
イタチザメ 64
1ガロン当たりの単価 261
一眼レフ・カメラ 235
イチゴ 109
イチゴの断面図 109
イチジク 113
一時停止ボタン 239
1度 222
位置灯 203
1番管 231
1番車 169
1番ピン 281
1リットル当たりの単価 261
1塁 290
1塁手 290
1階 138
イッカク 89
一貫輸送車 196
一蹄 85
一般家庭ユーザー 249
一般観覧席 280
一般的な案内標識 319
一般名 109, 110, 111, 112
糸受け 227, 228, 229
移動住宅 189
移動爪 161
糸切り歯 94

糸倉　227
糸蔵　227
糸巻き　227, 228, 229
糸巻き箱　227
糸枕　227, 228, 229
糸楊枝　133
稲妻　36
稲光　36
イヌの形態図　78
イヌの前節　78
イヌの品種　78
命綱　17
イブニング・グラブ　123
居間　138, 309
イモリ　66
イモ類　104
イヤ(ー)パッド　245
イヤホン　241, 243
イヤホン・ジャック　246
イヤホン端子　246
イラクサ　106
入り江　22
入り口　182, 219, 272
医療班　305
衣料品店　258
医療用酸素ガス配管端末器　266
医療用ベッド　266
衣類　116
衣類と身の回り品　116
イルカ　89
イルカの形態図　88
色鉛筆　212
岩小島　31
印環　129
陰極　175
インクジェット・プリンター　247
イングリッシュ・ホルン　231, 234
陰茎　90
インゲン(マメ)　108
インサイド・ラインバッカー　296
インジェクター　131
飲食店　258
インスタント食品　257
インターネット　248
インターネット・サービス・プロバイダー　249
インターネットの利用　249
インターネット・ユーザー　248
インド洋　19
インナー　125, 286
インナー・テーブル　315
インナー・ブーツ　307
インナー・ブル　316
インナー・ボード　315
インナー・ミラー　188
インナー・ミラー・バンド　243
陰嚢　90
インバウンズ・ライン　296
インブルービウム　218
陰門　90
イン・ライン・スケート靴　307
飲料　256
飲料自動販売機　261

う

ウィール　307
ウイキョウ　105
ウィグワム　215
ウィケット　292
ウィケットキーパー　292
ウィツィロポチトリ神殿　219
ウィッシュボーン・ブーム　278
ウインカー　187, 191
ウインカー・スイッチ　188
ウイング　306

ウイングレット　207, 208
ウインター・スポーツ　284
ウインチ　193
ウインチ操作用ハンドル　193
ウインドー　278
ウインドサーフィン　278
ウインドシールド　191, 192
ウインド・シンセサイザー・コントローラー　233
ウインドブレーカー　117
ウーファー　241
ウェーブ・クリップ　130
上側シーツ　142
植木鉢　164
ウエストゴム　117
ウエストバンド　117
ウエストバンド留め　116
ウエスト・ベルト　312
ウエスマン　116
ウェット・スーツ　279
ウェブカム　247
ウェブカメラ　247
ウォークイン・クロゼット　139
ウォークイン・ワードローブ　139
ウォーター・キー　230
ウォーター・ハザード　282
ウォーター・ポンプ・プライヤー　162
ウォール　307
ウォール・テント　309
ウォッシャー・ノズル　184
迂回誘導路　204
浮きクレーン　200
浮き橋　183
受付　259, 263, 264
受け骨　128
右舷　200
動き方の種類　314
ウサギ　77
ウサギ目の動物　77
羽状中裂の　49
後脚　61, 62
後肢　66
後ろ足　76
後ろディレーラー　194
後ろブレーキ　194
後ろ変速機　194
右心室　98
右心房　98
薄のみ　213
薄刃のみ　213
渦巻き　227
渦巻き雲の帯　37
渦巻き状の若葉　47
渦巻きの腕　11
ウズラの卵　114
歌口　230, 231
打ち上げロケット　16
打ち上げロケットの断面図　16
打ち上げロケットの例　16
宇宙実験室　15
宇宙探査　13
宇宙探査機　13, 32
宇宙服　17
ウッド　282
腕　83, 91
腕木　179
腕輪　129
ウナギ　65
項　91
ウニ　56
右肺　97
右肺静脈　98
羽片　97
ウマの形態図　84
ウマの蹄　84
海　9, 22, 30

埋め立て　46
羽毛掛け布団　142
右翼　291
右翼手　290
裏当て　125, 126, 286
裏打ち　126
裏地　116, 126
ウラン燃料が核分裂を起こす　178
売上票　170
雨量記録計　38, 39
雨量測定　39
鱗　65, 67, 73
上框　137
上着　305
上駒　227, 228, 229
上皿天秤　170
上皿秤　147
上瞼　66, 79, 102
運転室　196, 198
運転席　306
運転台　196, 209, 210
運搬用手袋　123
ウンブリエル　7
雲母　25

え

柄　47, 109, 110, 111, 133, 146, 161, 162, 163, 214, 285, 311
絵　313
エア・クッション　122
エア・クラクション　192
エア・コン　188, 189
エア・コンプレッサー　197
柄穴　161
エアフィルター　197
エア・ブレーキ　179
エア・ホーン　192
エア・マット(レス)　310
エア・ユニット　122
エア・ロック　15
AMアンテナ　241
映画　272
映画館　258, 272
鋭角　171
映画撮影セット　273
映画セット　273
映画名と上映スケジュール　272
嬰記号　223
エイコーンスクワッシュ　107
映写機　272
映写室　272
映写スクリーン　269
映写ヘッド　269
映写幕　272
英数キーパッド　245, 261
英数キーボード　261
英数字キーパッド　245
英数字キーボード　261
衛星　16
衛星地上局　249
衛星通信アンテナ　201
映像スクリーン　239
衛兵所　220
泳法監察員　276
泳法審判員　276
泳法の種類　277
エウロパ　6
エース　313
絵柄　313
腋窩　90
液果　109
腋芽　97
腋窩静脈　99
腋窩動脈　99

液果の例　109
液材　53
液晶ディスプレイ　168, 233
液体酸素タンク　16
液体水素タンク　16
液柱計　267
液胞　56
駅舎　254
エクリン汗腺　101
餌台　72
餌箱　72
エシャロット　103
エスカレーター　254, 272
S状結腸　96
エスパドリーユ　125
エゾネギ　103
枝　52, 55
X接点　235
エッジ　286, 287, 289
エッジ・カバー　286
エナメル質　94
エネルギー　173
FMアンテナ　241
f字孔　227
絵筆　212
FD　246
エプロン　191, 304
F1カー　306
エベレスト山　32
エメラルド　129
エメリー・ボード　132
鰓蓋　65
襟　116
襟先　116
L型定規　161
エルボー・パッド　285, 298, 307
エルロン　206
エレキ・ギター　228
エレベーター　207
エレボン　15
延音記号　223
宴会場　218
円花窓　221
沿岸州　31
円環面　172
演技台　274
円鋸歯状の　49
園芸　164
円形の　49
円形パノラマ　238
園芸用手袋　164
縁甲板　67
円周　171
エンジン　191
エンジン回転計　188
エンジン支柱　207
エンジン・スイッチ　188
エンジン・フード　184, 192
円錐　172
延髄　97
円錐火山　27
塩水湖　29
円錐図法　21
延声記号　223
掩体壕　220
エンダイブ　106
エンタブラチュア　217
演壇　268
円柱　172, 217
延長記号　223
延長はしご　163
円筒図法　21
エンド・ゾーン　296, 298
煙突　135, 201
エンド・ライン　295, 296, 299
円の部分　171
円盤　11

日本語索引

322

縁板 67
円盤部 11
鉛筆 271
鉛筆型紙巻き消しゴム 271
鉛筆型消しゴム 271
鉛筆削り 270

お

尾 67, 76, 77, 78, 79, 82, 84, 88, 207
オアシス 29
追い越し車線 182
オイル・パステル 212
王 314
凹角 171
横隔膜 97
応急処置解説書 267
横行結腸 96
欧州実験モジュール 14
応接室 218
応接間 138, 219
王台 61
横断歩道 317, 318
応答メッセージ録音カセット 244
応答メッセージ録音ボタン 244
王の間 217
王妃 314
王妃の間 217
大顎 60, 62
大雨 36, 37
OHP 269
大枝 52
大型衣装だんす 141
大型貨物自動車等通行止め 317, 318
大型ジェット機 206
大型バス・タオル 132
オオカミ 80
狼爪 78
扇形 171
扇形筆 212
オーク 54
大皿 145
大太鼓 234
オーディオ・コンソール 237
オーディオ・システム 188
オーディオ・モニター 237
大道具係 273
大道具主任 272
大通り 250
オオトカゲ 69
オート・スコアラー 281
オート・ダイヤル・インデックス 244
オー・ド・トワレ 132
オートバイ 191
オートバイの例 191
オートバイ・レース 306
オート・リバース・ボタン 243
オーバーオール 121, 287
オーバーコート 119
オーバー・テーブル 266
オーバーフロー 154
オーバーベッド・テーブル 266
オーバーヘッド・プロジェクター 269
オオハシ 74
オービター 14, 15
オオブドウホオズキ 107
オープン 143, 153
オープン・カー 186
オープン調節つまみ 153
オーボエ 231, 234
大物車 196
オオヤマネコ 81
オールの種類 278

オールロック 279
丘 28
オカビ 87
小川 30
オクターブ 222
オクターブ・レバー 231
オクトパス 279
オクラ 107
送り錘 170
おくるみ 121
押さえ 130
押さえレバー 130
オサガメ 68
押し圧チューブ 270
押し出し装置 270
雄しべ 50, 111
押しボタン 270
オジロジカ 86
雄バチ 60
雄ミツバチ 60
オセアニア 19
汚染 44
汚染ガス放出 44
オゾン層 32
オタマジャクシ 66
落ち込み穴 30
オッズ表示板 280
オットマン(チェア) 140
大人の頭蓋 93
緒止め 227
緒止め板 227
オドメーター 188
緒止め掛け 227
緒止めボタン 227
踊り場 139
鬼目やすり 213
尾根 28
オパール 129
尾羽 73
帯 305
尾びれ 64, 65, 88
オフィス・タワー 250
オフィス・ビル 251
オフ・ロード車 186
オフ・ロード・バイク 191
オベロン 7
オポッサム 76
オマールエビ 58
おむつ替え用テーブル 141
重さ 170
おもちゃ屋 258
表板 227, 229
表底 122, 125
主な動き 315
主な国際道路標識 317
主な静脈と動脈 99
主な部屋 138
主な骨 92
錘 26, 168
親知らず 94
親骨 128
親指 101, 123, 291
親指掛け 230, 231
オランウータン 83
オリーブ 107
折り返し 116
折り返し壁 116
折り返し監察員 277
折り返し審判員 277
折り畳み椅子 140
折り畳み式傘 128
折り畳み式爪やすり 132
折り畳み式ドア 136
折り畳み式ベッド 310
折り畳み寝台 310
折り目 116
オルガン 226

オールロック 279
オレンジ 112
オレンジ色 211
オレンジの断面図 112
下ろし金 147
オン・エア・ランプ 237
音階 222
音楽 222
音楽室 268
音響技師 273
音響調整卓 237
音響発生器 237
温室効果 43
温室効果ガス 43
温室効果ガスの濃縮 43
音声再生装置 241
音声編集ボタン 233
音声モニター 237
温帯気候 34
温帯林 40
音程 222
温度切り替えスイッチ 131
温度切り換えボタン 160
温度計 169
温度センサー 152
温度測定 39, 169
温度調節ダイヤル 158
温度探査 151
温度表示器 130
温度目盛り 32
オンドリ 75
音符 223
温風機 158
温風吹き出し口 199
音部記号 222
オン・ボード・コンピューター 188
オンライン・ゲーム 249
音量指示計 237
音量調節つまみ 233, 242, 243, 244, 246
音量調節ボタン 239
音量つまみ 229, 242, 243, 244, 246
音量ボタン 239

か

カ 63
ガーキン 107
カーゴ・ベイ 14
カーゴ・ベイのドア 14
ガーゼの巻き包帯 267
カーディガン 120
ガーターヘビ 68
ガーデニング 164
カーテン 238
カード 313
ガード 168
カートウィール 124
カート道路 282
カード読み取りスロット 261
カード読み取り装置 245
カートリッジ 270
カートリッジ・テープ・レコーダー 237
カートリッジ・フィルム 235
ガード・レール 152, 307
カーナビ 188
カーネーション 51
ガーネット 129
ガーメント・バッグ 127
カール 9
カール・アイロン 130
カー・レース 306
外陰部 90
外縁堆積原 29

海王星 7
回音 223
外核 24
絵画と線画 211
外果皮 109, 110, 111, 112
絵画用画材 212
海岸線の例 31
海岸断崖 31
海岸の地形 31
外気圏 32
会議室 263, 269
皆既食 8, 9
階高 60
外球 156
階級型 60
階級記章 265
海峡 22
外頸静脈 99
外鰓 66
外鰓孔 64
改札係 253
改札ブース 254
外趾 72
碍子 176
外耳 100
外耳道 93, 100
海上スポーツ 278
海上探査 180
海上輸送 181, 200
海食崖 31
海棲哺乳動物 88
海棲哺乳動物の例 88
外側広筋 95
階段 135, 138, 182, 219, 254, 272, 304
階段座席 218
階段状の観覧席 218
階段吹き抜け 139
階段吹き抜けの天窓 139
懐中電灯 265
回腸 96
海底ケーブル 248
海底パイプライン 181
回転運動のローターへの伝送 176
回転器 167
回転コード 130
回転式改札入り口 254
回転式改札出口 254
回転軸 150
回転台 183
回転灯 263
回転ドラム 26
回転ブラシ 130
回転翼 179, 203
ガイド 151
外套 57
街灯 157, 251
外套膜 57
ガイド・ローラー 243
外半規管 100
外皮 112
外鼻 102
外鼻孔 66
外腹斜筋 95
解剖学 96
外部電源入力端子 242
外部燃料タンク 14
解放レバー 289
カイマン 69
海面 24, 32
海綿 132
買い物袋 127
外野フェンス 291
海洋 42
海洋気象観測船 38
海洋気象観測ブイ 38
海洋性気候 34

日本語索引

323

| カイラン　105
街路　250
回廊　179
カイワレダイコン　106
カウンター　143, 260
カエデ　54
替え刃インジェクター　131
カエル　66
カエルの一生　66
カエルの形態図　66
顔　83, 90
家屋　215
家屋の外観　134
家屋の構成要素　136
抱え鞄　126
抱えバッグ　126
下顎　65
科学　166
科学機器　15
下顎骨　92, 93
化学肥料散布　44
下顎鬚　60
踵　91, 122, 125, 286, 291
鏡　154, 269
鏡板　136
花冠　50
下眼瞼　102
鉤　170, 214
鉤竿　263
鉤爪　72, 73, 76, 77, 78, 82
鉤針　214
鉤棒　263
鍵屋　259
蝸牛　100
蝸牛神経　100
核　8, 10, 11, 56
萼　50, 109
架空(送)電線　176
核エネルギー　177
核エネルギーによる電気発生　178
隔壁板　61
角氷ディスペンサー　143
拡散板　273
角質の口　67
学習障害児用教室　268
学術名　109, 110, 111, 112
萼状総苞　109
核小体　56
角錐　172
学生休憩室　269
学生室　269
学生食堂　269
拡大鏡　167, 311
殻頂　57
家具調度　140
格闘技　304
角度の例　171
格納式取っ手　126
格納式握り　126
格納部　16
格納容器　178
核廃棄物　45
攪拌器取り付け部　150
各部　142
楽譜記号　222
額縁　137
隔壁　137
隔壁付き長物車　196
萼片　50, 109, 111
核膜　56
楽屋　272
影　168
崖　9
掛け金　127, 152
カケス　74
下弦の月　10
河口　22, 31

火口　27
花梗　50, 109, 110, 111
花崗岩　25
花崗岩層　24
下行結腸　96
下降通廊　217
傘　47, 128
笠　157
火災予防　262
花菜類　105
果菜類　107
笠木　140
傘立て　128
傘とステッキ　128
傘布　128
飾り穴　122, 125
飾り板　153, 224
飾りステッチ　123
火山　24, 27
過酸化物　267
火山弾　27
火山のタイプ　27
火山灰層　27
火山灰の雲　27
花糸　50
舵　278
カ[華]氏度　169
カ[華]氏目盛り　169
貨車の例　196
カシューナッツ　113
花床　50, 109
火床　158
家事用品と家電製品　159
下歯列弓　102
下唇　102
下唇髭　62
下唇鬚　62
ガス　156
ガスケット　152
カスタネット　232, 234
ガス・バーナー　166
カスピ海　19
ガス・レンジ　153
風　45
火星　6
火成岩　24
化石エネルギー　180
化石燃料　43
カセット　243
カセット収納部　240
カセット挿入部　240
カセットテープ　243
カセット・テープ・デッキ　241
カセット・デッキ　237, 241
カセット取り出しボタン　240
カセット・プレーヤー　242, 243
カセット・プレーヤー操作ボタン　242, 244
風の作用　42
架線　198, 199
加線　222
下層雲　35
下層土　53
加速車線　182
家族用テント　309
ガソリン　181
ガソリン・スタンド　261, 319
ガソリン・タンク　191
ガソリンの種類　261
ガソリン・ポンプ　261
肩　78, 85, 90, 227
ガター　281
肩当て　285, 298
下腿　98
下大静脈　98, 99
肩掛けかばん　271

花托　50
カタツムリ　57
カタツムリの形態図　57
肩吊り紐　119
片手鍋　311
片手鋸　161
肩紐　119, 127, 265
片眼鏡　128
花壇　135
下段部　16
家畜車　197
花柱　50, 109, 110, 111
ガチョウ　75
カチンコ　273
楽器　224
学校　268
学校あり　317, 318
学校用文房具　270
滑車　163
活栓付きビュレット　166
滑走面　289
滑走路　204
カッター　150
勝手口　260
ガット　302
カップ　119, 144, 311
カップ台　119
家庭汚染　44
家庭ごみ　44, 45
家庭用品　256
家電製品　150
可動あご　162
可動橋　183
可動式搭乗橋　205
可動照明　157
可動性の上顎　67
金槌　161
カナディアン・フットボール　298
カニ　58
果肉　109, 110, 111, 112
カニグモ　59
ガニメデ　6
カヌー　279
曲尺　161
加熱ハム　115
カバ　87
カバー　128, 155, 158, 282, 312
カバーオール　121
カバノキ　54
下尾筒　73
画鋲　270
カフ　125
カブ　104
カフェテリア　269
カブカンラン　104
カフス　116
ガフ・トップスル　201
カフ・ボックス　237
下部マントル　24
かぶり物　124
花粉かご　61
花粉塊　61
花粉房　61
花柄　50, 109, 110, 111
壁　9, 309
壁キャビネット　143
壁雲　37
壁通気口　134
花弁　50
可変噴射ノズル　208
可変翼　206
カボチャ　107

カマキリ　63
がま口　126
釜状凹地　28
紙とボール紙の選別　46
紙とボール紙の分別　46
紙の回収箱　46
紙のリサイクル用コンテナ　46
仮眠室　192
カメ　67
カメの形態図　67
カメムシ　63
カメラ　238, 267, 306
カメラ支持台　238
カメラ・ボディー　235
カメラ本体　235
カメラ用アクセサリー　235
カメラ用ビューファインダー　238
カメラ用付属品　235
カメレオン　69
画面　239
貨物機　208
貨物室　14, 207
カヤック　279
下葉　97
殻　57
カラー　278
カラー・サークル　211
カラー・テレビ・カメラ　17
ガラガラヘビ　68
空締めボルト　136
カラス　74
ガラス　173
ガラス・カバー　152
ガラス管　156
ガラス器　144
ガラス球　156
ガラスの回収箱　46
ガラスの分別　46
ガラスのリサイクル用コンテナ　46
ガラス屋根　138
カラッフェ　144
空手　305
空手衣　305
空手家　305
空手着　305
カラフェ　144
カラマツ　55
カランドリア　177
カランポーラ　113
刈り込み鋏　164
カリスト　6
カリフォルニア・ミラー　192
カリブ海　18
カリフラワー　105
下流ゲート　279
火力調節つまみ　153
カルドン　105
カール氷河　29
カレイ　65
ガレージ　134, 264
涸れ谷　29
カロン　7
川　22, 30
皮　109, 110, 111, 112
側板　229
カワウソ　80
カワカマス　65
革鞘　312
革製品　126
革製品店　258
カワセミ　75
革の端　116
皮むき器　147
瓦　217, 218
瓦端飾り　217
間　222
簡易寝台　267

簡易ベッド 267
岩塩 25
乾果 113
感覚器官 100
感覚毛 77
管楽器 230
カンガルーの形態図 76
汗管 101
雁木車 169
換気口 217
換気扇 197
柑橘果物 112
柑橘果物の例 112
換気フード 158
眼球 66
眼球保護ゴーグル 263
缶切り 147, 150, 311
玩具店 258
間欠泉 27
岩圏 41
管弦楽団 234
汗孔 101
看護士 266
寛骨 92
看護婦 266
監査役 305
かんじき 288
鑑識課 264
患者 266
干出岩 31
環礁 31
岩漿 27
岩礁 31
緩衝装置 199
環状道路 23
冠状縫合 93
観賞用樹木 134
完成 213
管制室 204, 264
管制塔 204
岩石 25
岩石砂漠 29
岩石と鉱石 25
幹線道路 23, 182
幹線道路番号 23
肝臓 96
乾燥機 160
乾燥気候 34
乾燥した空域 30
乾燥タイマー 160
観測窓 15
寒帯気候 34
カンタループ（メロン） 113
カンチレバー橋 183
缶詰食品 257
感電の危険あり 320
監督 273, 295
監督の椅子 273
乾ドック 200
貫入岩 24
貫入岩床 27
岩盤 26, 53
幹部用寝室 262
幹部用トイレ・シャワー室 262
眼柄 57
岸壁クレーン 200
ガン・ベルト 265
灌木林 40
岩脈 27
顔面保護シールド 263
管理室 263
管理事務所 200, 264
管理人室 269
眼輪筋 95
カンロメロン 113

き

木 52
黄 211
気圧測定 39
キー 224, 226, 231, 233
キーウィ（フルーツ） 113
キー・ガード 231
キー・グリップ 273
キー・ケース 126
キーボード 233, 246, 281
キー・レバー 231
キー・ロック 126
キオスク 255
機械作業の電気への変換 176
機械式時計 169
機械室 174, 175
器械体操 274
幾何学 171
幾何学的な形 171
気管 97
基岩 53
機関室 201
機関車 198
企業 249
器具庫 268
キクイモ 104
キクゴボウ 104
キクヂシャ 106
危険区域 305
危険地帯 305
危険物 320
気閘 15
気候 33
き甲 78, 85
きさげ 163
刻み付きナット 163
刻み目 170
騎士 314
気室 72
機首 206
騎手 280
技術室 182
記章 265
気象衛星 38
気象学 32
気象観測航空機 38
気象現象 35
気象測定機器 39
気象予報 38
気象レーダー 38, 206
貴石 129, 169
季節の移り変わり 33
季節の循環 33
基線 312
北 23
北アメリカ 18
北アメリカの主な道路標識 318
黄橙 211
北回帰線 20
北半球 20
基壇 217
着付け係 272
切っ先 146
喫茶店 259, 319
キッチン・タオル 159
キツネ 80
キツネザル 83
軌道 253, 254
軌道修正用エンジン 15
軌道輪 14, 15
起動輪 210
砧骨 100
機能キー 170, 245
機能選択ダイヤル 235
機能選択ボタン 244

機能表示画面 233
機能表示窓 233
キノコ 47
木の構造 52
キノコの構造 47
牙 59
キバナスズシロ 106
黄パプリカ 107
基部 312
基部 103
起伏シリンダー 193, 263
ギフト・ショップ 258
キブラ 227
キブラ壁 219
木彫 213
気密室 182
黄線 211
気門 62
ギヤ 229
脚 142
客室 201, 203, 207
客車 198, 199
脚鎧 59
客船 200
客用入り口 260
客用クローク 260
客用トイレ 260
キャスケット 124
キャスター 127, 141
脚立 163
キャタピラー 210
キャッサバ 104
キャッチャー 290, 291
キャッチャー・ミット 291
キャップ 270, 276
キャディー・バッグ 283
キャノピー 208, 210
キャビネット 239
キャビン 203
キャブ 209, 210
キャベツ 106
キャリア 194
ギャロップ 85
キャンバス 304
キャンピング・カー 189
キャンプ 309
キャンプ可 319
キャンプ禁止 319
キャンプ用品 311
球 172
吸引器 267
吸引装置 267
球芽 103
嗅覚と味覚 102
吸気 277
球技 290
給気管 263
給気筒 263
救急 319
救急資材 267
救急室 319
救急車 182, 267
救急隊員席 267
救急箱 265, 267
救急ヘリコプター 203
キュウケツコウモリ 82
救護所 319
球根の断面図 103
給仕長 260
厩舎 280
吸収管 267
吸収された日射 43
90度 171
球状星団 11
球状船首 200
弓状動脈 99

弓身 227
球審 290
球節 84
球体 172
球体平面図 18
弓身 227
吸入器 267
牛乳パック 114
吸盤 57
休符 223
救命浮き輪 265
救命ブイ 265
救命ボート 201
給油口蓋 185
給油車 205
給油場 261
給油装置 197
給油ノズル 261
給油ホース 261
給油ポンプ 261
キュウリ 107
キュロット 119
教育 268
教育機関 249
競泳コース 276
頬窩 67
教会 251
鉄角 59
胸郭 90
鏡基 167
競技委員 293
競技者 305
競技場 218, 305
供犠の石 219
胸脚 58, 62
鏡脚 167
凝結 42
響孔 227
胸骨 92
頬骨 92, 93
胸鎖乳突筋 95
教師 268
教室 268, 269
橋床 183
教師用机 268
橋床部 183
行政区画図 22
鏡台 141, 167
橋台 183
教卓 268
鏡柱 167
橋柱 183
鏡筒 12, 167
共同住宅 216
鏡筒スリーブ 167
鏡筒バンド 12
響板 226, 227, 229
胸部 60, 62
挟壁ダム 174
強膜 102
共鳴管 229
共鳴板 226, 229, 241
橋門 183
恐竜 70
魚介類 257
極気候 34
極光 32
極軸クランプ 12
極軸微動ハンドル 12
棘条 65
曲線あご 162
極低温主ステージ 16
鋸歯 161
鋸歯状の 49
居城 220
鋸刃 161, 162
霧 36

錐 311
折り返し壁 277
切り株 53
切り込み角度調節装置 162
霧雨 36
ギリシャ神殿 217
切り出しナイフ 213
切妻壁 134
切妻換気口 134
切り刃 150, 214
キリン 87
記録員 294, 299, 305
記録エリア 243
記録係と計時係 305
記録保管室 265
記録領域 243
際削り刃 131
金 25
銀 25
銀河 11
キンカン 112
金管楽器群 234
金管楽器の仲間 234
金環食 8
銀器 146
緊急ステーション 182
緊急待避所 182
緊急ブレーキ 199
キング 313, 314
キング・サイド 314
キング・ピン 281
金庫 265
銀行 259
菌糸 47
キンシウリ 107
菌糸体 47
金星 6
金属の分別 46
金的 281
キントキマメ 108
筋肉 95
キンポウゲ 51

く

クイーバー 281
クイーン 313, 314
クイーン・サイド 314
杭上住居 215
クイック・ターン 277
空気圧縮機 197
空気入れ 194
空気入れポンプ 310
空気孔 270
空気呼吸器 263
空気取り入れ口 203
空気抜きポンプ 310
空気フィルター 197, 210
空気袋 224
空気ホース 279
空気ボタン 224
空気ポンプ 261, 310
空港 23, 204
空港地上支援機材 204
空港特殊車両 204
グーズベリー 109
空腸 96
空調システム 43
空調装置 188, 189
空白 313
クーペ 186
クーラー・ボックス 311
空力ブレーキ 179
クール・チップ 130
クォーター・ウインドー 185
クォーターバック 297
区間距離計 188

茎 47, 48
釘 161
釘頭 161
釘先 161
釘抜き 161
釘抜きハンマー 161
供犠の石 219
草地 40
草取り 164
楔形テント 309
鎖 168
クサリヘビ 68
クジャク 74
孔雀石 25
苦情相談室 264
苦情相談窓口 264
クズイモ 104
グズベリー 109
薬指 101
管 84
果物 109
口 57, 66, 88, 90, 102
口金 156
口先ノズル 131
嘴 72
嘴の例 73
唇 79, 85
口紅 133
靴 125
靴踵締め具 289
クッキー 115
クッキー型 148
靴先締め具 289
掘削 180
掘削機 209
掘削装置 180
靴下 119
クッション 142
クッション・ブラシ 130
屈折(式)望遠鏡 12
屈折(式)望遠鏡の断面図 12
靴店 259
靴の各部 125
靴紐 122, 125
駆動軸 203
駆動輪 210
国 22
首 67, 85, 91, 146, 227
頸 72
首カバー 263
首枕 142
くびれ 227
熊手 165
組み鐘 234
組子 137
雲 32, 35, 36
クモ 59
雲による吸収 43
クモの形態図 59
クモの巣 59
蜘蛛類 59
蜘蛛類の例 59
鞍 280
クラウン 124
グラウンド 290, 293, 297, 298, 300
グラウンド・シート 309
鞍覆い 280
クラクション 188, 196
鞍敷き 280
クラシック・ブラウス 118
グラス 144
クラスター・フード＆ラック 281
クラッシュ・ヘルメット 287
クラッチ・バッグ 126
クラッチ・ペダル 188
クラブ 313

グラフィック・イコライザー 241
クラブサン 226
クラブ・チェア 140
クラブハウス 280, 282
クラリネット 231, 234
グランド・シート 309
グランドファーザー・クロック 168
クランプ 155
クランプ・ホルダー 166
クランベリー 109
クランポン 288
クリ 113
グリース 181
クリーニング店 259
クリーマー 144
クリーム入れ 144
グリーン 282
グリーンピース 108
グリーンランド海 19
繰り返し記号 222
クリカボチャ 107
クリケッター 292
クリケット 292
クリケット・シューズ 292
クリケット・ボール 292
繰り出しはしご 163
クリップ 245
グリップ 130, 278, 282, 288, 289, 291, 292, 293, 302
グリップ・エンド 291, 302
クリップ式スポットライト 157
クリップ・テープ 307
クリップレス・ペダル 308
グリドル 151
クリュー 278
グリル 153, 184, 224
グリンピース 108
クルーズ・コントロール 188
クルー・ネック・セーター 120
クルック 231
クルック・キー 231
踝 90
車椅子 266
車椅子乗り入れ可能 319
車椅子乗り入れ禁止 319
クルミノキ 54
クルミ割り器 147
郭 220
クレーター 9
グレート・デーン 78
グレービー(ソース)入れ 144
グレープフルーツ 112
クレソン 106
クレバス 29
クレビドーマ 217
黒石 315
黒イチゴ 109
クロオオコウモリ 82
クローバー型インターチェンジ 182
クロー・ハンマー 161
グローブ 17, 284, 287, 288, 292, 304, 306, 308
グローブ・ボックス 188
クローラー・トラクター 210
クロール泳法 277
クロールのキック 277
クロコダイル 69
黒駒 314
クロス・カントリー・スキー 288
クロス・カントリー・スキーヤー 288
クロス・カントリー用自転車とサイクリスト 308
クロス・カントリー用スキー板 288

クロス・カントリー用スキー靴 288
黒スグリ 109
クロゼット 138
黒ダイコン 104
クロッカス 51
クロッチ 117
黒桝 314
クロマチン 56
黒マメ 108
クロメマメ 108
クロワッサン 114
くわえ部 162
グワッシュ・ケーキ 212
グワッシュ・チューブ 212
群島 22
群葉 52
軍用ナイフ 311

け

毛 83, 101, 131, 133
警音器 188
景観道路 23
計器コンソール 279
計器盤 188
計器板 188
蛍光管 156
蛍光管固定クリップ 156
蛍光灯 263
蛍光塗料 156
蛍光ペン 271
警告帯 291
警告灯 188, 265
警告表示地帯 291
脛骨 82, 92
茎菜類 105
警察 319
警察官 265
警察署 264
警察バッジ 265
計時員 276, 294, 305
計時主任 276
掲示板 268
傾斜路 217
芸術 211
軽食カウンター 272
形成層 53
計測機器 168
携帯用酸素ボンベ 267
携帯電話機 245
携帯用消火器 262
携帯ランプ 263
競馬 280
競馬場 280
軽飛行機 208
警報器 196, 263
警棒ホルダー 265
軽油 181
鶏卵 114
渓流 28
頸領 48
頸領 48
計量カップ 148
計量皿 170
計量スプーン 148
ケーキ 115
ケース 156, 161, 162, 168, 243
ケータリング車 204
ゲート審判員 279
ケープ 118
ケーブル 162, 193, 238, 246
ケーブル回線 249
ケーブル・スリーブ 162
ケーブル・モデム 249
ゲーム 313

ゲーム機　316	鍵盤台　226	後檣縦帆　201	コーヒー・ポット　151, 311
ゲーム・コンソール　316	顕微鏡　167	交信音量調節つまみ　17	コーヒー・マグ　144
ケール　106	玄武岩　25	降水　36, 42	コーラ　225
毛皮　76, 83	玄武岩層　24	香水店　258	氷　42
激流　279		鉱石　25	氷自動販売機　261
ケシ　51	**こ**	高積雲　35	ゴール　280, 285, 293, 296, 298, 300
夏至　33		鉱石ホッパー車　197	コール・アングル　231, 234
消しゴム　270	弧　171	高層アパート　216, 251	ゴール・エリア　300
化粧　133	碁　315	高層雲　35	ゴールキーパー　284, 293, 300
化粧石鹸　132	小顎　60	後側頭泉門　93	ゴールキーパー・グローブ　301
化粧品店　258	コアラ　76	高速道路　182, 250	ゴールキーパー用スティック　284, 285
化粧ミラー　188	コイル・スプリング　142	高速誘走路　204	ゴールキーパー用胸当て　284
桁橋　183	降圧　176	高速列車　198	ゴールキーパー用レッグガード　284
血圧計　266, 267	高圧域　37	後退灯　187	ゴール・クリーズ　285
血液の組成　98	高圧送電　176	後退翼　206	ゴール・ジャッジ　285
血管　82, 98, 101	甲当て　125	高地　9	ゴールポスト　296
結合組織　101	更衣室　262, 268, 272	拘置室　265	ゴール・ライン　284, 293, 296, 298
欠刻状の　49	後縁　206	後中央板　67	コールラビ　105
血漿　98	後縁フラップ　206	校長室　269	ゴール・ランプ　285
決勝線　280	高音域用鍵盤　224	交通島　182	コーンサラダ　106
血小板　98	高音域用スピーカー　241	工程　213	ゴーントリット　123
月食　33	高音調節つまみ　242	校庭　269	小型草かき　164
齧歯類　77	高音用鍵盤　224	光電セル　235	小型クッション　142
齧歯類動物　77	高音用スピーカー　241	喉頭　97	小型バス　190
齧歯類動物の例　77	高音用レジスター　224	喉頭蓋　97	小型モーターボート　202
蹴爪　84	紅海　19	後頭骨　93	小形ライマメ　108
ケツルアズキ　108	口蓋垂　102	高度目盛り　32	コガネグモ　59
月齢盤　168	口蓋舌弓　102	構内入り口　254	呼気　277
毛止め　227	甲殻　58	口内洗浄機　133	呼吸系　97
ケトル・ドラム　232	口角　102	口内洗浄剤　133	黒鉛　25
毛箱　227	光学式スキャナー　247	公認のごみ埋立地　44	漕ぐこととスカーリング　278
ゲル　215	光学スキャナー　257	コウノトリ　75	漕ぐこととスカリング　278
ケラ　217	光学ステージ　269	香箱車　169	漕ぐことと幅寄せ　278
鍵　224, 226, 233	光学的分別　46	後半規管　100	国際宇宙ステーション　14
弦　226, 227	甲殻類　58	甲皮　58	穀食鳥　73
牽引車　209	甲殻類の例　58	後尾　288	黒板　268
牽引装置　193	光学レンズ　269	後部滑走部　287	穀物食品　114
牽引トラクター　205	高架交差路　182	後部緩衝器　191	穀物ターミナル　200
牽引棒　204	硬貨挿入口　245	後部ショック・アブソーバー　191	国立公園　23
巻雲　35	硬貨投入口　245	後部デッキ　201	苔　47
弦押さえ　226	硬貨バケット　114	後部バケット　209	固形パウダー　133
圏界面　43	硬貨返却口　245	後部ランナー　287	コケモモ　109
顕花植物　48	甲冑　125	高棒　274	ココット皿　144
弦楽器　227	口器　60	硬棒　274	ココナッツ　113
弦楽器群　234	後脚　140	硬膜　163	腰　73, 84, 91, 227
玄関　138, 218	光球　8	硬膜終糸　97	腰当て　298
玄関広間　138	工業汚染　44	剛毛　163	腰革中部　125
玄関ホール　138	交響楽団　234	肛門　96	こしき　59
現金自動支払機　259	口峡部　102	噴門　200	ゴシキヒワ　74
健康　266	咬筋　95	肛門括約筋　96	ゴシック様式の大聖堂　221
原稿ガイド　245	口腔　96, 97	広葉樹　54	腰ベルト　141
肩甲骨　91, 92	航空輸送　203	広葉樹林　40	腰巻き壁　220
原稿挿入口　245	工具綱　17	高翼　208	腰巻きスカート　118
健康美容グッズ　257	工芸　214	小枝　48, 52	５０ヤード・ライン　297
圏谷　9	合計額　170	コエビ　58	胡椒入れ　144
圏谷氷河　29	高原　22, 28	ゴーグル　276, 287, 289, 306, 308	コショウソウ　106
検索　249	高原気候　34	コース　276, 282	個人識別章　265
犬歯　94	口腔　96, 97	コース計時員　276	梢　52
玄室　217	硬口蓋　102	コース・ゲート　279	小銭入れ　126
研修医　266	航行灯　207	コース・ライン　277	跨線橋　182
原色　211	広告パネル　254	コース・ロープ　277	小太鼓　232, 234
原子力発電所　177	硬骨魚　65	コーチ　285, 293, 295	固体ブースター・ステージ　16
原子炉　177, 178	硬骨魚の例　65	コーチス・ボックス　290	古代ローマの円形競技場　218
原子炉格納容器　178	虹彩　102	コート　294, 299, 302, 316	古代ローマの住宅　218
原子炉建屋　177	交差点につき一時停止　317, 318	コード　243	固体ロケット・ブースター　14, 16
原子炉容器　177	交差部　221	コードレス電話機　245	木立　282
懸垂氷河　29	交差部尖塔　221	コーナー　304	小タマネギ　103
巻積雲　35	高山気候　34	コーナー・アーク　301	黒海　19
舷窓　201	後趾　73	コーナー椅子　304	骨格　92
舷側　62	後肢　76	コーナー・パッド　304	国境　22
巻層雲　35	格子　175, 217	コーナー・フラッグ　293, 301	コックス・シート　278
舷側　201	甲締め具　289	コーニス　217	コックピット　203, 206, 306
減速車線　182	公衆電話　259, 260, 319	コーヒー・ショップ　319	小粒インゲンマメ　108
建設　215	公衆電話機　245	コーヒー・スプーン　146	
建築物の作品　217	高周波アンテナ・ケーブル　208		
券売機　272	後檣　201		
鍵盤　226, 233			
鍵盤楽器　226			

こて 281
固定あご 162
固定橋 183
固定ジャッキ 189
固定装置 163
固定点 59
固定バンド 39
固定ベルト 288
5度 222
小道具係 273
小道具助手 273
子供の頭蓋 93
子供服 121
子供用三輪車 195
コニーデ 27
小荷物取扱所 253
小鉤 169
碁盤 315
小瓶類 115
コブラ 68
ゴボウ 104
コマ 10
駒 227, 229, 315
鼓膜 66, 100
ごみの分別 46
ごみ箱 159
コミュニケーション・プロトコル 248
ゴム編みカフス 120
ゴム入りウエストバンド 117
ゴム入りレッグ・ホール 117
ゴム・ケーブル 275
ゴム手袋入れ 265
ゴム長靴 263
ゴム・バンド 142
ゴム・ロープ 309
米 114
5メートル・ライン 293
こめかみ 90
小物入れ 188, 281
小指 101
小指掛け 230
コヨルシャウキの石板 219
コラード 106
娯楽 272
コラム 217, 227
コランダー 147
コリー 78
ゴリラの形態図 83
コリント式の片蓋柱 218
コリント式の付け柱 218
コルク栓抜き 311
ゴルジ装置 56
コルネット 230, 234
ゴルフ 282
ゴルフ・カート 283
ゴルフ・グローブ 283
ゴルフ・シューズ 283
ゴルフ手袋 283
ゴルフ道具と小物 282
ゴルフ・バッグ 283
ゴルフ・ボール 282
ゴレンシの実 113
コロナ 8
根冠 48
ゴング 234
コンクリート・ミキサー・トラック 193
根茎 47
根系 48
コンゴウインコ 74
混交樹林 40
コンサート・グランド 226
根菜類 104
コンソリ 104
コンセント 155
コンソール・ゲージ 279

昆虫 60
昆虫の例 63
コンテ担当 273
コンテナー 150
コンテナ・クレーン 200
コンテナ車 197
コンテナ船 200
コンテナ・ターミナル 200
コンテナ・パレット・ドーリー 205
コンデンサー 167
コンデンサー上下動ハンドル 167
コンデンサー調節ハンドル 167
ゴンドラ車 196
コントラバス 227, 234
コントラバスーン 234
コントラファゴット 234
コントローラー 316
コントローラー・ポート 316
コントロール・キー 245
コントロール・パネル 152, 153, 160
コントロール・ボタン 246
コントロール・ルーム 237
コンバーチブル 186
コンパクト・ディスク 243
コンパクト・フラッシュ・メモリー・カード 235
コンパス・カード 23, 312
コンパス子午線 312
コンピューター 268
コンピューター・サイエンス室 268
コンピューター・スクリーン 17
コンピューター・モニター 17
コンブルービウム 218
コンベヤー・ベルト 46
コンベンション・センター 250
梱包 46
根毛 48
根毛部 52
コンヨウセロリ 104

さ

サード 290
サーバー 248, 249, 303
サービス・エリア 23, 205
サービス・ジャッジ 302
サービス道路 204
サービス・ライン 303
サービス・ライン・ジャッジ 302
サーモスタット 158
サーモスタット制御ノブ 152
サイ 86
菜園 134
サイクル・ヘルメット 194
サイクロマ 238
鰓孔 64
最高温度計 39
さいころ 315
さいころとドミノ 313
岩柵 220
再生ヘッド用窓 243
再生ボタン 239, 243, 244
彩層 8
細断 46
最低温度計 39
サイト 281
サイド・コンプレッション・ベルト 312
サイド・ジャッジ 297
サイド・スクリーン 292
サイド・ステップ 197
サイド・テーブル 266
サイド・ドア 199
サイド・ハッチ 14

サイド・フェアリング 306
サイド・マーカー・ライト 187
サイド・マーカー・ランプ 187
サイド・モール 185
サイドライン 293, 294, 296, 299
再熱器 177
サイ・バッド 298
砕氷船 202
サイ・ブーツ 125
載物台 167
細胞質 56
裁縫と編み物 214
細胞膜 56
再利用できない残留ごみ 46
鰓裂 64
座金 153
砂岩 25
魚 115
魚皿 145
魚のうろこ落とし 311
砂丘 31
作業手順チェックリスト 17
朔 10
柵 134, 141
サクソフォン 231
サクソルン 230
サクラソウ 51
サクランボ 110
ザクロ 113
左舷 200
鎖骨 92
座骨 92
鎖骨下静脈 99
鎖骨下動脈 99
支えケーブル 274
支え綱 179
支え棒 166
支えワイヤー 274
ササゲ 108
差し込み口金 156
砂じょう 112
左心室 98
左心房 98
砂州 31
サスペンション 199
サスペンダー 116
サスペンダー・クリップ 116
座席 272
サソリ 59
サターン5 16
撮影監督 273
撮影主任 273
サッカー 300
サッカー・シューズ 301
サッカー・プレーヤー 301
サッカー・ボール 301
殺菌器 44
雑穀パン 114
サッシ窓 137
殺虫器 44, 45
サツマイモ 106
サテライト・ターミナル 205
サトイモ 104
砂糖入れ 144
ザトウクジラ 89
サドル 194, 280

サドル支柱 194
サドルバッグ 194
蛹 61, 62
サニーレタス 106
左肺 97
左肺静脈 98
砂漠 29, 40
砂漠気候 34
サハン 219
サバンナ 40
サファイア 129
サブ調整室 237
サボイキャベツ 106
ザボン 112
さまざまな食品 114
サム・レスト 231
サメ 64
サメの形態図 64
座面 140
鞘 312
サヤインゲン（マメ） 108
左翼 290
左翼手 290
皿 170, 238, 311
皿洗い機 143
サラウンド 316
皿鉤 170
サラダ 115
サラダ皿 145
サラダ・スピナー 147
サラダ取り皿 145
サラダ菜 106
サラダ・ボウル 145
サラダ用水切り(器) 147
ザリガニ 58
サロペット 121
サロン 118
座枠 140
桟 137, 140
三角筋 95
三角巾 267
三角形 172
三角小間 217
三角定規 271
三角州 30, 31
三角破風 217
三角板 12
三角フラスコ 166
三角翼 206, 208
三脚 12, 232
山脚 28
産業廃棄物 44, 45
サングラス 128
散光器 273
サンゴヘビ 68
35mm静止カメラ 17
32分音符 223
32分休符 223
30秒タイマー 294
三出の 49
三小葉ある 49
散水タンク 177, 178
散水バルブ 177
散水弁 177
酸性雨 45
酸素アウトレット 266
酸素圧つまみ 17
サンダル 125
山地 22
山頂 28
三蹄 85
サンデッキ 201
3度 222
サンドイッチ 115
サンド・バッグ 304
サンド・バンカー 282
サン・バイザー 188

三番車 169	試験管挟み 166	シトロン 112	車幅灯 187, 192
360度 171	視父叉 97	市内バス 190	シャフト 128, 278, 282, 285, 288, 302, 316
山腹 28	時刻表 253	歯肉 94, 102	
散歩用ステッキ 128	指骨 92	芝切り 164	シャベル 158, 164
3枚垂直型 207	趾骨 92	芝生 135	シャムネコ 79
3枚羽根プロペラ 208	歯根 94	芝縁刈り 164	車翼 179
山脈 9, 22, 24	歯根管 94	指板 227, 228, 229	車両進入禁止 317, 318
山稜 28	歯根膜 94	師部 53	車両待機所 182
三塁 290	自在スパナ 162	ジブ 209	車両転回禁止 318
三塁手 290	自在レンチ 162	4分音符 223	車輪 164, 192, 307, 308
	支軸 214	4分休符 223	車輪止め 204
し	翅室 62	四分円 171	斜路 217
シ 222	歯質 94	シフター 195	シャロット 103
試合者 305	磁石による選別 46	シフト・ペダル 191, 226, 233	シャワー 139, 266
試合場 305	耳小骨 100	シフト・レバー 188, 195	シャワー室 154
仕上げ 213	指針 158, 170	四分円 171	シャワー・ヘッド 154
C型クランプ 161	地震 26	四辺形 172	シャンデリア 157
シーケンサー・コントロール 233	磁針 312	子房 50	シャンパン・グラス 144
ＣＤ 243	地震記象 26	脂肪組織 101	シャンプー 132
ＣＤ・ＤＶＤプレーヤー 316	地震記録 180	絞り紐 127	ジャンプスーツ 121
ＣＤプレーヤー 237, 241, 242	地震計 26	絞り紐付きフード 121	ジャンベ 225
ＣＤプレーヤー操作ボタン 242	視神経交叉 97	島 22	州 22
ＣＤ・レコード店 258	地震波 26	シマウマ 87	重要記号 223
ＣＤ－ＲＯＭイジェクト・ボタン 246	歯髄 94	シマリス 77	州界 22
	歯髄腔 94	翅脈 62	銃眼 220
ＣＤ－ＲＯＭドライブ 246	システム・コンポ(ーネント) 241	ジム 263	銃眼付き胸壁 220
ＣＤ－ＲＯＭプレーヤー 247	システム・ボタン 233	事務室 219, 253, 261	銃眼壁の凹部 220
シート 191, 194, 201	シストルム 232	事務所 260	銃眼壁の凸部 220
Ｃ部 227	姿勢制御推進器 14	締め金 155, 304	重機 209
シーリング・ライト 157	姿勢制御スラスター 14	締め金 127, 155, 231	従業員用クローク 260
ジーンズ 121	自然環境 40	締め具 289	重鋸歯状の 49
シェーク 223	自然の温室効果 43	下弾き 128	集光器 167
シェード 157	歯槽 94	ジャージー 308	十五日月 10
シェービング・カップ 131	歯槽骨 94	シャープ 223	ジューサー 150
シェービング・フォーム 131	舌 96, 102	シャープ・ペンシル 271	終糸 97
シェービング・ブラシ 131	下顎 85	シャーレ 166	十字型 207
ジェット燃料 181	下絵 213	車庫車 197	終糸の硬膜部 97
ジェンベ 225	舌革 122, 125, 286, 289	ジャガー 81	私有車道 135
塩入れ 144	下側シーツ 142	社会 250	収集トラック 193
ジガー・トゲルン・ステースル 201	下キャビネット 143	ジャガイモ 104	シューズ 293, 295, 308
	下駒 227	ジャガ芋つぶし器 148	縦線 222
ジガー・トップマスト・ステースル 201	シダの構造 47	遮眼帯 280	集草箱 165
ジガーマスト 201	下穿き 305	車間距離制御装置 188	集草レーキ 165
耳介 76, 77, 100	下枕 227	弱音器 230	従端 116
市街電車 199	下瞼 66, 79, 102	弱音ペダル 226	シューティング・サークル 293
視覚 102	下見所 280	尺側皮静脈 99	充電残量表示ランプ 131
鹿(の飛び出し)に注意 317	下ろくろ 128	蛇口 154	充電灯 131
歯冠 94	シチメンチョウ 75	射撃練習場 265	柔道 305
指管 224	七面鳥 115	ジャケット 118	柔道衣 305
耳管 100	シチュー 115	車庫 134, 262, 264	柔道着 305
時間測定 168	支柱 26, 39, 140, 163, 166, 198, 199, 227, 238, 275, 286	遮光板 198	十二指腸 96
敷居 136		車軸 196, 307	収納家具 141
自記気圧計 39		視野絞りつまみ 167	収納庫 192, 263
磁気コンパス 312	指柱 168	射手 281	収納室 138
色彩円 211	室 111	車掌車 197	周波数表示画面 242
自記湿度計 39	膝蓋骨 92	写真 235	周波数表示窓 242
磁気動装置 170	実験器具 166	写真館 258	秋分 33
色相環 211	実際温度 158	写真屋 258	10分の1秒針 168
指揮台 234	湿潤大陸性気候 34	車体 184, 189, 287	重変記号 223
敷地平面図 135	湿度測定 39	車体の例 186	襲歩 85
磁気テープ 243	室内サーモスタット 158	遮断機 198	柔毛 79
色灯 198	ジッパー 127	遮断機可動装置 198	重油 181
色灯板 198	指定方向外進行禁止 317, 318	遮断機警告灯 198	収容用シャワー室 264
趾球 78	支点 59, 214	遮断機支持腕 198	修理場 261
指球 78	自転車 194	シャチ 89	終了キー 245
仕切り 126, 265, 309	自転車競技 308	斜張橋 183	重量測定
仕切りカーテン 266	自転車通行止め 318	シャツ 116, 295	重力拡散の部屋 217
仕切り壁 265	自転車の例 195	ジャケッ 263	重力(式)ダム 174
軸 161, 214, 270, 312, 316	自転車用チャイルドシート 194	ジャック 228, 313	ジュウロクササゲ 108
ジグソー・パズル 313	自動温度調節器 152	ジャッジ 274, 275, 304	16分音符 223
シグネット・リング 129	自動改札ドア 252	シャッター・レリーズ・ボタン 235	16分休符 223
軸箱 196	自動車 184		ジュエリー・ショップ 258
歯茎 94	自動車排気ガス汚染 45	車道 182	主エンジン 15
歯頸 94	自動車レース 306	シャドー・ロール 280	シュガー・ポット 144
試験管 166	自動速度制御装置 188	シャトル列車 252	主火道 27
	自動点火数表示機 281	蛇腹 224	
	自動二輪車通行止め 317, 318		

樹幹 52	小核果 109	蒸発 42	女性バーテンダー 260
樹冠 52	上顎骨 92, 93, 94	定盤 162	女性用衣類 118
主管抜き差し管 230	小花梗 109	消費者への送電 176	女性用下着 119
主脚 207	消火栓 262	上尾筒 73	除雪車 193
主鏡 12	浄化槽 45, 135	商品コード 170	除草器 164
縮梯防止装置 163	松果体 97	商品陳列棚 44	除草剤 44
主根 48, 52	小花柄 109	上部安全ガード 162	助走路 274, 281
手根関節部 78	消火(用)ホース 262	上部デッキ 206	書棚 268
手根球 78	上眼瞼 102	上部マントル 24	処置室 182
手根骨 92	上甲板 201	城壁 220	署長室 263, 264
種子 48, 109, 110, 111, 112	定規 271, 311	消防士 263	触角 60, 62
主車輪 207	蒸気圧がタービンを駆動させる 178	消防車 262	触覚 101
主樹 201	蒸気が凝縮して水になる 178	消防署 262	食品 144
主審 279, 290, 292, 293, 294, 297, 299, 300, 302, 305	蒸気発生器 177	消防士用共同寝室 262	ジョッキー 280
樹心 53	焼却 46	消防士用トイレ・シャワー室 262	食器洗浄器 143
主寝室、カテドラル型天井 139	掌球 78	情報処理室 268	食器棚 260
受信トレイ 245	小臼歯 94	小胞体 56	食器戸棚 138, 143
取水口 175	商業企業 249	消防長室 263	ショッピング・カート 257
受水漏斗 39	商業サービス 256	情報普及 249	ショッピング・センター 258
主端 116	商業ビル 251	消防服 262	ショッピング・バッグ 127
主柱 218	消極地帯 304	消防ヘリコプター 203	書店 258
出国審査 253	渉禽 73	錠前 136, 141	ショベル 288, 289
出国審査場 253	衝撃波 180	照明 155	女優 273
出糸突起 59	小剣 116	照明係 273	ショルダー 227, 302
出走ゲート 280	小剣通し 116	照明器具 157	ショルダー・ストラップ 119, 283
出発合図員 276	上弦の月 10	照明グリッド 238, 273	ショルダー・バッグ 127
出発ロビー 253	礁湖 31	証明写真ボックス 259	ショルダー・パッド 285, 298
出力端子 228	漏斗 148	照明主任 273	ショルダー・ベルト 312
首都 22	上行結腸 96	照明装置 167	白太 53
主塔 183	小後陣 221	照明灯 199	シラミ 63
主塔基礎 183	昇降ステップ 203	照明と暖房 155	尻 84, 91
シュノーケル 279	昇降舵 15, 207	錠面 136	シリアル食品 114
主発電機 196	昇降段 192	正面入り口 221, 269	臀べり 64, 65
主帆 201	掌骨 92	正面玄関 269	資料室 265
種皮 110	錠箱 136	正面図 221	資料センター 262
樹皮 53	蒸散 42	上葉 97	指輪 214
守備位置 290	上趾 78	小翼 207, 208	シリンダー・タイプの電気掃除機 159
守備的ミッドフィルダー 300	上趾球 78	上流ゲート 279	汁受け皿 153
珠柄 109	小室 111	如雨露 165	シルク・スクリーン・プリント 121
主脈 49	照準 312	鐘楼 221	シルク・ハット 124
樹木 52	照準器 281	小惑星帯 6	司令管制室 263
種目別得点掲示板 275	照準鏡 312	上腕骨 92	司令室 264
主要な筋肉 95	照準線 312	上腕動脈 99	城 220, 314
主翼 207	ショウジョウコウカンチョウ 74	上腕二頭筋 95	シロアリ 63
シュラ(ー)フ 310	上昇通廊 217	女王 220, 314	白石 315
シュラウド 201	掌状の 49	女王バチ 60	シロイルカ 89
首陸輪 206	小触角 57, 58	ジョーカー 313	白キャベツ 106
狩猟帽 124	上歯列弓 102	ショーツ 295, 301, 308	シロクジラ 89
酒類 256	上唇 60, 102	ショーティ 123	白駒 314, 315
受話音調節パネル 244	渉水鳥 73	ショート 290	シロタマゴテングタケ 47
受話器 244	使用済み注射器入れ 265	ショート・ソックス 119	白タマネギ 103
受話口 244	使用済み燃料貯蔵室 177	ショート・パンツ 121, 293	白パン 114
潤滑油 181	使用済み燃料廃棄室 177	助監督 273	シロフォン 232, 234
循環系 98	小尖塔 221	職員室 269	白樺 314
準貴石 129	小泉門 93	職員通用口 269	白ワイン用グラス 144
巡視路 220	上層雲 35	職員用出入り口 269	芯 110, 111
春分 33	上大静脈 98, 99	食事 115	仁 56
瞬膜 79	上段部 16	食事コーナー 138, 143	震央 26
ジョイスティック 247, 316	小腸 96	植生と生物圏 40	シン・ガード 287, 293, 301
署員休憩室 264	象徴 317	植生の垂直分布 40	深海底 24
ジョイント 270	上腸間膜静脈 99	植生分布 40	シンク 143
署員用クローク 264	上腸間膜動脈 99	食虫哺乳動物の例 76	シンク下キャビネット 143
署員用トイレ 264	小デカンター 144	食道 96, 97	ジングル 232
署員用ロッカー・ルーム 264	小塔 220	食堂 138, 201, 218, 260, 262	シングル・ジャケット 117
子葉 48	鐘塔 221	食の種類 8, 9	シングルス・サイドライン 303
錠 136, 141	消毒アルコール 267	植物界 47	シングル・スプロケット 308
昇圧 176, 178	消毒液 267	植物の構造 48	シングル・チェーン・ホイール 308
上衣 305	消毒剤 267	植物の構造と発芽 48	シングル・パドル 279
上映室 272	消毒用アルコール 267	触毛 79	シングル・ブル 316
省エネ電球 156, 173	衝突防止灯 206	食物連鎖 41	シングルブレード・パドル 279
消音ペダル 226	商取引 249	食料戸棚 138, 143	シングル・リード 231
場外 305	鍾乳石 30	食料品袋 257	神経 101
消火器 265, 319	小脳 97	蝕腕 57	神経系 97
消火器系 96	小刃 311	蹠骨 92	神経終末 101
城郭 220	乗馬スポーツ 280	書斎 139	
上顎 65		女子トイレ 272, 319	
		女子房 264	

神経線維 101	水源 30	スキー手袋 289	ステッチ 125
神経叢 94	吸いみみ穴 30	スキー・パンツ 118	ステップ 135, 192, 308
心形の 49	吸い込み口グリル 131	スキー・ブーツ 289	ステップ気候 34
腎形の 49	水彩絵の具ケーキ 212	スキー・ブレーキ 289	ステム 195
新月 10	水彩絵の具チューブ 212	スキー帽 288	ステレオ・モノ切り換えつまみ 242
震源(地) 26	水質汚染 45	スキューバ・ダイバー 279	ステンド・グラス 221
震源(地)の深さ 26	水準器 161	スキューバ・ダイビング 279	ストッキング 119, 284, 291, 301
人工衛星 32	水晶 25	スキューバ・タンク 279	ストッキング・キャップ 124
信号機あり 317, 318	垂唇 78	スクーター 191	ストック 288, 289
針広混交樹林 40	推進機 201	スクール・ゾーン 317, 318	ストック・リング 289
唇交連 102	推進装置 17	スクール・バス 190	ストッパー 300, 311
心材 53	スイス・アーミー・ナイフ 311	スグリ 109	ストップ 78
寝室 139, 218, 309	水星 6	スクリーン 131, 175, 246, 272, 316	ストップウォッチ 168
神室 217	彗星 10	スクリメージ 296, 297	ストップ・ウォッチ 237
紳士手袋 123	水槽 154	スクリメージ・オフェンス 297	ストップ・ボタン 168
伸縮警棒 265	膵臓 96	スクリメージ・ディフェンス 296	ストライカー 300
伸縮式アンテナ 242	吸い出し管 175	スクリメージ・ライン 297	ストラップ 291
伸縮自在筒 167	水中カメラ 236	スクリュー 201	ストラップ・ピン 229
伸縮ブーム 263	水中眼鏡 276	スクレイパー 163	ストレッチャー 267
伸縮包帯 267	水中翼船 202	スクロール 227	ストロークの種類 277
紳士用手袋 123	垂直安定板 203, 207	スクロール・ホイール 245, 246	ストロボ 235
腎静脈 99	垂直回転窓 137	スクロール・ボタン 246	ストロボ接点 235
シンセサイザー 233	垂直軸型風力タービン 179	スクワッシュパティパン 107	砂 299
心臓 97, 98	垂直地震計 26	スケーター 307	砂砂漠 29
心臓形の 49	垂直尾翼 203, 207	スケート 284, 286	砂島 31
腎臓形の 49	垂直方向の地面の動き 26	スケートボーダー 307	スナップ 117
身体 90, 91	垂直離着陸機 208	スケートボード 307	スナップ付き前身 121
寝台 142	スイッチ 152, 155	スケグ 278	スナップ付き前身頃 121
人体 90	スイッチ板 155	スケルトン 287	スナップファスナー 117
人中 102	スイッチ・プレート 155	スケルトン・ブラシ 130	スナップ・ボタン 123, 214
心土 53	水田 44	スケルトン・レーサー 287	砂箱 197
浸透 42, 44	水筒 195, 311	スコアボード 316	砂浜 31
振動板 241	スイバ 106	スコアラー 294, 299	スニーカー 125
腎動脈 99	水盤 218	スコート 303	脛当て 287, 292, 293, 301
芯取り器 147	水平安定板 201, 203, 207	スコップ 164	スネア・ドラム 232, 234
進入道路 204	水平回転窓 137	スズキ 65	スノーケル 279
進入ランプ 182	水平材 217	スズキの形態図 65	スノーシュー 288
芯抜き器 147	水平軸型風力タービン 179	スズメ 74	スノースーツ 121
シンバル 232, 234	水平地震計 26	スズメバチ 63	スノーボーダー 287
審判員 274, 275, 284, 292, 293	水平ターン 277	スズラン 51	スノーボーディング 287
審判スタンド 280	水平調節脚 160	裾 116	スノーボード 287
審判長 276	水平尾翼 203, 207	スターター 165, 276	スパークリング・ワイン・グラス 144
真皮 101	水平方向の地面の動き 26	スターティング・グリップ 276	スパイク 292
新聞スタンド 259	水泡水器 161	スターティング・ブロック 276	スパイク・シューズ 287, 291, 298
ジンベ 225	水門 175	スタート・キー 245	スパイク・タイヤ 306
心棒 307	水容器 151	スタート台 276	スパイラル・ノート 271
シンボル 313, 317	水流 30	スタート飛び込み 277	スパゲッティ 115
シンボルマーク 313	水力電気 174	スタート・ボタン 160, 168	巣箱 72
新芽 53	水力発電所 174	スターラップ 113	巣箱本体 61
震毛 77	水力発電所の断面図 175	スターラップ・ソックス 291	スパチュラ 148
針葉樹の例 55	スウィーパー 300	スターン 278	スパッツ 122
針葉樹林 40	スウェーデンカブ 104	スタジアム 251	スパット 281
人力散布機 164	スウェット・パーカー 122	スタジオ 237	スパンカー 201
森林火災 44	スウェット・パンツ 122	スタジオ・フロア 238	スパンカー・ブーム 201
森林破壊 44	数字キーボード 170	スタッド 122	スピーカー 241, 242, 244, 272
身廊 219	スーツ 118	スタビライザー 201, 281	スピーカー・カバー 241
	スーツ携帯用衣装バッグ 127	スタンド 130, 149, 166	スピーカー・グリル 241
す	スーツケース 127	スタンプ 292	スピード・スケート靴 286
巣 72	スーパーマーケット 256, 259	スチーム・アイロン 159	スピード調節つまみ 150
垂 102	スープ皿 145	スチ(ー)ル・カメラの例 236	スピード調節ボタン 150
水位 151	スープ・スプーン 146	スチール・カメラマン 273	スピードメーター 188
水位切り換えボタン 160	スープ・チューリン 145	スチ(ー)ル・ビデオ・フィルム・ディスク 235	スピノサウルス 70
スイートピー 108	スープ鉢 145	ズッキーニ 107	スプーン 146
スイープ用オール 278	スープ・ボウル 145	スティック 227, 232, 293	スプリング 196, 270, 275
水泳 276	ズーム・ダイヤル 240	スティック・タイプ電気掃除機 159	スプリング・ノート 271
水泳パンツ 122, 276	ズーム・レンズ 235, 238, 240	スティック糊 270	スプリンクラー 178
水泳プール 201, 277	据え置き式プール 135	スティミュレーター・チップ 133	スプレー・スカート 279
水泳帽 276	据え付けの棚 143	ステーキ 115	スプレー・ノズル 165
水温計 188	スカート 118	ステーキ・ナイフ 146	スプレー・ホース 154
スイカ 113	頭蓋骨 90	ステージ 106	スペア・タイヤ 189
水解小体 56	スカル用オール 278	ステージ・ストッパー 167	スペース・シャトル 14, 32
水管 57	スカンク 80	ステーション・ワゴン 186	スペースラブ 15
水銀球 169	スカンポ 106	ステープラー 270	スペード 313
水銀柱 169	スキー板 288, 289	ステゴザウルス 70	
水圏 41	スキー・ウエア 288, 289		
	スキー靴 289		
	スキー・グローブ 289		

滑り軸 162
滑り止め 275
滑り止め付き石付き 163
スベリヒユ 106
滑りやすい 317, 318
スポイト 148
スポイラー 206
巣房 61
スポーク 195
スポーツ 274
スポーツウエア 122
スポーツ・カー 186
スポーツ用品店 259
スポット 281
スポットライト 157, 238, 263, 273
ズボン 116, 122, 284, 291, 305, 306
ズボン下 117
ズボン吊り 116
隅金具 127
隅金 127
隅塔 220
スミレ 51
童色 211
スモール・ブレード 311
スモッグ 45
スモモ 111
スライディング・シート 278
スライディング・ドア 154
スライド映写機 269
スライド・ガラス 167
スライド式カバー 245
スライド式サンルーフ 185
スリーパー・キャブ 192
スリーピング・バッグ 310
スリーブ 203, 278
スリップ・ジョイント 162
スリップ・ジョイント・プライヤー 162
スリップ注意 317, 318
擂り鉢穴 30
スレイ・ベル 232
スローイング・ライン 316
スロート 302
スロート・ガード 291
スロー・モーション・ボタン 239
スロットル・コントロール 247
巣枠 61

せ

背 73, 78, 84, 140, 141
セイウチ 88
青果 256
正確さを競うスポーツ 281
税関 200, 253
税関検査場 253
制汗剤 132
正九角形 172
制御室 174, 177
西経 20
制限区域 295
制限サークル 294
正五角形 172
生産企業 249
生産者 41
精算所 257
生産プラットフォーム 180
正七角形 172
正十角形 172
精製 181
成層圏 32
成層圏界面 32
声帯 97
成長線 57
生徒 268

制動スイッチ 162
制動灯 187
生徒(用)机 268
生徒用ロッカー 269
西南西 23
生肉売り場 256
正八角形 172
整髪 130
整備壇 219
整備格納庫 205
整備員 261
整備トラック 204
製氷皿 152
製品番号領域 243
政府機関 249
生物圏 40
生物圏の構造 41
生物分解できない汚染物質 44
正方形 172
西北西 23
聖母礼拝堂 221
生命維持装置 17
生命維持装置制御装置 17
声門 67
精油所 181
精油製品 181
西洋カボチャ 107
西洋ゴボウ 104
西洋将棋 315
西洋双六 315
西洋だんす 141
西洋ナシ 111
西洋ニラネギ 103
整流板 192
セイル 278
セイル・スリーブ 278
正六面体 172
正六角形 172
セーター 120
セーフティー・バインディング 289
背泳ぎ泳法 277
背泳ぎのスタート 277
背泳ぎ用取っ手 276
背泳ぎ用標識 277
世界の気候 34
セカンド 290
セカンド・アシスタント・カメラマン 272
セカンド・レベル・ドメイン 248
赤緯クランプ 12
赤緯微動ハンドル 12
赤緯目盛り環 12
積雲 35
石果 110
赤外線 43
石果の例 110
石筍 30
脊髄 97
石炭 25
石柱 30
脊柱 92, 97
赤道 20
石畳 25
石油 180
石油汚染 45
石油化学製品 181
石油基地 200
石油鉱床 180
石油貯蔵基地 181
石油流出 45
セコンド 304
セ氏度 169
セ氏目盛り 169
節 48
絶縁器 176

石灰海綿 56
石灰岩 25
節間 48
接眼部アダプター 12
接眼レンズ 12, 167
説教壇 219
赤経目盛り環 12
赤血球 98
ゼッケン 295
ゼッケン番号 284, 298
切歯 94
摂氏度 169
摂氏目盛り 169
舌鞘 67
設定温度 158
接点 175
セット 273
セットアップ 281
セット・デザイナー 272
セット・ドレッサー 273
雪量計 38
背中 91
背中洗い用ボディー・ブラシ 132
背ビレ 140
背びれ 88
背骨 92, 97
ゼブラ 87
セミ 63
セミクジラ 88
セミ・タイト・スカート 118
セミトレーラー 192
セミ・マミー型 310
ゼム・クリップ 270
セメント質 94
背もたれ 141
背もたれ椅子の各部 140
セラ 217
セラック 29
迫台 221
セルタス 106
セルフ・インフレーティング・マット(レス) 310
セルリアク 104
セロリ 105
線 222
前縁 207
全縁の 49
前縁フラップ 207
顫音 223
全音符 223
船外活動装置 17
旋回橋 183
旋回塔 209
線間 222
洗岩 31
洗浄タオル 132
全顔用マスク 263
前脚 140
船客ターミナル 200
全休符 223
前脛骨筋 95
前脛骨動脈 99
線形の 49
閃光管 235
仙骨 92
浅根 52
センサー・プラグ 152
前翅 62
船室 201
前室 217
洗車場 261
セコンド 304
選手椅子 299
船首 200, 201
船首甲板 200
船首斜檣 201
船首推進機 200

戦術輸送ヘリコプター 203
選手番号 295
船首プロペラ 200
選手(用)ベンチ 285, 293, 297, 298, 299
船首楼 200
前檣 201
前上頭 65
前檣縦帆 201
洗浄タンク 154
前照灯 184, 187, 192, 195, 197, 198
洗浄瓶 166
染色質 56
線審 274, 284, 299, 301, 302
全身の手入れ 132
前側頭泉門 93
センター 284, 290, 291, 294, 297, 304
センター・アタッカー 299
センター・コンソール 188
センター・サークル 285, 294, 300
センター・サービス・ライン 303
センター・ストラップ 303
センター・スポット 300
センター・ハーフ 293
センター・バック 299
センター・ピラー 185
センター・フォワード 293
センター・フラッグ 300
センターボード 278
センター・マーク 302
センター・ライン 285, 293, 294, 298
センター・ライン・ジャッジ 302
蘚苔類 47
前打音 223
洗濯機 160
選択キー 245
洗濯室 138
洗濯タイマー 160
先端 316
泉亭 219
前庭 100
前庭神経 100
剪定鋏 164
宣伝ポスター 199
尖塔 219, 221
前頭筋 95
前頭骨 92, 93
セント・バーナード 78
栓抜き 147, 311
船舶用ディーゼル油 181
前半規管 100
船尾 201
船尾甲板 201
前鼻棘 93
船尾楼 201
前部滑走部 287
前部ランナー 287
前房 217
前方道路工事中 317, 318
前方優先道路 317, 318
ゼンマイ 105
千枚通し 311
洗面所 138, 139
繊毛 56
繊毛状の 49
専門医学実習生 266
専用回線 248
専用ライン 248
前輪 206
蘚類 47
線路 253, 254
前廊 217
線路番号札 198

前腕 78, 85, 91
前腕当て 298

そ

ソ 222
藻 47
ゾウ 87
層雲 35
痩軀 109
双眼顕微鏡 167
送気ダクト 182
送迎デッキ 253
総頸動脈 99
象牙質 94
草原気候 34
倉庫 268
走行エリア 204
走行距離計 188
走行クレーン 175
走行車線 182
走行体 209, 210
総合得点掲示板 274
総菜 257
操作解説図 261
操作キー 245
操作盤 153, 160
操作棒 316
操作ボタン 240, 246
操作レバー 262
巣室 61
操縦桿 203
操縦区域 204
操縦室 14, 203, 206
操縦者 287
僧正 314
装飾音 223
装飾帯 141
草食動物 94
装飾用品店 259
送信済みトレイ 245
層積雲 35
総腸骨動脈 99
送電 176, 178
送電網へのエネルギーの統合 176
操帆索 201
装備 264
送風ファン内蔵部 131
増幅器 241
僧帽筋 95
総務部 269
ソウメンカボチャ 107
巣門 61
巣門スライド 61
ゾウリムシ 56
僧侶 314
藻類 47
藻類, 地衣類, 蘚類, シダ類 47
送話器 244
送話口 244
副え木 267
ソースパン 149, 311
ソール 286, 289
側径間 183
足根骨 92
側スパン 183
側切歯 94
側線 65, 182
側堆石 29
側対速歩 85
側柱 136
測定管 39
側頭骨 92, 93
速度計 188
速度調節つまみ 165
足背動脈 99

側壁 276
鼠径部 90
ソケット・コンタクト 155
底 286, 289
注ぎ口 159
粗調整棹 170
ソックス 119, 284, 298, 303
測候所 38
側衛 48
ソテー・パン 149
袖口 116
粗動ハンドル 167
外側カウンター 125
外底 122, 125
外箱 168
外袋 128
外ポケット 126
その他の記号 223
ソファー 140
ソフト・ペダル 226, 233
ソムリエ 260
反らせ板 158
そり 203
橇 287
剃り角度設定つまみ 131
橇の鈴 232
ぞろ目 313

た

ターゲット 281
ダーツ 316
ダーツボード 316
ダート 316
タートルネック 120, 288
ダービー・ハット 124
タービン 177
タービンからの排水 176
タービン軸が発電機を回転させる 178
タービン建屋 177
タービンの回転 176
ターボジェット・エンジン 207
ターミナル 155
ターミナルと駅 252
ターン 223
ターン・シグナル 187
ターンテーブル 209, 237, 263, 304
タイ 223
台 26, 130, 157, 166, 247, 275
体育館 268
体育館事務室 268
第1コーナー 280
第一趾 72
第一次消費者 41
第一小臼歯 94
第一触角 58
第1スペース 295
第一背びれ 64
第一大臼歯 94
第1トリガー 230
第1抜き差し管 230
第1バイオリン 234
第一葉 48
第一趾 73
第一指 82
ダイオウ 105
ダイオード 173
体温計 169
体温制御装置 17
大河 22, 30
大回廊 217
耐火煉瓦の背壁 158
大気汚染 44
大気汚染物質 45

大気圏 32, 41
大気圏の構造 32
大臼歯 94
大臼歯の断面図 94
大胸筋 95
大工ハンマー 161
台形 172
大剣 116
ダイコン 104
台座 129, 141, 158, 168, 170
第3コーナー 280
第三趾 72
第三指 82
第三次消費者 41
第三色 211
第三大臼歯 94
第3トリガー 230
第3抜き差し管 230
台車枠 196
体重計 170
大槽 201
大状在静脈 99
帯状装飾 141
大触角 58
ダイス 315
ダイス 108
ダイス・カップ 315
ダイスとドミノ 313
ダイス・ボックス 315
大聖堂 221, 250
大西洋 18
堆積岩 24
大泉門 93
体操 274
ダイボード 278
大草原 22
大腿 78, 84, 91
橙 211
大腿筋膜張筋 95
大腿骨 92
大腿静脈 99
大腿直筋 95
大腿動脈 99
大腿部 76
タイタン 7
タイタン4 16
大腸 96
大動脈 98
大動脈弓 98, 99
タイト・エンド 297
台所 138, 143, 218
台所用スポンジ 159
台所用品 147
第2コーナー 280
第二趾 72
第二指 82
第二次消費者 41
第二小臼歯 94
第二色 211
第二触角 58
第2スペース 295
第二背びれ 64
第二大臼歯 94
第2トリガー 230
第2抜き差し管 230
第2バイオリン 234
第2レベル・ドメイン 248
ダイニング・キッチン 138, 143
ダイニング・ルーム 138
耐熱膜 14
大脳 97
大刃 311
堆肥箱 165
ダイビング・グローブ 279
対物レンズ 12, 167, 235
太平洋 18
タイマー 152, 153

タイマー付きラジオ 242
タイムキーパー 294, 304
タイム・コード 273
タイヤ 185, 192, 195, 308, 313
タイヤ・バルブ 195
ダイヤフラム 241
タイヤ・ポンプ 194
ダイヤモンド 25, 129, 313
ダイヤル・ロック 126
太陽 6, 8, 33
大洋 9, 22
太陽エネルギー 173
太陽系 6
太陽黒点 8
太陽電池 173
太陽電池の仕組み 173
太陽電池パネル 14, 173
太陽の構造 8
太陽の黒点 8
太陽放射 173
第4コーナー 280
第四趾 72
第四指 82
大陸の配置 18
大理石 25
対流圏 32
対流圏界面 32
対流式電気暖房器 158
対流セル 37
対流層 8
台輪 140, 217
唾液腺 96
タオル掛け 154
タカ 74
ダガーボード 278
ダガーボード・トランク 278
高さ調節パイプ 274
高さ調節ハンドル 275
打楽器 232, 234
多角形 172
高められる温室効果 43
高床(式)住居 215
滝 30
抱き 136
抱き石 158
打球面 291
卓122
卓越風 37
タクシー乗り場 319
託児所 259
タグ車 205
タグボート 202
托葉 49
打撃用手袋 291
タケノコ 105
タコ 57
蛇行 30
タコメーター 188
打者 290, 291, 292
打者線 292
打者用ヘルメット 291
多汁葉 103
舵手席 278
畳 305
ダチョウ 75
タック 278
ダッグアウト 290
タック・プリーツ 116
脱脂綿 267
脱臭剤 132
ダッシュボード 188
タッチ・ターン 277
タッチ・ライン 301
手綱 280
ダッフル・コート 117
竪穴 217

縦糸　59
竪型ピアノ　226
縦框　137
たてがみ　85
縦材　163
縦樋　134
縦長の瞳孔　67
縦に発達する雲　35
縦の動き　314
縦笛　231
棚　152
棚板　152
棚脇の陣列台　257
谷　28, 30
ダニ　59
多肉果　109
種　109, 110, 111, 112
種なしキュウリ　107
タバコ屋　258
タブ　126
タブリーヌム　218
ダブリング・キューブ　315
ダブル・クリップ　270
ダブル・シックス　313
ダブル・シャープ　223
ダブル・ジャケット　117
ダブルス・サイドライン　302
ダブル・スラッシュ　248
ダブル・パドル　279
ダブル・フラット　223
ダブル・ブランク　313
ダブル・ブル　316
ダブルブレード・パドル　279
ダブル・ベース　227, 234
ダブル・ホルン　230, 234
ダブル・リード　231
ダブル・リング　316
ダブレット　313
食べ物　103
打棒　232
卵　61, 66, 72
卵泡立て器　148
卵立て　152
卵と乳製品　114
玉杓子　148
タマネギ　103
玉縁ポケット　120
ダム　174
タム・タム　232
ダムの頂上　174
ダムの例　174
溜め池　174, 175
打面　161, 232
タラップ　252
タラップ車　252
ダルマシアン　78
ダルメシアン　78
垂れ布　142
タロイモ　104
タワー　179
タワー・ケース　246
タワー・ラダー　263
単価　170
担架　267
タンカー　181, 200
断崖　28, 31
単眼　60, 62
弾丸入れ　265
タンク　15, 262
タング　116
タンク・車　181, 193, 196
タンク・トップ　122
タンク・トラック　181, 193
タンク・ローリー　181, 193
短骨　93
短駒　226
探査　180

単細胞動物，海綿動物，棘皮動物　56
端子　155
男子トイレ　272, 319
男子房　264
端子ボックス　173
単純な植物　47
単純な生物と棘皮動物　56
弾性帯　116
男性用衣類　116
男性用下着　117
男性用ショルダーバッグ　127
断層　26
探測気球　38
端堆石　29
段違い平行棒　274
単蹄　85
タンデム自転車　195
タンデム・トレーラー　193
断熱材　14
胆嚢　96
ダンパー・ペダル　226, 233
タンバリン　232
ダンプ・カー　192, 210
ダンプ・トラック　192, 210
タンブラー　144
端壁　276
暖房　158
暖房油　181
タンポポ　51, 106
弾薬入れ　265
男優　272
単葉　49
断裂ホモサイン図法　21
暖炉　138, 158
暖炉用鉄器具　158

ち

地衣　47
チーズ　114
チーズ売り場　257
チーズ・ナイフ　146
チーター　81
チーム・エンブレム　284
チーム・シャツ　291, 293, 295, 298, 301
地衣類　47
チェーン　194
チェーン・ホイール　308
チェス　314
チェス駒　314
チェスト・プロテクター　291, 298
チェスの座標式表記法　314
チェス盤　314
チェスボード　314
チェッカー　315
チェッカー盤　315
チェッカーボード　315
チェリートマト　107
チェロ　227, 234
チェンジ・ペダル　191
チェンジ・レバー　188
チェンバロ　226
地階　138
地殻　24, 26
地殻断面図　24
地下茎　103
地下室　217
地下水面　30, 45
地下水流　30
地下鉄　199
地下鉄駅　254
地下鉄車両　199, 254
地下鉄路線（系統）図　199, 255
地下トンネル　254
地下窓　135

地下流出　42
地球　6, 8, 9
地球温暖化　43
地球儀　268
地球座標とグリッド法　20
地球の軌道　8, 9
地球の構造　24
地球の地形　28
地峡　22
蓄電池　173
畜糞　45
チケット売り場　272
チケット・カウンター　252
チケット係　272
恥骨　90
チコリ　106
智歯　94
地質学　24
地質学的現象　26
地上気象観測所　38
地上気象台　38
地上探査　180
地上標識　254
地上輸送　181
地図　22, 268
地図作成法　20
地図投影法　21
地勢図　22
チター　225
チタニア　7
地中海　19
地中海性亜熱帯気候　34
地表による吸収　43
地表流出　42
乳房　90
チャージ・ライト　131
チャージ・ランプ　131
チャーム・ブレスレット　129
チャイブ　103
チャイム　234
着順審判員　276
着脱式の車体　192
着地台　61
着氷性雨　36
チャク・モル　219
着陸舷窓　203
着陸灯　203
チャック　162
チャット・ルーム　249
チャパティ　114
チャンター　224
チャンネル送りボタン　239
チャンネル・スキャン・ボタン　239
チャンネル選局ボタン　239
中圧配電線　176
中央アメリカ　18
中央径間　183
中央スパン　183
中央尖塔　221
中央側板　67
中央板　67
中央氷域　284
中央分離帯　182, 250
中央ホール　218
中音（域）用スピーカー　241
中華鍋　149
中華鍋セット　149
中果皮　109, 110, 111, 112
中間圏　32
中間圏界面　32
中間帯　217
駐機場　205
中堅　291
中堅手　290
中国ブロッコリ　105
中趾　72

中耳　100
注射器　266
駐車場　182, 251, 252, 269, 282
中手骨　92
虫食鳥　73
中心　59, 171
柱身　217
中心街　250
中心柱　179
虫垂　96
中枢神経系　97
沖積岩　30
中舌　60
中切歯　94
中層雲　35
中足骨　92
中堆石　29
柱頭　50, 227
チューナー　241, 242, 243
中二階　138, 139, 254
中二階への階段　139
チューニング・スライド　230
チューニングつまみ　242, 243
チューニング・ピン　226
チューニング・ペグ　228, 229
チューニング・ボタン　239
チューバ　230, 234
厨房　263
中葉　97
チューリップ　51
駐輪場　269
柱列（廊）　218
柱廊　218, 219
中廊　219
中助　49
チョウ　62
長円形スノーシュー　288
頂芽　48
聴覚　100
頂冠帯　217
長距離ジェット機　206
長距離バス　190
蝶形晶　93
調号　223
調光スイッチ　155
超高層ビル　251
超小型車　186
彫刻　213
彫刻具の例　213
彫刻刀　213
腸骨　92
長骨　93
長座　136
長指伸筋　95
聴取室　264
聴小骨　100
聴診器　266
調整可能な肩紐　121
調製食品　256
調整ねじ　227
調節クランプ　157
調節スライド　116
調節つまみ　153
調節ねじ　162
調節バンド　241
調節溝　162
朝鮮アザミ　105
ちょうちんばね　142
蝶番　126, 136, 137, 141
手斧　263, 312
蝶ネクタイ　116
蝶ねじ　162
チョウの形態図　62
跳馬　274, 275
長腓骨筋　95

長方形　172
蝶結び　124
帳面　271
調理器具　149
調理室　206, 269
調理台　143
調理場　263
調理ハム　115
鳥類　72
直線翼　206
直腸　96
直読式雨量計　38, 39
貯水器　39
貯水池　174, 175
貯蔵可能推進剤上段ステージ　16
貯蔵室　260
直　171
直角定規　271
直角の動き　314
直径　171
チョロギ　104
地理学　18
ちり取り　159
塵の尾　10
チリメンキャベツ　106
チルド・ケース　152
チンゲンサイ　106
チン・ストラップ　298
チンパンジー　83
陳列準備区域　256

つ

ツイーター　241
椎甲板　67
ツイスト・ハンドル　247
通気口　217
通常型　207
通信　235
通信衛星　249
通信装置　199
通信プロトコル　248
ツー・ドア・セダン　186
通風装置　196
ツーリング・バイク　191
通路　256, 258
通廊　221
通話(開始)キー　245
通話終了キー　245
使い捨てかみそり　131
使い捨てカメラ　236
つかむ棒　199
つかむのに適した指　83
月　6, 8, 9
ツギ　315
月形芯　125
突き出し狭間　220
継ぎ足しはしご　163
月の軌道　8, 9
月の相　10
月の地形　9
継ぎ目ゲージ　214
継ぎ環　131
ツケ　315
槌骨　100
土小屋　215
つっかけ　125
繋ぎ　84
つば　47, 124
翼　15, 72, 82, 207
唾抜き　230
ツバメ　74
つぼ　47
蕾　48
爪革　125
爪先金具　288
爪先革　125

爪先の飾り革　125
積み込み機　209
積み荷ターミナル　200
爪　58, 67, 101, 129, 161, 225
爪掛け　311
爪切り　132
爪切り鋏　132
爪磨き　132
爪やすり　132
冷たい下降気流　37
露　36
露先　128
釣り合い錘　209
吊り腕　209
釣り鐘状の鈴　232
吊りケーブル　183
吊り材　183
吊り下げ灯　157
吊り橋　183
吊元框　136
吊り輪　275
ツルコケモモ　109
ツンドラ　40
ツンドラ気候　34

て

手　83, 91, 101
手洗い　259, 269
低圧域　37
低圧配電線　176
ティー　282
T型　207
ティー・グラウンド　282
ティースプーン　146
ディーゼル・エンジン　197
ディーゼル・エンジン収納部　209, 210
ディーゼル電気機関車　196
ディーゼル油　181
DVD　240
DVDプレーヤー　240
DVD-ROMイジェクト・ボタン　246
DVD-ROMドライブ　246
ティーポット　145
ディオネ　7
低音域用指盤　224
低音域用スピーカー　241
低音域用ボタン部　224
低音調節つまみ　242
低音用指盤　224
低音用スピーカー　241
低音用ボタン部　224
低音レジスター　224
蹄冠　84
定期航空機　32
蹄叉　84
抵抗板　206
停止ボタン　239
艇首　278
蹄踵　84
ディスク・カメラ　236
ディスク・ドライブ　233
ディスク・トレー　240
ディスク・ブレーキ　191
ディスプレイ　243, 244, 245, 246, 316
蹄尖　84
蹄側　84
低速車線　182
艇体　278
底堆石　29
ディッシュ　238
ディッシュ・アンテナ　238
ディッパー・アーム　209

ディッパー・アーム・シリンダー　209
蹄鉄　84
底土　53
ディナー皿　145
ディノニクス　71
艇尾　278
ティピー　215
ディフューザー　273
ディフレクター　158
ディプロドクス　70
蹄壁　84
低棒　274
ティラノザウルス　71
テイル　278
ディレーラー　308
ディレクトリー　248
ティンパニ　232, 234
ティンパヌム　217, 221
ディンプル　282
データ・エントリー・スライダー　233
データ・エントリー・ダイヤル　233
データ処理　38
データ表示画面　240
データ表示窓　240, 245
データベース　249
テーパー翼　206
テープ　161, 293
テープ・ガイド　243
テープ・ディスペンサー　270
テープ・ホルダー　270
テーブル　141
テーブル・ランプ　157
テープ・ロック　161
テール　287, 288, 289
テール・コーム　130
テールバック　297
テールピース　227
テール・ブーム　203
テールライト　187, 191, 194
テールランプ　187, 191, 194
手押し車　164, 253
手斧　263, 312
デオドラント　132
デカンタ(一)　144
デキャンタ(一)　144
出口　61, 182
手首　78, 82, 91, 101
手首丈グラブ　123
手先框　136
手作業による分別　46
デジタル・オーディオ・テープ・レコーダー　237
デジタル・カメラ　236
デジタル多用途ディスク　240
デジタル時計　168
手錠ケース　265
デスクトップ・コンピューター　248
デスク・ランプ　157
テスト・パターン　238
手すり　138, 139, 192
手摺り綱　183
テチカトル　219
デッキ　288
デッキ・チェア　140
デッキ・テープ　307
鉄格子　217
鉄骨　226
鉄枝　84
鉄唇　84
鉄頭　84
鉄道駅　250

鉄道線路　250
鉄道輸送　196
デッド・ボルト　136
鉄尾部　84
鉄棒　274
鉄砲狭間　220
テテュス　7
テナー・ドラム　232
テナガエビ　58
テナガザル　83
テニス　302
テニス・シューズ　303
テニス・プレーヤー　303
テニス・ボール　302
テニス・ラケット　302
手荷物一時預かり所　253
手荷物受取所　252
手荷物カート　253
手荷物検査(場)　253
手荷物室　253
手荷物とハンドバッグ　127
手の甲　101
手のひら　101, 291
デパート　259
手挽き鋸　161
手袋　17, 306, 308
手袋型洗顔タオル　132
手袋型浴用タオル　132
手袋着用　320
手袋の手の甲側　123
手袋の手のひら側　123
手袋の指　123
デミタス　144
手元　128
手元ボタン　128
テラス　134
テラス・ドア　138, 143
デルタ(地帯)　30, 31
デルタ2　16
デルタ　206, 208
テレスコピック・フロント・フォーク　191
テレビ　268
テレビ受像機　268, 239
テレビ電源ボタン　239
テレビ・ビデオ切り替えボタン　239
テレビ・モード　239
テレプロンプター　238
電圧降下　176
電圧上昇　176, 178
電気回路　175
電気かみそり　131
電気乾燥機　160
電気ケーブル　162
電気コード　131
電気鋸　130
天気図　38
電気洗濯機　160
電器店　258
電気ドリル　162
電気ナイフ　150
電気発生の過程　176
電球　156
電極　156
電気レンジ　153
天元　315
電源・音量つまみ　242
電源・機能スイッチ　240
電源コード　131
電源スイッチ　130, 131, 151, 157, 233
電源表示灯　130
電源ボタン　239, 240, 243, 245, 246
電源ランプ　244
臀甲板　67

日本語索引

335

電子安定器　156
電子楽器　233
テンジクネズミ　77
電子決済端末　257
電子商取引　249
電子ドラム・パッド　233
電子秤　170
電子ピアノ　233
電子ビューファインダー　240
電車ホーム　252
天井灯　157
電子レンジ　143, 152
天体観測　3
デンタル・フロス　133
電池　175
天頂プリズム　12
点滴スタンド　266
テント　309
伝統楽器　224
電動ゴルフ・カート　283
電動式工具　162
伝統的な家屋　215
テントウムシ　63
テント・トレーラー　189
天然橋　7
天王星　7
伝票　260
伝票発行口　261
臀部　91
テンプル　128
店舗　218
テンポ・コントロール　233
テンポ調節つまみ　233
天幕　218
天窓　135
天文学　6
臀裂　91
電話　244, 245
電話機　244
電話器コード　244
電話線　248
電話通信　244
電話番号インデックス　244
電話ボックス　319

と

ド　222
ドア　136, 185, 206
ドア・ウインドー　185
ドアガスケット　152
ドア・ストッパー　152
ドアの取っ手　136
ドアの握り　136
ドアノブ　136
ドアの例　136
ドア・ハンドル　185
ドア・ミラー　184
ドア・ロック　185
トイレ　138, 139, 218, 259, 266, 269
トイレット・ペーパー・ホルダー　154
塔　179, 221, 314
胴　66, 161, 228, 229, 316
トウ・ガード　291
頭蓋骨　90
塔型風車　179
トウガラシ　107
唐辛子スプレー　265
塔岩　31
トウガン　107
投球　292
頭胸甲　58
頭胸部　58, 59
洞窟　30
トウ・クリップ　194

峠　28
東経　20
洞穴　30
瞳孔　79, 102
橈骨　82, 92
搭載機器ベイ　16
冬至　33
投手　290, 292
投手部　292
搭乗橋　205
同乗者用足載せ台　191
同乗者用フットレスト　191
塔状氷塊　29
導水路　174, 175
導線　175
橈側皮静脈　99
胴体　179, 207
胴体部　169
頭頂骨　93
頭頂部　179
東南東　23
導入線　156
トウ・バー　204
トウ・バインディング　288
塔はしご　263
頭髪　91
トウヒ　55
トウピース　289
トウ・ピック　286
頭部　10, 60, 62, 79, 133, 228, 229
胴部　130
動物界　56
動物細胞　56
東北東　23
透明中隔　97
灯油　181
東洋ゴキブリ　63
動力式芝刈り機　165
動力車　199
道路　23
道路清掃車　193
道路地図　23
道路トンネル　182
道路番号　23
道路標識　317
道路網　182
道路輸送　182
等和色　211
十日月　10
トーキング・ドラム　225
トーク　124
トークバック・ボックス　237
トースター　151
ドーム形テント　309
トーラス　172
通り　250
ドーリス式の付け柱　218
ト音記号　222
トーン・コントロール　228
トカゲ　69
尖り岩　29
トガリネズミ　76
毒牙　67
毒管　67
毒キノコ　47
読書用眼鏡　128
毒腺　67
得点掲示板　305
毒の導管　67
毒針　61
毒ヘビの形態図　67
トグル・ボタン　117
時計　152, 153, 168, 237, 268
都市　22

都市住宅　216
土壌汚染　44
土壌断面　53
土壌の肥沃化　44
図書館　268
図書室　268
土星　7
塗装　163
土壌断面　53
土台　179, 198
ドック　200
取っ手　126, 127, 130, 131, 142, 151, 152, 153, 159, 162, 199, 242, 311
トップ　232, 287, 288, 289
トップ・ベンド　288, 289
トップ・レベル・ドメイン　248
トナー・カートリッジ　247
トパーズ　129
鳶口　263
飛び込み台　135
飛び梁　221
扉　152, 153
扉パッキン　152
トマト　107
止まり鳥　73
ドミノ牌　313
止め板　142
ドメイン・ネーム　248
止め金具　127
留め金具　155
留め金　126, 155, 231, 312
止め金　127
鱊　201
共柄熊手　164
トラ　81
どら　234
トライアングル　232, 234
ドライバー　161, 287
ドライ・パステル　212
ドライブ・シャフト　203
トラック　307
トラック運送　192
トラック・トラクター　192
トラック・トレーラー　193
トラックの例　192
ドラムス　232
ドラム・セット　232
ドラムリン　28
トラロック神殿　219
トランク　127, 185
トランクス　117, 304
トランス　176
トランプ　313
トランペット　230, 234
トランポリン　275
鳥　72
ドリーネ　30
鳥打ち帽　124
トリガー　247
トリガー・スプレー　164
取り替え式スパイク　301
取り調べ室　264
取り出しボタン　316
取り付け脚　235
取り付け台　156
ドリップ式コーヒー・メーカー　151
トリップ・メーター　188
ドリップ・モール　185
トリトン　7
鳥の形態図　72
トリプル・リング　316
トリマー　131
トリル　223
ドループ・スヌート　208

トルコ石　129
トルティージャ　114
トルティーヤ　114
トルネード　37
トルマリン　129
トレイ　127, 141, 164
トレーナー　122, 293, 295, 304
トレーニング・パンツ　122
トレーラー　189
トレーラー・ハウス　189
ドレスオール　121
ドレッサー　141
トレブル・コントロール　229
トレブル・ピックアップ　228
トレブル・レジスター　224
トレモロ・アーム　228
ドローストリング・バッグ　127
ドロー・チューブ　167
トロール船　202
ドローン・パイプ　224
トロピカルフルーツ　113
泥除け　185, 192, 194
トロンボーン　230, 234
鈍角　171
鈍鋸歯状の　49
トング　148
ドングリカボチャ　107
トンネル　254
トンネル状アーチ　218
トンボ　63
トンボロ　31

な

内科医　266
内核　24
内果皮　110, 111
内頭静脈　99
内趾　72
内耳　100
内室　217
内陣　221
内側広筋　95
内腸骨動脈　99
ナイト　314
ナイト・テーブル　266
ナイト・モード切り換えスイッチ　240
ナイフ　146, 150, 213, 312
ナイフ・プリーツ　116
内部炉床　158
内野　290
内野手用グローブ　291
ナオス　217
中脚　60, 62
長椅子　140, 267
長柄ボディー・ブラシ　132
中折れ　124
長傘　128
長靴着用　320
長駒　226
流し　143, 154
中接　116
中庭　219, 220
中パネル　136
中棒　128
中方立て　141
長枕　142
長物車　196
中指　101
中枠　141
ナキウサギ　77
投げ矢　316
ナシ状果　111
ナシ状果の例　111
ナス　107
ナタウリ　107

ナチュラル 223
夏 33
ナット 227, 228, 229
ナツメヤシ 110
7度 222
斜めの動き 314
斜めのコーニス 217
ナビゲーション・ライト 207
名札 127
常歩 84
波形やすり 213
波目やすり 213
南極 20
南極圏 20
南極大陸 19
軟口蓋 102
軟骨魚 64
軟骨魚の例 64
軟条 65
南西 23
軟体動物 57
軟体動物の例 57
南東 23
南南西 23
南南東 23
ナンバー・プレート 306
ナンバー・プレート・ライト 187
ナンバー・プレート・ランプ 187

に

ニア 13
ニー・パッド 291, 298, 307
荷下ろし場 259
二階 138, 139
二階席 206
二階建て住宅 216
二階建てバス 190
ニガウリ 107
二級道路 23
握り 126, 127, 162, 278, 291
肉食動物 41
肉食哺乳動物 78, 79
肉食哺乳動物の例 80
西 23
虹 36
ニシキヘビ 68
西半球 20
二重鋸歯状の 49
二重鍋 149
22メートル・ライン 293
二十六日月 10
荷台 189, 191, 194, 210
荷台付き小型トラック 186
日曜大工 161
日曜大工店 258
日射 42, 43
日射計 38
日照計 38
日食 8
ニット・ベスト 120
ニット帽 124
二蹄 85
2度 222
二番管 231
二番車 169
240度 171
2分音符 223
2分休符 223
2分の2拍子 222
日本実験モジュール 14
二枚舌 67
2枚羽根プロペラ 208
荷物預かりカウンター 252
荷物受取所 253
荷物室 198, 203
荷物台 189, 194

荷物トレーラー 205
荷物発送所 253
入院患者 266
乳製品 256
乳製品室 152
乳製品搬入区域 256
乳頭 90
ニュートラル・ゾーン 284, 296
乳房 90
入浴台 154
二葉式跳開橋 183
二塁 290
二塁手 290
庭 218
庭木 134
庭の小道 134
庭の通路 134
人形型 310
人間 90
ニンジン 104
ニンニク 103

ぬ

貫 140

ね

根 103
ネイル・ハンマー 161
音色(選択)ボタン 233
ネーブ 219
ネギ 103
ネギの例 103
ネギ類 103
ネクスト・コール・ボタン 245
ネクスト・バッターズ・サークル 290
ネクタイ 116
ネクタリン 110
猫車 164
ネコの形態図 79
ネコの品種 79
ねじ 161, 214, 227
ねじ頭 161
ねじ頭の溝 161
ねじ込み口金 156
ねじ筋 161
ねじの溝 161
ねじ回し 161, 311
ねじ山 161
ねじれ錐 162
ネズミイルカ 89
ネズミの形態図 77
熱エネルギー 43
熱が発生する 178
ネック 227, 228, 229
ネック・スロート・プロテクター 285
ネック・ロール 298
熱圏 32
熱圏界面 32
熱シールド 14
熱遮蔽板 14
熱せられた冷却材 178
熱損失 43
熱帯雨林 40
熱帯雨林気候 34
熱帯気候 34
熱帯果物 113
熱帯サバンナ気候 34
熱帯性低気圧 37
熱帯林 40
ネット 295, 299, 303
ネット・アンパイア 303
ネット・バンド 303
ネット・ポスト 302

熱輸送ポンプ 177
熱を水に伝える 178
寝袋 310
練り歯磨き 133
粘着糸 59
粘着テープ 267
粘板岩 25
燃料残量警告灯 188
燃料装荷機 177
燃料タンク 191, 192, 196, 203
燃料注入口キャップ 165
燃料補給口 192
燃料補給車 205
年輪 53

の

脳下垂体 97
脳弓体 97
脳橋 97
農業汚染 44
ノウサギ 77
脳梁 97
ノーズ 287
ノート 271
ノートファイル 126
軒蛇腹 135, 136
軒樋 134
鋸刃 161, 162
伸し棒 148
ノズル 14, 16
載せ台 170
覗き窓 152, 153
ノチシャ 106
ノッチ 1/0
咽 72
喉当て 285, 291
喉彦 102
喉仏 90
ノネズミ 77
ノブ・ハンドル 162
登り蛇腹 217
ノミ 63
乗り継ぎ券売機 255
ノルウェー帽 124

は

葉 47, 48
歯 49, 64, 67, 94, 146, 162, 209
刃 132, 146, 150, 161, 163, 286
バー 258, 260, 315
バー・カウンター 260
パーキング・ブレーキ・レバー 188
バー・スツール 140, 260
パースニップ 104
パーソナル・コンピューター 246
バーティカル 307
ハート 313
ハード・パステル 212
ハード・ブーツ用バインディング 287
バーナー 149, 153
バーバー・コーム 130
ハーブ 227, 234
ハーフウェイ・ライン 301
ハーフ・グラス 128
ハーブシコード 226
ハーフ・スリップ 119
ハーフ・パイプ 307
ハーモニカ 224
パイ 115
ハイイロマングース 80
ハイエナ 80

パイオニア 13
バイオリン 227
バイオリンの仲間 234
バイオレット 211
排気ダクト 182
排気筒 192, 203, 210
廃棄物の層 44
廃棄物の分別 46
バイキング 13
バイク・ヘルメット 191
背甲 67
バイザー 17, 191, 284, 287
バイシクル・モトクロス 308
バイシクル・モトクロスとサイクリスト 308
胚珠 50
排障器 197, 198
肺静脈 99
廃水 45
バイス・プライヤー 162
配膳室 206
配膳台 260
配送傾斜路 250
バイソン 86
売店 255, 261
肺動脈 99
肺動脈幹 98
排土板 210
パイナップル 113
ハイパーリンク 248
ハイ・ハット・シンバル 232
胚盤 72
ハイ・ビーム 187
ハイ・ビーム表示灯 188
パイプ・バッグ 224
パイプライン 181
俳優の椅子 272
パイロット 287
パイロン 207
バインダー・クリップ 270
バインディング 288
バウ 278
ハウジング 131
ハウスプリット 201
ハウスボート 202
パウダー・パフ 133
バウ・ボール 279
ハエ 63
バオ 215
ハ音記号 222
秤台 170
脛 84
パキケファロサウルス 71
バキューム・カー 192
白亜 25
白菜 106
白帯 303
白熱電球 156
バグパイプ 224
爆発性の火山 27
爆発性物質 320
博物館 251
爆薬 180
刷毛 133, 163
バケツ 159
バケット 209
バゲット 114
バケット・ヒンジ・ピン 209
箱時計 168
箱ポケット 120
ハゴロモカンラン 106
破砕機 46
刃先 146, 161, 210
歯先 162
狭間 220
狭間胸壁 220
はさみ 58

鋏　214, 267, 311
橋形走行クレーン　174, 175
はしご　189, 210, 215
はしご車　263
はしごの頂部　263
ハシバミの実　113
パジャマ　119, 121
柱　179, 221
バス　190
バスーン　231, 234
バス・クラリネット　234
バスケット　295
バスケットボーラー　295
バスケットボール　294
バスケットボール用ボール　295
パスタ　114
バス・タオル　132
バスタブ　139, 154
バス・ドラム　232, 234
パスファインダー　13
バスルーム　139, 154
バス・レジスター　224
バスローブ　119
破線　182
刃線　214
パソコン　246
バター　114, 282
バター皿　144
バター室　152
バター・ナイフ　146
バターヘッドレタス　106
バタフライ泳法　277
バタフライ・ターン　277
バタフライのキック　277
働きバチ　60
ハタラキバチの形態図　60
砲　225
ばち　232
8度　222
ハチドリ　74
ハチの巣　61
8分音符　223
8分休符　223
爬虫類　67
爬虫類の例　68
発煙筒　265
発芽　48
ハツカダイコン　104
二十日月　10
バッグ　224
バック　285
バックアップ・ライト　187
バックギャモン　315
バックコート　303
バック・サスペンション　308
バック・ジャッジ　297
バックステー　125, 286
バックストップ　295
バックストレッチ　280
パック済み肉売り場　256
バック・ゾーン　299
バッグ立て　283
バックネット　290
バックパック　312
バック・パッド　284
バックホー　209
バックボード　295
バックボード支柱　295
バックホー・ハンドル　209
バック・ミラー　191
バック・ライト　187
バックル　116, 127, 289, 307, 312
パッケージ商品　256
白血球　98
発光管　156
パッシビティ・ゾーン　304

発射時のスペース・シャトル　14
パッションフルーツ　113
発信キー　245
パッセンジャー・ステップ　252
パッセンジャー・ステップ車　252
バッタ　63
バッター　290, 291
バッター用ヘルメット　291
ハッチバック　186
バッツマン　292
バッチ盤　237
発着案内板　253
バッティング・グリーン　282
バッティング・グローブ　291
バッテリー　173, 175, 196
発電機　177
発電器　194
発電機電圧でのエネルギー伝達　176
発電機による電気発生　176, 178
発電所　174
発電装置　175
発電ブレーキ　196
バット　291, 292
パッド　285
バット・アーム　128
バット・エンド　285
ハット・スイッチ　247
パッド付き壁　295
パッド付き土台　295
ハットバンド　124
バットレス　221
バットレス・ダム　174
バップ・テント　309
ハッブル宇宙望遠鏡　32
馬蹄　84
パティオ　134
パティパン　107
バテン　278
バテン・ポケット　278
ハト　74
パトカー　265
パドック　280
鳩目　122, 125, 127, 286
ハドロサウルス　70
花　48, 50
鼻　76, 77, 78, 79, 85, 90
鼻先　66
鼻面　64, 76, 78, 79, 85
バナナ　113
花の構造　50
パナマ帽　124
ハナマメ　108
花屋　259
離れ岩　31
バニティ・キャビネット　154
バニティ・ミラー　188
羽　61
翅　62
羽根　179
羽根板　141
ハネジューメロン　113
刎ね出し狭間　220
羽根止め　179
ばね枰　170
跳ね橋　220
パネル　136
葉の構造　49
歯の付いたあご　162
パパイヤ　113
はばき金　163
破風　168, 217
ハブ　179, 195
歯ブラシ　133
破片　37

ハボタン　106
ハマナ　106
歯磨き　133
歯磨き剤　133
ハムスター　77
はめ込み台　129
速歩　84
早送りボタン　239, 243
ハヤトウリ　107
早戻しボタン　239
腹　72, 84, 90, 146
バラ　51
腹帯　280
バラクラバ帽　124
パラサウロロフス　70
腹びれ　64, 65
パラフィン製品　181
パラボラ・アンテナ　238
パラボラ反射板　238
ばら窓　221
バラモンジン　104
バランサー　198, 229
バランシング・ベスト　279
バランス・ウエイト　12
パラライカ　225
バリカン　130
バリケード・テープ　265
ハリケーン・ランプ　311
針刺し　214
張り出し　158, 220
張り綱　309
ハリネズミ　76
針差し　214
針山　214
春　33
バルコニー　139
バルコニー窓　139
バルジ　11
春タマネギ　103
バルブ　230
バルブ・ケーシング　230
バルブ・ケース　230
バルブ・ボタン　230
バレー・シューズ　125
バレーボール　299
バレーボール用ボール　299
バレッタ　130
バレリーナ・シューズ　125
バレル　130, 316
ハロー（部）　11
バローリウス橋　97
ハロン棒　280
バン売り場　257
半影　8, 9
半円　171
半円筒ボールト　218
ハンガー・ループ　120
半返し縫い　123
パン・菓子屋　259
バン型トラック　193
バングル　129
半径　171
半月　101
番号灯　187
犯罪防止　264
パン皿　145
反射器　194
反射鏡　167
反射された日射　43
反射（式）望遠鏡　12
反射（式）望遠鏡の断面図　12
反射テープ　263
バンジョー　224
絆創膏　267
パンタグラフ　198, 199

パンタグラフ付きフラッドライト　238
パンチ穴　116
パンチング・ボール　304
パンツ　116, 122, 284, 291, 295, 298
パンティー・ストッキング　119
ハンディ(ー)・フード・プロセッサー　150
ハンティング・キャップ　124
バンド　128, 168
半島　22
パン投入口　151
バンド・エイド　267
ハンド・ガード　306
ハンド型リング　129
ハンド・スプレー　164
ハンド掃除機　159
ハンドソー　161
ハンド・ブレーキ・レバー　188
ハンド・ブレンダー　150
ハンド・プロテクター　306
ハンド・ミキサー　150
バンド・リング　129
ハンドル　131, 163, 164, 165, 188, 191, 195, 278, 287, 306
反トルク・ローター　203
ハンドル支柱　195
ハンドルバー　195, 308
ハンド・レスト　247
搬入区域　256
バンの笛　224
バンパー　192
バンパー・モール　184
バンバイブ　224
バンプ　125
バンプス　125
ハンマー　226
ハンマー・レール　226

ひ

ピアス・イヤリング　129
ピアノ　234
ビア・マグ　144
BMX自転車　195
ビーカー　166
ピーカンナッツ　113
ピー・コート　118
BC　279
ピー・ジャケット　118
ピース　313
ヒーター　153
ビーター　232
ビーチ・バレー（ボール）　299
ビーチ・バレー用ボール　299
ビーツ　104
ビート　104
ピーナッツ　108
ビーバー　77
ピーマン　107
ビーム　170, 275
ビーラー　147
ヒール　229, 285, 286
ヒール・グリップ　125
ビール・ジョッキ　144
ヒール・ストップ　307
ビールとワイン　256
ヒールピース　289
ヒールプレート　288
ビーン・バッグ（チェア）　140
ビオラ　227, 234
控え壁　221
控え柱　221
控えベンチ　301
火掻き棒　158

皮革製品店　258
東　23
東半球　20
皮下組織　101
光　12
ヒキガエル　66
引き出し　141, 143, 153
引き違い窓　137
引き戸　136, 154
曳き馬場　280
引き紐　127
引き船　202
尾脚　58, 62
鼻鏡　79
挽き割りエンドウ　108
鼻腔　97
ピクニック禁止　319
ピクニック地域　319
ひげ　79
ひげぜんまい　169
髭剃り　131
鼻孔　64, 65, 67, 72, 85, 102
鼻腔　97
飛行機　206
飛行機の例　208
鼻口部　76, 78, 79, 85
飛行哺乳動物　82
腓骨　92
尾骨　92
尾骨　93
鼻根　102
膝　78, 85, 90
ピザ　115
膝当て　291, 298, 307
ひさし　124
庇　189, 309
ピザパイ　115
ヒシ　103
肘　78, 82, 85, 91
肘当て　285, 298, 307
肘掛け椅子　140, 268
菱形　172
皮脂腺　101
ビジネス機　208
美術　211
美術監督　272
美術室　268
微小繊維　56
微小体　56
秘書室　269
ビショップ　314
披針形の　49
ビスケット　115
ピスタチオ　113
ピストル　265
ピストル型グリップ　162
ピストル・ケース　265
ピストン・バルブ　230
飛節　78, 84
尾節　58
鼻尖　102
尾そり　203
ひだ　47
額　90
ピタパン　114
左チャンネル　241
鼻中隔　102
微調整竿　170
ピック　225
ピックアップ　229
ピックアップ・セレクター　228
ピックアップ・トラック　186
ピックガード　228
ピッコロ　231, 234
ヒツジ　86
ピッチ　292
ピッチ・ホイール　233

ピッチャー　145, 290
ピッチャーズ・マウンド　290
ピッツァ　115
ピット　281
ヒップ　287
ヒップ・パッド　298
蹄　84
蹄の例　85
ピテ　154
ビデオカセット　240
ビデオカセット・レコーダー　240
ビデオ・ゲーム　316
ビデオ操作部　239
ビデオテープ操作ボタン　240
ビデオ電源ボタン　239
ビデオ・モード　239
ビデオ・レコーダー　240
ビデオ式打ち合わせ　240
尾灯　187, 191, 194
微動載物台　167
微動ハンドル　167
ビトー　306
日時計　168
ヒトコブラクダ　87
人差し指　101
ヒトデ　56
人の歯列　94
一人掛けシート　199
1人用テント　309
ヒナギク　51
避難所　182
避難路　182
火の粉止め（衝立）　158
鼻背　102
火箸　158
火鉢　219
脾腹　84
ヒヒ　83
響き穴　229
皮膚　101
尾部　58, 207
尾部支柱　203
皮膚の表面　101
ピペット　166
ピボット　278
飛膜　82
ヒマワリ　51
紐　286, 291
紐穴　122, 125, 286
紐先金具　122, 125
１３０度　171
百葉箱　38
冷やされた冷却材　178
ビュー・カメラ　236
ビューグル　230
ヒューズ　173, 176
ヒューズ・ホルダー　176
ビュラン　213
ヒョウ　81
鼻葉　82
病院　319
美容院　258
氷河　29, 30, 40
ヒョウガエル　66
錨鎖孔　200
表示画面　240, 243, 244, 245
表示画面設定ボタン　244
拍子記号　222
標識灯　198
病室　266
病室ベッド　266
表示　151, 153
表示パネル　235, 240
表示部　170
表示窓　240, 243, 244, 245, 261
苗条　48

氷晶雨　36
表示ランプ　239
秒針　168
氷舌　29
氷雪気候　34
氷堆丘　28
標的　281
表土　53
表皮　101
標本押さえ　167
表面遮水壁型ダム　174
比翼　116
鼻翼　102
尾翼　207
尾翼形状の例　207
比翼式打ち合い　121
比翼式打ち合わせ　121
火除け　158
日除け　309
ヒヨコ　75
ヒヨコマメ　108
平　123
ピラー　227
避雷器　175, 176
避雷針　135
平泳ぎ泳法　277
平泳ぎターン　277
平泳ぎのキック　277
ヒラガキ　57
開き戸　136
開き窓　137
開き窓枠　137
ピラミッド　217
ピラミッドの入り口　217
平屋住宅　216
鼻梁　85
鼻涙管　102
ひれ　158
広場　250
瓶　166
ピン　155, 156, 281
ピン板　226
ヒンジ　289
ヒンジ・ピン　209
ピンセット　267
ビンディング　288, 289
ビンディング・ペダル　308
ピント調節つまみ　12

ふ

ファ　222
ファースト　290
ファースト・クラス客室　206
ファースト・フード店　259
ファイル　173
ファイル・フォーマット　248
ファインダー　12
ファインダー脚　12
ファウル・ボール　291
ファウル・ライン　281, 290
ファクシミリ　245
ファゴット　231, 234
ファスナー隠し　293
ファンクション・キー　245
ファン内蔵部　131
ファン・ヒーター　158
フィード・チューブ　150
フィードホーン　238
フィールド　292
フィールド・プレーヤー　293
フィールド・ホッケー　293
フィギュア・スケート靴　286
Vネック　120
Vネック・カーディガン　120
VU計　237
VUメーター　237

フィヨルド　31
フィラー・キャップ　192
フィラメント　156
フィルター　135, 153
フィルター・バスケット　151
フィルター・ホルダー　151
フィルム感度設定ボタン　235
フィルム・ディスク　235
フィルム巻き上げモード・ボタン　235
フィルム巻き戻しボタン　235
フィルン　29
フィン　158, 278, 279
フィンガーボード　228, 229
フィンチ　74
封蓋巣房　61
風向計　38, 39
風向測定　39
風向板　158
風車軸　179
ブースター・シート　141
ブースター・パラシュート　14
ブーツ　279, 286, 306, 307
フード　12, 117, 131, 158, 184, 192, 279
封筒型　310
フード付きトレーナー　122
フード・プロセッサー　150
プードル　78
フープ・イヤリング　129
風防　208
風防ガラス　206
ブーム　193, 209
ブーム係　273
風量切り替えスイッチ　131
風力エネルギー　179
風力計　38, 39
風力測定　39
フェアウェイ　282
フェアリング　16
フェイス・オフ・サークル　285
フェイス・オフ・スポット　285
フェイス・マスク　284, 292, 298
フェース　282
フェースプレート　136
フェネック　80
フェリー（ボート）　200, 202
フェルト・ペン　212
フェルト帽　124
フェルマータ　223
フェンス　134, 285
フェンダー　184, 192
フェンネル　105
フォアアーム・パッド　298
フォア・アッパー・トゲルン・スル　201
フォア・アッパー・トップスル　201
フォアコート　303
フォアスル　201
フォアマスト　201
フォア・ロイヤル・スル　201
フォア・ロワー・トゲルン・スル　201
フォア・ロワー・トップスル　201
フォーカスつまみ　240
フォーカス・モード切替ボタン　235
フォーク　12, 146, 195, 306, 308
フォー・ドア・セダン　186
フォーム・パッド　310
フォーム・マット（レス）　310
フォーカス・スイッチ　240
フォッグ・ライト　187, 192
フォッグ・ランプ　187

日本語索引

339

フォボス 6
フォワード 300
フォンデュ・セット 149
フォンデュ鍋 149
フォンデュ・フォーク 146
深揚げ鍋 151
深型両手鍋 149
深皿 145
不活性ガス 156
深鍋 149
吹き口 230, 231
吹き込み管 224, 230, 231
吹き出し口 188
吹き出し口グリル 131
複打ち上げ構造 16
副火道 27
複眼 60, 62
腹脚 62
副鏡 12
複鋸歯状の 49
腹甲 67
輻射式暖房器 158
輻射層 8
副署長室 264
副審 294, 297, 299, 305
復水器 177
復水器逆洗水入り口 177
復水器逆洗水出口 177
復水器冷却水入り口 177
復水器冷却水出口 177
腹足 57
腹大動脈 99
腹直筋 95
腹部 58, 59, 61, 62
複葉 49
膨ら脛 91
袋 112
袋詰め係 257
フクロネズミ 76
ふ骨 92
フジマメ 108
ふ蹠 73
腐食性物質 320
腐植土 53
婦人(用)手袋 123
付随車 199
付属品 194
付属礼拝堂 221
蓋 149, 150, 151, 153, 159, 160
ブタ 86
舞台装置係 273
フタコブラクダ 87
二つ折り札入れ 126
二股の舌 67
二人掛けシート 199
2人用テント 309
フダンソウ 105
縁 128
ブチンゲン 108
プチオニオン 103
縁飾り 141, 229
縁取り 124
縁取り花壇 134
ふつうのさいころ 313
フック 131, 137, 170, 193, 214, 263
フック取り付け板 152
プッシャー 150
プッシュ・アーム 210
プッシュ式電話機 245
プッシュ・ボタン 128, 244, 245
プッシュ・ボタン電話機 245
フット 278
フットツール 140, 143
フット・ストラップ 278
フット・ストレッチャー 278

フット・フォールト・ジャッジ 303
フットボード 142
フットボーラー 298
フットボール用ボール 298
不定根 47
埠頭 200
ブドウ 109
ブドウの断面図 109
ブドウの葉 106
浮動肋骨 92
ブナノキ 54
譜表 222
部分食 8, 9
扶壁 221
踏み板 278
踏切 198
踏切警鐘 198
踏切警標 198
踏切板 274
譜面台 233
譜面立て 233
冬 33
腐葉土 53
フライト 316
フライト・デッキ 14, 206
フライ・パン 149, 311
フライング・ジブ 201
フライング・ロープ 276
ブラウザー 248
フラウト・トラベルソ 231
ブラキオサウルス 71
プラグ 241
プラグ・アダプター 155
ブラシ 159, 163
ブラジャー 119
ブラジルナッツ 113
プラスチックの分別 46
プラスねじ回し 311
ブラスの電極 173
ブラックビーン 108
ブラックベリー 108
フラッシュ 235
フラッシュチューブ 235
フラット 223, 307
フラット・スクリーン・モニター 246
フラット・バック・ブラシ 130
プラットフォーム 307
プラットホーム 255
フラッドライト 238
プラネタリウム 250
フラミンゴ 75
プラム 110
ブランク 313
フランスパン 114
フランス窓 137
フリーズ 217
フリー・スロー・サークル 294
フリー・スロー・ライン 295
フリー・ゾーン 299
フリー棚 152
ブリーチ 231
ブリーチ・ガード 231
プリーツ・スカート 118
フリー 117, 119
ブリーフケース 126
ブリーフス 119
振り子 168
プリセット・ボタン 239, 240
ブリッジ 128, 227, 228, 229
フリップ・ターン 277
プリム 124
浮力調節具 279
プリンセス型ワンピース 118
プリンセス・ドレス 118
フルーツジュース 115
フルート 231, 234

ブルーベリー 109
ブルー・ライン 284
ブルゴーニュ・グラス 144
ブルズ・アイ 316
ブルゾン 117
ブルドーザー 210
ブルドッグ 78
ブルバード 250
フルバック 297
フレア 8
ブレーカー 176, 287
ブレーキ 308
ブレーキ・キャリパー 191
ブレーキ・ペダル 188, 289
ブレーキマン 287
ブレーキ・ライト 187
ブレーキ・ランプ 187
ブレーキ・レバー 195, 289
ブレーキ・レバーとギャレバー 308
ブレーキ・レバーとシフトレバー 308
ブレーキ・ワイヤー 195
ブレード 155, 161, 210, 278, 284, 285, 286
ブレード・カバー 286
ブレード・リフト・シリンダー 210
フレーム 126, 127, 158, 173, 191, 209, 210, 275, 291, 302, 308, 309
フレーム・パッド 275
プレーヤー用スティック 285
プレーリー 22
フレスコ画 218
フレット 228, 229
プレパラート 167
ブレンダー 150
フレンチ・ホルン 230, 234
フロア・スタンド 157
フロア・タム 232
フロアボード 191
フロア・ランプ 157
ブロウ・ブラシとアイ・ラッシュ・コーム 133
ブローチ 129
フロート 208
フロート水上機 208
プログラマブル・ボタン 247
プログラム・セレクター 233
ブロッコリ 105
ブロッコリカブ 105
フロッピー・イジェクト・ボタン 246
フロッピー・ディスク 246
フロッピー・ディスク・イジェクト・ボタン 246
フロッピー(ディスク)ドライブ 246
プロテクション・エリア 304
プロデューサー 273
プロナオス 217
プロペラ 201
プロミネンス 8
プロムナード・デッキ 201
フロント・ウインド 184
フロント・エンド・ローダー 209
フロント・ガード 184
フロント・ガラス 184, 192
フロント・コンプレッション・ベルト 312
フロント・スポイラー 184
フロント板 136
フロント・バンパー・スポイラー 184

フロント・ビーム 170
フロント・ピックアップ 228
フロント・フェンダー 191
フロント・フォーク 308
フロント・ホーク 308
分解者 41
文化機関 249
噴火性の火山 27
噴火中の火山 27
噴気 27
噴気孔 88
分針 168
分水トンネル 174
吻端 66, 67
分鍋 170
分度器 271
分別工場 46
分別収集 46
分別センター 46
噴霧ホース 154

へ

ヘア・アイロン 130
ヘア・コンディショナー 132
ヘア・スタイリスト 272
ヘア・ドライヤー 131
ヘア・ピン 130
平均台 274, 275
平行四辺形 172
平行棒 275
平行六面体 172
米国居住モジュール 14
米国実験モジュール 14
餅盤 27
平面型ディスプレイ 246
平面鏡 12
平面交差 198
平面図法 21
平面投射図 18
平野 22, 30
ベイル 292
ベイロード 16
ベイロード・アダプター 16
ベインティング・ナイフ 212
ベーカリー 257
ベーグル 114
ベース 162, 247
ベース・ギター 229
ベース・コントロール 229
ベース・ピックアップ 228
ベース・プレート 162, 289
ベースライン 303
ヘーゼルナッツ 113
ペーパー・ガイド 245
ペーパー・クリップ 270
ベーリング海 19
ヘ音記号 222
ベカンナッツ 113
壁龕 219
壁塔 220
ペグ 227, 228, 229
ベゴニア 51
舳 201
ベダル 129
臍 90
ペダル 194, 227, 232, 308
ペダル・レール 226
ペチコート 119
ヘチマカボチャ 107
ヘチマスポンジ 132
へちまたわし 132
ヘッド 131, 228, 229, 282, 293, 302
ベッド 142, 189, 275
ヘッド・カバー 283
ヘッドギア 284, 304

ベット・ショップ 258
ヘッド・セット 245
ベッドとマット(レス) 310
ヘッドバンド 241, 243
ヘッドピン 281
ペット・フードとペット用品 257
ヘッドボード 141, 142
ヘッドホン 241, 243
ヘッドホン・ジャック 242
ヘッドホン端子 233, 242
ヘッドホン・プラグ 243
ベッド用テーブル 266
ヘッドライト 184, 187, 192, 195, 197, 198
ヘッドライト・スイッチ 188
ヘッド・ラインズマン 297
ヘッドランプ 187, 192, 195
ベッド・ランプ 266
ペディメント 168, 217
ペトリ皿 166
ペナルティ・アーク 300
ペナルティ(ー)・ボックス 284
ペナルティ(ー)・ボックス係員 284
ペナルティ・エリア 300
ペナルティ・エリア・ライン 300
ペナルティ・キック・マーク 300
ペニス 90
ベニテングタケ 47
ベニバナインゲン 108
ペパロニ 115
ヘビ 67
ベビー・チェア 141
ベビー・ベッド 141
ペポカボチャ 107
へら 148
へら形の 49
ヘラコウモリ 82
ペリカン 75
ヘリコプター 203
ヘリコプターの例 203
ベル 230, 231
ペルオキシソーム 56
ベルガモット 112
ベル支柱 231
ベルシャネコ 79
ベルト 116
ベルト・コンベヤー 252
ベルト通し 116, 312
ベルト・ループ 312
ベルト・ローダー車 205
ヘルメット 17, 263, 280, 284, 287, 289, 292, 298, 306, 307, 308
ヘルメット接続リング 17
ベレー帽 124
ベロ 122, 125, 126, 286, 289
ペン 26
変圧器 157, 175, 176, 177
変圧器塔 174, 175
便器 154
変記号 223
ペンギン 75
便座 154
辺材 53
ペン先 270
便所 218
変成岩 24
弁足 73
変速機 308
変速レバー 188, 195
ペンダント 129, 157
ペンダントライト 157
ベンチ 140, 255, 259, 290
ベンド 128
扁桃 102
ベント・ブラシ 130

ペン・ブレード 311
扁平骨 93
ペン・ホルダー 126
弁膜 73

ほ

帆 179, 278
ボア 68
保安炎筒 265
ホイール 164, 245, 246
ホイール・カバー 185
ホイール・キャップ 185
ホイール・トラクター 209
ホイール・マウス 246
ホイール・ローダー 209
ホイッパー 148
ポインター 158, 170
ポイント 286, 315, 316
ポイント・ガード 294
望 10
ボウ 281
方位線 312
防火着 262, 263
防火室洗濯室 262
防火帽 263
帯 158, 159
防御柵 220
防具 285, 298
棒グラフ型ピーク・メーター 237
防眩ミラー 188
方向キー 316
縫工筋 95
方向指示灯 187, 191
方向指示表示灯 188
方向舵 15, 179, 201, 207
方向ボタン 316
防護カップ 285, 298
報告書作成室 264
防護服 306
防護ヘルメット 191, 194
防護眼鏡 306
防災教育担当官室 263
胞子 47
帽子 265
蜂児圏 61
胞子嚢群 47
帽子のリボン 124
蜂児脾 61
放射糸 59
放射性物質 320
放射層 8
放射暖房器 158
宝飾店 258
宝飾品 129
防塵マスク着用 320
放水管 175
放水銃 263
放水ノズル 263
放水路 174
包装商品 256
帽体 191
膨張室 169
防毒マスク着用 320
放熱 14, 197
放熱パネル 15
放物面鏡 12
ボウラー 281, 292
ボウリング 281
ボウリング・アレー 281
ボウリング・クリース 292
ボウリング・ボール 281
ボウリング・レーン 281
ボウル 148
ホウレンソウ 106
頬 78, 90
ボー 124

ポーカー・ダイス 313
ホーク 308
ホーザリー 119
ホオジロザメ 64
ホース 262
ホース掛け 262
ホース乾燥機 262
ホオズキ 109
ホース車 165
ホースラディッシュ 104
ボーダー花壇 134
ボー・タイ 116
ポータブル音響機器 242
ポータブルＣＤプレーヤー 243
ポータブルＣＤラジカセ 242
ポータブル・シャワー・ヘッド 154
ポータブル・デジタル・オーディオ・プレーヤー 243
ポータブル・ラジオ 242
ポータブル・ラジカセ 243
ポーチ 135, 219
ポーチ・ドーム 219
ボード 278, 285, 313
ボートと船の例 202
ボートの部分名称 278
頬紅 133
ホーム 255
ホームストレッチ 280
ホームの縁石 255
ホーム・ユーザー 249
ボーリング場 258
ホール 282
ボール 281, 166
ボール・パーソン 302
ボール・ペン 270
ボール・ボーイ 302
ボール・ライト 157
ボール・リターン 281
ホーン 188
ボーン 314
保温トレイ 151
保温ヒーター 151
捕獲 315
ほかの指に対して向かい合わせになる親指 83
保管室 265
ボギー台車 196
歩脚 59
補強材 179
補強壁 219
ボクサー 304
ボクサー・ショーツ 122
ボクサー・パンツ 122
ボクシング 304
北西 23
踝部 73
火口 149, 153
火口格子 153
北東 23
北北西 23
北北東 23
踝膜 73
帆桁 179, 201
ポケット 126, 281, 283
ポケット・カメラ 236
ポケット・クリップ 270
保健機関 249
歩行者通行止め 317, 318
保護ガラス 284
保護具 320
保護歯周組織 94
保護層 7
保護板 306, 316
保護帽着用 320
保護眼鏡着用 320
星 315

ポジション 294, 300
ポジション・マーク 228, 229
捕手 290, 291
補助椅子 141
補助コンセント 153
補助ハンドル 162
補助目盛り 170
補助翼 206
ポスター 272
ボタン 116, 120, 150, 224
ボタン穴 116
ボタン付き前開き 116, 120
ボタン留め 116
ホチキス 270
ホチキス芯 270
ホチキス針 270
ホチキス・リムーバー 270
北極 19
北極海 18, 19
ホッキョクグマ 81
北極圏 20
北極地方 18
ホック 286
ボックス・スプリング 142
ボックス席 260
ホッケー 293
ホッケー・ボール 293
ホッチキス 270
ホッチキス芯 270
ホッチキス針 270
ホッチキス・リムーバー 270
ホット・シュー接点 235
ホット・プレート 151
ポッピング・クリース 292
ポップ・アップ・テント 309
ボディー 226, 228, 229, 287
ボディー・ケア 132
ボディー・スーツ 119
ボディー・フラップ 15
ボディ・スーツ 119
ホテル 251
ホテル予約カウンター 252
ホテル予約デスク 252
歩道 135
歩道橋 220, 255
ボトム 307
ボトル 166, 195, 311
ボトル・ケージ 195
哺乳動物 76
帆布 179
骨 128
骨受け 128
骨の種類 93
ホバークラフト 202
帆柱 278
ボビー・ピン 130
ボブスレー、リュージュ、スケルトン 287
ポプラ 54
歩兵 314
歩法 84
歩様 84
ポラロイド・カメラ 236
濠 220
ボリューム・コントロール 228, 233
ボリュームつまみ 229
ホルスター 265
ホルダー 166
ポロ・シャツ 120, 303
ボロ・ドレス 118
ボロ・ワンピース 118
ボワロー 103
本位記号 223
本影 8, 9
ボンゴ 232

本締めボルト 136
本初子午線 20
本底 122, 125
本体 131, 226, 288
ポンチョ 118
ポンツーン 183
ボンネット 184, 192
本部席 284
ポンプ番号 261
本丸 220
本屋 258

ま

マーカー 271, 281
マーカー・ライト 192
マーシュ 106
マーモット 77
マイク 237, 238, 240, 244, 245, 247, 265
マイク係 273
マイク付きヘッドホン 245
マイク・ブーム 238
マイク・ブーム・スタンド 238
マイクロ・コンパクト・カー 186
マイクロバス 190
マイクロ波中継局 248
マイクロホン 237, 238, 240, 244, 245, 247, 265
マイクロホン・ブーム 238
マイクロホン・ブーム・スタンド 238
埋設式プール 135
マイナスの電極 173
マウス・パイプ 230
マウス・パッド 246
マウスピース 230, 231, 233
マウス・ピース 298
マウスピース・レシーバー 230
マウンテン・バイキング 308
マウンテン・バイク 195
前脚 60, 62
前肢 66, 76
前足 76
前髪 85
前華 125
前立て 116, 117, 121
前ディレーラー 194
前ブレーキ 195
前変速機 194
前ポケット 116, 127
前身 116
前身頃 116
マカク 83
まき 124
巻き上げ機 193
巻き上げ装置 169
巻き上げロープ 163
巻き尺 161, 214
巻き線 227
巻き取りリール 243
薪箱 158
薪運び台 158
巻き戻しボタン 243
まぐさ 136, 158
幕壁 220
マグマ 27
マグマ溜り 27
枕 142
枕カバー 142
枕木 198
枕ばね 199
枕用クッション 142
マグロ 65
摩擦防止パッド 289
マス 65
マスク 279, 291

マスクメロン 113
マスト 238, 278
マスト・スリーブ 278
マスト・フット 278
マストヘッド 278
股 117
股下 305
股下スナップ・ボタン 121
股布 117
襠 117
待合室 264
襠付きの折り鞄 126
マチネ・レングス・ネックレス 129
マツ 55
マッコウクジラ 89
マッサージ・グローブ 132
マッシャー 148
末端堆石 29
マット・チェアマン 304
マッド・フラップ 185, 192
マットレス 141, 142
マットレス・カバー 142
マツの実 55, 113
マテガイ 57
的 281
窓 137, 139, 152, 153, 189, 199, 206
窓ガラス 137
窓の例 137
窓枠 137
マノメーター 267
マフィン型 148
瞼 67
マフラー 191
マフラー・フェルト 226
マフラー・ペダル 226
魔法瓶 311
ママー型 310
マメモヤシ 108
豆類 108
マラカイト 25
マランガ 104
丸座 136
丸底フラスコ 166
丸太小屋 215
丸鋸 162
丸鋸刃 162
マルハナバチ 63
丸筆 212
マルメロ 111
マレット 232
マンクス 79
満月 10
マンゴー 113
マンダリン 112
マンドリン 225
マントルピース 158
万年筆 270
万年雪 28, 29
万力 161

み

ミ 222
三日月 10
身柄拘束室 265
幹 52
ミキサー 150
ミキサー・ボトル 150
ミキシング・ボウル 148
右チャンネル 241
幹の断面図 53
ミクロフィラメント 56
岬 22, 31
ミシガン・スノーシュー 288

ミシン 214
湖 9, 22, 28, 30
水掻き 66, 73
水掻きのある足 66
水が蒸気になる 178
水が使用済みの蒸気を冷却する 178
水着 122
水切りボウル 147
水差し 144, 145
水タンク 197, 311
水鳥 73
水の循環 42
水の備蓄 176
水は蒸気発生器に送り戻される 178
水辺の鳥と海辺の鳥の例 75
ミズン・スル 201
ミズンマスト 201
未成年者房 264
溝 146, 281, 289
霙 36
蜜入れ 61
ミット 123
ミッド・ソール 122
ミツバチ 60
ミツバチの巣の断面図 61
ミツバチの巣箱 61
蜜房 61
ミトコンドリア 56
緑 211
ミドル・ピックアップ 228
ミドル・ラインバッカー 296
ミトン 123
港 200
南 23
南アメリカ 18
南回帰線 20
南シナ海 19
南半球 20
ミナレット 219
ミニバン 186
峰 28, 146
身の回り品 123
ミフラーブ 219
ミフラーブ・ドーム 219
ミマス 7
耳 79, 82, 90, 140
耳当て 128
耳覆い 124
耳隠し 124
耳栓着用 320
耳の構造 100
ミヤコドリ 75
ミュート 230
ミラー 269
ミランダ 7
ミンク 80
民族楽器 224
ミンバル 219

む

ムールガイ 57
無蓋車 196
無機物 41
ムクドリ 74
蒸し器用かご 149
虫眼鏡 311
無線アンテナ 200, 306
無線機 265
鞭 280
霧灯 187, 192
胸びれ 64, 65, 88
胸 72, 85

胸当て 121, 291, 298
胸ポケット 116
棟割り住宅 216
ムフロン 86
紫 211
ムラサキウマゴヤシ 108

め

目 37, 57, 58, 59, 67, 79, 88, 90, 102, 313
芽 103
冥王星 7
メイキング・シーツ 142
名所 23
明滅灯 198
メインクーン 79
メイン・スタンド 191
メイン・スル 201
メインマスト 201
メウシ 86
メーキャップ 133
メーキャップ係 272
メカジキ 65
メカニカル・ステージ 167
メカニカル・ステージ前後動ハンドル 167
眼鏡 128
眼鏡ケース 126
眼鏡店 259
眼鏡の各部 128
眼鏡レンズ 128
メキャベツ 106
雌しべ 50
メス・シリンダー 166
目出し帽 124
メッカの方向 219
滅菌圧定布 267
滅菌ガーゼ 267
メッシュ窓 309
メニュー 260
目の壁 37
メモ・パッド 270
目盛り 161, 169, 170, 271, 312
メモリー・カード差込口 316
メモリー・カード・スロット 316
メモリー・ボタン 244
目盛り盤 170, 312
メロンくり抜き器 147
メロン類 113
メンズ・バッグ 127
免税店 253
面体 263
メンドリ 75
麺棒 148
綿棒 267

も

毛衣 77
毛縁の 49
毛幹 101
毛球 101
猛禽 73
毛細管 169
毛細血管 101
盲腸 96
猛毒キノコ 47
毛乳頭 101
毛嚢 101
毛髪 91
毛布 142
毛包 101
モーター 162, 165
モーター・スポーツ 306
モーター付きボギー台車 199

モーター内蔵部　150
モーター部　198
モーター・ホーム　189
モーター・ヨット　202
モード切り換えスイッチ　242
モーペッド　191
モカシン　125
木材　217, 218
木星　6
木炭　212
木部放射組織　53
モグラ　76
モザイク　218
文字盤　168
モジュレーション・ホイール　233
モスク　219
モダン　128
持ち送り　220
持ち送り台　141
持ち手　131, 132, 133, 214, 242
木管楽器群　234
木管楽器の仲間　234
木琴　232, 234
木工用工具　161
モップ　159
モデム　248
モトクロス・スーパークロス用のオートバイ　306
モニター　246
物置　134
モノクル　128
モミ　55
モモ　110
腿　73
股当て　298
モモの断面図　110
霧　36
モルデント　223
モルモット　77
モンキー・レンチ　162

や

矢　281
ヤード・ライン　296
ヤエナリ　108
やかん　151
夜間撮影モード切り換えスイッチ　240
ヤギ　86
焼き網　153
焼き色調節つまみ　151
野球　290
野球ボール　291
薬　50
ヤク　86
役員席　284
薬品収納庫　267
野菜　103
野菜ブラシ　147
野菜ボウル　145
野菜保存室　152
ヤシ　54
椰子林　29
野手用グローブ　291
やすり　311
薬局　258, 319
矢筒　281
ヤナギ　54
柳材　292
屋根　61, 135, 189
屋根飾り　217
屋根窓　134
ヤベトゥス　7
山　28
ヤマアラシ　77
山高帽　124
ヤマトシビレエイ　64
ヤムイモ　104
矢来　220
ヤリイカ　57

ゆ

油圧式ショベル　209
有蓋車　197
遊撃手　290
U字管　231
雄蕊　111
Uターン禁止　318
有袋動物の例　76
有袋哺乳動物　76
有蹄哺乳動物　84
有蹄哺乳動物の例　86
誘導路　204
誘導路線　205
有毒性物質　320
融氷水　29
郵便局　259
ユーフォニウム　230
遊歩デッキ　201
ユーラシア　18
床　179
床板　191
床運動マット　274
床部　179
床マット　274
雪　36
行き先表示板　255
油性パステル　212
湯煎鍋　149
輸送　181
輸送館　208
輸送と重機　182
ユニフォーム　291, 293, 295, 298, 301
指　66, 77, 291
指当て　214
指貝　231
指掛け（リング）　230
指時計　168
指なしアーム・ロング　123
指貫き　214
指輪の各部　129
弓　227, 281
弓毛　227
弓竿　227
弓先　227
弓鋸　312
弓元　227
ユリ　50
揺り椅子　140
ユルト　215
揺れ止め　209

よ

与圧服　17
葉腋　49
葉縁　49
溶岩岩　27
溶岩流　27
容器　150
陽極　175
用具库　268
用件再生ボタン　244
用件メッセージ録音カセット　244
幼児　48, 52
葉菜類　106
葉鞘　49
幼児用家具　141
葉身　47, 49
幼虫　61, 62
巣頂　49
ヨウトウ　113
腰部　91
葉柄　47, 49
葉脈　49
ヨーグルト　114
ヨーロッパ　19
ヨーロッパ型コンセント　155
ヨーロッパ型プラグ　155
ヨーロッパバイ　57
ヨーロッパヤマウズラ　74
翼　207
翼形状の例　206
翼桁　206
翼小骨　206
翼支柱　208
浴室　139, 154, 266
浴室の天窓　139
浴槽　139, 154
翼端小翼　208
浴用タオル　132
横板　140, 229
横糸　59
横木　140, 292
横桟　163
横の動き　314
横揺れ防止構造　306
汚れ除け　153, 160
余水導水路　174
余水門扉　174
余水路　174
4人乗りボブスレー　287
四番車　169
呼び出し音量調節パネル　244
予備レギュレーター　279
読み出し面　243
読み取り鏡　17
鎧板　221
鎧戸　137
鎧窓　137
45度　171
四蹄　85
4度　222
4分の3拍子　222
4分の4拍子　222
4本マスト・バーク　201
4本マスト・バーク型帆船　201

ら

ラ　222
ラージ・ブレード　311
雷雨　36
ライオン　81
ライチ　113
ライティング・ケース　126
ライト　290, 291
ライト・アタッカー　299
ライト・インサイド　293
ライト・インサイド・フォワード　293
ライト・ウィング　284, 293
ライト・ガード　297
ライト・コーナーバック　296
ライト・サービス・コート　303
ライト・セーフティ　296
ライト・タックル　297
ライト・ディフェンシブ・エンド　296
ライト・ディフェンシブ・タックル　296
ライト・ディフェンス　285
ライト・ハーフ　293
ライト・バック　293, 299, 300
ライト・フォワード　294
ライト・ミッドフィルダー　300
ライニング　125, 286
ライマメ　108
ライム　112
ライン　299
ライン・ジャッジ　274, 297
ラインズマン　284, 299, 301, 302
ラウド・ペダル　226, 233
落石注意　317, 318
落石の恐れあり　317, 318
ラクレット・グリル　151
ラケット・スポーツ　302
ラコリス　27
ラジエーター　197
ラジエーター・グリル　192
ラジオ　237
ラズベリー　109
ラズベリーの断面図　109
螺旋　172
螺旋錐　162
螺層　57
ラダー　15, 207, 278
ラダー・ロープ　278
落下防止用柵　141
ラッチ・ボルト　136
ラッパズイセン　51
ラディッキョ　106
羅牌　23
ラピス・ラズリ　129
ラフ　278, 282
ラブ・シート　140
ラブ・チェア　140
ラマ　87
ラムカン皿　144
ラン　50
卵黄　72
卵殻　72
卵形の　49
ランジェリー・ショップ　258
乱層雲　35
ランドセル　271
ランナー　315
ランニング・シャツ　117
ランニング・シューズ　122
卵白　72
ランプ　167, 182
ランプ・ソケット　156

り

リアス式海岸　31
リア・ビーム　170
リア・ピックアップ　228
リーキ　103
リーチ　278
リード　231
リード・イン・エリア　243
リード・イン領域　243
リード・ピックアップ　228
リール　240
理科室　268
リガチャー　231
リキッド・アイライナー　133
リキッド・ファンデーション　133
リキッド・マスカラ　133
陸繋島　31
陸生鳥類の例　74
リコーダー　231
リサイクリング　46
リサイクル容器　46
リス　77
リスト・ガード　307
リスト・ストラップ　288, 289
リストバンド　298, 303
リズム設定ボタン　233

リズム・セレクター 233
リズム・ピックアップ 228
リセット・キー 245
リセット・ボタン 168, 246, 316
リソゾーム 56
リターン・クリース 292
立体 172
リッパー 210
リッパー・シャンク 210
リップ 307
立方体 172
立面図 138
リネン類 142
リブ 210
リフト・アーム 209
リフト・シリンダー 193, 263
リブ・パッド 298
リベロ 299, 300
リボソーム 56
リボゾーム 56
リム 128, 191, 195
リムーバー 270
リムジン 186
リモート・マニピュレーター・システム 14
リモコン 239
リモコン受光部 239
リモコン受信部 239
リモコン端末 235
竜骨 64
リュージュ・レーサー 287
竜頭 168
流星 32
流通倉庫 200
留点 169
流木路 174
梁 215
両替所 319
料金表示窓 261
両生類 66
両生類の例 66
両刃かみそり 131
量表示窓 261
両開き窓 137
料理包丁 148
旅客駅 253
旅客ターミナル 205, 252
旅客搭乗橋 253
旅客ホーム 253
旅客列車 196, 253
リョクトウ 108
旅行鞄 127
旅行代理店 258
リラ 225
リリース・レバー 162, 289
輪環面 172
リンク 284
リング 168, 170, 295, 304
リンク・コーナー 284
リングサイド 304
リング・バインダー 271
リング・ファイル 271
リング・ポスト 304
リンゴ 111
リンゴの断面図 111
臨時記号 223
リンネル類 142
鱗片葉 103

る

涙丘 102
涙小管 102
涙腺 102
塁壁 220

ルーク 314
ルーズ・リーフ 271
ルーター 248
ルーフ 185, 189
ループ 182, 309
ルーフ・ラック 189
ルーペ 167, 311
ルーペと顕微鏡 167
ルーム・ミラー 188
留守番電話機 244
ルッコラ 106
ルバーブ 105
ルビー 129
ルピナス 108

れ

レ 222
レア 7
冷蔵庫 143, 152, 260
冷蔵室 152, 256, 257
冷蔵室ドア 152
冷蔵車 196
冷蔵倉庫 200
冷蔵陳列ケース 260
冷帯気候 34
霊長類 83
霊長類の動物の例 83
0度 171
冷凍庫 143, 152, 260
冷凍室 152
冷凍室ドア 152
冷凍食品 257
冷凍食品保存庫 257
冷凍陳列棚 256
礼拝堂 219, 220
レインコート 117
レーキ 165
レーキング・コーニス 217
レーザー・プリンター 247
レードル 148
レール 198
レーン 276
レオタード 122
レガーズ 287, 291, 292
レコード・プレーヤー 241
レジ 257
レシーバー 245, 302
レジ係 257
レジスター 257
レジデント 266
レジャーとゲーム 309
レスト・エリア 23
レストラン 251, 258, 260, 319
レスラー 304
レスリング 304
レスリング・エリア 304
列 133
レッカー・クレーン 193
レッカー車 193
レッグ 164
レッグ・ウォーマー 122
レッグ・ガード 291, 292
列車時刻表 253
列島 22
裂片状の 49
レバー 132, 151, 162
レバー式コルク抜き 147
レバノンスギ 55
レフェリー 284, 293, 297, 299, 300, 304
レフト 290
レフト・アタッカー 299
レフト・インサイド 293

レフト・インサイド・フォワード 293
レフト・ウィング 284, 293
レフト・ガード 297
レフト・コーナーバック 296
レフト・サービス・コート 303
レフト・セーフティ 296
レフト・タックル 297
レフト・ディフェンシブ・エンド 296
レフト・ディフェンシブ・タックル 296
レフト・ディフェンス 285
レフト・ハーフ 293
レフト・バック 293, 299, 300
レフト・フォワード 294
レフト・ミッドフィルダー 300
レフリー 284, 293, 297, 299, 300, 304
レボルバー 167
レモン 112
レモン搾り器 147, 151
連音 223
連結突起 198
連結器ヘッド 197
連結装置 192
連結バス 190
レンジ上面 153
レンジ上面の縁 153
レンジファインダー・カメラ 236
レンジ・フード 143, 152
レンジ・プレート 143
レンジ窓 152, 153
練習グリーン 282
レンズ 235, 247
レンズ・キャップ 235
レンズ付きフィルム 236
レンズマメ 108
連接バス 190
連棟住宅 216
連絡 315
連絡通路 14, 182
連絡板 268
連絡路 182

ろ

ロア・シェル 289
漏斗 57
漏斗雲 37
ローイングとスカーリング 278
ローイングとスカリング 278
ローイングと幅寄せ 278
ロースト鍋 149
ローター 203
ローター・ハブ 203
ローター・ブレード 203
ローター・ヘッド 203
ロード・レース 308
ロード・レース用自転車とサイクリスト 308
ロー・ビーム 187
ロープ 304, 309
ローファー 125
ロープ・ネックレス 129
ローマンシャン 108
ローラー・カバー 163
ローラー・スポーツ 307
ローラー刷毛とトレイ 163
ローラー・ブラシ 307
ローラー・フレーム 163
ロール・ブラシ 130
録音装置 273
録音テープ 243
録音用竿持ち 273

録画テープ 240
録画編集ボタン 240
録画ボタン 239, 240
64分音符 223
64分休符 223
6度 222
ロケット 106, 129
ロケット・エンジン 16
ロシア・モジュール 14
露出モード・ボタン 235
路線図 254
路線表示板 199
炉棚 158
ロッカー・ルーム 262
ロッキング・チェア 140
ロッキング・プライヤー 162
ロック 194
肋甲板 67
肋骨 92
肋骨当て 298
ロッジ型テント 309
ロバ 87
露盤 217
ロビー 252
ロブスター 58
ロブスターの形態図 58
ロボット・アーム 14
ロメインレタス 106
路面電車 199
ロング・ブーツ 125
ロンパース 121

わ

ワードローブ 139
ワイド・レシーバー 297
ワイパー 184
ワイパー・スイッチ 188
ワイヤー・ブラシ 232
ワイン・セラー 260
ワイン貯蔵庫 260
和音 223
若芽 53
腋の下 90
脇柱 136
脇腹 73, 84
湧き水 30
枠 137, 275
枠糸 59
枠框 141
惑星と衛星 6
惑星の軌道 6
ワゴン車 186
ワゴン・テント 309
ワサビダイコン 104
ワシ 74
ワジ 29
山 128
ワックス・クレヨン 212
ワッシャー 153
ワッフル焼き器 150
藁葺き小屋 215
割りエンドウ 108
湾 9, 22
腕骨 92
腕橈骨筋 95
ワン・ピース 287

ENGLISH INDEX

0° 171
1/10 second hand 168
130° 171
22 m line 293
240° 171
35 mm still camera 17
360° 171
45° 171
5 m line 293
90° 171

A

A 222
abdomen 58, 59, 61, 62, 72, 90
abdominal aorta 99
abdominal rectus 95
abdominal segment 62
ablutions fountain 219
above ground swimming pool 135
absorbed solar radiation 43
absorbent cotton 267
absorption by clouds 43
absorption by Earth surface 43
abutment 183, 221
Abyssinian 79
acceleration lane 182
accent mark 223
access road 204
access server 249
accessories 194
accessory pouch 281
accessory shoe 235
accidentals 223
accordion 224
accuracy sports 281
ace 313
achene 109
acid rain 45
acorn squash 107
acoustic guitar 229
acoustic meatus 100
acroterion 217
action buttons 316
action of wind 42
actor 272
actors' seats 272
actress 273
actual temperature 158
acute angle 171
Adam's apple 90
adhesive bandage 267
adhesive tape 267
adipose tissue 101
adjustable channel 162
adjustable clamp 157
adjustable lamp 157
adjustable strap 121
adjusting band 241
adjusting buckle 307
adjusting catch 289
adjusting screw 162
adjusting tube 274
adjustment slide 116
administration 269
administrative office 263, 264
adobe house 215

adult's skull 93
adventitious roots 47
advertising panel 254
advertising sign 199
adzuki bean 108
aerial ladder truck 263
aerodynamic brake 179
Africa 19
Afro pick 130
after shave 131
agricultural pollution 44
aileron 206
air compressor 197
air concentrator 131
air conditioner 189
air conditioning system 43
air filter 197
air hole 270
air horn 192
air hose 279
air inlet 203
air mattress 310
air pollutants 45
air pollution 44
air pre-cleaner filter 210
air pressure, measure 39
air pump 261
air shaft 217
air space 72
air transport 203
air unit 122
air-inlet grille 131
air-outlet grille 131
air-supply tube 263
aircraft maintenance truck 204
aircraft weather station 38
airliner 32
airplane 206
airport 23, 204
aisle 256
ala 102
albumen 72
alcohol bulb 169
alcohol column 169
alfalfa 108
alga 47
alga, lichen, moss, and fern 47
alighting board 61
alkekengi 109
alley 302
alligator 69
allosaurus 70
almond 110, 113
alphanumeric keyboard 261
alphanumeric keypad 245
alpine salamander 66
alpine skier 289
alpine skiing 289
alpine snowboard 287
altitude clamp 12
altitude fine adjustment 12
altitude scale 32
altocumulus 35
altostratus 35
aluminum frame 288
aluminum recycling container 46
alveolar bone 94

AM antenna 241
ambulance 267
ambulance attendant's seat 267
ambulance helicopter 203
American football 296
American plug 155
American shorthair 79
amethyst 129
ammunition pouch 265
amoeba 56
amphibians 66
amphibians, examples 66
amphitheater, Roman 218
amplifier 241
anal clasper 62
anal fin 64, 65
analog camcorder 240
analog watch 168
anatomy 96
anatomy, human being 96
anchor point 59
anchor-windlass room 200
anchorage block 183
anemometer 38, 39
angles, examples 171
animal cell 56
animal dung 45
animal kingdom 56
ankle 90
ankylosaurus 71
announcer turret 237
annual ring 53
annular eclipse 8
anorak 122
ant 63
Antarctic Circle 20
Antarctica 19
antefix 217
antenna 58, 60, 62, 185, 203, 206, 241,
   242, 245, 265
antennule 58
anterior fontanelle 93
anterior nasal spine 93
anterior tibial 95
anterior tibial artery 99
anther 50
anti-torque tail rotor 203
anticollision light 206
antifriction pad 289
antiseptic 267
antislip shoe 163
anus 96
aorta 98
aorta, arch 98, 99
apex 57
apocrine sweat gland 101
Apollo 13
apparatus room 262
apple 111
apple corer 147
apple, section 111
appoggiatura 223
approach 281
approach ramp 183
approach runs 274
apricot 110
apron 140, 191, 204, 304

apsidiole 221
aquamarine 129
aquatic bird 73
arachnids 59
arachnids, examples 59
arbitration committee 305
arc 171
arcade 218, 221
arch bridge 183
arch dam 174
arch of aorta 98, 99
arch of foot artery 99
archer 281
archery 281
archipelago 22
architectural works 217
architecture 215
architrave 217
archives 265
Arctic 18
Arctic Circle 20
Arctic Ocean 18, 19
arena 218
Ariane IV 16
Ariane V 16
Ariel 7
arm 83, 91, 157, 167, 209
arm guard 281, 298
armchair 140, 268
armless chair 268
armoire 141
armpit 90
arpeggio 223
arrow 281
art director 272
art room 268
arteries 99
artichoke 105
articulated bus 190
artificial satellite 32
arts 211
arugula 106
ascending colon 96
ascending passage 217
ash layer 27
Asia 19
asparagus 105
asphalt 181
aspirator 267
aspirin 267
assistant camera operator 272
assistant coach 285, 295
assistant director 273
assistant property man 273
asteroid belt 6
astronomical observation 12
astronomy 6
athletic shirt 117
Atlantic Ocean 18
atmosphere 32, 41
atoll 31
atrium 218
attaché case 126
attack line 299
attack zone 299
attitude control thrusters 14
audio console 237

345

audio monitor 237
audio system 188
auditory meatus, external 93
auditory ossicles 100
auger bit, solid center 162
auricle 100
authorized landfill site 44
auto-reverse button 243
automatic dialer index 244
automatic drip coffee maker 151
automatically controlled door 252
automobile 184
automobile car 197
autumn 33
autumn squash 107
autumnal equinox 33
auxiliary handle 162
avocado 107
awl 311
axillary artery 99
axillary bud 48
axillary vein 99
axle 196, 307
azimuth clamp 12
azimuth fine adjustment 12
Aztec temple 219

B

B 222
baboon 83
back 73, 78, 84, 91, 101, 140, 141, 146, 161
back brush 132
back judge 297
back of a glove 123
back suspension 308
back zone 299
backboard 295
backboard support 295
backcourt 303
backgammon 315
backguard 153, 160
backhoe 209
backhoe controls 209
backpack 312
backstay 286
backstop 290, 295
backstretch 280
backstroke 277
backstroke start 277
backstroke turn indicator 277
backward bucket 209
bactrian camel 87
badge 265
badger 80
bag well 283
bagel 114
baggage cart 253
baggage check-in counter 252
baggage claim area 252
baggage compartment 198, 203
baggage conveyor 205
baggage room 253
baggage trailer 205
bagger 257
bagpipes 224

baguette 114
bail 292
bailey 220
bakery 257
balaclava 124
balalaika 225
balance beam 274, 275
balancer 229
balcony 139
balcony window 139
baling 46
ball 281
ball boy 302
ball return 281
ball sports 290
ball stand 281
ballerina 125
ballpoint pen 270
bamboo shoot 105
banana 113
band ring 129
bangle 129
banjo 224
bank 259
bar 128, 258, 260, 315
bar counter 260
bar line 222
bar stool 140, 260
barber comb 130
bargraph-type peak meter 237
bark 53
barmaid 260
barograph 39
barrel 130, 131, 270, 316
barrel vault 218
barrette 130
barrier 141
barrier barricade tape 265
barrier beach 31
basalt 25
basaltic layer 24
base 103, 156, 157, 158, 166, 167, 170, 179, 198, 247
base cabinet 143
base plate 162, 289, 312
baseball 290, 291
baseline 303, 312
basement 138
basement window 135
basic source of food 41
basilic vein 99
basket 151, 289, 295
basketball 294, 295
basketball player 295
bass bridge 226
bass clarinet 234
bass drum 232, 234
bass guitar 229
bass keyboard 224
bass pickup 228
bass register 224
bass tone control 229, 242
bassoon 231
bassoons 234
baster 148
bat 291, 292
bat, morphology 82

bath sheet 132
bath towel 132
bathrobe 119
bathroom 139, 154, 266
bathroom scale 170
bathroom skylight 139
bathtub 139, 154
baton holder 265
bats, examples 82
batsman 292
batten 278
batten pocket 278
batter 290, 291
batter head 232
batter's helmet 291
battery 173, 175, 196
batting glove 291
battlement 220
bay 9, 22
bayonet base 156
beach 31
beach volleyball 299
beaker 166
beam 170, 215, 275
beam bridge 183
bean bag chair 140
beans 108
beauty care 257
beaver 77
bed 142, 275, 310
bed chamber 218
bedrock 26, 53
bedroom 139, 309
bedside lamp 266
bedside table 266
beech 54
beer 256
beer mug 144
beet 104
begonia 51
belfry 221
Belgian endive 106
bell 230, 231
bell brace 231
bell tower 221
bellows 224
bells 232
belly 84
belt 116, 305
belt highway 23
belt loop 116
beluga whale 89
bench 140, 255, 259, 267
bend 128
beret 124
bergamot 112
Bering Sea 19
berries 109
bezel 129
bib 121
biceps of arm 95
bicycle 194
bicycle bag 194
bicycle parking 269
bicycle, accessories 194
bicycles, examples 195
bidet 154

bilberry 109
bill 72
bills, examples 73
binding 124, 288
binocular microscope 167
biosphere 40
biosphere, structure 41
birch 54
bird 72
bird feeder 72
bird of prey 73
bird, morphology 72
birdhouse 72
birds 72
bishop 314
bison 86
bitter melon 107
Black 314
black bean 108
black bear 81
black board 268
black currant 109
black flying fox 82
black gram 108
black radish 104
black salsify 104
Black Sea 19
black square 314
black stone 315
black-eyed pea 108
blackberry 109
blackboard 268
blade 47, 49, 150, 155, 161, 162, 163, 179, 210, 214, 278, 284, 285, 286, 293
blade injector 131
blade lift cylinder 210
blade tilting mechanism 162
blank 313
blanket 142
blasting charge 180
blastodisc 72
blender 150
blending attachment 150
block cutter 213
blocking glove 284
blood pressure monitor 266
blood vessel 98, 101
blood vessels 82
blood, composition 98
blow pipe 224
blowhole 88
blue 211
blue line 284
blue mussel 57
blue-green 211
blueberry 109
BMX 308
BMX and cyclist 308
BMX bike 195
boa 68
board 278, 313, 315
boarding room 253
boarding step 203
boarding walkway 205
boards 285
boats 202
bobby pin 130

bobsled, luge and skeleton 287
bodies, examples 186
body 168, 184, 189, 228, 229, 231, 288
body (anterior view) 90
body (posterior view) 91
body care 132
body flap 15
body of fornix 97
body side molding 185
body suit 119
body temperature control unit 17
body tube 167
bole 52
bolster 142
bones, types 93
bongos 232
bony fishes 65
bookcase 268
booking room 265
bookstore 258
boom 193, 209
boom operator 273
booster parachute 14
booster seat 141
boot 279, 286, 288, 306, 307
booth 260
border 134
boreal forest 40
bottle 166, 311
bottle opener 147, 311
bottom 289
bottom line 277
bottom-fold portfolio 126
boulevard 250
bow 124, 200, 227, 278, 281
bow ball 279
bow saw 312
bow thruster 200
bow tie 116
bow-winged grasshopper 63
bowl 150
bowler 281, 292
bowling 281
bowling alley 258, 281
bowling ball 281
bowling crease 292
bowsprit 201
box car 197
box office 272
box spring 142
boxer 304
boxer shorts 117, 122
boxing 304
boxing trunks 304
bra 119
brachial artery 99
brachioradialis 95
brachiosaurus 71
bracket base 141
brake 308
brake arm 289
brake cable 195
brake caliper 191
brake lever 195, 308
brake light 187
brake pedal 188, 289
brakeman 287

branch 52, 55, 84
branches 52
brass family 234
brattice 220
brazier 219
Brazil nut 113
bread and butter plate 145
bread guide 151
breast 72, 90
breast pocket 116
breaststroke 277
breaststroke kick 277
breaststroke turn 277
breathing in 277
breathing out 277
breech 231
breech guard 231
bridge 128, 227, 229
bridge assembly 228
bridges 183
briefcase 126
briefs 117, 119
brim 124
bristle 131, 133
bristles 163
broad beans 108
broadleaved trees, examples 54
broccoli 105
broccoli rabe 105
broken line 182
brooch 129
brood chamber 61
brook 30
broom 158, 159
brow brush and lash comb 133
browser 248
brush 159, 163, 212
Brussels sprouts 106
bubble 191
bucket 209
bucket hinge pin 209
buckle 116, 127, 289
bud 103
buffet 260
bugle 230
bulb 84, 156
bulb vegetables 103
bulb, section 103
bulbil 103
bulge 11
bulk terminal 200
bulkhead flat car 196
bull's-eye 281, 316
bulldog 78
bulldozer 210
bulletin board 268
bumblebee 63
bumper 192
bumper molding 184
bunk 189
bunker oil 181
bunting bag 121
buoy weather station 38
buoyancy compensator 279
burdock 104
burgundy glass 144
burial 46

burner 149, 153
burner control knobs 153
burner ring 149
buses 190
bush-cricket 63
bushing 174, 175
business aircraft 208
business transactions 249
butt 302
butt end 285
butter 114
butter compartment 152
butter dish 144
butter knife 146
buttercup 51
butterfly 62
butterfly kick 277
butterfly stroke 277
butterfly turn 277
butterfly, morphology 62
butterhead lettuce 106
buttock 91
button 116, 120, 224
button loop 116
buttoned placket 116, 120
buttress 221
buttress dam 174
by-pass taxiway 204

C

C 222
C clef 222
C degrees 169
C-clamp 161
cab 209, 210
cabbage 106
cabin 201, 203
cabinet 143, 239
cable 162, 193, 243, 246
cable line 249
cable modem 249
cable sleeve 162
cable-stayed bridge 183
cables 238
caboose 197
cafeteria 269
caiman 69
cake 115
calandria 177
calcareous sponge 56
calf 91
Callisto 6
calyx 50, 109
cambium 53
camcorder 240
camel 87
camera 235, 238, 267, 306
camera body 235
camera pedestal 238
camera viewfinder 238
camping 309
camping (tent) 319
camping (trailer and tent) 319
camping (trailer) 319
camping equipment 311
camping prohibited 319

can opener 147, 150, 311
Canadian football 298
canal lock 200
canine 94
canned goods 257
cannon 84
canoe 279
canoe-kayak 279
canopy 128, 189, 208, 210
cantaloupe 113
canteen 311
cantilever bridge 183
canvas 304
canvas divider 309
cap 47, 124, 150, 179, 265, 270, 276
cape 22, 118
capillary blood vessel 101
capillary tube 169
capital 22
captain 287
capture 315
car racing 306
car wash 261
carafe 151
carambola 113
carapace 58, 67
caravans 189
card reader 245
card reader slot 261
cardigan 120
cardinal 74
cardoon 105
cards 313
cargo aircraft 208
cargo bay 14
cargo bay door 14
Caribbean Sea 18
carina 64
carnation 51
carnivores 41
carnivorous mammals (cat) 79
carnivorous mammals (dog) 78
carnivorous mammals, examples 80
carpal pad 78
carpenter's hammer 161
carpentry tools 161
carpus 92
carrier 194
carrier bag 127
carrot 104
cart path 282
cartilaginous fishes 64
cartography 20
cartridge 270
cartridge film 235
cartridge tape recorder 237
cartwheel hat 124
carving 213
case 161, 168, 226
casement 137
casement window 137
cash dispenser 259
cash register 257
cashew 113
cashier 257
casing 137
Caspian Sea 19

cassava 104
cassette 243
cassette compartment 240
cassette deck 237
cassette eject switch 240
cassette player 242, 243
cassette player controls 242, 244
cassette tape deck 241
castanets 232, 234
caster 141
castes 60
castle 220
cat breeds 79
cat, morphology 79
catcher 290, 291
catcher's glove 291
catching glove 284
catenary 198, 199
catering vehicle 204
caterpillar 62
cathedral 221, 250
cathedral ceiling 139
cathedral roof 139
caudal fin 64, 65, 88
cauliflower 105
cave 30, 31
CD radio cassette recorder, portable 242
CD/DVD player 316
CD/DVD-ROM drive 246
CD/DVD-ROM eject button 246
CD/ROM player 247
cecum 96
cedar of Lebanon 55
ceiling fitting 157
celeriac 104
celery 105
cell 61, 62, 264
cell membrane 56
cello 227
cellos 234
cellular telephone, portable 245
Celsius scale 169
celtuce 106
cementum 94
center 171, 284, 294, 297, 315
center attacker 299
center back 299
center circle 294, 300
center console 188
center face-off circle 285
center field 291
center fielder 290
center flag 300
center forward 293
center half 293
center line 285, 293, 294, 298
center line judge 302
center mark 302
center post 141, 185
center service line 303
center span 183
center spot 300
center strap 303
center wheel 169
Central America 18
central column 179

central incisor 94
central nave 219
central nervous system 97
central wrestling area 304
cephalic vein 99
cephalothorax 58, 59
cereal products 114
cerebellum 97
cerebrum 97
cesspit emptier 192
Chac-Mool 219
chain 168
chain wheel 308
chaise longue 140
chalk 25
chameleon 69
champagne flute 144
chandelier 157
changing table 141
channel scan button 239
channel selector controls 239
chanter 224
chapati bread 114
chapel 220
charcoal 212
chard 105
charge indicator 131
charging light 131
charm bracelet 129
Charon 7
chat room 249
chayote 107
check 260
checker 315
checkerboard 315
checkers 315
checkout 257
checkouts 257
cheek 78, 85, 90
cheese 114
cheese counter 257
cheese knife 146
cheetah 81
chemise 220
cherry 110
chess 314
chess notation 314
chess pieces 314
chessboard 314
chest 85
chest protector 291, 298
chestnut 113
chick 75
chick peas 108
chief judge 279
chief officer's office 264
chief timekeeper 276
chief's office 263
chiffonier 141
child carrier 194
child's skull 93
child's tricycle 195
children's clothing 121
children's furniture 141
chimney 135
chimpanzee 83
chin 72, 90

chin guard 263, 287
chin protector 191
chin rest 227
chin strap 263, 298
chipmunk 77
chive 103
choir 221
chord 223
chromatin 56
chromosphere 8
chrysalis 62
chuck 162
church 251
cicada 63
ciliate 49
cilium 56
cinema 272
circle, parts 171
circular saw 162
circular saw blade 162
circulatory system 98
circumference 171
cirque 9
cirque, glacial 29
cirrocumulus 35
cirrostratus 35
cirrus 35
citron 112
citrus fruits 112
citrus juicer 147, 151
city 22
city bus 190
city houses 216
clam 57
clamp 130, 155
clamp lever 130
clamp spotlight 157
clamp/holder 166
clapper/the slate 273
clarinet 231
clarinets 234
clasp 126
classic blouse 118
classroom 268, 269
classroom for students with learning disabilities 268
clavicle 92
claw 58, 67, 72, 76, 77, 78, 82, 129, 161
claw hammer 161
clear space 299
cleated shoe 298
cleated shoes 287
clefs 222
clew 278
click 169
cliff 9, 28, 31
climate 33
climate control 188
climates of the world 34
clinical thermometer 169
clip 245, 270
clipless pedal 308
clippers 130
clock 237, 268
clock operator 294
clock radio 242
clock timer 152, 153

clog 125
closed to bicycles 318
closed to motorcycles 317, 318
closed to pedestrians 317, 318
closed to trucks 317, 318
closeness setting 131
closet 138
clothing 116
clothing and personal objects 116
clothing store 258
cloud 32, 36
cloud of volcanic ash 27
clouds 35
clouds of vertical development 35
cloverleaf 182
club 313
club chair 140
clubhouse 280, 282
clubhouse turn 280
clutch pedal 188
coach 190, 285, 293, 295
coach's box 290
coal 25
coarse adjustment knob 167
coastal features 31
cobra 68
coccyx 92
cochlea 100
cochlear nerve 100
cockpit 306
cockroach 63
coconut 113
coffee maker 151
coffee mug 144
coffee pot 311
coffee shop 259, 319
coffee spoon 146
coin purse 126
coin return bucket 245
coin slot 245
colander 147
cold coolant 178
cold shed 200
cold storage chamber 256, 257
cold temperate climates 34
collar 48, 116, 131, 278
collar point 116
collards 106
collecting funnel 39
collection truck 193
collie 78
color circle 211
color television camera 17
colored pencils 212
colors 211
column 30, 217
column of mercury 169
coma 10
combat sports 304
combination lock 126
comet 10
comforter 142
command control dial 235
commercial concern 249
commercial premises 251
commercial services 256
commissure of lips of mouth 102

common carotid artery 99
common coastal features 31
common frog 66
common iliac artery 99
common plaice 65
common stingray 64
common symbols 319
common toad 66
communication by telephone 244
communication protocol 248
communication set 199
communication tunnel 14
communications 235
communications volume controls 17
compact disc 243
compact disc player 237, 241, 242
compact disc player controls 242
compact disc player, portable 243
compact flash memory card 235
compacting 46
compass 312
compass card 23, 312
compass meridian line 312
competition area 305
competitive course 276
complaints office 264
compluvium 218
composition of the blood 98
compost bin 165
compound eye 60, 62
compound leaves 49
compressed air reservoir 197
compressed-air cylinder 263, 279
computer 246, 268
computer science room 268
computer screen 17
concave primary mirror 12
concert grand 226
concrete mixer truck 193
condensation 42
condensation of steam into water 178
condenser 167, 177
condenser adjustment knob 167
condenser backwash inlet 177
condenser backwash outlet 177
condenser cooling water inlet 177
condenser cooling water outlet 177
condenser height adjustment 167
condominiums 216
conductor's podium 234
cone 27, 55, 172
configuration of the continents 18
conic projection 21
coniferous forest 40
conifers, examples 55
connecting gallery 182
connection 175, 315
connective tissue 101
constriction 169
contact 315
container 39, 150
container car 197
container ship 200
container terminal 200
container-loading bridge 200
container/pallet loader 205
containment building 178

contest area 305
contestant 305
continents, configuration 18
continuity person 273
contrabassoons 234
control button 246
control center 263
control keys 245
control knob 153, 160
control panel 152, 153, 160, 235
control room 174, 177, 237, 264
control stand 196
control stick 203
control tower 204
control tower cab 204
controller 316
controller ports 316
controls 240
convection zone 8
convective cell 37
convenience food 257
convention center 250
conventional door 136
convertible 186
conveyor belt 46, 252
cook's knife 148
cooked ham 115
cookie cutters 148
cookies 115
cooking utensils 149
cooktop 143, 153
cooktop edge 153
cool tip 130
cooler 311
coping 307
coral snake 68
corbel 220
corbel piece 158
cordate 49
cordless telephone 245
core 8, 111
Corinthian column 218
Corinthian pilaster 218
corkscrew 311
corn salad 106
corner 304
corner arc 301
corner flag 293, 301
corner judge 305
corner pad 304
corner stool 304
corner tower 220
cornerpiece 127
cornet 230, 234
cornice 135, 136, 141, 217
corolla 50
corona 8
coronal suture 93
coronet 84
corpus callosum 97
corrosive 320
costal shield 67
costume 272
cot 267
cotton applicators 267
cotyledon 48
countertop 143

counterweight 12, 198, 209
country 22
coupler head 197
coupling guide device 198
course 282
course gate 279
court 294, 299, 302
courtyard 219, 269
cover 128, 155, 158, 282, 312
coveralls 287
covered parapet walk 220
cow 86
cowl 184
coxswain's seat 278
Coyolxauhqui stone 219
crab 58
crab spider 59
cradle 12
crafts 214
crampon system 288
cranberry 109
crash helmet 287
crater 9, 27
crawl kick 277
crawler tractor 210
crayfish 58
creamer 144
crease 116
crenate 49
crenel 220
crepidoma 217
crescent wrench 162
crest 28
crevasse 29
crew neck sweater 120
crib 141
cricket 292
cricket ball 292
cricket player 292
cricket shoe 292
crime prevention 264
crisper 152
crochet hook 214
crocodile 69
crocus 51
croissant 114
crook 231
crook key 231
crookneck squash 107
crosne 104
cross rail 140
cross section of a hydroelectric power plant 175
cross section of a molar 94
cross section of a reflecting telescope 12
cross section of a refracting telescope 12
cross-country bicycle 308
cross-country cyclist 308
cross-country ski 288
cross-country skier 288
cross-country skiing 288
cross-tip screwdriver 311
crossbuck sign 198
crossing 221
crossing gate mechanism 198

crotch 117
croup 84
crown 52, 94, 124, 168, 227
cruise control 188
crusher 46
crustaceans 58
cube 172
cucumber 107
cuff 116, 125
culottes 119
cultural organization 249
cumulonimbus 35
cumulus 35
cup 119, 144, 311
curled endive 106
curled kale 106
curling iron 130
currant 109
currant tomato 107
currency exchange 319
current event scoreboard 275
curtain 238
curtain wall 220
curved jaw 162
customers' cloakroom 260
customers' entrance 260
customers' toilets 260
customs control 253
customs house 200
cutting blade 150
cutting edge 146, 210
cycling 308
cyclone 37
cyclorama 238
cylinder 172
cylinder vacuum cleaner 159
cylindrical projection 21
cymbal 232
cymbals 234
cytoplasm 56

D

D 222
daffodil 51
daggerboard 278
daggerboard well 278
daikon 104
dairy compartment 152
dairy products 114, 256
dairy products receiving area 256
daisy 51
dalmatian 78
dam 174
damper pedal 226, 233
dandelion 51, 106
danger area 305
dangerous materials 320
dart 316
dartboard 316
darts 316
dashboard 188
data display 240, 245
data processing 38
database 249
date 110
day-care center 259

dead bolt 136
deadly poisonous mushroom 47
debris 37
decagon 172
decanter 144
deceleration lane 182
deciduous forest 40
deck 183, 288
declination setting scale 12
decomposers 41
decorative articles store 259
dedicated line 248
deep fryer 151
deep-sea floor 24
deer crossing 317
defensive midfielder 300
deflector 158
deforestation 44
Deimos 6
deinonychus 71
delicatessen 256
delivery 292
delivery ramp 250
delta 30, 31
Delta II 16
delta wing 206, 208
deltoid 95
demitasse 144
dental alveolus 94
dental care 133
dental floss 133
dentate 49
dentin 94
deodorant 132
department store 259
depressed-center flat car 196
depth of focus 26
derailleur 194, 308
derby 124
dermis 101
descending colon 96
descending passage 217
desert 29, 34, 40
desired temperature 158
desk lamp 157
desktop computer 248
destroying angel 47
detachable body 192
dew 36
dew pad 78
dew shield 12
dewclaw 78
diagonal movement 314
dial 168, 170
diameter 171
diamond 25, 129, 313
diaphragm 97, 241
dice 313
dice cup 315
die 315
diesel engine 197
diesel engine compartment 209, 210
diesel motor compartment 210
diesel oil 181
diesel-electric locomotive 196
diffuser 273
digestive system 96

digit 66, 76, 77
digital audio player, portable 243
digital audio tape recorder 237
digital camera 236
digital pad 78
digital versatile disc 240
digital watch 168
dike 27
dimmer switch 155
dimple 282
dinette 138, 143
dining room 138, 201, 218, 260, 262
dinner plate 145
dinnerware 144
dinosaurs 70
diode 173
Dione 7
diplodocus 70
dipper arm 209
dipper arm cylinder 209
direct-reading rain gauge 38, 39
direction of Mecca 219
direction to be followed 317, 318
directional buttons 316
directional sign 255
director 273
director of photography 273
director's seat 273
directory 248
disc brake 191
disc tray 240
dish 238
dish antenna 238
dishwasher 143
disk 11
disk camera 236
disk drive 233
diskette 246
display 170, 240, 243, 244, 245, 261
display panel 240
display preparation area 256
display setting 244
disposable camera 236
disposable razor 131
diversion tunnel 174
divider 126
diving board 135
diving glove 279
djembe 225
do-it-yourself 161
do-it-yourself shop 258
dock 200
document-to-be-sent position 245
documentation center 262
dog breeds 78
dog's forepaw 78
dog, morphology 78
dolphin 89
dolphin, morphology 88
domain name 248
dome tent 309
domestic appliances 150
domestic pollution 44
dominoes 313
donkey 87
door 136, 152, 153, 185, 206, 219
door handle 185

door lock 185
door shelf 152
door stop 152
doorknob 136
doors, examples 136
Doric column 218
dormer window 134
dorsal fin 88
dorsalis pedis artery 99
dorsum of nose 102
double bass 227
double basses 234
double boiler 149
double flat 223
double reed 231
double ring 316
double seat 199
double sharp 223
double virgule 248
double-bladed paddle 279
double-blank 313
double-breasted jacket 117
double-deck bus 190
double-edged razor 131
double-leaf bascule bridge 183
double-six 313
doubles sideline 302
doublet 313
doubling die 315
doubly dentate 49
dousing water tank 177, 178
dousing water valve 177
downspout 134
downstream gate 279
downtown 250
draft tube 175
dragonfly 63
draw tube 167
drawbridge 220
drawer 141, 143, 153
drawers 117
drawing 211, 213
drawing supplies 212
drawstring 127
drawstring bag 127
drawstring hood 121
dresser 141, 272
dressing room 268, 272
drilling 180
drilling rig 180
drinks 256
drip bowl 153
drip molding 185
drive chain 194
drive shaft 203
driver's cab 196, 198
driveway 135
driving glove 123
drizzle 36
dromedary camel 87
drone 60
drone pipe 224
droop nose 208
drug storage 267
drum 232
drumlin 28
drums 232

drumstick 225
drupelet 109
dry cleaner 259
dry climates 34
dry dock 200
dry fruits 113
dry gallery 30
dry pastel 212
dual launch structure 16
dual seat 191
duck 75
duffle coat 117
dugout 290
dump body 210
dump truck 192, 210
dune 31
duodenum 96
dura mater 97
dust tail 10
dustpan 159
duty belt 265
duty-free shop 253
DVD 240
DVD player 240
dynamic brake 196

E

E 222
e-commerce 249
e-mail 249
e-mail software 248
eagle 74
ear 79, 82, 90, 140
ear drum 100
ear flap 124
ear protection 320
ear, structure 100
earbud 245
earphone 241
earphone jack 246
earphones 243
earpiece 128
Earth 6, 8, 9
Earth's atmosphere, profile 32
earth's coordinates and grid systems 20
Earth's crust 24, 26
Earth's crust, section 24
Earth's features 28
Earth's orbit 8, 9
Earth, structure 24
earthquake 26
East 23
East-Northeast 23
East-Southeast 23
Eastern hemisphere 20
Eastern meridian 20
eau de toilette 132
eccrine sweat gland 101
echinoderms 56
eclipses, types 8, 9
edge 214, 286, 287, 289, 312
edit search button 240
education 268
educational institution 249
eel 65

effusive volcano 27
egg 61, 72
egg beater 148
egg tray 152
eggplant 107
eggs 66, 114
eighth note 223
eighth rest 223
eject button 316
elastic 142
elastic strainer 309
elastic support bandage 267
elastic waistband 117
elastic webbing 116
elasticized leg opening 117
elbow 78, 82, 85, 91
elbow pad 298, 307
elbow pads 285
electric baseboard radiator 158
electric circuit 175
electric drill 162
electric dryer 160
electric golf cart 283
electric guitar 228
electric knife 150
electric range 153
electric razor 131
electric wire 175
electrical hazard 320
electrical tools 162
electricity transmission 176, 178
electrode 156
electronic ballast 156
electronic drum pad 233
electronic flash 235
electronic instruments 233
electronic payment terminal 257
electronic piano 233
electronic scale 170
electronic viewfinder 240
electronics store 258
elements of a house 136
elephant 87
elevating cylinder 193, 263
elevation 138
elevation zones 40
elevator 207
elevon 15
elliptical snowshoe 288
embankment dam 174
emerald 129
emergency brake 199
emergency regulator 279
emergency station 182
emergency truck 182
emery boards 132
enamel 94
end aisle display 257
end button 227
end key 245
end line 295, 296, 299
end moraine 29
end zone 296, 298
endocarp 110, 111
endoplasmic reticulum 56
energy 173

energy integration to the transmission network 176
energy transmission at the generator voltage 176
energy-saving bulb 156, 173
engaged Corinthian column 218
engaged Doric column 218
engaged Ionic column 218
engine 191
engine mounting pylon 207
engine room 201
English horn 231
English horns 234
enhanced greenhouse effect 43
entablature 217
enterprise 249
entertainment 272
entire 49
entrance 61, 182
entrance doors 272
entrance hall 138
entrance slide 61
entrance to the pyramid 217
entrance turnstile 254
environment 40
epicalyx 109
epicenter 26
epidermis 101
epiglottis 97
Equator 20
equestrian sports 280
equipment 264
equipment storage room 268
eraser 270
eraser holder 271
Erlenmeyer flask 166
escalator 254, 272
escape wheel 169
escarole 106
escutcheon 136
esophagus 96, 97
espadrille 125
Eurasia 18
Europa 6
Europe 19
European experiment module 14
European outlet 155
European plug 155
Eustachian tube 100
evacuation route 182
evaporation 42
evening glove 123
event platform 274
examples of airplanes 208
examples of amphibians 66
examples of angles 171
examples of aquatic and shorebirds 75
examples of arachnids 59
examples of bats 82
examples of berries 109
examples of bicycles 195
examples of bills 73
examples of bodies 186
examples of bony fishes 65
examples of broadleaved trees 54
examples of bulb vegetables 103
examples of carnivorous mammals 80

examples of cartilaginous fishes 64
examples of citrus fruits 112
examples of conifers 55
examples of crustaceans 58
examples of dams 174
examples of doors 136
examples of feet 73
examples of flowers 50
examples of freight cars 196
examples of helicopters 203
examples of hoofs 85
examples of insectivorous mammals 76
examples of insects 63
examples of marine mammals 88
examples of marsupials 76
examples of mollusks 57
examples of motorcycles 191
examples of pome fruits 111
examples of primates 83
examples of reptiles 68
examples of rodents 77
examples of shorelines 31
examples of space launchers 16
examples of still cameras 236
examples of stone fruits 110
examples of tail shapes 207
examples of terrestrial birds 74
examples of tools 213
examples of trucks 192
examples of ungulate mammals 86
examples of windows 137
examples of wing shapes 206
exhaust air duct 182
exhaust pipe 191, 203
exhaust pipe stack 210
exhaust stack 192
exit 182
exit cone 61
exit turnstile 254
exocarp 109, 110, 111, 112
exosphere 32
expandable baton 265
expandable file pouch 126
expansion chamber 169
explosive 320
explosive volcano 27
exposure mode 235
extension ladder 163
exterior of a house 134
exterior pocket 126
exterior sign 254
external auditory meatus 93
external ear 100
external fuel tank 14
external gills 66
external jugular vein 99
external nose 102
external oblique 95
eye 37, 57, 58, 59, 67, 79, 88, 90, 102, 161
eye guard 263
eye protection 320
eye wall 37
eyeball 66
eyecup 240
eyeglasses 128
eyeglasses case 126
eyeglasses parts 128

eyelahes 79
eyelash 102
eyelashes 79
eyelet 122, 125, 127, 286
eyelet tab 125
eyelid 67
eyepiece 12, 167
eyepiece holder 12
eyeshadow 133
eyestalk 57

F

F 222
F clef 222
F degrees 169
façade 221
face 83, 90, 161, 282
face mask 284, 292, 298
face-off circle 285
face-off spot 285
faceplate 136
facsimile (fax) machine 245
Fahrenheit scale 169
fairing 16
fairway 282
falcon 74
falling rocks 317, 318
false start rope 276
family tent 309
fan brush 212
fan heater 158
fan housing 131
fang 59, 67
fantail 179
far turn 280
fast data entry control 233
fast-food restaurants 259
fast-forward button 239, 243
faucet 154
fault 26
feed tube 150
feedhorn 238
feet, examples 73
felt hat 124
felt tip pen 212
femoral artery 99
femoral vein 99
femur 92
fence 134
fender 184, 192, 194
fennec 80
fennel 105
fern, structure 47
ferrule 163
ferry boat 202
ferryboat 200
fertilizer application 44
fetlock 84
fetlock joint 84
fibula 92
fiddlehead 47
fiddlehead fern 105
field 290, 292
field hockey 293
field lens adjustment 167
field mouse 77

ENGLISH INDEX

351

field player 293
fielder's glove 291
fifth 222
fifth wheel 192
fifty-yard line 297
fig 113
figure skate 286
filament 50, 156
file 248, 311
file format 248
filler cap 165, 192
film advance mode 235
film disk 235
film rewind knob 235
film speed 235
filter 135, 153
fin 158, 203, 207, 279
fin-mounted tail unit 207
final drive 210
finch 74
finderscope 12
fine adjustment knob 167
fine arts 211
fine data entry control 233
finger 291
finger button 230
fingerboard 227, 228, 229
fingernail 101
finish line 280
finish wall 276
finishing 213
fir 55
fire extinguisher 265, 319
fire extinguisher, portable 262
fire hose 262
fire hydrant 262
fire irons 158
fire prevention 262
fire prevention education officer's office 263
fire station 262
fire truck 262
firebrick back 158
firefighter 263
firefighters' dormitory 262
firefighters' toilets and showers 262
fireplace 138, 158
fireplace screen 158
firmer chisel 213
firn 29
first aid 319
first aid kit 265, 267
first aid manual 267
first aid supplies 267
first base 290
first baseman 290
first dorsal fin 64
first floor 138
first leaves 48
first molar 94
first premolar 94
first quarter 10
first referee 299
first space 295
first valve slide 230
first violins 234
first-class cabin 206

fish 115
fish platter 145
fish scaler 311
fishes, bony 65
fishes, cartilaginous 64
fission of uranium fuel 178
fitted sheet 142
fittings 127
fixed bridges 183
fixed jaw 162
fjords 31
flageolet 108
flamingo 75
flammable 320
flank 73, 84
flanking tower 220
flare 8
flashing light 198
flashlight 265
flashtube 235
flat 223, 307
flat bone 93
flat car 196
flat oyster 57
flat part 214
flat screen monitor 246
flat sheet 142
flat-back brush 130
flea 63
flesh 109, 110, 111
fleshy leaf 103
flews 78
flight 316
flight deck 14, 203, 206
flight information board 253
flip turn 277
float 208
float seaplane 208
floating bridge 183
floating crane 200
floating rib 92
floodlight 238
floodlight on pantograph 238
floor 179
floor exercise area 274
floor lamp 157
floor mats 274
floorboard 191
floppy disk drive 246
floppy disk eject button 246
florist 259
flower 48, 50
flower bed 135
flower bud 48
flower, structure 50
flowering plants 48
flowers, examples 50
fluorescent tube 156
flutes 234
fly 63, 116, 117, 121
fly agaric 47
fly front closing 121
flying buttress 221
flying jib 201
flying mammals 82
FM antenna 241
foam pad 310

focus 26
focus mode selector 235
focus selector 240
focusing knob 12
fog 36
fog light 187, 192
folding chair 140
folding cot 310
folding door 136
folding nail file 132
foliage 52
fondue fork 146
fondue pot 149
fondue set 149
fontanelle 93
food 103
food chain 41
food processor 150
food, basic source 41
foods, miscellaneous 114
foot 57, 76, 82, 83, 90, 141, 278
foot fault judge 303
foot pegs 308
foot protection 320
foot strap 278
foot stretcher 278
football 298
football player 298
football, American 296
football, Canadian 298
footboard 142
footbridge 220, 255
footless tights 122
footrest 141
footstool 140, 143
fore royal sail 201
forearm 78, 85, 91
forearm pad 298
forecastle 200
forecourt 303
forehead 90
foreleg 60, 62
forelimb 66, 76
forelock 85
foremast 201
foresail 201
forest fire 44
forewing 62
fork 12, 146, 195, 306, 308
forked tongue 67
formula 1 car 306
fortified wall 219
forward 300
fossil energy 180
fossil fuel 43
foul line 281, 290
foul line post 291
foundation of tower 183
fountain pen 270
four-door sedan 186
four-four time 222
four-masted bark 201
four-person bobsled 287
four-toed hoof 85
fourth 222
fourth wheel 169
fox 80

frame 61, 126, 127, 158, 173, 191, 209, 210, 275, 291, 302, 308, 309
frame stile 141
framing square 161, 271
free throw line 295
free zone 299
freeway 182, 250
freezer 143, 260
freezer compartment 152
freezer door 152
freezing rain 36
freight cars, examples 196
freight expedition 253
freight hold 207
freight reception 253
French horn 230
French horns 234
French window 137
frequency display 242
fresco 218
fresh air duct 182
fresh meat counter 256
fret 228, 229
frieze 141, 217
frog 66, 117, 227
frog, life cycle 66
frog, morphology 66
frond 47
front 116
front apron 116
front beam 170
front brake 195
front compression strap 312
front crawl stroke 277
front derailleur 194
front fascia 184
front fender 191
front fork 308
front leg 140
front pocket 127
front runner 287
front top pocket 116
front-end loader 209
frontal 95
frontal bone 92, 93
frozen food storage 257
frozen foods 257
fruit juice 115
fruit vegetables 107
fruits 109, 256
fruits, tropical 113
frying pan 149, 311
fuel indicator 188
fuel tank 192, 196, 203
fueling machine 177
full face mask 263
full moon 10
fullback 297
fumarole 27
function display 233
function keys 170, 245
function selectors 244
fungicide 44
funiculus 109
funnel 148, 201
funnel cloud 37
fur 76, 77, 79, 83

fuse 173, 176
fuse cutout 176
fuse holder 176
fuselage 207
fuselage mounted tail unit 207

G

G 222
G clef 222
gable 134
gable vent 134
gaff sail boom 201
gaff topsail 201
gaffer 273
Gai-lohn 105
gaits, horse 84
galaxy 11
gallbladder 96
gallery 179, 221
galley 206
gallop 85
game console 316
games 309, 313
gantry crane 174, 175
Ganymede 6
garage 134, 264
garden 218
garden cress 106
garden path 134
garden sorrel 106
garden spider 59
gardening 164
gardening gloves 164
garlic 103
garment bag 127
garnet 129
garter snake 68
gas 156
gas burner 166
gas pedal 188
gas range 153
gas tank 191
gas tank door 185
gaskin 84
gasoline 181
gasoline pump 261
gasoline pump hose 261
gastrocnemius 95
gate 175
gate arm 198
gate arm lamp 198
gate arm support 198
gate judge 279
gauntlet 123
gauze roller bandage 267
gearshift lever 188, 191
generator 177, 194
generator unit 175
gentlemen's toilet 272
geographical map 268
geography 18
geological phenomena 26
geology 24
geometrical shapes 171
geometry 171
germination 48

geyser 27
gherkin 107
gibbon 83
gift store 258
gill 47
gill slits 64
giraffe 87
girth 280
glacial cirque 29
glacier 29, 30, 40
glacier tongue 29
glass 173
glass collection unit 46
glass cover 152
glass lens 128
glass protector 284
glass recycling container 46
glass slide 167
glass sorting 46
glassed roof 138
glassware 144
global warming 43
globe 268
globular cluster 11
glottis 67
glove 17, 284, 287, 288, 292, 304, 306, 308
glove compartment 188
glove finger 123
glove, back 123
glove, palm 123
glue stick 270
gnomon 168
go 315
goal 285, 293, 296, 298, 300
goal area 300
goal crease 285
goal judge 285
goal lights 285
goal line 284, 293, 296, 298
goalkeeper 284, 293, 300
goalkeeper's gloves 301
goalkeeper's pad 284
goalkeeper's stick 284, 285
goalpost 296
goat 86
gob hat 124
goggles 287, 308
gold 371
goldfinch 74
golf 282
golf bag 283
golf ball 282
golf cart 283
golf cart, electric 283
golf equipment and accessories 282
golf glove 283
golf shoes 283
Golgi apparatus 56
gondola 257
gondola car 196
gong 234
goose 75
gooseberry 109
gorge 30
gorilla, morphology 83
Gothic cathedral 221
gouache cakes 212

gouache tube 212
gour 30
government organization 249
grab handle 192
graduated cylinder 166
graduated dial 312
graduated scale 170
grain terminal 200
grand gallery 217
grandfather clock 168
grandstand 280
granite 25
granitic layer 24
granivorous bird 73
grape 109
grape leaf 106
grape, section 109
grapefruit 112
graphic equalizer 241
graphite 25
grassbox 165
grasshopper 63
grassland 40
grate 153
grater 147
gravity dam 174
gravy boat 144
greases 181
Great Dane 78
great green bush-cricket 63
great horned owl 74
great saphenous vein 99
great white shark 64
greater pectoral 95
Greek temple 217
green 211, 282
green bean 108
green cabbage 106
green onion 103
green peas 108
green sweet pepper 107
greenhouse effect 43
greenhouse effect, enhanced 43
greenhouse effect, natural 43
greenhouse gas 43
greenhouse gas concentration 43
Greenland Sea 19
griddle 151
grille 184, 217, 224
grip 278, 282
grip tape 307
grocery bags 257
groin 90
groove 289
ground airport equipment 204
ground moraine 29
ground transport 181
groundhog 77
grounding prong 155
growth line 57
guard 138, 139, 294
guard rail 152, 307
guardhouse 220
guide roller 243
guinea pig 77
guitar 228, 229
gulf 22

gum 94, 102
gun range 265
gusset 126
gutter 134, 281
guy cable 274
guy line 309
guy wire 179
gymnasium 263, 268
gymnasium office 268
gymnastics 274

H

hadrosaurus 70
hair 91, 101, 227
hair bulb 101
hair conditioner 132
hair dryer 131
hair follicle 101
hair shaft 101
hair stylist 272
hairdressing 130
hairdressing salon 258
hairspring 169
half note 223
half rest 223
half-glasses 128
half-slip 119
halfway line 301
hall 138
halo 11
hammer 226
hammer rail 226
hamster 77
hand 83, 91, 101
hand blender 150
hand cultivator 164
hand lamp 263
hand mixer 150
hand protection 320
hand protector 306
hand rest 247
hand vacuum cleaner 159
handbags 127
handcuff case 265
handgrip 191
handicap spot 315
handle 126, 127, 128, 130, 131, 133, 142, 146, 151, 152, 153, 159, 161, 162, 163, 164, 165, 214, 227, 242, 287, 289, 291, 292, 293, 302, 311
handlebars 195, 308
handrail 199
handsaw 161
handset 244, 245
handset cord 244
hang-up ring 131
hanger loop 120
hanging glacier 29
hanging pendant 157
hanging stile 136, 137
harbor 200
hard palate 102
hare 77
harmonica 224
harness 288
harp 227

harps 234
harpsichord 226
hasp 127
hat switch 247
hatband 124
hatchback 186
hatchet 263, 312
hazelnut 113
head 10, 57, 60, 62, 79, 82, 91, 131, 133, 161, 214, 227, 228, 229, 282, 302
head cover 283
head linesman 297
head protection 320
head, bat 82
headband 241, 243
headboard 141, 142
header 136
headgear 124, 304
headland 31
headlight 184, 192, 195, 197, 198
headlight/turn signal 188
headlights 187
headphone jack 233, 242
headphone plug 243
headphones 241, 243
headpin 281
headset kit 245
health 266
health and beauty care 257
health organization 249
hearing 100
heart 97, 98, 313
heartwood 53
heat energy 43
heat loss 43
heat production 178
heat ready indicator 130
heat selector switch 131
heat shield 14
heat transport pump 177
heating 158
heating grille 199
heating oil 181
heavy machinery 182, 209
heavy rain 36
heavy rainfall 37
hedge 135
hedge shears 164
hedgehog 76
heel 84, 91, 122, 125, 227, 229, 285, 286, 291
heel grip 125
heel stop 307
heelpiece 289
heelplate 288
height adjustment 275
helicopter 203
helicopters, examples 203
helix 172
helmet 17, 263, 284, 287, 289, 292, 298, 306, 307, 308
helmet ring 17
hen 75
hen egg 114
heptagon 172
herbicide 44
herbivores 41

hexagon 172
high beam 187
high beam indicator light 188
high chair 141
high clouds 35
high frequency antenna cable 208
high wing 208
high-back overalls 121
high-hat cymbal 232
high-pressure area 37
high-rise apartment 216, 251
high-speed exit taxiway 204
high-speed train 198
high-tension electricity transmission 176
highland 9, 34
highland climates 34
highlighter pen 271
highway 23, 182
highway crossing 198
highway crossing bell 198
highway number 23
hill 28
hind leg 62
hind leg, honeybee 61
hind limb 66, 76
hind toe 73
hind wing 62
hinge 126, 136, 137, 141, 289
hinge pin 209
hip 91
hip pad 298
hippopotamus 87
hitting area 291
hive 61
hive body 61
hock 78, 84
hockey 284
hockey ball 293
hockey skate 286
hoisting rope 163
holder 166
hole 282
holster 265
home user 249
home-plate umpire 290
homestretch 280
honey cell 61
honeybee 60
honeybee, hind leg 61
honeybee, middle leg 60
honeycomb 61
honeycomb section 61
honeydew melon 113
hood 117, 158, 184, 192, 279
hooded sweat shirt 122
hoof 84
hoofs, types 85
hook 137, 161, 170, 193, 214, 286
hoop earrings 129
hopper ore car 197
horizontal bar 274
horizontal ground movement 26
horizontal movement 314
horizontal pivoting window 137
horizontal seismograph 26
horizontal stabilizer 203, 207

horizontal-axis wind turbine 179
horn 188, 196
horny beak 67
horse racing 280
horse's hoof 84
horse, gaits 84
horse, morphology 84
horseradish 104
horseshoe 84
hose 119, 262
hose dryer 262
hose holder 262
hose trolley 165
hospital 319
hospital bed 266
hot coolant 178
hot pepper 107
hot-shoe contact 235
hotel 251
hotel reservation desk 252
hour hand 168
house 134
house furniture 140
house, elements 136
house, elevation 138
house, exterior 134
houseboat 202
household equipment and appliances 159
household products 256
household waste 44, 45
houses 215
houses, city 216
houses, traditional 215
housing 131, 156, 162, 243
hovercraft 202
hub 59, 179, 195
Hubble space telescope 32
Huitzilopochtli, Temple 219
human being 90
human body 90
human denture 94
humerus 92
humid continental—hot summer 34
humid continental—warm summer 34
humid subtropical 34
humidity, measure 39
hummingbird 74
humpback whale 89
hunting cap 124
hurricane lamp 311
hut 215
hydraulic shovel 209
hydroelectric complex 174
hydroelectric power plant, cross section 175
hydroelectricity 174
hydrofoil boat 202
hydrologic cycle 42
hydrosphere 41
hyena 80
hygrograph 39
hyperlinks 248
hypha 47

I

Iapetus 7
ice 42
ice breaker 202
ice cream 114
ice cream scoop 148
ice cube dispenser 143
ice cube tray 152
ice dispenser 261
ice hockey 284
ice hockey player 284
iceberg lettuce 106
identification badge 265
identification section 264
identification tag 127
igloo 215
igneous rocks 24
ignition key 165
ignition switch 188
iguana 69
ileum 96
ilium 92
impluvium 218
in-ground swimming pool 135
in-line skate 307
inbounds line 296
incandescent lamp 156
incineration 46
incisors 94
incoming message cassette 244
incus 100
index finger 101
Indian chapati bread 114
Indian Ocean 19
indicators 239
industrial pollution 44
industrial waste 44, 45
industry 249
inert gas 156
inferior dental arch 102
inferior vena cava 98, 99
infield 290
infiltration 42
inflated carrying tire 199
inflated guiding tire 199
inflator 310
inflator-deflator 310
inflorescent vegetables 105
information 319
information booth 259
information console 279
information counter 252
information desk 264
information spreading 249
infrared radiation 43
inkjet printer 247
inner boot 307
inner core 24
inner hearth 158
inner table 315
inner toe 72
inorganic matter 41
insectivorous bird 73
insectivorous mammals, examples 76
insects 60
insects, examples 63

354

inside 146
inside linebacker 296
inside-leg snap fastening 121
instrument panel 188
instrument shelter 38
insulator 176
intensive farming 43, 45
intensive husbandry 43, 44
interchangeable studs 301
intermodal car 196
internal boundary 22
internal ear 100
internal filum terminale 97
internal iliac artery 99
internal jugular vein 99
international boundary 22
international road signs 317
international space station 14
Internet 248
Internet service provider 249
Internet user 248
Internet uses 249
internode 48
interrogation room 264
interrupted projection 21
intervals 222
intravenous stand 266
intrusive filtration 44
intrusive rocks 24
Io 6
ion tail 10
Ionic column 218
iris 102
iron 282
isba 215
ischium 92
island 22, 143, 182
ISS 14
isthmus 22
isthmus of fauces 102

J

jack 313
jack field 237
jacket 117, 118, 305
jaguar 81
jalousie 137
jamb 136, 158
Japanese experiment module 14
Japanese plum 111
jaw 132, 162
jay 74
jeans 121
jejunum 96
jersey 308
Jerusalem artichoke 104
jet fuel 181
jet refueler 205
jewel 169
jewelry 129
jewelry store 258
jicama 104
jigger topgallant staysail 201
jigger topmast staysail 201
jiggermast 201
jigsaw puzzle 313

jingle 232
jockey 280
joint 270
joker 313
journal box 196
joystick 247
joysticks 316
judge 304, 305
judge's stand 280
judges 274, 275
judo 305
judo-gi 305
juice sac 112
jumpsuit 121
junior officer's office 264
Jupiter 6
juvenile cell 264

K

kale 106
kangaroo, morphology 76
karate 305
karate-gi 305
karate-ka 305
kayak 279
keep 220
kerosene 181
kettle 28, 151
kettledrum 232
key 224, 226, 231
key case 126
key cutting shop 259
key finger button 231
key grip 273
key guard 231
key lever 231
key lock 126
key signature 223
keybed 226
keyboard 226, 233, 246, 281
keyboard instruments 226
keys 233
killer whale 89
king 313, 314
king's chamber 217
king's side 314
kingfisher 75
kiosk 255, 261
kitchen 138, 143, 218, 263, 269
kitchen scale 147
kitchen towel 159
kitchen utensils 147
kiwi 113
knee 78, 85, 90
knee pad 291, 298, 307
knife 146, 213, 312
knife pleat 116
knight 314
knit shirt 120
knitting 214
knitting needle 214
knob 291
knob handle 162
knurled bolt 163
koala 76
kohlrabi 105

kora 225
kumquat 112

L

labial palp 60, 62
lablab bean 108
laboratory equipment 166
laccolith 27
lace 286, 291
lachrymal canal 102
lachrymal caruncle 102
lachrymal gland 102
ladder 189, 210, 215
ladder pipe nozzle 263
ladies' toilet 272
ladle 148
Lady chapel 221
ladybird beetle 63
lagomorphs 77
lagoon 31
lake 9, 22, 28, 30
lamp 167
lamp socket 156
lanceolate 49
land pollution 44
land station 38
landfill site 44
landing 139
landing light 203
landing window 203
lane 276
lane rope 277
lane timekeeper 276
lapis lazuli 129
larch 55
large blade 311
large intestine 96
larva 61
larynx 97
laser printer 247
last quarter 10
latch 127, 152
latch bolt 136
lateral great 95
lateral incisor 94
lateral line 65
lateral moraine 29
lateral semicircular canal 100
latex glove case 265
latrines 218
laundry room 138
lava flow 27
lava layer 27
lawn 135
lawn edger 164
lawn rake 165
lead-in wire 156
leading edge 207
leaf 48, 49
leaf axil 49
leaf lettuce 106
leaf margin 49
leaf node 48
leaf vegetables 106
leaf, structure 49
leather end 116

leather goods 126
leather goods shop 258
leather sheath 312
leatherback turtle 68
ledger line 222
leech 278
leek 103
left atrium 98
left attacker 299
left back 293, 299, 300
left channel 241
left cornerback 296
left defense 285
left defensive end 296
left defensive tackle 296
left field 290
left fielder 290
left forward 294
left guard 297
left half 293
left inside forward 293
left lung 97
left midfielder 300
left pulmonary vein 98
left safety 296
left service court 303
left tackle 297
left ventricle 98
left wing 284, 293
leg 67, 83, 90, 141, 142, 164, 275
leg guard 291
leg-warmer 122
legumes 108
leisure activities 309
lemon 112
lemur 83
length post 280
lens 247
lens cap 235
lentils 108
leopard 81
leotard 122
lettuce 106
leveling foot 160
lever 132, 151, 162
lever corkscrew 147
libero 299
library 268
license plate light 187
lichen 47
lid 149, 150, 151, 153, 159, 160
life buoy 265
life cycle of the frog 66
life support system 17
life support system controls 17
lifeboat 201
lift arm 209
ligature 231
light 12, 199
light aircraft 208
light bar 265
lighting 155
lighting and heating 155
lighting grid 238, 273
lighting technician 273
lightning 36
lightning arrester 175, 176

lightning rod 135
lights 157
lily 50
lily of the valley 51
Lima bean 108
limb 52
limb top 167
lime 112
limestone 25
limousine 186
line 222, 299
line judge 274, 297, 299
line map 254
line of scrimmage 297
linear 49
linen 142
linesman 284, 299, 301, 302
lingerie shop 258
lining 116, 125, 126, 286
lintel 158
lion 81
lip 79, 85
lipstick 133
liquid eyeliner 133
liquid foundation 133
liquid hydrogen tank 16
liquid mascara 133
liquid oxygen tank 16
liquid-crystal display 168
listen button 244
litchi 113
lithosphere 41
little finger 101
little finger hook 230
liver 96
livestock car 197
living room 138, 309
lizard 69
llama 87
loafer 125
lobate 49
lobate toe 73
lobby 252
lobe 73
lobster 58
lobster, morphology 58
lock 136, 141, 194
locker room 262
locket 129
locking device 163
locking pliers 162
locomotive, diesel-electric 196
loculus 111
log carrier 158
log chute 174
log tongs 158
loin 84, 91
long bone 93
long extensor of toes 95
long peroneal 95
long-range jet 206
loop 116, 182
loophole 220
loose-leaf paper 271
lost and found articles 319
loudspeakers 241
louse 63

louver-board 221
louvered window 137
love seat 140
low bar 274
low beam 187
low clouds 35
low-pressure area 37
low-tension distribution line 176
lower eyelid 66, 79, 102
lower fore topgallant sail 201
lower fore topsail 201
lower lip 102
lower lobe 97
lower mantle 24
lower section 16
lower shell 289
lubricating oils 181
lubricating system 197
luff 278
luge racer 287
luggage 127
luggage rack 189, 191
lunar eclipse 9
lunar features 9
lung 97
lunula 101
lupine 108
lynx 81
lyre 225
lysosome 56

M

macaque 83
macaw 74
machicolation 220
machine hall 174, 175
magma 27
magma chamber 27
magnesium powder 275
magnetic compass 312
magnetic damping system 170
magnetic gasket 152
magnetic needle 312
magnetic separation 46
magnifier 311
magnifying glass 167
main cryogenic stage 16
main engine 15
main entrance 138, 269
main generator 196
main landing gear 207
main rooms 138
main sail 201
main stand 191
main tube 12
main vent 27
Maine coon 79
mainmast 201
maintenance 261
maintenance hangar 205
maître d'hôtel 260
major international road signs 317
major motions 315
major North American road signs 318
makeup 133
makeup artist 272

malachite 25
malanga 104
mallet 232
mallets 232
malleus 100
mammals 76
mandarin 112
mandible 60, 62, 65, 92, 93
mandolin 225
mandown alarm 263
mane 85
maneuvering area 204
maneuvering engine 15
mango 113
manned maneuvering unit 17
manometer 267
manrope 183
mantel 158
mantel shelf 158
mantid 63
mantle 57
manual release 289
manual sorting 46
Manx 79
map projections 21
map, physical 22
map, political 22
map, road 23
maple 54
maps 22
maquis 40
marble 25
marbled electric ray 64
margin 49
marginal shield 67
marine 34
marine diesel 181
marine mammals 88
marine mammals, examples 88
maritime transport 181, 200
marker 271, 281
marker light 192
Mars 6
mars light 263
marsupial mammals 76
marsupials, examples 76
mask 279, 291
mass 26
massage glove 132
masseter 95
mast 198, 218, 278
mast foot 278
mast sleeve 278
masthead 278
mastoid fontanelle 93
mat 305
mat chairperson 304
matinee-length necklace 129
mattress 141, 142, 310
mattress cover 142
maxilla 60, 65, 92, 93
maxillary bone 94
maximum thermometer 39
meals 115

meander 30
measure of air pressure 39
measure of humidity 39
measure of rainfall 39
measure of temperature 39, 169
measure of time 168
measure of weight 170
measure of wind direction 39
measure of wind strength 39
measuring cup 148
measuring devices 168
measuring spoons 148
measuring tube 39
meat keeper 152
Mecca, direction 219
mechanical pencil 271
mechanical stage 167
mechanical stage control 167
mechanical watch 169
mechanics 261
medial great 95
medial moraine 29
median 182
median strip 250
medical team 305
Mediterranean Sea 19
Mediterranean subtropical 34
medium-tension distribution line 176
medulla oblongata 97
meeting room 263, 269
melon baller 147
melons 113
meltwater 29
memo pad 270
memory button 244
memory card 235
memory card slots 316
men's bag 127
men's cell 264
men's clothing 116
men's gloves 123
men's rest room 319
men's underwear 117
menu 260
Mercury 6
mercury bulb 169
merlon 220
mesocarp 109, 110, 111, 112
mesopause 32
mesosphere 32
metacarpal, 2nd 82
metacarpal, 3rd 82
metacarpal, 4th 82
metacarpal, 5th 82
metacarpus 92
metal frame 226
metal rod 232
metal sorting 46
metamorphic rocks 24
metatarsus 92
meteorological forecast 38
meteorological measuring instruments 39
meteorological station 38
meteorology 32

meteorology, measuring instruments 39
mezzanine 254
mezzanine floor 138, 139
mezzanine stairs 139
mica 25
Michigan snowshoe 288
micro compact car 186
microfilament 56
microphone 237, 238, 240, 244, 245, 247, 265
microphone boom 238
microphone boom tripod 238
microscope 167
microscope, binocular 167
microscopes 167
microwave oven 143, 152
microwave relay station 248
middle clouds 35
middle ear 100
middle finger 101
middle leg 62
middle leg, honeybee 60
middle linebacker 296
middle lobe 97
middle panel 136
middle sole 122
middle toe 72
midrange 241
midrange pickup 228
midrib 49
midriff band 119
Mihrab 219
Mihrab dome 219
milk carton 114
Milky Way 11
Mimas 7
minaret 219
Minbar 219
minerals 25
minibus 190
minimum thermometer 39
minivan 186
mink 80
minute hand 168
Miranda 7
mirror 154, 167, 191, 269
mist 36
mitochondrion 56
mitt 123
mitten 123
mixed forest 40
mixing bowls 148
mizzen sail 201
mizzenmast 201
moat 220
mobile passenger stairs 252
moccasin 125
mode selectors 242
modem 248
modulation wheel 233
molar, cross section 94
molars 94
mole 76
mollusks 57

mongoose 80
monitor lizard 69
monocle 128
Moon 6, 8, 9
Moon dial 168
Moon's orbit 8, 9
Moon, phases 10
mop 159
moped 191
moraine 29
mordent 223
morphology of a bat 82
morphology of a bird 72
morphology of a butterfly 62
morphology of a cat 79
morphology of a dog 78
morphology of a dolphin 88
morphology of a frog 66
morphology of a gorilla 83
morphology of a honeybee 60
morphology of a horse 84
morphology of a kangaroo 76
morphology of a lobster 58
morphology of a perch 65
morphology of a rat 77
morphology of a shark 64
morphology of a snail 57
morphology of a spider 59
morphology of a turtle 67
morphology of a venomous snake 67
mosaic 218
mosque 219
mosquito 63
moss 47
motocross motorcycle 306
motor 162, 165
motor bogie 199
motor car 199
motor home 189
motor scooter 191
motor sports 306
motor unit 150, 198
motor vehicle pollution 45
motor yacht 202
motorcycle 191
motorcycles, examples 191
motorcycling 306
mouflon 86
mountain 28
mountain bike 195
mountain biking 308
mountain mass 22
mountain range 9, 22, 24
mountain slope 28
mountain torrent 28
mounting foot 235
mounting plate 156
mouse pad 246
mouth 57, 66, 88, 90, 102
mouthparts 60
mouthpiece 230, 231, 233
mouthpiece receiver 230
mouthpipe 230
mouthwash 133
movable bridges 183

movable jaw 162
movable maxillary 67
movable stands 268
movie set 273
movie theater 258, 272
movies' titles and schedules 272
Mt Everest 32
mud flap 185, 192
muffin pan 148
muffler felt 226
muffler pedal 226
multigrain bread 114
mummy 310
mung bean 108
muntin 137
muscles 95
museum 251
mushroom 47
mushroom, structure 47
music 222
music room 268
music stand 233
music store 258
musical instruments 224
musical instruments, traditional 224
musical notation 222
muskmelon 113
mussel 57
mute 230
muzzle 78, 79, 85
mycelium 47

N

nacelle 179
nail 161
nail cleaner 132
nail clippers 132
nail nick 311
nail scissors 132
naos 217
nape 72, 91
narwhal 89
nasal bone 93
nasal cavity 97
national park 23
natural 223
natural arch 31
natural greenhouse effect 43
natural sponge 132
nautical sports 278
navel 90
navigation light 207
NEAR 13
near/far dial 240
neck 67, 85, 91, 94, 146, 227, 228, 229
neck end 116
neck guard 263
neck pad 298
neckroll 142
necktie 116
nectarine 110
needle 29
negative contact 173
negative pole 175

Neptune 7
nerve 101
nerve fiber 101
nerve termination 101
nervous system 97
nervous system, central 97
nest 72
net 295, 299, 303
net band 303
net judge 303
nettle 106
neutral zone 284, 296
new crescent 10
new moon 10
newspaper shop 259
newt 66
next call 245
nib 270
nictitating membrane 79
nightshot switch 240
nimbostratus 35
nipple 90
no entry 317, 318
no U-turn 318
no wheelchair access 319
nonagon 172
nonbiodegradable pollutants 44
nonreusable residue waste 46
North 23
North America 18
North American road signs 318
North Pole 0, 20
North Sea 19
North-Northeast 23
North-Northwest 23
Northeast 23
Northern hemisphere 20
Northern leopard frog 66
northern right whale 88
Northwest 23
nose 77, 85, 90, 102, 206, 287
nose landing gear 206
nose leaf 82
nose leather 79
nose of the quarter 125
nostril 64, 65, 66, 67, 72, 85
notation, musical 222
notch 170
note symbols 223
notebook 271
nozzle 14, 16
nubby tire 306
nuclear energy 177
nuclear energy, production of electricity 178
nuclear envelope 56
nuclear generating station 177
nuclear waste 45
nucleolus 56
nucleus 10, 11, 56
number of tracks sign 198
number plate 306
numeric keyboard 170
nurse 266
nut 113, 227, 228, 229
nutcracker 147

O

oak 54
oarlock 279
oars, types 278
oasis 29
Oberon 7
obi 305
objective 167
objective lens 12, 235
oboe 231
oboes 234
observation deck 253
observation window 15
obtuse angle 171
occipital bone 93
ocean 9, 22, 42
ocean weather station 38
Oceania 19
oche 316
octave 222
octave mechanism 231
octopus 57
odometer 188
off-road motorcycle 191
office 253, 260, 261
office building 200, 251
office tower 250
officers' dormitory 262
officers' toilets and showers 262
officials 293
officials' bench 284
offshore prospecting 180
oil 180
oil paint 212
oil pastel 212
oil pollution 45
oil spill 45
oil terminal 200
okapi 87
okra 107
old crescent 10
olive 107
on-air warning light 237
on-board computer 188
on-deck circle 290
on-off button 243
on-off indicator 130
on-off light 244
on-off switch 130, 131, 151, 157
on-off/volume 242
one-person tent 309
one-piece suit 287
one-story house 216
one-toed hoof 85
onion 103
online game 249
opal 129
operating instructions 261
operculum 65
opossum 76
opposable thumb 83
optic chiasm 97
optical lens 269
optical scanner 247, 257
optical sorting 46
optical stage 269

optician 259
oral cavity 96, 97
orange 112, 211
orange, section 112
orange-red 211
orange-yellow 211
orangutan 83
orbicular of eye 95
orbiculate 49
orbiter 14, 15
orbits of the planets 6
orchestra 234
orchid 50
ordinary die 313
organ 226
oriental cockroach 63
ornamental kale 106
ornamental tree 134
ornaments 223
ostrich 75
other signs 223
ottoman 140
outer bull 316
outer core 24
outer table 315
outer toe 72
outfield fence 291
outgoing announcement cassette 244
outlet 155
output jack 228
outrigger 209, 263, 279
outside counter 125
outside linebacker 296
outside mirror 184
outsole 122, 125
outwash plain 29
ovary 50
ovate 49
oven 143, 153
oven control knob 153
overall standings scoreboard 274
overbed table 266
overcoat 119
overflow 154
overhead connection 176
overhead projector 269
overpass 182
ovule 50
owl 74
oxygen cylinder, portable 267
oxygen outlet 266
oxygen pressure actuator 17
oystercatcher 75
ozone layer 32

P

pace 85
pachycephalosaurus 71
Pacific Ocean 18
packaging products 256
pad 292
pad arm 128
padded base 295
padded upright 295
paddle, double-bladed 279
paddle, single-bladed 279

paddock 280
paddy field 44
pads 285
pail 159
paint roller and tray 163
painting 211
painting knife 212
painting supplies 212
painting upkeep 163
pajamas 119, 121
pak-choi 106
palatoglossal arch 102
palm 101, 123, 291
palm grove 29
palm of a glove 123
palm tree 54
palmar pad 78
palmate 49
pan 170
pan hook 170
panama 124
pancreas 96
pane 137
panel 136
panpipe 224
pantograph 198, 199
pantry 138, 143
pants 116, 122, 284, 291, 298, 306
panty hose 119
papaya 113
paper clips 270
paper collection unit 46
paper guide 245
paper recycling container 46
paper separation 46
paper sorting 46
paperboard separation 46
paperboard sorting 46
papilla 101
paraffins 181
parallel 20
parallel bars 275
parallelepiped 172
parallelogram 172
paramecium 56
parapet walk 220
parasauroloph 70
parcels office 253
parietal bone 93
park 250
parking 282
parking area 205, 269
parking brake lever 188
parking lot 251, 252
parsnip 104
partial eclipse 8, 9
partition 265
partridge 74
parts 142
parts of a boat 278
parts of a circle 171
parts of a ring 129
parts of a shoe 125
parts of a side chair 140
pass 28
passenger cabin 207
passenger car 198, 199

passenger liner 200
passenger platform 253
passenger station 253
passenger terminal 200, 205, 252
passenger train 196, 253
passenger transfer vehicle 253
passing lane 182
passion fruit 113
passivity zone 304
passport control 253
pasta 114
pastern 84
pastry shop 259
patella 92
Pathfinder 13
patient 266
patient room 266
patio 134
patio door 138, 143
pattypan squash 107
pause 223
pause/still button 239
pawn 314
pay phone 245, 259, 260
payload 16
payload adaptor 16
pe-tsai 106
pea jacket 118
peach 110
peach, section 110
peacock 74
peak 28, 124
peanut 108
pear 111
peas 108
pecan nut 113
pectoral fin 64, 65, 88
pedal 194, 227, 232, 308
pedal rod 226
pedestrian crossing 317, 318
pedicel 109
pediment 168, 217
pedipalp 59
peduncle 50, 109, 110, 111
peeler 147
peg 227, 229
peg box 227
pelican 75
pelvic fin 64, 65
pen 26, 270
pen blade 311
pen holder 126
penalty arc 300
penalty area 300
penalty area marking 300
penalty bench 284
penalty bench official 284
penalty spot 300
pencil 271
pencil sharpener 270
pendant 129
pendulum 168
penguin 75
peninsula 22
penis 90
penstock 174, 175
pentagon 172

penumbra shadow 8, 9
pepper shaker 144
pepper spray 265
pepperoni 115
perch 65
perch, morphology 65
perching bird 73
percussion instruments 232, 234
perforated toe cap 125
perfume shop 258
periodontal ligament 94
peristyle 218
peroxide 267
peroxisome 56
perpetual snows 28
Persian 79
personal articles 123
personal computer 246
personal radio cassette player 243
pesticide 44, 45
pet food 257
pet shop 258
petal 50
petiole 47, 49
Petri dish 166
petrochemicals 181
petroleum trap 180
phalanges 92
pharmacy 258, 319
pharynx 97
phases of the Moon 10
philtrum 102
phloem 53
Phobos 6
phosphorescent coating 156
photo booth 259
photoelectric cell 235
photographer 258
photographic accessories 235
photography 235
photosphere 8
photovoltaic arrays 14
physical map 22
physician 266, 304
piano 226, 234
piccolo 231, 234
pickguard 228
pickling onion 103
pickup selector 228
pickup truck 186
pickups 229
picnic area 319
picnics prohibited 319
picture 313
pie 115
piece 313
pierced earrings 129
pig 86
pigeon 74
pika 77
pike 65
pike pole 263
pile dwelling 215
pillar 26, 221, 227
pillion footrest 191
pillow 142
pillow protector 142

pillowcase 142
pilot 197, 198
pin 156, 262, 281
pin base 156
pin block 226
pin cushion 214
pine 55
pine nut 113
pine seeds 55
pineal body 97
pineapple 113
pinna 47, 76, 77
pinnacle 221
pinnatifid 49
pinto bean 108
Pioneer 13
pip 109, 111, 112, 313
pipeline 181
pistachio nut 113
pistil 50
pistol 265
pistol grip handle 162
pit 67, 281
pita bread 114
pitch 292
pitch wheel 233
pitcher 290
pitcher's mound 290
pith 53
Pitot tube 306
pituitary gland 97
pivot 214, 312
pivot cab 209
pizza 115
placing judge 276
plaice 65
plain 22, 30
plane projection 21
planetarium 250
planets 6
planisphere 18
plant litter 53
plant, structure 48
plasma 98
plastics sorting 46
plastron 67
plate 311
plate binding 287
plateau 22, 28
platelet 98
platform 170, 252, 255, 276, 307
platform edge 255
platform ladder 163
platter 145
play button 239, 243
player positions 290, 294, 300
player's number 284, 295, 298
player's stick 285
players' bench 285, 293, 297, 298, 299
players' chairs 299
playing area 201, 316
playing field 293, 297, 298, 300
playing window 243
pleated skirt 118
plectrum 225
plexus of nerves 94
plinth 168

plug 155, 241
plug adapter 155
plum 110
Pluto 7
pocket 126, 281, 283
pocket camera 236
podium 268
point 146, 214, 227, 270, 286, 315, 316
point guard 294
point of interest 23
pointer 158, 170
poison 320
poisonous mushroom 47
poker 158
poker die 313
polar bear 81
polar climates 34
polar ice cap 34
polar lights 32
polar tundra 34
Polaroid® camera 236
pole 238, 302
pole grip 288
pole shaft 288
police 319
police car 265
police officer 265
police station 264
political map 22
pollen basket 61
pollen cell 61
pollutants, non-biodegradable 44
polluting gas emission 44
pollution 44
pollution, agricultural 44
pollution, air 44
pollution, domestic 44
pollution, industrial 44
pollution, land 44
pollution, motor vehicle 45
pollution, oil 45
pollution, water 45
polo dress 118
polo shirt 303
polygons 172
pome fruits 111
pomegranate 113
pomelo 112
pommel horse 274
poncho 118
pond 282
pons Varolii 97
pontoon 183
poodle 78
poop 201
pop-up tent 309
poplar 54
popping crease 292
poppy 51
porch 135, 219
porch dome 219
porcupine 77
pore 101
porpoise 89
port hand 200
portable CD radio cassette recorder 242

portable cellular telephone 245
portable compact disc player 243
portable digital audio player 243
portable fire extinguisher 262
portable oxygen cylinder 267
portable radio 242
portable shower head 154
portable sound systems 242
portal 221
porthole 201
position light 198, 203
position marker 228, 229
positive contact 173
positive pole 175
post lantern 157
post office 259
poster 272
posterior fontanelle 93
posterior rugae 91
posterior semicircular canal 100
potato 104
potato masher 148
pouch 76
pouring spout 159
powder blusher 133
powder puff 133
power button 239, 240, 245, 246
power car 198
power mower 165
power plant 174
power plug 242
power supply cord 131
power switch 233
power/functions switch 240
practice green 282
prairie 22
prayer hall 219
precious stones 129
precipitation 42
precipitations 36
precision sports 281
prehensile digit 83
premaxilla 65
premolars 94
prepared foods 257
preset buttons 239, 240
pressed area 243
pressed powder 133
pressure bar 226
pressure cooker 149
pressure demand regulator 263
pressure regulator 149
pressurized refuge 182
prevailing wind 37
price per gallon/liter 261
primary colors 211
primary consumers 41
primary root 48
primate mammals 83
primates, examples 83
prime meridian 20
primrose 51
princess dress 118
principal bones 92
principal muscles 95
principal's office 269
printer, ink jet 247

ENGLISH INDEX

359

printout 170
prisoners' shower 264
privacy curtain 266
private dressing room 272
probe receptacle 152
proboscis 62
procedure checklist 17
producer 273
producer turret 237
product code 170
production designer 272
production of electricity by the generator 176, 178
production of electricity from nuclear energy 178
production of electricity, steps 176
production platform 180
profile of the Earth's atmosphere 32
program selector 233
programmable buttons 247
projection booth 272
projection head 269
projection room 272
projection screen 269, 272
projector 272
proleg 62
promenade deck 201
prominence 8
pronaos 217
propeller 201
property man 273
prospecting 180
protection 320
protection area 304
protection layer 17
protective cup 285, 298
protective equipment 285, 298
protective goggles 306
protective helmet 191, 194
protective plate 306
protective suit 306
protective surround 316
protractor 271
province 22
pruning shears 164
pubis 90
puck 285
pull strap 127
pulley 163
Pullman case 127
pulmonary artery 99
pulmonary trunk 98
pulmonary vein 99
pulp 94, 112
pulp chamber 94
pump 125
pump island 261
pump nozzle 261
pump number 261
pumpkin 107
punch hole 116, 122, 125
punching bag 304
punching ball 304
pup tent 309
pupa 61
pupil 79, 102
purfling 229

purse 126
purslane 106
push button 128, 150, 245
push buttons 244
push frame 210
push-button 270
push-button telephone 245
pusher 150
putter 282
pygal shield 67
pyramid 172, 217
pyramid, entrance 217
pyranometer 38
python 68

Q

Qibla wall 219
quadrant 171
quadrilateral 172
quail egg 114
quarter 84
quarter note 223
quarter rest 223
quarter window 185
quarter-deck 201
quarterback 297
quartz 25
quay 200
quayside crane 200
queen 60, 313, 314
queen cell 61
queen excluder 61
queen's chamber 217
queen's side 314
quick ticket system 272
quince 111
quiver 281

R

rabbit 77
raccoon 80
racetrack 280
rack 149, 153
racket sports 302
raclette with grill 151
radial passenger loading area 205
radial thread 59
radiant heater 158
radiation zone 8
radiator 197
radiator grille 192
radiator panel 15
radiators 14
radicchio 106
radicle 48, 52
radio 237
radio (studio and control room) 237
radio antenna 200, 306
radioactive 320
radish 104
radius 82, 92, 171
rail 198
rail transport 196
railing 139
railroad shuttle service 252

railroad station 250
railroad track 250
rain 36
rain gauge recorder 38, 39
rainbow 36
raincoat 117
rainfall, measure 39
rake 165
ramekin 144
ramp 182, 217, 307
rampart 220
range hood 143, 153
rangefinder 236
rank insignia 265
rasp 213
raspberry 109
raspberry, section 109
rat, morphology 77
ratchet wheel 169
rattlesnake 68
raven 74
razor clam 57
reach-in freezer 256
reactor 177, 178
reactor building 177
reading mirror 17
reading start 243
rear apron 116
rear beam 170
rear brake 194
rear derailleur 194
rear leg 140
rear light 194
rear runner 287
rear shock absorber 191
rearview mirror 188
receiver 244, 245, 302
receiver volume control 244
receiving area 256
receiving tray 245
receptacle 50, 109
reception area 263
reception hall 219
record announcement button 244
record button 239, 240
record player 241
recorder 231
recording tape 240, 243
rectangle 172
rectangular 310
rectum 96
recycling 46
recycling bin 46
Red 315
red 211
red blood cell 98
red cabbage 106
red kidney bean 108
red onion 103
Red Sea 19
red sweet pepper 107
red whortleberry 109
red-violet 211
reed 231
reel 240
reentrant angle 171

referee 276, 284, 293, 294, 297, 299, 300, 304, 305
refinery 181
refinery products 181
refining 181
reflected solar radiation 43
reflecting telescope 12
reflecting telescope, cross section 12
reflective stripe 263
reflector 194
refracting telescope 12
refracting telescope, cross section 12
refrigerated display case 260
refrigerator 143, 152, 260
refrigerator car 196
refrigerator compartment 152
refrigerators 260
refuse container 159
regular decagon 172
regular heptagon 172
regular hexagon 172
regular nonagon 172
regular octagon 172
regular pentagon 172
reheater 177
rein 280
release lever 162
relieving chamber 217
remote control 239
remote control sensor 239
remote control terminal 235
remote manipulator system 14
renal artery 99
renal vein 99
reniform 49
repeat mark 222
report writing room 264
reptiles 67
reptiles, examples 68
reservoir 151, 174, 175
reset button 168, 246, 316
reset key 245
resident 266
residue waste, non-reusable 46
resonator 241
respiratory system 97
respiratory system protection 320
rest area 23
rest symbols 223
restaurant 251, 258, 260, 319
restaurant, fast-food 259
restricted area 295
restricting circle 294
resurgence 30
retractable handle 126
return crease 292
reverse light 187
revolving nosepiece 167
rewind button 239, 243
Rhea 7
rhinoceros 86
rhizome 47
rhombus 172
rhubarb 105
rhythm selector 233
rias 31
rib 128, 210, 229

rib joint pliers 162
rib pad 298
ribbing 120
ribosome 56
ribs 92
rice 114
ridge 28
riding cap 280
riding crop 280
riffler 213
right angle 171
right ascension setting scale 12
right atrium 98
right attacker 299
right back 293, 299, 300
right channel 241
right cornerback 296
right defense 285
right defensive end 296
right defensive tackle 296
right field 291
right fielder 290
right forward 294
right guard 297
right half 293
right inside forward 293
right lung 97
right midfielder 300
right pulmonary vein 98
right safety 296
right service court 303
right tackle 297
right ventricle 98
right wing 284, 293
rim 128, 191, 195, 295
rim soup bowl 145
rind 112
ring 47, 128, 168, 170, 230, 304
ring binder 271
ring post 304
ring step 304
ring, parts 129
ringing volume control 244
rings 275
ringside 304
rink 284
rink corner 284
ripper 210
ripper shank 210
rising warm air 37
river 22, 30
river estuary 22, 31
river otter 80
road 23
road flare 265
road map 23
road number 23
road racing 308
road signs 317
road system 182
road transport 182
road tunnel 182
road-racing bicycle 308
road-racing cyclist 308
roadway 182
roadwork ahead 317, 318
roasting pans 149

Roberval's balance 170
rock salt 25
rocket engine 16
rocking chair 140
rocks 25
rocky desert 29
rocky islet 31
rod 166
rodents 77
rodents, examples 77
roll structure 306
roller cover 163
roller frame 163
rolling pin 148
romaine lettuce 106
Roman amphitheater 218
roman bean 108
Roman house 218
rompers 121
roof 61, 135, 185, 189
rook 314
room thermostat 158
rooms, main 138
rooster 75
root 94, 103
root canal 94
root cap 48
root hairs 48
root of nose 102
root rib 206
root system 48
root vegetables 104
root-hair zone 52
rope 129, 304
rose 51, 136, 229
rose window 221
rotating drum 26
rotation of the turbine 176
rotor 179
rotor blade 203
rotor head 203
rotor hub 203
rough 282
roughing out 213
round brush 130
round-bottom flask 166
route sign 199
router 248
row 133
rowboat, parts 278
rowing 278
rubber boot 263
rubber sheath 278
rubbing alcohol 267
ruby 129
rudder 15, 201, 207, 278
rudder cable 278
ruler 271, 311
rump 73
runabout 202
rung 163
runner 315
running shoe 122
Russian module 14
rutabaga 104

S

sacrum 92
saddle 280
saddlecloth 280
safe 265
safety 262
safety area 305
safety belt 306
safety binding 289
safety handle 165
safety lighting 265
safety line 255
safety niche 182
safety officer 279
safety pad 275
safety pin 214
safety rail 196
safety symbols 320
safety tether 17
safety valve 149, 178
sail 179, 278
sail cloth 179
sailbar 179
sailboard 278
Saint Bernard 78
salad 115
salad bowl 145
salad dish 145
salad plate 145
salad spinner 147
saline lake 29
salivary glands 96
salsify 104
salt shaker 144
sand 299
sand bunker 282
sand island 31
sandal 125
sandbox 197
sandstone 25
sandwich 115
sandy desert 29
sapphire 129
sapwood 53
sarong 118
sartorius 95
sash frame 137
sash window 137
satchel 271
satellite 16
satellite earth station 249
satellites 6
Saturn 7
Saturn V 16
saucepan 149, 311
sauté pan 149
savanna 40
savanna climate 34
savoy cabbage 106
saxhorn 230
saxophone 231
scale 65, 67, 73, 161, 169, 222, 271, 312
scale leaf 103
scallion 103
scampi 58
scapula 92

scarlet runner bean 108
scatter cushion 142
scenic route 23
schedules 253
school 268
school bus 190
school supplies 270
school zone 317, 318
science 166
science room 268
scientific air lock 15
scientific instruments 15
scissors 214, 267, 311
sclera 102
score console 281
scoreboard 305, 316
scoreboard, current event 275
scoreboard, overall standings 274
scorekeeper 305
scorer 294, 299
scorers 305
scorpion 59
scouring pad 159
scraper 163
screen 131, 175, 239, 292
screen door 189
screen print 121
screen window 309
screw 161, 227
screw base 156
screwdriver 161, 311
scrimmage (defense) 296
scrimmage (offense) 297
scroll 227
scroll wheel 245, 246
scrotum 90
scuba diver 279
scuba diving 279
sculling 278
sculling oar 278
sea 9, 22, 30
sea kale 106
sea level 24, 32
sea lion 88
sea urchin 56
seafood 257
seal 88
sealed cell 61
seam gauge 214
search 249
seasons in the cold temperate climates 33
seasons of the year 33
seat 140, 154, 191, 194, 272
seat post 194
seats, side chairs, and armchairs 140
sebaceous gland 101
second 222, 304
second assistant camera operator 272
second base 290
second baseman 290
second dorsal fin 64
second floor 138, 139
second hand 168
second molar 94
second premolar 94
second referee 299

ENGLISH INDEX

361

second space 295
second valve slide 230
second violins 234
second-level domain 248
secondary colors 211
secondary consumers 41
secondary mirror 12
secondary road 23
secondary root 48
secretaries' office 269
section of a bulb 103
section of a grape 109
section of a peach 110
section of a raspberry 109
section of a strawberry 109
section of an apple 111
section of an orange 112
section of the Earth's crust 24
sector 171
security check 253
sedimentary rocks 24
seed 48, 109, 111, 112
seed coat 110
seedless cucumber 107
segment 112
segment score number 316
seismic wave 26
seismogram 26
seismograph, vertical 26
seismographic recording 180
seismographs 26
selection key 245
selective sorting of waste 46
self-contained breathing apparatus 263
self-inflating mattress 310
self-service meat counter 256
semi-mummy 310
semicircle 171, 294
semicircular canal, lateral 100
semicircular canal, posterior 100
semicircular canal, superior 100
semidetached cottage 216
semiprecious stones 129
semitrailer 192
sense organs 100
sensor probe 152
sent document tray 245
sepal 50, 109, 111
separate collection 46
septic tank 45
septum 102
septum pellucidum 97
sequencer control 233
serac 29
serological pipette 166
server 248, 249, 303
service area 23, 205
service judge 302
service line 303
service provider, Internet 249
service road 204
service room 219
service station 261, 319
service table 260
set 273
set dresser 273

set of bells 232
setting 129
setup 281
seventh 222
sew-through buttons 214
sewing 214
sewing machine 214
sewn-in floor 309
shade 157
shadow 168
shadow roll 280
shady arcades 219
shaft 217, 278, 282, 285, 302, 316
shallot 103
shallow root 52
sham 142
shampoo 132
shank 128, 161, 214
shark 64
shark, morphology 64
sharp 223
shaving 131
shaving brush 131
shaving foam 131
shaving mug 131
sheath 49, 312
shed 134
sheep 86
sheet 201
shelf 152
shelf channel 152
shell 57, 72, 287
shelter 182
shield bug 63
shifter 195
shin guard 287, 293, 301
ships 202
shirt 116, 295
shirttail 116
shock wave 180
shoe 293, 295, 308
shoe store 259
shoe, parts 125
shoelace 122, 125
shoes 125
shoot 48, 53
shooting star 32
shop 218
shopping carts 257
shopping center 258
shore cliff 31
shorebirds, examples 75
shorelines, examples 31
short bone 93
short glove 123
short sock 119
shorts 121, 293, 295, 301, 308
shortstop 290
shoulder 78, 85, 90, 227, 302
shoulder bag 127
shoulder blade 91
shoulder pad 298
shoulder pads 285
shoulder strap 119, 127, 265, 283, 312
shovel 158, 164, 288, 289
shower 139, 266
shower head 154

shower stall 154
shredding 46
shrew 76
shrimp 58
shroud 201
shutter 137
shutter release button 235
shutting stile 136
Siamese 79
side 146, 201
side chapel 221
side compression strap 312
side door 199
side fairings 306
side footboard 197
side handrail 199
side hatch 14
side judge 297
side lane 182
side marker light 187
side rail 163
side span 183
side vent 27
side wall 84
sideline 293, 294, 296, 299
sidewalk 135
sidewall 276
sight 102, 281, 312
sighting line 312
sighting mirror 312
sigmoid colon 96
signal ahead 317, 318
signal background plate 198
signal lamp 151, 153
signet ring 129
sill 27
silos 200
silver 25
silverware 146
simple eye 60, 62
simple leaves 49
simple organisms 56
simple vegetables 47
single chain wheel 308
single reed 231
single seat 199
single sprocket 308
single-bladed paddle 279
single-breasted jacket 117
single-lens reflex (SLR) camera 235
singles sideline 303
sink 143, 154
sinkhole 30
siphon 57
sistrum 232
site plan 135
sitting room 138
sixteenth note 223
sixteenth rest 223
sixth 222
sixty-fourth note 223
sixty-fourth rest 223
skate 284, 286
skate guard 286
skateboard 307
skateboarder 307
skater 307

skating 286
skeg 278
skeleton 92, 287
skeleton sledder 287
skerry 31
ski 288, 289
ski boot 289
ski glove 289
ski goggles 289
ski hat 288
ski pants 118
ski pole 288, 289
ski suit 288, 289
ski tip 288
skid 203
skin 101, 109, 110, 111
skin surface 101
skirt 118, 303
skull 90, 93
skunk 80
skylight 135, 139
skyscraper 251
slat 141
slate 25
sled 287
sleeper-cab 192
sleepers 121
sleeping bags 310
sleet 36
sleeve 203
sleigh bells 232
slide projector 269
sliding cover 245
sliding door 136, 154
sliding folding door 136
sliding folding window 137
sliding seat 278
sliding sunroof 185
sliding weight 170
sliding window 137
slip joint 162
slip joint pliers 162
slip presenter 261
slippery road 317, 318
sloping cornice 217
slot 146, 151, 161
slow lane 182
slow-motion button 239
small decanter 144
small hand cultivator 164
small intestine 96
small jars 115
smell 102
smog 45
smoke shop 258
snack bar 272
snail 57
snail, morphology 57
snake 67
snap 214
snap fastener 117, 123
snap-fastening front 121
snare drum 232, 234
snorkel 279
snout 64, 66, 76
snow 36
snow gauge 38

snowblower 193
snowboard 287
snowboard, alpine 287
snowboarder 287
snowboarding 287
snowshoe 288
snowshoe, elliptical 288
snowshoes 288
snowsuit 121
soap dish 154
soccer 300
soccer ball 301
soccer player 301
soccer shoe 301
society 250
sock 119, 298, 301, 303
socket-contact 155
sofa 140
soft palate 102
soft pedal 226, 233
soft ray 65
soft-drink dispenser 261
soil fertilization 44
soil profile 53
solar cell 173
solar eclipse 8
solar energy 173
solar radiation 42, 43, 173
solar shield 17
solar system 6
solar-cell panel 173
solar-cell system 173
sole 286
solid booster stage 16
solid center auger bit 162
solid rocket booster 14, 16
solids 172
sorting plant 46
sorus 47
sound box 229
sound engineer 273
sound hole 227
sound recording equipment 273
sound reproducing system 241
sound systems, portable 242
soundboard 226, 227, 229
sounding balloon 38
soup bowl 145
soup spoon 146
soup tureen 145
South 23
South America 18
South China Sea 19
South Pole 20
South-Southeast 23
South-Southwest 23
Southeast 23
Southern hemisphere 20
Southwest 23
soybean sprouts 108
soybeans 108
space 222
space exploration 13
space launcher 16
space launchers, examples 16
space probe 32
space probes 13

space shuttle 14, 32
space shuttle at takeoff 14
space telescope 32
spacelab 15
spacesuit 17
spade 313
spaghetti 115
spaghetti squash 107
spanker 201
spar 206
spare tire 189
sparkling wine glass 144
sparrow 74
spatula 148
spatulate 49
speaker 242, 244, 272
speaker cover 241
spear-nosed bat 82
speed control 165
speed selector 150
speed selector switch 131
speed skate 286
speedometer 188
spent fuel discharge bay 177
spent fuel storage bay 177
sperm whale 89
sphenoid bone 93
sphenoidal fontanelle 93
sphere 172
sphincter muscle of anus 96
spider 59
spider web 59
spider, morphology 59
spiked shoe 291
spillway 174
spillway chute 174
spillway gate 174
spinach 106
spinal cord 97
spindle 140, 150
spinneret 59
spinosaurus 70
spiny lobster 58
spiny ray 65
spiracle 62
spiral arm 11
spiral binder 271
spiral cloud band 37
spiral thread 59
spire 221
spirit level 161
spit 31
splints 267
split peas 108
spoiler 206
spoke 195
sponge 56
spoon 146
spores 47
sport-utility vehicle 186
sporting goods store 259
sports 274
sports car 186
sports on wheels 307
sports, combat 304
sports, equestrian 280
sportswear 122

spot 157
spotlight 238, 263, 273
spray hose 154
spray nozzle 165
spray skirt 279
sprayer 164
spreader 128, 164
spring 26, 30, 33, 157, 162, 196, 270, 275
spring balance 170
springboard 274
sprinklers 178
spruce 55
spur 28
square 172, 250
square movement 314
squash 107
squid 57
squirrel 77
stabilizer 281
stabilizer fin 201
stabilizer jack 189
stable 280
stack 31
stadium 251
staff 222
staff cloakroom 260, 264
staff entrance 260, 269
staff lounge 264
staff toilet 264
stage 167
stage clip 167
stained glass 221
stairs 138, 182, 254, 272
stairways 219
stairwell 139
stairwell skylight 139
stake loop 309
stalactite 30
stalagmite 30
stalk 109, 110, 111
stalk vegetables 105
stamen 50, 111
stanchion 286
stand 26, 130, 149, 157, 166
stapes 100
staple remover 270
stapler 270
staples 270
star diagonal 12
starboard hand 200
starfish 56
starling 74
start button 168
start key 245
start switch 160
starter 165, 276
starting block 276
starting dive 277
starting gate 280
starting grip (backstroke) 276
state 22
station 252
station entrance 254
station name 254
station wagon 186
steak 115
steak knife 146

steam generator 177
steam iron 159
steam pressure drives turbine 178
steamer basket 149
steelyard 170
steering wheel 188, 306
stegosaurus 70
stem 47, 48, 169, 195, 201
stem bulb 200
step 192
stepladder 163
steppe 34
steps 135, 138, 213
steps in production of electricity 176
stereo control 242
sterile pad 267
stern 201, 278
sternocleidomastoid 95
sternum 92
stethoscope 266
stew 115
stick 227, 293
stick holder 271
stick umbrella 128
sticks 232
stifle 84
stigma 50
stile 140
still video film disk 235
stills photographer 273
stimulator tip 133
sting 61
stingray 64
stipule 49
stirrup sock 291
stitch 125
stitching 123
stock 179
stock pot 149
stockade 220
stocking 119, 284
stocking cap 124
stomach 96
stone 110, 129
stone for sacrifice 219
stone fruits 110
stop 78
stop at intersection 317, 318
stop button 168, 239
stop watch 237
stopper 300, 311
stopwatch 168
storable propellant upper stage 16
storage compartment 192, 263
storage door 152
storage furniture 141
storage room 265
store room 260
storeroom 268
stork 75
stove oil 181
straight muscle of thigh 95
straight skirt 118
straight stopcock burette 166
straight wing 206
straightneck squash 107
strait 22

363

strap 168, 291
strap loop 312
strap system 229
stratocumulus 35
stratopause 32
stratosphere 32
stratus 35
strawberry 109
strawberry, section 109
street 250
street sweeper 193
streetcar 199
streetlamp 251
stretcher 267
striker 300
striking circle 293
string 227
stringed instruments 227
stringing 302
strings 226
stroke judge 276
strokes, types 277
structure of a fern 47
structure of a flower 50
structure of a leaf 49
structure of a mushroom 47
structure of a plant 48
structure of a plant and germination 48
structure of a tree 52
structure of the biosphere 41
structure of the ear 100
structure of the Earth 24
structure of the Sun 8
strut 179
stud 122, 292
student 268
student's desk 268
students' lockers 269
students' room 269
studio 237
studio floor 238
studio, television 238
study 139
stump 53, 292
style 50, 109, 110, 111
subarctic 34
subclavian artery 99
subclavian vein 99
subcutaneous tissue 101
submarine line 248
submarine pipeline 181
subsiding cold air 37
subsoil 53
substitute's bench 301
subterranean stream 30
subway 199
subway map 199, 255
subway station 254
subway train 199, 254
sucker 57
sudoriferous duct 101
sugar bowl 144
suit 118
summer 33
summer solstice 33
summer squash 107
summit 28
Sun 6, 8, 9, 33

sun visor 188
Sun, structure 8
sundeck 201
sundial 168
sunflower 51
sunglasses 128
sunshine recorder 38
sunspot 8
super 61
supercross motorcycle 306
superior dental arch 102
superior mesenteric artery 99
superior mesenteric vein 99
superior semicircular canal 100
superior vena cava 98, 99
supermarket 256, 259
supersonic jet 32
supersonic jetliner 208
supervisor's office 269
supply of water 176
support 12, 39, 140
support thread 59
surface element 153
surface insulation 14
surface prospecting 180
surface runoff 42
suspender 183
suspender clip 116
suspenders 116
suspension 199
suspension bridge 183
suspension cable 183
swallow 74
swallow hole 30
sweat pants 122
sweat shirt 122
sweater vest 120
sweaters 120
sweep oar 278
sweeper 300
sweet peas 108
sweet pepper 107
sweet potato 104
swept-back wing 206
swimming 276
swimming goggles 276
swimming pool 201, 277
swimming pool, above ground 135
swimming pool, in-ground 135
swimming trunks 122
swimsuit 122, 276
swing bridge 183
Swiss Army knife 311
Swiss chard 105
switch 152, 155
switch plate 155
swivel cord 130
swordfish 65
symbols 313, 317
symbols, common 319
symbols, dangerous materials 320
symbols, protection 320
symphony orchestra 234
synthesizer 233
syringe 266
system buttons 233
system components 241

T

T-shirt dress 121
T-tail unit 207
tab 126, 128
table lamp 157
tablinum 218
tachometer 188
tack 278
tactical transport helicopter 203
tadpole 66
tag 122, 125
tail 58, 67, 76, 77, 78, 79, 82, 84, 88, 207, 287, 288, 289
tail assembly 207
tail boom 203
tail comb 130
tail feather 73
tail shapes, examples 207
tail skid 203
tailback 297
taillight 187, 191
taillights 187
tailpiece 227
tailrace 175
take-up reel 243
talk key 245
talking drum 225
talon 73
tambourine 232
tandem bicycle 195
tandem tractor trailer 193
tank 15, 262
tank car 181, 196
tank farm 181
tank top 122
tank truck 181, 193
tanker 181, 200
tape 161, 293
tape dispenser 270
tape lock 161
tape measure 161, 214
tape-guide 243
tapered wing 206
taproot 52
target 281
taro 104
tarsus 73, 92
taste 102
taxi transportation 319
taxiway 204
taxiway line 205
teacher 268
teacher's desk 268
teachers' room 269
team shirt 291, 293, 298, 301
team's emblem 284
teapot 145
teaspoon 146
technical identification band 243
technical room 182
technical terms 109, 110, 111, 112
tee 282
teeing ground 282
teeth 94
telecommunication antenna 201
telecommunication satellite 249

telephone 319
telephone answering machine 244
telephone index 244
telephone line 248
telephone set 244
telephone, communication 244
teleprompter 238
telescopic boom 263
telescopic corridor 205
telescopic front fork 191
telescopic umbrella 128
telescoping antenna 242
television 238
television set 239, 268
telson 58
temperate forest 40
temperature control 151, 158
temperature indicator 188
temperature scale 32
temperature selector 160
temperature, measure 39, 169
temple 90, 128
Temple of Huitzilopochtli 219
Temple of Tlaloc 219
tempo control 233
temporal bone 92, 93
tendon guard 286
tennis 302
tennis ball 302
tennis player 303
tennis racket 302
tennis shoe 125, 303
tenor drum 232
tensor of fascia lata 95
tent trailer 189
tentacle 57
tents 309
tepee 215
terminal 155, 252
terminal box 173
terminal bud 48
terminal filament 97
terminal moraine 29
termite 63
tern 75
terrestrial birds, examples 74
tertiary colors 211
tertiary consumers 41
test pattern 238
test tube 166
Tethys 7
thermometer 169
thermopause 32
thermosphere 32
thermostat 158
thermostat control 152
thigh 73, 76, 78, 84, 91
thigh pad 298
thigh-boot 125
thimble 214
third 222
third base 290
third baseman 290
third finger 101
third valve slide 230
third wheel 169
thirty-second note 223

thirty-second rest 223
thistle 51
thoracic legs 58
thorax 60, 62, 90
thread 161
three-blade propeller 208
three-four time 222
three-toed hoof 85
threshold 136
throat 72, 302
throat protector 285, 291
throttle control 247
thrust device 270
thrust tube 270
thruster 17
thumb 82, 101, 123, 291
thumb hook 230
thumb rest 231
thumb tacks 270
thumbscrew 162
thunderstorm 36
tibia 82, 92
tick 59
ticket clerk 272
ticket collecting booth 254
ticket collector 253
ticket counter 252
tie 128, 198, 223
tier 218
tiger 81
tiger shark 64
tight end 297
tightening band 39
tightening buckle 312
tile 217, 218
timber 217, 218
time code 273
time signatures 222
timed outlet 153
timekeeper 294, 304, 305
timekeepers 305
timpani 234
tine 146
tip 49, 128, 146, 161, 162, 288, 289
tip of nose 102
tire 185, 192, 195, 308
tire pump 194
tire valve 195
tissue holder 154
Titan 7
Titan IV 16
Titania 7
Tlaloc, Temple 219
toad 66
toaster 151
toe 73, 78, 84, 90
toe binding 288
toe box 286
toe clip 84, 194
toe guard 291
toe pick 286
toepiece 288, 289
toggle fastening 117
toilet 138, 139, 154, 266, 269
toilet soap 132
toilet tank 154
toilets 259

tom-tom 232
tomatillo 107
tomato 107
tombolo 31
tone control 228
tone leader generator 237
toner cartridge 247
tongs 148
tongue 60, 96, 102, 116, 122, 125, 286, 289
tongue sheath 67
tonsil 102
tool tether 17
tools, wood carving 213
tooth 64, 67, 161, 162, 209
tooth guard 298
toothbrush 133
toothed jaw 162
toothpaste 133
top 52
top bar 274
top flap 312
top hat 124
top ladder 263
top of dam 174
top rail 140
top rail of sash 137
top-level domain 248
topaz 129
topsoil 53
toque 124
tornado 37
tortilla 114
torus 172
total 170
total eclipse 8, 9
total sale display 261
tote board 280
toucan 74
touch 101
touch line 301
touring motorcycle 191
tourmaline 129
tow bar 204
tow tractor 205
tow truck 193
towel bar 154
tower 179, 183, 221
tower case 246
tower ladder 263
tower mill 179
towing device 193
town houses 216
toy store 258
trachea 97
track 210, 253, 254
track lighting 157
traditional houses 215
traditional musical instruments 224
traffic island 250
traffic lane 182
traffic lanes 182
trailer 189
trailer car 199
trailing edge 206
trailing edge flap 206
train 196, 253

trainer 295, 304
trampoline 275
transept spire 221
transfer dispensing machine 255
transfer of heat to water 178
transfer ramp 182
transformation of mechanical work
  into electricity 176
transformer 157, 175, 176, 177
transit shed 200
transmission of the rotative movement
  to the rotor 176
transmission to consumers 176
transmitter 244
transpiration 42
transport 181
transport, air 203
transport, maritime 200
transportation 182
transverse colon 96
transverse flute 231
trapezius 95
trapezoid 172
travel agency 258
traveling crane 175
trawler 202
tray 127, 141, 164
treble bridge 226
treble keyboard 224
treble pickup 228
treble register 224
treble tone control 229, 242
tree 52
tree frog 66
tree, structure 52
tree, trunk 53
trees 282
triangle 172, 232, 234
triangular bandage 267
triceratops 71
trifoliolate 49
trigger 247, 262
trigger switch 162
trill 223
trim 127
trim ring 153
trimmer 131
trip odometer 188
triple ring 316
triple tail unit 207
tripod 12
tripod accessories shelf 12
tripod stand 232
Triton 7
trombone 230
trombones 234
Tropic of Cancer 20
Tropic of Capricorn 20
tropical climates 34
tropical cyclone 37
tropical forest 40
tropical fruits 113
tropical rain forest 34, 40
tropical wet-and-dry (savanna) 34
tropopause 32, 43
troposphere 32
trot 84

trousers 305
trout 65
trowel 164
truck 196, 307
truck frame 196
truck tractor 192
truck trailer 193
trucking 192
trucks, examples 192
trumpet 230
trumpets 234
trunk 52, 66, 127, 185
trunk, cross section 53
tub platform 154
tuba 230, 234
tube retention clip 156
tuber vegetables 104
tubular bells 234
tug 202
tulip 51
tumbler; glass 144
tuna 65
tundra 40
tuner 241, 242, 243
tuning control 242
tuning controls 239
tuning dial 243
tuning peg 228, 229
tuning pin 226
tuning slide 230
tunnel 254
turbine 177
turbine building 177
turbine shaft turns generator 178
turbined water draining 176
turbojet engine 207
turf 280
turkey 75, 115
turn 223
turn signal 187, 191
turn signal indicator 188
turnbuckle 304
turning judges 277
turning wall 277
turnip 104
turnouts 262, 263
turnouts' cleaning 262
turnstile 254
turntable 183, 209, 237
turntable mounting 263
turquoise 129
turret 220
turtle 67
turtle, morphology 67
turtleneck 120, 288
TV mode 239
TV power button 239
TV/video button 239
tweeter 241
tweezers 267
twig 48, 52
twist bit 162
twist handle 247
two-blade propeller 208
two-door sedan 186
two-person tent 309
two-story house 216

365

ENGLISH INDEX

two-toed hoof 85
two-two time 222
tympanum 66, 217, 221
type of fuel 261
types of bones 93
types of eclipses 8, 9
types of movements 314
types of oars 278
types of strokes 277
types of volcanoes 27
tyrannosaurus 71

U

U.S. habitation module 14
U.S. laboratory 14
ulna 92
umbra shadow 8, 9
umbrella 128
umbrella and walking stick 128
umbrella stand 128
Umbriel 7
umpire 292, 297, 299, 302
under tail covert 73
underarm portfolio 126
underground chamber 217
underground flow 42
underground stem 103
undershirt 291
underwater camera 236
underwear 117, 119
uneven parallel bars 274
ungulate mammals 84
ungulate mammals, examples of 86
unicellulars 56
uniform resource locator 248
uniform resource locator (URL) 248
uniforms 262
unison 222
unit price 170
universal step 252
unloading dock 259
uphaul 278
upper blade guard 162
upper deck 206
upper eyelid 66, 79, 102
upper fore topgallant sail 201
upper fore topsail 201
upper lip 60, 102
upper lobe 97
upper mantle 24
upper section 16
upper shell 289, 307
upper strap 289
upper tail covert 73
upright 275
upright piano 226
upright vacuum cleaner 159
upstream gate 279
Uranus 7
URL 248
uropod 58
used syringe box 265
usual terms 109, 110, 111, 112
utensils, kitchen 147
uvula 102

V

V-neck 120
V-neck cardigan 120
vacuole 56
vacuum bottle 311
vacuum cleaner, cylinder 159
vacuum cleaner, hand 159
vacuum cleaner, upright 159
valance 142
valley 28, 30
valve 230
valve casing 230
vamp 125
vampire bat 82
van straight truck 193
vanity cabinet 154
vanity mirror 188
variable ejector nozzle 208
variable geometry wing 206
vaulting horse 274, 275
VCR controls 239
VCR mode 239
VCR power button 239
vegetable bowl 145
vegetable brush 147
vegetable garden 134
vegetable kingdom 47
vegetable sponge 132
vegetables 47, 103, 256
vegetables, bulb 103
vegetables, fruit 107
vegetables, inflorescent 105
vegetables, leaf 106
vegetables, root 104
vegetables, stalk 105
vegetables, tuber 104
vegetation 40
vegetation regions 40
vehicle equipment bay 16
vehicle rest area 182
vein 49
veins 99
velarium 218
venom canal 67
venom gland 67
venom-conducting tube 67
vent 188
vent brush 130
ventilating fan 197
ventilator 196
Venus 6
vermiform appendix 96
vernal equinox 33
vernier 170
vertebral column 92, 97
vertebral shield 67
vertical ground movement 26
vertical movement 314
vertical pivoting window 137
vertical pupil 67
vertical section 307
vertical seismograph 26
vertical take-off and landing aircraft 208
vertical-axis wind turbine 179
vestibular nerve 100

vestibule 100, 218
vibrato arm 228
vibrissa 77
video entertainment system 316
video monitor 246
videocassette 240
videocassette recorder (VCR) 240
videotape operation controls 240
view camera 236
Viking (lander) 13
Viking (orbiter) 13
viola 227
violas 234
violet 51, 211
violet-blue 211
violin 227
violin family 234
viper 68
visor 191, 198, 284, 287
visual display 316
vocal cord 97
voice edit buttons 233
voice selector 233
volcanic bomb 27
volcano 24, 27
volcano during eruption 27
volleyball 299
volleyball, beach 299
voltage decrease 176
voltage increase 176, 178
volume control 228, 229, 233, 239, 242, 243, 244, 246
volume display 261
volume unit meters 237
volva 47
vulva 90

W

wadi 29
wading bird 73
waffle iron 150
wagon tent 309
waist 91, 227
waist belt 141, 312
waistband 116, 117
waistband extension 116
waiting room 264
walk 84
walk-in closet 139
walk-in wardrobe 139
walkie-talkie 265
walking leg 59, 62
walking stick 128
walkway 258
wall 9, 112, 309
wall cabinet 143
wall cloud 37
wall tent 309
wallet 126
walnut 54
walrus 88
waning gibbous 10
wardrobe 139
warm temperate climates 34
warming plate 151
warning lights 188

warning track 291
wash bottle 166
washcloth 132
washer 160
washer nozzle 184
waste layers 44
waste water 45
waste, selective sorting 46
water bomber helicopter 203
water bottle 195
water bottle clip 195
water carrier 311
water chestnut 103
water cools the used steam 178
water hazard 282
water intake 175
water is pumped back into the steam generator 178
water key 230
water level 151
water pitcher 145
water pollution 45
water spider 59
water strider 63
water table 30, 45
water tank 197
water turns into steam 178
water under pressure 176
water-level selector 160
watercolor cakes 212
watercolor tube 212
watercourse 30
watercress 106
waterfall 30
watering can 165
watermelon 113
wave clip 130
wax bean 108
wax crayons 212
wax gourd 107
waxing gibbous 10
weasel 80
weather map 38
weather phenomena 35
weather radar 38, 206
weather satellite 38
web 66, 73, 291
webbed foot 66
webbed toe 73
Webcam 247
weeder 164
weighing platform 170
weight 168, 170
weight, measure 170
welt pocket 120
West 23
West Coast mirror 192
West-Northwest 23
West-Southwest 23
Western hemisphere 20
Western meridian 20
wet suit 279
whale 88, 89
wheel 127, 164, 192, 307, 308
wheel chock 204
wheel cover 185
wheel loader 209

wheel mouse 246
wheel tractor 209
wheelbarrow 164
wheelchair 266
wheelchair access 319
whelk 57
whisk 148
whiskers 79
White 314, 315
white blood cell 98
white bread 114
white cabbage 106
white onion 103
white square 314
white stone 315
white wine glass 144
white-tailed deer 86
whitewater 279
whole note 223
whole rest 223
whorl 57
wicket 292
wicketkeeper 292
wide receiver 297
wigwam 215
willow 54, 292
winch 193
winch controls 193
wind 45
wind deflector 192

wind direction, measure 39
wind energy 179
wind instruments 230
wind strength, measure 39
wind synthesizer controller 233
wind vane 38, 39
windbag 224
windbreaker 117
winder 169
window 137, 139, 152, 153, 185, 189, 199, 206, 278
window canopy 309
windows, examples 137
windshaft 179
windshield 184, 191, 192, 206
windshield wiper 184
wine 256
wine cellar 260
wine steward 260
wing 15, 61, 62, 72, 82, 207, 306
wing covert 72
wing membrane 82
wing rib 206
wing shapes, examples 206
wing slat 207
wing strut 208
wing vein 62
winglet 207, 208
winter 33
winter solstice 33

winter sports 284
wiper switch 188
wire brush 232
wisdom tooth 94
wishbone boom 278
withers 78, 85
wok 149
wok set 149
wolf 80
women's cell 264
women's clothing 118
women's gloves 123
women's rest room 319
women's underwear 119
wood 282
wood carving 213
wood ray 53
woodbox 158
woodwind family 234
woofer 241
worker 60
wrestler 304
wrestling 304
wrestling area 304
wrist 78, 82, 91, 101
wrist guard 307
wrist strap 288, 289
wrist-length glove 123
wristband 298, 303
writing case 126

X

xylophone 232, 234

Y

yak 86
yam 104
yard line 296
yellow 211
yellow onion 103
yellow sweet pepper 107
yellow-green 211
yellowjacket 63
yield 317, 318
yogurt 114
yolk 72
yurt 215

Z

zebra 87
zest 112
zipper 127
zither 225
zoom lens 235, 238, 240
zucchini 107
zygomatic bone 92, 93

オールカラー 英語百科大図典

2006年4月20日　初版第1刷発行

著　者　　ジャン＝クロード・コルベイユ
　　　　　アリアーヌ・アルシャンボ
編　集　　小学館外国語辞典編集部
発行者　　大澤　昇

発行所　　〒101-8001
　　　　　東京都千代田区一ツ橋2-3-1
　　　　　株式会社　小　学　館
　　　　　電話　編集　東京 (03) 3230-5169
　　　　　　　　販売　東京 (03) 5281-3555

印刷所(カバー)　凸版印刷株式会社

Shogakukan 2006

Printed and Bound in Singapore　ISBN4-09-505082-9

本書の一部あるいは全部を無断で複製・転載することは、法律で認められた場合を除き、著作者および出版者の権利の侵害となります。あらかじめ小社あてに許諾を求めてください。

Ⓡ ＜日本複写権センター委託出版物＞
本書の全部あるいは一部を無断で複写（コピー）することは、著作権法上での例外を除き、禁じられています。本書からの複写を希望される場合は、日本複写権センター（☎03-3401-2382）にご連絡ください。

造本には十分注意しておりますが、万一、落丁・乱丁などの不良品がありましたら、「小学館制作局」（☎0120-336-340）あてにお送りください。送料小社負担にてお取り替えいたします。（電話受付は土・日・祝日を除く9:30～17:30です）

★小学館外国語辞典のホームページ
http://www.l-world.shogakukan.co.jp/

Japanese translation rights arranged with QA International, Montréal through Tuttle-Mori Agency, Inc., Tokyo